MW00811465

HOC MVNIMINE TVTVS
VERO NIL VERIVS.
WF fec.

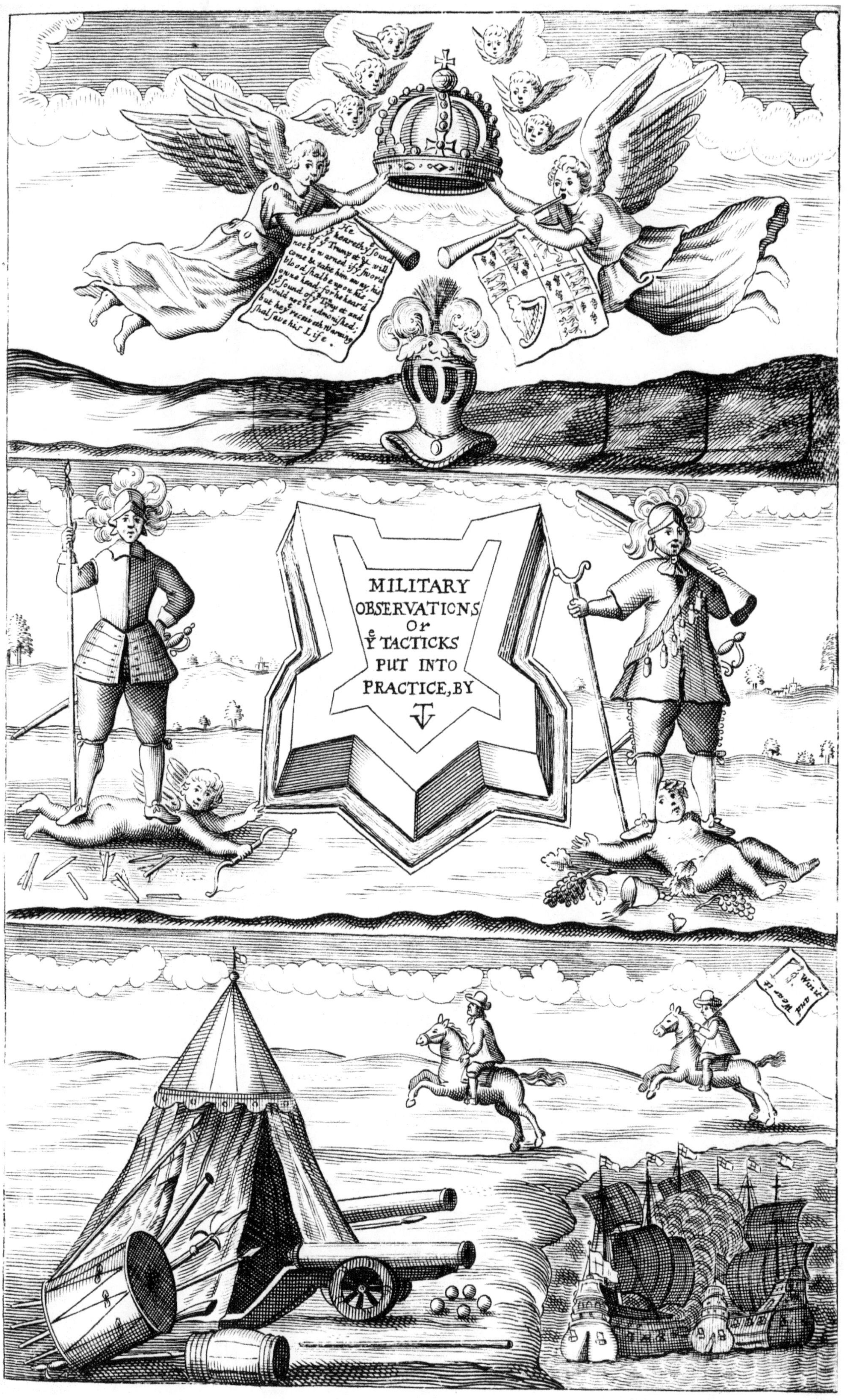

He yt heareth ye sound of ye Trumpet & will not be warned if ye sword come & take him away, his blood shall be upon his owne head; for he heard ye sound of ye Trumpet and would not be admonished; but he yt receiveth warning shal save his Life.
MILITARY
OBSERVATIONS
Or
Ye TACTICKS
PUT INTO
PRACTICE, BY
Win it and Wear it

Military & Maritine DISCIPLINE

IN

THREE BOOKS.

Book I.

Military Obſervations or Tacticks put into Practice for the Exerciſe of Horse and Foot; the Original of Ensignes; the Poſtures of their Colours: With Sir *Francis Veres* Directions for Officers; And a ſmall Treatiſe of Invasion.

By Captain *Thomas Venn.*

Book II.

An exact Method of Military Architecture, the Art of Fortifying Towns; with the wayes of Defending and Offending the ſame.

Rendred into *Engliſh* by *John Lacey*, out of the Works of the late Learned Mathematician *Andrew Tacquet.*

Together with Corrections made by the *Count de Pagan* and Sr *Sam. Moreland's* Methods of Delineating all manner of Fortifications.

Book III.

The Compleat Gunner in three Parts, Shewing the Art of Founding of Great Ordnance; making Gun-powder; the taking of Heights and Diſtances either with or without Inſtruments; with the nature of Fire-works.

Tranſlated out of *Caſimir, Diego, Uffano* and *Hexam,* &c.

To which is added the Doctrine of Projects applied to Gunnery by *Galilæus* and *Torricellio.* And Obſervations out of *Merſennus* and other Authors.

The Naval & Military Press Ltd

Published by

The Naval & Military Press Ltd
Unit 5 Riverside, Brambleside
Bellbrook Industrial Estate
Uckfield, East Sussex
TN22 1QQ England

Tel: +44 (0)1825 749494

www.naval-military-press.com
www.nmarchive.com

Military Obſervations,

OR THE

TACTICKS

PUT INTO

PRACTICE,

Collected and Compoſed for the EXERCISE

BOTH OF

Horſe and Foot,

To our preſent mode of Diſcipline.

WITH

The Original of ENSIGNES their duties, and Poſtures of their COLOURS.

Hereunto is added Sr. FRANCIS VEARES notes of Direction for Officers,

---

By Capt. *Thomas Venn.*

TO THE
Right Noble JOHN DUKE
OF

SOMERSET,

MARQUES and EARLE
OF

HARTFORD,

VICOUNT BEAUCHAMP
AND

Lord Seymour.

May it pleaſe your Grace.

IN vacant hours my Genius guiding me to ſome thoughts upon Art Military, *and having made ſome Collections of part thereof, out of the chiefeſt Authors both Ancient and Modern, but finding in them many Motions to be of little uſe, and may well be ſpared according to our preſent Mode of Diſcipline, which is to Exerciſe and fight our*

Horse but three in File, and the Foot six. I have according to the several Commands for the Exercise thereof, drawn the platforms, and directions for the performance of the same, and now they want nothing but your Graces protection, for which, being your Servant and Tenant, I have presumed to implore; knowing that there is in your Right Noble self, Wisdome and Potency enough to allow hereof for the use of the young Souldrie of this Kingdom: Sir, *next to my Sacred* KING *be assured of my dutiful affections, and Command the Life of him who is in all humlity*

Your Graces

most obliged Servant

Tho. Venn.

TO

TO
All such of the
Deputy Lieutenants
For the County of
SOMERSET
That have faithfully managed his MAJESTIES affairs in the well ordering of the Militia of the said County.

Right worshipful, and truly Honoured.

I Am to crave your pardons for my boldness, that (being Comissionated to obey your Commands) have presumed thus far without them; but your Honours love to this Art, and my own experience of you, is the cause thereof; and as the Country can testifie the same, so it is my endeavour (if it were possible) the whole world should know it: But your splendid carriages in the activeness of your proceedings in the Militia, do shine most glorious in your effectual managements; for your diligence hath drawn obedience, your wisdom reverence, your vertuous education makes a willingness in all to serve you, and a readiness in your Honours (in all your actions) to equallize the same. These Collectives are but shaddowes your Noble minds are adorned withall, being but little more than the Accidence of Military Discipline, yet useful in this Warlike age. My Lord Duke's Patronizing hereof I hope may not be denied by you to suffer these to march and quarter within the precincts of your Honours Commands, assuring that in quality I am

Your Honours Servant to be Commanded.

Tho. Venn.

A List of the names of those worthy Gentlemen as are concerned in the affairs of the County of *Somerset*, as Deputy Lieutenants, and Colonels, both of Horse and Foot.

The Lord *Fitzharding*, Colonel of Horse.
Lord *Pawlett*, Colonel of *Crewkerne* Regiment, 1.
Sir *William Portman.*
Sir *John Syddenham.*
Sir *William Wyndham.*
Sir *Thomas Bridges.*
Sir *Hugh Smith.*
Sir *George Horner.*
Sir *Edmond Windham* Knight Marshall.
Sir *John Coventrey* Colonel of *Taunton* Regiment, 2.
Edward Phillips Esq.
Ralph Stawell, Esq. Colonel of *Bridgwater* Regiment. 3.
Peregrine Palmer Esq.
Henry Rogers Esq.
George Speake Esq.
Francis Windham Esq. Colonel of *Wells* Regiment, 4.
Samuel Gorges Esq.
Robert Hunt Esq.
Thomas Peggot Esq. Colonel of *Bath* Regiment, 5.

To

TO THE
Right worshipful, and truly honoured
Sir COPLESTONE BAMPFIELD *Knight*,
And one of the Knights of
PARLAMENT
For the County of DEVON, *&c.*

SIR,

ALthough I am a stranger to you, yet the Gallantry of your Vertuous inclinations, together with the nearness of affections to my never to be forgotten Cammander Sir Hugh Wyndham *Knight, late deceased, forceth me to present you with a Lively Portraicture of his worth. As to his Military concerns, he made his Souldiers Commanders of the chiefest principles of War (that is) to be Faithful, Obedient, Resolute to fight, loving to their Country, and loyal to their Soveraign: So likwise in the private Exercises of his Troops, those under his Command were as Ornaments in peace, and a guard in War: This only was not the heighth of his ambition, for he made it a principle to himself in Warlike combates, not to have many names, but many hands:*

hands: And for his deportments, I am ſure none was more beloved in his Country, nor could command more able and ſtouter Souldiers for his Majeſties ſervice than himſelf: And I hope the Heavens have moſt largely rewarded him for his blood ſpilt in his late Majeſties ſervice (of ever bleſſed memory.)

Sir, *I humbly beg I might by your favour indicate to the world my Obligements to his deceaſed perſon, which was accepted of by him when he was alive, as an Epiſtle to my Obſervations for the* Military Exerciſe of Horſe and Foot. *And what I have truely ſaid of him, your own worth falls not ſhort, in your Paternal affections to your Country, which hath of late appeared (notwithſtanding great oppoſition) in their clear affections to you again, eſpecially in that unparallel'd Election of you for* Knight of the Shire: *And give me leave to declare to the World your Countries further Eſteems of you, to be one of his* Majeſties *chiefeſt Cittadels (or fort Royall) for their ſafety: Not that I declare this to leſſen any of the beames of thoſe other worthy Heroes that ſhall joyn with you, when ever his* Majeſty *ſhall Command.*

Sir, *I crave your Pardon for my boldneſs, and conclude (with my deſired wiſhes for your Worſhips tranquillity, the increaſe of Honour here, and what may be merited for you, to make you glorious in the world to come) ſubſcribing in the quality of*

July 29.
1671.

Your Humble Servant

Tho. Venn.

To

TO THE

Truly Generous Gentlemen and

CITIZENS of LONDON

Practiſing Armes in the

Artillery Garden.

Gentlemen,

ALthough I am a ſtranger to you, I muſt declare to the world that what I know in this *Art Military*, I received, as it were from your breaſt; from ſome who were Leaders in your ground: And 'tis a grief to me that I live at ſuch a diſtance from you, as not to be of your number; the leaſt amongſt you being of ability to be Commanders in Chief, when ever his MAJESTY may require it. There is in you ſtrength enough to ſhield a juſt cauſe; and a Royal cauſe is able to advance your power: give me leave to tell you there can be nothing done by you without it; it is that which giveth ſtrength and ſinewes, to all your motions.

Gentlemen, you may ſee, by my other Epiſtles, what Authors I have made uſe of, and if you find ſome of the words of Command, one and the ſame with others late before me, I could not help it, for this was finiſhed as to the Commands and directions above four or five years now laſt paſt, and in *Elton.*

b all

all that time I never ſaw any thing of the Gentlemans, nor his latter piece as yet.

This you'l find to be but methodical collections for the young Country Souldier; and in our rural exerciſes they can draw up but twelve files, in which I am ſtinted to a very ſmall number for ſo great a work; if there were a proportionableneſs in the Armes, the figures would have been better; yet not in the leaſt preſuming to teach you; but I hope with your favourable conſtructions you will allow it uſeful for us in the Country, although your abilities may teach the world ten times more. I aim'd at nothing but to ſhew how neceſſary the readyneſs and uſe of Armes is, and of men to be well exerciſed in them. Which hath been a benefit to Republicks, as Hiſtory and experience hath made to appear; for what Nation hath not found ſafety in the expert uſe of them, and in the neglect thereof ruin?

I hope there are none of you ſo diſloyal, as not to obey your Princes Commands; in Order to which I cannot but Commend your cloſe order to his Religion, (and not to be at open diſtances); it is that which will make your obedience free, your affections ſettled, your ſelves renowned, and as I may in ſome part ſay, the peace of the Kingdom ſecured.

I humbly crave your pardons for my boldneſs, and grant me not only to be in the number of the well wiſhers to this Art, but alſo to the proſperity of your ground, and I ſhall alwayes ſubſcribe,

March, 1671. Yours

Tho. Venn.

To

TO ALL MY

FELLOW-OFFICERS SOULDIERS

AND

LOVING COUNTRY-MEN

To whom the Exercise of

ARMES

Is delightful.

Gentlemen, and Fellow Souldiers.

ALthough there are discouragements enough to make you negligent in the exercise of Armes, not only to see this Art so little countenanced, but our late Enemies by sitting still, grow rich, and the Royal Sons of Mars, *in all their labours not able with one hand to wash the other; yet this one thing, in making our selves capable to do our Gracious King and Country service, should be the chiefest motive to labour after the* Theorick *part of this Art, by which we shall be the better able to perform the* Practick *when we shall be called thereunto.*

 But

But lest these few Collectives might meet with some objections, why that I should treat of the Horse in the first place, when Antiquity alloweth the precedency thereof to the Infantry; It was not to raise a dispute amongst the Novists, but I leave such to enquire of the precedencies in a Council of War, and who taking place there will resolve them: And it is well known to most of you I was a Commander of Horse my self; and then having finished my weak thoughts as to the Exercise thereof, which being viewed by some Gentlemen of our Country, I was desired by them to set out likewise some few Collections for the young foot Souldier.

It is true there have been many Books printed of this Art in our past ages, and some in our present; and as Solomon *saith of making many Books there is no end; yet if it had not been for Books this Art might have been buried in oblivion. And if I should set out at full how all that we practise is not only borrowed from Antiquity, but most of the very words of Command are kept still in use, it would be too large, and it being not my business, I shall acquiesce with what I intended for my private use, but being (as I have declared) requested hereunto, and now fearing that most of our books are consumed by fire, I am further perswaded to put these introductives to publick view. Let me perswade, you fellow Souldiers, although you meet with many discouragements and scoffs in your Country, although taxes lie heavy upon you, and your allowances do not answer your moderate expences, nay although not your due for your time spent herein, yet go on; for I*

When London *was burnt,* 1666. Sept. 3d. *&c.*

will

will boldly tell you that practical knowledge in this Art is the higheſt ſtep to preferment.

We read among the Romans *of* Lucullus, *and in our latter age of* M. Spinola, *who through maturity of judgement and great Learning became Generals as ſoon as Souldiers: Intimating that it is the Prerogative of Princes to be born leaders of Armies; But others muſt expect to aſcend this Mountain of Honour by many and difficult ſtepps. Therefore firſt lay a foundation of honeſt fame, labouring after the practice of private vertues; Then orderly proceeding to ſignalize thy ſelfe by ſome publique atchievements (which I doubt not, but every generous ſpirit will endeavour the aſcention thereof) you may be aſſured that paſſing once the brunt of it, even to the hazzard of life it ſelf, you'l find delightful pleaſures in following the exerciſes of this* Art Military.

Who is it that ſhall think ſo deſpicably of a Souldier, or his profeſſion ſo baſe, as ſome have ſo accounted them? When they that are the ſons of Mars *and have the true form of Military Diſcipline, are highly to be eſteemed as honourable, and as neceſſary members in a Kingdome; ſuch as no Kingdome can be without.*

It is honourable, becauſe it is compaſſed about with ſuch reaſons as that the contemners thereof by the judicious are much reproved; for that State that is not able to ſtand it out in Armes againſt the rage of inteſtine, and forraign violence, is ſure to fall into the hands of the deſtroyer. How can any particular intereſt pre-

 ſerve

ſerve it ſelf without it? I will boldly ſay that the Deſpiſers of the uſe of Armes, are not only diſloyal to their Prince but deſtructive to themſelves. What are the Laws and Civil Orders without defence for the maintenance of them? I may truly terme them like a Ship without a Rudder, which being let at liberty to every guſt of Wind will be ruined upon the Rocks of Rebellion: Or like ſome curious Edifice erected without a roof, which cannot withſtand the violence of any ſtorme. Conſtantine the Great, *by the perſwaſions of ſome peaceable Subjects caſhier'd his antient Legions, by which he overthrew the beſt of his Military Diſcipline, and ſo left an open gap for the barbarous Nations to invade the Empire.*

Solomon *in the time of Peace provided for War. What Nation dare to meddle with that People who are prepared, and well exerciſed in this Art of War?*

Therefore let every one, Gentlemen and Farmours, Rich and poor, that intend to approve themſelves true Engliſh *men and Loyal Subjects, not only imbrace, honour and cheriſh Armes, but alſo exerciſe (and be exerciſed) and diligently learn this Military Art: that in caſe any Rebellion or treachery may ariſe, they may be fit to defend His* MAJESTIES *perſon, with all his rights and Prerogatives: That ſuch as our late inteſtine ruines may be for ever hereafter prevented: That the Armed ſervant may no more command the unarmed Maſter: Nor the Rebellious armed Subject his unarmed Prince.*

Let us not be overwhelmed in ſecurity, but when

any

any ſuddain Alarme may ſound in our ears, there may be alwayes found ſuch ready and fit both to command and obey. Solomon *doth in effect tell us, that it is not the great number of untrained men that are ſufficient for defence when he ſaith,* A wiſe man is ever ſtrong; yea a man of underſtanding increaſeth in ſtrength; for with Wiſdome muſt War be taken in hand; and where there are many that give Counſel there is victory. *Pro. 14.*

It is impoſſible for any Kingdome or Dominion to live in peace, without the uſe of the Sword: As Idleneſs and the neglect of Warlike Diſcipline hath been the ruine of many States; ſo the Order of the antient Romans *reſolved not to lie as ſluggards, nor to delight in Idle, or wanton paſtimes, but at certain times allotted them in a year for the bettering of their experience in Warlike Exerciſes, they did it with delight and pleaſure, ſo that no labour herein was burdenſome to them: and being become by the practice thereof moſt ready and expert in the ſame, became at laſt, as Hiſtory hath declared, great and mighty Conquerours.*

I wiſh the ſame of us, that our reputation may not ſcornfully be laid aſide, as if we minded more our Carpets, and the following products thereof, than the Musquett; That through the Exerciſe of this Military Art, we may become ſo mighty and Valiant, as that we may be able to withſtand any oppoſition both Forraign and Domeſtick.

 Thus

Thus wishing prosperous successe in all Martial affairs that may be for the good both of King and Countrey; I conclude and subscribe not onely to be a well-wisher to all Military Arts, but in the quality of

Your fellow Souldier

and Servant

Tho. Venn.

Introductive

Introductive Collections;

OR

INSTRUCTIONS

For the Young Souldier,

IN

Art Military.

CHAP. I.

Military Observations for the Exercise of Horse.

Otwithstanding what these late Rebellious Times have made to appear, yet there is so much of self-willed Ignorance, with more than the common sort of people, not only to think, but to say, that in all services and Exercise of Arms, there needeth no more Action, but by these words of Command; *Make ready*, *Present*, and *Give fire*: All other words of Command to be but as tendances to them; and all other postures are by them judged to be but superfluous, and may well be spared; or but trifles of small consequence: Whereas the life and well being of every well ordered Troop of Horse, and Company of Foot, consisteth wholly of form; and those received Ceremonies belonging to every Posture, cannot in the least, in the prime of Exercise be neglected, but with the hazzard of Confusion; *Qu d si cœcus cœcum per viam duxerit ambo in foveam cadent*. The crooked deformity of the bones is covered with the flesh, for the better adorning of the body; so are Ceremonies which by experience (the Antient have made Reverent) *Math. 15. 14.*

 are

are the life and being of a Kingdom: And here by way of digression, give me leave to say, that which is but truth, that the neglect of Ceremonies formerly used and commanded, proved most injurious to this Kingdom, and yet to this day is an evident demonstration of Faction and Rebellion.

It is the ambition of many men striving to be Captains before they be Souldiers, labouring after Command, before they know how to obey; and being well considered, what more is the Mother of Errour, but Ignorance? It is well scited out of *Vegetius*, That knowledge in all things belonging to Warr, giveth Courage; *Nemo facere metuit quod se bene didicisse confidit*; No man feareth to do that which he hath well learned how to do: Without a true knowledge in the single Accidence, in this Art Military, (as I may term it) you will never be able to judge of the *Syntaxis* thereof; without experience in all the Postures belonging to Horse and Foot, none can be capable of exactness in that which is most of use in this Art; for Military Discipline (where with care it is observed) is but a true confirmation of Souldiers in their Valour and Vertue, and in short is performed

By { Exercise, Order Compulsion, & Example.

1. By Exercise: Good Instructions are nothing without they be followed by care and diligence; for what breeds more strong and resolved gallantry in Gentlemen than Industry? It excelleth nature it self: All the labour and exercise of a Commander from time to time, is not of any value as to the Execution of this Art, either in courage or strength in their Souldiers, without he be industrious to teach, and they also willingly labour after a perfection in the exercise of such Instructions as shall be commanded them; for experience with Instruction is the best way to perfection. *Vegetius* saith, *Paucos viros natura fortes procreat, bonâ Institutione plures reddit industria*; Nature brings forth very few strong men, but Industry by good Instruction breeds up many: None ought to be called for to exercise this Art, but such, who are able to produce what they know to action; for that Souldier that is not well taught, can never expect the fruit of his labour (to be couragious in his Enterprizes.)

Exercitium, Importeth nothing else but exercising an Army, *&c.* And it is most certain that the Souldery, who are often and well exercised, are much the better; as *Varro* saith, *Exercitus dicitur quòd melius fit exercitando*: Thus being willing to be exercised begetteth knowledge, knowledge begets courage; courage obtained, makes perils contemned, calamities despised, and death it self conquered.

2. By Order: There hath been so much writ of this by many Authours, that I shall only say in short, It consisteth in dividing, disposing and placing of men so fit; that upon all occasions they may be apt and ready to be commanded, by their Superiours as they shall direct.

Polibius, Vegetius, &c.

3. By Compulsion: That Souldier that makes not this Military Art his delight, but is given to other pleasures and pastimes, (and being accustomed thereunto) contracts an unmanly effeminacy, and degenerates from courage; as *Tacitus* saith, *Degenerat à robore ac Virtute miles assuetudine voluptatum*: Now all such Souldiers, as are vainly given, and mind pleasure more than commands, ought to be bridled and governed by compulsion.

4. By Example,

And they are either in { Reward or Punishment.

1. **In Reward**: That Souldier that expects advancement from his Commander, must be so stout in his resolutions, as perfectly to perform what is commanded: And when he shall answer his Commanders expectation, in the execution of some singular service, he ought to receive *Fame, Honour* and *Riches*, as a reward for it.

1. And first, That Souldier whose care is, that at all times his behaviour be such as to endeavour after all vertuous habits, and being so adorned, he ought to have that which vertuous Souldiers most desire and labour after; That is **Good Fame**: for it is the food of his reputation, and nourisheth towards Honour in the highest Atchievements.

2. There is a second reward, and that is **Honour**: It is not the nature of a true Souldier to hunt after Honour, or to buy it with Bribes; It is blood and not gold, that hath been the price of Honour: Therefore that Souldier that shall thus deserve, ought not to be voyded of it, but according to his merits and quality, ought to have his preferment.

3. And lastly; but not the least, the good, faithful, and stout Souldiers reward is **Wealth**; that when they are preferred they may not be despised, but to be in ability, as to the greatness and smallness of place, to hold up to his Rank and advancement; without These a Souldier can neither perform nor continue the duty of his calling; and therefore the bestowing thereof deserveth great consideration, that the well deserving Souldier at no time should be neglected. *M. D.* 1. *p.* 27.

It must be acknowledged that **Rewards** are seldome seen, for Offices are more often known to be bestowed for favour (if not for money) than for desert: What makes many brave spirits to give up their services; but when they see their way of Advancement cut off, and their pay it may be hard to come by; in regard that some Pay-Masters, or Treasurers have been corrupt, that the souldier shall not have his pay without some unknown fees? And rather than to commit any base action in his Country, he is forced to desert the service; or when their service is ended, without they'l give one part of their just dues, that they may have the other, they shall be delayed, *&c.* And this is one reason there are so many unwilling hearts to serve their Country; and what makes a Souldier so despicable in his Country, as to be forced to use extremity even for necessity sake? How base a thing is it for some Deputy Chieftains that make it their study to rob Honours Workmen of their hire? And if it be so in our Country affairs, and in times of Peace; What can be expected from such in times of trouble? Let such know that Honours trumpet shall never sound their prayses.

But to such as shall not in the least debar it from the deserved, but (as I may terme it) are rather willing to disburthen themselves of their Souldiers stipend; to such, I say, not only remains the obsequious diligence of their Souldiers to serve them in all hazzardous attempts; but also the glorious title of a faithful Steward, which draws after it both the affection of Prince and People.

2. There are also **Punishments** due to those that are Vicious and Cowardly; for nothing more holds a Souldier in his due obedience than the severity of Discipline.

Souldiers (as *Vegetius* saith) ought to stand more in awe of their Generals, than in fear of their Enemies: Discipline being once infringed, either by a slightment of Reward, or neglect of a Souldiers just pay, will cause the Vertuous to desist, and to others 'twill prove a spur, to necessitate them to base Actions; which with other corruptions, when seen by superiour Officers, and shall not according to Martial Law endeavour to punish such vicious Actions; I say the Souldier instead of submitting to the Commands of his Leader, oftentimes breaketh forth into Mutinies and Rebellions. I must confess when, and where *Reward* and *Punishments* are not slighted, the wellfare of a Country will be so supported, that no Vice shall be able to stagger it: So in an Army, what maketh a Souldier to forget obedience, more than the want of Pay and the execution of good Laws? which being duly performed, the Souldier will undoubtedly, the better know his Duty and Discipline.

Here, by the way, I cannot but insert some few things that are prejudicial to the Souldier, and Army, *&c.*

First, When the Publique Service of God is so neglected, that the whole Souldery, under a Christian Prince are not tyed to be Exercised in the same Religion his Prince is of; for Faction amongst them will do more hurt, than bullets against them.

Secondly, When high debauchery is not severely punished.

Thirdly, When Gaming is not most strictly forbidden; because it is not only a waste of Maintenance, and an Introduction to Quarrels, but a Prophanation of God's holy name.

And Fourthly, When Muster-masters are so careless in their Office, as to suffer any Captain, upon wilful absence of Souldiers, to receive some out of other Companies, or hired men out of the Town and Country; this being well considered will prove prejudicial both to King and Country.

And lastly, When those strict Laws against Duelling are not better observed, that for every trivial quarrel, the life of a stout spirited Gentleman must drop. For better satisfaction, read *Ward's* Discourse of unjust Valour against Duels. *Fol.* 183. &c.

Chap. II.

Of the Souldier, and Officers in General.

IT is not my intention to run through the description of every particular Officer at large, of his duty in his respective place; it being set forth at large in several Authours: I shall therefore briefly pass them over; hoping it will be the endeavour of all that undertake any Office Military, in the service of his King and Country, to labour after a true form of Discipline, that is now in exercise by Authority in general; That when it shall please our Gracious King to call for us, we may not be uncapable of Command: What greater dishonour can there be than for a Commander to be commanded by his inferiour Officers? Therefore it behoves all in their several Capacities, who are willing to win Honour; not to be wanting in their endeavours after the Exercise of Arms.

1. Of the private Souldier.

None were admitted Souldiers among the *Romans*, but such as were of an honest Tribe, (or Family, as being more likely to labour after Victory, not only for his Liberty, but for his goods, or estate.) As for those that were absolutely necessitous, they might have liberty promised by their Enemies, and so betray their Trust. Again, they would never take any Souldiers into their Armies, but such as were well exercised before-hand; and this did their work, and obtained them Victories against their Enemies, *Vegetius, Lib.* 1. *Chap.* 8. The private Souldiers duty is as followeth. Whensoever he is commanded for service, let him labour to be sober, and patient, enduring all hardships and travels; To know and observe all Orders Military, Compleatly Armed, and expert in the use thereof; *Horridum militem esse decet, non cælato auro argentóque, sed ferro.* (*Liv.*) It becometh a Souldier best to appear terrible; not to be garnished with gold and silver, but with steel. And Souldiers ought not only to be obedient to their Captains; but chiefly to Love God, and Honour their King. This being the duty of a Souldier in general, there are two particular duties belonging to him, that is, as a **Sentinel** and a **Scout**.

2. **Sentinels**; The further any Sentinels are set from the body of the Guard, it is thought necessary two should be placed, and there they are to endeavour both to hear and see, thereby to learn of their Enemy, what may be intended, and what they have discovered; that whilst one goeth to certifie the Captain of the Guard, the other

other may stand fixt, and observe what else might happen in his fellows absence. A Sentinel must not alight from his Horse unless it be for natural necessity, and but one of them at once. Near to the Body of the Guard there may be placed but a single Sentinel, to observe the moving of the double. If the distances be not too large, if there be any other Cross-ways or advenues, that each Sentinel may see the other, then there may be but a single set; for they must know that they are set there only to certifie the Body of the Guard concerning the several occurrances that may happen: Suppose a Sentinel should be provoked by any advantagious affairs; It is resolved he must not stir a foot; for that Sentinel that shall by day or night, remove from the place where he was set by his Corporal, before he shall be by him fetched off (or relieved) shall be punished with death. *Polyb. lib. 1.*

If the whole Troop be upon the Guard the Lieutenant is to set forth the first Sentinels with the Corporal, according to his directive Commands received, and to change them, conducting them to his Guard; (but the Cornet is not to forsake his Standard;) Then the Captain of the Guard is to go the first Round, to see not only that all things are safe, but also whether those Sentinels are vigilent: And upon his return, there are four other Rounders to be sent twice in a night, to discover round the Quarters. Observe, that no Sentinel is to have the Word, but Officers and Corporals. Directions.

3. **Scouts**; They are not only to discover the High-wayes, but also to scoure them: they are to be of a number, answerable to the danger of the Guard; for the hazzard of them, may prove dangerous, both to a private Guard or an Army in General. They are to give notice of the Enemies motion, of his approach, and of the number of them, that all suddain surprizes may be prevented.

4. **A Provost Martial**; For the badge of his Office he is to have in his hand a staffe or Truncheon; and having the same in his hand, it is death for any Souldier violently to lay hands on him: All Delinquents are to be delivered to him, by the Chief in Command. He is not to enter any quarter without the leave of the Chief Officer for any Prisoner; He is to clear all by-ways of Souldiers, that no prejudice may be done by them in their March; He is to see all Orders published, be duly executed; He must be an honest man, and take no Bribes.

5. **A Trumpeter**, ought to be a man skilful in all the sounds of the Trumpet distinctly; He ought to deliver all Embassies, &c. He ought to observe the Enemies Works, Guards, and Souldiers, that he may give a good accompt thereof at his return: And for the better performance thereof, he ought to be a man witty and subtle, and to manage it discreetly; He ought not in the least to discover any thing, as may prejudice his own party; He must not fail to sound the hours commanded: One Trumpet is to be with the Cornet, and he is to be allowed by the Captain for him; who is to receive a list of the Guards from the Cornet, and is privately to warn the Souldiers thereof.

6. **Corporals**, in a Troop of Horse, have been always allowed to be of great use; who ought to be of a civil carriage and stout spirit; they are to be three or more, according to the allowance of Horse, &c. They are to be assistant to the Lieutenant in placing of the Sentinels, each in their several squadrons when they are to perform duty: If any parties are to be sent abroad, either for discovery, or to scoure the high-wayes, a Corporal is to be sent with them; He is bound to keep a list of his Squadron.

7. **A Quarter-Master**, ought to be a man of much fidelity in regard of distributing of the *Word* and *Billets*; He is to have the Command of the Troop in the absence of his superiour Officers: Who in going to make his Billets is to have a Souldier along with him by the appointment of the Lieutenant, who is to return to the Troop to conduct them to their Quarters.

8. **A Cornet**, ought to be a man of gallant behaviour and undaunted courage; His place in the Troop upon a march is on the front of his own squadron; and to take the Standard himself, marching through any great Town or City (or when commanded) or into the field with it flying; and when any General shall appear in the field he is to drop the head of his standard towards the ground in obeysance to him. His

Place when the Troop is drawn up (to the opinion of some) is for to exercise upon the left of the Captain, somewhat behind the Captain; But in fight or skirmish, he is to place himself in the first rank of his own squadron; with his staffe sunkt or slopt; and in danger, it is more honour to break his Launce (or staff) himself, then to suffer his standard to be broken and taken from him: He is to keep a list of the Troop, and wait every day upon his Superiour Officers; and such Souldiers as his Captain and Lieutenant shall appoint he shall send to the Guard: In the absence of the Captain and Lieutenant he is to command the Troop.

9. **For the Lieutenant**; The Reer is assigned him for his place, and was antiently called *Tregidux*, that is a Reer Commander: And Lieutenant is a *French* word signifying one which supplyeth the place of another; for in the absence of the Captain he commands the Troop; appointing an Officer to be in the Reer: He ought to be a man well educated in Cavalry, and in the other parts of the Art Military. He ought to be strict to see the souldiers punctually to do their service, and to have a care to their Horses and Arms in the field and fight. He being in the Reer is not only to encourage the Souldiers, but to have his sword drawn, and to kill any that shall endeavour to flee, and not to fight. He ought to know the ability of his Souldiers, keeping the list of their names; that the Guards may be in a readiness, with the Captains consent, and by him delivered to the Cornet.

In the mounting of the Guard, he is to inform himself of the place for the Guard, and of the Sentinels for to set, the ways for to be scoured, and must go himself with the Corporal of the Guard, and see the first Sentinels placed; And when he hath the Guard himself, he must often visit them; always to be armed and to keep his bridle day and night upon his horse's head.

When the Troop is drawn up to lodge the Standard; He is to see the Quartermaster deliver to the Souldiers their respective Billets for their quartering, upon that Alt before they move, for then the Souldier will know thereby the better where to wait on the Cornet upon any occasion.

He ought to visit all Quarters, as to his list received, and see that the Souldiers be of civil bevaviour; and if any complaints be made of any disorder, he is to remedy it, by punishing the Offenders.

When the Trumpet sounds to Horse, he ought to be first mounted, and to cause all immediately to do the same; He must punish all lingring and lazie Souldiers that are not presently mounted with him. The good Examples of a Leader have ever been observed to be of a marvellous efficacy with the Souldiers.

10. **Every Captain** ought to be obedient, valiant, and resolute in the execution of all Commands with Judgement, discretion and Valour; that with vertuous nobleness and generosity he may win the love of his Souldiers, to their King, Country, and himself; and that by his own experience in the knowledge of Military Discipline, he may be able to govern his Souldiers accordingly.

11. **Colonels**, They ought to have an high respect with all Obedience to their higher Officers, faithfully to perform their Commands, and that with care, valour, affection and diligence they govern their Regiments.

12. **And when every General** shall make his whole Army to love and fear God, and shall govern with prudence, care, order and Justice; and knowing how to prevent, remedy and execute, as occasions shall offer themselves, with great skill and dexterity, will make himself no less loved than feared.

From these Officers, the Trained Bands of this Kingdom (with the Ships) are the defence thereof (or ought to be;) but to speak of the choice of the Souldiers, or of their being armed, or well disciplined, (as in many places is much neglected,) and where the fault is, as I am an inferiour Officer I must be silent: Pardon me to say it would be much better if his Majesties Deputies would cast their eyes and commands oftner amongst them.

I could wish that our *Militia* instead of celebrating their Feasts to *Mars*, did it not too much to *Bacchus* with carousing and drunkenness; which folly and detestable vice is an Enemy to all Vertues, both of soul and body; (and to all Military Discipline.)

pline.) It is the very Nurse of Effeminacy, of Cowardise, of Sensuality, of Rebellion, and of all other Vices that can be imagined.

This was a Forrain Vice brought in amongst us by our Neighbour Commanders, quaffing and carousing, until as the *Fleming* say, Doot Dronken.

It is a sad thing that any that bears affection to Military Affairs, should make such fruits the merchantable effects of that Discipline; I am sure he is no true Souldier (nor Subject) that shall follow such beastly ensamples; when it is the Command of our Soveraign to the contrary: All must know they are bound to obey Authority; and let all true hearts take that for his Card to steer the course of his Loyalty by.

Chap. III.

Of the Arming of the Cavalry.

THe Cavalry are required in their Persons, Arms, and Horses, to be suitable to their several ends and Imployments: There were among the *Græcians* and *Romans* two bodies of Horse, a light-armed body, and a heavy-armed body; the light-armed were to give the first onset to the Infantry, to make way (as I conceive) by disordering the Enemy; then the heavy-armed Horse were to take their advantages for Victory.

There were and are to be taken notice of five several kinds of men at Arms for the Horse service:
- Lanceirs,
- Cuirasiers,
- Harquebuziers,
- Carabiniers,
- Dragoniers.

1. Lanciers, they were offensive, but chiefly defensive, and were armed *Capa pe*, with *Swords* and *Peternels*, somewhat longer than our ordinary *Pistols* now in use, with a Lance of about sixteen or eighteen foot long. It hath been adjudged by our Royal Generals, and found by experience of late years not so serviceable, because not so nimble for any suddain enterprizes, or field services as our light-armed Horse-men are; therefore wholly laid aside: Besides they were not always of effectual use in a body, for execution, but in a straight line, upon a Carreer, and where they must have both leasure, and room enough to work their designs; which I leave to the Judicious to give their Verdicts herein: for if men in our days should be laden with such Arms, how would they be able to command a Lance at that length: If there were such inconveniences in the weight of the Armour and Weapons as the then after experienced found many; yet our men are much weaker, and wholly unable to undergo the burden thereof; upon these considerations the use of the Lance was then left off; so that the Horse were called

2. Curasiers, who were both for Horse and Armes in no wise inferiour to the Lanciers (his Lance excepted) and are also offensive but chiefely defensive; but not subject to those inconveniences as the former with their Lances: He is to have under his Armour (which is *Capa pe*) a good Buff coat, and good Peternels with a Sword whose point must be stiff, and sharp, his Sadle and bitt strong, and his bridle with an Iron chain to prevent cutting: he is to have a boy to carry his armes, and to forrage for him. These are the heavy-armed for the Horse service which are not used amongst us, especially in our settled Militia, nor but few of the next, which are termed

3. Harquebuziers, who are very serviceable and are to be armed defensive with a

good Buff coat, and to have a back, breast and pot, Pistoll proofe: and for his offensive armes, he is to have a good Harquebuz, hanging on a Belt, with a swivel, and serviceable Pistols, as is set forth in the Horse service by Act of Parliament for the service of the Militia, but rather somewhat larger, and a good cutting sword; His Horse should be somewhat better than the Militia Horses, as is set forth in the said Statute, with a strong Sadle, and bitt; and his bridle to be made with a chain that the cutting thereof may be prevented.

4. **Carabiniers** are to be armed defensive as the Harquebuziers, their Horses may be somwhat lesser, but for the offensive Armes instead of the Harquebuz, a good Carabine, hanging on a belt with a swivel, by the ring of the Carabine; but for Pistols and Swords, they must be according to the Act of Parliament for the Arming of a Militia Trooper, as in the said Act more at large appeareth.

The service of them in execution is not to be disputed; the Experienced Souldier can testifie enough of the singular benefit they are of in service; although it is not regarded in some places in the Country, I believe it is not their Judgements, but rather their unwillingness to put themselves (the rich men of the Country) to such a charge, and not to walk one step further than the bare words of the Act of Parliament will impower them.

I hope when his Grace the Duke of *Somersett* shall appear in the head of the Militia of the County of *Somersett* all defaults of Men, Horses and Armes will then be most regularly amended: And then the Souldrie in general and the Horse in particular, being made compleat Carabiniers, the men and horses to be one and the same, kept, preserved, managed, and made fit for service, his Majesty may the better trust to his Militia, who may be also capable of doing him and their Country service. Wounds are never feared by them, who are well horsed, well armed, and well exercised. I crave pardon of the Ingenious Reader if I digressively propound a question or two, and I wish the guilty would answer them by their good examples in better perfomances hereafter.

How many of those Gentlemen that should find Horses for his Majesty in the service of the Militia, will send no other, but such as are common for all uses? Instead of keeping them in their stables, well meating, and managing of them fit for service, they'l send them long journies, set them to plough, or other carriages and draughts, not regarding how suddainly they may be called for service.

How many send in their Armes restie and unfixed, not fit for service? some have sent base pads, ordinary hackney sadles; others for covetousness have sent their servants with snafle bridles; How many are there that borrow Horses and Armes one of another?

And I am truly sorry to see some sufficient Gentlemen that have taken so much paines to ride for to ease themselves, or to be freed from reasonable assessments upon them. I wish some could clear themselves that command us, whose Horses ought to be the first that should apear, and best equipt, from being the worst and last, nay not at all to some Musters; for this the Country murmurs at: And how can our returns of defaults be executed against the Criminal, when Justice it self is guilty of the same errors? It is the good examples of our Superiours, that should make the Inferiour tremble to do amiss, *&c.* I could wish that all neglects for the compleating of His Majesties Militia might be amended hereafter, according as Authority hath commanded; and for such as must be subject thereunto, they would most willingly be obedient, and to close with their Commanders in any thing that may advance the publique service, and not to be stupidly secure, and basely to undervalue the use of Armes: Let such know that I doe boldly affirme it for a truth to be a symptom of disobedience and disloyalty.

5. **The Dragonier.** Dragoones are but Foot, (to be) on horseback and are so mounted for the expedition of their march, who are to have large leather belts, for the more easie carriage of their Pikes and Musquets, in some extraordinary service, for making good of passes, linening of hedges, and other ambushments: But if you raise any Regiments of Dragoons, and so are to march, and to be in a readi-

ness

ness, for the like expedition; their Musquets are to be somewhat wider in the bore than the Field Musquet, and about two foot and nine inches in length, and Pikes (if allowed) not to be above thirteen foot in length; his Horse must be of a good mettle and nimble, but of a less price and stature.

And in the execution of any service (when commanded) they are to alight, and to every ten souldiers there is one to be allowed to hold their Horses. Some have been of an opinion that he is of such excellent service as that the duty of the Carabinier may be wholy laid aside; whose arguments have been judged frivolous by the judicious in this Art, that I need not trouble you any more with them, but do declare that Musquetiers on horsback to be made Dragooners upon some special service; or that the Dragooner himself may be very usefull for expedition and inclosed Countries, &c.

I have treated of the Souldier, and of arming of him. I humbly insert; Seeing the whole burden lyeth upon the Loyall hearted subject; and the discontented party sit still, grow rich and laugh at it, therefore it hath been the opinion of some Gentlemen, that the discontented party should be armed in the Trained Bands, and made to performe and execute all commands whatever. I am of an other opinion, but shall not presume a determination in this place.

CHAP. IV.

Of Military Signes.

IT is requisite that every Souldier should understand (or learn) all Military signes, and directions; for experience hath taught, that the neglect and errour in the right understanding of Signes, hath brought great inconveniences, and quite overthrown enterprises in hand.

There are three signes used in War { Vocal, Semivocal, A Mute.

1. A vocal Sign is that when a Captain shall so immediatly command, as that every Souldier shall heare him distinctly; or else by some inferiour officer to the ear of the Souldier.

A Semivocal Signe is that which is distinguished by the Trumpet, or other warlike instruments: In which as to the horse service; the Souldier is to take notice of six points of War, which are Commands to the ear by the sound of the Trumpet; And it ought to be performed with care and diligence. Those Commands that are by the Trumpet sounded out to them are as followeth.

The six points of war are { Butte Sella, Mounte Chaballo, A la Standardo, Tucquet, Charga, Auquet.

1. Butte Sella; Or *Boutez-selle*; when sounded is, *Clap on your Sadles*. The Souldier must then make himself ready, and horse with all expedition.

2. Mounte Chavallo; Or *Chevall*; when sounded is, *Mount on Horse-back*. The Souldier then bridles his Horse, leads him forth, and mounts him.

3. A la Standardo; Or *A Standart*; when sounded is, *Repair to your Colours*, or Cornet. Upon this the Souldier must go to his Colours, in order to his march: But when he heareth it sounded in the Field he must retire to them with all Speed.

4. Tucquet; Or, *March*: When this is sounded he is presently to March; in which he is to observe his right-hand man, and to follow after his Leader.

5. Charga; Or, *Charge*: When this is sounded, by and with the examples, or directions of his Commander, the Souldier is to give proof of his valour in the speedy charging of his Enemy.

6. Auquet; Or, *Watch*: When this is sounded at night the Souldier is to repaire to the place for mounting of the Guard for Watch; Or at the morning for dismounting of the Guards.

I have read of another sound called Attende Hoe, for *listening unto*, *A call for summons*, *A Senat for State*; and the like. This when sounded, the Souldier is to hearken unto it, that he may the better be able to perform those Edicts that shall be then commanded.

The third and last Military Signe is

3. A Mute; That is by signes to the eye, as by the Cornets Colours; or other motions by the hand of the Commander, &c. You see there are two principal senses of Advertisements, the Eare and the Eye; the true observation and use of these signes availeth much in Warr: for he that is negligent, in either, may not only lose himself, but be the cause of the loss of many others; so that by being careless herein, Victory it self is often lost: How careful ought every Souldier then to be, that by silence he may the beter hearken to all Commands; that by the Vigilancy of his eye, he may the better observe, every sign that may by given. For *Vegetius* saith, that nothing profiteth more to Victory than to obey the Admonitions of signes.

Vide Chap. 5.

Chap. V.

For the Marching and drawing up of a Troop of Horse.

Every Troop of Horse must be furnished with a Captain, Lieutenant, Cornet, and a Quartermaster, two Trumpeters, a Clark, a Sadler, a Chirurgeon and a Farrier. And every Troop is usually divided into three equal parts; each of which is called a Squadron; and are severally known by the Captain's, Lieutenant's and Cornet's Squadron; acordingly there are three Corporals.

There are as great diversitie of judgements almost as Authors about the placing of some Officers either in their marchings of a single Troop, or being drawn up into a *Battalia*.

Some would have the Captain and one Trumpet in the front; Then the Cornet leading of his Squadron, and the third to be lead by the Eldest Corporal; and the Junior Corporal in the reer, with the Lieutenant who hath the command of a Trumpet with him.

Ward fo. 26.

Markham

Markham varieth something from this and but little, only the two junior Corporals to be extravagant in the March, who are so ordered on purpose to keep the Souldiers in their Ranks and to be orderly in their March: Both *Ward* and *Markham* marcheth six in file, but *Ward* marcheth Five in Rank, and *Markham* Four only: Others again differ in placing of Officers both in March and *Battalia*; as, *Walhawsen* would have the Harquebuzier to March eight in File, and the Cuirasier ten in File. But *Markham* and *Ward* being later Disciplinerс in this Art Military, I shall only insert two platformes accordingly.

Captain

Trumpet Trumpet

Cornet

Markham. h h h h . h h h h . h h h h . h h h h

First Corporal.

h h h h . h h h h . h h h h . h h h h

h h h h . h h h h . h h h h . h h h h

Second Corporal. h h h h . h h h h . h h h h . h h h h

Third Corporal.

h h h h . h h h h . h h h h . h h h h

Fourth Corporal. h h h h . h h h h . h h h h . h h h h

Lieutenant

First Trumpet.

Captain

Second Corporal. Eldest Corporal. Cornet

Ward. h h h h h . h h h h h . h h h h h . h h h h h

h h h h h . h h h h h . h h h h h . h h h h h

h h h h h . h h h h h . h h h h h . h h h h h

h h h h h . h h h h h . h h h h h . h h h h h

h h h h h . h h h h h . h h h h h . h h h h h

h h h h h . h h h h h . h h h h h . h h h h h

Lieutenant. Second Trumpet. Third Corporal.

These of *Markham* and of Captain *Ward* are decyphered six in File; and a File so drawn is distinguished according to their dignity of Place, a Leader, a Follower, two Middlemen, a Follower, and a Bringer up.

The Ancient Dignity of a File.

	Dignity of place.			
1		1	H	Leader.
2		5	h	Follower.
3		4	H	Middle man to the front.
4		3	H	Middle man to the reere.
5		6	h	Follower.
6		2	H	Bringer up.

Cruso exerciseth eight deep, and therefore useless to our mode of fighting; for our Custome is to make the Horse but three in File. I shall not stand to answer the objections on both sides, but shall leave it to the most expert in this Art; I conceive it enough that our late experience hath taught otherwise; And our present discipline being in practice to the Contrary.

Accordingly here shall follow a Troop of threescore Horse marching with each Officer in his respective place, and also the form of a Troop drawn up in a body. And when you march through any City or Town, your Pistols must be loaded, and so fixed, that you may be in a readyness to fire when ever occasion may be offered and commandgiven; having one of your Pistols drawn forth of your Holster, mounting your muzzel, and resting the butt end thereof upon your Thigh.

Observe.

A Troop marching to our present mode.

Two Trumpeters.

Captain.

h h h h h
h h h h h
h h h h h

First Corporal.

h h h h h
h h h h h
h h h h h

Cornet.

h h h h h Third Corp.
h h h h h
h h h h h

Second Corpo.

h h h h h
h h h h h
h h h h h

Lieutenant.

Quartermaster.

A Troop drawn up.

Two Trumpeters.

2d. Corp. **Cornet.** First Corp. **Captain.**

3d. Corp.

h h h h h. h h h h h. h h h h h. h h h h h
h h h h h. h h h h h. h h h h h. h h h h h
h h h h h. h h h h h. h h h h h. h h h h h

Quartermaster. **Lieutenant.**

In

In the March some place the Quartermaster to lead up the Lieutenant's Squadron, and the two other Corporals to be extravagant, that is to view and see each Souldier to keep his place. In private exercises it is not denied but the Quartermaster may lead up the Lieutenant's Squadron; But it is conceived best to place the Quartermaster in the Reere; for it is presupposed that he is or may be to take up Quarters, *&c.*

Chap. VI.

The Exercising of a Troop, as Armed with a Carabine, and Pistol.

THe Horse being in a body to exercise, and to make the Souldier more able to handle his armes, when he shall be called forth to fight; The words of Command shall follow.

Notwithstanding there is but little difference between the words of Command for the Pistol with a Snaphans, and the Carabine; I shall however give them severally.

Although Mounting to Horse is no Posture of Arms, and but a preparative to exercise and Service, I shall presuppose the Souldiers to be dismounted, annd stand ready by their Horses in a body; The word of Command (according to our English mode is) To horse.

Now all being ready to Mount must be careful that his Horse be well girt, *&c.* And as a preparative to Exercise there is another word of Command [Silence] Without there be silence in the body, the Souldier in no wise can distinctly hear, what is commanded by the chief Officer; It is the Souldiers Ear, and care to preserve the body from fractions, and where Silence is not diligently performed, the Souldier doth not only fail in his motions, but the event will be naught, for it is the very footstep to rashness; And it is as *Livius* saith (*Temeritas præterquam quod stulta est etiam infœlix*) not only foolishness, but infortunate.

The words of Command for the Carabine.

All the Carabines being dropt (let fall) and hanging by their Swivells; The Postures are as followeth.

Silence being commanded.

Postures.

1. Handle your Carabine.
2. Mount your Carabine, placing your butt end upon your Thigh. (Some terme this Order; and others against that, because it's proper to the Pike.)
3. Rest your Carabine in your bridle hand.
4. Bend your cock, to half bent.
5. Guard (or secure) your cock.
6. Prime your Pan.
7. Shut your pan, (or fix your hammer.)
8. Sink your Carabine on your left side.
9. Gage your flask.
10. Lade your Carabine.
11. Draw forth your scouring stick (or Rammer.)
12. Shorten your Rammer.
13. Lade with Bullet and Ramm home.

14. With-draw your Rammer, (or scowring stick.)
15. Return your scowring stick.
16. Recover and rest your Carabine in your bridle hand.
17. Fix your Hammer, (or Steel.)
18. Free your Cock.
19. Present your Carabine.

In presenting of the Carabine, he must rest it upon his bridle Arm, placing the butt end to the right side near the shoulder; or at length with his right hand.

20. Give fire.

Note; That the Carabine is to be fired about twelve foot distance, and to be levelled at the knees of your Enemies Horse, because that by the strength of the Powder and motion of the Horse your shot may be at Random.

21. Drop (or let fall) your Carabine.

These Postures may serve for the Harquebuz; but observe, when at any time you make your Approaches towards an Enemy, your Carabine is to be mounted, with the butt end on your thigh, with your hand above the lock; and so when you march through any Town or City; otherwise to be dropt.

Here follow the Commands for the Pistols.

Postures.

1. Uncape your Pistols.
2. Draw forth your Pistols.

This must be performed with the right hand; the left Pistol first, and then to mount the Muzzel.

3. Order your Pistol.

Rest your Pistol a little in your bridle hand, and then immediately take your Pistol near the middle part of it, and place the butt end upon your thigh.

4. Sink or rest your Pistol in your bridle hand.
5. Bend your Cock (or draw up your Cock to half bent.)
6. Secure, or Guard your Cock.
7. Open your Pan.
8. Prime your Pan.
9. Shut your Pan, or, order your Hammer or Steel.
10. Cast about your Pistols.

Which is to be done against your left thigh, with your muzzel upwards in your bridle hand.

11. Gage your Flasks.
12. Lade your Pistols with Powder.

For your more speedy lading of your Pistols, there is lately invented a small powder flask, with a suitable charge; but it is not to be denied but your Cartroaches are very serviceable.

13. Draw forth your Rammer.
14. Shorten your Rammer.
15. Lade with Bullet and ram home.
16. With-draw your Rammer.
17. Shorten your Rammer.
18. Return your Rammer.

19. **Recover your Pistol.**
20. **Fix, or order your Hammer, (or Steel.)**
21. **Free your Cock.**
22. **Bend your Cock, at full bent.**
23. **Present your Pistols.**
24. **Give fire.**

In the firing of your Pistols, you are not to fire directly forwards, to your Enemies horses head, but towards the right hand with the lock of the Pistol upwards.

25. **Return your Pistol**, &c.

The Souldier having fired and returned his Pistol, (if time will permit him so to do) he is to take himself to the use of the sword, (his sword being drawn and placed in his bridle hand, near to the hilt of the sword) and having received it into his weapon hand for service, must place the pummel upon his right thigh, and so to raise his point to his mark, higher or lower, as occasion serveth, and therewith to endeavour to disable his Enemy, either by cutting his Horses bridle, or other his Arms, that he serveth in, which if discreetly managed will prove perilous to them.

And further, it is very requisite that the *Harquebuzier* and *Carabinier* be often exercised to shoot bullets at a mark, that in time they may be approved marks-men: In order to which they are to take special care not to over-charge their peeces with powder (as it is too much an errour in many, endeavouring more for a report, than for execution;) Wherefore there ought not to be in proportion for any peece, but almost half as much the weight in Powder, of the bullet; or, the Diameter and half of the peece is charge enough: And it ought to be the special care of every Commander to see that his Souldiers be served with good powder and well cast bullets; and that their bullets be directly fit to their Carabines and Pistols.

I should now come to shew you what is to be learned by a Souldier, for the better demeaning of himself being joyned in a body. But shall not in this place shew at large what is meant by a File, or Rank; half files or half ranks; front, flanks, or reer; because it will spend too much time, and our late unhappy differences have given some light thereunto: besides there is so much writ of them in several Treatises of the Infantry, that it would be too much trouble here to treat thereupon.

Read in the exercise of the foot, pag.

Chap. VII.

Of Distance.

Every Troop consisteth of Ranks and Files.

Note, That in drawing up of a Troop it must be performed by files (not by Ranks) and by squadrons; as *Chap.* 5.

In Order to distance, I must briefly declare what a File and a Rank is.

A File is a sequent Number certain, standing head to crupper in a straight line from the Front to the Reer; and according to our Mode of Discipline consisteth of three Persons.

See Foot, Ch. 3.

1	h
2	h
3	h

A Rank is a Row of men uncertain in Number; Pouldron to Pouldron; even in breaſt, be they more or leſs, according to the quantity of Souldiers, as it falls out, to make a Rank.

h h h h h. h h h h h. h h h h h. &c.

There are to be obſerved two ſorts of diſtances, or orders in File and Rank.

Viz. { Cloſe & Open } Order.

Cloſe Order in Files is three foot, or as occaſion ſerveth, cloſing knee to knee: Open Order in files is ſix foot; Cloſe Order in Ranks is three foot, or as occaſion ſerveth cloſing to the Horſes crupper: Open Order in Ranks is ſix foot.

And herein you muſt further know, that there is a difference between the manner of taking the diſtance, of the Cavalry and the Infantry: In the Foot the diſtance is taken from the Souldiers body; which cannot be underſtood in this place, but only of ſpace of ground between Horſe and Horſe.

Chap. VIII.

Of Motions.

There be four kind of Motions, { Facings, Doublings, Counter-marches, Wheelings.

But ſome of theſe being not of uſe to our preſent mode of Diſcipline; therefore I ſhall treat no more of them, but what may be uſeful.

1. Facings are uſed to make the Company perfect, and to be ſuddainly prepared for a Charge, on either Flank or Reer.

With 10. 8. *and* 6. *in depth.*

2. Doublings, There hath been uſed in the Horſe ſervice theſe following, as

1. As to ſtrengthen the Front.

1. Doublings of Ranks.
2. Doublings of half Files.
3. Doubling of the Front by bringers up.

There were uſed to ſtrengthen the Flanks

4. Doublings of Files.
5. Doublings of half Ranks.

The three firſt as to our Mode of Exerciſe may be wholly laid aſide, in regard they cannot be performed, the Troop being but three in depth.

It is conceived the other two may be neceſſary; either for Exerciſe ſake, or in regard of ſome ſuddain Onſet, on the Flanks, thereby to ſtrengthen them; but I otherwiſe think this may be prevented by a ſpeedy wheeling.

3. For Counter-marches, which is but the reducement of File-Leaders into the place of bringers up, or one flank into the place of another; which is more proper for the foot ſervice, than uſeful in the exerciſe of the Horſe: yet becauſe ſome have uſed it in their exerciſe; therefore I ſhall demonſtrate one Counter-march by Figure in his place.

4. For Wheelings; They are of moſt excellent uſe in the ſervice of the Horſe, and ought

ought to be very carefully exercised by every Commander; they serve in some respect to execute what is to be performed by Counter-marches; which is to bring the Frontiers, who are always supposed to consist of the ablest men, thereby to be ready to receive the Charge of the Enemy in either Flank or Reer; which by Counter-marches you cannot do.

Accordingly the Motions shall follow; that the untutoured Souldier may the better apprehend them; It shall be represented by the Letter h.

Front.

The left Flank

h h h h h . h h h h h . h h h h h . h h h h h
h h h h h . h h h h h . h h h h h . h h h h h
h h h h h . h h h h h . h h h h h . h h h h h

Right Flank

Reer.

All Motions are to be done intirely, at one and the same time: for in our Military Exercises they are the very life of an Army; and the only means being truly performed that giveth Victory; without which all preparations of Forces are in vain, and avail nothing in the field to the end for which they were levied: And this among experienced Souldiers is of inestimable reputation.

1. To the Right Hand.

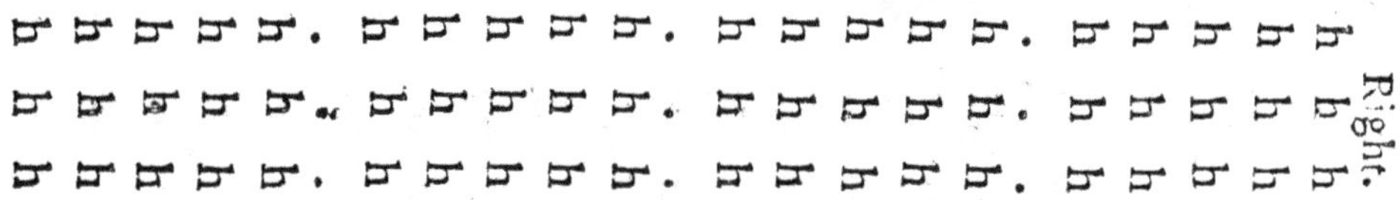

h h h h h . h h h h h . h h h h h . h h h h h
h h h h h . h h h h h . h h h h h . h h h h h
h h h h h . h h h h h . h h h h h . h h h h h

Right.

Note, That in all Motions, before a second be commanded (I mean in all single Motions) the body must be reduced to his first proper form.

To Reduce them command { **To the left,** or **To your Leader,** or **As you were.** }

2. To the Left Hand.

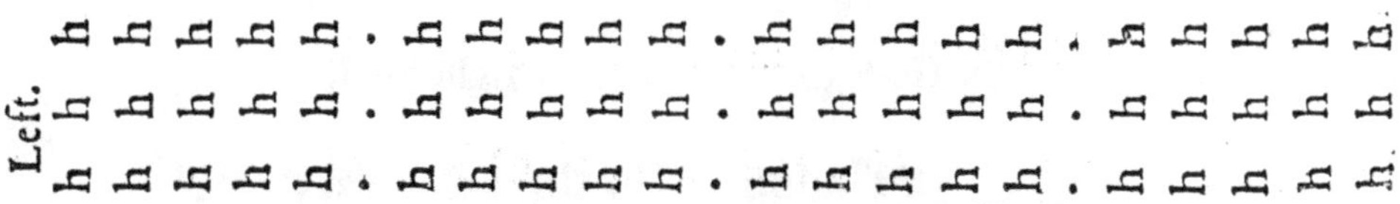

Left.

h h h h h . h h h h h . h h h h h . h h h h h
h h h h h . h h h h h . h h h h h . h h h h h
h h h h h . h h h h h . h h h h h . h h h h h

To reduce them command { **To the Right,** or **To your Leader,** or **As you were.** }

3. **To the right hand about.**
4. **To the left hand about.**

This is by turning to the left hand until their Faces front the Reer.

The proper Front.

q q q q q . q q q q q . q q q q q . q q q q q

q q q q q . q q q q q . q q q q q . q q q q q

q q q q q . q q q q q . q q q q q . q q q q q

Reer.

To reduce them. **To the right hand about.**

5. **Ranks open forward to your double distance.**

h h h h h . h h h h h . h h h h h . h h h h h

h h h h h . h h h h h . h h h h h . h h h h h

h h h h h . h h h h h . h h h h h . h h h h h

6. **Files to the right double.**
7. **Files to the left double.**

20 19 18 17 16 15 14 13 12 11 10 9 8 7 6 5 4 3 2 1

h o h o h o h o h o h o h o h o h o h o

h h h h h h h h h h

h o h o h o h o h o h o h o h o h o h o

h h h h h h h h h h

h o h o h o h o h o h o h o h o h o h o

h h h h h h h h h h

It is most convenient for the Horse to move from the right hand.

To reduce them. { **Ranks to the right double,** or **Files rank as you were.** }

8. **Files to the right hand Counter-march.**
9. **Files to the left hand Counter-march.**

Front.

Front.

. . . .
ч ч ч ч ч ч ч ч ч ч ч ч ч ч ч ч ч ч ч ч
h h h h h h h h h h h h h h h h h h h h
. . . .
h h h h h h h h h h h h h h h h h h h h
. . . .

Foot pa.60.

Reer.

To perform this *Direct*, That all the file Leaders move their Horses intirely a little forwards, and so likewise turning off to the left hand, they march even in rank down to the Reer; and none of the rest to turn off until he come to his Leaders ground.

To Reduce them. **Counter-march to the left.**

As this is for the maintaining of the same Ground, so there may be a Counter-march for the gaining of Ground; but I conceive them wholly useless but where you have not ground to make your *Wheels*: Therefore not knowing what necessity may force us unto, it is convenient the Souldier should be sometimes exercised therein.

Note, That in your Counter-marches for gaining of ground, the Souldier is to turn off the ground his Horse stands upon, and so passing through each is to follow his Leader.

10. **Ranks close forwards.**

h h h h h . h h h h h . h h h h h . h h h h h
h h h h h . h h h h h . h h h h h . h h h h h
h h h h h . h h h h h . h h h h h . h h h h h

11. **Files close to the left.**

h h h h h . h h h h h . h h h h h . h h h h h
Left. h h h h h . h h h h h . h h h h h . h h h h h
h h h h h . h h h h h . h h h h h . h h h h h

12. **Files close to the left to your close Order.**

hhhhh.hhhhh.hhhhh.hhhhh
hhhhh.hhhhh.hhhhh.hhhhh
hhhhh.hhhhh.hhhhh.hhhhh

Observe in closing to the left, the left File is to stand fixt, the next are to move to the left.

13. **Ranks close forward to your close Order.**

hhhhh.hhhhh.hhhhh.hhhhh
hhhhh.hhhhh.hhhhh.hhhhh
hhhhh.hhhhh.hhhhh.hhhhh

In performance of this Command the first Rank is to stand; the second moving, and taking its distance, stands likewise; and so the third.

It cannot be expected that any Wheeling of the Horse should be so exactly per-

formed

formed in ſo little a compaſs as is taken by the foot; therefore every Commander ought diſcreetly to take larger room for the compaſs of his motion, ſo that all his Wheelings may be performed intirely without diſtraction.

Note, That Wheeling to the left for the Horſe is the readieſt way, except you are prevented by ſome hinderances, *&c.*

14. **Wheel to the left hand.**

In this motion the whole body moveth to the left, upon the left hand file-leader as the center

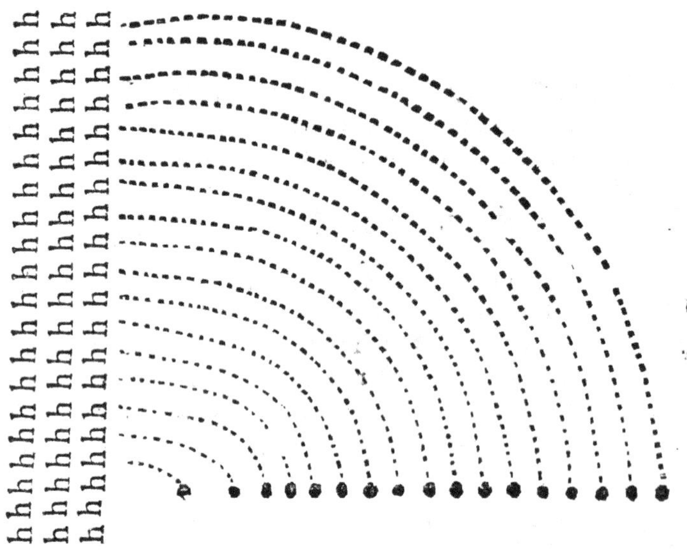

And ſo you may keep wheeling until you have brought them to their proper front: So if you wheel them to the left about, the Reer then will be their accidental Front.

15. **Wheel to the right and left by Diviſion.**

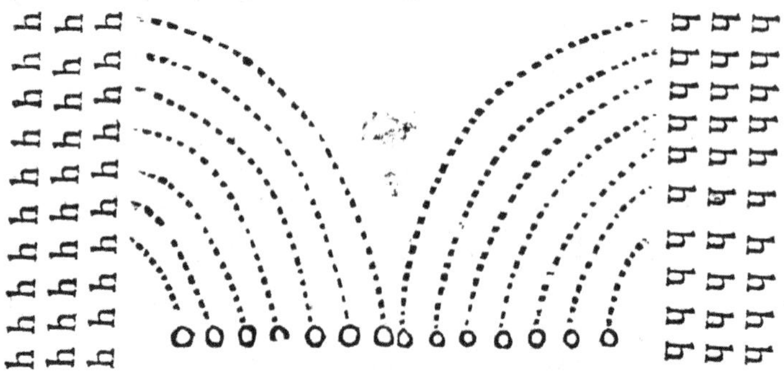

The Wheelings of the accidental Fronts upon both Wings into the proper Front, and cloſe their Diviſions, will reduce them.

16. **Trot large and wheel to the left.**

Wheeling to the right will Reduce them, or by a circular Wheeling of them until they are brought into their proper form.

17. **Trot and wheel to the left about.**

This bringeth the ableſt men to be in the Reer for any ſpeedy On-ſet; and Wheeling to the right about will reduce them, *&c.*

The word Alt *doth ſignifie to make a ſtand, and is derived from the Dutch word* Halt; *which is as we ſay, hold,* &c.

Obſerve that in all motions you make an *Alt*, that the Souldery may ſettle themſelves in their places, both in Rank and File, before you put any freſh Command upon them.

18. **Gallop**

18. **Gallop and wheel to the left.**

19. **Gallop and wheel to the left about.**

To reduce both these is by wheeling to the contrary: All these being performed to reduce them to their first form; **Open first your Ranks, and then your Files**: and in opening of your Ranks, the best way is to open them forwards.

CHAP. IX.

Of Firings.

I Had thoughts to have treated of Encampments and Embattelings, but that being not my work at present I shall pass them by, because it is my business to treat only of the exercise of a single Troop: In the first place I shall set out one firing of *Walhausens*; When your Enemy chargeth you in a full career, you are suddainly to open to the right and left, facing inwards and charge them in the flanks, and when the Enemy is past your body, you are to wheel to the right and left inward, and so charge him with a full career in the Reer; but here you must observe their files to be six, and eight in depth; and so his Figure is represented as followeth.

Cruso fol. 29.

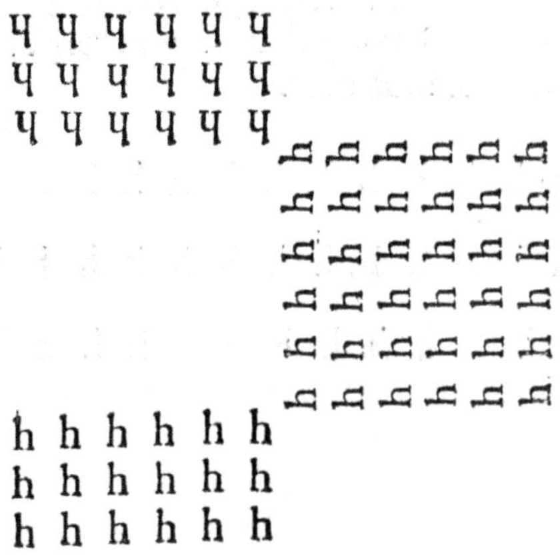

```
ɥ ɥ ɥ ɥ ɥ ɥ
ɥ ɥ ɥ ɥ ɥ ɥ
ɥ ɥ ɥ ɥ ɥ ɥ
            ⊏ ⊏ ⊏ ⊏ ⊏ ⊏
            ⊏ ⊏ ⊏ ⊏ ⊏ ⊏
            ⊏ ⊏ ⊏ ⊏ ⊏ ⊏
            ⊏ ⊏ ⊏ ⊏ ⊏ ⊏
            ⊏ ⊏ ⊏ ⊏ ⊏ ⊏
            ⊏ ⊏ ⊏ ⊏ ⊏ ⊏
h h h h h h
h h h h h h
h h h h h h
```

This he commends very much, for whilst the Enemy is upon his Career, you are but upon your Trot; and then opening to the right and left, either he must run through, and do but little execution, or else *Alt* in his career, and so disorders himself, which is advantageous to you. But I am of another opinion as to our Mode of fighting, being but three in depth; we must rather sink than suffer any Voluntary Breach.

This he speaks of Cuirassiers.

The same Author would have our *Harquebuziers* to give fire by Files, either right or left, advancing before the Body in a full career towards the Enemy; but many do wholly reject it, as being dangerous in Field service.

But now for the private exercise of a single Troop, which may be necessary to bring the Souldier to a more ready and complete use of his Arms, I shall demonstrate of Files firing in the Front and Reer, and then of firing by Ranks. And first of Files firing in the Front.

h h h . h h h

1 2 3 . 3 2 1

1. *Files firing in the Front.*

1 o o h h h h h h h h h h h h h h h h o o 1
2 o o h h h h h h h h h h h h h h h h o o 2
3 o o h h h h h h h h h h h h h h h h o o 3
h h
h h
h h

The right hand File and the left hand File March some distance before the head of the Troop, and Rank themselves to the right and left inward, and so *Present* and *Give fire*; which being performed, let them wheel off to the right and left outwards into the Reer of their first Station, and so set themselves in their respective places even with the remainder of the Body, leaving distance for every Rank to march into his proper place, after they have once fired over.

2. *Files firing in the Reer.*

o h h h h h h h h h h h h h h h h h h o
o h h h h h h h h h h h h h h h h h h o
o h h h h h h h h h h h h h h h h h h o

ı ᄅ Ɛ · Ɛ ᄅ ı

ɥ ɥ ɥ · ɥ ɥ ɥ

When they have thus fired they are immediately to fall off to the right and left, and March forth into their places. As you observe in each firing both the Files do rank themselves and then fire: Now a further exercise you may Command for each File to face in opposition, and fire each to the other.

Firing in the Front, & firing in the Reer.

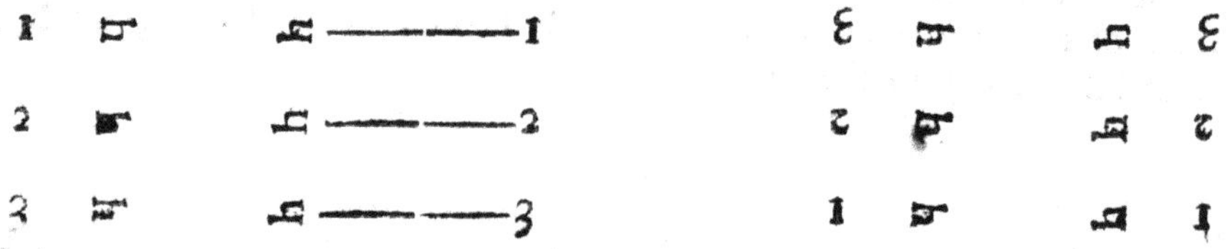

1 ——— 1 Ɛ Ɛ
2 ——— 2 ᄅ ᄅ
3 ——— 3 1 1

I

I shall now demonstrate one platforme of firing by Rank.

h h h h h h h h h h h h h h h h h h h h
20 1

h h h h h h h h h h h h h h h h h h h h. 2

h h h h h h h h h h h h h h h h h h h h. 3

20. h 19 1

But in firing by Rank, observe the first Rank may advance upon a larg Trot Gallop, or Carrere, as Command is given between thirty or fourty paces from the Body. The first Rank having fired wheels off to the left (if occasion will permit) and falls into the Reer; and immediatly upon the wheeling off of the first Rank, the second advanceth according to Command and fireth, and so the third.

You may fire also by divisions which is of singular use in the exercise of Horse; either by firing by single divisions both in Front and Reer, or in opposition both in Front and Reer also, as in firing of the Files before mentioned; so that I need not trouble you with any platformes of them.

After that these firings have been performed and the Souldier is grown expert in the handling of his Arms, and well managing of his Horse; there is one thing that ought not to be forgot by any Commander, which is of most excellent use; That is, for the Souldier to be well exercised, both with his Carabine and Pistol to shoote with Bullet at Marks; which if it be not well exercised and taught, it will be to little purpose as to the Executive part of this Art.

So it ought to be the care of every Chief Officer to exercise those Troops under his Command, sometimes, as occasion may serve, in a Regimental way; leaving sufficient distances betwen each Troop, that each other may be relieved orderly; and so to retreat in due order, to avoid Coufusion.

CHAP. X.

The Conclusion.

BEfore I conclude these few spent hours about the Exercise of the Horse, and that my demonstrating of them but three in depth; I hear many brave Souldiers (but old ones) to make some objections against me. As first, in medling with that which is of too high a concern for me.

My answer to that is breifly; That those that have writ Books of this Art, although they have been gallant Souldiers if they had been in Command now, and of late years to have seen what have been performed in the Executive part of the Horse service, they would correct their Judgements, and amend their Mode of Exercise, finding in it much error, and serviceable for nought, but to prolong Execution; as if all experienced *genus*'s in this Art should be tyed up to the *Low Country* services: And what I have done is but my duty if accepted, else for my own private use, also for my friends and relations that come after me; And because there ought to be a great deal of care had in a work of this nature, I leave the correction hereof to the better Learned and more Experienced in this Military Art.

And for the drawing of the Horse but three in File; I say, If the *Grecian* Writers were alive, and some of our Modern Writers that have Commented upon them and made Collectives out of them, which they have published for authentick Maximes in this Art, would now much admire to see our Mode of Exercise so changed for the better.

64 in a Troop. When as our late *Cruso* in his Military instructions in his platformes of Exercise demonstrates then Eight in depth, and Eight in rank: And Captain *Ward* in his Drilling and exercise of Horse is six in File and twenty in Rank, and alleadgeth it for the best, and is taken out of *Polibius*, General of the *Achæans* Horse: *Leo* writeth almost the same; *Leo Ch.7.Sect. 81, Ch.14. Sect. 78. 108, 109.* That if there be many horse to be exercised, they are to be ordered ten in File, and if but few no more but five, giving this reason; That if the Body be but shallow, the Body will be so weak, that it is subject it self to fraction: Then *Livie* verifieth that of *Leo*, and saith the Souldiers had then Speares of four and twenty foot in Length, which was to match the Pikes of the Infantry: But in some process of time as History makes it appear, the *Macedonians* found great inconveniency in the length of those Spears, and made some of them to be fifteen foot in length; and being then at that length determined that five Horse in depth was too many, as to be offensive to their Enemies: but notwithstanding these results endeavoured to make their *Battalias* seem to be square, and for their better advantage in shew, order ten in Rank and five in File to every Troop of Horse; And these depths were only in those dayes used when the Horse fought only with Spears, and Guns not at all used.

Now if they had the use of Guns so much as we, and should fire in Ranks, five, six, eight or ten in depth (and our mode of fighting being but three in File) their exercise would be so long in the performance thereof, that it would not only be tedious but hazzardous to us; for of late years it hath been experienced, and seldome known any Troops to stand it out, as may be thought that time, in competition for victory: for we know that the ordering of our Horse, in making a large Front, as occasion and ground will give leave, and thereby over-winging our Enemies *Battalia*, hath proved Victorious.

And whereas they alleadge when they are six and eight in File, they can make their body to shew powerful against their Enemy by commanding them to double their Fronts by their Middle-men (or half-file-leaders) and can if occasion serve take away a party in the reer, and fire the Enemy in their Flank, or Flanks, &c. But this I conceive to be dangerous and of ill consequence: for when we are settled in *Battalia* three deep, we are then fixed for service, and need not be troubled in doubling of the Front, thereby we are free from distraction, and other disturbances which are most incident by suddain motions to the breaking of Ranks and the like, which contrarywise is with us; for our fighting is not by wheeling off as formerly, but by charging at Pistols length, and so to charge through; every man betaking himself to his Sword; or otherwise as occasion shall serve: For when we assault our Enemy with our Carabines, and if time will permit it with one Pistol, what need have we of such tedious firing by Files or by Ranks, which the experienced Souldier thinks useless; for when our Horse are in a readiness for execution, they must fire intire, which I conceive to be most offensive: except the Enemy retreates, and wheels off, there will be but little use of a second Pistol. *I shewed those firings only for exercise sake.*

Tacticks of Ælian, 107. There was also among the *Grecians* used divers formes of *Battalia's*, called *Rombes* of Horse, and a wedge of Horse.

The

The *Rombes* were according to these Figures.

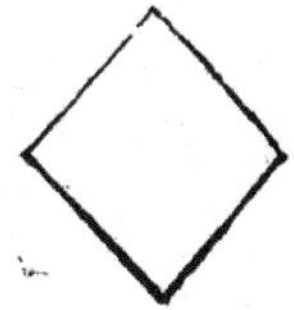
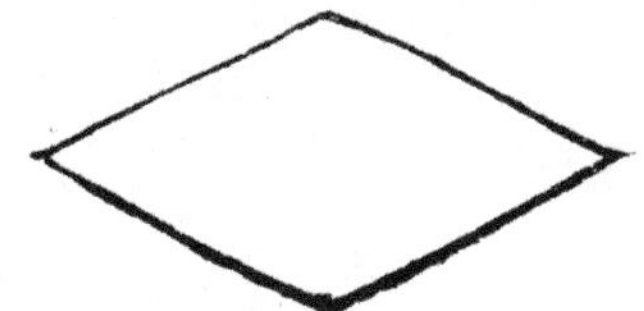

Some were made of Files and Ranks, some neither filing nor ranking, others rankiug but not filing; as Captain *Ward* hath set it out at large. Likewise in those dayes they used the Wedge, which they accounted to be of more singular service than the *Rombes*, and is thus described.

But neither of these being used in our Exercise and Mode of fighting, I shall give you *Euclid's* definition of a *Rombe. That a Rombe is a square figure that hath the sides equall, but the Angles not right, two of them become sharp and two of them blunt*, &c.

Thus I have passed over the several formes of the Exercise of the Horse, briefly, both in their facings and *Battalia's*: and I shall conclude these Collectives of the Cavalrie, as is needfull for the Exercise of a Country Troop; it being but one part as an Introduction to *Military Art.*

I need not plead any thing for this Art; In it selfe it is commendable. Empiredoms, Kingdomes, Nations, Princes and People can testifie enough: no Nation can subsist without experience in it.

It being asked the question; What part of the world brought forth the most Valiant men for War? Answer was made they were found to be in all places, where youth was bred up in the shame of Vice, and had audacity to undergo any Peril for Vertues sake. *Ælians Tacticks.* 38.

The *Lacedemonians* were accounted the most valiant People of *Greece*; History will tell you the reason: Therefore to conclude; None are born Souldiers, one may have an Inclination to War more than an other, but experience cometh not without Industry; and pardon me if I boldly affirme, that the *English* Nation are a Warlike Nation; which if we should neglect our duties herein, the Commander to be industrious, and the Souldier diligent, we shall make our selves a by word, (or scorn) to other Nations: And our Gracious Soveraign at a loss in his designes, and expectations: The more we ingrave this Art in our minds, the more courage we shall have, and the better enabled to fight for, and pray,

God save the King.

I cannot but give you the saying of *M. T. Cicero*, in Commendation of this Art, above any other Art whatsoever. *Rei Militaris virtus, præstat cæteris virtutibus*, and further saith after many other reasons to prove the same; That all other Arts do rest in safety under the Banners of this

Art Military.

THE ART OF DRILLING

Or New Mode of

EXERCISING A Foot-Company.

BEING

Collective Instructions Methodically composed, with their several Figures, for the young Souldier.

By Capt. *Thomas Venn.*

TO THE

Honourable RALPH STAWEL

ESQUIRE,

One of the Deputy Lieutenants of the County of SOMERSET, *and Colonel of a Regiment of Foot in the same.*

S it hath been your Pleasure to accept of the Command of a Regiment of Foot, so it is your design to have it complete, for Officers, Men (and Arms) that they should be well disciplin'd in *Military Art*; and being commanded to serve you in the same, I thought it my duty to present to your view some Collections and other Observations in the *Art Military*, for the Exercise of the Foot: and I am confident of your Honours care to see what ever is, or may be amiss in your Regiment, to be completed, not only in the certainty

of your men, but also for some certain days to be allotted over and above two or three days Musters, (that are only for the Muster-masters due,) for your Commanders to be impowred for to appoint some private Exercisings, for the better fitting and preparing of your souldiers for publick services: To which end I may presume to say, that what I have presented you with, is none of the least or worst parts of Military Order; which if it passeth my Countries acceptance, by your favourable countenancing of it, I may give it a Supplement to make it completer, not destroying my Title, as he who did supplement Mr *Elton's* complete Body: Yet I would not have the *Eltonist* take it amiss, that most of our Worthy *Cruso's* Works are *Verbatim* supplemented to his complete Body of *Art Military* to make it complete, *&c.*

Sir, I have not Embellished this with curiosity of Language, but rendered it for the meanest capacity, that none may be wanting in the Rudiments of Military Discipline; which diligently look'd into, will make the younger sons of *Mars* the better able to perform their Duty when ever his Majesty shall call for it. And now most *Noble Sir*, True Heir of Honour and Vertue; your Pardon for my boldness, and your favourable construction of my weak endeavours, commands me to subscribe an obligement by the title of

SIR,

Your faithful and

Obedient Captain,

T. V.

Verſes.

FOr your experience in this Art of War,
With ſilence hear what your Inſtructions are.
Perform your Poſtures with a manly grace,
Obſerve your diſtances, and learn to face
To right, and left about, and as you were,
By Diviſion, Intire and Anguler;
Then to your doublings of your depth and length,
When you perceive your Army wanteth ſtrength;
Inverting Files, converting of your Ranks,
Brings ableſt men in Front, or Reer, or Flanks:
Your Counter-marches, you muſt next perform
(Of dangerous uſe in fight in field, or ſtorm)
The Chorean *and* Lacedemonian,
And the faining Macedonian:
Then laſt of all your motions, learn to wheel,
Which doth conclude this Martial Art *to Drill.*
Wherein, were all our Trained Bands well skil'd,
They'd leave their Ground, to march into the Field;
And not be ſcar'd and frighted with Alarms,
For want of uſe in Handling of their Arms;
Which Bingham, Hexham, Barriff, Elton, Ward,
And many others too (as I have heard)
Beſides my ſelf, who now have written part,
That from us all, you may learn all this Art:

I 2 *And*

And were I worthy, humbly ſhould adviſe
Our Lord Lieutenant, and their Deputies,
To charge their Muſter-maſter, when they view
Defaults of Arms, contempt of Perſons too,
To ſee their Arms to be the Perſons own,
And not then borrow'd, only to be ſhown,
And muster in Perſon, to fight by ſpell
Against our Foes, or Traytors that rebel:
Of whom our Church, or State, can't be afraid
With fixed Arms, and ready men well paid;
Which will Reſtore to England *and its Crown*
The Subjects Honour, and their King's Renown.

Military

Military Obſervations FOR THE EXERCISE OF THE FOOT.

Chap. I.

By way of Introduction.

HAving paſſed ſome few Collectives to the ſervice of the Horſe, I was deſired to do the like for the foot; figuring out each Command, or platforme after the proportion of Six in File, which is according to our late Mode of diſcipline.

There have been many Books writ of this Military Art, in the Exerciſe of the Foot,both ancient andModerne; but of our later writers, I referr our new commiſſion'd Gentlemen to the peruſal of *Bingham*, *Hexham*, *Barriſe* and *Ward*; I would not have *Elton* (although a Parliament Officer) wholly to be laid aſide; for I have received informations of the great Worth and parts of the Gentleman.

To them whoſe experience have been their maſterpiece, I am ſilent; deſiring with all ſubmiſſion rather to learn from ſuch , than preſume to direct.

Thoſe Gentlemen are to be commended that will beſtow time in reading of this Art, but eſpecially ſuch as put in practice what they read; which is the readieſt way to make men fit for the ſervice of their King and Country: For what maketh a man more confidently Couragious, than knowledge?

There are many Gentlemen that are greater Readers of the Wars, than Practitioners of the ſame; who have had ſome cavelling diſputes, about the diſcipline thereof; not conſidering the great change that time hath made, and experience hath found out in Martial affaires.

In the reading of the Roman and Grecian Orders, Diſcipline, and Government of their Armies, I had thought to have given you a taſt thereof, but deſerving a better Pen than mine to ſet forth the Gallantry of them, I ſhall be ſilent: And yet if it were poſſible to renew them, it would never work the like effect, as it did againſt their Enemies; One great cauſe thereof is ſuppoſed, that they made better pay-men in thoſe dayes; Vice was ſeverely puniſhed, Vertue moſt bountifully rewarded: and when the Wars were ended, ſuch as deſerved well, were both regarded and rewarded; or elſe remained inrolled in penſionary pay; ſo by that meanes the Exerciſe of Armes continued. It is to be obſerved that where Payment and Reward ceaſe, there Diſcipline and good Order ceaſeth alſo.

As for the Exerciſe of Armes belonging to the Infantry, it is the part of the young Souldier to learn and practiſe, in the firſt place, the Poſtures, and well handling of Armes: Which I may term to be the ſingle Accidence of this Art, before he enters his Syntaxis: and it muſt be done by endeavouring to ſet ſome time apart for the exerciſe thereof.

There have been many that have not only diſputed, but have writ againſt the many Poſtures now uſed; but being ſhamefully confuted by our Moderne Writers I ſhall be ſilent; and proceede to thoſe *Poſtures* belonging to ſuch Armes that are now in uſe in the Country, which are far ſhort of what is compleat in Exerciſe in the Cities of *London* and *Weſtminſter*, and therein of thoſe Honourable Societies of the Artillery and Military Gardens, and alſo now of late (The Triple) with out *Criplegate*.

Chap. II.

Of the poſtures of the Pike and Muſquet.

Before I give you the poſtures of them both, I ſhall give you a brief definition of a *Poſture*.

A Poſture *is a mode or Garb that we are fixed unto, in the well handling of our Armes: In which there are motions attendant unto the ſame for the better grace.*

Preſuppoſing your company to be in the Field and drawn up in a ready way for Exerciſe, then the beſt way, is to Exerciſe them apart, by drawing of the body of Pikes from their Muſquets; that each may be Exerciſed in their particular *Poſtures* by themſelves.

Only there are ſome Poſtures of the Pike and Muſquet which are anſwerable to each other by conformity; which ought to be performed in a Body, or upon a March, as occaſion ſerveth: as for Example.

In Marching, All are to be ſhouldred; In Trooping, or in any other Motion, the Pikes are to be advanced, and the Muſquets poyſed: In Porting of the Pike, the Muſquet to be reſted; In Trailing of the Pike, the Muſquet to be reverſed; which is the Funeral Poſture: When the Pike is Cheek'd, the Muſquet is to be reſted at the Sentinel Poſture; when the Muſquet is preſented to fire, the Pike is to be charged; And when the Pike is Ordered, moſt commonly, (eſpecially in a ſtand or for Exerciſe) the butt end of the Muſquet is to be ſet to the Ground *&c.*

It is moſt proper for the Captain to Exerciſe the Pikes himſelf: I do not deny but he may Exerciſe both; as he ought ſometimes to do: and the Enſign and Lieutenant

nant are not to be negligent herein when they are commanded, or in the absence of their superior Officer.

The next for the Exercise of the Pike, in point of Antiquity and Honour, the Gentleman of the Pikes craveth the precedency.

I have declared in the Exercise of the Horse, what an excellent Vertue, *Silence* is; which ought in the first place to be commanded, and most diligently observed.

The Body of Pikes from their March, and standing all shouldered, Command as followeth.

1. **Order your Pikes, to your { 1. open / 2. close } order.**

This ought to be made use of always upon a stand: And in the daytime it may serve for a Sentinel Posture: And for the abatement of the fury of the Horse, having the butt end of the Pike on the inside of the right foot; Charge then to the Horse, drawing your swords over your left arm, having your Pike in your left hand, you may then receive them by Commanding; either to

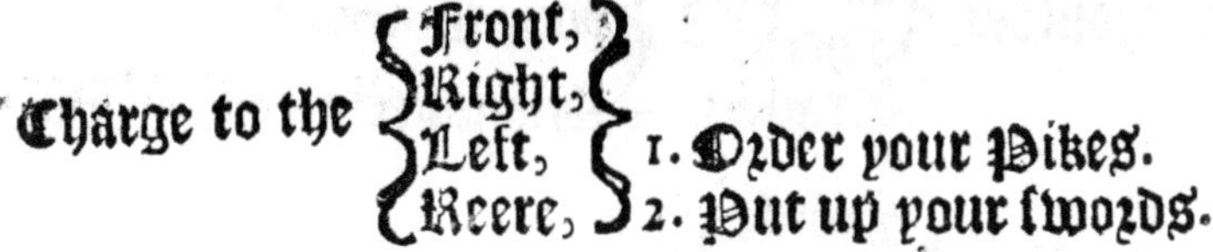

This is only useful upon a stand of Pikes; and by some able Souldiers it is not thought to be the securest charging against the Horse, or of strength to make the greatest resistance in their full Career. Therefore it hath been thought fit to be most convenient, to close your files to your close Order, and Ranks closing forward, and being thus semented (as it were) will be the better able to ward any resistance.

From your Order,
Advance
Shoulder
Port
Comport
Cheeke
Traile
your Pikes.
Order as you were.

From your Order charge to the
Front,
Right,
Left,
Reere.
Order as you were.

2. **Advance your Pikes.**

This is useful upon all occasions when the Drum shall beat a Troop. It is also useful in all motions of Doublings, *&c.* Only remember when they are reduced they put themselves, or be commanded into the same Posture the standing Party was in.

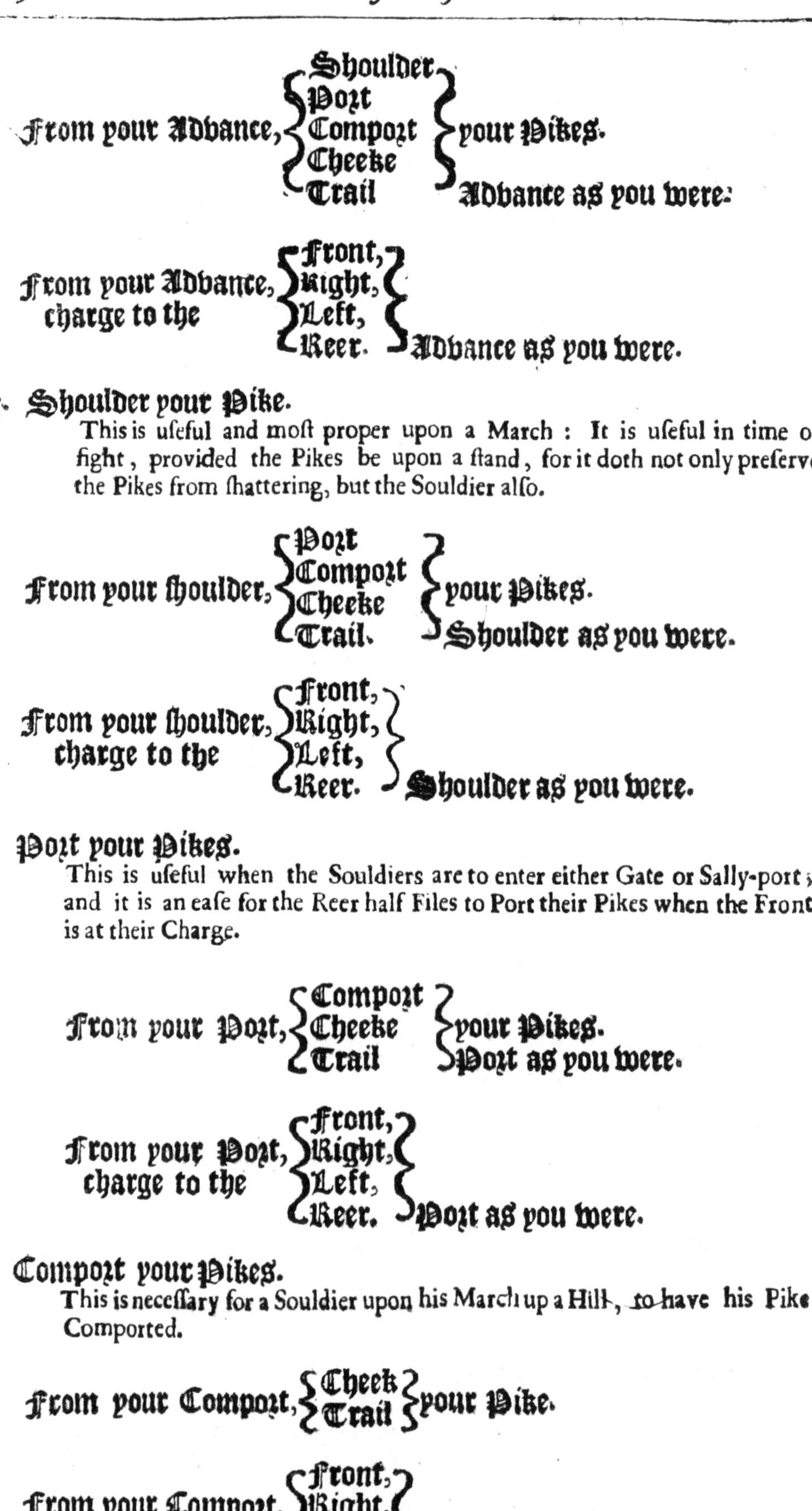

From your Advance, { Shoulder / Port / Comport / Cheeke / Trail } your Pikes.
Advance as you were.

From your Advance, charge to the { Front, / Right, / Left, / Reer. } Advance as you were.

3. **Shoulder your Pike.**

This is useful and most proper upon a March: It is useful in time of fight, provided the Pikes be upon a stand, for it doth not only preserve the Pikes from shattering, but the Souldier also.

From your shoulder, { Port / Comport / Cheeke / Trail. } your Pikes.
Shoulder as you were.

From your shoulder, charge to the { Front, / Right, / Left, / Reer. } Shoulder as you were.

4. **Port your Pikes.**

This is useful when the Souldiers are to enter either Gate or Sally-port; and it is an ease for the Reer half Files to Port their Pikes when the Front is at their Charge.

From your Port, { Comport / Cheeke / Trail } your Pikes.
Port as you were.

From your Port, charge to the { Front, / Right, / Left, / Reer. } Port as you were.

5. **Comport your Pikes.**

This is necessary for a Souldier upon his March up a Hill, to have his Pike Comported.

From your Comport, { Cheek / Trail } your Pike.

From your Comport, charge to the { Front, / Right, / Left, / Reer. } Comport as you were.

6. Cheeke

6. Cheeke your Pikes.
This is useful for the Sentinel Posture.

From your Cheeke, { Trail } your Pikes.
Cheeke as you were.

From your Cheeke, charge to the { Front, Right, Left, Reer. } Cheeke as you were.

7. Trail your Pikes.
This is useful in a Trench to move for security of any breach undiscovered; and is seldom used else, but marching through a Wood, *&c.*

From your Trail, charge to the { Front, Right, Left, Reer. } Trail as you were.

From your Trail, { Order } your Pikes.

8 Lay down your Pikes.

Oberve that if your Pikes be laid down when you begin your exercise, then your Command must be —— { 1. Handle / 2. Raise } your Pike to your { Open order, / Order, / Close order, *&c.* }

You may observe that the Postures of the Pike, some are for conveniency, and ease to the Souldier, as to expedition either in Marchings, or other services commanded; and the several charges serve either for defence or offence; none ought to slight any of these Commands, but to put them into practice; for at some one time or other they may be useful.

Here followeth the Postures of the Musquet, or Calliver.

In which, I do affirm, that the word of Command generally used (Make ready) is no Posture, but a word for brevity presupposing the Souldier to be expert in all, and doth include those postures precedent to that (Present your Musquet) and so from the Presenting of your Musquets the other postures following unto that (Give fire) which is the completement of all the rest of the Commands given.

Therefore for the better handling of Arms no Judicious Practitioner in this Art but will confess, it is better to be Instructed from Posture to Posture for more comely, and swifter execution thereof.

The Musquetteer being shouldered Command

Snap-haunce.

Sloop your Musquets.
Let slip your Musquets.
1. Unshoulder your Musquet, and Poyse.
2. Palm or rest your Musquet.

Match-lock.

I need not here insert every Command, but only add such as are used for the Match-lock, wholly laying aside the rest.

Snap-haunce.	Match-lock.
3. Set the Butt end of your Musquet to the ground.	
4. Lay down your Musquet.	Take your Match from between the fingers of your left hand.
5. Take off your Bandeliers.	
6. Lay down your Bandeliers.	Lay down your Match.
7. Face about to the left & march.	
8. Face about to the right and march to your Arms, (or stand to your Arms.)	
9. Take up } your Bandeliers.	Take up your Match with your right hand.
10. Put on } your Bandeliers.	Return (or place) your Match into your left hand.
11. Take up your Musquet.	
12. Rest (or Palm) your musquet.	Open } your Pan.
13. Secure (or Guard) your cock.	Clear } your Pan.
14. Draw back your hammer, (or steel.)	Prime } your Pan.
15. Clear your pan.	Shut } your Pan.
16. Prime your pan.	
17. Put down your steel, (or hammer.)	
18. Blow, or cast off your loose corn.	
19. Bring or cast your musquet about to your left side.	
Handle your Charger.	
Open your Charger.	
20. Charge with Powder.	
21. Draw forth } your scowring stick.	
22. Shorten } your scowring stick.	
23. Charge with Bullet.	
24. Put your scouring stick into your Musquet.	
25. Ram home your charge.	
26. Withdraw } your scouring stick.	
27. Shorten } your scouring stick.	
28. Return } your scouring stick.	
29. Bring forward your Musquet and poise.	
30. Palm (or rest) your Musquet.	
	Draw forth your Match.
31. Fit your hammer, or steel.	Blow your Coal.
	Cock } your Match.
	Fit } your Match.
32. Free your cock.	Guard your Pan.
33. Bend your cock.	Blow the ash from your Coal.
	Open your Pan.
34. Present your Musquet.	
35. Give fire.	
36. Palm (or rest) your Musquet.	
	Uncock, and return your Match.
37. Clear } your Pan.	
38. Shut } your Pan.	
39. Poyse your Musquet.	

40. Shoulder

40. **Shoulder your Musquet.**

So you are ready for a March; or in the Posture upon the first motion.

That which is called the Saluting Posture, is to be performed from the resting (or palming) of the Musquet; when he shall have an occasion: as a Souldier to salute his Friend, or to the honouring of any other person deserving.

And the Sentinel Posture, is for the Musquet to be in the Palm of the left hand, at his Resting posture: But his Musquet to be charged with Powder and Bullet, his Cock freed, and to be secured with his Thumb, so to be ready to execute his charge, and commands given, *&c.*

There is indeed a word of Command sometimes used, **Reverse your Musquet; which is the marching Funeral Posture**; That is to put the butt end of your Musquet upwards, under your left arm, holding it in your left hand, about the lock of your Musquet. Thus I have finished the Postures of the Musquet or Caliver with a Snaphance, and with a Match-lock without a Rest; for your further inquiry, if there need be, I refer you to Lieutenant *Barriffe* or Captain *Ward.*

If I should forget to say something of the excellency as to the use of the Half-Pike and Musquet, that is now of use in the Artillery Garden; first invented by Lieutenant *Barriffe* and Mr *John Davis* of *London*; whatsoever is performed in the exercise thereof, it is with greater ease than the Rest and Musquet is. *Half-Pike.*

And knowing how far it hath been the care of many Souldiers, by invention to make the Musquetteers, as well defensive as offensive, but none amongst many of their Projects was received like this, all falling to the ground, and this standing as the best, being of most excellent service; for it serveth as a Rest; as a *Pallisado* to defend the Musquetteer from the Horse: When the shot is all spent they may with that Weapon, fall in among the Enemy, and in the pursuit of an Enemy, by reason of the lightness thereof, and their nimbleness in Action, may do great execution; and in Trenches they are good seconds for the Souldiers preservation.

Those Souldiers that are thus Armed are the best to be commanded out upon any Party, because they are the best able to defend themselves and offend their Enemies: And when any hedges are to be lin'd with shot, that the Musquetteers by their forced service become silent, and the ways deep and narrow; then the Half-Pike will be of singular service. *West Country.*

And last of all the Souldier so marching with his Half-Pike and Musquet; It is not only a Grace to the Souldier but a Terrour to the Enemy: Besides this hath been ap-approved of by some of the ablest Souldiers in this Kingdom. If once the Countrey saw the practice of it, and what a strong preservation it is against the incursion of the Horse, and in all other respects rather an advantage to the Souldier than disadvantageous to him; it would be not only esteemed good but carefully put into practice. Vic. *Wimbaldon*, Sir *Tho. Genham.*

As the Musquetteer is secured by the gallant invention of the Half-Pike; any strange eye would think it very unjust that such Numbers of the Pike-men should be slain by the shot, and not able to resist and offend again; I could therefore say much for the Long Bow to be joyned with the Pike, how their showers of Arrows will gaul and terrifie the Horse, wound and hurt the Souldiers both on Horse and Foot; So if this should be duly performed all hands would be fighting, and all in a readiness for self preservation. History is full of the great slaughters and Atchievements in those days, when the Bow was most in use; but because it is laid aside I shall be silent, hoping the practice will never be forgotten. *Bow and Pike.*

CHAP. III.

The Places of Dignities both of Files and Ranks.

IN this Military Age, who would have thought that few or any could be so ignorant of the difference between a File and a Rank; but finding in our Annual Exercises many (Farmor like) Souldiers to be much guilty thereof, I shall speak a a little thereunto; shewing what is required to the making up of a File, and also of a Rank, with the dignity of each as they stand both in File and Rank.

A File. First, Know that a File is a sequent Number of men, standing one behind an other Front to the Reer.

Or from the first which is termed a File-Leader, unto the last which is termed a bringer up, which shall be demonstrated according to our mode of Discipline.

A Ranke. Secondly, A Rank is a Row of men be they more or less, standing or marching, shoulder to shoulder in a direct Line from the right hand to the left, (and from the left to the right) even a breast.

And by the way observe that in all preparations to exercise, Files must be made up first, and being then drawn forth, and the Files joyned together, Ranks are made.

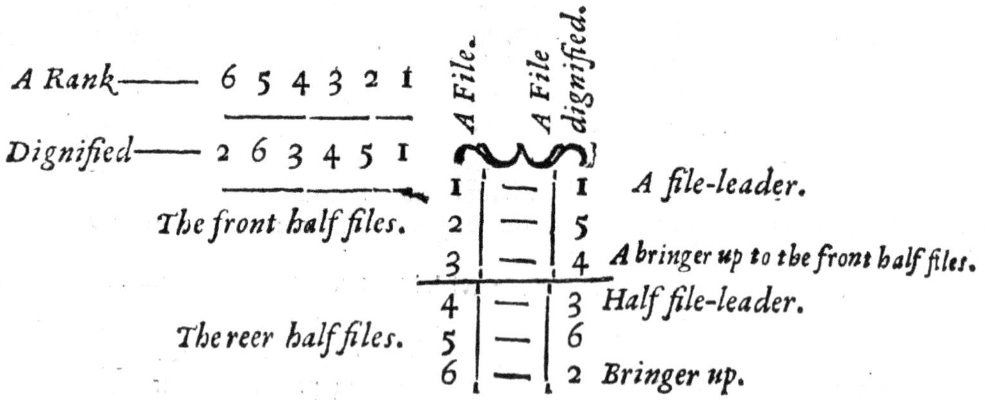

A Rank —— 6 5 4 3 2 1

Dignified —— 2 6 3 4 5 1

	A File.	*A File dignified.*	
The front half files.	1	1	*A file-leader.*
	2	5	
	3	4	*A bringer up to the front half files.*
The reer half files.	4	3	*Half file-leader.*
	5	6	
	6	2	*Bringer up.*

Both which are according to *Barriffe*, *Ward*, and others; but in giving their Dignities to a file of eight deep there are various opinions, yet all endeavouring after a Geometrical proportion; and it is that which Commanders should chiefly follow as near as possibly they can.

And because the Sages of our Times do differ in their Judgments, more in this particular than in any one thing that I know of; I shall set down what Rules I have know or heard, leaving it to the more experienced that can command better.

Here followeth the Rule of *Barriffe*, *Ward*, and others in placing the Dignities, for six, eight, and ten, both in File and Rank.

Dignities

Dignities of Ranks.

Number	10	9	8	7	6	5	4	3	2	1
Place	2	6	10	7	3	4	8	9	5	2
Number	8	7	6	5	4	3	2	1	9	3
Place	2	6	7	3	4	8	5	2	8	4
Number	6	5	4	3	2	1	8	3	4	5
Place	2	6	3	4	5	2	4	4	3	6
					4	3	3	5	7	7
					3	4	7	6	10	8
					6	5	6	7	6	9
					2	6	2	8	2	10
					Place	*Number*	*Place*	*Number*	*Place*	*Number*

Dignities of Files.

I shall here insert those various Opinions of the Dignities of Souldiers eight in File, and so for eight Companies in a Regiment; by all which you may dignifie each Officer in his due place of Honour; either in March, or in a Body: The consideration that there is, or ought to be an answerableness in the Reer to the Front, in the left flank to the right, by an equitable right in their true Dignity, is that which giveth life and being to orderly Discipline; for the worth of one must be answerable to the other in Skill, Valour, and in Number.

This amongst the *Grecians* was antiently put into practice, as you may see at large in the Notes of Captain *Bingham* upon the Tacticks of *Ælian*; and described after this proportion. 2——3 over 5 | 4——1 over 5. Two and three on the left hand, is equal in Number to four and one on the right, each making but five in Number; as it is thus in a little Number, so it may and ought to be made good in a greater.

Barriffe, *&c.* *In Battalia they oppose thus.*

2 6 7 3 | 4 8 5		1	*Colonel*
		5	*Capt.2.*
18	18	8	*Capt.5.*
		4	*Capt.1.*
(36)			
		3	*Major*
	18	7	*Capt.4.*
		6	*Capt.3.*
		2	*L. Col.*

L. Colonel	*Capt. 3.*	*Capt. 4.*	*Major.*
2	6	7	3
4	8	5	1
Capt. 1.	*Capt. 5.*	*Capt. 2.*	*Colonel*

The equality in this opposition is thus; As (1) and (4) makes five in the Colonels Division, so (3) and (2) in the Lieutenant Colonels Division makes five also: Then as in the first (5) and (8) makes thirteen; so the second (7) and (6) is thirteen, which is an equal opposition.

As inform'd Mr. Elton'*s Rule.* A Second Opinion for the Dignity of eight Companies, is as followeth.

In Battalia they oppose thus.

2 5 8 3 | 4 7 6		1	*Colonel*
		6	*Capt.3.*
18	18	7	*Capt.4.*
		4	*Capt.1.*
(36)			
		3	*Major*
	18	8	*Capt.5.*
		5	*Capt. 2.*
		2	*L. Col.*

L. Colonel	*Capt. 2.*	*Capt. 5.*	*Major*
2	5	8	3
4	7	6	1
Capt. 1.	*Capt. 4.*	*Capt. 3.*	*Colonel*

These oppose as the first, and somewhat more in the equality of their Number; as one and six is seven in the right Wing of the Colonels Division, so two and five is equal to that in the right Wing of the Lieutenant Colonels Division; and six and seven is equally thirteen, in the first, as five and eight in the second.

But

But according to the Rules for the Dignity of a File, the second Captain hath lost his place of Honour.

For those of that Opinion who place the second Captain in the Lieutenant Colonels Division, affirm that there may be a Geometrical equality (in length and breadth) in File and Rank; yet in point of Honour according to first Rule in the Colonels Division, the second Captain being placed loseth his Dignity; for if the eldest Captain in priority is placed upon the Head or first Division, Body or stand of Pikes, leading the Colonels Colours, then by the self same Rule of Equity, the second Captain *Numb.* (5) may and ought to be in the head of the Lieutenant Colonels Division, Body or stand of Pikes.

To which I conclude that the second Captain hath as much Honour to bring up the Reer of the Colonels own Division of Pikes when so marched; but if marched (intire) Regimentally, there to bring up the Reer of the whole Body or stand of Pikes is a greater Honour, and the second Captains Dignity.

A third Opinion for the Dignity of eight Companies.

In Battalia they oppose thus.

2 7 6 3 | 4 5 8		1	*Colonel*
		8	*Capt.* 5.
18	18	5	*Capt.* 2.
		4	*Capt.* 1.
(36)			
		3	*Major*
	18	6	*Capt.* 3.
		7	*Capt.* 4.
		2	*L. Col.*

L. Colonel	*Capt.* 4.	*Capt.* 3.	*Major*
2	7	6	3
4	5	8	1
Capt. 1.	*Capt.* 2.	*Capt.* 5.	*Colonel*

This is the most received Opinion of the other two of late years, and the Reasons may be as followeth: First, their opposement is more upon a direct equality than the former, as for example, 1 and 8 stands upon the right Wing of the Colonels Division which maketh 9; now equally to oppose this there is 3 and 6 on the left Wing of the Lieutenant Colonels Division, that maketh 9 also; then upon the Right Wing of the Colonels Division there is 4 and 5 that maketh 9; and to oppose that there is 2 and 7 which is 9 also; all this makes out the justness of this opposement, and in that particular exceeds both the former, for what can be said for the second may be alleadg'd for this third also.

The differences in them as to their opposements may hereby be discerned, and how that all three make equal in numbers, as in half Files and half Ranks, 18 is equal to 18, and in Rank and File making (36.)

Indeed when the Seignior Officers of a Regiment had more Souldiers in their respective Companies, there was then great reason to stand upon an equal opposement; or else one Wing might be too strong for the other.

All this being now laid aside and there being of Souldiers an equality of number in each company, why then should our first rule for the dignity of a File be laid aside for the marching of a Regiment either intire or divisional? In the second Opinion the second Captain is placed in the Lt. Colonel's division; in the third he is placed in the Collonels; although I conceive he ought to be in that Division yet he is there misplaced: for by the same rule in the second and third Opinion, as you place the Collonel in the Dignity of a file leader, the Lieutenant Collonel hath his Dignity in the place of a Bringer up, the Major in the place of the half File leader, the first Captain in the place of the Bringer up to the Front half-files: Thus far all three joyntly go together, and because there is no difference in number of men, but equal in both parties, they need not stand so much upon an equal opposement, but that the second Captain *Numb.* 5. may have his just place of honour immediately next unto his Collonel.

If it were not for this mode of Dignity according unto a File in the marching of a Regiment, and so unto a Rank in a Body, I might as well and better require satisfaction (the number of each Company being equal in Souldiers) why there may not be two field officers in the Collonels Division as well as in the Lieutenant Collonels; which I leave to better judgments.

For the proof of my assertion, as joyning with *Barrife, Ward* and others in apointing the second Captain, whose is the fift place of Honour next to the File leader, or next to the Collonels own company both in Rank and File.

Bar. pa. 17. 1. The File leader ought to be the worthiest because he hath the Command of his File, and marcheth first against the Enemie.

2. The Bringer up ought to be the second place of Honour, because his place of March is in the reer; and is in most danger, should the Enemie charge on that part.

3. The half file leader is the third place of Honcur, because when the Front half files are taken off upon any occasion, he is the leader unless he be commanded to face about.

4. The last man (or Bringer up) of the Front half files is the fourth man in dignity, for so he is when the Reer Division is taken of.

5. The next man to the File leader hath the fift place of honour, for one doubling brings him into the Front.

6. The sixt place of Honour is before the Bringer up, for if the Body be faced about, one doubling brings him into that accidental Front, or keeping of his proper Front by once doubling he becomes bringer up to the File leader.

7. The seventh Dignity of place is his who marcheth next after the half file leader, for when the half files double the Front, or march forth, then one doubling ranks him even with the Front.

8. The eight place of Honour (the File being but eight in depth) is the third from the front, for he may be made a File leader also, although it may be with more trouble, for by countermarching of the Front and Reere into the midst, and then facing to the first Front, and after doubling of Ranks makes him a File leader also.

I desire to speak nothing here to tye up the Ingenious to any particular fancy, when his own reason shall guide him in this Military Discipline, as may not be irregular and contrary to the rules of Art.

Now each Souldier being well exercised in the Postures of the Pike and Musquet, and knowing their Dignity both in File and Rank, will not stand still here, but must be labouring to march farther in this field of Military Discipline, that by the knowledge thereof his undaunted courage might conduct him to some higher worth or place of Dignity.

CHAP.

Chap. IV.

Of the Drum.

I Come in the next place to advise every Souldier to be careful and endeavour to know the several Beates thereof, or else he may often fall short of his Captains Commands.

There are these several Beates to be taken notice of as Military signs, for the Souldier to walk or guide his actions by; and are termed Semivocall signes, as you may see in the Horse service, *pa.9.*

The several Beates or poynts of War, are

1. A Call.
2. A Troope.
3. A March.
4. A Preparative.
5. A Battalia.
6. A Retreit.

Besides these six there are two other Beats of the Drum,

7. A Ta-to. 8. A Revally.

The *Ta-to* is beaten when the Watch is set at the discretion of the Governour; after which in most places or Garrisons of note, there is a Warning piece discharged, so that none are to be out of their houses, without the word is given them, *&c.*

A Revally is beaten in the morning by day light, at which time the subofficers are to take off their out Sentinels. This, when by reason of the great noyse of Guns, men, armes, and Horses, the Commanders voyce for it can neither be heard or obeyed without the beat of the Drum: And the action of the Souldier whether valiant or otherwise is to be guided by it.

And For the better performance hereof it is the Captains duty to teach his Souldiers distinctly the several beats of the Drum, that they may be the better able to perform their respective duties, when ever they shall be so commanded by the Drum.

Chap. V.

Of Distances.

HErein I shall shew you what distance is, and the several sorts of distances: Without distance no motion can be performed: Although distance in it self is not motion; yet there is a motion in that action, that produceth our several distances of place, between man and man, or that space or intervall of ground, either in File, or Rank.

And I may truly assert that the Discipline of a Foot Company, *&c.* consisteth so much in distance, and motion, that there is great necessitie of learning this very principle; for they are not fixed in one station, but are mutually interchanged one with another, as occasion is offered by command, and so are all brought into Order by their distances; for if a perfect form of order be not observed, disorder must necessarily follow; the effect of which produceth confusion.

In our Modern discipline there are these four distances in use.

1. **Close Order.**
2. **Order.**

3. **Open Order.** & 4. **Double distance.**

	which is both in File & rank	
1. **Close Order**		**one foot and half.**
2. **Order**		**three foot.**
3. **Open Order**		**six foot.**
4. **Double distance**		**twelve foot.**

There are several distances to be performed in 1. **March.** 2. **Motion.** 3. **Skirmish.**

1. The distance of marching { between File and File is three foot. between Rank and Rank is six foot.

2. The distance for motion as for doubling of Files, and Ranks, for facings and Countermarches——— } between File and Rank is six foot.

3. Distances for intire doublings and skirmishes between Rank and File is——— } three Foot.

4. Distances for prevention of Cannon shott is { 12 Foot, or 24. Foot, the double double distance.

Note that the close Order is useful {
1. To the Files of Pikes to the charge of Horse.
2. Before you Command any Wheelings.
3. When the Commander is to deliver somewhat to the Souldier that all may hear.

Observe. **Before** you open or close your body by command to Distance to action; let every Captain or chief Officer Command his Souldiers to streighten their Files, and to even their Ranks: In the next place to be silent that thereby they may be attentive to the words of Command,

Which for the several Distances are as followeth.

Commands.	Reducements.
1. Files. 2. Ranks. } to your close Order.	
1. Files open to the right. { 1. To your Order. 2. To your open Order. 3. To your double distance.	1. Files close to the right. { 1. To your open Order. 2. To your Order. 3. To your close Order.
2. Ranks open forward. { 1. To your Order. 2. To your open Order. 3. To your close Order.	2. Ranks open forward. { 1. To your open Order. 2. To your Order. 3. To your close Order.

there might be abreviated into a shorter method but my intents is for plain capacities.

3. Files

3. Files open to the Left.
1. To your Order.
2. To your open Order.
3. To your double distance.

4. Ranks open to the reer, (or) backwards.
1. To your Order.
2. To your open Order.
3. To your double distance

5. Files open to the right and left.
1. To your Order.
2. To your open Order.
3. To your double distance.

6. Ranks open to the right and left.
1. To your Order.
2. To your open Order.
3. To your double distance.

3. Files close to the left.
1. To your open Order.
2. To your Order.
3. To your close Order.

4. Ranks close to the reer. *&c.*
1. To your open Order.
2. To your Order.
3. To your close Order.

5. Files close to the right and left inward, (or) to the midst.
1. To your open Order.
2. To your Order.
3. To your close Order.

6. Ranks close to the right and left inward.
1. To your open Order.
2. To your Order.
3. To your close Order.

These are useful and may be used at the discretion of the Commander.

And for your better performance in the closing and opening of Files and Ranks, take these following Observations.

1. When Files open to the right, the left, hand File must stand fast; every File taking his distance from the File next his left hand.

2. When they open to the left the right hand File stands fast, *&c.*

3. When Ranks open forward, the last rank stands; every rank taking his distance from the rank next behind him.

4. When they open backward, (or to the reer) the first rank stands; *&c.*

5. When Files close to the right, the right hand file stands, the rest close to the right, taking their distance from the right hand file,

6. And if Files close to the left, the left hand file stands; the rest of the Files close to the left, and take their distance, *&c.*

7. When Files close to the right and left, then they close inward, taking their distance from those Files within them, nearest to the midst of the Body.

8. When files close to the right and left by Division, it must be outwards, according to the fift and sixt observation.

9. When Ranks close to the front and reer, then the first and last Ranks stand; the other taking their distance.

10. If Ranks close to the midst then they close towards their two midlemost Ranks.

I have not used the word [Center] in any of these Commands, because it is conceived that the word is more proper to a circle, and not to a square, (or a broader fronted body.)

It is not of absolute necessity that a Commander in the exercise of a private Company shall use all these openings, and closings to those several distances mentioned; but so many of them, as may be thought fit for his present Exercise intended; although it cannot be denied but that they may be useful at some time or other.

CHAP. VI.

Of Marching and Drawing up of a Company.

THe Souldier being informed of the Dignity of Place, together with the several Beats of the Drum; and their respective distances: I shall march a Company of Foot, and draw them up: which Company shall consist of twelve Files; four Files of Pikes, and eight Files of Musqueteers.

But the Deputy Lieutenants for the County of *Sommerset* have allotted some files more to each Company, and it is a rare thing to have them compleat in the Field, so that it hath been too apparent, because there hath not been an equality in Files, their Companies have been wholly unfit for Exercise; but I hope these errors will be better looked into and amended hereafter.

A Company marching.		A Company drawing up.	
	Captain.		Captain.
	m m m m 2d. Ser.		m m m m
Files are to be at their Order, and Ranks at their open Order.	m m m m		m m m m
	D		
	m m m m		m m m m
	m m m m		m m m m
	m m m m		m m m m
	m m m m		m m m m
	Ensign.	Ensign.	
	P P P P	P P P P	
	P P P P	P P P P	
	P P P P	P P P P	
	P P P P	P P P P	
	P P P P	P P P P	
	P P P P	P P P P	
	1. Serjeant.	1. Serjeant.	
	m m m m	m m m m	
	m m m m	m m m m	
	D	D	
	m m m m	m m m m	
	m m m m	m m m m	
	m m m m	m m m m	
	3d.S. m m m m	3d. S.m m m m	
	Lieutenant.	Lieutenant.	

When the Company is drawing up, the Drum is to beat a Troop, the Pikes to be advanced, the Musquets to be poised; and being in a Body are ready for Command.

A

A Company drawn up.

Captain.

					D		E.		D				
2. S.	m	m	m	m	p	p	p	p	m	m	m	m	1. S.
	m	m	m	m	p	p	p	p	m	m	m	m	
	m	m	m	m	p	p	p	p	m	m	m	m	
	m	m	m	m	p	p	p	p	m	m	m	m	
	m	m	m	m	p	p	p	p	m	m	m	m	
3d.S.	m	m	m	m	p	p	p	p	m	m	m	m	

Lieutenant.

A number of Men being thus drawn up, and completed (consisting of Pikes and Musquets) there is in them according to the rules of Art; a Front, a Reer, a right and left Flank; Front half files; Reer half files; Right half ranks, and left half ranks; there is the length and depth of the Battel, and these are extended in their number of men.

Front.

Captain.

E

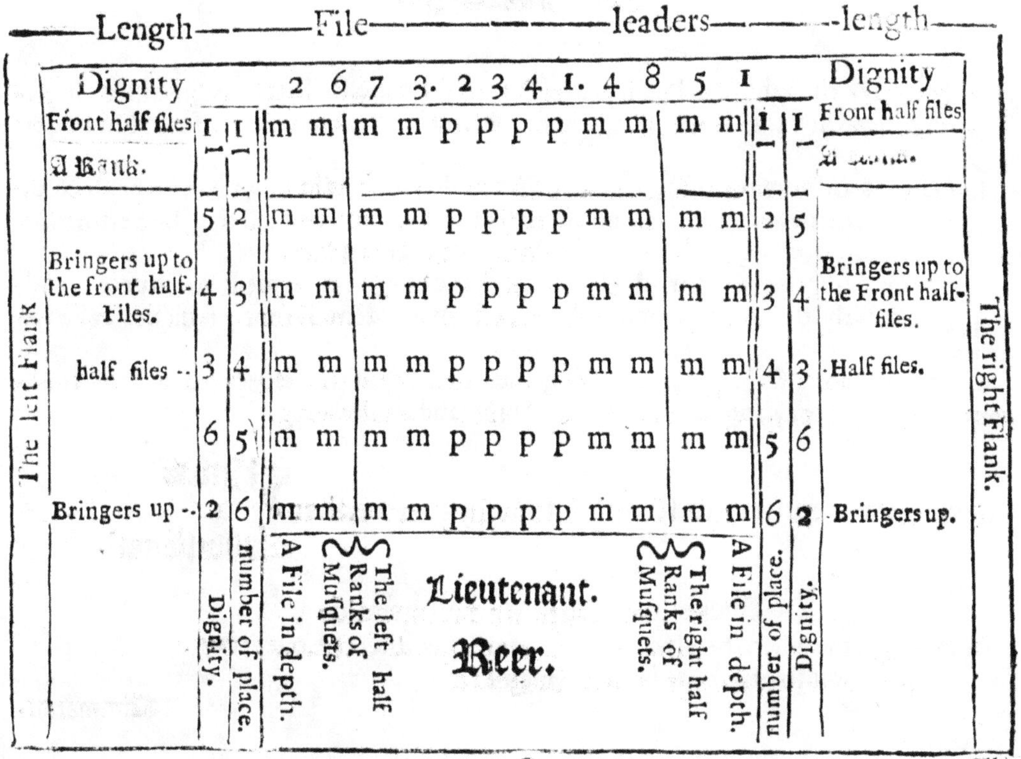

——Length———File——————leaders————length——

The left Flank

Dignity			2	6	7	3.	2	3	4	1.	4	8	5	1			Dignity
Front half files	1	1	m	m	m	m	p	p	p	p	m	m	m	m	1	1	Front half files
A Rank.																	A Rank.
	5	2	m	m	m	m	p	p	p	p	m	m	m	m	2	5	
Bringers up to the front half-Files.	4	3	m	m	m	m	p	p	p	p	m	m	m	m	3	4	Bringers up to the Front half-files.
half files --	3	4	m	m	m	m	p	p	p	p	m	m	m	m	4	3	Half files.
	6	5	m	m	m	m	p	p	p	p	m	m	m	m	5	6	
Bringers up --	2	6	m	m	m	m	p	p	p	p	m	m	m	m	6	2	Bringers up.
	Dignity.	number of place.	A File in depth.	The left half Ranks of Musquets.			Lieutenant. Reer.					The right half Ranks of Musquets.		A File in depth.	number of place.	Dignity.	

The right Flank.

The

The front in this Figure is first of all to be taken notice of: There are in all exercises a proper Front and an accidental Front: the Company being drawn up and standing in a body, with faces to their leader, maketh a proper Front.

Vide Chap. of facings. And the accidental front is as the Cheifetains shall command the face of the whole body: In short the front is where the faces of the Company are directed one way.

The first Rank, or row of men, they are termed File leaders; who have the command of their respective Files, and are to Exercise them severally.

Observe, that from, and with the right hand file leader, to and with the left hand file leader, is the extent of the Front, and is termed the length of the Battel.

And the Souldiers standing severally from and with their File leaders in a sequence to and with their Bringers up are termed Files, or the depth of the Battel.

The Reer of the body is so termed, where ever the back of the Company are turned.

Every File leader hath his bringer up, that by death or other absence, next in point of honour is to succeed them, both in Place and power: The extent and length of the Reer (last rank or bringers up) is the same with the Frontiers.

The right and left Flanks, are the outmost Files upon either hand of the body from the Front to the bringers up.

There is in a body drawn up front half files and Reer half files; the Front half files extend themselves (three in depth) to and with the third Rank; and the Reer half files is the fourth Rank to and with the last, both which have their extents divided in the whole length, and depth of the body.

Half Ranks are from the midst of the Files so taking their length, or bounds to the outmost man or file leader, either upon the right or left hand.

Chap. VI.

Of Facings.

Some have thought that Facings are but of little use, so that a commander might dispence with the Exercise thereof. There being a mistake in such, I must declare,

That facings are very necessary, and of such excellent use, as in no wise to be neglected; for in service, their executions are quicker than other motions, and may be performed when other commands cannot be used both for time and place.

The Body being faced (or the faces of the Body) is termed an aspect, and being particularly turned by command maketh an accidental front, which is called a facing.

So that in short, facing is the turning and altering of the aspect to either hand, Front or Reer, as may appear in the several commands following.

In which we must understand that facings are either { Intire or Divisional.

There are Angular facings also.

1. Intire Facing is when the aspect of the company is directed one way. There are four intire facings, besides Angular.

Command.

Command. Face to the { 1. Right. 2. Left. 3. Right about. 4. Left about.

Each man is to turn upon that foot to which hand the facing is commanded, wheeling the Body to that Aspect. When you face to any hand, you may reduce them to the contrary.

To reduce them, Command: *As you were*: or, *To your Leader*.

Angular, facings are when directed to make their Aspects to the right or left corner men; (that is, to the right or left Angle.) And so if you command to the four corners, it is to face them to their four Angles, which is Divisional.

Command: Face to the { Right / Left } Angle.

To reduce them, Command: *As you were*: or, *To your leader*.

These Angular facings are not so much in use as formerly.

Divisional facings are contrary to the Intire, for they look divers wayes. Which are

Command: Face to the { 1. Right and left. 2. Right and left inward. 3. Four Angles.

To reduce them: *As you were*: or, *To your leader*.

It is necessary that the half files doe many of these commands by themselves, that they may the better understand it, when the body shall come to be subdivided. For *Angular facings*, they are out of use, or not so much in use as formerly.

By most Authors facings are to be performed at open order both in Rank and File: But it is also necessary to exercise the Souldier in these facings at close Order: for if a Souldier should be assaulted in a straight or narrow passage that he hath neither time, nor ground to receive it, either by doublings, Counter-marches or wheelings, they stand at their Order, or close Order; may then by their particular facings defend themselves against any such assault and with wore ease so charge their Enemy by some of these facings, than by any other motion.

Facings are not to be slighted, but carefully to be observed and practised; they are the ground-work of Military discipline, for all motions have relation in one respect or another to them.

There are two facings, square as followeth, set down in their platformes, because they are not only useful but may serve as demonstrations of the former.

See Barrife & Ward, &c.

Command: The two first Ranks stand; the two last Ranks face about; the rest of the body face to the right and left, and march all.

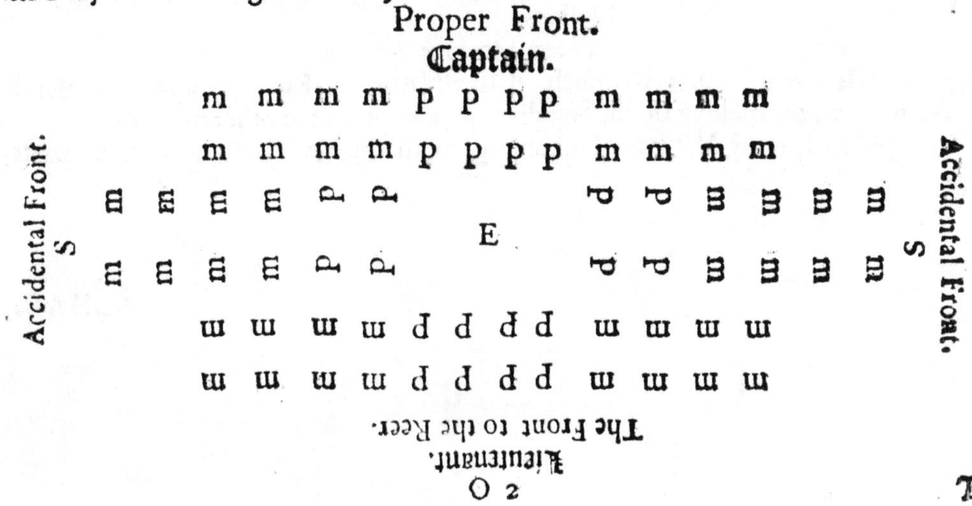

Proper Front.

Captain.

m m m m p p p p m m m m

m m m m p p p p m m m m

Accidental Front. S

m m m m p p   p p m m m m

E

m m m m p p   p p m m m m

S Accidental Front.

m m m m p p p p m m m m

m m m m p p p p m m m m

The Front to the Reer.

Lieutenant.

To reduce them; **Command.** 1. Face about to the right, march and close your Divisions.
2. Face to your leader, who standeth at his proper front.

Figure 2.

Command. 1. Musquetteers face to the right and left.
2. Half Files of Pikes face about to the right.
3. March all.

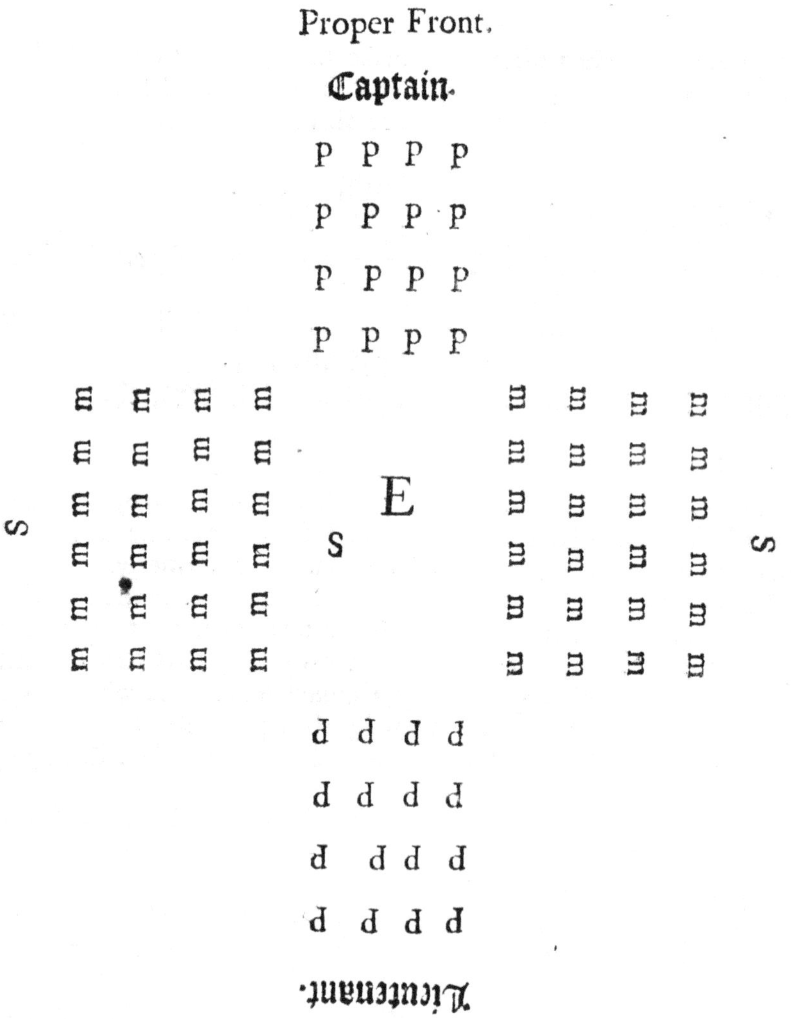

Proper Front.

Captain.

P P P P

P P P P

P P P P

P P P P

m m m m   m m m m

m m m m   m m m m

m m m m   E   m m m m

S   m m m m   S   m m m m   S

m m m m   m m m m

m m m m   m m m m

d d d d

d d d d

d d d d

d d d d

Lieutenant.

To reduce them. **Command.** 1. Face all about to the right, march and close your divisions.
2. Face all to your Leader.

By this little you may perceive much of the Nature of Facings, and how useful they are towards the making of the Souldier apt and perfect in other motions.

I shall proceed to the Nature of doublings with the several branches, or parts of them.

CHAP.

CHAP. VII.

Of Doublings.

IT is allowed by the Judicious that they are most necessary and completely useful for the strengthening any part of the Battle as occasion and discretion shall command.

All which consist in these two Generals. { 1. **Doublings of Length,** 2. **Doublings of Depth,** } All times in quantity of Number; sometimes in Number and place.

The several sorts of doublings are as followeth, {
1. **Of ranks.**
2. **Of half files.**
3. **Of bringers up.**
4. **Of the reer.**
5. **Of files.**
6. **Of half ranks.**
}

1. The doubling of Ranks is when every Rank double the odd.
2. Half Files } are said to be doubled, when they shall double their Ranks into
3. Bringers up } the Front.
4. The doubling of the Reer is when the Front half file doubles the Reer.
5. The doubling of files is when even files double the odd.
6. The doubling of half ranks is when one rank shall double the other.

And that is performed by { **Passing through.** **Countermarches.** **Intire, or divisional doublings.** }

The doubling of Ranks, half files or bringers up into the Front is a doubling of quantity, or number, and not of place.

But the doubling of ranks intire, or for to double the front by half files intire, either to the right or left; or by Division; It makes not only a doubling in quantity and of place, but lengthens the battle also.

The doubling of files and half files, or half ranks, or doubling to either flank, is a doubling in quantity, and not of place.

But the doubling of files, and right half ranks intire, and the depth of the left flank intire, is not only a doubling of number, but of place and depth of the battle.

Observe, that all divisional doublings are to be at open Order both in Rank and File.

Observe, that in all motions they must be performed in three steps; and first by stepping forth of that foot, which is next to the place named: And for reducement to return by the contrary hand.

Observe, that in doubling of Ranks, the doubling of Files reduceth them; so in the doubling of Files to any hand, the doubling of Ranks to the contrary hand reduceth them also.

Observe, that in all motions of doublings, that they who are to double, before they move from their places, are to Advance and Poyse their Arms; and when they have performed their Commands they are immediately to conform to the same posture that those whom they double are in; whether it be at shoulder or advance.

Observe, that all intire doublings are to be performed at Order both in Rank and File: And in all motions observe your right hand man.

I shall not only give you the words of command for most particular doublings that may be useful for service with directions for the performance of the same; with their reducements: And as I have been importuned by some of the Deputy Lieutenants to add to them their several platforms(or Figures) it is accordingly performed.

But my chief aim is to demonstrate how a *Battalia* may be strengthned by doublings.

And that is either in the { 1. Front, 2. Reer, or 3. Both Flanks.

The Front may be strengthned by { Intire Doublings, Divisional Doublings, Intire Wheelings, & Divisional Wheelings.

Of these I shall proceed in their several Orders, shewing how intire Doublings do strengthen the Front.

And that is by { 1. Ranks, 2. Bringers up, 3. Half Files.

1. The Front is strengthned by intire Doublings of Ranks.

1. Command. Ranks to the { 1. Right or 2. Left } Doubles.

Directions for doubling to the Right, from the left, the even Ranks from the Front move forward to the Right into the odd Ranks.

Front.

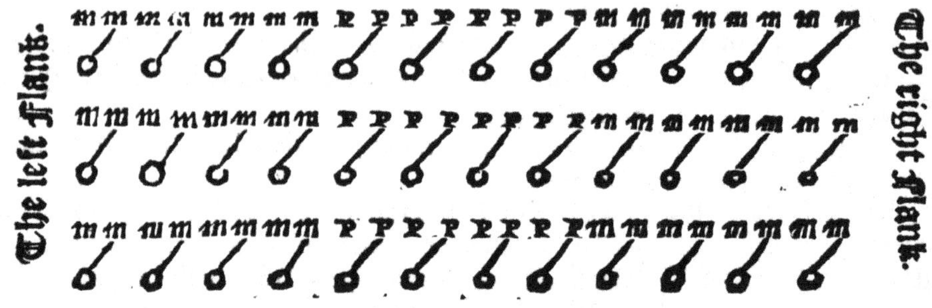

The left Flank. The right Flank.

Reer.

To reduce them Command

Files to the left double, (or) Ranks as you were.

The doubling of this Figure to the right doth easily make appear what is meant by doubling to the left, that I need not demonstrate it.

2. Command. Ranks to the right and left double { 1. Outward, or 2. Inward.

1. Directions:

1. **Directions Outward.** Even Ranks move outward from the Flanks with three steps forward into the odd Ranks.

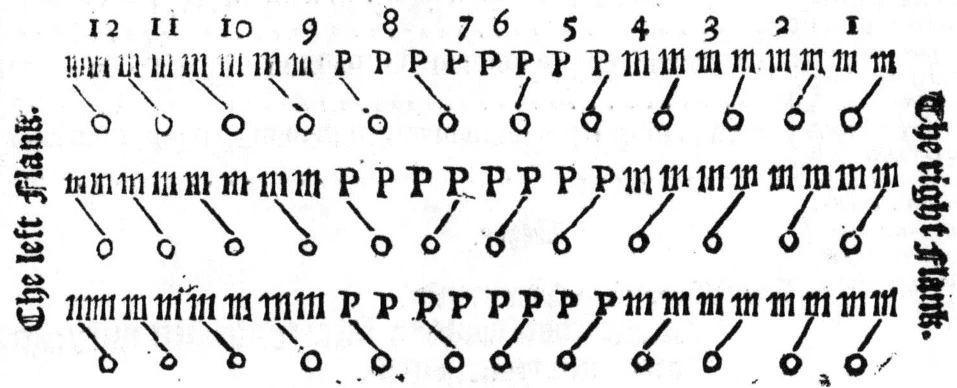

To reduce them: **Ranks as you were**: Or, **Files to the right and left double inward.**

2. **Directions inward.** The even Ranks move inward from the Flanks with three steps forward into the odd Ranks.

To reduce them: **Ranks as you were**; Or, **Files to the right and left double outward.**

3. **Command.** Double your Ranks to the {1. **Right** / 2. **Left**} **Intire.**

Directions to the right.

Even Ranks from the Front, face to the right, and march forth until they be clear of the standing Ranks; then face them to their Leader, and double the odd Ranks that are standing.

Front.

If you command them to close their Ranks forward it will be the same Figure as may be produced by commanding half files to double the front to the right, the difference being only in quality, not quantity, vide Fig. 3.

```
  12                       1 .12                        1
  1 mmmm pppp mmmm . mmmm pppp mmmm
  2 ..........................................
  3 mmmm pppp mmmm . mmmm pppp mmmm
  4 ..........................................
  5 mmmm pppp mmmm . mmmm pppp mmmm
  6 ..........................................
```

The left Flank. The right Flank.

Reer.

To reduce them **Command.**

Ranks that doubled, face to the left and march forth into your places.

Or,

Half Ranks of the right, face to the left and double your left Flank.

Or,

Ranks as you were.

4. **Command:** Double your Ranks inward intire.

Directions. Every even Rank from the Reer, face to the right and left out wards, and march until they be clear of the standing part; then let every even Rank from the Front (which is the standing part) move forwards into the Front.

Front.

```
12 11 10 9 8 7                                         6 5 4 3 2 1
1 m m m m P P m m m m P P P P m m m m P P m m m m 1
              2  o o o o o o o o o o o o  2
3 m m m m P P m m m m P P P P m m m m P P m m m m 3
              4  o o o o o o o o o o o o  4
5 m m m m P P m m m m P P P P m m m m P P m m m m 5
              6  o o o o o o o o o o o o  6
```

Reer.

5. **Command.** Double your Ranks to the { 1. **Right** / 2. **Left** } Intire.

Every man placing himself on the outside of his right hand man.

This doubling is the same in Figure with the third, they differ only in place, the quantity being the same.

Directions. Every even Rank from the Front, face to the right and march, placing your selves on the outside of your right hand men.

Front.

```
12 11 10 9 8 7 6 5 4 3 2 1 . 1 2 3 4 5 6 7 8 9 10 11 12
mmmm pppp mmmm . mmmm pppp mmmm

o o o o o o o o o o o o
```

To

To reduce them **Command.** **Right half ranks double your left flank each placing your selves on the inside of his left hand man.**

2. Intire doublings for the strengthening of the Front by Bringers-up.

6. **Command.** Bringers-up double your Front to the { 1. **Right.** 2. **Left.**

Directions for doubling to the right: Bringers up move forwards with your right legs, and pass through ranking themselves even with the Front, the rest following successively and placing themselves even with the standing ranks.

Front.

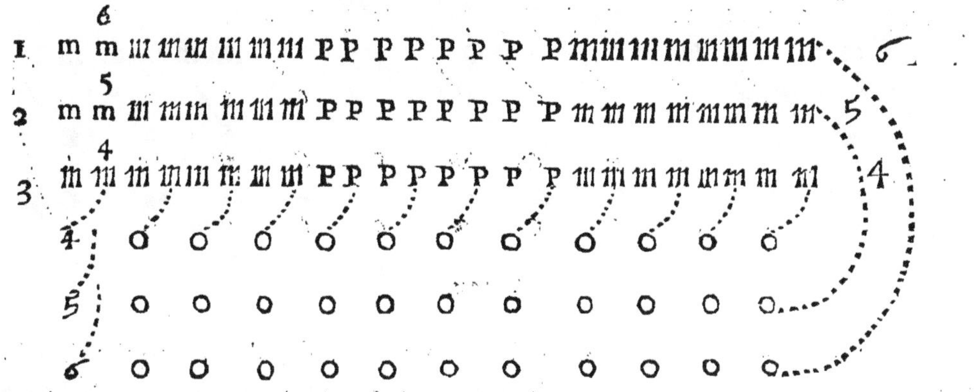

```
    6
1 m m m m m m m m P P P P P P P P m m m m m m m m m m   6
    5
2 m m m m m m m m P P P P P P P P m m m m m m m m m m   5
    4
3 m m m m m m m m P P P P P P P P m m m m m m m m m m   4
4   o o o o o o o o o o o
5   o o o o o o o o o o o
6   o o o o o o o o o o o
```

Reer, or Bringers-up.

To reduce them **Command.** Bringers up, or Reer half files face about to the left, and march into your places.

O R,

Even files from the left double your depth to the left, each fall behind his accidental bringer-up (or half file-leader.)

When they march into their places, the half file-leaders who were the last that took their places, now in this reducement must be the first to take their places.

7. **Command.** Bringers-up double your Front to the right and left { 1. **Outward.** 2. **Inward.**

This I never saw but once in a private Exercise, but I conceive it more out of curiosity than of necessity. And because it is suitable to the second Command of Ranks, I need not demonstrate them in Figures; as the even ranks move and take their respective places in the second Figure, in this the bringers-up are to be the first movers to the right and left either outwards or inwards.

If outwards; then it is to be performed from the midst of the Reer from the right and left into the Front.

To reduce them **Command.** The odd files from the right and left flank double your depth to the right and left inwards, every man falling behind his accidental bringer-up.

If inwards; then it ought to be performed from the flanks to the right and left inwards even into the Front.

To reduce them **Command.** The even files from each flank double your depth to the right and left inwards, all falling behind his accidental bringer-up.

3. Intire doublings for the strengthening of the Front by half-files.

8. **Command.** Half files double your Front to the { 1. **Right.** 2. **Left.**

Directions. If to the right, the half file-leaders must pass through (or move forwards) to the right into the Front, and the succeeding ranks are to follow them.

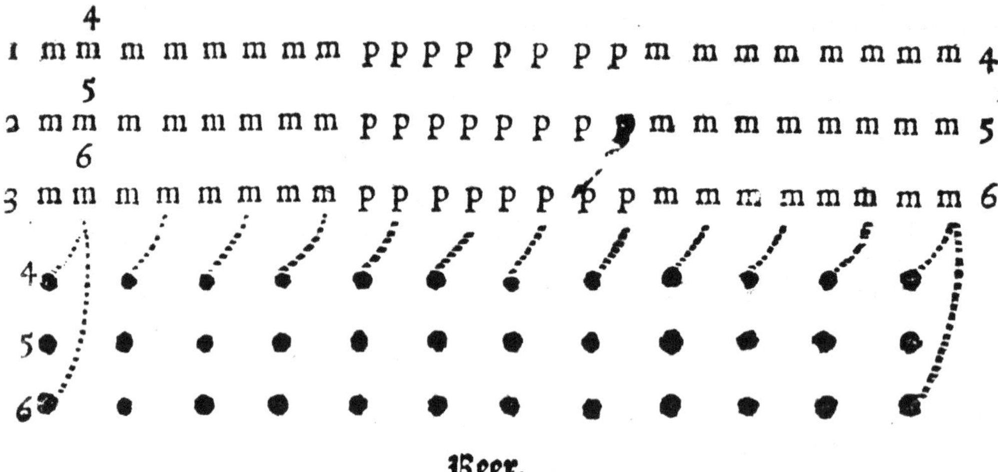

To reduce them **Command.** Even files from the left, double your depth to the left. Or, Half files face about to the left and march forth into your places. Or, Half files as you were.

9. **Command.** Half files double your Front to the right and left { 1. **Outwards.** 2. **Inwards.**

What I have declared in the seventh Command, I do the same here: However I shall demonstrate the Command by doubling outwards.

1. **Directions.** It is to be performed from the midst of the half files to the right and left into the Front.

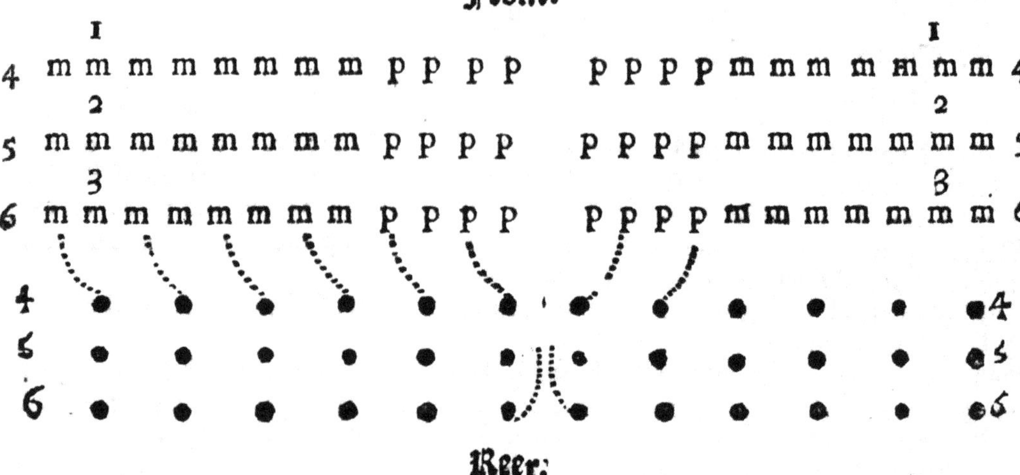

To reduce this **Command.** The odd files from the right and left flank double your depth to the right and left inward.

OR,

OR,

Halfe files face about to the right, and march forth into your places.

2. **Directions.** If the command be inward, then it is to be performed from the flanks of the half files, marching even into the Front.

To reduce them **Command.** Even files from each flank, double your depth to the right and left outwards.

OR,

Half files as you were.

10. **Command.** Half files double your Front to the { 1. **Right** / 2. **Left** } Intire.

Directions to the right. Half files face to the right and march, until they be clear of the front half files, then face them to their Leader, and march them up even with the Front.

Front. **Half Files in motion.**

mmmm pppp mmmm : mmmm pppp mmmm
:
mmmm pppp mmmm : mmmm pppp mmmm
:
mmmm pppp mmmm : mmmm pppp mmmm
:
. . . . ————————————
. . . . ————————————
. . . . ————————————

Reer.

To reduce this **Command.** Half files face about to the right and march forth into your places.

OR,

Half ranks of the right double the depth of your left flank intire.

11. **Command.** Half files double your Front inward intire.

Directions. Front half files face to the right and left outwards, and march until they be clear of the Reer half files; then face them to their Leader and stand. Then let the reer half files march up even into the Front.

Front.

mmmm pp . . . . pp mmmm
mmmm pp . . . . pp mmmm
mmmm pp . . . . pp mmmm

Half files in motion.

mmmm pppp mmmm
mmmm pppp mmmm
mmmm pppp mmmm

Reer.

To reduce them. Half files upon the intire motion face about and march; Front half files face to the right and left inward and close your Divisions.

OR,

Reer half files, double the depth of your Front half files intire, face all to the right and left inward, and close your Divisions.

I have shewed you how the Front may be strengthened by intire doublings; I shal briefly shew how it may be by divisional.

The Front is strengthened by divisional Doublings as followeth.

12. **Command.** Double your Ranks to the right and left by Division.

To perform this, **Command.** Even Ranks from the Front face to the right and left outwards; march forth and double the odd.

Front.

```
              1
2 m m m m p p m m m m p p p p m m m m p p m m m m 2
  :           2                                 :
  . . . . . . . . . . . . . . . . . . . . . . . . . .

              3
4 m m m m p p m m m m p p p p m m m m p p m m m m 4
  :           4                                 :
  . . . . . . . . . . . . . . . . . . . . . . . . . .

              5
6 m m m m p p m m m m p p p p m m m m p p m m m m 6
  :           6                                 :
  . . . . . . . . . . . . . . . . . . . . . . . . . .
```

Reer.

To reduce this; half ranks that doubled, face to the right and left inwards, and march into your places.

13. **Command.** Half files double your Front by Division.

To perform this: Half files face to the right and left outwards, and march until they be clear of the Front half files, then face them to their Leader; then move forward and double the Front.

Front.

```
          1 m m m m p p p p m m m m 1

          2 m m m m p p p p m m m m 2

          3 m m m m p p p p m m m m 3
  Motion : :                       : : Motion.
4 m m m m p p . . . . . . . . . . . . p p m m m m

5 m m m m p p . . . . . . . . . . . . p p m m m m

6 m m m m p p . . . . . . . . . . . . p p m m m m
```

Reer.

To

To reduce this Command. Half files face about to the Reer, and march until they be clear of the Front half files; then, face to the right and left inward, close your Divisions and face to your Leader.

OR,

The half files that moved double the depth of the Front half files.

14. **Command.** Double your Ranks to the right and left by Division, every man placing himself on the outside of his right and left hand man.

To perform this Command. Every even Rank from the Front move forth to the right and left outward, each man placing himself according as is commanded.

Front.

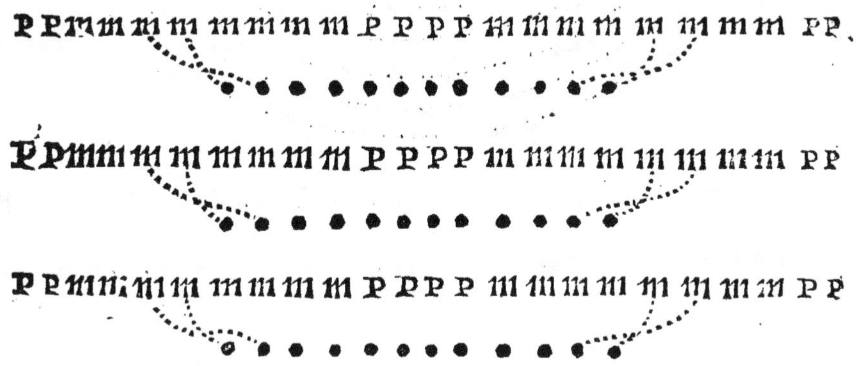

P P m m m m m m m m m m P P P P m m m m m m m m m m P P

● ● ● ● ● ● ● ● ● ● ● ●

P P m m m m m m m m m m P P P P m m m m m m m m m m P P

● ● ● ● ● ● ● ● ● ● ● ●

P P m m m m m m m m m m P P P P m m m m m m m m m m P P

● ● ● ● ● ● ● ● ● ● ● ●

Reer.

To reduce this Command. The half Ranks that moved double your Files to the right and left inward; every man placing himself on the inside of his right and left hand man.

I have hitherto shewed how the Front may be strengthened by divisional Doublings. Now followeth how

The Front may be strengthened by intire and Divisional Wheelings.

15. **Command.** Wheel off your reer half files to the { 1. **Right** / 2. **Left.** } Intire into the Front.

To perform this to the right, Command. Half files face about to the right, and wheel them to the left about, until they be even with the Front.

1 m m m m p p p p m m m m.m m m m p p p p m m m m 6

2 m m m m p p p p m m m m.m m m m p p p p m m m m 5

3 m m m m p p p p m m m m.m m m m p p p p m m m m 4

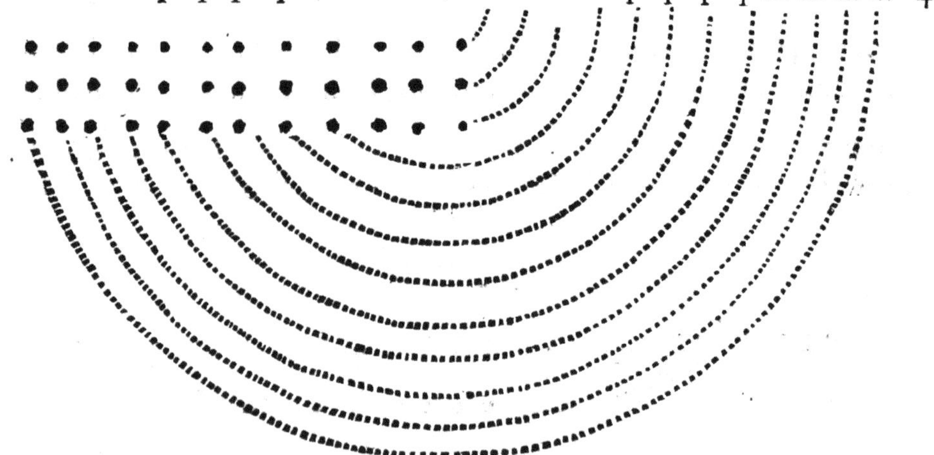

To reduce this; Wheel off your half ranks, and double your left flank intire to the left.

To perform this reducement, let them face to the right; then **Command**: Right half ranks, wheel about to the right until they be even a breast with the front half files: To your Leader.

16. **Command.** Wheel your Flanks into the Front.

There are diversities of Commands for the production of this Figure, and much according to the opinion of the Commander. I shall insert them, and leave the choice thereof to the judicious in this Art.

Wheel your { **Flanks into the front.**
Wings into the front.
Front into the battle.
Front into the midst.
Reer into the flanks.

Front.

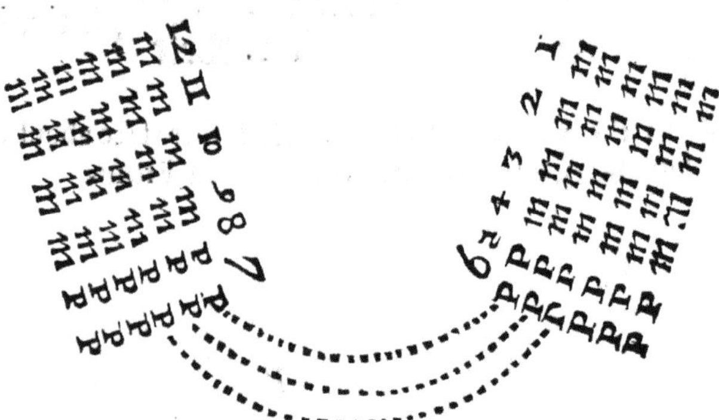

To reduce any one of them **Command**. Wheel your flanks into the Reer.

17. **Command.**

17. **Command.** Reer half files wheel and double your Front by Division.

To perform this **Command.** Half files face about to the right, and so wheel off to the right and left about; moving forwards until they be even with the Front.

Front.

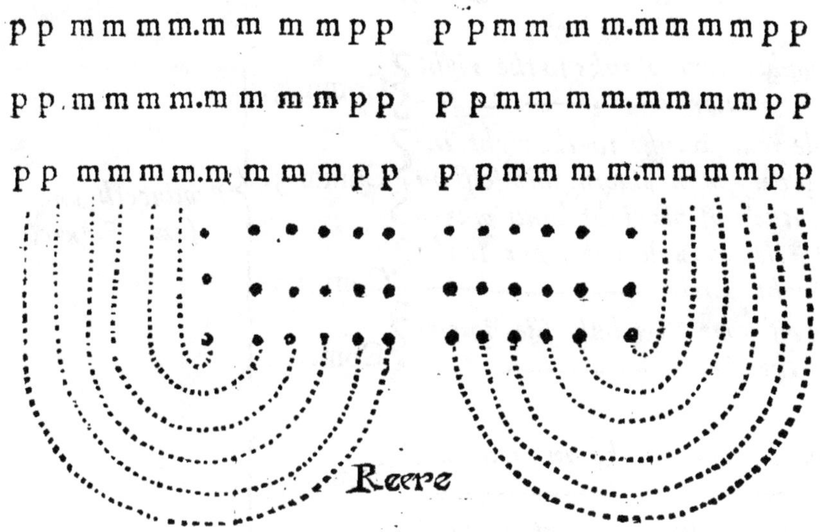

p p m m m m.m m m m p p   p p m m m m.m m m m p p

p p m m m m.m m m m p p   p p m m m m.m m m m p p

p p m m m m.m m m m p p   p p m m m m.m m m m p p

Reere

To reduce this **Command.** Half files that doubled, wheel about to the right and left inward, and march into your places.

OR,

Half ranks face to the right and left outward; then wheel to the right and left inward, and double the depth of your Front half files, and face them to their Leader.

There is some other Wheelings, but I shall not trouble you with them, because they are more for curiosity than for service, &c.

CHAP. VIII.

I Shall here insert the several preceding Commands for the strengthening of the Front, wherein, in the closing of some of the Ranks, as may be seen by them severally, the Figures are one and the same *Battalia*, in quantity but not in quality; in number but not in place.

Ranks to the right Double.	Command 1.	*Produceth one and the same Figure.*
1. *Bringers up double your Front to the right.* ————	Comm. 6.	
Half files double your Ranks forward to the right. ————	Comm. 8.	

Ranks to the right and left double first outward and then inward —	Comm. 2.	*Produceth one and the same Figure.*
Bringes up double your Front to the right and left { 1. *Outward.* 2. *Inward.* } —	Comm. 7.	
Half Files double your Front to the right and left { 1. *Outward.* 2. *Inward.* } —	Comm. 9.	

2. *Double your Ranks to the right intire* —	Comm. 3.	*Produceth one and the same Figure.*
Double your Ranks to the right intire, every man placing himself on the outside of his right hand man —	Comm. 5.	
Half Files double the front to the right intire —	Com. 10.	
Wheel off your Reer half files intire into the Front —	Com. 15.	

3. *Double your Ranks inward intire* —	Comm. 4.	*Produceth one and the same Figure.*
Half files double your Front inward intire —	Com. 11.	
Double your Ranks to the right and left by division —	Com. 12.	
Half files double your Front by division —	Com. 13.	

Double your Ranks to the right and left by division, every man placing himself on the outside of his right hand man —	Com. 14.	*Produceth one and the same Figure.*
Reer half files wheel and double your Front by division —	Com. 17.	

Vide { Chap. 11. Chap. 14.

CHAP.

CHAP. IX.

How Battalias may be strengthened in the Reer.

HAving ended with most of those doublings that do strengthen the Front, I proceed to some few that may strengthen the Reer: I might be as large in them as the former; but the labour and pains would be of no great necessity; because all what hath been commanded in the Front may by counterchange of them be performed in the Reer. Therefore I shall only for example sake set down four **Commands**, and demonstrate them by their respective figures, and they only shall be performed by the doubling of half Files, leaving the rest for the delightful Artist in this pleasing exercise.

1. **Command.** Front half files double your Reer to the { 1. **Right.** 2. **Left.** }

To perform this: (to the right) **Command.** Front half files face about to the left and march directly forwards to the left of the standing part in opposition even in each rank according to their several places.

Front.

1 1
2 2
2 3
1 ɯ 4 m ɯ m ɯ m ɯ m d p d p d p d p ɯ m ɯ m ɯ m ɯ m 4
ᘔ ɯ 5 m ɯ m ɯ m ɯ m d p d p d p d p ɯ m ɯ m ɯ m ɯ m 5
Ɛ ɯ 6 m ɯ m ɯ m ɯ m d p d p d p d p ɯ m ɯ m ɯ m ɯ m 6

Reer.

If this be commanded for service then face the Reer half files also about to the left. Then

To reduce them. Face them all to their proper Front, and **Command**: Double your files to the right intire advancing.

If it be for a private exercise, **Command.** Half files face about to the left and march forth into your places.

2 **Command.** Front half files double your Reer to the { 1. **Right** 2. **Left** } intire.

To perform this to the right intire, **Command.** Front half files face to the right, march until they be clear of the Reer half files; then face them all to the Reer, and march them even in breast with the Reer.

Front.

. . . .

. . . .

. . . .

Right flank.

m m m m p p p p m m m m · w w w w d d d d w w w w

m m m m p p p p m m m m . w w w w d d d d w w w w

m m m m p p p p m m m m . w w w w d d d d w w w w

Reer.

To reduce this, **Command.** Front half files, face about to the right and march into your places.

OR,

Face all to your leader, then right half ranks double your left flank intire advancing.

3. **Command.** Front half files double your Reer by Division.

To perform this, **Command.** Front half files face to the right and left, and march until they be clear of the Body, then face them to the Reer, and move down to the Reer even in breast with the last Rank.

Front.

. . . .

. . . .

. . . .

w w w w d d m m m m p p p p m m m m d d w w w w

w w w w d d m m m m p p p p m m m m d d m w w w

w w w w d d m m m m p p p p m m m m d d w w w m

Reer.

If this be for service you may face them all to the Reer. If only for Exercise you may reduce them, as they now stand; by Commanding,

Front half files face about to the right and advance forwards, until they are clear of the standing part, then face them to the right and left inwards; and close your Divisions.

4. **Command.** Front half files double your Reer to the { 1. **Right** / 2. **Left** } by Countermarch.

To performe this; If the Command given for the left; face the standing half files to the Reer, and the rest Countermarch to the left and lose ground.

But

But if it be only for Exercise you need not face the standing part to the Reer at all.

Front.

```
1     .  .  .  .  .  .  .  .  .  .  .  .  .  .
2     .  .  .  .  .  .  .  .  .  .  .  .  .  .
3     .  .  .  .  .  .  .  .  .  .  .  .  .  .
      :                                        :
  Ɛ ɯ   ɯ   ɯ   ɯ   d   d   d   d   ɯ   ɯ   ɯ   ɯ
4    m   m   m   m   p   p   p   p   m   m   m   m
  ᘔ ɯ   ɯ   ɯ   ɯ   d   d   d   d   ɯ   ɯ   ɯ   ɯ
5    m   m   m   m   p   p   p   p   m   m   m   m
  1 ɯ   ɯ   ɯ   ɯ   d   d   d   d   ɯ   ɯ   ɯ   ɯ
6   :m: m:m :m : p : p: p:  p :m :m : m: m
```

Reer.

To reduce this (as being only for Exercise) **Command.** Front half files face about to the left and march forth into your places.

But if it be upon service that they are all faced to the Reer, then all upon the Reducement, are to face about to the left; and the front half files to march into their places.

Object. But Some may object here, and say; that this is a countermarch, and no doubling, and so ought not to be demonstrated in this place.

Answ. To which I answer; that what is done by the Front half files, in short is a *Lacedemonian* Countermarch, (of losing ground;) but if it were a direct countermarch, they ought not to stand mixed with any other part of the body, by passing through to the Reer, but only to Countermarch into the midst and there remain; so that now passing through into the Reer makes it an absolute doubling.

What I have mentioned in the beginning of this Chapter may be sufficient to the ingenious Artist, having concluded what I intended for the strengthening of the Reer.

I thought to have inserted here a strengthening of the Front and Reer, but being in the Chapter of Wheelings, Command the tenth, the inquisitive may be better satisfied.

CHAP. X.

Which is the last in order to shew, how a Battalia may be strengthened in both Flanks.

THe Flanks are doubled by { 1. **Files.** 2. **Half ranks.** 3. **Division.** 4. **Wheelings.** }

1. First by Files.

1. **Command.** Files to the { **Right** or **Left** } double.

If to the left to perform this, **Command**. Every even ranks from the left, move with three steps into the odd.

Front.

Left flank

1 m m P P m m
m m P P m m
2 m m P P m m
m m P P m m
3 m m P P m m
m m P P m m
4 m m P P m m
m m P P m m
5 m m P P m m
m m P P m m
6 m m P P m m
m m P T m m

Right flank

Reer.

To reduce this, **Command**. Ranks to the right double.

OR,

Files as you were. *In all motions observe to move that leg first, to which the Command guideth.*

2. **Command**. Files to the { 1. **Right.** or 2. **Left.** } double advancing.

To perform this, if to the right, **Command**. Every even file from the right advance three steps forward and double the odd.

Front.

m m P P m m
1 m m P P m m
m m P P m m
2 m m P P m m
m m P P m m
3 m m P P m m
m m P P m m
4 m m P P m m
m m P P m m
5 m m P P m m
m m P P m m
6 m m P P m m

Reer.

To reduce this **Command**. Ranks to the left double.

OR,

Files as you were.

3. **Command.**

3. **Command.** Files to the right and left double outward.

In doubling outward, the outmost File of each Flank stands, and the even File of each flank doubles the odd.

Front.

m m P P m m
m m P P m m
m m P P m m
m m P P m m
m m P P m m
m m P P m m
m m P P m m
m m P P m m
m m P P m m
m m P P m m
m m P P m m
m m P P m m

Reer.

To reduce this **Command.** Double your Ranks to the right and left inwards.

OR,

Ranks as you were.

4. **Command.** Files to the right and left double Inward.

Front.

m m P P m m
m m P P m m
m m P P m m
m m P P m m
m m P P m m
m m P P m m
m m P P m m
m m P P m m
m m P P m m
m m P P m m
m m P P m m
m m P P m m

Reer.

To reduce this **Command.** Double your Ranks to the right and left outwards.

OR,

Ranks as you were.

5. **Command.** Double your Ranks to the { 1. **Right** & 2. **Left** } { 1. Outwards advancing. 2. Inwards.

 This

This will be performed as in the third and fourth Command, only instead of falling behind their right or left hand men, here they are to advance before them as in the second Command.

6. **Command.** Double your Files to the { 1. Right or 2. Left } intire advancing.

To performe this, to the right. The even files from the right advance so far until they be clear and double the odd files to the right.

Front.

m	m	p	p	m	m	1
m	m	p	p	m	m	2
m	m	p	p	m	m	3
m	m	p	p	m	m	4
m	m	p	p	m	m	5
m	m	p	p	m	m	6
m	m	p	p	m	m	1
m	m	p	p	m	m	2
m	m	p	p	m	m	3
m	m	p	p	m	m	4
m	m	p	p	m	m	5
m	m	p	p	m	m	6

Reer.

To reduce this, **Command.** Files that doubled face about to the left and march forth into your places.

OR,

Front half Files double your Reer to the left.

OR,

Half Files double your Front to the right.

7. **Command.** Double your files to the { 1. Right or 2. Left } Intire advancing, every man placing himself before his leader.

To perfom this, to the right.

Front.

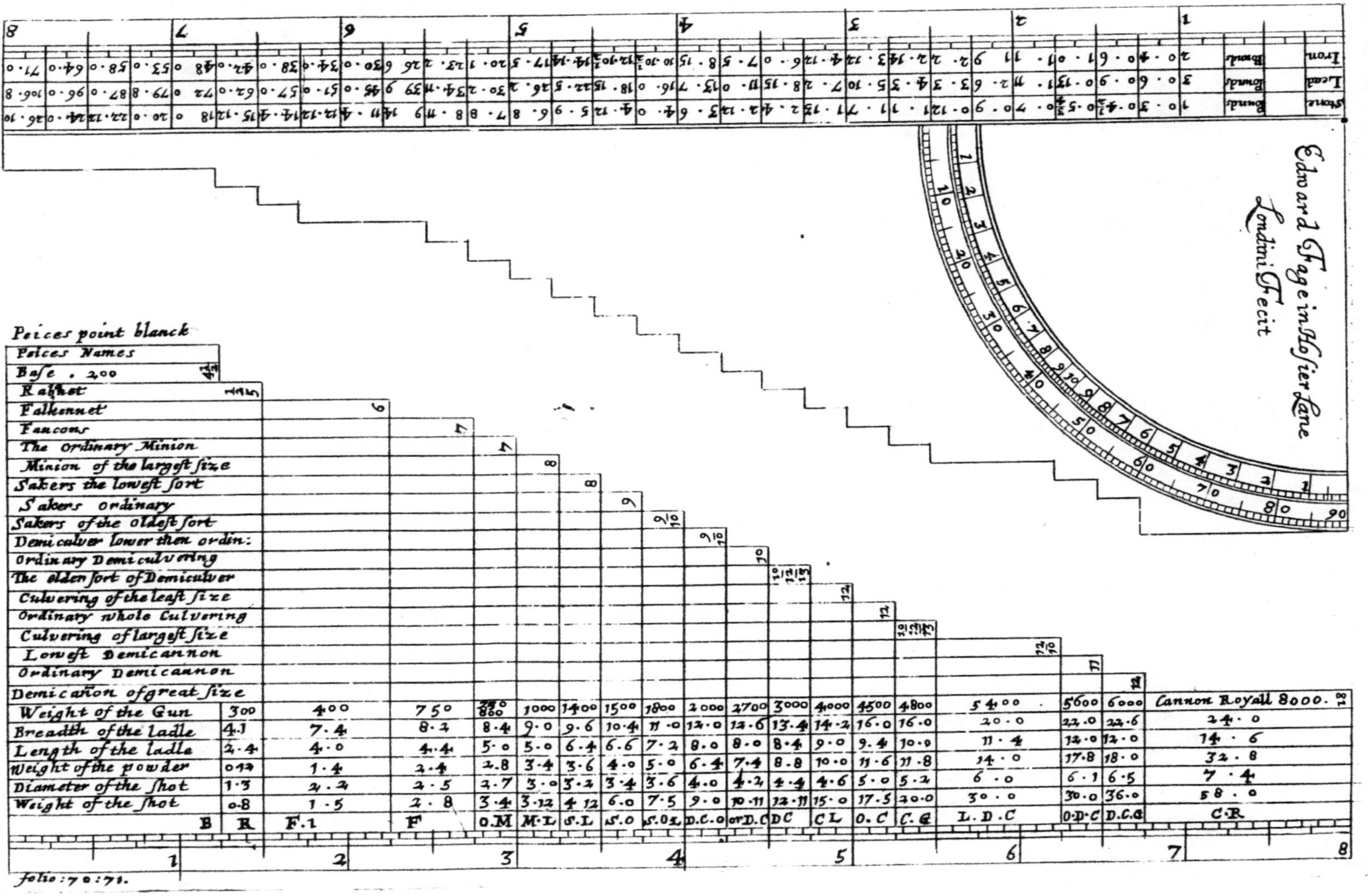
Edward Fage in Hosier Lane
Londini Fecit
Stone
Lead
Iron
Peices point blanck
Peices Names
Base . 200
Rabbet
Falkonnet
Faucons
The Ordinary Minion
Minion of the largest size
Sakers the lowest sort
Sakers ordinary
Sakers of the oldest sort
Demiculver lower then ordin:
Ordinary Demiculvering
The olden sort of Demiculver
Culvering of the least size
Ordinary whole Culvering
Culvering of largest size
Lowest Demicannon
Ordinary Demicannon
Demicañon of great size
Weight of the Gun 300 400 750 1000 1400 1500 1800 2000 2700 3000 4000 4500 4800 5400 5600 6000 Cannon Royall 8000.
Breadth of the ladle 4.1 7.4 8.2 8.4 9.0 9.6 10.4 11.0 12.0 12.6 13.4 14.2 16.0 16.0 20.0 22.0 22.6 24.0
Length of the ladle 2.4 4.0 4.4 5.0 5.0 6.4 6.6 7.2 8.0 8.0 8.4 9.0 9.4 10.0 11.4 12.0 12.0 14.6
Weight of the powder 0.12 1.4 2.4 2.8 3.4 3.6 4.0 5.0 6.4 7.4 8.8 10.0 11.6 11.8 14.0 17.8 18.0 32.8
Diameter of the shot 1.3 2.2 2.5 2.7 3.0 3.2 3.4 3.6 4.0 4.2 4.4 4.6 5.0 5.2 6.0 6.1 6.5 7.4
Weight of the shot 0.8 1.5 2.8 3.4 3.12 4.12 6.0 7.5 9.0 10.11 12.11 15.0 17.5 20.0 30.0 30.0 36.0 58.0
B R F.1 F O.M M.L S.L S.O S.O.L D.C.O or D.C DC CL O.C C.G L.D.C O.D.C D.C.G C.R

folio:70:71.

Front.

m	m	p	p	m	m	6
m	m	p	p	m	m	5
m	m	p	p	m	m	4
m	m	p	p	m	m	3
m	m	p	p	m	m	2
m	m	p	p	m	m	1
m	m	p	p	m	m	1
m	m	p	p	m	m	2
m	m	p	p	m	m	3
m	m	p	p	m	m	4
m	m	p	p	m	m	5
m	m	p	p	m	m	6

Reer.

The reducement. **Command.** Front half Files face about to the left and march forth into your places.

OR,

Front half files, turn off by countermarch, and double your Reer to the right: Face all to your leader.

8. **Command.** Files double your depth to the right intire.

To perform this, **Command.** Even files from the right face about to the right, and march until they are clear of the Reer, placing themselves after their bringers up; then face them to their leader.

Front.

1	m	m	p	p	m	m
2	m	m	p	p	m	m
3	m	m	p	p	m	m
4	m	m	p	p	m	m
5	m	m	p	p	m	m
6	m	m	p	p	m	m
1	m	m	p	p	m	m
2	m	m	p	p	m	m
3	m	m	p	p	m	m
4	m	m	p	p	m	m
5	m	m	p	p	m	m
6	m	m	p	p	m	m

Reer.

To reduce this, **Command.** Half files double your Front to the left.

OR,

Front half files double your Reer to the right.

9. **Command.** Files double your depth to the right placing your selves behind your bringers up.

To perform this **Command**. Every even File from the right, face about to the right and double the remaining files behind their bringers up.

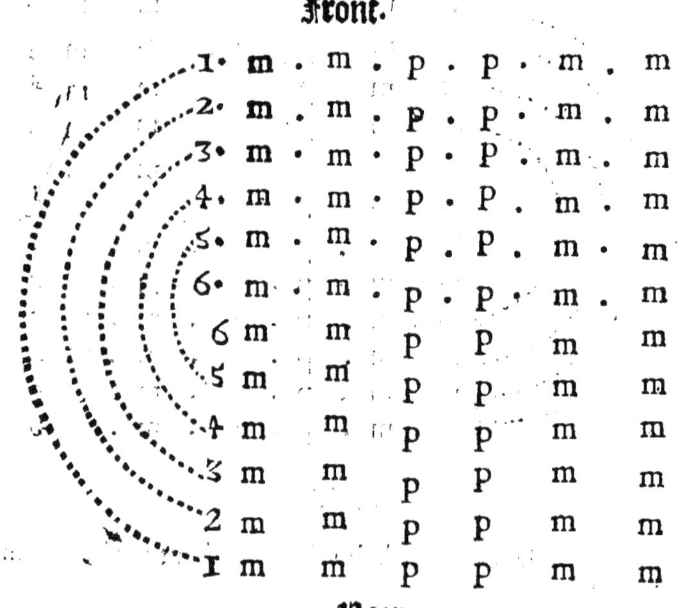

To reduce this **Command**. Bringers up double your Front to the left.

O R,

Half files double your Front to the left, each placing themselves before their half file Leaders.

There is but a small difference between the Figures of some of the precedent **Commands**, as some may at first sight guess them to be: yet if you would but well observe them the words of Command are several, and in the Battalia there is difference in the Dignity of place; but not in quantity (or number.)

Secondly. **How the flanks are doubled by half ranks.**

10. **Comand.** Half ranks of the left, double your right flank to the { 1. **Right**, or 2. **Left**.

To perform this to the right. Left half ranks face to the right and move to the right forward and double your right flank.

Front.

. . . . p p m m m m
m m m m p p
. . . . p p m m m m
m m m m p p
. . . . p p m m m m
m m m m p p
. . . . p p m m m m
m m m m p p
. . . . p p m m m m
m m m m p p
. . . . p p m m m m
m m m m p p

Reer.

To

To reduce this **Command.** Face to the left and march forth into your places.

O R,

Double your Ranks to the left intire. You may face them at discretion.

I shall demonstrate another Figure to the left, shewing how it may be performed without mixture of Arms, *&c.*

11. **Command.** Half Ranks of the right, double your left flank to the right.

To perform this **Command.** Half ranks of the right face to the right, turn off to the right and double your left flank.

Front.

```
    m  m  m  m  p  p  . . . . . . . .  1
   .. .. .. .. .. .. .. .. .. .. .. ..
1   m  m  m  m  p  p
    m  m  m  m  p  p  . . . . . . . .  2
2   m  m  m  m  p  p
    m  m  m  m  p  p  . . . . . . . .  3
3   m  m  m  m  p  p
    m  m  m  m  p  p  . . . . . . . .  4
4   m  m  m  m  p  p
    m  m  m  m  p  p  . . . . . . . .  5
5   m  m  m  m  p  p
    m  m  m  m  p  p  . . . . . . . .  6
6   m  m  m  m  p  p
```

Reer.

To reduce the 11. **Command.** Ranks double to the right intire, every man placing himself on the outside of his right hand man.

12. **Command.** Half ranks double your right flank to the right and left { 1. **Outward.** 2. **Inward.**

1. To perform this **Outward.** Face all to the right, then the left half ranks move to the right and left outwards, doubling your right flank; face to your Leader.

Front.

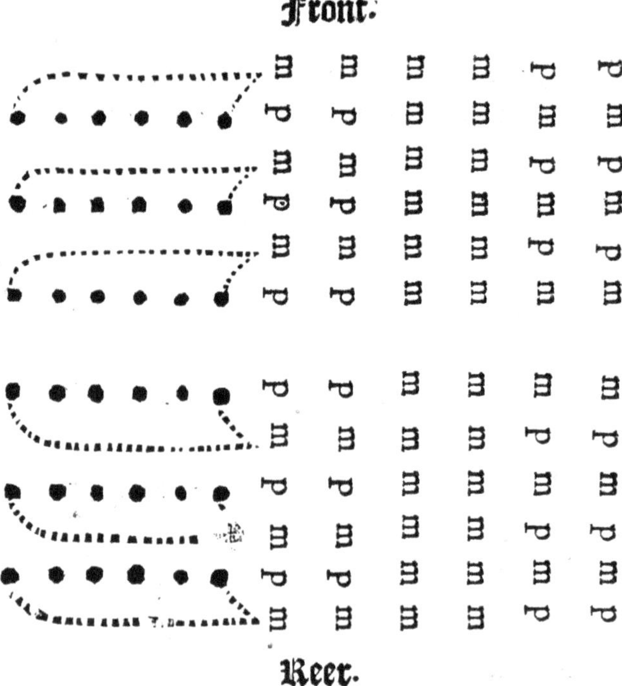

Reer.

To reduce this **Command.** 1. Front and Reer half files double your ranks intire to the left flank.

OR,

Half ranks that doubled face about to the right, and march forth into your places.

OR,

Half ranks face about to the right, and the even ranks from the midst move forth and double your left ranks intire to the left flank; face to your Leader.

2. To perform the 12. **Command inward.** Face all to the right, then the left half ranks move forwards to the right and left inwards, and double the right flank; face all to your Leader.

Front.

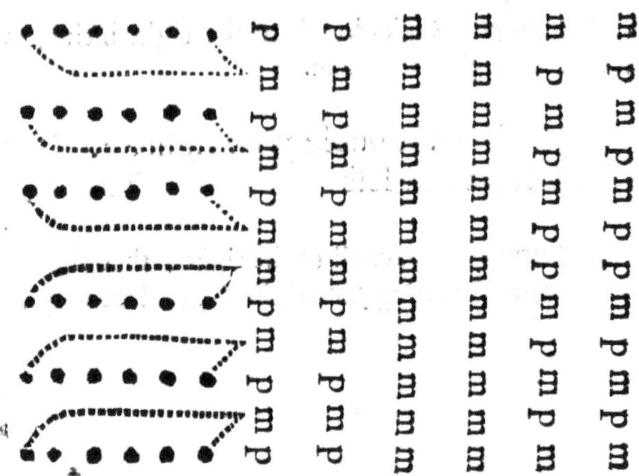

Reer.

To reduce the 12. **Command inward.** Front and reer half files, double your Ranks intire to the left.

By direction, you may **Command.** Half files face about, and every even rank from

from the ſront and reer move forth, and double your ranks intire to the left flank; then face to your Leader.

13. **Command.** Half ranks double your right flank to the { 1. **Right** or 2. **Left** } by Countermarch.

OR,

Half ranks to the right by Countermarch double your left flank.

To perform this. Half ranks of the right, face to the right and Countermarch into the left flank loſing ground.

This produceth the ſame Figure as the 11. Command.

To reduce this. Double your Ranks to the left intire, every man placing himſelf on the outſide of your right hand men, and face to your Leader.

OR,

Ranks that doubled, face to the right and march forth into your places.

In like manner if you would double the right flank by countermarch, the right flank is then to ſtand, and you are to inſert the left into the right flank, as before, the right will be by this Command inſerted into the left.

And by the reducement of the one by the contrary hand, you may reduce the other alſo.

14. **Command.** Left half ranks double your right flank to the right and left { 1. **Outwards** 2. **Inwards** } by countermarch.

Theſe inſertions I ſhall not demonſtrate by Figure, becauſe the three laſt being but well obſerved, will give you a light to the execution of theſe; only I ſhall briefly give you the performances and reducements thereof.

If Outward, Command. Half ranks of the right face to the right, and left half ranks face to the left, then move forward and double your right and left flank to the right and left outwards; face to your Leader.

To reduce this **Command.** Front and Reer half files double your Ranks intire to the left flank, every man placing himſelf, on the outſide of his right and left hand man.

By direction you may **Command.** The Front half files to face about, and the even ranks from the midſt, move forth to the left flank and double the odd, placing your ſelves on the outſide of your right hand men.

And every even rank from the reer half files, move forth and double the odd, placing your ſelf on the outſide of your left hand men; face to your Leader.

If Inwards, Command. Ranks face to the right and left outwards, and the left half ranks turn off to the right and left inward, moving forward, until you have doubled the right flank; face to your Leader.

To reduce this **Command.** Front and reer half files double your ranks intire to the left flank, every man placing himſelf on the outſide of his right and left hand man.

For direction you may **Command.** Half files face about, and every even rank from the reer, move forward, and place your ſelves on the outſide of your right hand men, and every even rank from the front, move forth and double the odd, placing your ſelves on the outſide of your left hand men; face to your Leader.

15. **Command.** Left half ranks double your right flank intire advancing.

To perform this **Command.** The left flank (or the left half ranks) march forth until they be clear of the remaining party; then face them to the right and double the right flank, and face them to their Leader.

Front.

```
m m m m p p —
m m m m p p —
m m m m p p —
m m m m p p —
m m m m p p —
m m m m p p —
. . . . . . . p p m m m m
. . . . . . . p p m m m m
. . . . . . . p p m m m m
. . . . . . . p p m m m m
. . . . . . . p p m m m m
. . . . . . . p p m m m m
```

The right Flank.

Reer.

To reduce this. The left flank that doubled, face to the left, and march into your places.

OR,

Front half files double your Reer to the right.

16. **Command.** Left half Ranks double intire the depth of your right Flank.

To perform this **Command**. The left half ranks to face about to the right, until they are clear of the standing part; then face to the left and double the right flank; face to your Leader.

Front.

```
. . . . . . . p p m m m m
. . . . . . . p p m m m m
. . . . . . . p p m m m m
. . . . . . . p p m m m m
. . . . . . . p p m m m m
. . . . . . . p p m m m m
m m m m p p —
m m m m p p —
m m m m p p —
m m m m p p —
m m m m p p —
m m m m p p —
```

The right Flank.

Reer.

To

To reduce this Command. Half files double your Front to the left intire.

OR,

Half files that doubled face about to the left and march forth into your places.

3. How the Flanks may be strengthened by divisional Doublings.

17. Command. Double your Files to the right and left by Division.

To perform this Command. Half files of the even files from the right, face to the Reer; then, even files march clear of the standing part; then move to the right and left, and double the odd files.

Front.

1 m m p p m 1 m
2 m m p p m 2 m
3 m m p p m 3 m

1 . m . m . p . p . m . m 1
2 . m . m . p . p . m . m 2
3 . m . m . p . p . m . m 3
4 . m . m . p . p . m . m 5
5 . m . m . p . p . m . m 5
6 . m . m . p . p . m . m 6

4 m m p p m 4 m
5 m m p p m 5 m
6 m m p p m 6 m

Right Flank.

Reer.

To reduce them Command. Face to the right and left inward, march forth and take your places, and face to your Leader.

18. Command. Half Ranks of the left double your right flank by Division.

To perform this Command. Half files of the left half ranks face about to the right; then, Front and Reer half ranks of the left flank move clear of the standing body, face all to the right flank, and move even in breast with the right flank.

Front.

m m m m p p
m m m m p p
m m m m p p
. . . . p p m m m m
. . . . p p m m m m
. . . . p p m m m m
. . . . p p m m m m
. . . . p p m m m m
. . . . p p m m m m
ɯ ɯ ɯ ɯ d d
ɯ ɯ ɯ ɯ d d
ɯ ɯ ɯ ɯ d d

Right Flank.

CAPT.

The accidental Front.

Reer.

To reduce them. Front and Reer half files that doubled, face about inwards and march into your places.

OR,

The half files that doubled may double the depth of their right flank.

Obs. You may in the Command, when they are marched clear of the standing party, Countermarch them with this Command. Front and Reer half files of the left flank countermarch to the right and left, losing of ground into the right flank, which will produce the same Figure, *Com.* 18. only in place. *Vide Com.* 13.

4. The Flanks are strengthened by Wheelings.

18. Command. Left half ranks wheel off, and double your right flank to the { Right or Left } Intire.

To perform this, Command. Right half ranks face outwards; left half ranks wheel about to the left, and keep wheeling until you have doubled the right flank; face the moveants to their Leader.

Front proper.

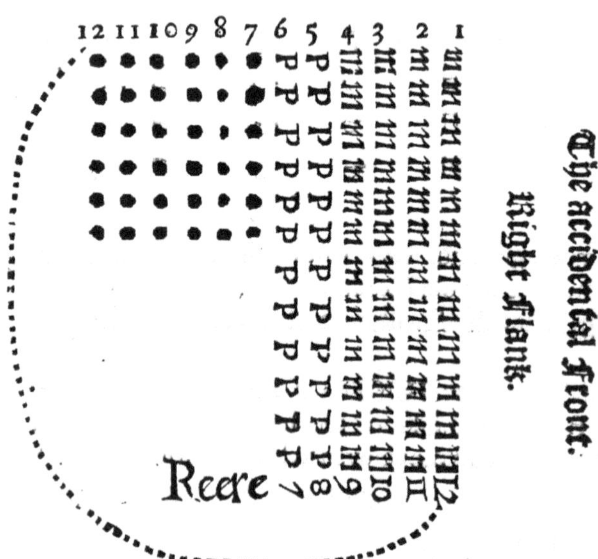

To reduce them. Face them to their proper Front; then Command, Reer half files double your Front to the left intire.

But if you countermarch them, then the reducement of the 13. Command will give you light to it also.

19. Command. Wheel Front and Reer into the { 1. Right or 2. Left } Flank.

OR,

Front and reer half files wheel off into the right Flank by Division.

To perform this, Command. Face all to the right.

Wheel off to the right and left, and so keep moving until the Bringer up of the right hand file, meet with the right hand file leader.

Front.

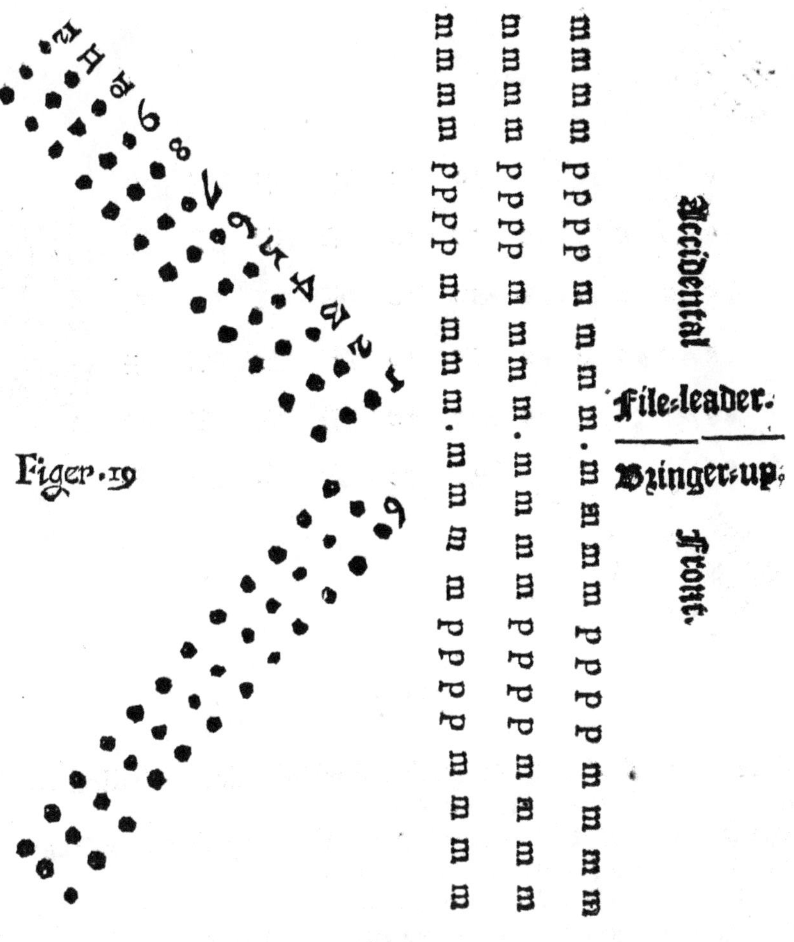

Reer.

To reduce them if faced to the right Flank.

Wheel both Flanks into the Reer, and face them to their Leader,

But if faced to their proper Front, then Command. Wheel Front and Reer into their left Flank, and face them to their Leader.

20. Command. Left half Ranks wheel off to the right and left, and double your right Flank by Division.

To perform this, Command. Half ranks of the right face to the right, then the half files of the left half rank face to the Reer.

Front and Reer half files wheel off to the right and left about; and more forwards until you are even a breast, then double your right flank and face them to their accidental Front.

Front.

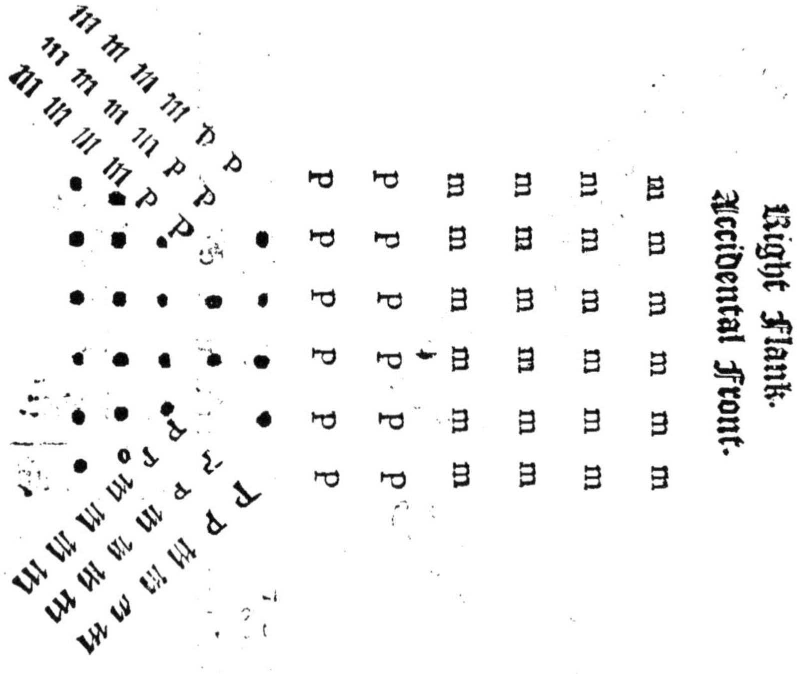

Reer.

To reduce them, Command. Files that doubled, double the depth of the standing files intire to the right and left inwards.

2. If you face them to their proper Front, then to reduce them Command. The three first and the three last Ranks double your left flank intire.

That is, The three last Ranks face about and wheel to the right, and the three first Ranks wheel about to the left, all moving and meet in opposition in the midst of the left flank; then face them to their Leader.

I have ended those Doublings whose Battalia's are strengthened in the Front, Reer, and both Flanks. Although they may not be useful at all times in the field service, yet it is not amiss for every Commander to be well grounded in the knowledge of them, that by his experience therein he may not be silent, when occasion serveth, nor the Souldier seeking what to do, when he may be commanded: They are so necessary, that some are delightful in private Exercises, and most of them profitable in Field (or Garrison.) I am sure the Ingenious if once experienced herein will confess them to be of such absolute necessity as not in the least to be slighted by any.

And further, it is adjudged to be most convenient for all the Chief Officers to bend their thoughts before the time of Service, to make their Commands as short as possible may be, in order to which see *Chapt.* 8. and 11.

I do declare that I have heard some of our late young *Eltonists* to be too tedious in their Commands and Reducements; I shall advise the young Souldier to follow the Rules of *Barriffe*, *Ward*, *Bingham* and *Hexham*, for there is in them enough to direct for most Services, and then they may peruse *Elton* at last, whose worth (as I have been informed) is not to be laid in the dust without the due respects belonging to a Souldier, and I hope now a Loyal Subject.

CHAP.

Chap. X.

YOu may perceive in those several Commands for the strengthening of the Flanks, and their Figures being produced, and have closed some of their Files, as occasion may offer it self, they are one and the same in Number but not in Place.

As in the 8. Chapter, I have also in this set down the several Commands that produce one and the same Figure, yet the Commands are distinct and several; all which if the Officer please to endeavour the remembring of: How that such and such Commands will produce such a Figure, he may in the hottest disputes take the shortest Commands to expedite his motions, having respect to his Ground for the execution of them.

1. *Files to the right double.* Command 1.
Files to the right double, advancing — Comm. 2.
Files to the right and left double
1. *Outward.* — 2. *Inward.* — Comm. 3. *and* 4.
Double your Ranks to the right and left
1. *Outward* 2. *Inward* — *advancing* — Comm. 5.
Double your Files to the right intire advancing. — Comm. 6.
Double your Files to the right intire advancing, every man placing himself before his Leader — Comm. 7.
Files double your depth to the right intire — Comm. 8.
Files double your depth to the right, placing your selves behind your Bringers-up — Comm. 9.
Double your Files to the right and left by Division. — Com. 17.

Produceth one and the same Figure.

2. *Half Ranks of the left, double your right flank to the right* — Com. 11.
Half Ranks double your right flank to the right and left outwards —

Produceth one and the same Figure.

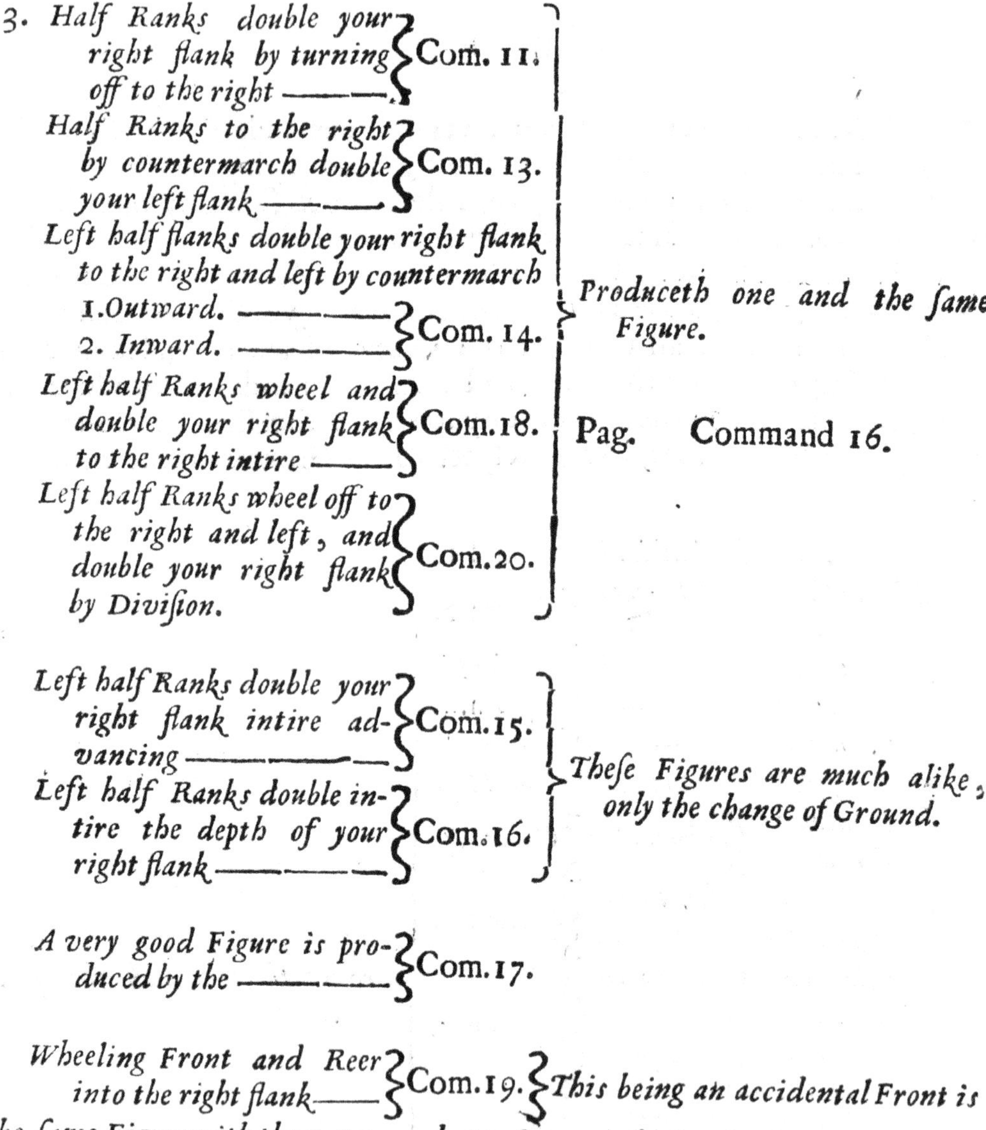

3. *Half Ranks double your right flank by turning off to the right* — Com. 11.

Half Ranks to the right by countermarch double your left flank — Com. 13.

Left half flanks double your right flank to the right and left by countermarch
1. *Outward.* —
2. *Inward.* — Com. 14.

Left half Ranks wheel and double your right flank to the right intire — Com. 18.

Left half Ranks wheel off to the right and left, and double your right flank by Division. — Com. 20.

} *Produceth one and the same Figure.*

Pag. Command 16.

Left half Ranks double your right flank intire advancing — Com. 15.

Left half Ranks double intire the depth of your right flank — Com. 16.

} *These Figures are much alike, only the change of Ground.*

A very good Figure is produced by the — Com. 17.

Wheeling Front and Reer into the right flank — Com. 19. *This being an accidental Front is the same Figure with the* 5. 10. *and* 15. *Command, for the strengthening of the proper Front by the doubling of Ranks.*

CHAP.

CHAP. XII.

I **Shall** now treat of that which is called in a more particular manner **Inversion** and **Conversion**, shewing you what is meant by them; And the nature and use of those several Commands, most in practice belonging to each of them.

1. **Inversion produceth a File, or Files;**

That is either by { *Files filing,* or *Ranks filing.* }

2. **Conversion produceth a Rank, or Ranks.**

That is either {
By increase of File ranking by { *Even,* or *Uneven* } *Parts.*
Of Ranks ranking to the { *Right,* or *Left.* }
Of Ranks wheeling to the { *Right,* or *Left* } *Flank.*
}

Observe, That in the performance of most of these Works, there must be either a double or twice double distance of Ground. But it must be the Commanders care so to open his Ranks or Files at such distances as the quantity of Ground will give leave.

I shall not demonstrate the Commands in the same method, as I have the Doublings for the strengthening of the Front, but shall insist in that method already set down; because I find the reception hereof to be somewhat of difficulty with some of our Rural Officers.

First, Inversion of files, or tiles filing in sequence.
Secondly, Files filing by countermarch.

1. **Command.** Files, file to the { 1. **Right.** / 2. **Left.** }

To perform this, to the right, **Command.** The right hand file to march away single, clear of the body, then the File leader of the next File is to fall in after the bringer up of the first File, and so all the rest, until the whole Body become one single file.

Captain.

1 m a
m
m
m
m
m
2 m
m
m
m
m
m
3 m
m
m
m
m
m
4 m
m
m
m
m
m
5 p
p
p
p
p
p

To reduce this, **Command.** File leaders lead up you Files to to the left.

O R,

Files, file six to the left.

Front.

12	11	10	9	8	7	6	5	4	3	2	1
m	m	m	m	p	p	p	.	.	.	.	.
m	m	m	m	p	p	p	.	.	.	.	.
m	m	m	m	p	p	p	.	.	.	.	.
m	m	m	m	p	p	p	.	.	.	.	:
m	m	m	m	p	p	p	.	.	.	.	.
m	m	m	m	p	p	p	.	.	:	.	.

Reer.

2 **Command**

2. **Command.** Files file to the { Right. or Left. } intire advancing.

To perform this to the right. The right hand file ſtand, the ſecond from the right advanceth into the Front of the firſt, the third into the Front of the ſecond, and the reſt ſucceſſively into the Front of each other, until they may be made one direct file.

p 5 a
p
p
p
p
p
m 4
m
m
m
m
m
m 3
m
m
m
m
m
m 2
m
m
m
m
m

To reduce this, **Command.** Face all about to the right, Files, file ſix to the right into the Reer.

OR,

As they ſtand without facing, **Command.** File ſix to the right gathering towards the Front.

Front.

p
m m m m p p p . . . . . m 1
m m m m p p p . . . : m
m m m m p p p . . . . m
m m m m p p p ; . . . m
m m m m p p p . : . . m
m m m m p p . . . . . . m

Reer.

Z 3. Command.

3. **Command.** Files, file inward into the right Flank.

To perform this **Command.** Half files face about, then file leader and bringer up of the left flank advance forward, and each file of the half files from the left, are to fall successively into the Reer of each file until they have made one intire, then face them to their leader.

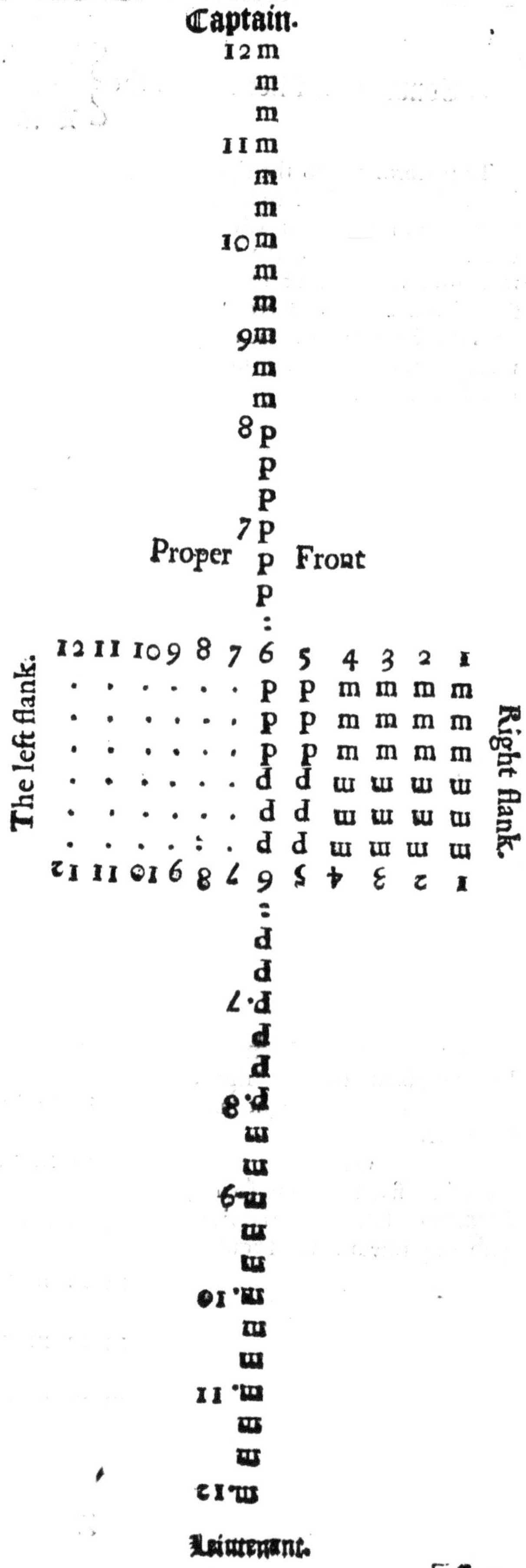

To reduce them **Command.** Reer half files face about to the left.

Front half files, file three to the left: and the Reer half files file three to the right;

Face all to your leader, and close your divisions.

```
                         Captain.
                           12m
                             m
                             m
                           11m
                             m
                             m
                           10m
                             m
                             m
                            9m
                             m
                             m
                            8p
                             p
                             p
                            7p
                     Proper  p  Front
                             p
                             :
              12 11 10 9 8 7 6  5  4  3  2  1
 The left     .  .  .  . . . p  p  m  m  m  m    Right
 flank.       .  .  .  . . . p  p  m  m  m  m    flank.
              .  .  .  . . . p  p  m  m  m  m
              .  .  .  . . . d  d  w  w  w  w
              .  .  .  . . . d  d  w  w  w  w
              .  .  .  . . : d  d  w  w  w  w
              12 11 10 9 8 7 6  5  4  3  2  1
                             :
                             d
                             d
                           d.7
                             d
                             d
                           d.8
                             w
                             w
                           w.9
                             w
                             w
                          w.10
                             w
                             w
                          w.11
                             w
                             w
                          w.13
                       Leiutenant.
```

4. **Command.** Files file to the right and left by Division.

To perform this, **Command.** The file leaders of each flank march away with your files until they are clear of the Body, then the next file leaders from the right and left are to fall in after the bringers up of the first moveants, until the Body become two files upon each wing.

Captain.

m. m
m m
m m
m m
m m
m m
m. m
m m
m m
m m
m m
m m
m m
m m
m m
m m
m m
m m

Proper Front.

11 10 9 8 7 6 5 4 3 2

. . . m p p p p m . . .
. . . m p p p p m . . .
. . . m p p p p m . . .
. . . m p p p p m . . .
. . . m p p p p m . . .
. . . m p p p p m . . .

Reer.

To reduce them, **Command** : File leaders lead up your files to the right and left.

OR,

Files file six to the right and left.

5. **Command.** Files, file inward into the right and left flank by Division.

You may the better understand this by the directions for the third **Command**: But

To perform this, **Command.** Half files face about, then file leaders and bringers up of each file, both from the right and left, and fall successively into the reer of each other, until they have made two intire files on each flank; Face to your leader.

To reduce this, **Command.** Reer half files face about to the right: Front and Reer half files file three to the right and left inwards; Face to your leader and close your Divisions.

Figure. 5.

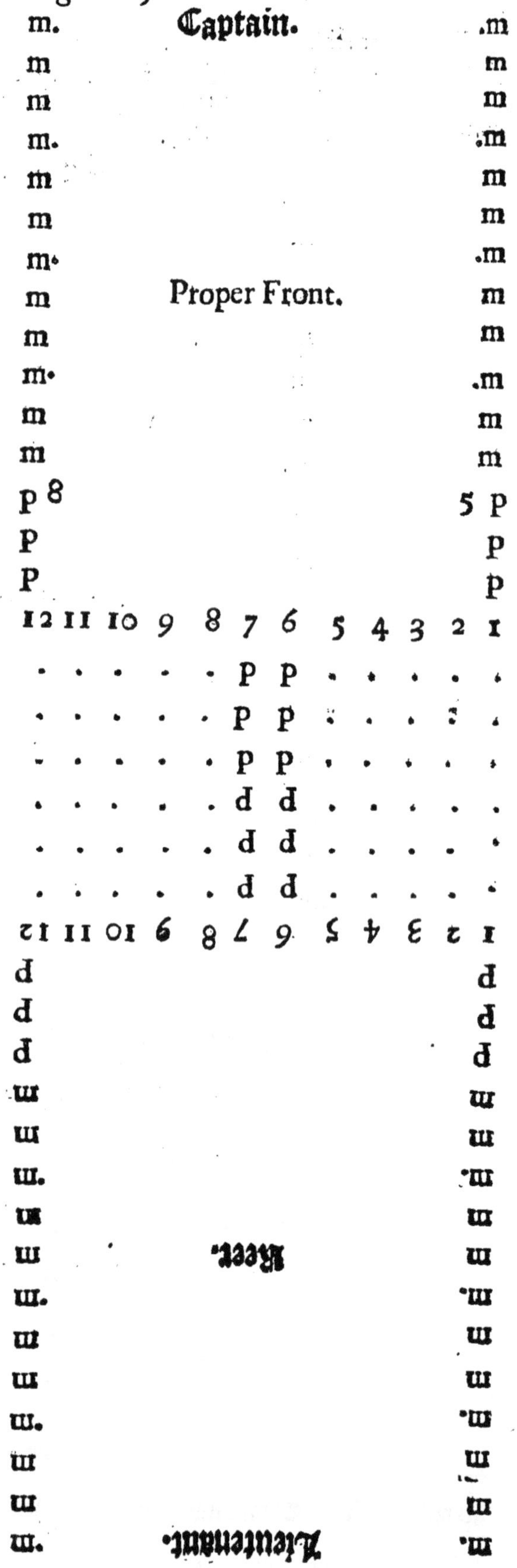

```
m.        Captain.        m
m                         m
m                         m
m.                        m
m                         m
m                         m
m.                        m
m       Proper Front.     m
m                         m
m.                        m
m                         m
m                         m
p 8                     5 p
p                         p
p                         p
12 11 10 9 8 7 6 5 4 3 2 1
 .  .  . . . p p . . . . .
 .  .  . . . p p . . . . .
 .  .  . . . p p . . . . .
 .  .  . . . d d . . . . .
 .  .  . . . d d . . . . .
 .  .  . . . d d . . . . .
12 11 10 9 8 7 6 5 4 3 2 1
d                         d
d                         d
d                         d
m                         m
m                         m
m.                        m
m                         m
m          Reer.          m
m.                        m
m                         m
m                         m
m.                        m
m                         m
m                         m
m.      Lieutenant.       m
```

6. **Command.**

Figure 5.

Captain

Proper Front.

Command, Files the in-[illegible] into the right and left Flank by Division.

You may the better understand [illegible] the directions for the third [illegible] mand. — But

To perform this Command, [illegible] [illegible] march, then the Leaders [illegible] up on each side both from the right and left and fall successively into the rear of each other until they have made three intire files on each flank; Face to your leader.

5. **Command.** Files, file inward into the right and left flank by Division.

You may the better understand this by the directions for the third **Command**: But

To perform this, **Command.** Half files face about, then file leaders and bringers up of each file, both from the right and left, and fall successively into the reer of each other, until they have made two intire files on each flank; Face to your leader.

To reduce this, **Command.** Reer half files face about to the right: Front and Reer half files file three to the right and left inwards; Face to your leader and close your Divisions.

Figure. 5.

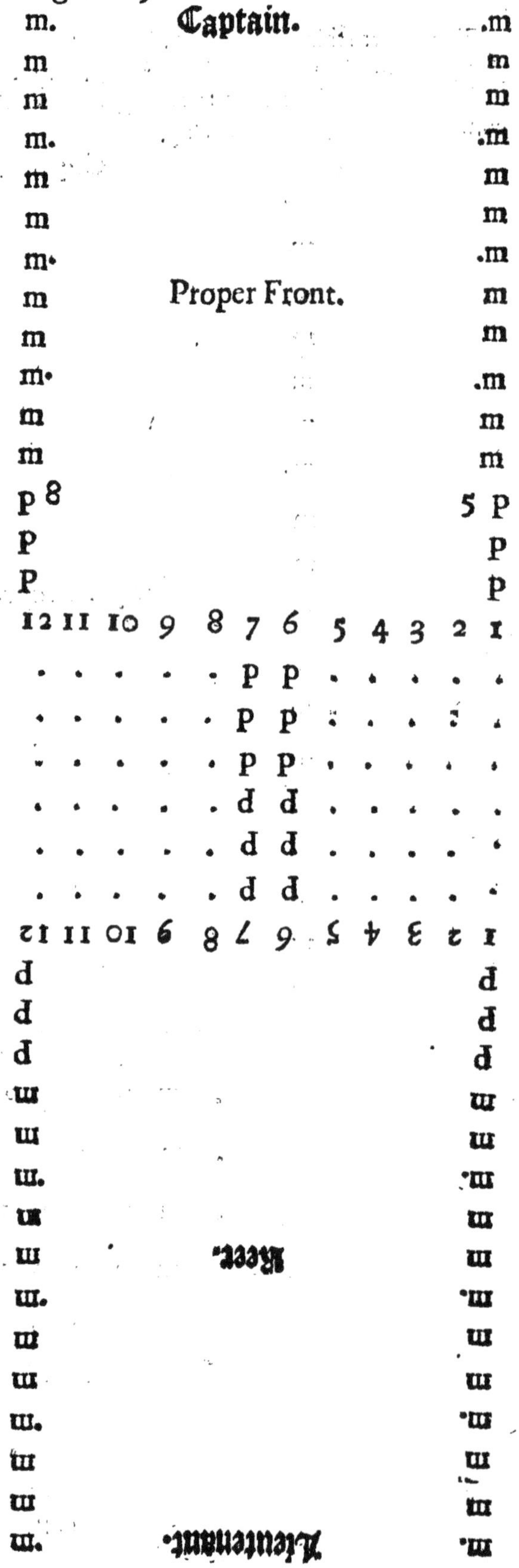

m. **Captain.** m
m m
m m
m. m
m m
m m
m. m
m Proper Front. m
m m
m. m
m m
m m
p 8 5 p
p p
p p
12 11 10 9 8 7 6 5 4 3 2 1
. . . . . . p p . . . . . .
. . . . . . p p . . . . . .
. . . . . . p p . . . . . .
. . . . . . d d . . . . . .
. . . . . . d d . . . . . .
. . . . . . d d . . . . . .
12 11 10 9 8 7 6 5 4 3 2 1
d d
d d
d d
m m
m m
m. m
m m
m **Reer.** m
m. m
m m
m m
m. m
m m
m m
m. **Lieutenant.** m

6. Command.

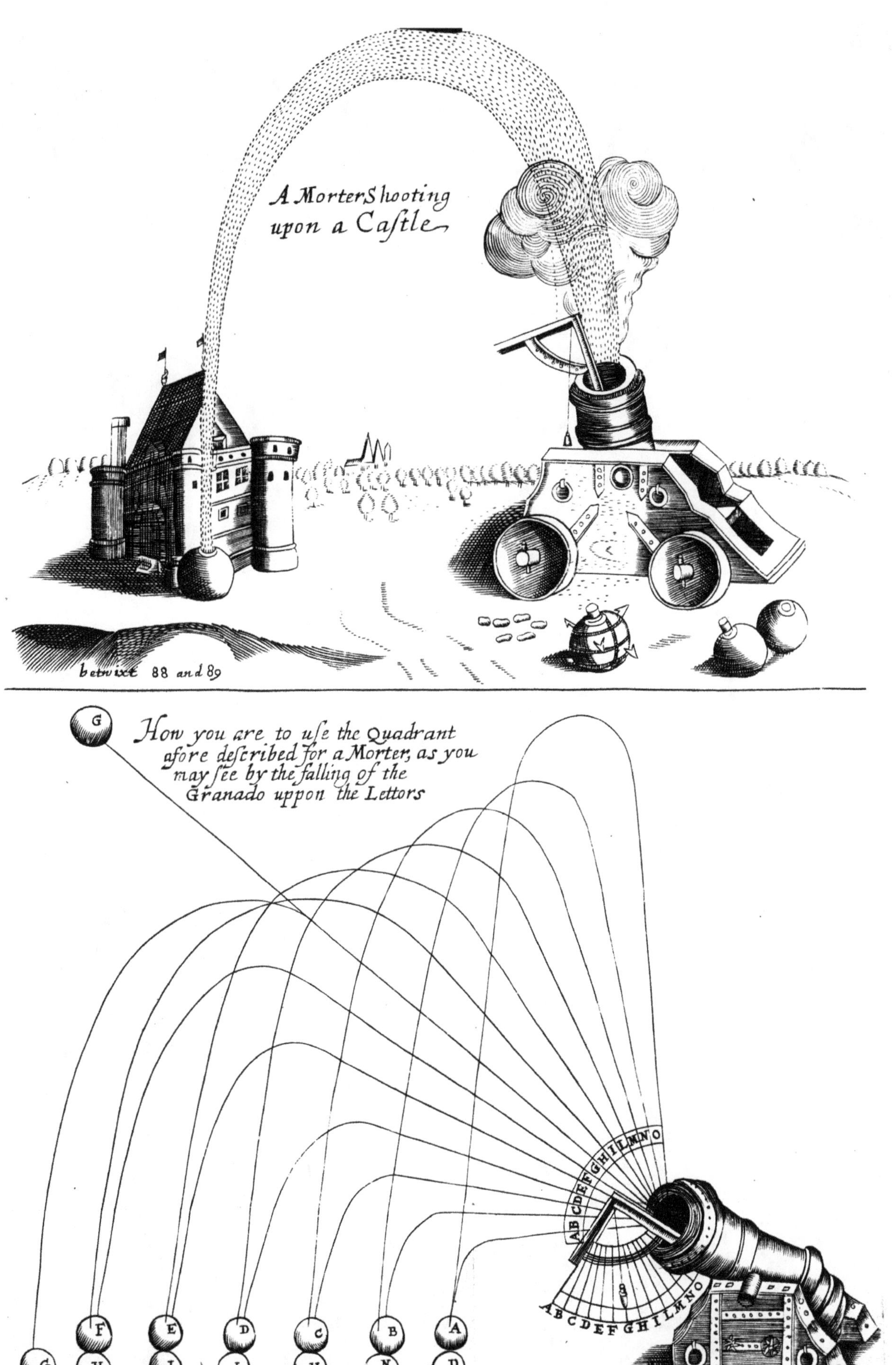
A Morter Shooting upon a Castle
betwixt 88 and 89
How you are to use the Quadrant afore described for a Morter, as you may see by the falling of the Granado uppon the Lettors
G
F
E
D
C
B
A
G
H
I
L
M
N
D
ABCDEFGHILMNO
ABCDEFGHILMNO

6. **Command.** Files, by countermarch file to the right, every man placing himself in the reer of the right hand file.

To perform this, **Command.** The right hand file stand, the rest of the Body face about to the left, then every particular file march forward to the left, and place themselves behind the bringers up of the right hand file.

To reduce this, **Command.** Files file fix to the left, each placeing themselves before their leader.

Figure. 6.

Front.

12 11 10 9 8 7 6 5 4 3 2 1

w w w w d d d . . . . . m a

w w w w d d d . . . . . m

w w w w d d d . . . . . m

w w w w d d d . . . . . m

w w w w d d d . . . . . m

w w w w d d d . . . . . m

2 m

Reer.

m

m

m

m

m

3 m

m

m

m

m

m

4 m

m

m

m

m

m

5 P

P

P

P

P

P

7. **Command.** Files by countermarch file to the right by division, each placing himself before his leader and bringer up.

To perform this, **Command.** Reer half files face about, the right hand file is to keep his ground, the rest moving forwards to the right, placing themselves before their File leaders and Bringers up.

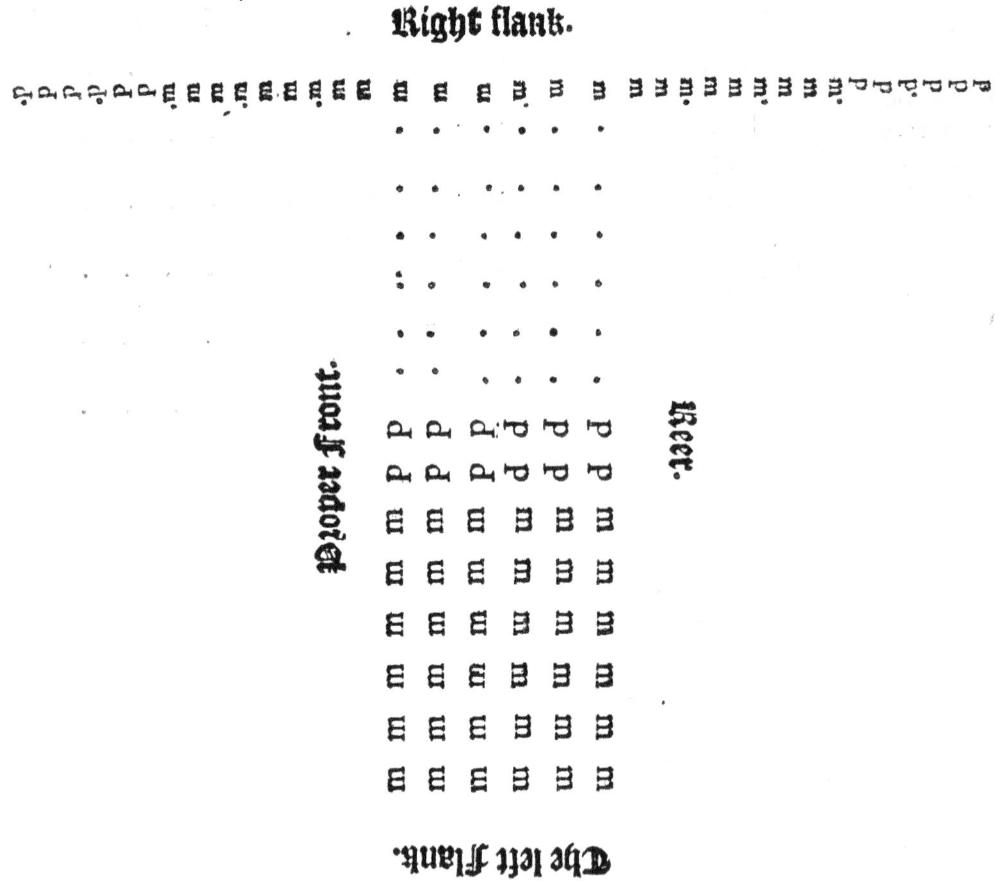

Right flank.

Proper Front.

Reer.

The left Flank.

To reduce this, **Command.** Front half files face about, and file three to the right, every man placing himself before his bringer up: And the Reer half files, file three to the left, placing your selves before your leaders.

I have with as much brevity, as conveniently I could, set forth by demonstration the first part of Inversion which is **of Files filing.**

Iproceed to the **second part of Inversion which is of Ranks filing.**

For the performance of which, observe that in all these motions, your files are to be at their **Order**, or otherwise as may be thought most convenient, and their Ranks to be opened either forwards or backwards at the discretion of the Commander, but at twice double distance (or more) as may be required to his number of men.

The distances being set, let every rank move according to Command.

8. **Command.**

8. **Command.** Ranks file to the right, placing your selves before your right hand man.

To perform this, **Command.** The right hand man of each rank is to stand, the rest are to move forwards with their right leg, and so place themselves before their right hand men.

8. Figure.

Front.

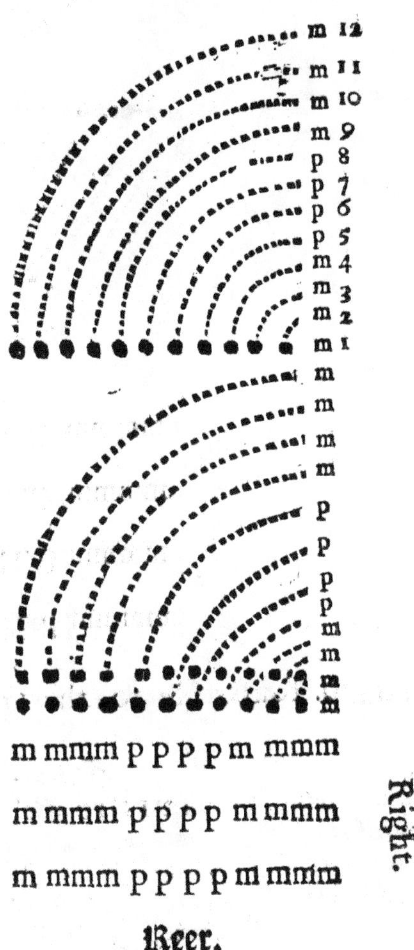

Reer.

To reduce them, **Command.** Files rank twelve to the left :

O R,

Ranks as you were.

Observe, Ranks filing are sooner executed in the commands and reducements, than files filing: For they will sooner be in readiness to receive any opposition with a suteable resistance in the Front: for in files filing it will be some long time before the file leaders will be able to do it.

9. **Command.** Ranks file to the right, placing your selves behind your right hand men.

To perform this, Direct. If they be upon a stand, they may open backwards to their distance for the work as by example.

But if they be upon a march, then the right hand man marcheth first, and all his rank so facing as to march to the right, file-wise after their leader: The right hand man of the second rank is so to do, and fall in the reer of the left hand man of the first Rank.

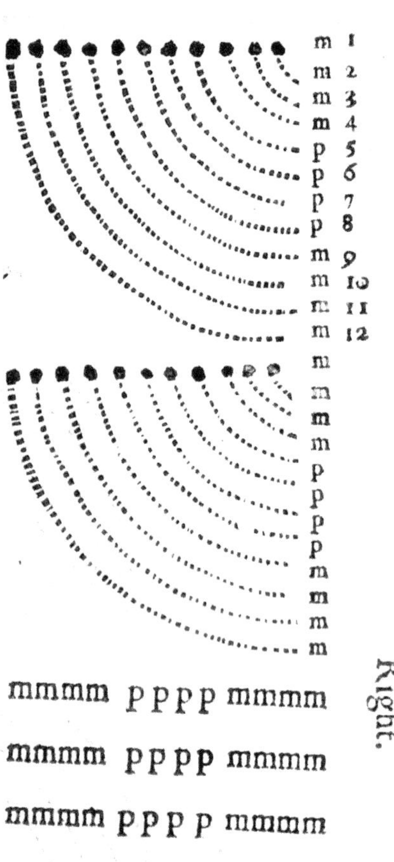

To reduce this, **Command.** Files rank twelve to the left:

OR,

Ranks as you were.

Ælian Tact. Ch. 30. p. 6. 10. **Command.** Ranks file to the right and left by Division.

The two former are directions enough for this. And may also be performed with the two former, either before their right hand men or otherwise.

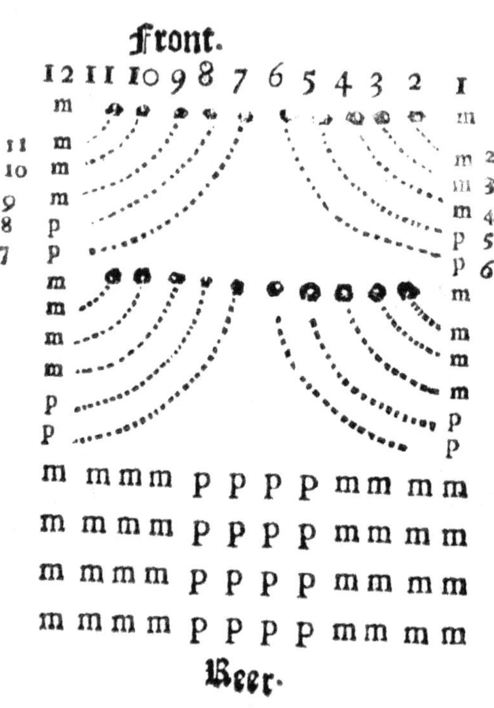

To reduce this, **Command.** Files convert into Ranks as you were.

OR,

Files Rank to the right and left inward as you were.

OR,

Files rank twelve to the right and left inward.

This

This Figure as by the Notes of Captain *Bingham* hath been of great use amongst the *Græcians*, and judged by our ingenious Artists not to be slighted by us for the avoydance of the great Ordinance or showers of small shot: In Cities I have seen it often used for lodging of the Colours: It is also a large Interval for the reception of any Honourable Person.

Some may dislike, in this last Inversion of Ranks filing, because there is a promiscuous mixture of Arms: This may be easily prevented by bringing both Divisions of Musquetteers into the Front of Pikes, or otherwise upon a march at the discretion of the Commander.

There yet remain divers words of Command of Ranks filing; By wheeling your Ranks into the right Flank, or into both Flanks, &c. But the prolixity of them have made me to abbreviate, and being more out of curiosity than of necessity. *Vide Conversion.*

I have shewed what is meant by Inversion both in Files and Ranks, and have demonstrated them by their Figures, so many as I conceive may be sufficient for the knowledge thereof.

Many I have heard to use the word *Inversion* to some of the precedent Commands; but I think it very convenient to be left out in the Exercisings of our Rural *Militia's*; It is a word not suitable to a Rustick capacity, and a word that may be spared.

Chap. XIII.

Of Conversion, and the several Parts thereof.

Conversion, I have declared to consist of a Rank or Ranks.

And that is performed either by

1. *Increase of Files ranking by* { *Even*, or *Uneven* } *Parts.*
2. *Increase or decrease of Files ranking by uneven Parts.*
3. *Files ranking intire into the Front, and wheeling into the same.*
4. *Ranks ranking to the right or left.*
5. *Wheeling into both Flanks.*

And of these I shall declare unto you, as briefly as I may, that your delight in the true understanding of them may not be neglected, by the least obscurity. Now the reason that I have demonstrated most with Figures, is that the young Souldier may see how many Commands produce one and the same Figure, their difference being only in quality, and not in quantity.

1. I shall begin with Files ranking by even parts, that is when they rank two, three, or four, keeping the same number in Rank, all being in an equal proportion; and if more, what is wanting to make up the Ranks in the Command, must be made good by the next Rank.

Front. **Captain.**

1. **Command.** Files rank three to the right.

Observe, in this motion, the File leader is first to move unto that hand the **Command** is given: And if six deep, the half file leader is to advance the same way.

1. { m m m **File-leader.**
   { m m m **Half file-leader.**
2. { m m m
   { m m m
3. { m m m
   { m m m
4. { m m m
   { m m m
5. { p p p
   { p p p
6. { p p p
   { p p p

p p p 7

7 p p p

To reduce this, **Command.**
Ranks file (or invert) to the right:
Then every File-leader, lead up his File, and rank to the right:
OR,
As you were.

12	11	10	9	8	7	6	5	4	3	2	1
m	m	m	m	p	.	.	.	.	.	.	.
m	m	m	m	p	.	.	.	.	.	.	.
m	m	m	m	p	.	.	.	.	.	.	.
m	m	m	m	p	.	.	.	.	.	.	.
m	m	m	m	p	.	.	.	.	.	.	.
m	m	m	m	p	.	.	.	.	.	.	.

Reer.

2. **The** uneven parts of Files ranking, is when there is such an increase either of two, three, or more in each Rank so exceeding the Rank before it: (and these exceedings are termed in Arithmetick, A Progressional Increase) Or else by the decrease of each Rank following after.

2. **Command.** Files rank three first, then by increase to the right two, in each Division of Musquetteers and Pikes.

m m m	p p p	m m m
m m m m m	p p p p p	m m m m m
m m m m m m m	p p p p p p p	m m m m m m m
m m m m m m m m m	p p p p p p p p p	m m m m m m m m m

These are termed half Rombes, or Wedges.
For Exercise sake you may make a Wedge, or half Rombe of all twelve by

3. **Command.**

3. **Command.** Files rank first two, and by increase two, from the whole Body.

You may alter the mixture of Armes at your discretion.

C

m m

m m m m

m m m m m m

m m m m m m m m

E

m m m m p p p p p p

p p p p p p p p p p p p

p p p p p p m m m m m m m m

m m m m m m m m m m m m m m m m

L

4. **Command** [is in the nature of a Rombe.]

Files rank first two, and by increase, and decrease two in each Rank, Divisionally both of Musquetteers and Pikes.

m m	p p	m m
m m m m	p p p p	m m m m m
m m m m m m	p p p p p p	m m m m m m
m m m m m m	p p p p p p	m m m m m m
m m m m	p p p p	m m m m
m m	p p	m m

The reducement of these three last **Commands** is, Ranks file as you were.

These Rombes, and half Rombes or Wedges were much of use in the *Græcian* Wars; Read the *Tact.* of *Ælian*, *pag.* 108. But being not now so much in use, I shall not spend much time in them, but leave the desirous to the view of Captain *Ward.*

5. & 6.

5. **Command.** Files rank to the { **Right,** or **Left** } into the Front.

6. **Command.** Files rank to the { **Right,** or **Left** } by wheeling into the Front.

I shall demonstrate both in this by Wheeling; only observe there must be so much distance between each file, as will contain each in rank.

To perform them **Command.** Files open to the left to your double distance; Ranks close forward to your close Order, face to the right, wheel all to the left until the whole Body be brought into one intire Rank.

5. & 6. Figure.

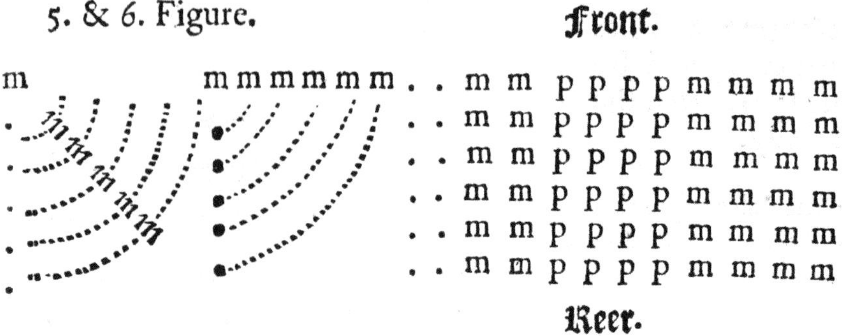

To reduce this, **Command.** Face to the Reer; then the first six to the right wheel to the right:

(When all have wheeled by sixes to the right) then face them to their Leader, and close their Files at discretion.

7. **Command.** Files rank into the Front and Reer by Division.

To perform this, **Command.** Files open to the left to your order; Ranks close forward to your close order; Half files face about to the right, and face to the left, then move all into the Front and Reer, and make two intire Ranks.

When the distance is set, *Observe* that those in motion are to face to the right flank.

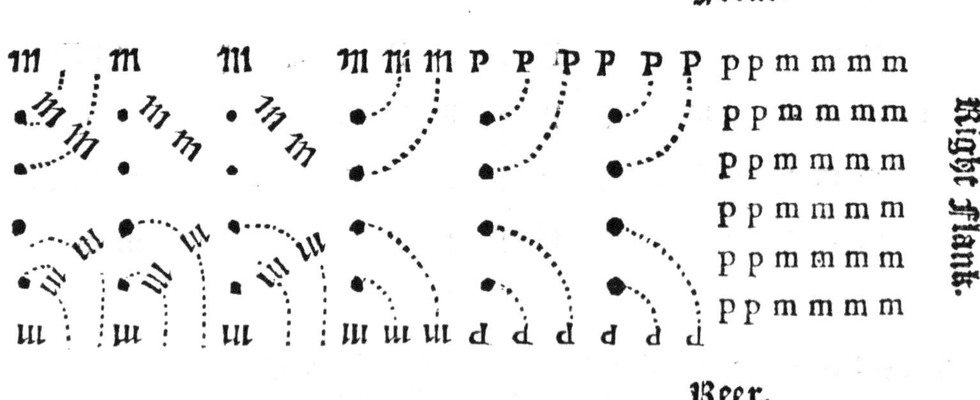

To reduce this, **Command.** Front half files face about to the left, rees half files face about to the right, then wheel all into their respective Files, then face them to their Leader, and close their files at discretion.

Here might be inserted for variety and curiosity some more words of **Command** of Conversion, of files ranking into the midst; by Countermarches, and by Wheelings.

But by what is demonstrated already you'l find enough in them, and I must look to be censured by some for what is done: and conceiving the remainder to be useless, I shall omit them to avoid a further censure, and proceed to the Conversion of Ranks ranking in equal Parts.

1. Conversion of Ranks ranking in equal Parts.

Observe, that in Ranks ranking, you may perform it with any number, more or less, as place and occasion may serve; containing in every Rank an equality in Number.

And it is to be understood after this manner: When there is twelve more or less marching

marching a breast, and by reason of some narrowness of passage, or some other intent, the Commander causeth his Souldiers to rank either two, three, five or seven, &c. according to the place or occasion.

8. **Command.** Ranks, rank two to the right.

To perform this, **Command.** The two first in Rank, to the right advance forwards, the next two of the same Rank in the Reer of them, until the first Rank have made six Ranks, and in all 36 Ranks.

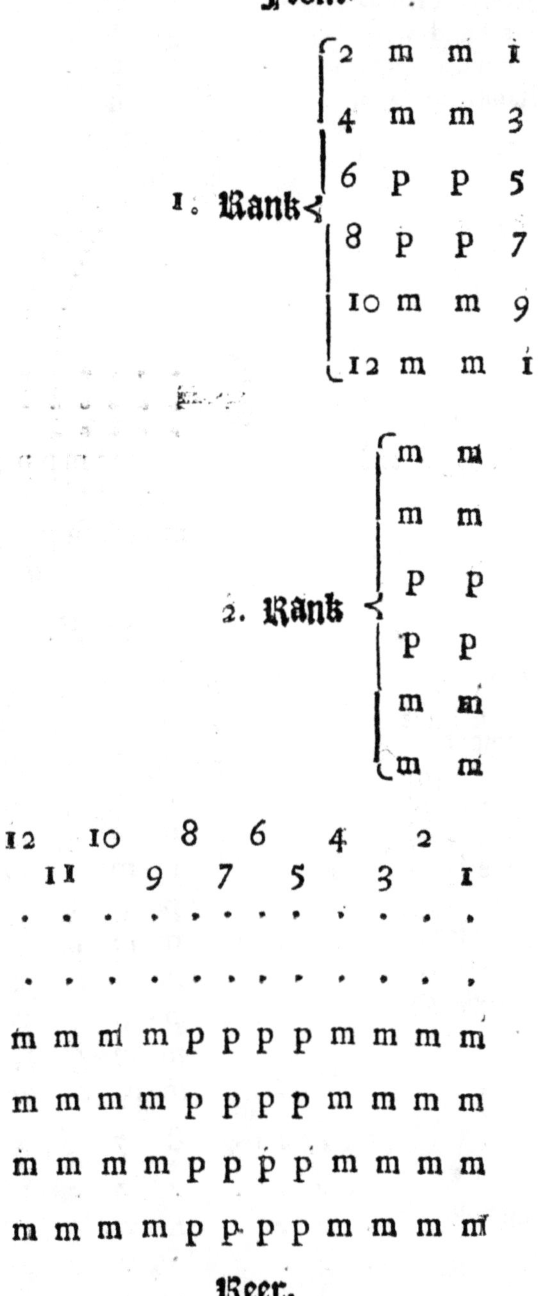

To reduce this, **Command.** Ranks, rank twelve to the left.

Observe, that the first rank stands, the rest are to advance, two and two, until the whole rank of twelve be complete in one rank.

9. **Command.** Rank two to the right and left { 1. **Outward,** then 2. **Inward.**

To perform this outward, **Command.** The two outmost men, upon the right and left hand, advance forwards, the next in the same Rank are to follow, dividing themselves two to the right hand, and two to the left hand; so when the Work is finished there will be eighteen Ranks in each Division.

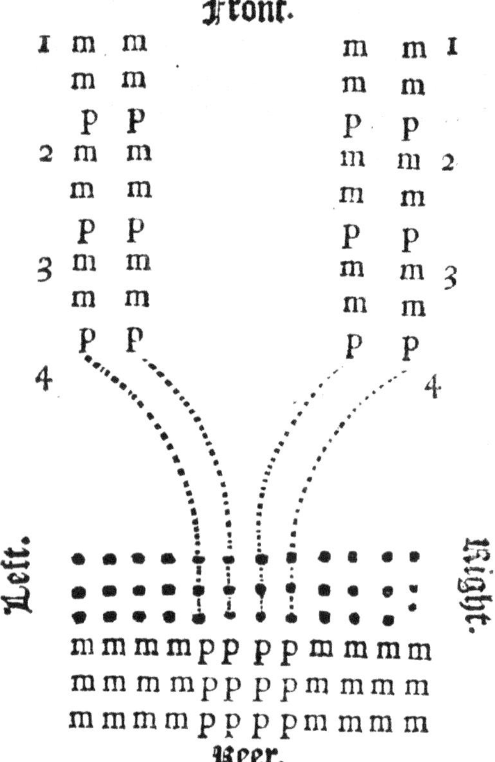

To reduce this:
Ranks as you were.

OR,

Rank twelve to the right and left inward.

Front.

2. To perform it **Inward.**
Ranks rank two to the right and left inwards. **Command.**
The two inmost men of the right and left hand in the midst of the Battail, advance forwards, the next in the same Rank are to follow, two from the right hand, and two from the left, until the Work be finished, making eighteen Ranks.

8 p p p p 5
10 m m m m 3
12 m m m m 1
p p p p
m m m m
m m m m 2
p p p p
m m m m
m m m m 3
p p p p
m m m m
m m m m 4

12 11 10 9 8 7 6 5 4 3 2 1
. . . . 1
. . . . 2
. . . . 3
. . . . 4
m m m m p p p p m m m m 5
m m m m p p p p m m m m 6

Reer.

To reduce this, **Command.**
Ranks as you were.

OR,

Ranks twelve to the right and left outwards.

I shall

I shall demonstrate one Figure of Ranks ranking in unequal parts which is rather to satisfie the curious than of any absolute necessity. *Unequal Parts.*

10. **Command.** Ranks, rank 1, 3, 5, 7, 9, 11. by increase and decrease as they stand in a Body.

To perform this.

The right hand man of the first rank march forth, then the three next of the same rank follow in the reer of him, then five more out of the same rank to make the third, and what is wanting in the first rank of the Body to make good the fourth in Figure, must be taken out of the second in body, and so to proceed in the remainder both for its increase and decrease, until your **Command** be produced.

To reduce this, **Command.** Right hand men rank, twelve as you were.

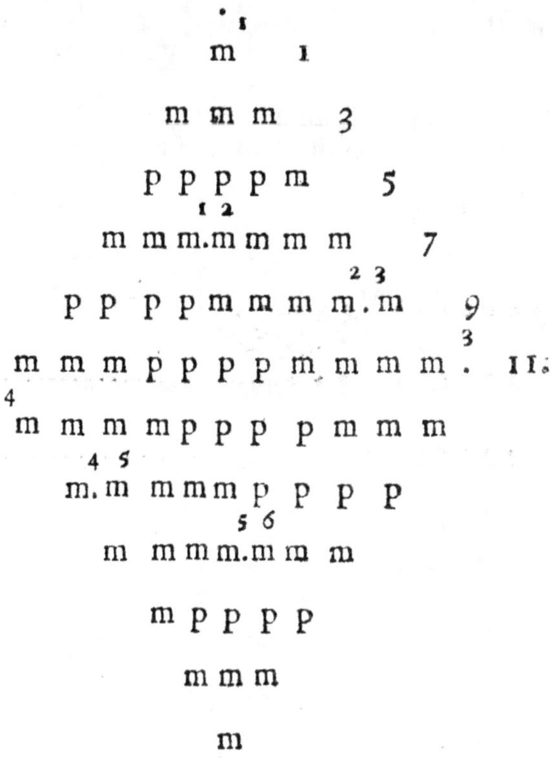

```
            1
            m      1
         m m m       3
      p p p p m        5
          1 2
   m m m.m m m m         7
                  2 3
p p  p p m m m m m.m        9
                          3
m m m p p p p m m m m .   11.
4
m m m m p p p  p m m m m
  4 5
m.m  m m m p  p p p
           5 6
   m  m m m.m m m
     m p p p p
       m m m
         m
```

11. **Command.** Ranks rank intire to the { **Right,** or **Left** } into the Front.

To perform this, Let the first rank stand, every rank else face to the right, and move away to the right successively placing themselves on the right hand of each rank, until they all stand in one intire rank in the Front.

Figure 11.

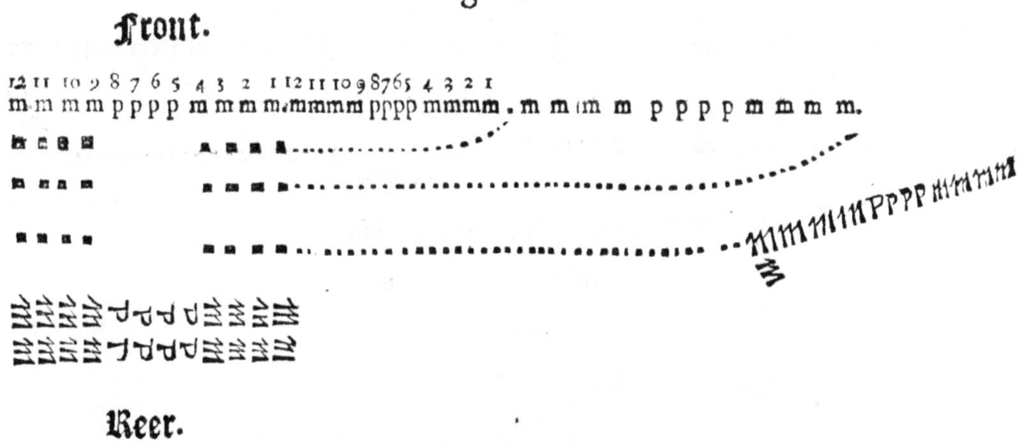

Front.

```
12 11 10 9 8 7 6 5 4 3 2 1 12 11 10 9 8 7 6 5 4 3 2 1
m m m m p p p p m m m m.m m m m p p p p m m m m . m m m m p p p p m m m m.
```

Reer.

To reduce this, **Command.** Ranks rank as you were.

OR,

Ranks rank twelve to the left; the second falls into the reer of the first, the third into the reer of the second, and so all successively until they be reduced.

12. **Command.** Ranks, rank intire into the Front, every man placing himself on the outside of his { Right, or Left } hand man by Countermarch.

To perform this, to the right hand man. The first rank stands, the rest moves away to the right on the outside of the right hand man.

Front.

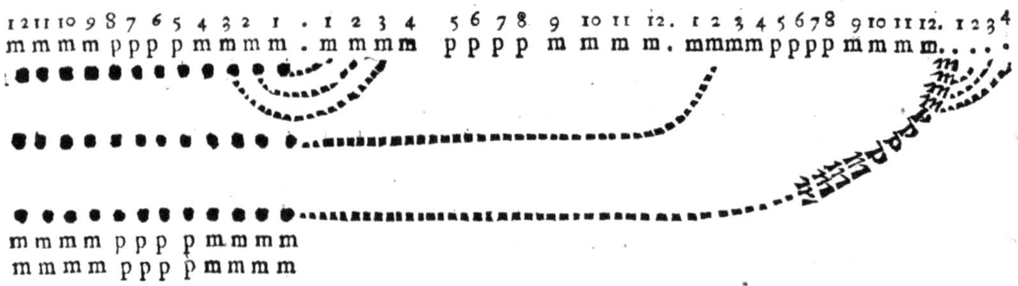

12 11 10 9 8 7 6 5 4 3 2 1 . 1 2 3 4 5 6 7 8 9 10 11 12. 1 2 3 4 5 6 7 8 9 10 11 12. 1 2 3 4
m m m m p p p p m m m m . m m m m p p p p m m m m. m m m m p p p p m m m m. . . .

m m m m p p p p m m m m
m m m m p p p p m m m m

Reer.

The precedent reducement will reduce this.

OR,

Ranks, rank twelve to the left, each placing himself on the outside of his left hand man.

13. **Command.** Ranks, rank { 1. Outward 2. Inward } into the Front.

1. To perform it outwards, **Command.** The first rank to stand, the rest to face to the right and left outwards, the second rank to advance clear of the first, and then to move forth even with the Front in breast, and all the rest successively do the same, until they be all even with the Front in one intire rank.

Front.

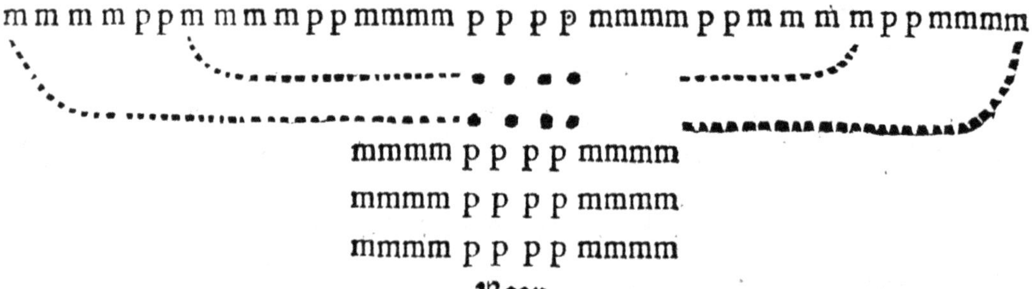

m m m m p p m m m m p p m m m m p p p p m m m m p p m m m m p p m m m m

m m m m p p p p m m m m
m m m m p p p p m m m m
m m m m p p p p m m m m

Reer.

To reduce this; Ranks as you were.

OR,

The first 12, or 12 middlemost stand, the rest face to the right and left inwards; the second to move into the reer of the first rank, the third into the reer of the second, and successively the rest into the reer of the remainder, and being faced to their Leader, and even in their ranks, they are reduced.

2. To perform it **Inwards. Command.** Ranks, rank inward into the Front.

To produce it, the first rank to move to the right and left outwards, and so to keep moving,

moving, (or opening) then the second rank is to advance into the ground of the first, and the second is then to move with the first to the right and left outwards; then the third is to advance into the place of the second rank, so all are to do until the last rank is advanced intire into the Front.

Front.

12 11 10 9 8 7   12 11 10 9 8 7 6 5 4 3 2 1   6 5 4 3 2 1
m m m m p p . m m m m p p . . . . p p m m m m . m . p p m m m m

m m m m p p p p m m m m
m m m m p p p p m m m m
m m m m p p p p m m m m
m m m m p p p p m m m m

Reer.

To reduce this; The first six upon the right, and left hand stand; then **Command**; Ranks, rank six to the right and left outwards; And close your Divisions.

Lastly, the Conversion of Ranks by wheeling into the Flanks.

14. **Command.** Ranks wheel to the { **Right,** or **Left** } into the right Flank.

To perform this, **Command.**

Every particular rank to be at double Distance in rank; and at close Order in file: Then Wheel them to their right hand, until they have brought their Faces (or Aspects) unto the right Flank.

After you may face them to the Front.

Front. **C.**

To reduce this, **Command.**

Files rank twelve to the right.

The first man is to stand, the rest is to move forward to the right successively twelve in rank.

But if you wheel them to the left hand into the right flank, you must command them to face about and wheel your ranks to the left hand, until their Faces (or Aspects) be brought to the right Flank.

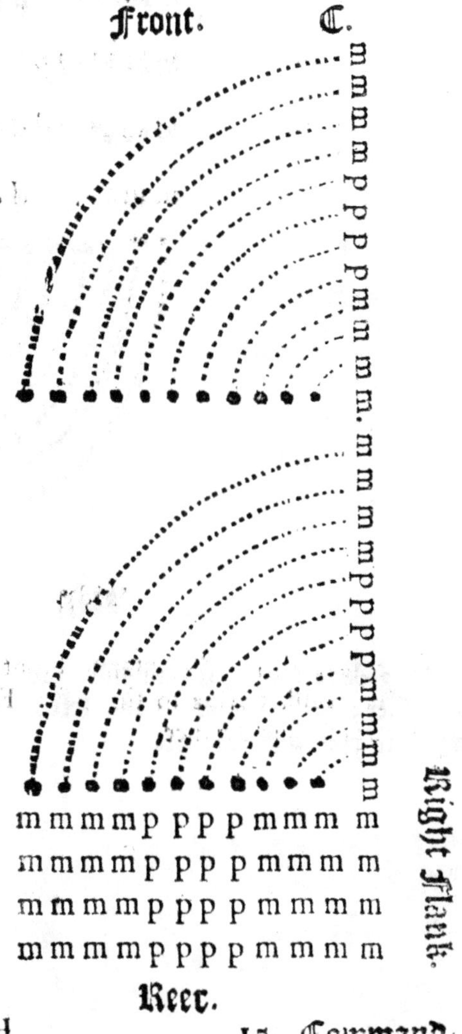

m m m m p p p p m m m m
m m m m p p p p m m m m
m m m m p p p p m m m m
m m m m p p p p m m m m

Right Flank.

Reer.

15. **Command.** Ranks of your Front and Reer half files, wheel outwards to your right Flank.

I shall put in execution but two Ranks, one in the Front half files, and the other of the Reer half files, which is sufficient for Demonstration.

To perform this, **Command.** Ranks open all to your twice double distance; then Front half files wheel to the right; and Reer half files wheel to the left. And face to your Leader.

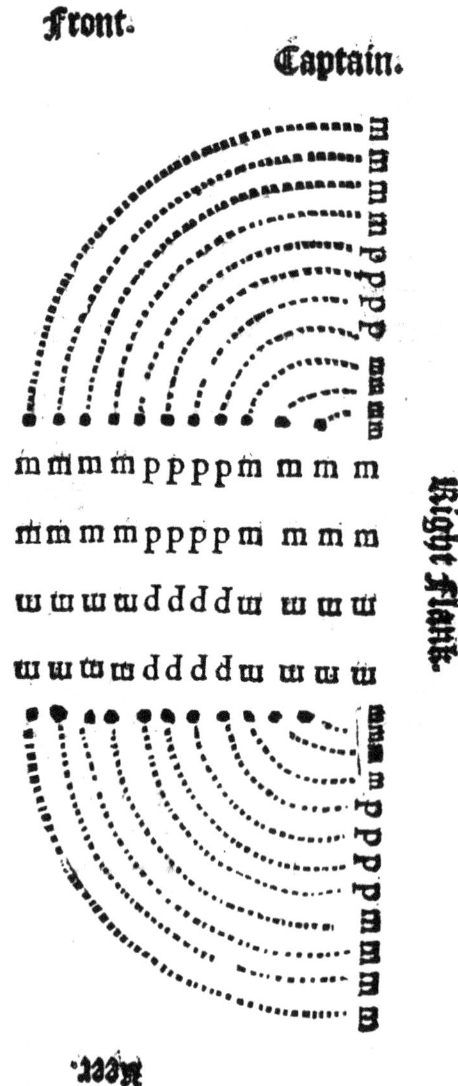

To reduce them, **Command.** Front half files, rank twelve to the right; Reer half files, rank twelve to the left: Face to your Leader; march up and close forwards to your due distance.

16. **Command.**

16. **Command.** Ranks of your Front and Reer half Files, wheel inwards into your right Flank.

To perform this, **Command.** Front and Reer half files march clear to your twice double distance; Front and Reer half files face about.

Front half files wheel your Ranks to the left, and Reer half files, wheel your Ranks to the right; Face to your Leader.

Front.

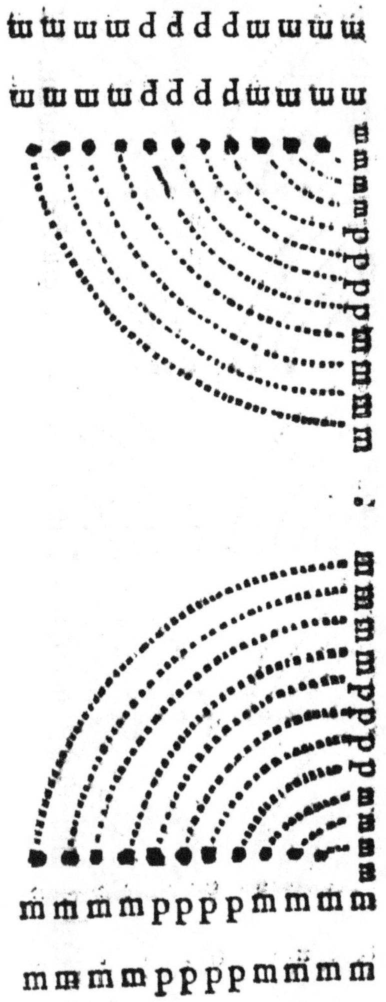

ɯ ɯ ɯ ɯ d d d d ɯ ɯ ɯ ɯ

ɯ ɯ ɯ ɯ d d d d ɯ ɯ ɯ ɯ

m m m m p p p p m m m m

m m m m p p p p m m m m

m m m m p p p p m m m m

m m m m p p p p m m m m

Reer.

To reduce this, **Command.** Front half files, rank twelve to the left: Reer half files face about and rank twelve to the right: Face to your Leader, and close your Divisions.

17. **Command.** Ranks, rank to each Flank, by wheeling to the right and left into the same by Division.

OR,

Ranks wheel to the right and left by Division into both Flanks; advancing (or placing) themselves before their right and left hand men.

Observe, they are to be at double distance in Rank, and at Order in File.

Figure 17.

Front.

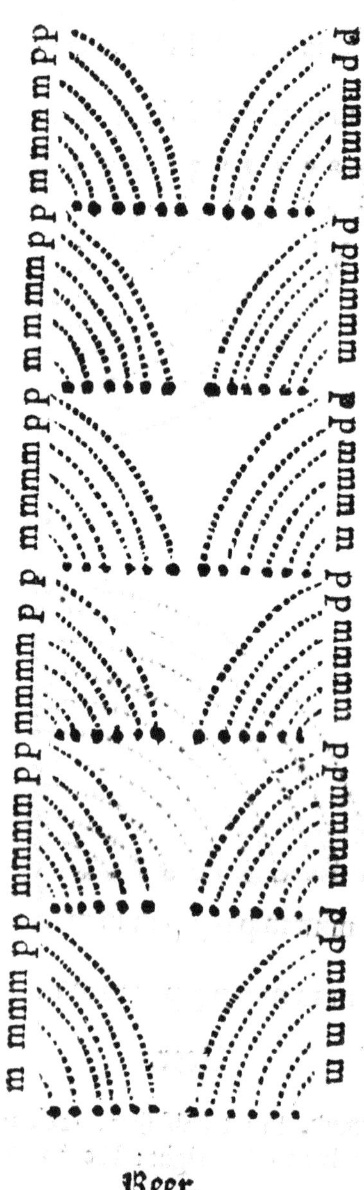

Reer.

To reduce them, **Command** them to face to the Reer, and wheel into their places.

OR,

Files, rank twelve to the right and left inward into the Reer, and close them to their order; then face them to their Leader.

But if you would avoid mixture of Arms, you may place all your Musquetteers either in Front and Reer.

Or

Or else, wheel only the Musquetteers first, and leave the Pikes standing.

Or else it may be performed in marching; and then the Reducement is; Ranks as you were.

18. Command. Ranks of your Front and Reer half files, wheel outwards to your right and left Flank by Division.

They are to observe the same distance as in the former.

To perform this, **Command.** Half files face about. Ranks open to your double distance, then Front and Reer half files wheel to the right and left outwards into both Flanks.

Front.

Figure 18.

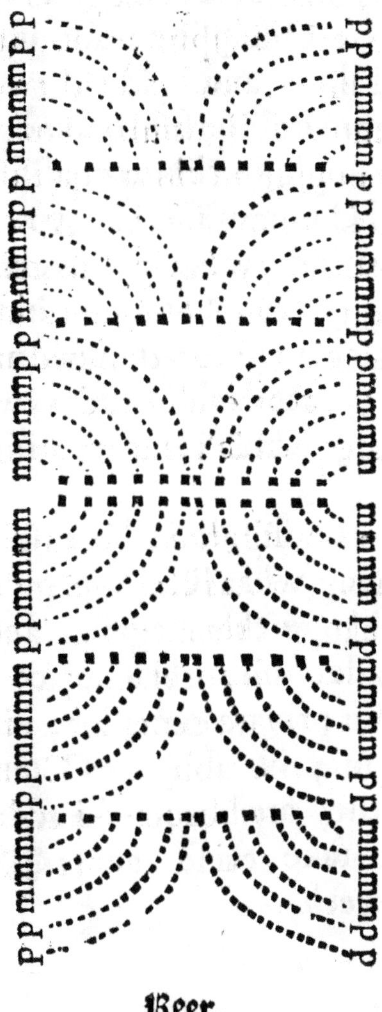

Reer.

To reduce this, **Command.** Who being faced to their Leader. Front half files face to the Reer, rank twelve to the right and left inwards. And Reer half files face about and rank twelve to the right and left inward, Files close to the midst to your order: Face to your Leader.

Chap. XIV.

Of making File-Leaders successively both of Number and Place in a File, and so for a Whole Body.

The Sweedish *Mode also.*

AS I have stinted my self to a set Number of Files, so I have also to a set Number in a File, not exceeding six, being according to our present Mode of Discipline; for if I had gone to a various Number in Files, and added two to each File, my Figures had been more delightful to some Spectators; others I hope will find enough in this to qualifie, or make them fit to do their King and Country service, *&c.*

And now the Souldery having marched sometimes together, and so loving (being Souldiers indeed) by reason of such experiences as they have attained unto in the exercise of this *Military Art*, that each Leader is willing his follower should take his place; which is a great incouragement to an ingenious Souldier.

This ought not to be slighted, because it is profitable to a Commander to bring what Ranks he pleaseth to lead in the Front, and to exchange them again, and at last to bring the proper File-Leaders into their places; Besides the incouragement it hath in private exercises, it makes men studious, whereby they may be able to Command in their respective Files, when they are become Leaders.

In the first place take these short **Commands** to produce them, as followeth.

Command

1. *A File-Leader.*
2. *Rank two to the left, and Files to the left double.*
3. *Countermarch Front and Reer into the midst, and face to that part which was the Reer.*
4. *Face about to the right.*
5. *Countermarch from the Reer into the midst, and face to that which was the Reer.*
6. *Files rank two to the right, and Files to the right double.*

This being performed they are reduc'd.

I ſhall demonſtrate by Tables the ſucceſſion of each man's Leading, and give you ſome, or ſeveral Words of **Command** according to my own and others, ſeverally, that ſhall produce ſuch Leader into his place, as they ſhall ſtand in ſequence, and as they ſhall alſo ſtand in their reſpective Dignities.

The Front and standings of each File as they come to be Leaders according to various Commands.

A File.
1
2
3
4
5
6.

A File						To make the	If upon a single File, Command.	
1	2	3	4	5	6	2	File-Leader with the odd men from the Front, face about to the right, and interchange Ground.	2
2	1	4	3	6	5	3	Front half file double your depth to the left.	3
3	6	5	2	1	4	4	File rank six to the left; then, Rank file six to the left.	4
4	1	2	5	6	3	5	Half file double your Front to the right; and Files double your depth to the right.	5
5	6	3	4	1	2	6	Rank two to the left, and Files to the left double.	6
6	5	4	3	2	1	1	Reducement. Bringer-up stand, the rest pass through to the left, and place your selves behind your Bringer-up.	
1	2	3	4	5	6	2	File rank two to the left; Files to the left double.	2
2	1	4	3	6	5	3	Half double your Front to the right; Files double your depth to the left.	3
3	6	5	2	1	4	4	Bringers-up double your Front to the right, and double your Files to the left intire advancing.	4
4	1	2	3	6	5	5	Bringers-up double your Front to the left, and double your Files to the right intire advancing.	5
5	6	3	4	1	2	6	File rank two to the right, and Files to the right double.	6
6	5	4	3	2	1	1	Reducement. File rank to the left into the Front; Rank file six to the left.	
							If more Files than one Command.	
1	2	3	4	5	6	2	Ranks to the left double, and Files to the left double.	2
2	1	4	3	6	5	3	Half double your Front to the right, and Files to the right double.	3
3	2	6	1	5	4	4	File-Leaders stand, the rest pass through to the right, and place themselves before their Leaders.	4
4	5	1	6	2	3	5	Ranks to the left double, and Files double your depth to the left.	5
5	6	3	4	1	2	6	Ranks to the right double, and Files to the right double.	6
6	5	4	3	2	1	1	Reducement. File Leaders stand, the rest pass through, and place your selves before your Leaders.	

This I saw *July*, 1671.

The

The front and standing of each file as they come to be leaders in their respective dignities

Dignity. / The dignity of a file. / Dignit y.

1.a 5.e 4.d 3.c 6.f 2.b

1	5	4	3	6	2	1	a	Countermarch front and Reer into the midst. Front and Reer half files interchange ground.	N. 2.
2	6	3	1	5	4	2	b	Bringers up double your Front to the right, & files to the right double advancing, & placing your selves before your leaders.	N. 3.
3	6	2	4	5	1	3	c	Front half files double your Reer to the right intire advancing.	N. 4.
4	5	1	3	6	2	4	d	Ranks to the right double, and Files to the right double.	N. 5.
5	4	3	1	2	6	5	e	Face about into the right and Countermarch your Reer into the Front.	N. 6.
6	2	1	3	4	5	6	f	**Reducement.** Rank two to the left and files to the left double, then Front half files double your Reer to the left intire advancing, every one placing himself behind his leader.	

						Dignity			
1	5	4	3	6	2	1	a	Bringers up double your front to the right, and files double your depth to the right.	N. 2.
2	6	3	1	5	4	2	b	File leaders & half file leaders stand, the rest pass through to the left, & place your selves before your leaders.	N. 3.
3	6	2	4	5	1	3	c	Front and Reer half files interchange ground.	N 4.
4	5	1	3	6	2	4	d	Ranks to the right double; Files to the right double.	N. 5.
5	4	3	1	2	6	5	e	File leaders stand, the rest pass through to the left and place your selves before your leaders.	N. 6.
6	2	1	3	4	5	6	f	**Reducement.** Ranks to the left double, files to the left double: then, half files double your Front to the right; then, Bringers up face about to the right and march forth into your places.	

						I much quaftion the dignity of this; how ever I have incerted it,		
1	6	4	3	5	2		Half files double your Front to the left. Files double to the right intire advancing, every man placing himself before his leader.	N. 2.
2	5	3	1	6	4		Front half files double the Reer to the left. Files double to the left intire advancing, every man placing himself before his leader.	N. 3.
3	5	2	1	6	4		Bringer up double your Front to the right, and files double your depth to the right, every man placing himself before his leader.	N. 4.
4	6	1	2	5	3		Half files double your Front to the right. Files double to the left intire advancing. Files rank two to the right. Files to the left double.	N. 5.
5	2	4	3	1	6		Bringer up double your Front to the left. Files double your depth to the left, every man falling behind his bringer up.	N. 6.
6	1	3	4	2	5		**Reducement.** Files rank two to the left; files to the left double.	

1 6 4 3 5 2.

CHAP. XV.

Of Countermarches.

WE read in the *Tacticks* of *Ælian* of three kinds of Countermarches uſed amongſt the *Græcians* and *Perſians* ;

And are termed, the { 1. Chorean, 2. Lacedemonian, 3. Macedonian } Countermarches,

There is another Countermarch that is of uſe in our modern exerciſes and is termed the Baſtard Countermarch, and ſo called becauſe it participates ſome times of one, and ſome times of another, but always, of two, and may in many reſpects be more uſeful than the former.

Moſt Authors place this amongſt the other Countermarches, therefore I ſhall not now alter it ; although in my opinion, it may be very well ranked amongſt the doublings.

I thought to have been large in demonſtrating the ſeveral natures of Countermarches ; but being conceived of all motions in this art the leaſt beneficial to our lateſt mode of diſcipline, I ſhall not be tedious to your Patience : But if the skilful Souldier will put them into practice (eſpecially the Baſtard Countermarch) he will not only find ſome of them ſerviceable but all delightful in private Exerciſes.

Obſerve the { Chorean, Lacedemonian, Macedonian } is { 1. Maintaining, 2. Loſing, 3. Gaining } Ground.

Firſt, The maintaining of Ground is a Countermarch commanded without any addition to it ; and is termed the *Chorean*, or *Cretan* Countermarch.

Secondly, The loſing ground is a Countermarch commanded when the Souldier is to take his ground from the Reer, and this is termed the *Lacedemonian* Countermarch.

Thirdly, The gaining of ground, that is a Countermarch taking of ground next before the front, and forſaking the ground it firſt ſtood upon, and this is termed a *Macedonian* Countermarch.

In all which there is Countermarchings of { Files. Ranks. The Front. The Reer half files. Half Ranks. }

And theſe may all be performed by intire or diviſional Countermarches.

1. The Countermarchings of Files is when every Souldier followeth his leader.
2. The Countermarchings of Ranks is when every Souldier followeth his ſide man.
3. The Front and Reer half Files Countermarchings is when the Souldier ſhall follow their File leaders or Bringers up.
4. The Countermarchings of half Ranks is when the Souldier ſhall follow their outſide men.

I ſhall

I shall in the first place shew how Intire and Divisional Countermarches are performed by files, and Ranks.

1. Observe, That in the execution hereof your distance is to be at six foot in rank and file.

2. When you are to Countermarch to the right, the file leaders are to step forward with their right legs, and face about to the right, passing down to the Reer with their respective File following them, keeping even a breast with their right handmen, and to be sure not to turn before they be advanced to the ground of their File leaders.

3. All Intire Countermarches of Files or ranks may be reduced by contrary Countermarches: If the Command be to the right, reduce them to the left: And so for Contermarchings of the Front, Reer or flanks into the midst, reduce them back from the midst.

It shall be my endeavour to demonstrate how all Intire and divisional Countermarches shall lye under these three heads.

Of { Mantaining, Losing, and Gaining of } ground.

First, of Countermarches maintaining Ground.

In the second precedent rule it will not be amiss to cast your eye back, for your better direction, by which you'l be able to pass these Countermarches with greater delight and Order.

1. **Command.** Files to the { 1. Right, or 2. Left } hand Countermarch.

To perform this, Let the file leaders step forward with their right legs, and march even in Rank to the Reer, and none to turn off until he come to his File leaders Ground.

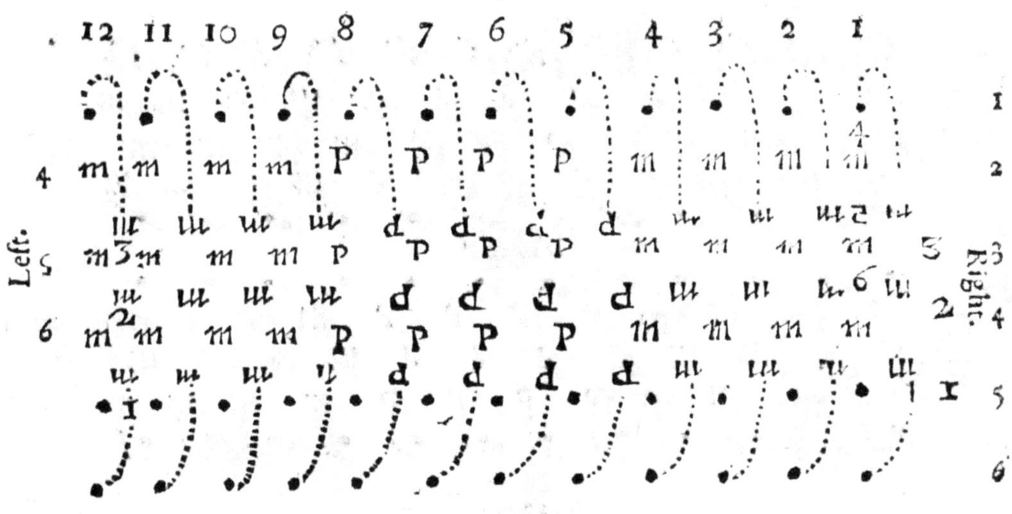

To reduce this, **Command.** Files to the left hand Countermarch.

 2. Command.

2. **Command.** Ranks to the {1. **Right** or 2. **Left**} hand Countermarch.

To perform this, Face them to the Right; and the right hand file is to turn off to the right, and to march even to the Ground of the left hand file.

Front.

12 11 10 9 8 7 6 5 4 3 2 1

Left. Right.

Reer.

You may reduce this, by Ranks Countermarching to the left.

3. **Command.** Countermarch your Front and Reer into the midst.

To perform this, **Command.** Half files, face about and turn to off the left. Front half files turn off to the right; and face to your leader.

Front

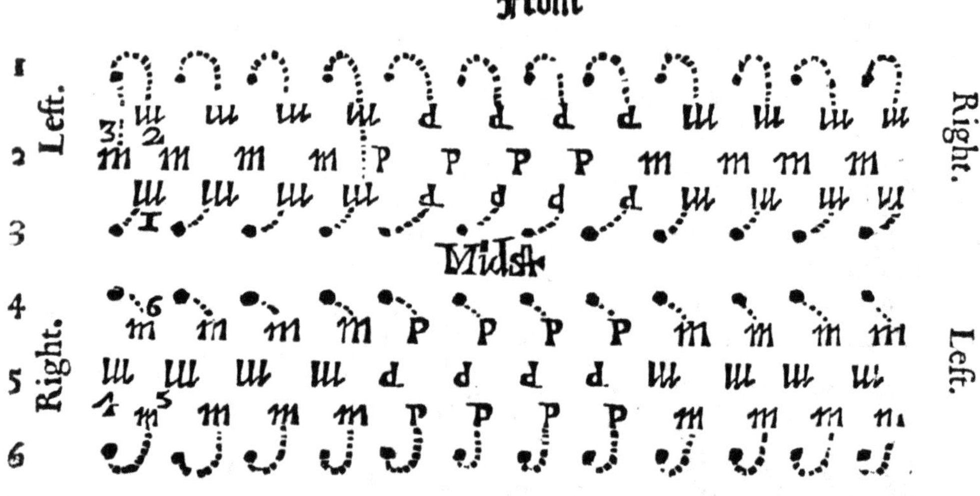

Reer.

You may reduce this figure by doing the same over again.
Or else, by any other divisional Countermarch.

4. **Command.**

4. **Command.** Front and Reer half files countermarch to the { 1. Right or 2. Left.

Reer.

You may reduce this Figure by doing the same over again,

OR,

By Countermarching Front and Reer into the midst.

5. **Command.** Countermarch your Front and Reer half files to right and left from the midst.

To perform this, **Command.** Front half files face about and turn off to the right, and Reer half files turn off to your left; then, face to your leader.

Front.

Midst.

Reer.

To reduce this, **Command**: To Countermarch from the midst into the Front and Reer.

The three last figures by command are several, but the figures are still one and the same in quantity, but not in quality, or motion, as you may perceive, &c.

 6. **Command.**

6. **Command.** Countermarch your flanks into the midst.

To perform this, **Command;** them to face to the right and left outwards; the right flank turn off to the right, and left flank turn off to the left until they meet in the midst.

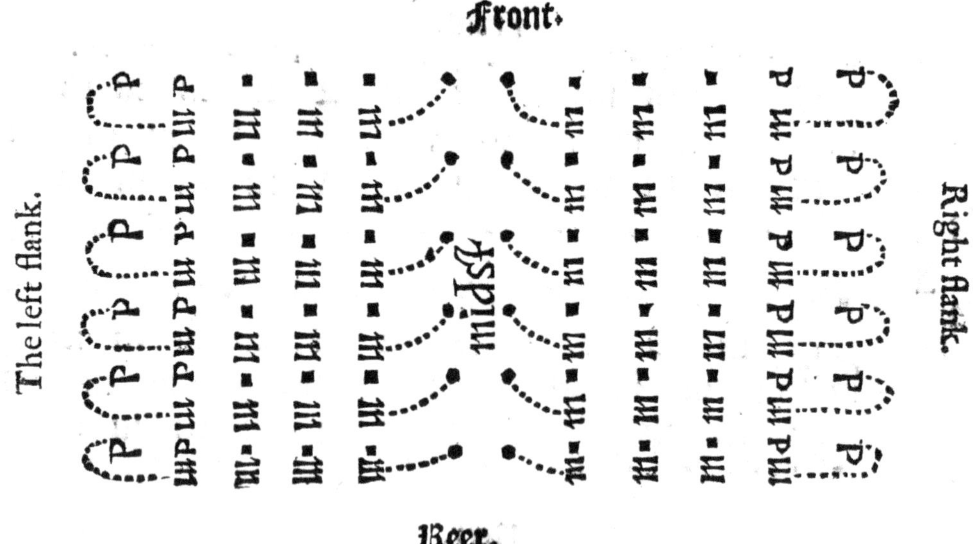

To reduce them, **Command.** Countermarch from the midst to the right and left into both flanks.

7. **Command.** Right and left half Ranks interchange your ground.

To perform this, Face to the right and left inward (and march all) and interchange your ground.

Front.

12 11 10 9 8 7 6 5 4 3 2 1

Reer.

This is of no great use except it be when the right (or left) flank hath fought, that then the reserved flank may come into service also.

You

You may reduce them by interchanging of them back again.

O R,

Divisionally to Countermarch their flanks into the midst of the Battel.

Secondly, **Countermarches losing ground.**

1. Command. Files to the	**Right,** or **Left,**	hand Countermarch placing your selves before your bringers up.

To performe this, **Command.** The bringers up to face about to the right, then the file leaders with the rest successively to turn off upon the same ground he stands; And on the same hand the Command is given, so to place themselves accordingly.

Front.

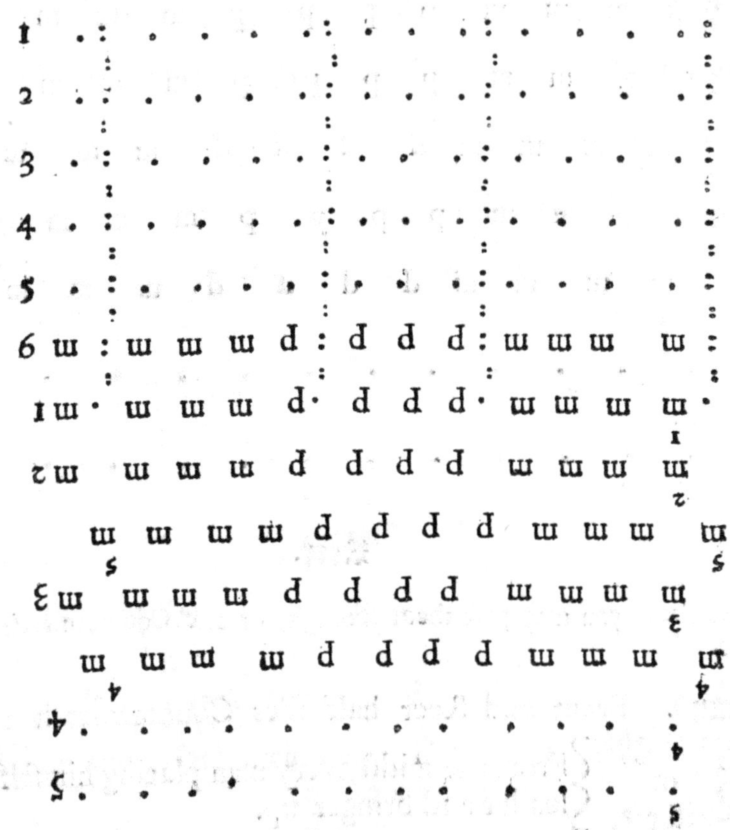

```
1  . : . . . . . : . . . . : . . . . . :
2  . : . . . . . : . . . . : . . . . . :
3  . : . . . . . : . . . . : . . . . . :
4  . : . . . . . : . . . . : . . . . . :
5  . : . . . . . : . . . . : . . . . . :
6 m : m m m d : d d d : m m m   m :
1 m . m m m d . d d d . m m m m .
2 m   m m m d   d d d   m m m m
   m m m m d  d d d  m m m  m
3 m   m m m d   d d d   m m m m
   m m m  m d  d d d  m m m  m
4 . . . . . . . . . . .
5 . . . . . . . . . . . .
```

Reer.

You may easily reduce them by any other Countermarch of files.

2. Command.	The last Rank stand the rest pass through to the	**1. Right** or **2. Left**	placing your selves behind your bringers up.

To perform this: As the last Rank is to stand and keep their first aspect; let all the rest face about to the right, and march all turning successively behind their bringers up.

 Front.

Front.

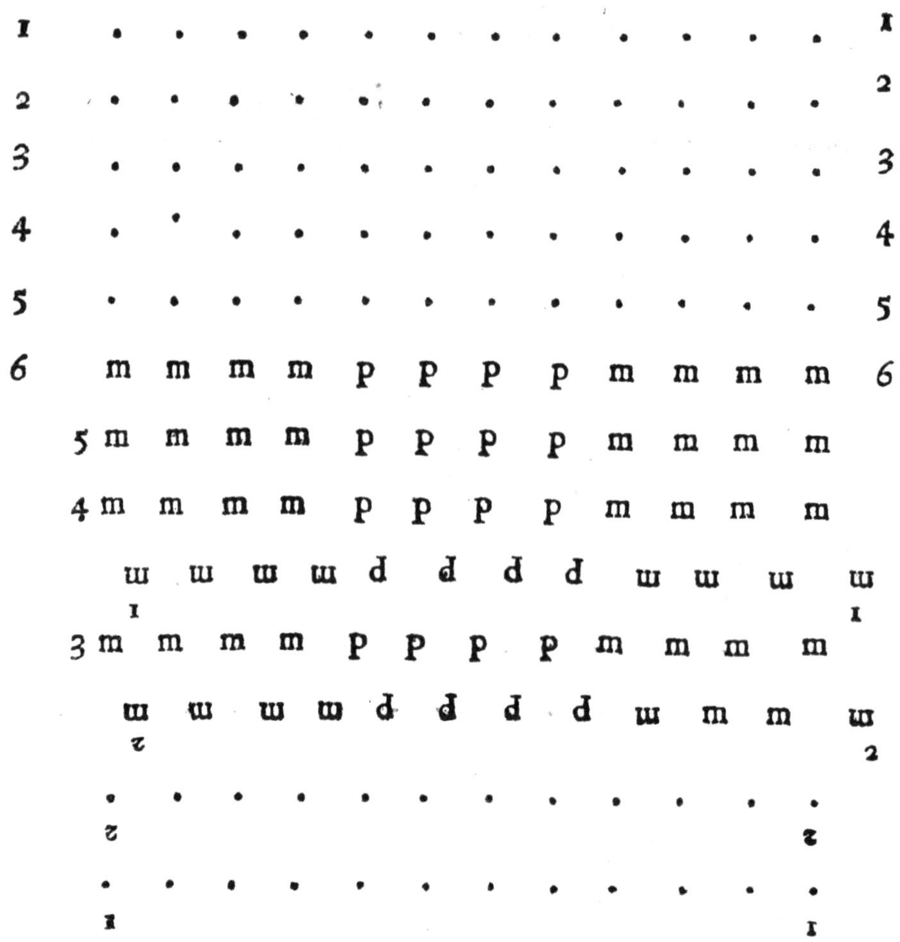

1 1

2 2

3 3

4 4

5 5

6 m m m m p p p p m m m m 6

5 m m m m p p p p m m m m

4 m m m m p p p p m m m m

ɯ ɯ ɯ ɯ d d d d ɯ ɯ ɯ ɯ

1 1

3 m m m m p p p p m m m m

ɯ ɯ ɯ ɯ d d d d ɯ m m ɯ

2 2

. . . .

2 2

. . . .

1 1

Reer.

To reduce them, you may pass them through, or else Countermarch by file into their places.

3. **Command.** Front and Reer half files Countermarch to the 1. **Right,** or 2. **Left,** From the midst, every man placing himself before his leader and bringer up.

To perform this, **Command.** The first rank of the front half files to stand, the rest to face about and turn off to the right; half file leaders face about and turn off to the left, and both to march clear of the Front and Reer, following their half file leaders, and bringers up of the front half files.

Front.

. . . .

3
m m m m p p p p m m m m 3

2
m m m m p p p p m m m m 2

1
1 m m m m p p p p m m m m 1

2 . . . .

3 . . . .

4 . . . .

5 . . . .

6 ɯ ɯ ɯ ɯ d d d d ɯ ɯ ɯ ɯ 9

9
ɯ ɯ ɯ ɯ d d d d ɯ ɯ ɯ ɯ ϛ

ϛ
ɯ ɯ ɯ ɯ d d d d ɯ ɯ ɯ ɯ ᔭ

ᔭ
. . . .

Reer.

To reduce this by an other Countermarch.

4.**Command.** Ranks to the { 1.**Right** or 2.**Left** } hand Countermarch, losing ground.

To perform this to the right. As in maintaining ground, upon their turning off, the rest march into the same place (or ground) and turn off also; as in figure 2.

Now this of losing ground, altereth only in this, the outmost file is to face to the right about, until he hath directly faced the left flank, and so to gain so much ground upon the left flank as they have lost upon the right;

OR,

That they have placed themselves on the outside (or before) of their left hand men.

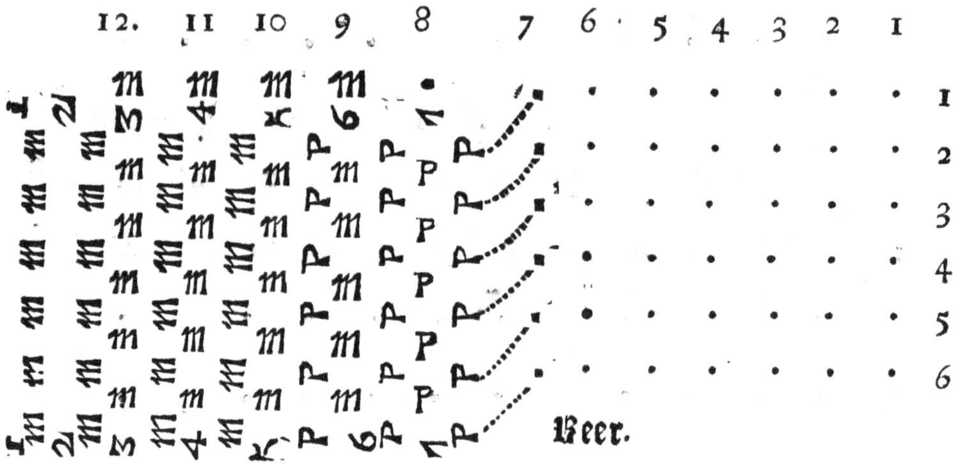

Front.

12. 11 10 9 8 7 6 5 4 3 2 1

m m m m 1

m m m m P P P P 2

m m m m P P P P 3

m m m m P P P P 4

m m m m P P P P 5

m m m m P P P P 6

1 2 3 4 5 6 1 Reer.

5. **Command.** Ranks to the right hand Countermarch, each following his right hand man; and place himself on the outside of his left hand man.

Front.

1 2 3 4 5 6 7 8 9 10 11 12 11 10 9 8 7 6 5 4 3 2 1

m m m p p p p m m m m m . . . .

m m m p p p p m m m m m . . . .

m m m p p p p m m m m m . . . .

m m m p p p p m m m m m . . . .

m m m p p p p m m m m m . . . .

m m m p p p p m m m m m . . . .

Reer.

To perform this, **Command.** The left hand file to stand; the out most file to the right turn about to the right as to make his aspect (or face) to the left, then move forward until he be clear of the second file, losing the ground he stood upon, and gain it again on the outside of the left flank.

To reduce this figure; may be done by a contrary Countermarch.

6. **Command.** The right and left hand file upon each flank face to the right and left outwards, the rest pass through, placing your selves before your outmost files.

Observe, files become ranks by their faceing.

To performe this, **Command.** The right hand file to face to the right, and the left hand file to the left, and then the rest of the body to turn their aspects, accordingly, & place themseves before their right & left hand men.

Front.

Front.

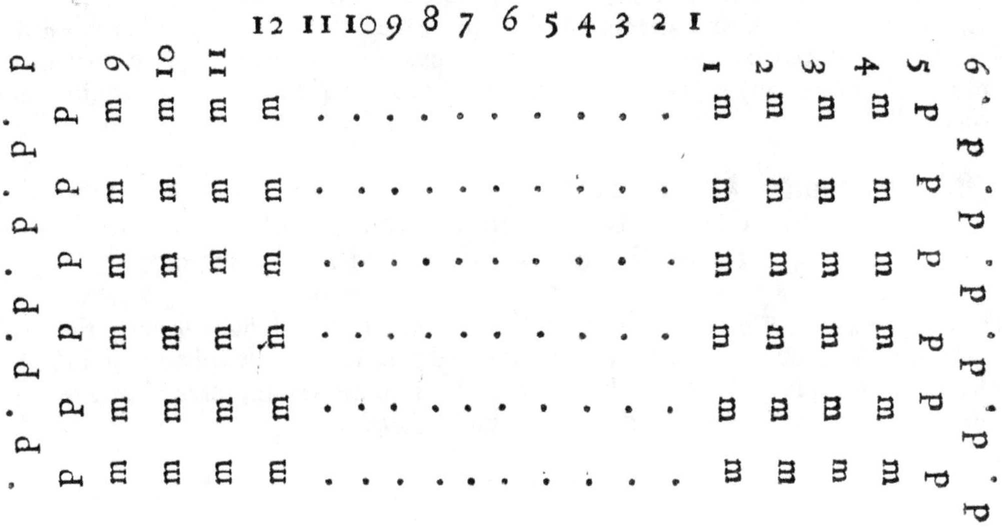

12 11 10 9 8 7 6 5 4 3 2 1

p 9 10 11 . . . 1 2 3 4 5 6

p . p m m m m . . . . m m m m p . p
p . p m m m m . . . . m m m m p . p
p . p m m m m . . . . m m m m p . p
p . p m m m m . . . . m m m m p . p
p . p m m m m . . . . m m m m p . p
. p m m m m . . . . m m m m p . p

Reer.

To reduce them, **Command**, them to Countermarch to the right and left into the midst of the Battel.

OR,

If they be faced to the proper Front, } **Command**. The two inmost files to stand, the rest pass through to the right and left inward, and close their divisions.

8. **Command**. The two outmost files of each flank face to the right and left inward, the rest pass through to the right and left, and place your selves behind your outside men.

To perform this, **Command**. The right and left hand file of each flank face inward, and the rest of the Body are to face to the right and left outwards, then all are to move forwards, and to place themselves behind their right and left hand men. (Else the motion is the same as the former.)

Front.

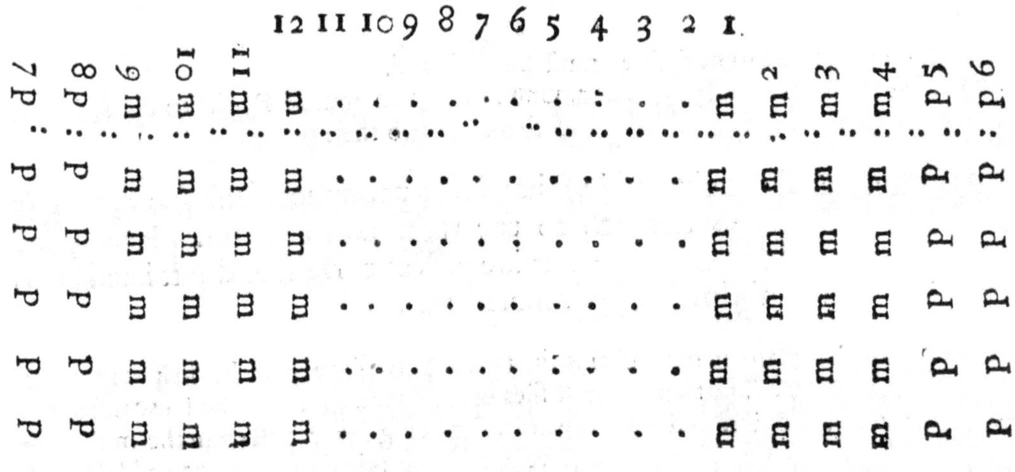

12 11 10 9 8 7 6 5 4 3 2 1.

p7 p8 m9 m10 m11 m . . . . m m2 m3 m4 p5 p6
p p m m m m . . . . m m m m p p
p p m m m m . . . . m m m m p p
p p m m m m . . . . m m m m p p
p p m m m m . . . . m m m m p p
p p m m m m . . . . m m m m p p

Reer.

To reduce this, Command. The two innermost files face to the right and left outwards, and the rest pass through to the right and left inwards, placing themselves behind their right and left hand men; Then, face them to their leaders.

Now if it be the Commanders pleasure to reduce them by any other word of Command, it may be done by the precedent words of Command, or of the next following, or of any other divisional Countermarch (except interchanging of ground.)

8. **Command.** The outmost file of each flank stand, the rest pass through to the right and left, and place your selves on the outside of your right and left hand men.

The ninth figure is the same as this, if faced to their leader.

To perform this. The outmost files of each flank stands; the rest of the body faceth to the right and left outwards, and so passing forwards through the intervalls into each flank, place themselves on the outside of their right and left hand men.

Front.

12 11 10 9 8 7 6 5 4 3 2 1

7 8 9 10 11 . . . . 2 3 4 5 6

p p m m m m . . . . m m m m p p

p p m m m m . . . . m m m m p p

p p m m m m . . . . m m m m p p

p p m m m m . . . . m m m m p p

p p m m m m . . . . m m m m p p

p p m m m m . . . . m m m m p p

Reer.

To reduce this, may be performed by any of the foregoing Countermarches of ranks: Or else, being faced to any of the flanks, then the Ranks, become files, and by divisional Countermarches of files, you may reduce divisional Countermarches of Ranks.

OR,

By Ranks files only some facings must be observed.

For the proper Reducement Command: The two inmost Ranks to stand, the rest to face to the right and left inward, and so march into their places.

9. **Command.** The right and lelft hand files upon each flank stand, the rest pass through to the right and left, and place your selves on the outside of your right and left hand men, following your inmost files.

Observe in the performance of this the two inmost files are to be first in motion; But first, Command, The two outmost files of each flank to stand, and the rest of the Body to face to their right and left outwards, so moving away first from the midst until they have successively placed themselves on the outside of their right and left hand men: (you may close their files into the midst to open Order.

Front.

Front.

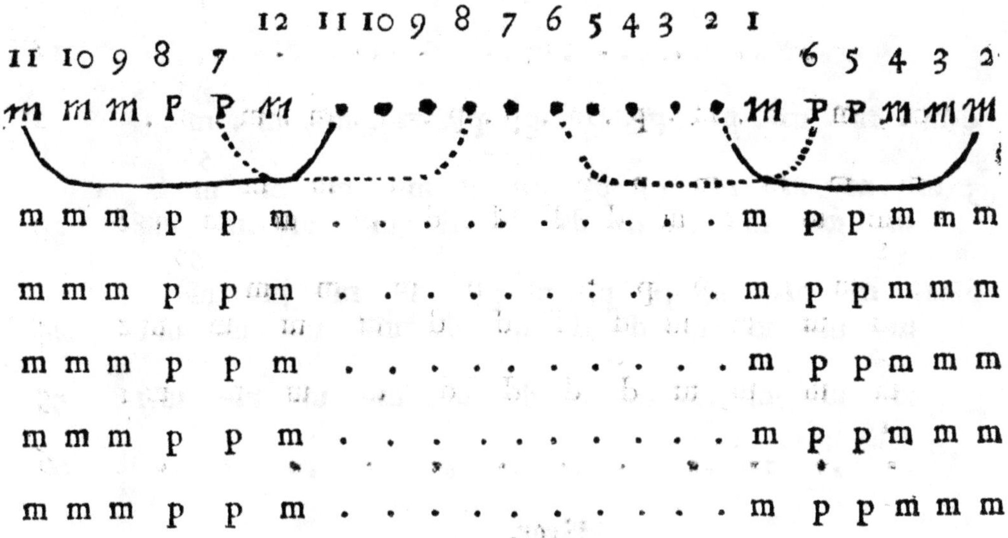

12 11 10 9 8 7 6 5 4 3 2 1

11 10 9 8 7 . . . . 6 5 4 3 2

m m m P P m . . . . m P P m m m

m m m p p m . . . . m p p m m m

m m m p p m . . . . m p p m m m

m m m p p m . . . . m p p m m m

m m m p p m . . . . m p p m m m

m m m p p m . . . . m p p m m m

Reer.

The reducement of the eight figure will reduce this also.

10. **Command.** Front and Reer half files Countermarch to the {1. **Right** or 2. **Left**} hand interchanging ground.

To perform this, **Command.** Half files to face about and turn off to the right, front half files doing the like move forwards until they be clear one of an other, six foot; then face to their leader if you please and close their divisions.

Front.

6m m m m p p p p m m m m6 1

5m m m m p p p p m m m m5 2

4m m m m p p p p m m m m4 3

3m m m m p p p p m m m m3 4

2m m m m p p p p m m m m2 5

1m m m m p p p p m m m m1 6

Reer.

A Countermarch interchanging of ground will reduce them and then close &c.

11. **Command.** Front and Reer half files to the right hand interchange ground.

Front.

. . . . 1

4 m . m . m . m . p . p . p . p . m . m . m . m . 2

5 m m m m p p p p m m m m

ɯ ɯ ɯ ɯ d d d d ɯ ɯ ɯ ɯ ɛ 3

6 m m m m p p p p m m m m

ɯ ɯ ɯ ɯ d d d d ɯ ɯ ɯ ɯ ʒ 4

ɯ ɯ ɯ ɯ d d d d ɯ ɯ ɯ ɯ 1 5

. . . . 6

Reer.

You may reduce this, interchanging of ground as they were, or by some other word of Command.

Thirdly, Countermarches to gain ground.

1. **Command.** The file leaders stand, the rest pass through to the
{1. **Right** or 2. **Left**,} and place your selves before your leaders.

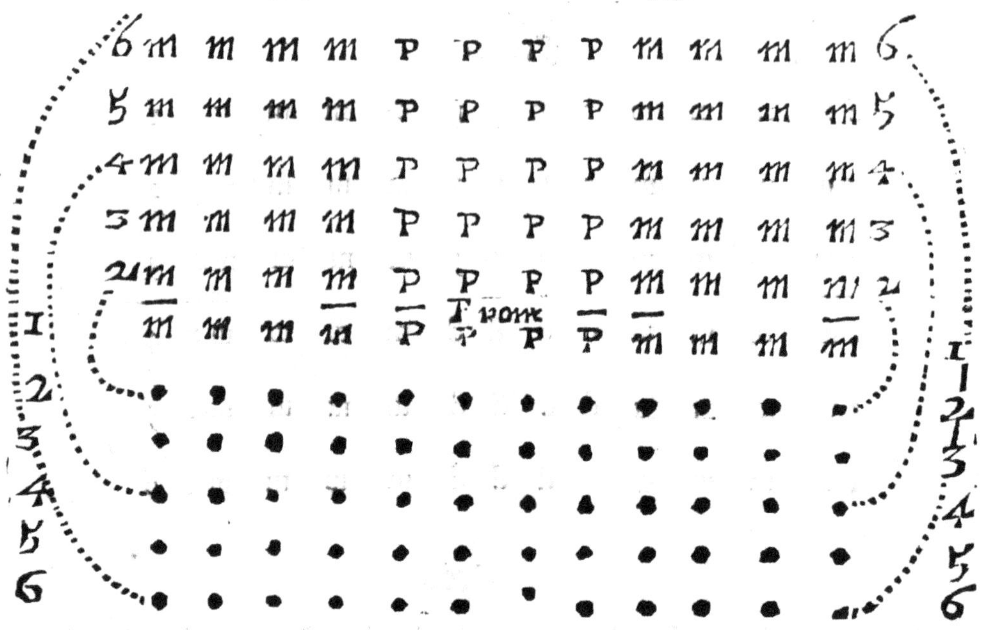

Reer.

The **Command** is so plain that there needeth no directions. Only if your command be to place your selves behind your leaders, then the file leaders are to face about,

about, and the rest are to execute it as the former, only in placing themselves they are to turn their aspect behind their leaders.

And then Commanding them to place themselves before their leaders will reduce them.

2. **Command.** File leaders face about to the right and stand. Bringers up with the rest following them, pass through to the right, and place your selves behind your leaders.

Face to your leaders.

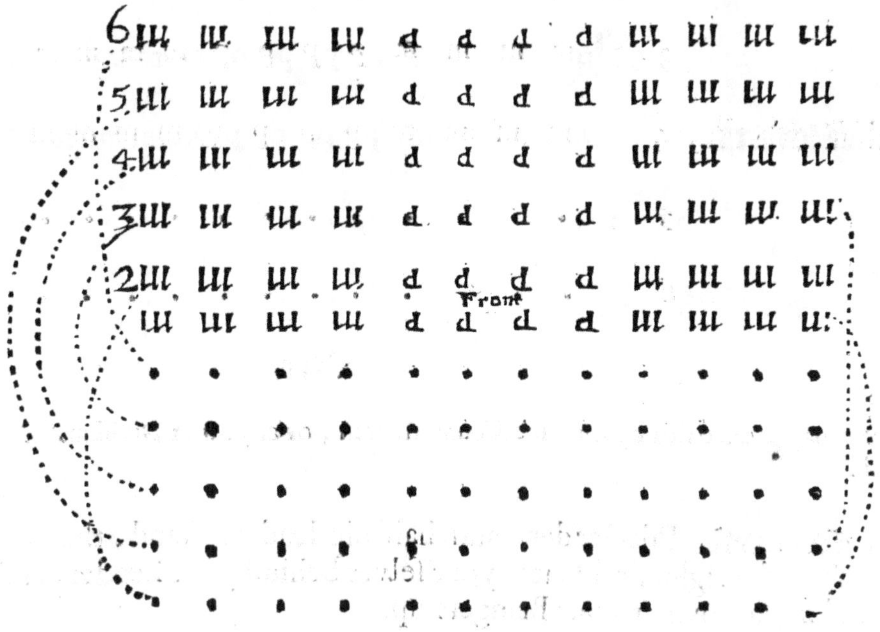

Front

Reer.

To reduce this you may do it by the same **Command**, or by the first **Command**.

3. **Command.** File leaders stand and the rest pass through to the {1. **Right**, or 2. **Left**,} placing your selves before your file leaders, following your Bringers up.

This is the same with the second figure, only in their work they are to keep their aspect to the Front: And the reducement the same also.

4. **Command.** File leaders and half file leaders stand, the rest pass through to the right and place your selves before your file leaders and half file leaders.

	3	m	m	m	m	p	p	p	p	m	m	m	m	3	
	2	m	m	m	m	p	p	p	p	m	m	m	m	2	
						Front.									
File leaders.	1	m	m	m	m	p	p	p	p	m	m	m	m		1
	2 . 6	m	m	m	m	p	p	p	p	m	m	m	m	6	2
	3 . 5	m	m	m	m	p	p	p	p	m	m	m	m	5	3
Half file leaders.	4	m	m	m	m	p	p	p	p	m	m	m	m		4
	5	.	.	.	.	.	.	.	.	.	.	.	.		5
	6	.	.	.	.	.	.	.	.	.	.	.	.		6
						Reer.									

You may reduce this by the same Countermarch, or any other Divisional Countermarch.

5. **Command.** File-leaders and half file-leaders stand, the rest pass through to the right, and place your selves behind your Leaders and half file-leaders, following your Bringers-up.

The file-leaders and half file-leaders are only to face about to the right and to stand, the motion is the same with the fourth Figure, but in taking their places they are to face to the Reer. The Reducement as the former.

6. **Command.** File-leaders and half file-leaders stand, the rest pass through to the right and left, and place your selves behind your Leaders and half file-leaders, *&c.*

I need not demonstrate this, it being the same with the fifth and sixth, only in the motion they are to pass to the right and left outwards. And is reduced as the former.

7. **Command.** File-leaders to face about, the rest pass through to the right, and place your selves behind your Leaders and Bringers up.

To perform this, **Command.** The first Rank is to face about and stand; then the two last Ranks from the Reer, (*i. e.* the fourth and fifth Ranks) are to face to the Reer and move all, *&c.*

ɛ ɯ ɯ ɯ ɯ d d d d ɯ ɯ ɯ ɯ ɛ

ᘔ ɯ ɯ ɯ ɯ d d d d ɯ ɯ ɯ ɯ ᘔ

Front.

1 ɯ ɯ ɯ ɯ d d d d ɯ ɯ ɯ ɯ **File leaders.**

2 . . . .

3 . . . .

4 . . . .

5 . . . .

6 m m m m p p p p m m m m **Bringers up.**

Reer.

5 m m m m p p p p m m m m 5

4 m m m m p p p p m m m m 4

The former Directions upon any Divisional Countermarch will reduce this.

8. **Command.** The outmost File of the right face to the right, the rest pass through to the { **Right,** or **Left,** } { and place your selves } { **Before,** or **Behind** } { your right hand men.

Front.

12 11 10 9 8 7 6 5 4 3 2 1 2 3 4 5 6 7 8 9 10 11 12

. . . . m m m m p p p p m m m m

. . . . m m m m p p p p m m m m

. . . . m m m m p p p p m m m m

. . . . m m m m p p p p m m m m

. . . . m m m m p p p p m m m m

. . . . m m m m p p p p m m m m

Right Flank.

Reer.

If your **Command** be behind your right hand men, then the right hand file is but to face to the left. I shall not trouble you with them, conceiving them of no great use: You may reduce these by a contrary Countermarch.

9. **Command.** The outmost File of the right hand stand, and the right hand File of the left half Rank stand, and the rest pass through, and place your selves on the outside of your right hand men.

Face to your Leader.

The ſame is done on the left hand.

And if you place them before their left hand men, then face them all to the right, and ſo let them paſs through obſerving the motion: And if you place them behind their right hand men; then let the right hand men face about to the left, and the reſt paſs through and fall behind them.

Figure 9.

12 11 10 9 8 7 6 5 4 3 2 1

. . . . . . p p m m m m m m m m p p

7 8 9 10 11 12 1 2 3 4 5 6

. . . . . . p p m m m m m m m m p p

. . . . . . p p m m m m m m m m p p

. . . . . . p p m m m m m m m m p p

. . . . . . p p m m m m m m m m p p

. . . . . . p p m m m m m m m m p p

The right hand file upon the left flank.

The outmoſt file up‑on the right hand.

A Counter word of Command will reduce them, &c.

There are many Countermarches that produce one and the ſame Figure: provided you cloſe your Diviſions, and face them to their proper Front; only they differ in place.

Firſt, therefore you may briefly obſerve that in thoſe Countermarches that Maintain their Ground, the firſt, ſecond, third, fourth, and fifth Commands; then in loſing of ground, the firſt, ſecond, third, fourth, fifth, tenth, and eleventh Commands; and in gaining of Ground, the firſt, ſecond, third, fourth, fifth, ſixth, and ſeventh do and will produce one and the ſame Figure.

Secondly, Alſo for maintaining of Ground, the ſixth and ſeventh; and in loſing of Ground the ſixth, ſeventh and eighth; and alſo in gaining of Ground the ninth Commands produce one and the ſame Figures.

Oserve, For the Countermarchings of half Ranks, ſee in the doublings of the Flanks, thirteenth and fourteenth Commands, they producing the ſame Figures as the eleventh and twelfth Figures; by all which you will the better underſtand the one for the other.

Although Countermarches are of great Antiquity, and uſed amongſt the *Græcians*; yet it is not much of uſe in our preſent Mode of Diſcipline: Therefore to conclude, though knowledge of them be no burthen, yet to be exerciſed in the face of an Enemy may prove prejudicial; and the beſt expert in this Art, allow that they may be beſt ſpared of any motions whatever.

CHAP.

Chap. XVI.

Of Wheelings.

I Am to treat of Wheelings, and the several uses of them, as to the strengthening of the Front, Reer, and both Flanks.

Before you enter upon them, take these four Observations.

1. That you close your Ranks and Files to your Order. 3. *Foot,*

2. That in all your Wheelings, you keep a due distance to your Leader.

3. That in all Commands for Wheelings, such moderation is to be used in their motions, that they on the contrary flank be not forced by running to disorder themselves.

4. That your Arms be at such Postures as may be equivalent to each other; (This is) If the Musquets be poysed, the Pikes are to be advanced (which are the Postures best to be used in these Motions.)

There are two sorts of Wheelings.

First, Angular Wheelings.

Secondly, Wheelings on the midst (or Center.)

I shall not use the word Center, for it is more proper to a Circular body than to a square.

These in their Motions (or Actions) are termed either Intire or Divisional.

1. Intire Wheelings, are for the gaining of ground upon the Enemy, or to fight him with your best men, as occasion serveth, turning the first Aspect wholly to the Command given.

2. Divisional Wheelings, being performed, extend the Battle either in length or depth: And may for the most part of them be called Doublings.

I have in the exercise of Doublings demonstrated some of them by Figures, and shall not recite them here again, but quote them by their several numbers of Commands.

First, I shall begin with Angular Wheelings.

And they so called, because the corner man to which the Aspect is commanded, is the main hinge of the motion.

Observe, the Wheelings to the right and to the left, To the right and left about are termed Angular. And for the Wheelings to the right and left, and to the right and left about on the same Ground are Wheelings on the midst of the Front, all which are Intire, the other Divisional. *Center.*

1. **Command.** Wheel	your ——— your	**Body** all, or **Battle**	to the	1. **Right,** or 2. **Left.**	*Intire Angular Wheelings.*

This Wheeling moves the main Body from the Ground whereon it first stood, and placeth it on the right Flank, causing the Aspects of the proper Front to be upon the same.

Observe, that the right hand man is to move to the right hand with a very small Motion, and every man else to remember that the farther off he is from the Right Angle, the swifter must his motion be.

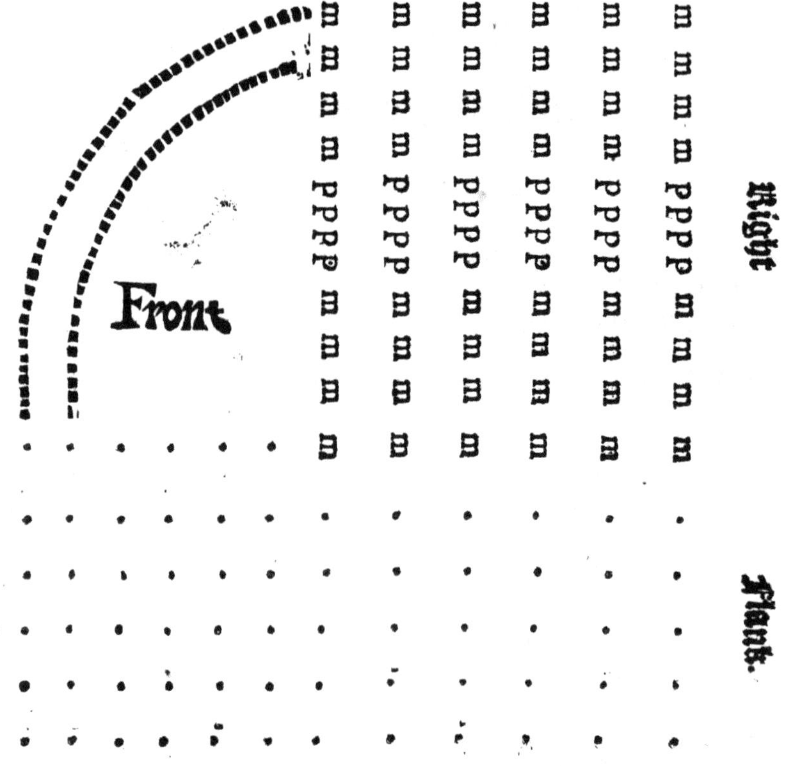

Reer.

To reduce them. Wheel to the left.

But this will not transfer them to the same Ground: But to reduce them to their first Aspect on the same Ground; you must face them all to the right, then wheel them to the left, and facing them to the left, it is compleated.

2. **Command.** Wheel—— your Body / all, or / your Battle } to the { 1. Right, / or / 2. Left } about.

This turneth the Aspect towards the Reer: Now by reason the motion is twice as much as the former, there ought to be the greater care had in the performance of it; observing so much the motion of the right hand man, that they fail not of being even in Rank with him.

Front.

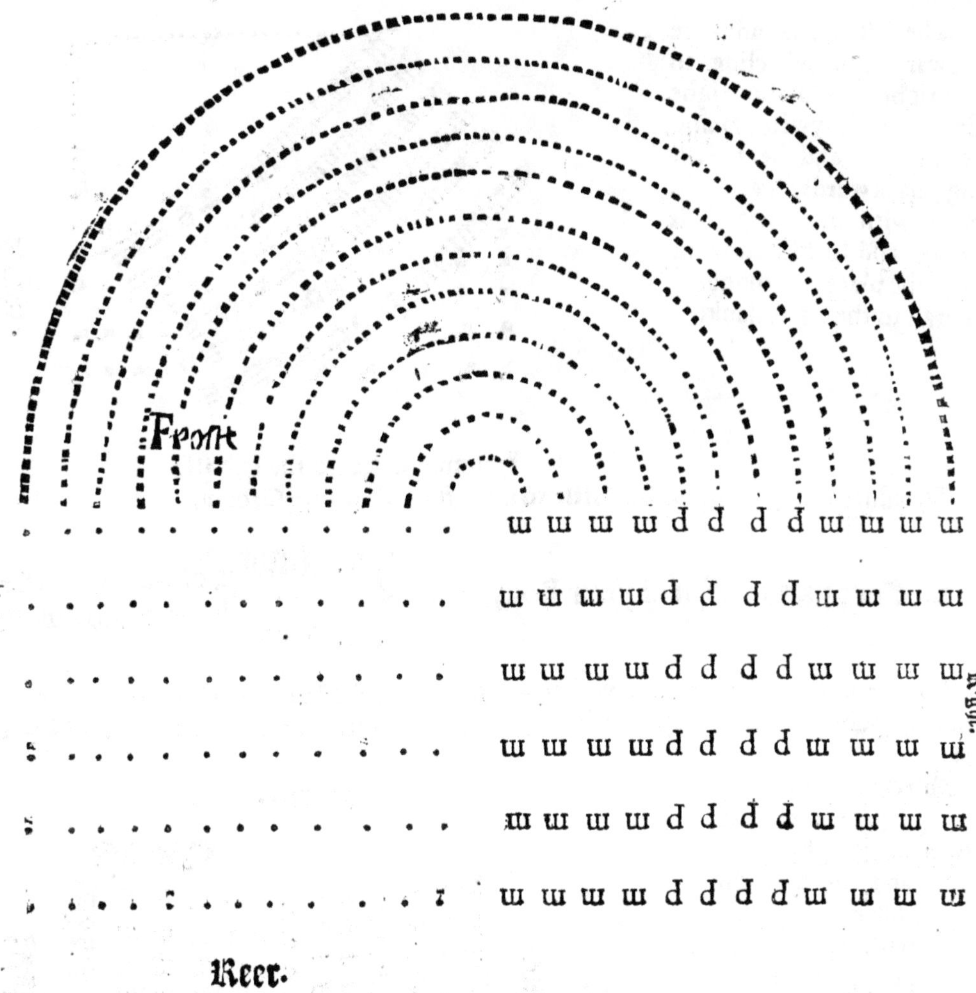

To reduce them to their first Ground, face to the right, wheel to the left about, then face them to the left: Although to the left about may reduce them, but not on the same Ground.

You may observe that Wheelings are the most facil for their Reducements; as for Example, Wheel your Flanks into the Front, is reduced by wheeling your Flanks into the Reer.

OR,

To wheel your Front and Reer into both Flanks, is reduced by Wheeling both Flanks into your Front and Reer, *&c.*

Secondly, I proceed to Wheelings on the midst (or Center) of the Front, which are Intire and Divisional, and are quicker in their motions, and performed on less Ground.

1. **Command.** Wheel your battle to the { 1. **Right** 2. **Left** } on the same ground. *Intire.*

This is termed *Grave Van Nawsaw*'s Wheeling.

But it is a wonder to me why our Antient and Modern Writers call these **Commands** Wheelings on the same Ground, when I am sure there will be ground lost (in the motion) from the first they stood upon: In a direct square this may be better performed and less loss of Ground.

To perform this, Command.

The left Flank advance forward still wheeling to the right, and the right flank contrarywise facing to the left, and keep falling backwards even in Reer with the left half ranks, and so still moving unto the place commanded, face all to the right flank.

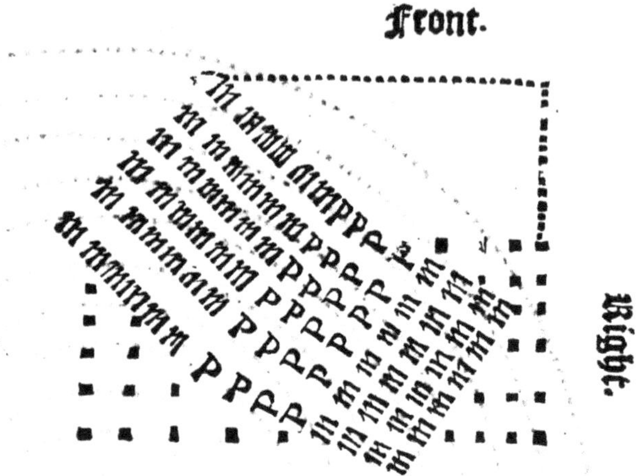

You may wheel to the left also.

To reduce this, Wheel your Battle to the left on the same Ground.

2. Command. Wheel your Body to the { 1. Right, or 2. Left } about on the same Ground.

The direction to the former will serve for the performance of this, only the motion is double as much, and their faces are turned from the first Front toward the Reer.

Observe in this motion, every man on the left flank his right hand man; and the men on the right flank must keep even with their left hand men, who are their Leaders until they have attained their Ground, after which they are to face as before, making an even Front.

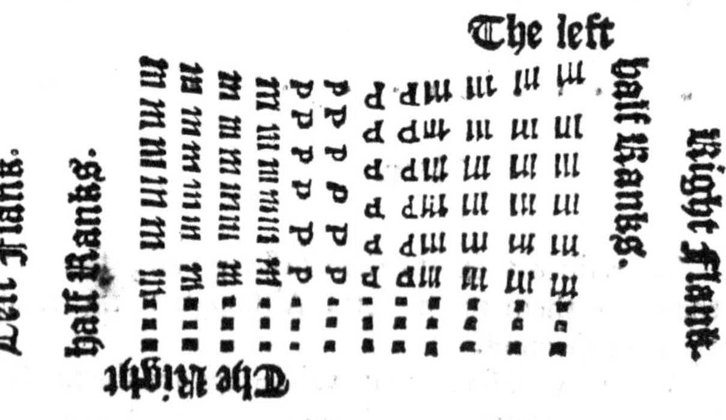

To reduce this, wheel your Battle to the left about on the same Ground.

Divisional Wheelings, Bingham 2. part Tactic. pag. 92.

3. Command. Wheel to the right and left from the Front,

OR,

Wheel off your Front by Division. Or if you will not go so far, then wheel your Front into the Flanks by Division.

This wheeling your Front into the Flanks by Division produceth the same Figure with Figure 8.

If upon occasion Musquetteers be on the Front of the Pikes, by this motion they will flank their Pikes: But otherwise being to be performed in a standing Body, the Pikes will flank the Musquetteers, and may easily be performed.

The File-leaders of the right flank with their respective Files are to wheel about to the right, and the File-leaders of the left flank are to wheel about to the left and close their Divisions.

Front.

Front.

In motion.

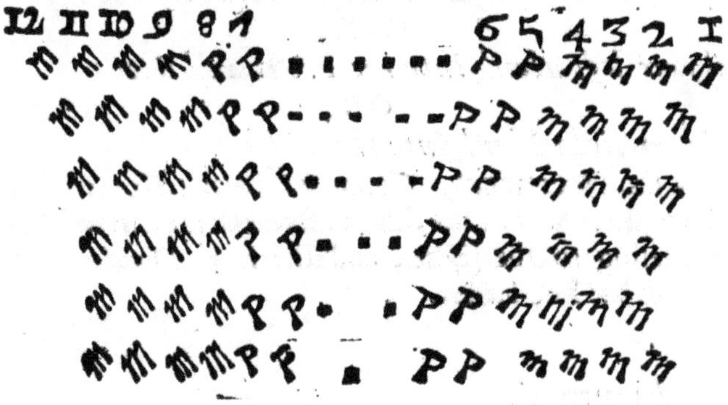

```
12 11 10 9 8 7          6 5 4 3 2 1
m m m m p p . . . . . . p p m m m m
m m m m p p . . . . . p p m m m m
m m m m p p . . . . p p m m m m
m m m m p p . . . p p m m m m
m m m m p p .  . p p m m m m
m m m m p p  .  p p m m m m
```

Reer.

Figure performed.

Front.

```
d d ɯ ɯ ɯ ɯ ɯ ɯ ɯ ɯ d d
d d ɯ ɯ ɯ ɯ ɯ ɯ ɯ ɯ d d
d d ɯ ɯ ɯ ɯ ɯ ɯ ɯ ɯ d d
d d ɯ ɯ ɯ ɯ ɯ ɯ ɯ ɯ d d
d d ɯ ɯ ɯ ɯ ɯ ɯ ɯ ɯ d d
d d ɯ ɯ ɯ ɯ ɯ ɯ ɯ ɯ d d
7 8 9 10 11 12 1 2 3 4 5 6
```

Reer.

To reduce them, wheel them off by Division again from the Reer, or by the fourth **Command.**

4. Command. Wheel your Body inward to the Reer.

If this be to reduce the former, it is presupposed the Commander is in the head of the first proper Front, then the Pikes will be in the midst of the Battle, as at first again: But if reduced without this **Command**, the Pikes will be in the Flanks ready to defend the Musquetteers from the fury of the Horse.

To perform this, **Command**, the Body to open from the midst to the right and left, to such a distance, as they may turn off to the right and left.

This I shall not demonstrate to you in Figure, because the precedent Figure performed will give light to the execution of this, and so for the next **Command.**

5. Command. Wheel off your Body from the Reer into the Front.

To perform this, face them to the Reer, then to the right and left, and wheel them inward to the Front.

To reduce the fourth **Command**, and this also:

Wheel them off again to the right and left by Division.

6. **Command**. Wheel off your Front and Reer into the right Flank.

These Commands following will produce the same Figure.

Wheel off your Body by Division from the left Flank.

O R,

Wheel your left Flank into the Front and Reer.

O R,

Wheel your right Flank into the midst.

To perform this sixth Command. Command them to face to the right; this done they must wheel together about the third and fourth men in the right hand File, the Front Division wheeling to the right, and the Reer Division to the left, until the Bringers-up meet with the File-leader.

Figure 6.

Front.

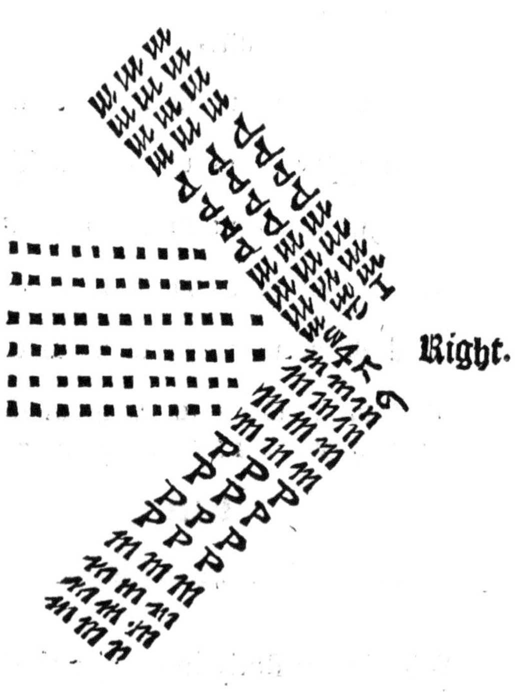

Reer.

To reduce this, it may be performed several ways, as the Body may be faced.

If they stand faced to the right, then wheel your Flanks into the Reer; and being faced to their proper Front they are reduced.

But if faced to the Front, then wheel the Front and Reer into the left Flank.

But for the performance of the same Command into another Figure; It is but to pass through your Musquetteers from the left Flank to the right, then the same Command will bring all the Pikes into the Front.

7. **Command**. Wheel your Body inward to the right Flank from the left.

To perform this, Command, To face to the right; then open to the right and left to a convenient distance, &c.

Figure 7.

Figure 7.

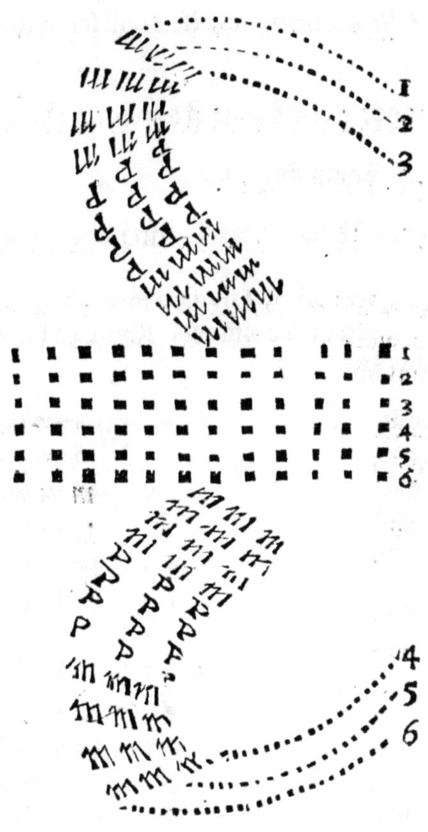

To reduce this, it may be done several ways as the former at the discretion of the Commander.

This produceth the same Figure as the sixth, only it is altered in motion, therefore I thought good to demonstrate it; although Wheelings in this nature is difficult.

8. Command. Wheel off to the right and left inward to the Front.

To perform this, let them open to the right and left from the midst, and then wheel, *&c.*

m m m m p p ■ ■ ■ ■ ■ ■ ■ ■ p p m m m m
m m m m p p ■ ■ ■ ■ ■ ■ ■ ■ p p m m m m
m m m m p p ■ ■ ■ ■ ■ ■ ■ ■ p p m m m m
m m m m p p ■ ■ ■ ■ ■ ■ ■ ■ p p m m m m
m m m m p p ■ ■ ■ ■ ■ ■ ■ ■ p p m m m m
m m m m p p ■ ■ ■ ■ ■ ■ ■ ■ p p m m m m
■ ■ ■ ■ ■ ■ ■ ■

This Figure when performed is serviceable against the Horse, because all the Pikes are in the Front, and stand according to this Figure.

P P P P P P P P P P P P
P P P P P P P P P P P P
m m m m m m m m m m m m
m m m m m m m m m m m m
m m m m m m m m m m m m
m m m m m m m m m m m m

To reduce them, is by wheeling them off to the Reer.

9. Command. Wheel your Flanks into the Front.

This is perform'd *folio* 62. Command 16. where you may see the diversity of words of Command for the producement of it.

10. **Command.** Wheel your Flanks into the Reer.

The former **Command** *folio* 60. being reversed will serve for your better intelligence herein.

11. **Command.** Wheel Front and Reer into the right Flank.

This is performed *folio* 78. **Command** 19.

12. **Command.** Wheel both Flanks into the Front and Reer.

OR,

Front and Reer half files wheel off by Division inwards into the midst of Ranks.

To reduce it, by another word of **Command.** Right and left half Ranks wheel from the midst inward to the Front and Reer.

To perform this **Command.** Half files face to the Reer; Front half files and Reer half files move all together, and wheel off your Divisions to the right and left.

Then face them to their proper Front and close their Divisions.

To reduce them,

The reducement of the next Figure will serve for both.

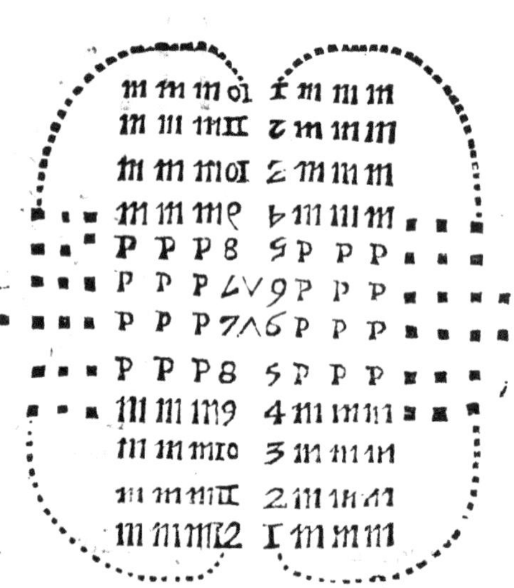

13. **Command.** Wheel Front and Reer into both Flanks.

To perform this from the precedent Figure, Face to the right and left outward, observing the former direction, and giving due distance for the motion.

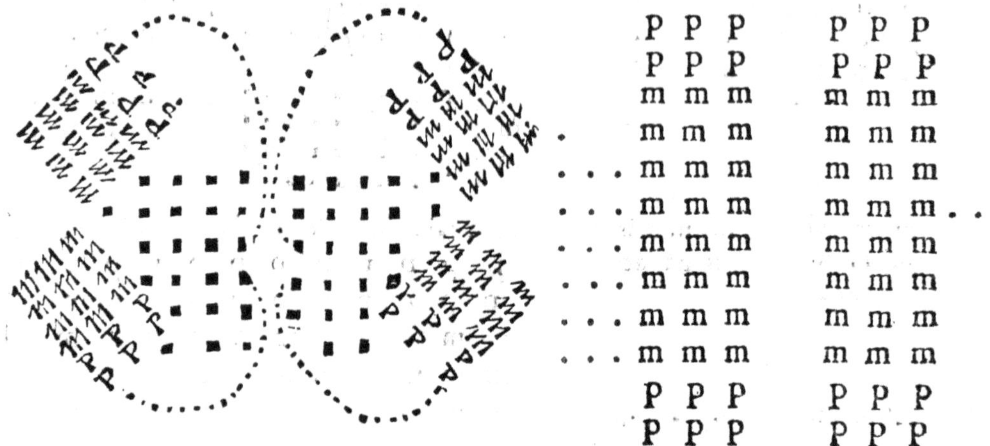

There are several **Commands** that will produce this Figure.

Wheel off your Body by Division from the midst of the Battle into the right and left Flank.

OR,

Wheel the midst of your Body by Division into the Front and Reer.

OR,

OR,

Wheel your right and left Flank into the midst.

OR,

Right and left Ranks wheel off by Division to the midst of Files.

To reduce this, Wheel Front and Reer into the midst of the Battle.

OR,

By Wheeling the Flanks into the midst of the Battle, if faced.

OR,

If you please to face the Body to one of the Flanks; then wheel Front and Reer into both flanks, and face them to their proper Front, and close their Divisions.

14. **Command.** Left half Ranks, wheel off to the right and left, and double your right Flank by Division. *Folio* 79. *Command* 20.

15. **Command.** Front and Reer half Files, wheel off by Division. *Folio* 78. and *Command* 19.

16. **Command.** Right and left half Ranks, wheel off by Division from the midst of Files.

To perform this, **Command** them to face to the right and left inwards, and then let them move backwards to such a convenient distance as to wheel off from the midst of Files.

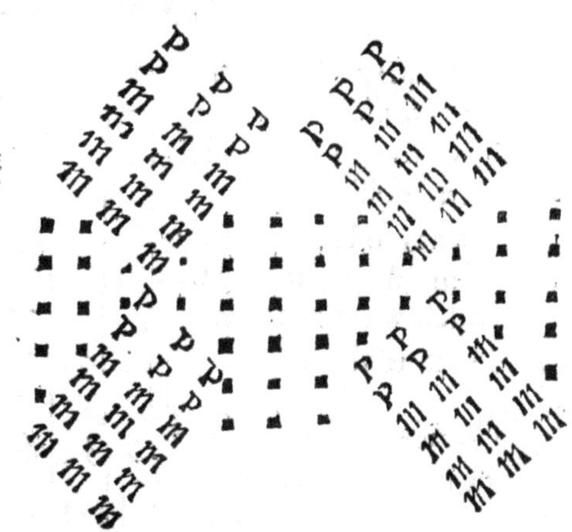

To reduce them, wheel off to the right and left inwards.

I need not trouble you with more Angular Wheelings, either wheeling them outwards to the right and left about from the midst of the Battle; or inwards to the midst, because the demonstration of the former may give light unto all such, &c. and I conceive them not of such absolute necessity.

Part of Ælian's Tacticks. chap. 36. 34. 46.

But I must advise that those Intire and Divisional Wheelings may be diligently learnt and practised, as being of great use in this Military Art.

I have in all my method demonstrated the **Commands** by their Figures to the right hand, you may easily command the same to the left hand, and the Reducements accordingly.

You will find to several Countermarches and Wheelings no Reducements directed for them, because they may be reduced the same way back as was commanded, or by some other **Command** as directed.

I know but little more to be invented for the secure Exercise of a Foot Company, (and because I would not be singular) I have demonstrated some that may be better spared than practised in service; however here is for all: Some may make use of what is necessary to the fitting of the Souldier for field services; and others at their pleasure what their fancy may guide them unto. And thus I have passed over the Grounds of Discipline for the Foot, I expect Censures; by the Ingenuous I submit to a correction; but for the Carper, let him remain in his own mud, he shall never be complemented to a cleared fountain by me.

Chap. XVII.

Of making file leaders successively both in number and place in a file, six in depth, and so for a whole body.

The Souldiers having passed thus many dayes exercise in these principles of Art Military; and now each Souldier is loving to his Comrade; every file leader to the rest of his file; being willing that their files should successively demonstrate some experiences as they have attained unto, in the exercise thereof: which will prove a great incouragement to the Ingenious: Also it is profitable to a Commander to bring what Ranks he pleaseth into the Front, and to exchange them, and to reduce them to their proper file leaders.

A File to be made file leaders successively according to Number; or by commanding as followeth.

Commanding by the file leader.							
	1	File leaders.					
Rank two to the left, and file to the left double.	2	2	Ranks to the left double, and Files to the left double.				
Countermarch Front and reer into the midst, and face to that part which was the Reer.	3	1	3	Half files double your front to the right, and files to the right double.			
Face about to the right.	4	4	2	4	File leaders stand, the rest pass through to the right, and place themselves before their leaders.		
Countermarch from the Reer into the midst, and and face to that which was the Reer.	5	3	6	5	5	Ranks to the left double, and Files double your depth to the left.	
Files Rank two to the right, and file to the right double: face them about and it will reduce them.	6	6	1	1	6	6	Ranks to the right double and Files to the right double.
		To	Re	du	ce		
		5	5	6	3	5	1. File leaders stand, the rest pass through and place your selves before your Leader.
			4	2	4	4	
				3	1	3	
					2	2	
						1	

A file

A File to be made file leaders successively according to their Dignity.

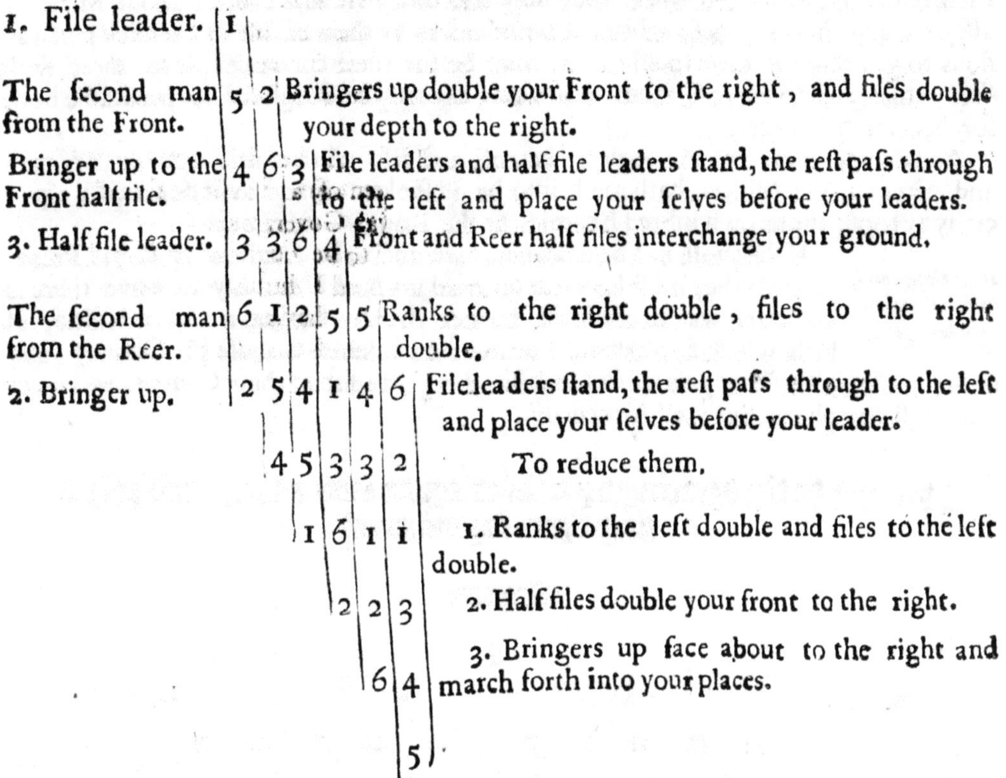

1. File leader.
The second man from the Front.
Bringer up to the Front half file.
3. Half file leader.
The second man from the Reer.
2. Bringer up.
Bringers up double your Front to the right, and files double your depth to the right.
File leaders and half file leaders stand, the rest pass through to the left and place your selves before your leaders.
Front and Reer half files interchange your ground.
Ranks to the right double, files to the right double.
File leaders stand, the rest pass through to the left and place your selves before your leader.
To reduce them.
1. Ranks to the left double and files to the left double.
2. Half files double your front to the right.
3. Bringers up face about to the right and march forth into your places.

Chap. XVIII.

Of certain Firings in the Front.

Having passed over the grounds of this Art Military, I am now come to the executive part of the *Tacticks*; and shall not here exceed the exercise of a single Company, shewing the Souldier the use of some few Firings, that they may the better perform their respective duties when they shall be commanded thereunto.

None can positively say, this or that figure shall be, or serve this day, time or place *&c.* because of the diversity of formes occasioned by situation of ground, he number of men, the order of the Enemy; with many other observable Stratagems, for the obtaining both of Wind and Sun.

I shall therefore according to my allotment of twelve files demonstrate by figure some Firings, which being well understood may enable such for higher preferment as time and place may fortune them unto.

By way of digression; I am sure it is a trouble to most ingenious spirits to see some Gentlemen chosen Captains in the Militia, that are but prisoners to their own reasons; and instead of being experienced in this Art have been wholly Ignorant of the least part thereof.

It is no wonder then if his Majesty may lose his expectation of a well disciplined Militia; and the Souldier in hazzard of his life and Country too.

How easily might this be remedied, if our Commanding power would but authorize the Commission officers to meet once in a moneth to exercise each other, by their respective turns, &c. where they may also discourse and consult about Military affairs; and then for these private Commanders by their affable and heroick perswasions to get some of their souldiers as may be for their conveniencie to meet with their armes, and to exercise them; this would not only be delightful but profitable both for King and Country.

And on the contrary, the neglect hereof, and also of the full number of men and Armes in the Militia, hath made it to be ill spoken of, and so little feared; especially by those of our own inbred Enemies to the Royal Government.

these things will be better looked into hereafter. If they will not be drawn to love and to be obedient to Royal Prerogatives, they must be made to dread it; And I humbly conceive there is no better way to effect the former than by having a choice Militia, of such whose spirits should account it a baseness to abuse the Country; and make not their Musters, pass times for debauchery; and that their Companies be not only well disciplined, but well Armed also.

I proceed to the drawing up of files again into a body, and preparing them for skirmish.

Captain.

E

2. S. D D 1. S.

m m m m p p p p m m m m

m m m m p p p p m m m m

m m m m p p p p m m m m

m m m m p p p p m m m m

m m m m p p p p m m m m

m m m m p p p p m m m m

L

3. S.

A Company of Foot being thus drawn up for service and the Colours flying in the head of the Company, and there they are to remain, until all forlorne firings are ended: But so soon as the Drumm shall beat his further preparatives for a close skirmish, the Ensign is to furle his Colours and retreit to the half files of Pikes.

Observe, That all firings are either direct, or oblique; and the manner how they are to be performed, are either Advancing, Receiving, or Retreiting: otherwhiles there may be firing in the Reer, marching from the Enemy; or in the flank marching by an Enemy: and also at several places, for an Enemy may at one and the same time charge, either in the Front or Reer, in Front and Reer, also in Front, Reer and Flank: and of these I shall demonstrate some that I at first learnt, and some amongst others that are most convenient to be learnt.

Now

Now that the Souldier might be expert in his firings against the Enemy, let him be often exercised with firings only, in the pan, falling off and on as shall be Commanded.

All which being well performed by the Musquetteers is a full accomplishment of what hath been before taught him, by which the Commander shall be credited, and the Souldier preferred to his merit.

Of firing by follorne files.

1. That which is to be used in our modern exercise is two manner of wayes; the two outmost files of each flank of Musquetteers to march with two Serjeants so far as shall be commanded, and there to stand: and the foremost ranks are to give fire and to fall into the Reer of themselves, either by wheeling off to the right, or to the right and left: Then let the remaining do the like and fall into their places.

m m S. 2. 1. S. m m

m m m m

m m m m

m m m m

m m m m

m m m m

Captain.

Those that have fired are to fall off on the inside of the Musquetteers between them and the Pikes; and as they are thus trooping back (after firing) to their places, the rest are in like manner to move away, and fire, and fall in next the Pikes.

E

D D

. . m m p p p p m m . .

. . m m p p p p m m . .

. . m m p p p p m m . .

. . m m p p p p m m . .

. . m m p p p p m m . .

. . m m p p p p m m . .

L

2. Accordingly as you draw out two files, so you may draw out more files to the number of Musquetteers; and so to fire and fall into the Reer of themselves, and places &c.

3. You may move them all clear of the Pikes, and let them open from the midst, leaving sufficient Intervals for their wheelings in the Reer of themselves, and then to place themselves even with their Pikes, the second having fired as before place themselves in the Reer of the first division &c.

m m   m m

m m   3   m m

m m   m m

m m   m m

m m   m m

m m   m m

Captain.

. . m m p p p p m m . .

. . m m p p p p m m . .

. . m m p p p p m m . .

. . m m p p p p m m . .

. . m m p p p p m m . .

. . m m p p p p m m . .

L

4. **Advance** the two outmost files by the Serjeants, who are to lead them to the place for execution as by order received; **Commanding**

1. Files to rank inward; to present and give fire all together.

2. You may rank inward two Files, or more, and fire as before.

And having fired are to wheel off to the right and left by their respective file leaders, placing themselves next the Pikes.

m m m m m m   m m m m m m

m   m

m   m

m   m

m   **Captain.**   m

m   E   m

D   D

. m m m p p p p m m m .

. m m m p p p p m m m .

. m m m p p p p m m m :

. m m m p p p p m m m .

. m m m p p p p m m m .

. m m m p p p p m m m .

L

I proceed to a second way of firing and that is by Ranks.
First, By advancing before the Front.

Secondly,

Secondly, firing even with the Front.

Thirdly, firing even with the half files.

Advancing before the Front may be performed by advancing of single ranks, and so firing in the Front; or by advancing of both flanks into the Front before the Pikes, and so to fire by single ranks. Which is performed by Commanding

Demyhearse.

5. Pikes stand, Musquetteers move forward and place your selves before in the Front of your Pikes, and close your Divisions.

I mention nothing to tye up the hand of the ingenious to any stinted form, whose ablities may command his figures at pleasure.

Observe, that when the forlorn files or Ranks march out, they are to give fire as upon a retreit (that is) to stand and fire, and wheel off that their followers may do the like, unless the Enemy give ground.

```
       S m m m m   m m m m S

 m                            m
 m                            m
 m  m m m m   m m m m         m
 m                            m
 :  m m m m   m m m m         :
 :                            :
 :  m m m m   m m m m         :
 :                            :
 :  m m m m   m m m m         :
 :                            :
 . . . . . . . . . . . . . . .
    . . . . . . . . .

           Captain.
           P P P P
           P P P P
           P P P P
              E
           P P P P
           P P P P
           P P P P
              L
```

And when the two last ranks were presented, the next two ranks must be ready to march forward being fixed to present and give fire also: Thus having fired in the Front by one single Rank, or more, they are by wheeling off to place themselves in the Reer of their own divisions before the Pikes; the rest doing the like until they have all fired round.

A second way of firing by this figure shall be a reducement to it.

First, The Frontiers having performed their firing are to wheel off by division until they come down so low as to be even to the first ranks of Pikes, and so to rank even a breast: All the Musquetteers are so to do successively and flank themselves even with the Pikes.

In this firing you are to take notice, when there are not above two Ranks to give fire, the Pikes may then Port, and when all the Musquetteers have fired they may charge, and then advancing their Pikes the Battel stands, which brings me to the next firing which is

S : m m m m m m m m m : S
: :
: m m m m m m m m m :
: :
: m m m m m m m m m :
: :
: m m m m m m m m m :
: :
: Capt. :
: D D :
m m m m : p p p p : m m m m
: :
m m m m : p p p p : m m m m
: :
. . . . . p p p p . . . . .
E
. . . . p p p p . . . .
. . . . p p p p . . . .
. . . . p p p p . . . .
L

6. Ranks advancing from the Front of a standing Battalia.

A Serjeant from each Flank leading up the two formost Ranks (according to order) the first Rank is to give fire, wheel off, and place themselves in the Reer of their own divisions: the second in order is to execute the same with speed, being not above three foot distance from the first, being ready with his Musquett palm'd, his Cock bent, and Muzzel mounted; so to Present and give fire; and so to wheel off and place themselves as their Leaders had done before them.

S S
m m m m m m m m

m m
m Capt. m
m D D m
m m m m m p p p p m m m m m
: :
: m m m m p p p p m m m m :
: :
: m m m m p p p p m m m m :
: :
: m m m m p p p p m m m m :
: :
. . . . . p p p p . . . . .
. . . . p p p p . . . .
L

7. Ranks

7. Ranks firing even with the Front.

The first Rank having fired and wheeled off placing themselves in the Reer of their Divisions, the next ranks are to move forwards at three motions into their places (making good their leaders ground) and there to present and give fire; wheeling off and placing themselves as by the former directions. By the way you must observe, if the body be upon a march the Pikes must be shouldered; and when they come to charge, they are to close forward at their close order.

Captain.

```
S          D          D          S
   m m m m  p p p p  m m m m
ɯ  m m m m  p p p p  m m m m  ɯ
ɯ  m m m m  p p p p  m m m m  ɯ
ɯ  m m m m  p p p p  m m m m  ɯ
ɯ  m m m m  p p p p  m m m m  ɯ
:                             :
:. . . . .  p p p p  . . . . .:
                L
```

It is presupposed ere one firing or two be performed (or past) over, the bodies are almost close; Then the Pikes are to be at their Port; and at length to be at their absolute Charge and push home: and being so near they may do great execution with their Musquets, firing upon the half files of Pikes as if they were even with the Front. Which brings me to

8. Ranks firing even with the half files.

When the Pikes are charging then the musquetteers may perform this who are to advance no further than the half files of Pikes, and there you may either fire one Rank or more at the discretion of the Commander; and as soon as every Rank hath fired successively they are to wheel off and place themselves in the Reer of their own leaders.

When the firing is ended, and each Souldier in his proper place, the Musquetteers marching up even in breast with the Front of Pikes they are reduced.

But in this firing the Musquetteers are to make good their leaders ground, except it be upon a retreit, then they are to fire upon the same ground and to wheel off, that their followers may doe the like, unless the Enemy give ground.

Captain.

```
            p p p p
            p p p p
S           p p p p           S
   m m m m  p p p p  m m m m
ɯ               E             ɯ
ɯ  m m m m  p p p p  m m m m  ɯ
ɯ                             ɯ
ɯ  m m m m  p p p p  m m m m  ɯ
:                             :
:  m m m m      L    m m m m  :
:                             :
:  m m m m           m m m m  :
:                             :
:. . . . .           : . . . .:
```

Horn.Bat. 9. **Command.** Pikes stand; Musquetteers march until the bringers up rank even with the Front.

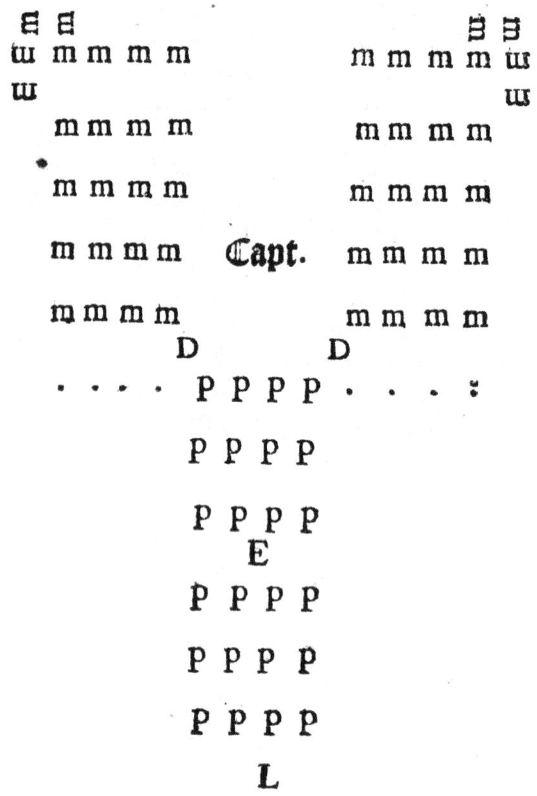

You may in this as with some of the former fire two Ranks ten paces advanced before the Front, and so whel off and place themselves in the Reer of their own files.

O R,

Secondly, let the first Rank of Musquetteers present and give fire and wheel off to the right and left, placing themselves in the Reer of their own files: then the second Rank firing are to advance into their leaders place, firing and wheeling off in the same manner, and so they are all successively to do the like.

Then Thirdly, when they have all given fire, let them begin again, and the file leaders having fired they are to wheel off to the right and left & flank themselves even with the Pikes; the second Rank now is to fire upon the same ground he stands and must not at all advance into his leaders ground as before, and having once fired all over they are reduced.

```
m m                          m m
m m m m m           m m m m m
m                                  m
 m m m m              m m m m

 m m m m              m m m m

 m m m m    Capt.     m m m m

 m m m m              m m m m
      D                 D
 . . . .   P P P P   . . . :
           P P P P
           P P P P
              E
           P P P P
           P P P P
           P P P P
              L
```

O R,

You may reduce them by Commanding the Musquetteers to face about to the right and march down into their respective places,

O R,

Command the Pikes to march up and even the Front with the file leaders of Musquetteers.

A triple firing. 10. Front half files of Musquetteers double your Front of Pikes by division: 2. Reer half files of Musquetteers open to the right and left and Rank even with the Pikes.

To perform this, direct the Front half files to advance clear of the body of Pikes, then face them to the right and left inwards, and so close their divisions before the Pikes.

Now

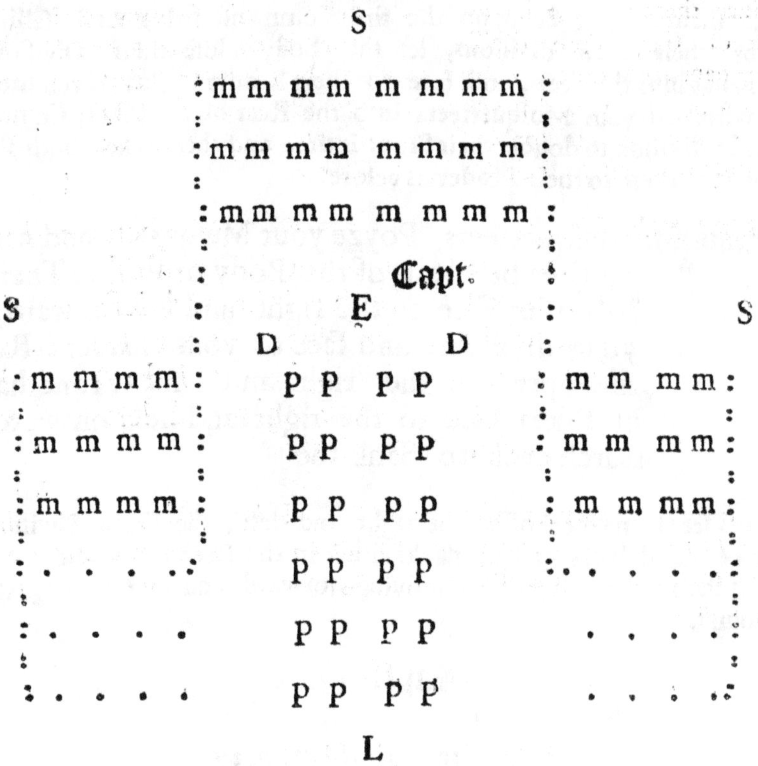

S

:m m m m m m m m :

:m m m m m m m m :

:m m m m m m m m :

Capt.

S : E : S

D D

:m m m m: p p p p :m m m m:

:m m m m: p p p p :m m m m:

:m m m m: p p p p :m m m m:

:. . . . .: p p p p :. . . . . .:

:. . . . p p p p . . . . .:

:. . . . . p p p p . . . . .:

L

You are to observe in this firing that the Musquetteers of the Front and both flanks are to present and give fire together; the Musquetteers of the Front division after firing are to wheel off to the right and left between their intervals, and place themselves even in Rank in the Reer of the Reer divisions of Musquetteers.

Then the Musquetteers that fired in the flanks march directly down and place themselves even in breast with the Reer of Pikes.

Thus they are reduced: Or else you may continue firing at your pleasure; and arging of your Pikes.

11. Wheel your flanks by division into the Front.

When they have fired let them march (or pass) down through the intervals, and place them in the Reer of their own divisions; And then upon an other firing they may place themselves in the Reer of the Pikes. The Pikes here may charge either at hand or foot, the Musquetteers may also fire over them.

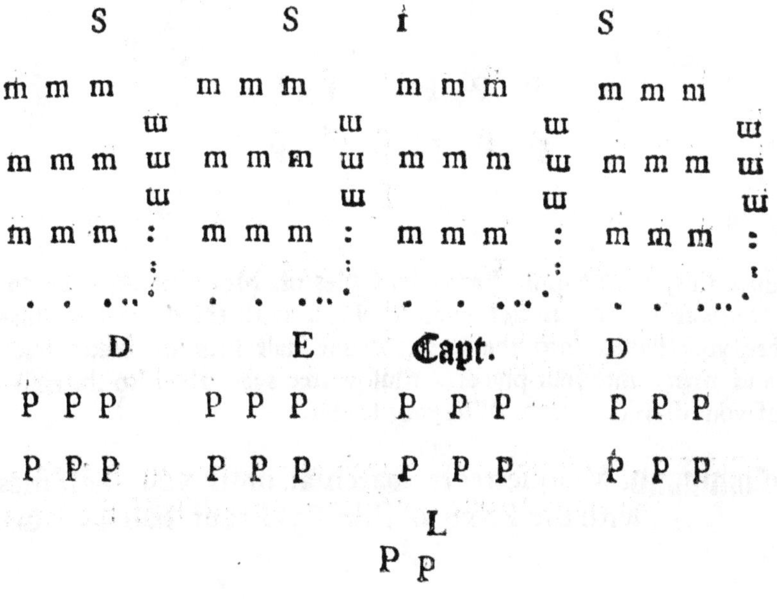

S S I S

m m m m m m m m m m m m

m m m m m

m m m m m m m m m m m m m m m m m m m m m m

m m m m

m m m : m m m : m m m : m m m :

: : : :

. . . .

D E Capt. D

P P P P P P P P P P P P

P P P P P P P P P P P P

L

To reduce them: if it be upon the first Command firing and falling off in the Reer of their own divisions, let the Body close their Divisions, and wheel their flanks into the Reer, and face to their Leader. But if you fire a second time, and wheel off your Musquetteers into the Reer of the Pikes, Command the musquetteers by division to double their Front intire, and then wheel both flanks into the Reer, and face them to their Leader as before.

12. **Command.** Musquetteers, Poyze your Musquetts, and march until theybe clear of the Body of Pikes: Then, Front half files face to the right and left inward, close your divisions, and face to your leader; Reer half files open to the right and left; Front half files of Pikes face to the right and left outwards, and march even to flank the

Having fired let them wheel off to the right and left, the Front Divisions falling in the Reer of themselves; and the flanks either in the Reer of themselves, or else in the Reer of their Pikes, the Pikes moving forward and maintaining the Musquetteers ground.

```
                    Capt.
           S                        S
           :m m m m  m m m m:
           :                :
           :m m m m  m m m m:
           :                :
           :m m m m m m m m:
         S ...              ...      S

m m m m:                         m m m m :
      :                                 :
m m m m :                        m m m m:
      :                                 :
m m m m :           E            m m m m:
     ...         D      D               ...
   P P                           P P
   P P                           P P
   P P                           P P
            P P P P P P
            P P P P P P
                  L
```

To reduce this, **Command.** Front half files of Musquetteers face to the right and left outwards, and march even in flank with the Reer half files of Pikes: Then wheel your flanks into the Reer. Front half files of Pikes face in opposition, and march into your places. Musquetteers face about to the right and march closing of your divisions: face all to your leader.

13. **Command.** Musquetteers march all until your half files be even with the Front of Pikes; Front half files march three paces

paces forward and ſtand: Reer half files of Muſquetteers face to the right and left outward and march clear of the Front half files. Reer half files of Pikes open to the right and left outward, and march clear of the Front Diviſion of Pikes.

```
                S              S
         m m m m            m m m m

         m m m m            m m m m
                   Capt.
         m m m m            m m m m

S               D          D               S
m m m m . . . . p p p p . . . . m m m m
                    E
m m m m . . . . p p p p . . . . m m m m

m m m m . . . . p p p p . . . . m m m m

             p p . . . . p p

             p p . . . . p p

             p p . . . . p p

                   L
```

The firſt Ranks of all diviſions having fired they may in the firſt place fall in the Reer of their own diviſions.

And for a ſecond firing ſo ſoon as the firſt ranks have fired in the Front, they are to wheel off to the right and left, and flank the Pikes as they were: then the Reer diviſion of Muſquetteers after firing fall off to the right and left, and place themſelves even abreaſt with the Reer diviſion of Pikes: Then Reer half files of Pikes face to the right and left inwards and march into your places: By this they are Reduced.

14. **Command.** Muſquetteers march until your two laſt Ranks are equal with the two firſt Ranks of Pikes. The two ſecond Ranks of Pikes, face to the right and march into the Reer of the right flank of Muſquetteers. The two laſt Ranks of Pikes face to the left and march into the Reer of the left flank of Muſquetteers.

Having fired let them whel off to the right and left falling in the Reer of themselves; and so having fired once or twice over, they may fall in the Reer of their own Pikes, every Musqueteer as he fireth to advance unto his leaders place, and the Pikes to advance also, who are to be ported, and when the two last Ranks are firing they are to charge at the discretion of the Commander; which Figure I have here set down, because from it the fourteenth shall be reduced.

```
S                          S
m m m m              m m m m
m m m m              m m m m
m m m m    Capt.     m m m m
m m m m      E       m m m m
m m m m   P P P P    m m m m
m m m m   P P P P    m m m m
P P P P              P P P P
P P P P              P P P P
             L
```

The Reducement. The two ranks of Pikes upon the right flank face to the left and march *&c.* then march the four ranks direct; The two Ranks on the left flank face to the right, and place your selves as you were facing them to their Leader, the Musquetteers to advance and flank the Pikes; they are reduced.

```
           Capt.
             E
          P P P P
          P P P P
P P P P              P P P P
P P P P      L       P P P P
m m m m              m m m m
m m m m              m m m m
m m m m              m m m m
m m m m              m m m m
m m m m              m m m m
m m m m              m m m m
```

15 **Command.** Front half files of Musquetteers, and the two first Ranks of Pikes march three foot: The four Ranks of Pikes wheel your flanks into the front by division, and face to the right and left, and march even in the Reer of the Front Division of Musquetteers; Then the Reer half files of Musquetteers face to the right and left, and march them clear of the division of Pikes, facing them to their Leader, and march up even with the flanks of Pikes.

Having

Capt.

E

m m m m p p p p m m m m

m m m m p p p p m m m m

m m m m m m m m

m m m m p p p p p p p p m m m m

m m m m p p p p p p p p m m m m

m m m m L m m m m

Having fired and wheeled off in the Reer of their own divisions of Musquetteers, then for a second firing let the Front divisions of Musquetteers fire and wheel into the Reer of Pikes, the pikes porting, and charge as in the figure and retreit; and upon the retreit the Pikes to fall all even in breast; And the front division of Musquetteers to sleeve up even in breast with the Reer division of Musquetteers; Then the Pikes to charge on again, and the reer division of Musquetteers to fire, wheeling off to the right and left, and fall into the Reer of the front division of Musquetteers: who will then stand after this form.

To reduce them, Command. The Pikes to advance and march all to a convenient distance, then march the middle division of Pikes six foot; then the two divisions of pikes upon the flanks to face in opposition and close their divisions; Then Wheel their flanks into the Reer and face them to their leader, which being done the Pikes are reduced. The Musquetteers are to march up and flank the Pikes.

p p p p · p p p p · p p p p

p p p p · p p p p · p p p p

m m m m m m m m

m m m m m m m m

m m m m m m m m

m m m m m m m m

m m m m m m m m

m m m m m m m m

Many firings the ingenious might invent to the Front more than what I have demonstrated: I shall only mention the

Introductive, and Extraductive firings.

I must give my judgement with those who do not allow the firings by way of Introduction to be useful in our modern Wars; nor are they secure to the Souldier unless when the Commander shall find his Souldiers to be well exercised, then amongst other various curiosities these may be performed.

By the word Introduction is meant a passing through, or between, and by its motion doth advance and gain ground upon an Enemy.

16. Command. Make ready to give fire by Introduction: Then Command the files of Musquetteers to open by division to their open order, and to pass through to the right, *&c.*

S Capt. S

2 m m m m . . m m m m

1 m m m m p p p p m m m m

m m m m m m m m

2 m m m m p p p p m m m m

m m m m m m m m

3 m m m m p p p p m m m m

E

4 . . . : p p p p . . . .

5 . . . : p p p p . . . .

6 . . . . p p p p . . . .

L

The first rank of each flank presents and gives fire, so done they stand and make ready again. The second rank so soon as the first have fired, passeth through, and placeth it self before the first, and do their fire, and stand also and make ready again. The third is to pass forward and stand in rank even with the first, and when the second rank hath fired, they must step before the second, and having fired are to stand and make ready again; and thus every rank is to follow his Leader successively, until the Bringers up of each Division are to give fire, and stand in the Front of all.

Observe, in this firing you may keep your Pikes shouldered, still moving slowly forwards (if there be no danger of Horse) and so keep even with the Front of Musquetteers: This done twice over will reduce them.

A Second way of Introductive firing.

The first Rank is to fire and stand, as in the forementioned Figure; then the Bringers-up (or last Rank) whilst the File-leaders are firingshall, march up and place themselves even with the second Rank, and when they have fired, the Bringers-up are to step before them, and immediatly to present and give fire; and when the rest have followed their Bringers-up, and fired once over, be sure that the File-leaders fire twice; who ought to be the first and the last, and so stand: the Pikes are to march up even with the Front of Musquetteers as in the former direction and they are reduced.

Both produce the born battle.

Extraductive.

17. Firing. There have been in use two Extraductive firings, I shall speak but of one which is allowed somewhat useful, especially in narrow passages, and in case your Enemy be too powerful, either in Horse or Foot; that then the passage might be filled up with the Pikes: but if your Pikes be not sufficient to do it (as you will perceive by my Figure) then double your Ranks, let your Pikes be in such posture and motion accordingly as occasion shall offer it self.

Command. Musquetteers face about to the right, and march until you are clear of the Body of Pikes; then face inward and close your Divisions: for the Pikes command them to double their Ranks to the right; Or, half Files double their Front to the right.

To

To perform this **Command**. The first rank of Musquetteers next after the Pikes, face to the right; then to march forth file-wise, close up by the right flank of Pikes; and when the Leader is advanced into the Front of Pikes, he is to lead them athwart the whole Front of Pikes; after which they are all to stand, present and give fire, and having fired they are to wheel off to the left, and fall into the Reer of Musquetteers; and whilst the first Rank is firing, the second is to be marching so as to be ready to fall into their Places.

m m m m m m m m
C
P P P P P P P P
P P P P P P P P m
P P P P P P P P m
• • • • m m m m m m
m m m m m m m m
m m m m m m m m
m m m m m m m m
m m m m m m m m
L

To reduce them, **Command** the Pikes to advance six foot (if they be doubled their Ranks to the right) let them now double their Files to the left; then **Command**:

I could have mentioned a great many more firings to the Front: but through my confinement to such a small number of men, and not an equality in arms, Art compleated cannot be expected from me.

Must of these firings are solid and serviceable; yet it cannot be conceived that three Ranks can make any abidement of Battle for continuance against any Enemy: although sometimes they may be forced to be reduced into less Numbers, yet by shewing the nature hereof you will be the better able to manage a greater, &c.

CHAP. XIX.

Of firing in the Front and Reer; And Reer alone.

BEfore I demonstrate the firings in the Reer, I thought it fit to give one Figure of firing to the Front and Reer, which may serve also for a firing to each Flank, when the Commander pleaseth.

1. **Command**. Front half Files of Musquetteers march until your Bringers-up be even in breast with the Front of Pikes: Reer half Files of Pikes face about to the right. Reer half Files of Musquetteers face about to the right, and march, until the half File-leaders are even in breast with the Bringers up of Pikes.

m m m m   m m m m
m m m m   Capt.   m m m m
m m m m I D   E   D m m m m
p p p p
p p p p
p p p p
d d d d
d d d d
d d d d
w w w w   I   w w w w
w w w w   w w w w
w w w w   w w w w

For the first firing by this Figure, so soon as the Ranks upon each Division have fired, they are to wheel off to the right and left, and fall into the Reer of their own Divisions: And having so fired all over they are to wheel off and place themselves even in breast with the Pikes, as now they stand faced; then being faced to their Leader they are reduc'd.

This is not our drift of firing in the Reer; but if in a March an Enemy eagerly pursues and assaults, then by facing about and firing in the Reer, or by Countermarching, or Wheeling about, and so firing; these repulses orderly performed may cause a disorder in the pursuants: And it is good sometimes as occasion may offer to keep an Enemy in play, whilst he may advantage himself in his Ground, either for his Embattlement, or Ambushes, or for the conveyances of Gunns or other Carriages, &c.

2. Firing. Upon a March the last Rank is to face about, and so to give fire, wheeling off in File by Division, and marching up towards the Front, and placing themselves before their File-leaders.

1. Observing, that they rank even with the second rank of Pikes.

2. In the performance of this, you will lose one rank in the Front.

3. Observe, that whilst the rank of Musquetteers are firing in the Reer, the next rank although he be marching, he ought to be preparing with his cock bent and garded, that with his three motions, he may next fire so soon as his precedent rank is wheeled off.

Capt.
E
D   D
. . . . P P P P . . . .
:   :
: m m m m p p p p m m m m :
m   m
m m m m p p p p m m m m
m   m
m m m m p p p p m m m m
m   m
m m m m p p p p m m m m
m   m
w w w w p p p p w w w w
S   I   S

4. Although

4. Although you are upon a march, yet you are to fall one rank nearer to the Reer, that the Body may be preserved intire.

5. Observe further in the performance of all this, your preparations and firings ought to be at three motions: Let the first be with the right leg advancing, the second with the left leg advancing, bending your cock; then a little advancing forward with the right foot, to present and give fire. *Cock your match, Blow your coal, Present, &c.*

Now I give these Reasons for the Observations of some motions in these firings to the Reer; because so soon as the Souldier hath fired, if the last rank should immediatly face about and present, *&c.* there would be a present incumbrance; This experience hath discovered, and that firing upon motion to be the most speediest and safest way for firing in the Reer.

Now for a Publick Exercise, when you have fired over once, you may then face them to their Leader, and fire in the Front.

But if you be upon a march, and should be pursued by an Enemies Horse, then Wheel your Flanks into the Front, and face to the Reer; your Pikes will defend your Body, so your Musquetteers may fire over them as in the 17. Figure by extraduction, and reduced accordingly.

Secondly, In firing to the Reer, the Musquetteers may be in the Reer of the Pikes. And first having fired they are to wheel off and place themselves between the Front of Musquetteers and Reer of Pikes. And secondly, having fired in the Reer they may wheel off by Division and march into the Front of Pikes, the Body still marching. Or, if both flanks be in the Reer, they may fire & wheel off by Division, and double both flanks.

This last hath reduced it self; and for the second you may for exercise, fire them in the Front, and in their wheeling off to flank their Pikes; or for expedition, for the Musquetteers to open to the right and left, and march the Pikes up in the interval, and they are reduced as at first.

You may perceive the use of firings in the Reer, and that the Souldier ought to be very well exercised in them: For a true experience herein doth not only add to the perfection of the Souldier, but his safety also.

Before I conclude this Chapter, I shall add two Figures of firing in Front and Reer marching.

3. **Command.** Front half Files of Musquetteers, march until you be clear of the Front of Pikes; Face in opposition and close your Divisions.

So for the reer half files, face about to the right, and march until you be clear of the Reer of Pikes; face them in opposition, and close their Divisions.

Having fired their first and last Ranks, they wheel off to the right and left by Division, the Front Division are to place themselves even in Rank with the Front of Pikes, and the Reer Division of Musquetteers are to place themselves even in Rank with the Bringers-up, and so each Rank successively after each other, will reduce this Figure.

```
        m m m m m m m m
        m m m m m m m m
             Capt.
m m m m p p p p m m m m
. . . . p p p p . . . .
. . . . p p p p . . . .
           E
. . . . p p p p . . . .
. . . . p p p p . . . .
m m m m p p p p m m m m
           T
        w w w w w w w w
        w w w w w w w w
```

4. Command. Half Files of Musquetteers, fire to your Front and Reer placing your selves between your Divisions.

Capt.

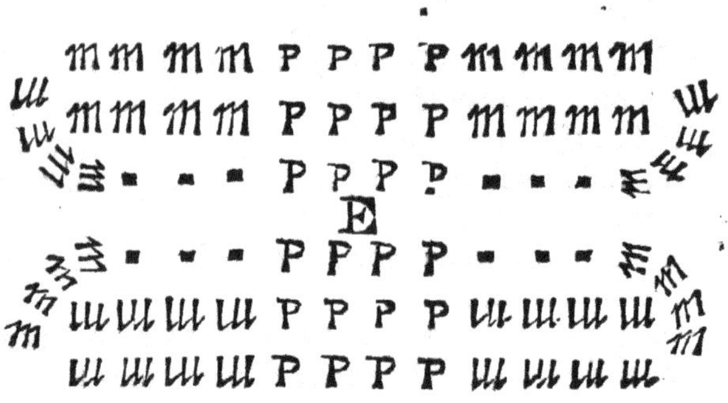

mm mm P P P P mm mm
m m mm mm P P P P mm mm m m
m m ▪ ▪ ▪ P P P P ▪ ▪ ▪ m m
E
m m ▪ ▪ ▪ P P P P ▪ ▪ ▪ m m
m m mm mm P P P P mm mm m m
mm mm P P P P mm mm

L

This firing is plain without direction, and the firing being ended they are reduced.

Chap. XX.

Of Firings in the Flanks.

THere are reasons to be given, and Experience hath found it necessary, for firing in the Flanks: When you are upon a March, an Enemy may endeavour an assault to molest you in your passages, that your disadvantages may be the greater, either by ambushments laid against you, or to frustrate your designs.

Now in the performance hereof there are several circumstances that are to be taken notice of, as the strength of your Enemy, the time, number and place; all for your own security, or advantages against him.

I shall begin with some Exercises upon the right flank, and what is performed there by Figure, may also be performed upon the left hand.

In order hereunto pass all your Musquetteers into your right flank by Commanding:

Musquetteers of the right Flank open to the right, and being opened to a convenient distance, stand; then Musquetteers of the left Flank, pass through your Ranks of Pikes to the interval of the right Flank, then stand, and face to your Leader.

Your facings to the right or left, is that, by which the flanks become accidental fronts, and then for the firings thereupon, you may to your discretion use such as are most convenient; being already shewn *Chapter* 18. I shall not here take up any room with the demonstrations thereof, and shall shew but some few firings in the right flank, as the Body shall be marching, in all which you are to observe the Pikes are to be shouldered.

1. Command.

1. **Command.** Musquetteers give fire to the right, and wheel after your Bringers-up, between your Divisions.

And this at the discretion of the Commander is done two wayes, either by commanding to be lead into their places by their File-leader, or by their Bringers-up, and to place themselves before them, *&c.*

```
        E                    C

p p p p D   m m m m m m
p p p p     m m m m m m   ɯ   1
p p p p     m m m m m m   ɯ   2
p p p p     m m m m m m   ɯ   3
p p p p     m m m m m m   ɯ   4
p p p p D . m m m m m m   ɯ   5
          :          L    ɯ   6
     6m
       5m
        4m 3m 2m 1m
```

Here by this Figure, they in the first place, as the Body is marching, face to the right (the outmost File) presents and gives fire: after their firing, they face to the right, and after their Bringer-up, who leads them off in the Reer of the Musquetteers, and up into the Interval between the Pikes and Musquets, until the Bringer-up of the File hath placed himself even in breast with the Frontiers; and so the marching Party, as **Command** shall be given, are to open, that the Files of Musquetteers after they have fired may march up between the Divisions, and so every File is successively to fire, and wheel off and place it self. This firing being performed twice over they are **Reduced**: If but once, you must countermarch your files of Musquetteers to reduce them.

2. **You** may secondly after they have fired, **Command** them to face to the right, and to wheel off, every man placing himself before his Bringer up (or present Leader) hereby the Bringer up will be in his due place and the file-leader in his proper place, also.

3. **A Third** way of firing upon this Figure, is to fire in the right flank, and to be lead off into their places by their respective File-leaders.

The Body marching, the outmost File faceth to the right and fires, and when the body is marched clear of the standing file, then the next file presents to the right and fires, and whilest he is firing, the first file that is fired faceth to the left, and marcheth up between the Musquetteers and Pikes. Observing the former directions in their march, that there may be space enough in the Interval for the several Files successively to march into their places.

```
        E                    C
            D.
p p p p     m m m m m m
p p p p     m m m m m m   ɯ   1
p p p p     m m m m m m   ɯ   2
p p p p     m m m m m m   ɯ   3
p p p p     m m m m m m   ɯ   4
p p p p  .  m m m m m m   ɯ   5
          D               ɯ   6
S          1m          L
            2m
             3m
              4m 5m 6m
```

 4. **There**

4. There is a fourth way of firing, that is, to give fire to the right and gather up your Files.

The Body marching the outmoſt file faceth to the right, fires, then ſtands, and faceth to their Leader: Then when the Body is clear of the ſtanding file, the ſecond file faceth to the right, and fires and ſtands alſo, facing to their Leader; then the firſt file is to advance up to the ſecond, and ſo when the firſt and ſecond have fired they are to be lead up to the third. Thus having fired, they are to be lead up even in breaſt to the file that laſt fired, and having all fired, they are to be marcht up even with the Front of Pikes.

```
E          C
           8 7 6 5 4 3 2 1
p p p p D  m m m
p p p p    m m m
p p p p    m m m
p p p p    m m m
p p p p    m m m
p p p p D  m m m
             L m

                 5
                 m
                 m 4           S
                 m m 3 2 1
                 m m m m m
                 m m m m m
                 m m m m m
                   m m m m
                   m m m m
                     m m m
```

To reduce this, Command: Left half Ranks of Muſquetteers, face to the left; Pikes face to the right, paſs through interchanging of Ground; Face to your Leader.

How beneficial this may be to the ſecurity of the Souldier, they that will make uſe of it that are ingenious will better judge: but I am of opinion it is more fit for a private Exerciſe, than for publick Service.

5. **Command.** Give fire to the right, and place your ſelves even in Front with the Pikes, marching up between the midſt of the Pikes.

Obſerve

Observe, in the performance hereof, the Pikes as they march are to open to the right and left, and the fired Musquetteers are to be lead up according to **Command**.

E C

12 11 2 1 10 9 8 7 6 5 4 3 2 1

p p . m p p m m m m m . . .

p p . m p p m m m m m ɯ . .

p p . m p p m m m m m ɯ . .

p p . m p p m m m m m ɯ . .

p p . m p p m m m m m ɯ . .

p p . m p p m m m m m ɯ . .

m L ɯ

m

m

m

m

m

To reduce this, **Command**. 1. Pikes to face inwards. 2. Musquetteers face to the right and left outwards. 3. Pass all through and interchange Ground. 4. Face to your Leader.

6. **Command**. Musquetteers give fire to the right, placing your selves on the outside of the left Flank of Pikes.

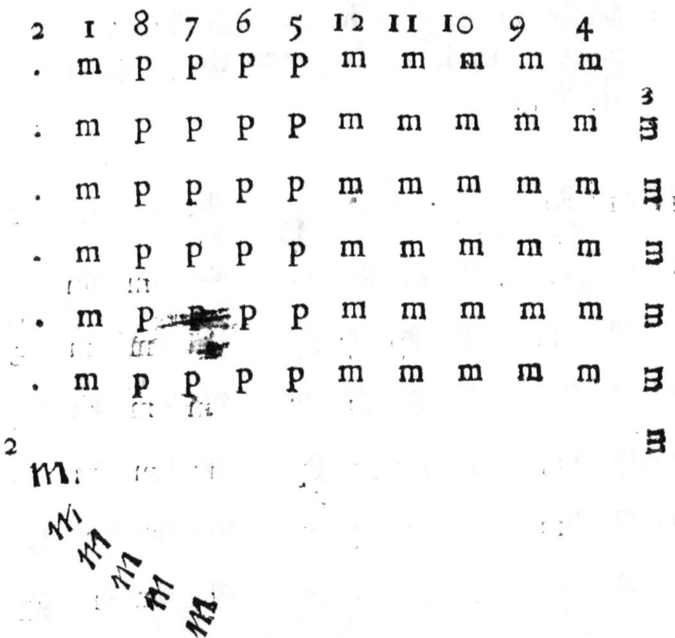

If you will reduce this without any firing, you may **Command** the right half Ranks to pass through your Ranks of Pikes.

(The Ingenious may find many ways for the Reducement.) Or, when all the Musquetteers are on the left flank, you may fire them over again, and they are reduced.

 7. **Command**.

7. **Command.** Musquetteers give fire to the right and to the Reer; placing your selves between the Pikes and your own Divisions.

A useful firing.

Having placed your left flank of Musquetteers in the Reer, then **Command,**

The outmost file upon the right flank, are to face to the right, and the last rank of Musquetteers in the Reer are to face about, and both are to present and give fire together; and having fired the outermost file upon the right hand faceth to the left, and marcheth after their Leader in the interval between the Musquets and the Pikes; and the rank fired in the Reer is to wheel to the right, placing it self in the Reer of Pikes, *&c.*

This is easily reduced, by commanding the Musquetteers to draw off into the left flank again.

Observe, that flank that is farthest from the Enemy ought to be drawn into the Reer.

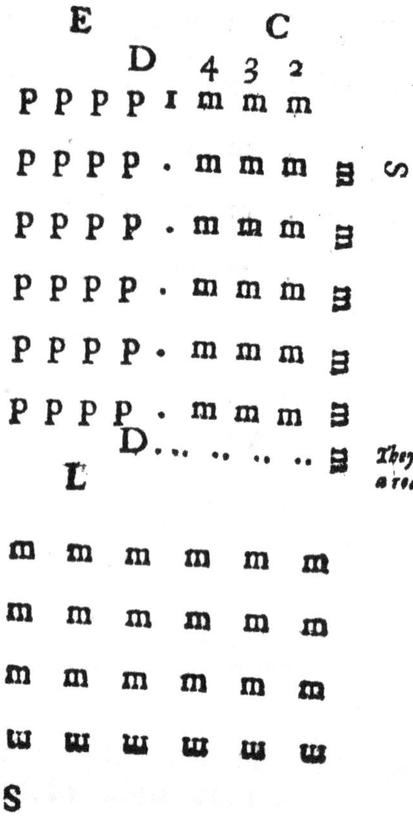

```
E           C
      D  4 3 2
P P P P 1 m m m
P P P P . m m m  m  S
P P P P . m m m  m
P P P P . m m m  m
P P P P . m m m  m
P P P P . m m m  m
     D.. .. .. .. m
  L
m m m m m m
m m m m m m
m m m m m m
w w w w w w
S
```

They are to march a reasonable pace.

8. **Command.** Musquetteers give fire to both Flanks (marching) and place your selves between the Pikes and your own Divisions.

```
                                              C
12 11 10 9           E              4  3  2  1
        12   D              D       1
     m  m  :  .  P P P P            m  m  m
S  m  m  m  m    P P P P            m  m  m  m  S
   m  m  m  m    P P P P            m  m  m  m
   m  m  m  m    P P P P            m  m  m  m
   m  m  m  m    P P P P            m  m  m  m
   m  m  m  m    P P P P            m  m  m  m
   m        m .  L             .                m
 .. .. .. .. .. .. :           : .. .. .. .. .. ..
```

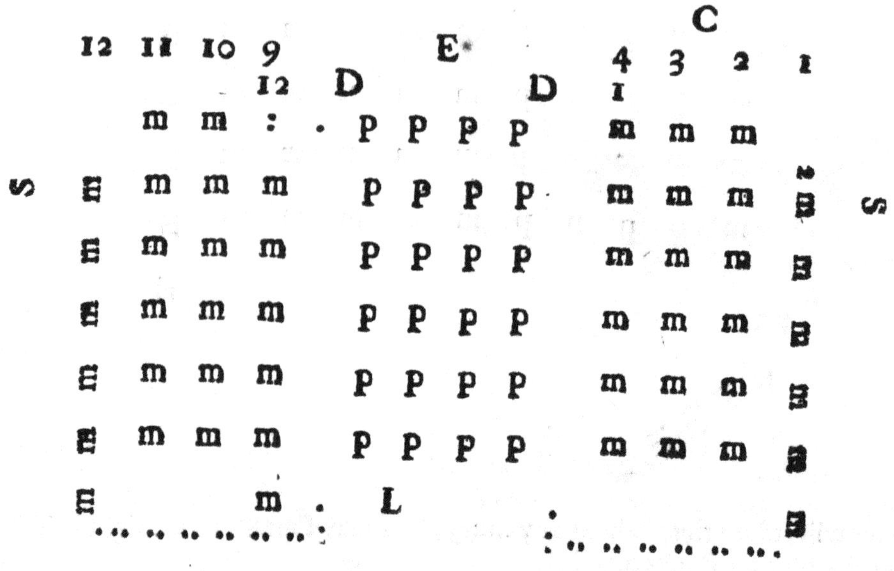

To perform this, the outermost file of each flank presents outward.

9. **Command.**

9. **Command.** The Body standing, Advance your Pikes; Musquetteers and Pikes face to the right and left; Musquetteers present and give fire to both flanks, and flank your Pikes.

The outermost file upon the right and left flank presents and fires, wheeling off by Division, ranking or flanking the Pikes, as they stand faced, leaving such a distance as the rest may securely follow them, every rank is to fire upon the same Ground, and wheel off by Division after the same manner.

From this Figure as they will stand after firing, there may be produced a great many brave Figures; but now I must leave them to the skilful Artist.

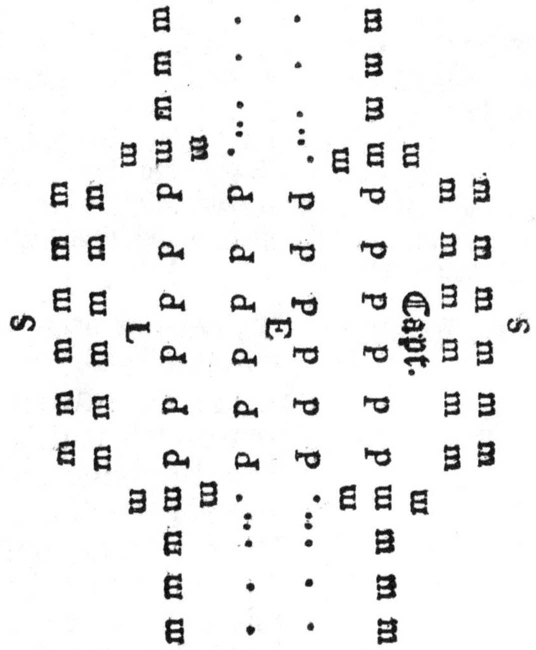

To reduce this **Command.** The Musquetteers to march all until they are clear of the Pikes; then face them to the right and left inwards, and close their Divisions, and face them to their Leader.

10. **Command.** Because it may easily be produced from the precedent Figure; it shall be from the first Figure of firing in the Front and Reer, *Chap.* 19. the Body being faced to the right and left will be a firing to both Flanks.

11. **Command.** Shall be a firing to right Flank and to the Front and Reer.

Left half Ranks double your right Flank by Division.

You may face the Divisions any way, which you intend for their firing.

After firing they are to wheel off into their own Divisions, every Rank moving into his Leaders Ground.

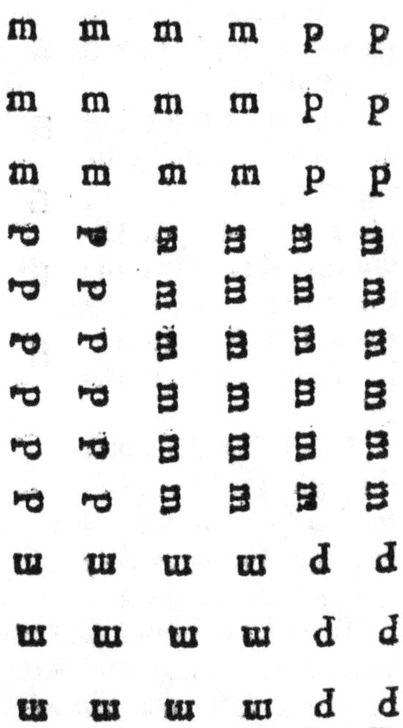

To reduce them, face them to their proper Front, then **Command** half Ranks that doubled face to the left, and so march into your places. See the doubling of Flanks Figure 17.

Chap. XXI.

Of several Divisional Firings.

I Might here make mention of a great many Figures for firings, some serviceable, and others not, but all left to the judicious for censure, and to make use of the best; yet none useless for delight or Garden Exercises: The Figures cannot be perfect because I am tied to the exercise but of twelve Files, four of them Pikes and eight Musquetteers; it being a Number that our Western Commanders can make use of, and no more; yet any who may be capable to perform them, will be able to invent others; and command the production of such like in geater Numbers, and with better delight.

1. **Command.** The two outmost Files upon each Flank stand; the two inmost half Ranks of the Reer face about to the right: the two inmost half Ranks both of Front and Reer, march until you are clear of the Body of Pikes; then half Files rank to the right and left inwards by wheeling into the Front.

For the Pikes, open them to the right and left from the midst; then **Command** the right and left hand File of Pikes to stand; the Reer half Files of the remainder face about to the right, then both half Files rank to the right and left inward into the Front and Reer.

This Figure in great Bodies must be performed otherways, and may be very serviceable against the Horse; the Pikes may advance into the Front of Musquetteers to secure them against the Horses fury if occasion shall serve.

After their first firing and wheeling off to the right and left in the Reer of their own Divisions, then when the Pikes are defending them from the Horse, let them fire over the Pikes.

This being done pass through the Musquetteers before the several Fronts of Pikes, as they were before any firing.

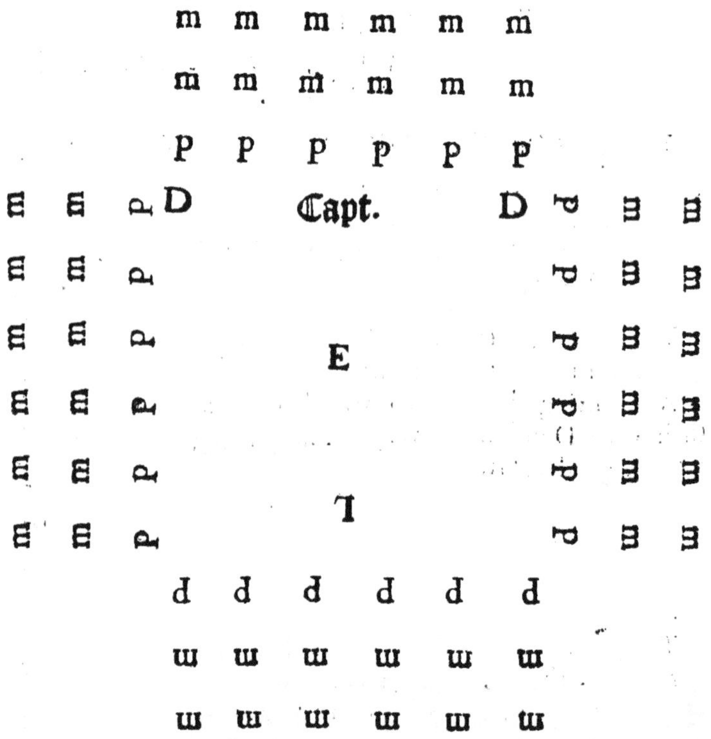

m m m m m m
m m m m m m
P P P P P P
m m p D Capt. D p m m
m m p p m m
m m p E p m m
m m p p m m
m m p p m m
m m p T p m m
d d d d d d
ɯ ɯ ɯ ɯ ɯ ɯ
ɯ ɯ ɯ ɯ ɯ ɯ

To reduce them, **Command.** Face the Front and Reer to the right and left inwards: The Front and Reer Ranks of Pikes file to the right and left inwards; the right and left hand files of Pikes close to the right and left inwards; and close all to the

the midſt: Then Command the Front and Reer Ranks of Muſquetteers, file to the right and left inward, face in oppoſition and march into your places; cloſing the whole Body to their cloſe Order; and open them again to their Order: Evening of their Ranks and ſtreightning of their Files they are reduced.

2. **Command** and **Direction.** Muſquetteers open ſix foot to the right and left: Front half Files of the right Flank of Muſquetteers, Advance intire into the Front of Pikes: The Reer Diviſion of the left Flank of Muſquetteers face about to the right, and double intire the Reer of the Pikes: The Front Diviſion of Muſquetteers of the left, face about to the right, and march even in breaſt with the Reer half Files of Pikes: The Front half Files of Pikes face to the right and left outwards, and march until you are clear, *&c.* Face them to their Leader.

```
                      m  m  m  m  S
                      m  m  m  m
                      m  m  m  m
              p p         C          p p
              p p         E          p p
              p p                    p p
S                                                 S
m m m m               p  p  p  p            m m m m
m m m m               p  p  p  p            m m m m
m m m m               p  p  p  p            m m m m

                      m  m  m  m
                      m  m  m  m
                      m  m  m  m
                          L
```

To reduce them. The Front Diviſion of Muſquetteers face to the right, and march into your places: Reer Diviſion of Muſquetteers face to the left, and march forth into your places: Front half Files of Pikes face in oppoſition and cloſe your Diviſions: The left flank of Muſquetteers advance even with the Front of Pikes: Muſquetteers cloſe to the right and left inward, and face them to their Leader. And they are reduced.

3. **Command.** Front half Files face to the right and left, and march clear of your Reer half Files: Face them to their Leader, and march them until their Reer be even in Front with their Pikes: The two first Ranks of each Division face to the right and left, and march them clear of their own Divisions; face them to their Leader: The four first Ranks of Pikes open to your open Order, and double your Ranks to the right, the two last Ranks of Pikes face about to the right and march clear of the Reer of Musquetteers: Face to your Leader.

Front.

m m S m m C m m S m m

m m m m E m m m m

m m m m P P P P P P P P m m m m

P P P P P P P P

m m m m m m m m

m m m m m m m m

m m m m m m m m

P P P P

P P P P

S L

To reduce them, **Command.** The first Body of Pikes to double their Files to the left, the two last Ranks of Pikes march and close your Divisions.

The two first Ranks of Musquetteers face in opposition, and close your Divisions.

Then the Front Divisions of Musquetteers face to the right and left inwards, and march even to the Front of Pikes, then face them to their right and left, and close their Divisions: Face them to their Leader: evening their Ranks and streightning of their Files, they are reduced.

4. **Command.**

4. **Command.** Front half files march clear from your Musquetteers: The Reer half files of Musquetteers face about to the right and march clear of your Pikes; and face to your leader.

```
                 Capt.

               P  P  P  P
               P  P  P  P
               P  P  P  P
S                                    S
m m m m                        m m m m
m m m m                        m m m m
m m m m           E            m m m m
               P  P  P  P
               P  P  P  P
               P  P  P  P
m m m m                        m m m m
m m m m                        m m m m
m m m m                        m m m m
          S           L
```

The Reducement. The Front Division of Pikes, face about to the right, and march into your places; the Reer Division of Musquetteers march up into your places.

5. **Command.** Wheel both your Flanks of Musquetteers into the Front, both flanks of Musquetteers open to the right and left: Front division of Pikes march clear of the Front of Musquetteers, and open to the right and left, until you are clear of the Angles of the Reer half files: The two inmost files of Musquetteers march until you are clear of the Front of Pikes: The next two inmost files of Musquetteers face in opposition, march and close your divisions in the Front of the Reer division of Pikes; face all to your leader.

m m   m m

m m   C   m m

m m   E   m m

P P   P P

P P   P P

P P   P P

m m m m . . : . m m m m . . . . m m m m

m m m m   m m m m   m m m m

m m m m   m m m m   m m m m

P P P P

P P P P

P P P P

L

To reduce this; The four middle files of Musquetteers face to the right and left and march into your places. The files of Musquetteers in the Front face about to the right & march into your places. Face them to their leader. The Front half files of Pikes face in opposition, and close your divisions facing them to the Reer and march them into their places; then close the Front of Musquetteers as at first, and wheel the Front into your flanks &c. they are reduced.

The two next figures are almost one and the same, and with but a little alteration in their Commands they may be either produced, or reduced.

6. **Command.** Pikes stand; The Reer half files of Musquetteers face about to the right: Musquetteers march all until you are clear both of your Front and Reer of Pikes, face in opposition and close your divisions: The four inmost Ranks of Musquetteers march clear of the remainder both in Front and Reer. The two last Ranks of Pikes stand, the rest to the right and left by division march clear of the Musquetteers, and wheel to the right and left outwards.

6. Figure

6. Figure.

```
            m m m m
            m m m m
            m m m m
       m m           m m
       m m           m m
       m m           m m
P P P P      . . . .       P P P P
P P P P      . . . .       P P P P
            P P P P
            P P P P
       m m           m m
       m m           m m
       m m           m m
            m m m m
            m m m m
            m m m m
```

Directions for firing upon this or others I must leave to the ingenious; wishing the unskilful to fire only as the Figure lyeth, lest it may prove trouble to them to reduce.

The Reducement. The two ranks upon the flanks wheel to the right and left inwards and march into your places: Front and Reer Musquetteers face about to the right and march forth into your places (provided they are faced to the Reer) only then the Front Musquetteers are to face about. Then Musquetteers face to the right and left outwards, and march clear of the Pikes; face in opposition and close your divisions, and face all to their leader they are reduced.

It is but marching up of the two last ranks of Pikes into the Reer of the Front division of Musquetteers, and the Musquetteers even to the Reer of the Pikes, which produceth this next figure.

m m m m

m m m m

m m m m

m m m m

m m m m

m m m m

p p p p p p p p p p p p

p p p p p p p p p p p p

m m m m

m m m m

m m m m

m m m m

m m m m

m m m m

7. **Command.** Half files double your Front to the right, the two outmost files of Musquetteers of each flank march ten paces direct and stand. The two next files of Musquetteers of each flank march to the Reer of the first, and the two next Ranks in the Reer of the second, until they are clear of the Front of the battel: And thus is this figure produced.
Or by Commanding. The two outmost in each flank to stand, the rest of the Body face about to the right and march, and so leaving the two outmost files in the Reer of the first, and the third in the Reer of the second, and the remainder of the Body in the Reer of the third; facing all to their proper Front.

S 7. Figure. S

m m m m

m m m m

m m m m

m m m m

m m m m

m m m m

m m **Capt.** m m

m m E m m

m m m m

m m p p p p p p p p m m

m m p p p p p p p p m m

m m p p p p p p p p m m

L

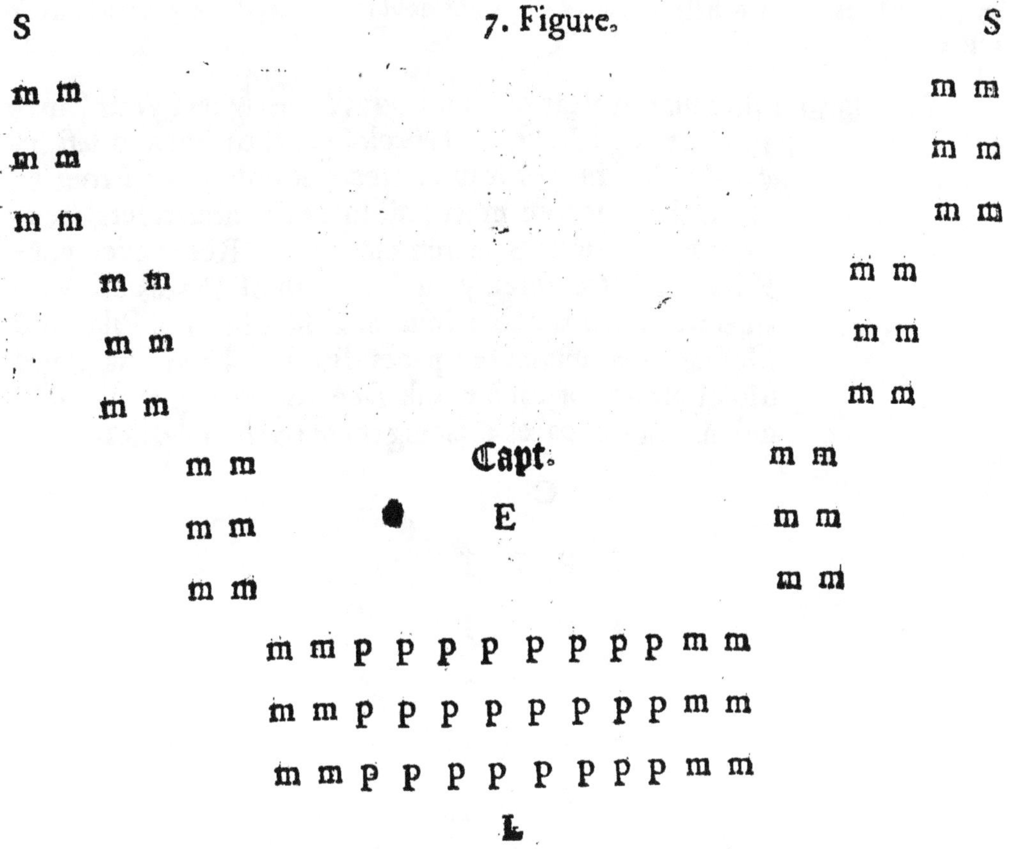

To reduce them, **Command.** Musquetteers face about to the right and march into your places; Then half files that doubled face about to the right and march forth into your places. Or, Even files from the left, double your files to the left.

8. **Command.** Half files double your Front to the right intire, then command the two outmost files of Musquetteers of each Flank to march until they are clear of the Front and stand; the four inmost files march until they are clear of the Battels also and stand.

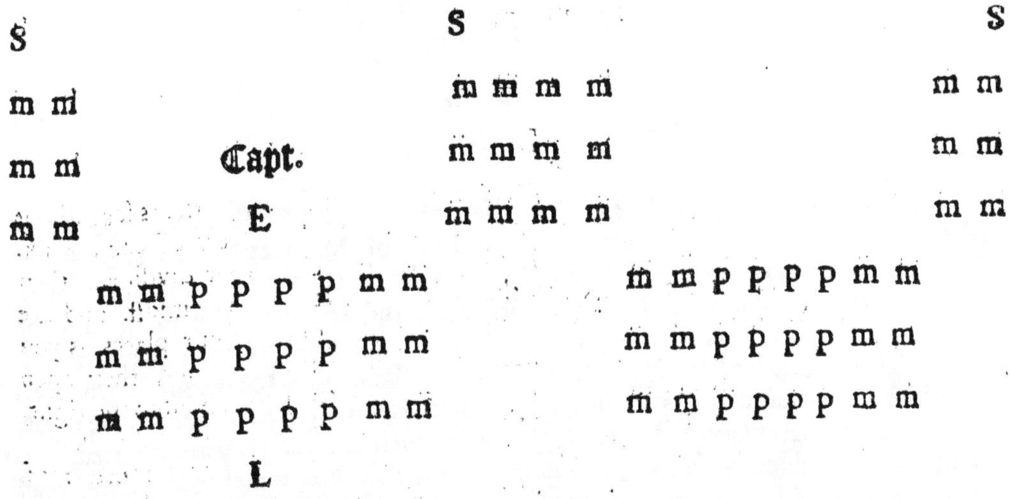

S S S

m m m m m m m m

m m **Capt.** m m m m m m

m m E m m m m m m

m m p p p p m m m m p p p p m m

m m p p p p m m m m p p p p m m

m m p p p p m m m m p p p p m m

L

To reduce them. Musquetteers face about to the right, and march forth into to your places. Then half ranks of the right double the depth of your left flank intire.

9. **Command.** Pikes march clear of your body; Pikes wheel your flanks into the Reer; Musquetteers close to the right and left inward: Half files of Musquetteers double your Front to the right: The four innermost files of Musquetteers face about to the right & march clear of the Reer: even your Ranks and streighten your files both of Pikes and Musquetts: Then the four innermost files both of Pikes and Musquetteers march ten paces direct. Then Pikes and Musquetteers of each Flank face to the right and left, and march ten paces; facing them to their leader.

```
              C

          P  P  P  P
          P  P  P  P
          m  m  m  m
          m  m  m  m
          m  m  m  m

P  P  P  P     E      P  P  P  P
P  P  P  P            P  P  P  P
m  m  m  m            m  m  m  m
m  m  m  m            m  m  m  m
m  m  m  m            m  m  m  m

          m  m  m  m
          m  m  m  m
          m  m  m  m

              L
```

To reduce this, **Command.** The front division of Pikes and Musquetteers face about to the right and march even in breast with the Reer of Musquetteers of each flank. Then face the division to the right and left inwards, and close your divisions, then Command the Musquetteers to open to the right and left from the midst, and the Reer divisions of Musquetteers march into the intervails (or into your places as you were. Then Command the Pikes to wheel their flanks into the Front, then open the divisions of Musquetteers to the right and left, facing the Pikes about to the right, and march into their places: so facing of them to their Leader they are reduced.

I might have added more, as the *Plinthium* Battel. For which and more read Captain *Bingham* Chap. 42. pa. 55. as also *Barrif*, *Ward*. And *Elton* as I am informed has written at large, but I never saw his works.

GHAP.

Chap. XXII.

IT may be expected I should treat, also of large Battalia's, or great numbers of men, demonstrating of them likewise by their several Plat-forms: But having my Number proportioned, as you see by my several exercises, I have stretched them as far as is convenient, that by their figures they may be so well understood, that when larger numbers are before you, your Commands may be performed with more delight and security.

But before the Drum beates a march to depart the field, I shall briefly declare, That in grand Battalias (or field services) the Souldier fires by vollies, or (as termed by some) Salves of shott; that is, when they are to fire intirely by two or three Ranks, or more, as your number will permit, and occasion require; thereby powring showers of lead upon your Enemy: Now this way of firing, and those also of gaining ground I could wish the Souldier should be often experienced in: The Commander in taking pains with his Souldier cannot be the worse for it, and I am sure the Souldier much the better; being fitted thereby to meet his Enemy in any field service, when his Majesty shall have occasion to Command him. For that Commander that is experienced in this Art Military finds that those, who know but little more than the Theory part, are oftimes pusled (or at a stand.)

What can such who are but meer Bookleidgers do? when their Number of men is wanting; or nature in place sparing to their advantage or intentions; such when they are forced to action, they will fail of their expectation, and at last must be beholding to others that are better Artists, or else it may prove a fatal ruin to both.

Some of my friends might think that I should treat also somewhat concerning the dignities of Officers in marching & in placing of them in field services: but that belonging to Commanders of an higher degree, it would be presumption in me to lay down rules for them to follow; for any Minor Officer that for his satisfaction will be pleased to view the third Chapter of these Obsevations, he may understand the method and mode thereof; and I hold it in my judgment, that all dignitie in marching of a Regiment is from a file; and the drawing up of Companies for a Battalia, is from a Rank.

In the next place I come to shew the necessity of the exercise of Armes, *&c.*

Chap. XXIII.

Shewing the necessity of the Exercise of Armes with their Antiquity.

BEcause I have heard it sounding in my ears; what needeth all this trouble and expences, in the exercise of Armes? We are now in times of Peace what need we to make provision, *&c*? I shall lay down some examples shewing.

First, How Antient the use of Armes have been.

Secondly, A complaint for want of Arms. And

Thirdly, The end and use of them.

For the first, *Abraham* had three hundred and eighteen men in his House fitted for War, upon short warning. *Moses* shewed the people how to encamp by their Standards,

dards, under the Ensigns of their fathers Houses. *Joshua* and the *Judges*, under whom of *Reuben* and *Gad* and the half Tribe of *Manasseh* were four hundred and forty thousand, seven hundred and sixty men exercised in Wars. You may read of *Dovid*, of *Solomon*, of *Jehosaphat*, of *Asa*, of *Uzziah*, whose care in this particular is most plentifully declared.

Secondly, Of the complaint for want of Arms. We read in the History of the *Judges*, *Was there a shield or a Spear seen among forty thousand in Israel?* This question is a plain negative, there was not; here is that *Defectus Remedii*, the want of help: Great was their misery, but no remedy; not a Spear to offend, nor not so much as a Shield to defend; War was at their Gates, yet neither offensive nor defensive weapon to assist: Such an extremity as this was will cause all to be lost; either present possessions, or in future possibilities, so that hope and help in such extremities must be laid aside.

There was likewise a great distress in the time of *Saul*; when the spoilers were come out from the Philistins, there was neither Sword nor Spear found in any of the hands of the people that were with *Saul* and *Jonathan* (but with *Saul* and *Jonathan* only) yet although here was a great want they had victory. It is well known that God can give victory by small means, (and as the Apostle said to Christ, Master, here are two Swords; he answered it is enough. He can give your Enemies into your hands with two Swords, with one Sword, with no Sword.) All this was to convince the Children of *Israel*, that God fought for them, to move them to bless the Lord,

Fifth monarchy men. Although some have been such audacious Rebels to think their zeal should even beck God Almighty, or to command power and aid from him to fight for them; therefore boldly attempted of late, saying that ten should chase an hundred and an hundred a thousand: But through the unjustness of their undertakings (and fewness in Number) they must sink; to convince them and all others upon any pretence of Religion that will be such Rebellious dissenters, God Almighty will not only fight against them, but will deliver them into the hands of Justice, to magnifie his own power in bringing such to condign punishment.

Thirdly, For the end and use of Armes; It is for the recovery of our just rights which wrongfully have been detained; or for the preservation of them, against any opposer either forraign or domestick: For these ends Armes may be used, and War proclaimed; yet not by any other way or pretence, but by and with his Majesties consideration thereof whether just or unjust; by which we are to be either incouraged or discouraged.

A just cause may be farther considered in the Peace of the People, the safety of the Countrey, and the Glory of the Kingdom: As to the first, there was never any War intended but to make way for Peace, (it is a base end to desire Peace, by which to leavy a force against an unjust War) but so to desire a just War that thereby may be settled a well grounded peace.

A second thing that may be considered is the health and safety of the Countrey: some must be endangered that all may not be destroyed: I could wish that our Chiefetains and Gentlemen with those dull, leaded spirits of our rotten Country —— and miserable worldlings would consider for whose sakes the worthy Souldier spares neither time nor purse in this Noble Exercise; but even for them and theirs, theirs and their Children; yet they must be judged most contemptible; rather than to countenance them, some will burden them in their rates and taxes, and keep their just dues and payes from them: yet consider who it is that must preserve your Cities and Countries, Temples and Pallaces, Trafficks and Marketts, Ships and Shops, from ruine, desolation and destruction; but the Souldier under God.

Thirdly, The Glory of a Kingdom lyeth much in a people well disciplin'd in the Art of War. That Prince that maketh it his designes to have his people instructed and trained up in Military exercises, will make his Enemies to fear him both at home and abroad: And that people that shall justly be called forth upon these principles, need not fear of being conquerours.

A just

A just cause may be spoiled through the ill management thereof, or through perfidious dealings.

A Rebellious Conquerour may make lawes even to death it self, to maintain his Victory; as our late Usurpation hath experienced: But at last the whole world beheld with an eye of admiration, to see how miraculously God restored his Majesty to his Crown and Dignities; the Church and People to their just rights and liberties.

I do affirme and truly say of Soveraign Power, Kingdomes, Lawes and Armies, as was said of *Hippocrates*'s Twins, they laugh and weep together, they live and die together; for as without Lawes the Soveraign power and the Common-wealth cannot subsist by reason of disorders within; so without Armes, and the exercise of them they cannot be safe by reason of dangers without.

I shall further and briefly prove that the safety both of King and people is much advanced by the exercise of Armes: although *Solomon* saith *In the multitude of people is the honour of a King, and for want of people cometh destruction.* Notwithstanding I may affirm that safety is not in a multitude of men without weapons, and skill to manage them. It is asserted *That Counsel and strength are for War*; Then, how shall Counsell and strength be established, without education and instruction to service? and how shall a man be instructed without Military Exercises? There are some disadvantages that happen in Wars, partly by reason of the suddainness of the War, and partly in respect of the inequality and odds betwixt party and party; Now Souldiers without dexterity and skill, can never be able to extricate themselves out of such difficulties as may befall them: All which proves that the exercise of Armes is to be allowed and Commanded.

Isa. 36.

And as I told you at first I have heard some say, that we live in Gospel times, which are to be times of Peace, and not of war, therefore there needeth not those Exercises of Armes as you reason for &c. This is argued by some out of covetousness to save their expences; but are ready to declare when there is occasion, then they will be in a readiness to do their best: There are others of a Fanatick humour, unwilling to set forward any thing that may be commanded them, & argue from that in *Isaiah, They shall beat their swords into plough shares and their Spears into pruning hooks. Nation shall not lift up a Sword against Nation, neither shall they learn War any more.*

He speaketh not against the use of weapons or lawfull War. Whereas before Christ they were enemies, but now there shall be love &c.

Now in answer hereunto we must oppose it by another saying in *Joel*, where the people were called upon *to beat their plough shares into swords, and their pruning hooks into Spears.*

For the reconciling hereof the learned say that *Isaiah* was to distinguish between the purpose and intent of Christs coming into the world, and the other sheweth the success and event which was accidental in respect of mans malice: Again to the first of these they argue what Christ said to Saint *Peter*, *Put up thy Sword, for he that strikes with the Sword, shall perish by the Sword.* But I pray you observe what he saith to his Disciples, *That he that hath no Sword, let him sell his coat and buy a Sword.*

Although the end of Christs coming was to reconcile things in Heaven and things on earth; I have been further taught by the Learned that this is attained unto between God and us in our Justification; and will be accomplished between man and man in the day of Redemption: Yet as long as there is a Sathanical Spirit in the children of disobedience, and so long as there is a remnant of sin in the heart of any, there will be Divisions, *Familists*, *Quakers*, *Anabaptists*, *Independents*, and *Presbyterians*; All being refractory to the present commands &c. Which sheweth a necessity to have a care and prepare for the exercise of Armes; That none of these by their Usurpation may for ever hereafter snatch the Trumpets out of *Moses*'s hands; nor the Trumpet only, but the Sword also, nor the Sword alone but the Crown and Scepter also: Now by this mutual exercise of Armes I doubt not but in a litttle time God Almighty will unite the affections of most against such as shall exalt themseves above all that is called God.

Let me excite all to be diligent, in the use of the meanes, to make themselves able and fit Souldiers and Commanders, by often Exercising, and willing to get compleat Armes, to be exercised in Martial dispipline; considering how ill it was with *Israel* when there was not a shield to be found amongst 40000 men; And consider again how worthy of praise it was to Martial Discipline in *Israel*, when they had 170000 every one able to lead an Army, *&c.*

I must tell you we have not our peace by Patent, we know not how long it may continue, Let war therefore be provided for, as to train up some to military practises: If War should come, it is labour well spent; If not, it is a labour well lost. Long preparations make a short and quick victory.

Some are apt to say we have Souldiers enough, we will all fight when occasion shall serve; Let me tell such that they that never tried it, think it a pleasure to fight, and they will fight strangely, if they have no weapons, and use their weapons more strangely if they have no skill: It is a saying of *Vegetius*, *Non de pugna, sed de fuga cogitant, qui nudi in acie exponuntur ad Vulnera.* Their minds are not so much on fighting as fleeing, that are exposed to War without weapons; and a Souldier may be almost as well without them as not to know how to use them.

Re Milita. lib. 1. c. 20.

Now that the Souldier may not be failing herein, and that his Majestie may never want able Souldiers in the Country as well as in the City; I most humbly beg, and crave pardon in presuming to present it, That the Muster master i every Countrey should be a careful unbyassed person, an able Souldier, and one whom the Commanders and Gentlemen love and affect, who should be alwayes by authority to attend at such times and places, as shall be thought convenient to exercise and teach the Art of Military discipline to all that shall willingly imbrace it; And if his pay be too little for him, to make it his business and to attend upon it: It may be then augmented without any trouble; and the Souldier will be found much more capable for service when commanded.

There must be exercise or else mens spirits will grow restie: what turnes to putrefaction sooner than standing water? what is Vertue without Action? Idleness doth neither get, nor save; but lose: If exercise be good then those are best that tend to the most good: The exercises of War step in to challenge their deserved praise, which I leave to the most Judicious to give them their due in time and place.

The antient *Gaules* were said to be the most Warlike and Valiant men of all Nations: But how became they such? It was by the continual exercise and use of Armes; for it was their Custome, to come Armed to their Councils.

Casars Com. l. 5. & 7.

Their applause of any Oration was signified by clattering of their Armes, and their Oathes taken were upon their Armes.

The *Germaines* were wont to go Armed about their negotiations, and to their Banquets.

The most Warlike Nations in the world have accounted it a piece of policy, to be frequent in the use of Armes: Why should not the laudableness of such martial exercises perswade men to love and imbrace the use of them?

We read some presidents for it; of *Jonathans* shooting for sport that he might be thereby fitted fo War. And without doubt the *Benjamites* attained that dexterity in casting stones out of a fling at an haires breadth by frequent exercise for recreation.

And may I not affirm, by the Exercise of Arms that Empires, Kingdoms and Common-wealths have come to their heigth and Soveraignty, and have so maintained their State in happiness and prosperity? and by neglecting of the same, they have declined and decayed, and at last have been made Preys to their Enemies: How were those Empires and Monarchies of the *Egyptians*, *Medians*, *Parthians*, *Persians* and *Romans*, established and greatly augmented by this *Military Art*; And how was the Dominion of the *Grecian* Empire preserved and wonderfully inlarged by the Art and Discipline of great *Alexander* with small Armies of well ordered and exercised Souldiers? How did he vanquish most great and huge Armies of his Enemies? Nay a great part of the World even contrary then to expectation?

Even

Even so on the other side, the forgetting and neglecting of this *Art Military*, hath not been only the decay but the ruine of many Empires and Kingdoms.

Now that people that is not incouraged, or rather compelled by good Laws to practise and exercise Arms, or any thing else belonging to this *Military Art*; they will in a short time for want of such Manlike, Martial Orders and Exercises, grow into Sloth, to Covetousness, to Drunkenness, and Vicious Effeminacies, and to all other Evils as Nature shall incline them unto; by the which they in a short time do become unfit to be imployed in any War offensive, and unable to defend themselves if they should be invaded.

Did not God for the sins of the *Jews* deprive them of understanding of this *Military Art*? Among other Priviledges he deprived them of, he took from them the valiant men of War, the Prudent and the Captains of fifty, *&c.* When he made them thus uncapable, then they were first of all conquered and utterly subdued and ruined by the *Romans*, under their Emperours *Vespasian* and *Titus* his Son: I might tell you of many Nations and Kingdoms that have been ruined for want of Order and Exercise: *Spain* by the *Moors*: King *Don Roderigo*, and many thousands of his Nobility and people were slain by the *Arabians* and *Moors*.

And about the Year 1353. we read that the Princes of *Greece*, aided by the *Despote* or Duke of *Bulgaria* did revolt against *John Paleologus* at that time Emperour of *Constantinople*; who for his safety against those Revolters entered into a League with *Amurat* the first, and third King of the House of *Ottoman*, and had his Assistance with ten thousand of his Horse-men; who by their good order and well disciplined Souldiers did prevail against his Revolters, and brought them to obedience: But what followed? *Amurat* being informed of the great riches those *Græcians* had, together with their weakness, by reason of their disorder in Military Affairs, transported an Army over the *Asian* Seas into *Greece*, and by that Invasion took many Cities and Towns, and did afterwards by battle slay the Duke of *Bulgaria* and *Servia*, with many others, *&c.* and there placed himself over a great part of their Dominion: So about fourscore years after, *Mahomet* the second Emperour of the Turks seeing *Constantine Paleologus* then Emperour of *Constantinople* without any settled *Militia*, and his people grown luxurious and not able to resist him by Battle, did in the Year 1453. besiege the Emperial City of *Constantinople*, who within two Months by assault won the said City, and put the Emperour, Empress, and their young Princes, with an infinite number of Men, Women and Children to the sword.

I might give a great many more Instances as to our own Country from the *Saxons* to the *Normans*; and what History speaks later of our selves, I must leave that to our Reformers to consider how useful and necessary the exercise of Arms is to the wellfare of a Nation and people.

The Emperour *Alexander Severus* that Excellent Prince being very skilful in Government, both in War and Peace, speaking to his Men of War said; The Military Discipline of our Ancestours doth maintain and preserve out State and Commonwealth; but if we do neglect the same, and make no account of the Orders and Exercises of it, We, our name and Reputation of *Romans*, and therewith all the *Roman* Empire, are lost and forgotten.

Though the frequent use of Arms in Exercise is most commendable, because of the special helps it hath in making us fit and serviceable Instruments of the Publick wellfare: Yet I advise it with these Cautions.

First, have a respect to your particular Calling. God Almighty feeds us, as well as defends us; so if any man under pretence of his Exercise shall waste his time and means, to the dammage or undoing of his Family; I say, such will bring a scandal, and an ill report upon this worthy design: He that would manage his Country Affairs with delight and profit, to his preservation and not to his ruine and destruction, must imitate those Builders under *Nehemiah*, who held their Swords in one hand, and their Trowel in the other; so mind your Military Exercises, as not to forget your necessary Affairs at home; without your dependances be wholly upon it, then to mind nothing more.

Yet Secondly, To have ſuch an intent upon their private and particular concernments, making them unfit for Imployments, as to impede them in the ſeeking the Publick Good, or make themſelves the main end of their Enterpriſe in what they undertake, doth degenerate ſo much from being true Souldiers, as to diſhonour themſelves in all their Services, and will be the ſole jet to hinder preferment when it ſhall fall.

And laſtly, *Sparta*'s Souldiers (I have read) were *Sparta*'s Walls, by reaſon of their Concord and Unity amongſt themſelves; therefore let every Souldier reſpectively preſerve Unity in the Bond of Peace, and in ſo doing we ſhall be the better able to pray with our Church, *To give peace in our time*, *O Lord*, *for there is none that fighteth for us*, *but only thou*, *O God.*

Chap. XXIV.

Concluſion.

I Humbly crave pardon for what is here undertaken, knowing my own inabilities for ſo great a Work; If I had ſeen any part of *Elton*'s Pieces, before I had concluded theſe my *minor* Lines; they ſhould have been turned into oblivious duſt: But being commanded by ſome of our Chieftains, and deſired by others of my Friends to proceed thus far (and no farther) accordingly I have both granted and obeyed: It is not in the leaſt to condemn any Perſon that hath gone before me, or to boaſt in the leaſt for what is done, or what I know: I have obſerved that ſome are moſt excellent for their Pen; ſome in their *Lingue*, and others for execution; now what I do want in either of the two firſt, the laſt with my blood ſhall witneſs to all the true zeal I bear to my Sacred King, and Countries good, when Commands and Occaſions preſent themſelves: In the mean time, to him who is the great King of Kings, Lord of Lords, preſerve to his Honour, good of his People, and confuſion of his Enemies.

CHAP. I.

The Original and beginning of Ensigns and Colours.

Of this Subject I never thought to have spoken any thing, but this last Summer perceiving most Ensigns (having that Honour assigned them by Commission) knew but little what belonged to their Office; and think it a thing of little or no difficulty, but only a Rag or Mark, which any man may carry, so it be born up, or swung about mens ears, and sometimes in the teeth of such which are next unto them. 1670.

And for the Election of these Officers by some new Commissionated Captains; It is not by the greatness of his skill, but the largeness of his body; not how able he is in his mind, but how strong he is in his Arms; not what is his Spirit, Activity, Dexterity, but what is his wealth, and how near he is allyed to the Captain in blood, friendship, or service; or some other beholdingness to him, for this piece of Honour: As if this Place deserved nothing else, but a meer Man, or some Friend: For when shall you see an Ensign almost in any Imployment, more than in ordinary Marches, or standing still, and observing other mens Actions? When shall you see either Captain or Lieutenant, teach the Ensign his Postures, or the Dignity of his Place, his demeanour before Kings, Princes and Potentates; and other his subjection to his Superiours; his State and Gard to his Equals, and his Humanity and Courtesie to his Inferiours.

I am sure that some are so far from making inquiry after these discoveries that you shall see some Ensigns let fly their Colours, when they should sink them; and some to stoop them to Pesants or Comrades, when Superiours have gone unsaluted: There are a great many other absurdities, but I shall hereby endeavour a Reformation; although it may not be to the satisfaction of all, yet I will lay open and plain what I know of these Concerns, as not to puzzle him who is desirous to learn, nor lull asleep with amazement the weakest capacity.

Therefore in the first place I shall endeavour to declare the Original and first beginnings of Ensigns (or Colours) in the Wars, and how they have grown up by succession, and continue as now they are.

It's true, that the Antient Historians and Heathen Writers, hold divers Opinions, touching the first beginning of Ensigns: Some deriving of them (especially the old Poets) from *Hercules*; in imitation of his Lyons skin: Others take the beginning from *Perithous*, the Companion of *Hercules* in Imitation of his inchanted shield; whereon was painted the head of the Monster *Gorgon*; on which whosoever gazed was instantly transformed into a stone: But these fictions are more moral than true. *Persius.*

There be others which suppose, that the first Ensign was born or carried before *Theseus*, when he went to combate with *Hippolyta*, Queen of the *Amazons*, whom he bravely conquered and afterward married.

Now as these, so many other Writers suppose divers other beginners of this Mystery: Some lay it upon *Mercury*, because of his *Caduceus*: Some upon *Vulcan*, when he forged *Mars* a Shield, and an Armour; and some upon *Jupiter*, whose Ensign was Thunder and Lightning.

But those which go much nearer the Truth ascribe the beginning of this Dignity unto *Tubalcain* the Son of *Lamech*, who painted in an Ensign the whole History of his Fathers Actions and Conquests, when he conquered (or rather tyrannized over) his weaker Neighbours: And that after him *Japhet* the Son of *Noah*, did the like, and caused his Actions to be painted out, and born before him in an Ensign.

But upon the credit of these old Poets, Historians and Rabbins, we may not rely, but must fly to the truth it self; which is ever a faithful and a constant Warrant.

We find in holy Writ that the greatest Chieftain that ever led Army upon the Earth was *Moses*, the great servant of the great God; He was truly *Dux* a Duke, a Leader, such a Duke and such a Leader, as after him (Christ excepted) was never the like seen in the World; and the Army which he lead, was the greatest, strongest, and most fortunate in Number, Power, and in all manner of hazardous Actions, that ever the World saw, or the Sun shined upon.

Now we find this Duke, this Prince over *Israel*, by the holy appointment of God himself was the first that began true *Martial Discipline*; for as himself was General over that huge Body; so for the well disposing and governing of every particular member, he constituted and appointed several Colonels over the several Tribes, and under every Colonel several Captains, as Commanders in Chief over particular Companies, who as Inferiours did execute the Commands of their Superiours, and had also executed under them, by others, whatsoever they lawfully commanded, that was for the good and benefit of the Army. As thus he divided the twelve Tribes into twelve war-like Bodies; so also he ordained them several Ensigns or Banners, charged with twelve several Marks or Divisions, under which they marched; which by solemn oath and protestation they were bound to guard and follow in all places and all dangers.

By these Ensigns and tokens of Honour, the Tribes were first of all distinguished and known one from another; and by the carriage of them in the field, and their waving and prospects in their several places, was the dignity of place and precedency of greatness first known; the Elder being distinguished by his Ensign or Mark from the younger, the greater from the less, and the eminent and more superiour from those of lower rank and inferiour.

Although we have a large *Basis* to superstruct our imitations upon, yet there was not the general use of Ensigns then, as now there is; for these Ensigns were due only to the great Colonel, or chief head of the Tribes, not to every particular Company, but to one Tribe was allowed but one Ensign, and after one manner and form; so as *Simeon* may not carry that of *Levi*, nor *Levi* that of *Judah*; but were tied to their own Colours: Also if that one Tribe were divided into many Bodies, yet did they not carry several Ensigns, but every Body the Ensign of his own Tribe; so that Companies were not distinguished by their Captains or Chiefs, but by their Tribes; nor could they say there goes such a particular Commander, but there is such a Tribe; not there marches *Aaron*, but there marches the Tribe of *Levi*; and thus of the rest.

Hence, and from this ground was taken up the use of the Ensigns, or Banners of Kingdoms, by which several Armies display to the World their several Nations; as with us in *England*, we have the Ensign of St. *George*, (as we term it) which is a bloody Cross in a white field, which shews to the world not what private Company I follow, but what King I serve, and what Country I acknowledge; for howsoever private Captains are allowed their Ensigns for private respects or distinctions; yet they are not allowed (or to be born on foot) without this general Ensign of this Kingdom: for thus it holdeth in all Christian Kingdoms, and amongst the Turks also, as appeareth by their Cressant or Half Moon in all their Armies, as the Ensign of their Universal Monarchy.

Thus you see *Moses* first (and that by the Commandment of God himself) began Ensigns, which by succession of time, descended and came down with a more general use, unto the days of *Maccabees*; for the Tribes then being dispersed far and wide, and made Kings of many spatious and fruitful Countries; they took liberty to alter their Ensigns, according to their own fancies: The glory thereof when it came to the eares of the *Græcians* and *Macedonians* (for *Alexander* is supposed to reign in the time of the *Maccabees*) they took to themselves a lawful imitation thereof, and so commanded their Captains, &c. to carry in their Ensigns, Devices in honour of their Renown and Conquests.

Then from the imitations of the *Græcians*, the *Romans* took to themselves the carriage

carriage of Ensigns; and because they found it the chiefest beauty and ornament of Armies, they made it therefore the noblest and richest spoil which could possibly be taken away from the Enemy; and so made it an hereditary right for any man that should take (in honourable fashion) such spoyls, ever after to bear them, as his own, to him and his Posterity for ever.

The *Romans* first brought this custom into the Monarchy of Great *Britain*, when *Cæsar* first invaded and got footing into the same: Howsoever there is an opinion taken that *Brute*, when he first conquered this Island, brought in the *Trojan* Ensigns, and other Ornaments of their Wars; yet it is certain that through Civil Dissentions, and other Forreign Combustions, all these Honourable Marks were lost and forgotten, and only the *Romans* renewed and brought them back unto memory, partly by their glory and example, and partly by their loss when they were repulsed back; who left behind them many of these spoyls to adorn the *Britains*: From these times hath the use of Ensigns remained amongst us; and as the Ages have succeeded, and proved wiser and wiser, and one time more than another, so hath the alteration of these Emblems (or Ensigns) changed and brought themselves into the form wherein they are at this instant carried; as the *Romans* varyed from the old *Britains*, so the *Saxons* from the *Romans*, and the *Danes* from the *Saxons*: But the *French* then being the most refined Nation of all other, altering from them all; and now the *English* having altered all into this present mode of Uniformity, they may display them to the World for their Gallantry.

Chap. II.

The Definition of Ensigns.

After the Original, Antiquity, and first beginning hath been endeavoured to be made to appear; I shall now descend to the definition and distinction of them; and by what proper names they were called in the best and most renowned Wars of Christendom, and for what reason they have held and retained them.

To begin with the first and most antient name belonging to Ensigns, I think it not amiss to borrow it from the *Romans*; for although the *Hebrews*, *Chaldeans* and *Græcians*, were the first Inventers, yet the Names and Attributes they gave them, were much incertain and unconstant, and as the experience of Wars grew great, and as the Invention dilated and spread further, so did the signification alter; for what was proper and substantial in this Age, in the next was utterly lost and forgotten, so as I shall not rest upon these Titles or significations.

The first then that retained a constant and firm settled name for those Trophies of Honour, is taken to be the *Romans*, who indeed being the greatest Schoolmasters in the Art of War, are the most worthy to be held for Imitation or Authority.

The name which the *Romans* first gave to the Ensign, or him that carried the Ensign (for to the man was ever attributed the Contents of the thing he carried) was *Insigne*, or Sign bearing, (and so Ensign-bearer) because they carried in those Ensigns, Marks, Empressaes or Emblems, best agreeing with their natures and condition, according to their own Inventions; or else the Pourtraictures of their former Battles and Conquests; either of which was so honourable, that indeed they were made Hereditary; descending down to their Children, from Generation to Generation: And no more were called Signs, &c. but Coat-Armour, or the Honour of the Families; nor were they of slight or ordinary esteem, as at first; neither had men liberty any longer to make election of them at their own Wills, but this power was incabinated within the breast of Emperours, Kings and Generals, who indeed (under God) are the unbounded Oceans of Honour, they only have the liberty of bestowing and confirming Honour at their own pleasures.

Hence it came that Ensigns thus carrying of Coat-Armours, were of such reverend esteem, that men took it for the honourablest place that might be, to fall near or about the Ensign; and for the defence of it, no hazzard could be too great, nor any torment insupportable: So that many times the Zeal of those that did defend these Ensigns, *&c.* and the inflamed desire or greedines of those which sought to conquer and atchieve them, was so immeasurable and unbounded, that an infinite of blood hath been shed, and many powerful Armies overthrown, only for the purchase of one of these honourable Trophies.

This when the wisdom of the *Romans* perceived, and that those *Insignias* were not Bugbears to affright, but rather fires, which did inflame their Enemies courage beyond their proper natures; they forthwith forbad the carrying of any Coat-Armour or Device in their Ensigns; but only such slight inventions, as might not make the Enemy much the richer by the enjoyment thereof, nor themselves much the poorer by the loss.

And hence it followed that the word *Insignia* was put out of use, and they then called the Ensign *Antesignia*, and made other Devices contrary to all Coat-Armour; intimating to the Enemy that whatsoever they got by those purchases, was dishonourable rather than any way worthy of Triumph: And from this word *Antesignia*, or *Antesigne*, (for it hath been so written in antient Records) it hath been judged that this word *Antient* in many places used amongst us, and given to our Ensigns, hath been corruptly retained by us; for it hath no coherence in signification, nor can any way be alluded unto this Officer, more than to his Antiquity and long standing in the Wars.

But this did not quench any flame in the Enemy, for the *Romans* found them every way as eager in pursuit of these weak and fained Devices, as the greatest hereditary Coat-Armour they could carry; for when in any skirmish Fortune made them Masters thereof, they took as great Pride, as if they had subdued whole Armies, and bare them with as much Pomp and Triumph, as if they had got all *Rome* in subjection: which the wisdom of the *Romans*, and other Nations looking into, it presently became a custom among all their Armies, that thence forth, no Foot Company or Chieftain of the Infantry should carry in his Ensign any Coat-Armour or other Device what ever, more than the mixture, or true composition of two colours, together with the general Ensign of the Kingdom in the most eminent corner thereof. And after this time the *Romans* called their Ensign-bearers no more *Antesignia*, or *Antesigne*; but of late only Signifier, from *Significo*, to signifie a thing, as being men of special note and regard; and that the thing signifying was only a Mark of much Honour, *&c.*

Read Markham's *Souldiers Accidence.*

The *Spaniards* and *Italians* that took all their imitation from the *Romans*, who were their great Lords and masters, do at this day call this Officer *Alferes*, and make account of him next unto their Captains, not suffering any second to step in between them.

The *Dutch* call this Officer *Vandragon*, or *Vandragar*, which holdeth with the same significations.

And we of *England* properly call him Ensign, and in some Countries Antient: The first from the thing he carrieth, and the latter from the Honour and Antiquity of the Institution: And both may well be agreeing with the first Titles, conceiving better cannot be invented.

CHAP.

CHAP. III.

The Original of Horse and Horse Colours.

HAving treated of the definition and signification of the several names which belong to the Ensignes of Foot, I will now take leave to speak a little to the Colours or marks of Honour that are born on Horseback; which I find by experienced Souldiers to be full as ancient or rather more than those which belong to the Foot Companies.

But omitting all prophane Opinions and vain circumstances, I find when the children of *Israel* passed through the Red Sea, how they were pursued by *Pharaoh*, and all his Host, which did consist most of Chariots (which in those dayes were accounted Horsemen) and very properly too) because being drawn by the violent force of Horse, and laden with the strongest and best experienced Souldiers, they had a double power to enter into Battalias to disrank and break their array, and to make their Enemies to run into a rout and confusion; and though they had not the use of our Discipline, nor the true managing of the Horse as we have, yet all their purposes and intents in the use of their Chariots, were to the same ends, to which at this day our Horse are applyed.

To these Chariots belonged Colours, or Ensignes of Martial Honour; which were called Standards or Standarts, or the Kings Emperial Trophie: Indeed these were nothing so general, as those on Foot, but more precious and reserved, as an Attribute only belonging to the King and not to any other.

These Standards were charged with the Kings Emperial Coat-Armour, and usually born by a Prince or some man of high place and dignity, the imitation whereof we still pursue and follow at this day, giving it a superiority above all other Ensignes.

After the use of Chariots was found out the use of Elephants a, warlike beast and of all other the strongest; for these cerried certain little artificial Houses (in the form of Castles) on their backs in which were some few experienced Souldiers placed with warlike Ensignes, and weapons by which they overthrew the Foot Companies and made passage through them in despight of all opposition; as you shall read in the History of *Porus* King of *India*.

Not long after the Exercise of Elephants, was found out the use of the single Horse, in those Countries where Horses were most frequent, as in *Arabia*, *Parthia*, *Persia*, and *Scythia*, for the *Asian* parts; in *Barbary*, *Egypt* and *Carthage*, for the parts of *Africa*; and with us in *Europe*, in *Russia*, *Muscovia*, *Poland*, *Hungary*, *Italie*, but principally and above all the rest in *France*, who were accounted in antient time the flower of warlike Horsemen, both in number and discipline; therefore from them hath been taken our Authority and examples: But now I conceive we may not go so far for either, referring for satisfaction to the present mode of Discipline in *England*, for his Majesties Horse now in Command it is thought none can exceed them.

I have read of a *Guydon* used with the light Horse in former times: Antiquity tells us of Gentlemen at Armes, Launciers and light Horsemen.

In the old Wars the Gentlemen at Armes belonged to the Kings own person, or in his absence to his General only; And the Empresa of honour that they followed was the Kings Standard Royall, being Damask and charged with his Coat-Armour.

The Launciers they had their Cornet to follow, which had Devices in them according to their commanders pleasures.

And then the Light-horsmen had their *Guydon* which was somewhat long and

 sharp

ſharp at the end but with a ſlit which made it double pointed much like to our late Dragooners; but for theſe Guydons I need not ſtand upon, only to ſhew all along there were Horſe Colours, as Enſignes of honour uſed. And now the Cornets being moſt in uſe with us in *England*, for the Horſe ſervice I need not decypher the length or breadth of them.

CHAP. IV.

Of the Dignitie of Enſigns.

1. THe Dignitie and eſtimation of Enſignes in all ages hath been held moſt Venerable, and worthy; they have been eſteemed the glory of the Captain, and his company; and indeed they are no leſs, for where they periſh with diſgrace there the Captains honour faileth, and the Souldier's in hazzard of Ruine; for if the loſs proceed either from their Cowardice (or miſgovernment) it hath been death by the law of Armes to all that ſurvive; and the beſt mercy that can be expected is that every Souldier ſhall draw a lot for his life (file by file) ſo that one out of every file periſheth for it.

2. The next Dignitie of the Enſign is, that every Souldier as ſoon as he is inrolled and hath received either pay or impreſs, they antiently took a ſolemne Oath to be faithful to their Colours, to attend them carefully, and to defend them valiantly; And that upon all ſummons, of the Trumpet or Drum, or Command of their Officers, to repair to them, whereſoever they ſhall be lodged, ſtand, or be; and not to depart or ſtragle from them until they have received orders.

3. The Enſign hath another dignity, that whenſoever he ſhall enter into City, Town, Garriſon, Campe, or other Randeſvouze of aboad, he is to be firſt lodged, before any other Officer or Souldier; And not in any mean place, but the beſt and moſt ſpacious for the drawng up of the Souldiers upon any Alarme; and his Quarter ought to be the moſt ſecure from danger.

4. The Enſign hath Dignity of place according to the Antiquity of his Captain: But in one particular caſe, it hath been judged to be greater than his Captain, and lendeth place to him; as thus, no Captain can receive his antiquity from his inrollment, but from the firſt hour in which his Colours flew; for if two be inrolled upon one day, and the latter marcheth before the face of his Enemy with his Colours flying, in this caſe the firſt hath loſt his priority, and the latter for ever after ſhall preceed him.

I have read of another reſolve; Three Captains (or more as occaſion happeneth) were all inrolled upon a day, and all their Colours flying; preſently upon a Truce, Compoſition or other occaſion there is ſome ſmall ceſſation of Armes, and theſe new inrolled Captains are Caſheer'd (or diſmiſt) for the preſent ſervice: Now the two firſt that had priority of place not only by inrollment but by flying of their Enſignes, becauſe they would not be out of action (to a Souldier the taſt of gain is pleaſant) took upon them the Commands as Lieutenants of two Colonels Companies &c. which are Captains places in courteſie, retaining thoſe titles, and in ſome Courts of War have had their Voyces; Now the third all this time taketh upon him no place, but remaineth in *Statu quo prius*; And in revolution of time all theſe three Captains aforeſaid are again Commiſſionated for three new Companies of their own, the Queſtion was whoſe Enſigne ſhould fly firſt, and which of theſe three ſhall have the priority of place? It was thus anſwered and adjudged by the old Earle of *Eſſex* and Sir *Francis Vere*, &c. that the two firſt who had taken upon them Lieutenancies had utterly loſt their Superiorities, and the third whoſe Honour ſlept, but diminiſhed

nished not, had precedencie of place, and his Ensign flew before the other ever after.

5. The Ensigne hath this Dignity to have a Guard ever about it, which no other Officer hath; neither is it to be disimbogued, or unlodged, without a special Guard, attending upon it both of Musquetteers and Pikes; (And so for a Cornet with his own Squadron of Horse) Also in the field if it be in particular Discipline or otherwise upon an Alt, or stand, at such time as the Army or Company are to refresh themselves with victuals or other rest, in this case the Ensigne shall by no means lay his Colours upon the ground, or put them in unworthy or base hands, but he shall first furle and fold them up and set the butt end on the ground supported with the Serjeants Holbearts, and the Ensign himself shall not go from the view thereof, unless he shall leave a sufficient guard for them.

6. An other dignity of an Ensign is, If a Noblemen or an Esquire will take upon him the Command of a private Company and have no other superiour place in an Army, and a mean Gentleman hath the like equal Command but a great deal more antient, although there ought to be a respect if they should happen in company unto the worth and quality of the person; yet the meaner Gentlemans Colours shall fly before the other.

As this hath been the antient practise in the Wars, how then do those Captains debase themselves, and their Ensigns, to suffer young Captains to step in, (either by greatness in quality or favour) to fly their Colours before them, *&c.*

7. Every Ensign hath his Dignity, although he is wholly to be at the Captains Command, yet in justice no Captain, nor other Officer can command the Ensign-bearer from his Colours, for they are as man and wife, and ought not to indure a separation; nor can he be commanded with his Ensign to any base (dishonourable) place or Action: And hence it is that to this day this place, and mark of Honour is held in such a venerable & worthy estimation amongst the *Spaniards* and *Italians* that they will not allow of any second between him and the Captain, as the name of a Lieutenant to be amongst them, thinking it to be a superfluous charge and command, because it is in their judgments a lessening and a bateing of the Ensignes Honour.

But in this although we esteem an Ensign very honourable, we in *England* differ from them, owning the place of a Lieutenant to be honourable and necessary, who ought to be a man of most approved experience; for he takes from the Captain those heavy burdens, which otherwise would make the Captains trouble insupportable, nor can the Ensign discharge them unless he neglects his care and duty to his Colours.

8. As for the dignity of the Ensign in *England* (not medling with the Standard Royal) to a Regimental dignity; The Colonels Colours in the first place is of a pure and clean colour, without any mixture The Lieutenant Colonels only with Saint *Georges* Armes in the upper corner next the staff; The Majors the same, but in the lower and outmost corner with a little stream Blazant, And every Captain with Saint *Georges* Armes alone, but with so many spots or several Devices as pertain to the dignity of their respective places.

But with us in *England*, placing and displacing is left to the Generalissimo, *&c.* and so to his substitutes, or deputies: It is to me a ridle that any person who cannot be stained with the least blemish should lose his advancing honour; But kissing goes by favour.

CHAP. V.

Of Disgraces to the Ensign.

THere are as many disgraces that belong to the Ensign as dignities; I shall for brevity sake mention but some few: all which must proceed from mistakes in one of these three, *Unskilful composure*, *Negligent government*, *or Rash actions*.

1. Touching *Unskilful composure*, either in false making, or bearing of Ensignes; and that you may be informed for the composures thereof, I cannot better it than to declare to you *Markhams* own words out of his Souldiers Accidence *pag.* 31. He saith, " There must be in Military honour nine several faces, or complexions, that is to say, " two which be called Mettals, as *Yellow* and *White*, figuring gold and Silver; and seven " which are called proper colours, as *Black*, *Blew*, *Red*, *Green*, *Purple*, *Tunnis* and *Ermine*.

" And here it is to be noted that no mettal is to be carried upon mettal: And for the " signification of those colours you shall understand that

" 1. Yellow betokeneth honour, or height of Spirit, which being never separated from " Vertue, of all things is most jealous of disgrace, and may not indure the least shad- " dow of imputation.

" 2. White signifieth Innocencie, or purity of conscience, Truth, and upright integrity " without blemish.

" 3. Black signifieth Wisdome, and sobriety, together with a severe correction of too " much Ambition, being mixed with *Yellow*, or with too much belief or lenity " being mixed with *White*.

" 4. Blew signifieth Faith, Constancy, or Truth in affection.

" 5. Red signifieth Justice, or Noble worthy Anger in defence of Religion, or " the oppressed.

" 6. Green signifieth good hope, or the accomplishment of holy and honourable " actions.

" 7. Purple signifieth fortitude with discretion, or a most true discharge of any " Trust reposed.

" 8. Tunnis or Tawny, signifieth merit, or desert, and a foe to Ingratitude.

" 9. Ermine, which is only a rich Furr, with curious spots, signifieth Religion, or " holiness, and that all aimes are not divine objects.

" Now from these colours and their mixtures are derived many bastard and dis- " honourable colours, as *Carnation*, *Orenge tawny*, *Popengie*, &c. which signifie *Craft*, *Pride* " and *wantonness*. So that all Commanders are left at their own pleasure for their mix- " tures, but with these considerations; As,

" 1. Not to put in his Ensign his full Coat-Armour.

" 2. Not to bear one black spot and no more in his Ensign, for it sheweth some " blemish in the owner, if the spot be round, square, or of equal proportion.

" 3. If the spot be unequal, it signifieth a Funeral or deadly revenge.

" 4. Not to carry words in his Colours without a Device; nor a Device without " words; but Device with words, and the words not to exceed four in number, for if " there be more it sheweth imperfection.

" 5. Not to carry more Colours than two; except it be for some special note, or " the Ensign of several Kingdoms, it is a Surcharge and esteemed folly.

2. Having shewed the true Colours, and the disgraces that may arise in the composure of them, as mentioned by Mr. *Markham*, I come to the next disgraces which proceed from *Negligence in Government*; as in carrying his Colours furl'd (or folded) up when they should be flying, or to let his Colours fly, when they should be folded up; or to display (or flourish them) when they should be carried without

any hand motion; or to carry them without motion when they should be displayed; or to vaile them when they should be advanced, or to advance them when they should be vailed.

To lodge or dislodge Colours without a Guard; or to suffer any man to handle them that hath not a lawful authority. Now the avoydance here of is sufficient to keep any man from gross errors.

3. The last disgrace as to the dignity of the Ensign is

1. From the rashness and unadvisedness of Actions; when he is in safety out of a phantastical bravado to thrust himself into danger; as to charge the Enemy when he should stand still: It is not only a disgrace; but the offence hath been adjudged worthy of death, although he may obtain victory by that forward action.

2. If in a March, Battalia, or setting of the Parade, or upon any other Military imployments, he shall misplace himself, it is a disgrace.

3. If in a battel, skirmish, or fight where the Ensign is put to retreit, his Colours shall be furled (or folded) up, or shouldred and not flying and held forth and extended with the left arm, and his Sword advanced in his right hand, his Colours are disgraced and such retreit is base and unworthy.

4. If the Ensign-Bearer shall happen either in battel or skirmish to be slain, and so the Colours fall to the ground, if those, or some of them next adjoyning threreunto do not recover and advance them up, it is not only a disgrace to the Ensign, but an utter dishonour to the whole Company; as I have declared, that if the Colours be lost, there must be a severe accompt given for them: And indeed a greater act of Cowardice cannot be found, than to suffer the Colours to be lost.

There is an antient president, but fresh in memory, that in great defeats when Armies have been overthrown, scattered and dispersed so that particular safety hath made men forget general observations; even then, the Ensign being wounded to death, and desperate of all relief, hath stript his Ensign from the staff and wrapt or folded it about his body, and so perished with it: This Ensign cannot be said to be lost, because the honour thereof was carried with his freed Soul into Heaven, to the possession of the eternal fort for ever: Now in this particular the Enemy cannot boast of any Triumph if then purchased, more than every Sexton may do when he robs the dead of his winding sheet.

Thus it hath been reported that *Sebastian* King of *Portugal* dyed at the battel of *Alcazar*: And I have read of many of our brave *English* that thus dyed at the renowned Battel at *Newport*, and have heard that many have so done in the Army of our late Soveraign of ever blessed memory.

5. And lastly, If any man shall recover the lost Ensign and bring it away flying, *&c.* no matter how low in condition the man is, if the Captain upon any after considerations bestow those Colours upon some other man; it is a disgrace both to the Captain and his Ensign, for he doth injury to Vertue and discourage Valour.

Obj. But some may object that upon composition with the party deserving, the Captain may dispose of his Colours where he pleaseth: I confess it true, but if this composition be forced it is injurious; And if it come by a voluntary consent of the party, it is base and most unworthy in him also.

Chap. VI.

Of the right use and ordering of the Ensign or Colours; with the Postures and Flourishes thereunto belonging.

As to my best Remembrance, I have given you a Catalogue of the Disgraces, so I shall here insert as to my knowledge the true use of the Ensign, whereby those injuries may be avoyded.

1. And first, you shall understand that in all extended Marches (and not drawn into a Body) as when they march either into a Friends or Enemies Country; or otherwise are conducted to some remote Randesvouz; here the Ensign (or Colours) ought to be half furl'd (or folded) up, and half flying, shall be shouldred and born a little cross the Ensign-bearers neck, with his hand extended a good distance from his body, and his left hand upon his side or hilt of his sword; this is termed a marching in State.

2. If he shall enter into any City or great Town; then he shall unfold or open his Colours, and let them fly at full length, and carry them in his right hand close under the hose, with a lofty hand and extended arm: This is a marching in Triumph; but if the wind blow stiff, or there is a weakness or wearisomness in the Ensign-bearer, then he may set the butt end against his waste and not otherwise; and is to have but one hand upon his staff in any march whatever.

3. In all Troopings the Ensign shall ever be furl'd and carried in the same Postures as the Pikes ought to be.

4. When the Company is drawn up into a Body, the Colours must be flying; and by the Way, in case the General or supreme of the Wars, or any Noble Stranger worthy of respect, do come, immediately upon his or their approach, the Ensign-bearer in all humility is to bow the head of his Colours, waving them with the bow of his body, and to raise both it and himself up again: And as the said person shall pass away, the Drum shall beat, and the Colours shall be displayed: This also the Ensign shall do in all Marchings, or other motions of Civil Exercises, where your Superiours pass by you, or you by them: Nay it is expedient and fit so to be done to any Gentleman, that is your familiar; for it is no more but as the vailing of your hat, or giving your friend a courtesie.

5. Now when the Body is drawn up into *Battalia* and the Enemy within view thereof, then every man being in his place is to express all the Gallantry he can, and especially the Ensign-bearer either in displaying his Colours *standing*, *marching*, *charging and retreiting* (or *retiring*;) and all these ought not to be done at one time, but when the bodies are joyning, and they must be done with great respect, for to use the Postures directly to the motion or standing of the Body; and not to do as I have seen some in ordinary *Militia Discipline*, that have but one or two motions of their Colours, upon and for all occasions; as if true Honour had such weak inventions; this without doubt is most base and unworthy.

To proceed to the Postures of the Ensign.

They are in general as followeth, so well as I can express them; for they are better in execution, and to be taught by example, than any pen can describe them.

1. To change them with a plain wave from hand to hand.

2. To change them with lofty turns from hand to hand; each hand performing their turns before you deliver them, as from the right to the left, and from the left to the right, as at first.

3. From

3. From the right hand with a wave and lofty turn jutting the Colours upon the left shoulder, and raising up with the same hand again, and with lofty turns to deliver it into the left hand, that so thereby you may execute the same upon the right shoulder, and after the turns, to deliver it into the right hand, as at first.

4. With (and from) the right hand with lofty turns throw your Colours under the left arm, recovering them speedily back with conceived Florishes, you deliver them into the left hand: you may execute the same with the left hand.

5. With turns or flourishes you bring the butt end of the staff to your left hand turning the palm of your left hand outwards (but not for the reception of it) and with the same hand only throw it off upon its turn with a flourish to deliver it into the left hand, and to perform the same with the left hand, and deliver the Colours into the right hand, as at first.

6. With lofty turns bring the Colours over the head down right (but not too low) before, and raising it again, with the fore-turn and back-turn over the head, changing of hands and delivering as before.

7. From the right hand deliver into your left hand with the palm of your hand, uppermost, the butt end of your staff turning it backwards upon the left shoulder; and turning it over the head with the same hand, you deliver it into the right hand after the same manner, which being performed with the right hand you proceed to the next.

8. From the right hand with lofty turns, fore-turns and back-turns, you deliver your staff into your left hind, and wheel it with the same hand on the same side, and after your recovery to deliver it into the right hand, performing of the same and proceed.

9. From the right hand upon the left shoulder, raising it and turning with its back-turn into the neck; with its returns and lofty florishes over the head, you deliver the Colours into the left, and with the left hand upon the right shoulder you execute the same, delivering them into your right hand as at first.

10. 'Tis by some termed the Figure of eighth; that is with the right hand the half wheel on the left side, and so back on the right side, and then delivering it into the left hand to perform the same.

11. To turn it round the head oftentimes upon the palm with your fingers of your right hand, so recovering it, with lofty florishes you deliver it into your left hand to perform the same, and so delivering of them into the right hand.

And if it be your pleasure to be compleat in the Exercise of them, you go back to the tenth, and so conclude with the first.

And in your conclusion I have seen some to furl them up as they display them, and so to open them again.

But to furl them up in the field it is most ridiculous.

Others there are that I have seen to round them oftentimes about their middles, but I cannot justifie it upon any *Military* account.

Others I have seen, that thinking to display their Colours bravely delivered them from hand to hand under leg; I must boldly inform such as use it, that 'tis a debasement to the Captains Colours, and an unworthy Act in the performers of it.

I told you of some particular Postures and proper for the Ensign-bearer to observe.

1. Standing, when the Body stands, you are to display the Colours, to and fro in a direct circle, and changing from hand to hand, and no more, without you are commanded to shew the excellency of your parts; but be sure to be well guarded when you shall be so commanded.

2. In marching, the Posture is to display the Colours with the right hand only, casting the Ensign still forwards, waving it close over and by the right shoulder, never crossing the Body, but still keeping it flying on the out-side of the right shoulder.

3. The charging Posture is to carry the staff extended streight forward before your body, waving it to and fro as high as your bosome, being ready to give the assistance or aid with the left hand for the preservation of your Colours, or to offend the Enemy if occasion require.

The retiring or retreiting posture is a mixture compounded of the three former; for in the first retreit, or drawing away of the Company, he shall use the posture of marching: but if the Enemy press near upon him, he shall stand upon his guard, and use the posture of charging; and in fine, having quit himself of danger, he shall use the standing posture a little, and then march or troop away, according to the directions of the commander.

And lastly, when the Ensign returns from the field, and is to be lodged; in former times the Lieutenant had the Vanguard; but that I shall not insist upon, because I have observed it to be left off by able Souldiers.

The Captain leading them out of the field, and coming near the place intended to lodge his Colours, Converts the ranks of Musquetteers of both divisions to the right and left outwards and joyns them; and being so fixed, the body of Pikes stand in the reer, and the Ensign in the head of them, the Captain before the Colours, with the Drums and Serjants guarding the Colours on each side, and the Lieutenant behind, the Ensign bearer, and all being advanced, shall troop up with the Colours furl'd to his lodging or quarters; and as he approacheth thereto, he shall with a bow to his Captain carry in his Colours; then the word shall be given to all the Musquetteers to make ready; that being done, they shall all present, and upon the beat of Drum, or other word of command, give one intire Volley; and then command every Officer to go to their quarters, and to be in readiness upon the next summons, either by Drum or Command.

It may fall out, that time will not permit this large circumstance; then the whole company being drawn up in a body shall troop up to the place, where the Ensign shall quarter, to see the colours safely lodg'd, which being effected, the Musquetteers shall with one intire Volley discharge their Musquets, and so depart to their respective quarters; commanding all upon the next summons to be in readiness, &c.

And I might here adde the funeral posture: if for a private souldier; the Ensign-bearer is to march in his place on the head of the Pikes, with the Pikes trailing revers'd, but the Colours furl'd and revers'd only: But if it be a commander that is to be interred, he is then to march just before the Hearse, with his Colours revers'd, &c.

If I have writ any thing amiss, or omitted any thing as may prejudice the honour of the Ensign, I beg your better advice, for it was in the years 1641. and 1642. that I minded any of these military actions; therefore for any error herein, let the length of time plead my excuse: However, I could wish that every Ensign would but observe these rules, he would then the better know his own worth, and what duty lieth incumbent upon him; and being careful in the performance of them, his own honour will be displayed in his Colours.

Sir Francis Vear's notes of Direction how far every mans office in a Regiment doth extend, and the duty of every Officer.

1. The Office of a Collonel.

1. Every Colonel is to command all his Officers, Captains and other; And all Souldiers, and men of War, of what degree soever they be, that do put themselves, or are by superior authority put and ranked under his Regiment, are all to respect his commands, and obey him as fully as they would the chiefest.

2. Also, He shall see all orders, commands and directions, which are delivered him, by the publick officers of the Army, for Guards, Watchings, or any thing else, for matter of justice, or for ordering of the Troops, executed. Furthermore, If he himself find any mutiny, or discontented humours tending to mutiny, or extream outrages, or

or disorders, or shall by any of his Captains, Officers or Souldiers be informed of any such, he shall forthwith advertise the Generals. And if he find any other fault, negligence or swerving from either directions given, or the policy of the Army set down; he shall straightway acquaint them, by whom such directions did come, or were brought unto him, or some other superiour Officer, if he can conveniently acquaint them with it, and shall produce the party so offending, with the Witnesses and Proofs, that order may be given forthwith, and justice done; and if he fail to give this information of any thing he knows or hears, he shall be deeply faulty: Or if any such thing pass without his knowledge, he shall be thought of worse Government than were fit for a man of his place and charge.

3. Also, In Lodging, every Colonel ought to lodge as near as he can in the midst of the quarter assigned for the Regiment, because he may best give directions for the whole.

4. In marching, he shall be at the end of the Regiment that is nearest the Enemy (that is to say) in the head of a Regiment going towards an Enemy, and in the rereguard going from the Enemy; and he shall not go from thence except it be for ordering of his Regiment or some extraordinary occasions.

5. Once every week the Colonel shall call together all his Captains, and shall enquire of all offences in his Regiment; and examine the nature and quality of such offences, to prepare the causes for a more speedy hearing in a Court Martial.

6. All Colonels shall repair to a Court Martial, as often as they shall be warn'd, and shall be assistant to the Lord Martial, in the causes that shall be there in question; or belonging to the justice of the Army.

2. The Office of a Lieutenant Collonel.

1. The Lieutenant-Colonel, when the Colonel is in presence, is to assist and obey him, in seeing all the directions that are delivered by any publick Officer, or such as shall be within the Authority of a Colonel to command, executed. And in the absence of the Colonel, he shall have the command that the Colonel hath himself.

2. He is to lodge ever on the right hand of his Colonels lodging, as near to the end of the quarter as conveniently he may.

3. In marching or imbattailing, whensoever the Colonel is in the head of the Regiment, he shall be in the reer; and when the Colonel shall be in the rereward, he shall be in the head.

Read Markham's *decads fo: 146. and* Ward, *fo: 200.*

3. Of the Office of a Serjant-Major.

2. He shall in the presence of his Colonel or Lieutenant Colonel be assistant to them, or either of them, in seeing all orders, and directions executed and performed, and in the absence of them both, to have the same authority as the Colonel himself: He shall lodge on the left hand of the Colonel, as near the end of the quarter as may be with conveniency.

2. In marching or imbattailing he shall keep as near the end of the Regiment as he can, sometimes on the side, that so he may overlook the order of the March.

3. He shall come to the Serjant-Major-General to receive the word from him, if there be no extraordinary cause to hinder him; And when he hath received the word, he shall deliver the word over to the Serjants of every company in the Regiment, who are to come to him for it.

4. As he doth receive directions for marching, imbattailing and placing of guards from the Major-General; so he is to deliver the same to the Captains of the Regiment, and call those to whom it doth pertain, and see them executed.

5. Every night he is to visit all the guards of that Regiment, and to keep turn of Watches, marches and going to the Wars; or sending Troops (or companies) upon service, to the end that both the labour and honour may be equally divided.

By the way you may obſerve: whereas the Serjants of every company are to be aſſiſtant to the Serjant-Major of that particular Regiment for the dividing of their ſeveral Corporalſhips or ſquadrons, files or half files, for the making up of any body, form or figure according to directions, *&c.*

So the Serjant-Majors of Regiments, are to aſſiſt the Serjant-Major of an Army, to bring in what diviſions or bodies ſoever ſhall be called for; and the Serjant-Major General is ſo to do to the Martial of the Field: And that his duty may be performed with all careful ſeverity, the Serjant-Major is allowed his Hakney to ſpeed it from Company to Company, to ſee that every Company be in his true form; and not to ſuffer any man whatever through Pride, Stubborneſs, Neglect, Covetouſneſs of Pillage, or by any other dilitory, and weak excuſe, to break out of his rank, or to diſproportion any part of the body, by any rude or uncomely poſture, but ſeverely to rebuke the ſame, and compel a ſpeedy reformation.

But out of an Army, both in field or otherwiſe, then the office both of a Serjant-Major and Marſhal ſhall be in himſelf; he ſhall ſummon Courts of War, with the aſſiſtance of his Captains, to proceed to trial againſt offenders, he ſhall proportion all allodgments, encampings, and with his beſt skill fortifie the ſame; and ſhall upon fight draw the battel (yet with this limitation, to take directions from his ſuperior Officer, *&c.*

And as you ſee he is to take care of all Watches and Guards about that Regiment: ſo if there be no greater Officer than himſelf, there to give the word, and to appoint the Court of guard and Sentinels; but if there be a ſuperior Officer, then the Serjant-Major ſhall receive it from him, and ſo give it to the Captains and other ſuch inferior Officers as ſhall have the guard that night.

In ſhort, a Serjant-Major ought to be dutiful to all his Superiours by whom he is to be directed: he ought to be an experienced Souldier, and of a valiant and undaunted behaviour.

4. The Office of a Quarter-maſter.

1. He ſhall in all changing of lodging, attend the Quartermaſter General, and take the place aſſigned by him for the quartering of the Regiment, in ſuch form as the Quartermaſter General ſhall direct him, and there he ſhall appoint lodgings to the Colonel and the Officers according to their places that they are to take in the Regiment, both in town and field.

2. He ſhall lodge ſuttlers of that Regiment in the hindermoſt part of the quarter, at ſuch diſtance as the Quartermaſter General ſhall appoint.

3. His place is to lodge on the back ſide of the Quarter, behind the lodgings of the Lieutenant-Colonel.

5. The Office of the Provoſt.

1. He ſhall ſee all Proclamations, Orders, or Decrees that ſhall be publiſhed by the Provoſt-Martial of the Army, likewiſe to be publiſhed in the Regiment whereof he is Provoſt.

2. Alſo he ſhall keep all the Priſoners committed to him; and once a week give notice to the Provoſt-Martial-General of all the Priſoners within his charge, and of the cauſe of their committance.

3. Furthermore, He ſhall overſee all the Victuallers of the Regiment, that they ſhall neither at unreaſonable prices, nor at unlawful hours ſell their victuals, and ſhall on the other ſide be watchful that no wrong be done, and if any be, that forthwith the party doing wrong, ſhall be brought before ſome officer that hath Authority to yield redreſs, and to that end he ſhall go about the Quarters once every forenoon, once in the afternoon, and once in the dead time in the night, if it may be conveniently performed.

4. He

4. He shall have an accompt given him every night of the Victualer, what victual is in the quarter, and he shall carry the notes thereof to the Provost-martial of the Army.

5. He shall when preys (or booties) are brought in, after the Provost-martial general hath divided them to the Regiments, divide them to the several Companies he is Provost-martial of.

6. He is to see the quarters kept clean and sweet; all garbage and filth buried; nothing that may annoy the quarters suffered to be at such a distance as shall be appointed by the Provost-martial of the Army.

7. He shall lodge in the midst of the Victuallers of the Regiment.

8. He shall come to the Carriage-master for directions where the baggage of that Regiment shall march, where they shall assemble, and what wayes they shall go, which directions he shall perform: and after he hath given the first place to the Colonels baggage he shall place by turn the rest as the Companies do march.

9. Also he shall see the wayes made for the Carriages accompanied with men sufficient, and with instruments to help and amend every thing that is amiss in the wayes, or Carriages, and if any carriages be unable to go, he shall provide that it may be no hindrance to the rest.

The Officers of a Foot Company.

1 The Office of a Captain.

1. He hath proportionably the same Command over his Company, as a Colonel hath over his Regiment; and so also all his Officers and Souldiers are to obey him.

2. When he receiveth his Company and his Arms he is to chose his men and to sort them to his Armes as he thinks fit, *&c.*

3. He shall chose his Officers such as either have had the like place before or are of Experience and good government, or such as have made themselves known to be fit for the like.

4. He shall divide his Company into Corporalships.

5. He shall take care and labour to teach all his Souldiers the carriage and use of their Armes, to keep their order in marchings and imbattailings, and to understand all manner of motions and the beat of the drum, and to this end he shall have usual times of Exercising, which shall be once a day at least, till his men be perfect.

6. In the marching of his Company alone he shall be in the head of his Company going toward the Enemy, and in the Reer-ward coming from an Enemy.

7. In Marching with the Regiment, he is to receive his directions from the the Serjant-major of the Regiment,(and to carry the several sorts of weapons as shall be by him directed: and to every one of the divisions of his Company appoint such an officer as the Serjeant-major shall direct:) and for his place it shall be where the Serjeant-major shall assign.

8. In imbattailing he is to order his Company as the Serjeant-major shall direct him, and to be himself where his Colonel or superiour Officer shall appoint him.

9. In lodging he shall take that according to his degree and place in the Regiment, and see that be ordered according to direction.

10. He shall have his quarter kept sweet for healthfulness, for quiet, for order, especially in the night.

11. If his whole company be to march he shall draw off his company and stand in arms, attending the directions of the Serjeant-major.

12. When he is brought to the place of his guard, he is to take the direction of the Serjeant-major of the Regiment, for the placing the *Corps du guard*; setting his

Sentinels, and ſending forth his rounds, and to ſee his directions performed, and not to abandon his Guard till he be returned, or whatſoever is diſcovered or brought to the Court of Guard where he is, ſhall by himſelf be ſent to the C.——of the Watch; and he ſhall make good his if he be not by a Superiour Officer commanded to retire.

13. If he hear or know of any mutiny, or diſcontented humour tending to mutiny, outrage, or diſorder committed by any of his company, or within the quarter, he ſhall forthwith advertiſe the Colonel of it, or if he be in the way, ſome publick Officer of the Army, and ſhall arreſt and bring forth the party ſo offending, and all ſuch witneſs and proofes as are to be produced, of which if he fail and know it, he ſhall be held very faulty, and if ſuch eſcape him he ſhall be held unworthy of his place.

14. He ſhall ſee thoſe of his Company that do better than their fellowes, advanced and incouraged accordingly, and to all he ſhall doe right, both in their place, and things that are due unto them, and ſhall as far as in him lieth take care for the comforting and preſerving them that are hurt and ſick.

15 In matter of ſervice he ſhall do all that is commanded by any ſuperiour Officer, that hath authority over him, in the beſt ſort he can; without either exceeding his Commiſſion or doing leſs.

16. When he is alone with his Company, he ſhall be very diligent and careful both in his march and lodgings, and if he be put to any extremity, he muſt look to make an accompt; therefore he ſhall do his uttermoſt both by judgment and by valour to free his Company, &c.

2. The Office of a Lieutenant.

1. He ſhall when the Captain is preſent be aſſiſtant to him in ſeeing all directions performed, that are commanded by a ſuperiour Officer, or all ſuch as his Captain hath authority to command; And in the abſence of the Captain he ſhall have the ſame authority as the Captain hath.

2. In a march if there be no Company but his own, he ſhall be at one end of the Company when his Captain ſhall be at the other, and if the Company ſhall march with the Regiment he ſhall take ſuch place as ſpuperiour Officers ſhal aſſign.

3. He is to lodge on the right hand of the Captain as near the end of the quarter as may be convenient; And ſhall in all ſervice, and at all times help to keep the Souldiers in diſcipline and obedience; and ſhall perform all things commanded him, or upon occaſion neceſſary to be done with valour and judgment.

3. The Office of an Enſign.

1. He ſhall when the Captain or Lieutenant be preſent be aſſiſtant to them, or either of them, and in their abſence he hath the ſame authority the Captain hath.

2. In his march he is to carry the Enſign, and to take ſuch place as ſhall be aſſigned him; and if his Company be alone, he ſhall upon entering the quarter, going out of his quarter, going upon the guard, or upon the ſight of an Enemy, carry his Enſign advanced and flying; and if he march with the Regiment, he and all other Enſigns of the Regiment ſhall do as the Colonels Enſign doth.

3. In fight he ſhall never carry his Enſign Advanced and flying, without offering to uſe it in any kind of offence, being a ſign for a Company to gather by, and therefore to be preſerved, for which cauſe he may uſe his ſword.

4 If he march with other Enſignes he ſhall take the place as ſhall be aſſigned him.

5. The

5 The Ensign shall never turn his face out of his order, or start from any danger, or forsake his Ensign upon pain of death.

6. Whensoever the Drum shall beat for the Companies gathering, he shall be in the place and shall see the Ensign well guarded, or be ready to march or do any thing for the service.

4. The Office of a Serjeant.

1. If all the Officers before named be out of the way by any accident, the Eldest Serjant is to Command the Company next.

2. In assembling the company he shall set every man in his place, and if any be missing he shall seek them out, and have power to correct them (in the absence of his superior officer) and if any be defective and cannot be found he is to acquaint his Captain (or chief officer) of it.

7. When the Company are assembled and set in order, he shall march on the outside, where he may best see the order of the march, and take care and charge of their several Corporalships.

4. Though it be usual to understand the use of Armes, and all things that belong to a Souldier, and though by custom he is to lead the Musquetteers to fight especially in a lone Company, (in all which cases he is to follow the directions of his Captain or the superior Officer in his absence,)

5. Yet for his more particular directions how to lead his Musquetteers after he hath brought them up to that ground, and in that number, and order, that his Captain, or superior officer hath commanded him; he shall make every man to come up close to him, and he shall see that they take their level and discharge to good purpose; And he shall see that they keep their order, as well in going on as retiring.

6. If he be joyned with other Companies, he shall follow the directions of him that commands in chief, and carefully look to that part on which he is assigned to attend.

7. The Eldest Serjeant shall lodge in the skirt of the quarter right behind the Captain, and the other in the same sort right behind the Lieutenant, and if more, right behind the Ensign: And in their Quarter they are to visit the Souldiers and their Lodgings, and to see them orderly and quiet.

8. He is to fetch the Word from the Serjeant-major of the Regiment and to deliver it to his Captain, Lieutenant, Ensign, and Corporal that is of the watch; and if the whole Company watch he is to attend, and to see the place where the Sentinels are put out, and to visit them all: If they watch by divisions or Corporalships, then he shall lead them, and bring them to their Guard, where he shall also attend upon any extraordinary accasions by the Command of the Captain of the watch.

9. And while he is there, to advertise the Captain of the watch if any extraordinary discovery or accident of importance happen.

10. He shall deliver such Munition either of Victuals, or of War to the Corporals of the Company, as he shall receive from the Serjeant-Major of the Regiment.

The Office of a Corporall.

1. Though it very seldom happeneth that he hath the charge of the Company, yet if such an accident should fall out that all the superiour Officers of a Company should be absent, then the Command doth belong to him.

2. To his place belongeth properly the charge of one division or squadron of the Company; he is to see them well exercised in their Armes, and that his deportment with them may be Souldier like: he is to deliver them Munition of Victuals or Armes, he is to govern the Watch, and to divide the labour of his Souldiers equally, either in watch, work or service, and to take care in every respect to do the duties of a good Souldier.

3. When the Drum beateth to gather the Company together the Corporals are immediatly to be in a readiness themselves, and to call together their Divisions, and with them he shall repair to their Ensign, and if any of them be wanting without leave, they shall give notice thereof to the Captain and shall prosecute their said absence to the puishment of them.

4. He shall have a third part or a fourth in his division, which being divided into files he shall himself be leader of the chief file; and is with the same alwayes to take place on the right hand of his division.

5. He shall in any case of default either of leaders or bringers up see that they be supplied by the next.

6. In marching or fighting the Corporals of a Company have no Command, but of the file that each of them leadeth: they are to see the opening of their files, or ranks, or to double the same, to follow the sound of the Drum, and to observe every other motion that shall be commanded by the chief Officer; Alwayes provided that he start not out of his place nor use any Command of himself.

7. He is to observe the beat (or sound) of the Drum, and shall see them fully furnished of their Arms, Powder, Bullets, Match (or Flints) and all things else that shall be necessary for the Armes they carry: whereof the Serjeant is to supply them.

8. He is to be lead by a Serjeant to the place of his watch, and from him to receive the word, and directions in what manner and where he shall place his Sentinels, as well by day as in the night, which he is to see performed.

9. His Sentinel being placed he is to let none to pass his Guard without the Word, unless it be to the Captain of the watch, or the Serjeant-major, to whom after he knoweth them, he is to deliver the word to the first Round. He shall direct the Sentinels that every one do the like; he shall see them changed at due time, and shall now and then visit them unlook'd for.

10. He must warn his Sentinel to give no false Alarms, but with as small a noyse as is possible to advertise his said Corporal, who upon an extraordinary occasion shall put his division in Armes and give notice of the danger discovered to the next Guards, and to the Captain of the watch.

11. He shall make good the place of his guard until he be called from thence, and not to suffer any of the Corporalships to leave the same till he be relieved; And he shall fullfil all commandements for the entring or going forth of any Souldiers.

12. At the coming of his relief he shall put all the Souldiers in his division into Arms, and stand ready to receive them, and when his Sentinels are relieved, march to his quarter.

13. If during the time of Watch, any of the Souldiers under his Corporalship shall offend, he is to commit him, or to acquaint his chief officer therewith.

14. If by any occasion the Company remove, and he be drawn from the guard before the twenty four hours be expired; and that the same Companies lodge again within the same time; then shall the said Corporal with his Souldiers be in readiness to watch out the residue of the time, and in such place as shall be appointed.

15. As a Corporal is next in degree to a Serjeant, so in behaving himself well he may pretend to the place of a Serjeant when by any accident it may be void.

The Office of Lansprizado.

1. Next to the Corporal is the Lansprizado, who is in the absence of the Corporal to do his office.

2. His own proper place is to lead the left hand file of the same division and to have his own and the files adjoyning to the same in care observing their orders, as is specified in the Corporals office.

The

The Office of a Drum.

There ought to be two Drummers at least in a Company, both of them perfect in every necessary beat (or sound) thereof, which by turns are to do all the service belonging to their place ; and therefore in the field or Garrison, one of them is to give attendance to the Quarter, though the Company were at that time free from any duty.

2. The Drum having warning to beat for the gathering of the company, shall go beating from one end of the quarter to the other, twice ; and then he shall repair to the Ensigns lodgings.

3. While the Company march the one must beat constantly and by turns ease each other.

4. When the Company shall be joyned with others, the Drums shall take place by the appointment of the Drum-major, and shall beat the same point of War, and observe the same time that Drum doth, that is next to the Colonel or Chief Officer.

5. It is the Office of a Drum, when any of the Company are taken prisoners, to inquire after them, and carry their Ransom, which he may do boldly, after he hath received a Passport from the General, or Commander in Chief of the Army where the Company is : And when he shall come near any place of the Enemies, he must beat (or sound) thrice, and not approach too near till he be by some of the Enemy fetched in.

6. He is only to make his errand known, and not to discover any thing of the estate of the place from whence he was sent which may be prejudicial to him.

A
Military diſcourſe,
Whether it be better for
ENGLAND
To give an Invader preſent battel, or to temporiſe and defer the ſame.

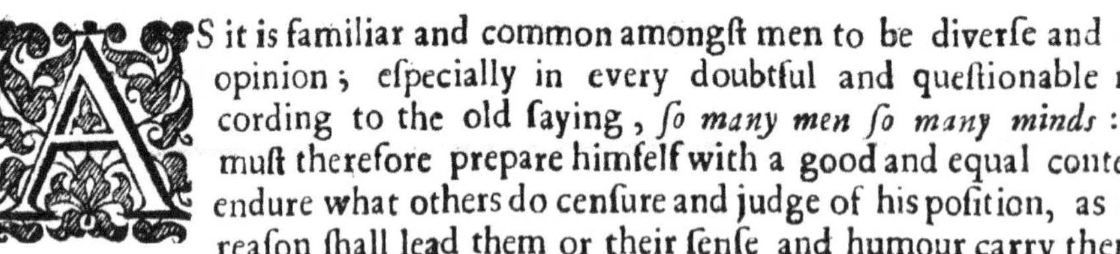

AS it is familiar and common amongſt men to be diverſe and contrarie in opinion; eſpecially in every doubtful and queſtionable matter, according to the old ſaying, *ſo many men ſo many minds*: every man muſt therefore prepare himſelf with a good and equal contentedneſs to endure what others do cenſure and judge of his poſition, as either their reaſon ſhall lead them or their ſenſe and humour carry them. Neither ought any man challenge greater prerogative to his opinion than he bringeth with him authority of reaſon for the ſame: And ſeeing that reaſon, joyned with experience, is the only guide to direct us in all affaires of Action, whereunto all our opinions and judgments muſt be reſtrained, we muſt ſubmit our private conceipts to be ruled by reaſon and experience. In things of great importance and weight, as it behoveth us to be very conſiderate, before we reſolve and ſet down a certainty which we intend to purſue; ſo in this matter of War, are ſome points ſo difficult as may miniſter occaſion and queſtion of long debate, unleſs thoſe controverſies be commended to men of ſtayed and approved Judgment, who are not carried away with corrupt and common opinion, but adviſed and perſwaded by the greater ſtrength of reaſon, confirmed by experience, and preſidents of the like examples: And by the way give me leave to declare my opinion, that no man can ſet down in writing a rule or method, preciſely to be obſerved in War, the ſame being rather to be printed by a long practice and experience in a Souldiers breaſt, to be executed, as time, matter and place may miniſter, that upon the accident of any (in which there may be then required a new form and order to be uſed accordingly) It is held for a maxime That a Prince cannot any way more dangerouſly hazard his Realm and Country, than by giving an Invader Battel at his firſt landing, as hath been heretofore an uſual cuſtome.

And ſince it is amongſt things of the greateſt importance that may concern a Prince and his kingdom, a people, their liberty and goods, it is to be conſidered and re-

ſolved

solved upon before-hand by what means an Army Royal coming to invaid and conquer, might be best prevented and defeated.

The accustomed Order hath been by firing of the Beacons to put the Shire in Arms, and presently all the forces to repair to the landing place, and there without delay to give them battel.

Short answers to the old accustomed Orders.

But because there are other opinions, the reasons of each opinion shall be set down, and then a resolve with submission to better Judgments shall follow.

Such as hold (or maintain) this old accustomed order alledge (besides the good success that many times it hath taken) in reason also it is the best dealing with the Enemy at his landing, before he hath firm footing, and before he shall have leisure to rank his men in due order of battel, and before he shall be able to land his Ordnance, Horse and Carriages, and that a very few men thus in time shall be able to give greater annoyance, and do greater service upon the Enemy than ten times so many, when the Enemy is landed and setled in strength and order with all his Horse, Ordnance and Carriages.

It might be so if the Enemy would acquaint you before where he would land.

They also adde these reasons ensuing for confirmation of their custome.

The Reasons.

First, The fury of the Countrey upon the first firing of the Beacons is great; every man (*pro aris & focis*) violently running down to the Sea side, to repel the disordered Enemy at the first confused landing; which fury, if suffered to grow cold, we shall not so easily inflame again.

The greater fury, the lesser reason; therefore to be suppressed in an Army, as a breach of Order, and not to be inflamed.

Secondly, While the Enemy is landing, if he find any difficulty or danger (being in boats) they are ready to retire to their ships again: But if they be once landed with their Artillery, &c. it is not then possible for them to retire to their Ships again, without extream danger of their lives upon the retreit, and the dishonourable loss of their Munition, &c. And therefore necessity compelling them to fight, and all hope of escape by flight being then taken away from them, they become ten times more dangerous Enemies to deal withall than before.

He is a silly Invader that upon a difficulty will make a retreit.

Thirdly, Every man knoweth what great advantage they have, that have a firm footing on land, to encounter an Enemy that must land out of boats, in confused stragling manner, and therefore ever, and speedily will go to enjoy the benefit of this advantage; whereas, if we suffer the Enemy to land, and put himself in Military order, he becometh more terrible unto us.

It is no great difficulty to land men both strongly and orderly.

Fourthly, There is in this Realm (as in all States divided in Religion) no small number of Trayterous minds; who having time to confer, and seeing an enemy of force then landed, may and then will discover their Malice, which on the suddain they dare not nor cannot.

It is not the sight of the Enemy which will cause them to discover themselves, but his prosperous success upon the first combat, which for that respect is to be avoided.

Another Opinion.

Some others hold this old custome of running to the Sea side to be but a barbarous custome, void of Order, and Warlike Discipline, very perillous to our selves, not hurtful to the Enemy, but rather a means to lose all; and therefore wish by special Command that order of repair to the Sea side be restrained and the Enemy suffered to land quietly: and in the mean time to drive and carry away all Cattel, Victuals, Forrage, Carriages, &c. and certain places of Randesvouze appointed, (some distance from the Sea side) from whence they may march in a Warlike manner and Order; and so by carrying away

Suffered to land quietly because the Enemy would land whether you would or no.

way all victuals and fortifying of Streights and Passages to weary the Enemy in time.

The Reasons of the Second Opinion.

First, It is said the invading Enemy bringeth a select Company of Disciplin'd and well train'd Souldiers whom we seek to encounter with a confused multitude of men untrain'd, in which match there is no comparison, but loss certain.

Secondly, It is said an Enemy of force meaning to land will do it in despight of us, and then the Countrey offering to repel them, and finding themselves not able, grow much more fearful, than if quietly without resistance we had suffered the Enemy to land.

Thirdly, Where we suffer the Enemy to land we may drive away all provision and Cattel further into the Countrey, and then maintain streights and passages well fenced and fortified; so as the Enemy shall be enforced to approach us upon our own strengths and fortifications to his great peril and danger.

Fourthly, They say, in this manner we keeping Victuals from him by land, and his Majesties Navy also in the mean time keeping the Seas, the Enemy for want of Victuals only shall be forced to retire, and glad to withdraw himself if he can.

Further, It is alledged how doubtful a thing Battel is, and how dangerous a thing for a King to commit his Crown upon it, and therefore is that temporizing course extolled.

These are thought most effectual reasons to impugn the speedy repair to the Sea side, and to maintain the other Opinion for suffering the Enemy to land quietly, and by driving and carrying away Victuals, and forrage and fortifying the streights and passages, by time and famine to weary the Enemy.

But having weighed the reasons on both sides, and by experience of former invasions examining the success and sequel of the like attempts, it is adjudged not safe, and therefore not to allow of confused and disorderly running to the Sea side, to encounter a select well trained Enemy invading; and secondly, neither is it safe to suffer the Enemy quietly to land all his forces, munition, *&c.* It is by some conceived that a middle (or a mean) course far more serviceable than either of them both may be taken, whereby the benefit of that old custome may be embraced, and the disorders of the other (well noted) may be reformed, and no advantage to annoy the invading Enemy omitted, as by these following reasons may be judged.

Reasons and Resolutions against the second Opinion.

It is subject to invasion notwithstanding: it is not meant but our Navy should annoy them both before, and in landing if they can.

First I say one of the chiefest forces of this famous Island of *England* consisteth in this, that it is fortified naturally with such a Trench (or ditch) as the Sea is, whereby it is not so subject to invasion as other Countries lying on the main; which singular benefit and peculiar advantage to our Countrey is utterly lost if we suffer the Enemy to land all his forces, *&c.* and take firm footing on the Main.

A reason made where there is no contradiction.

Secondly, Whereas this noble Island hath such a number of Mariners and good Shipping both of his Majesties Royal Navy, and also of Merchants, as may hope with good success to encounter on Sea the force of any forreign Enemy: Now if we suffer the Enemy quietly to land, and then temporize afterward (according to the second opinion) we lose a great part of this our strength.

Rather by supposition than by experience.

Thirdly, There is no man of any experience, but knoweth with what danger men land out of boats, if there be any ordinary force (before landing) to resist them; for if any storm arise the Sea alone fighteth for us, and with but small resistance on land may drown great numbers of our invading Enemy.

Fourthly,

Fourthly, Any small Trench on land shall lodge Musquetteers enough, to spoil as many of our Enemies as in boat shall offer to land, before they can approach the shoar.

No small work to entrench all the landing places about England.

Also, In landing, before they can have time to put themselves in Order, what an execution may a far less number of well armed men do on them, before they shall have time to unite their forces.

True, if the Enemy would not resist you with a far greater force than can possibly be gathered together on such a suddain to encounter him.

Again, After the Remnant shall land, if they be not all drown'd slain, or repel'd in or before their landing, how easie a matter shall it be for a few well Armed Souldiers, to put such a confused, dispersed, scattered, Sea-beaten Company to the sword, before they shall be able to advance a Standard, or put themselves in order of battel?

A strong Imagination upon a weak supposition.

Besides all this, if his Majesties forces should not in time be assembled of such strength as to be able before landing to give them battel, yet any mean force (assailing their Ships while their men are in landing) cannot but greatly annoy them, if not utterly defeat them.

No intendment but our Navy should impeach them upon all assays.

Again, In most places if (except the Enemy bring his tide justly with him) he cannot land, and then if part land, and any mean resistance made to give impediment to the rest, till the tide pass, their divided forces may more easily be defeated.

An Invador will both forecast and prevent those dangers.

Also, It is no small time that is requisite to land an Army with Horse, Carriage, and Ordnance, Munition, and Victuals: without which an Invader shall never be able to prevail: And then if any mean resistance be made at the landing, it much prolongeth the same time, so as any storm happening, the Winds, Tides, Shelves, Rocks, Bars, and Seas fight for us, (in our favour, and to the ruine of our Enemies;) and therefore I utterly disallow that opinion, to give an Enemy leave quietly to land, and then by device to temporize afterwards.

You grant him victuals enough if he can land, you say he shall find houses, and Barns full.

Further, If any such resolution by the Prince and people be taken, that the invading enemy should be suffered to land quietly to spoil and burn at his pleasure; and the inward forces of the Countrey not permitted, even at the first landing to come to their rescues, it would cause (no doubt) the Inhabitants of the Coasts to abandon their Towns, and leave the Frontiers desolate; which the wise Kings and grave Counsellers of this Land have ever to sought to make populous, by granting many privileges and immunities to allure Inhabitants on the Frontiers.

It behoveth an Invader to be as wary of burning and spoiling as your self, lest he make himself odious to his own party.

Let the Company come down to the Randesvouze as fast as they can so they give no battel.

But touching driving, or carrying away of Victuals, and leaving the Countrey waste, thereby to famish our landed Enemies, it is a thing more easily wished than performed.

No great difficulty, though not easily done as wished.

I confess in *Ireland* where most of their substance consisteth of Kine, it is easily done.

By which retreiting and driving away of Victuals and keeping of streights and passages they starve and weary them that follow them.

But in this rich and wealthy Countrey of England it is not possible but that the Enemy (if he be once landed with all his force) shall find houses full of provisions, and barns full of all kind of Forrage, and Corn all the Country over, unless the King should command all to be wasted with fire, which president we see seldome or never put in use, neither in the Wars in *France*, *Flanders*, nor in any former invasion that we read of, for it will make the Prince odious, and alienate the Subjects minds, therefore not to be used but upon a great extremity, when all other means fail: and here in *England* above all other Countreys it may worst be done, for our Towns be poor, weak, and unprovided and unfortified; the Countrey full of habitations, populous, rich, and abundance of all commodities.

That is where the prince is a Tyrant otherwise he shall be obeyed in all things that tend to the preservation of the Countrey.

dities. In the *Low Countries* by reason of their great store of strong well fortified Towns, they might much more easily drive and carry to their Cities (at hand) all victuals and forrage, *&c.* And yet when the great Army of the *States* and *Don John* were in the Field, notwithstanding all the Boars and Country People were fled and retired, to the next walled Town, and had knowledge long before of the approaching of the Armies, yet were they not able so to drive and carry away their Victuals and forrage, but that the Enemy found Barnes full in every place, as the Enemy was never forced to forrage four miles from their Camp: So difficult, or rather impossible a thing it is to carry away our victuals or forrage, or leave the Enemy a wast Country. But if here in *England* we should drive or carry away our Victuals or Forrage to the next walled Towns, the Enemy being quietly landed with all his Munition should have his chief desire, knowing not only how weak and unfortified our Towns are, but also how unprovided of all necessaries to abide a Siege; as if fortification on a suddain could be made.

I grant for Forrage because they came in harvest, but all other victuals came out of the Towns behind their backs.

Here he speakes as if the Enemy by his landing were straight master of the Field, and no place left us but walled Towns to guard our Cattel and Victualls.

Wherefore it is wished that all provident meanes should be used to give the Enemy all possible annoyance before and at his landing. And by no meanes to suffer him to land quietly, or to trust to that temporising course, which is rather to be practised when all other means fail, than to be relied upon at the beginning. It is granted perilous for a defendant Prince to hazard his Crown upon a Battel, and more dangerous for men untrayned to encounter expert Disciplined Souldiers, and most perilous to us that have no strong Towns to make head if we lose the Battel: Therefore it is no part of judgement to wish our Prince to give an invading Enemy Battel with all our forces, how well prepared and ordered soever they be; but the meaning is to have such provisions in every Shire, as we may be able readily on a sudden to give the Enemy all annoyance possible before, and at his landing, whilst the inward forces of our Country may the better assemble, and put themselves in Military order to proceed after as shall be most convenient.

By reasons and presidents it is proved that an invadours landing cannot be prevented.

Too late to shut the Stable when the Steed is stollen.

A Reply to the reasons aforesaid.

Now to come to the question, and matter propounded, whether it be better to fight with an Enemy at his landing or to defer battel.

I will first distinguish between an Enemy Invador, whom we do presuppose would be a conquerour to alter and change the state; and another Enemy Borderer, who either to procure a new quarrel, or to revenge an old wrong, may support some small company by shipping (or dwelling upon the maine) and make incursion into a Country only to burn, and spoyle some part thereof, such an Enemy may be fought withal at his first appearance or landing, because there is a means and likelyhood to repulse him again, with the only aid and strength of the Frontier forces, as hath been already alledged, *Viz.* That if the Enemy should intend but to land and burn some houses, and villages near the Sea coast; for the prevention thereof as much as may be, it were good to appoint only those, that dwell within two or three miles of the Sea side to repair thither to make resistance, and for their succour to appoint the Horse men to draw down to the Plains next adjoyning, who may also give them stop for stragling far into the Country, and though you should receive a foyl, there is no danger, for his intent is not to dwell and tarry by it. But for an Invadour as there is difference of his intention and force, so must you make also a difference in the incounter and prevention accordingly, who if he cannot

A Distinguisher betwixt an Enemy Invador, and an Enemy Borderer.

These may be termed the forelorn hope.

not be defeated by our Navy (is alwayes preferred by the first trial, although it be hardly gathered to the contrary against me) which either I say might by contrary winds or other accidents happen to miss each other, and so the Enemy come undiscovered upon our Coast, or otherwise might land in despight of our shipping, then my opinion was to restrain the Countries disorderly running down to the Sea Coast, as a thing very dangerous, being not able to withstand their landing; first, because it was said, such an Enemy would land more men within three hours, than would be meet in reason for you to fight in three dayes; such a while will it be, before the Country can come down to the Sea side, as hath been seen by many false Alarms given to the Country for trial of the readiness thereof.

As the Earl of Warwick *did out of* Normandy *in* Edward *the fourths time.*

Next because it is Impossible so to man the Sea coast round, as that an Enemy (meaning to land and burn only) might be prevented, for that he will make shew to land in one place, and (the Country being drawn down thither) may suddenly weigh Anchor and Saile further in few hours, than your Army that you have provided in a readiness, can march well in two dayes.

As for example, The *French* made a shew in King *Henry* the eighth's days as though they would Land in the Isle of *Wight* or *Portsmouth*, & finding the Country drawn down thither by means of the Kings being there, hoysed Sayles, landed & burnt at *Brighthemsteed* in *Sussex*, & in the Downs in *Kent*, and after returned and landed in the Isle of *Wight*. Then seeing the Enemies remove from place to place is so speedy, and his landing place so uncertain, and the knowledge thereof before hand impossible; I would fain know how strong a resistance the Country can be able to make upon the sudden, against an Invadour, that will land a thousand or two, at one instant, or rather which hath imbarqued his men in vessels of so small draught, as the men may leap a shoar out of them.

How your prepared forces may be prevented.

The Opponent meaning to sail safely betwixt the two Rocks of *Scylla* and *Charybdis*, imagineth he goes clear when as he striketh upon both; who seeming to dislike of giving Battel, would have the Country drawn down to make resistance and impeach their landing. I would thereupon ask this question; if the men you send down be once in fight, whether you think it not requisite to second them, and if you second them, what do you else, but ingage your self to Battel; if you will not second them, then do you most barbarously expose your men to the slaughter and butchery of your Enemy: How great a discouragement that would be to your people, and what inconvenience might follow, I leave to your Judgement to consider.

But from whence proceedeth this opinion of the necessity or convenience of a rash and suddain incounter with an Enemy at his landing, but from an excessive fear and doubtfulness conceived beforehand that all the Realm should be in hazzard to be lost, if the Enemy were but once suffered to land, and have firm footing. Which imagination groweth for want of skill and judgment in Martial actions, and therefore we seek to prevent that by a desperate and disorderly fight, which we might more safely remedy by a defensive, and less dangerous course, as may appear by the examples of a weak Ship, and a battered Town; which both by suffering themselves to be entered and assaulted, the one by her close fights, the other by new intrenchments, do give the entered Enemy the greater foyle, even then when they think themselves possest of all.

Besides a King that is in his own Country may be supplied with infinite Numbers of Pioniers, who in few hours may rear earth works to triple his force against an Invadour (as is well known to him that is a Souldier) whereof he should be utterly deprived, by that most barbarous custome heretofore used and yet maintained; I mean of that disorderly running down to the Sea side, to give an Invading Enemy battel, at his first landing.

What reason had *Spain* to attempt the Conquest and subversion of this Realm, but that they presumed, we would assuredly rely upon our old Custom of giving them Battel at their landing: which if we should do, there would be great likelihood; first

The only hope of an invador is to prevaile by Battel.

first that we should lose the same, and next having lost the Battel, I fear that the subversion of this famous Island would ensue. For an aspiring King that hath a great faction within a Contry may presume beforehand to carry the same, if he be assured, that the people thereof will give him battel at his firstlanding. Therfore if you will avoid an Invasion and the danger of a Conquest, let it be known to the world that it is an error, whereby you might imbrace those advantages, and the benefit that our Country affords, and you shall undoubtedly avoid the trouble of the first, and be free from the danger of the last. We read that *Scanderbegge* (never thelesse that he expected the Invasion of so puissant an Enemy, as was the *Turk*,) thought it not good to leave any great Army of Force to give him Battel; but only certain select bands (or Companies of Foot) with Troops of Horse, & the foot too lightly armed, & causing all the frontiers to withdraw themselves, their Cattel, Corn and Substance into the strong and fortyfied places of the Country, did with such select forces face the Enemy on the frontiers, by keeping of streights & passages, making suddain attempts in the night, & such other times as by Spies he found the Enemy carelesse, and so with a few people (or small force) by time, famine and expences he wearied the Enemy and caused him to retire, that otherwise in Battel might have gotten the victory, and so in short time commanded the whole Country. Wherefore I would not wish any Prince to adventure his Kingdom that way, unless he be weary of the same Battel being the only thing for an Invadour to seek, and on the contrary for the invaded to avoid and shun, for the one doth hazzard but his people, and hath a lot to win a Kingdom, and the other in losing of the Battel endangereth his Crown.

Scanderbegg *against the* Turk.

The Opponent disalloweth of a confused disorderly running down to the Sea side, and yet would fight with them in their landing, which is a thing impossible. For if you tarry time to put men in order, (which you must of necessity do by reason of the Countries slack assembly) then will the Enemy land in the mean time and frustrate your purpose, unless you were made acquainted long beforehand, when and where he intended to land, and where you may make your supposed Trenches you have declared, to lodge your men in. There be some also that conceive a great advantage of the Enemies weakness coming from the Sea, and of their landing out of Boates disorderly, which when it shall happen to come to trial, it will easily appear how far they are deceived of both: for who knoweth not that even all men coming near the shore, and smelling land, become well and sound again of their Sea sickness. Also, what numbers of men will be landed at one instant in Boats, Gallies and other Vessels of small draught, and that safe enough, those that have been imployed in like actions, can testifie. And as touching Rocks, Shelves, contrary Winds, &c. which is said may fight for us, we must not build upon such uncertainties, for an Enemy will beforehand so set down, and lay his plot, where he will make his descent, as that none of all those accidents shall give any impedement to the same. What other advantages our Country men may have either of their Courage, or goodness of their cause, without knowledge, and order, how to dispose thereof, will rather be an occasion of their overthrow, than means of the Victory. But especially a few to fight against many, disordered against ordered, Countrey men against experienced Souldiers; the odds that the Enemy hath of you therein, will be much greater than your imagined advantages. And albeit that I confess, our Country men have a shew of desire to fight, (as having as great, natural help of strength, courage and ability as any other Nation) yet can it not be denied, but that in the Artificial we must needs be defective, for want of use and Practice, therefore not to be suffered to run down to the Sea side, in that confused and accustomed manner unless it might be done with a compleat number of choyce men, conducted by a skilful leader that knoweth how to make his fight upon the best ad vantages, and to retire them orderly again to their least hurt and discouragement; otherwise I do altogether disallow, of that general repair to the Sea side. But rather to make your assemblies five or six miles distant with all your Foot forces, and

Strength and courage availeth much being joyned with skill and order to dispose of them.

to attend them in the plaines, with your Horse; for whatsoever men resolve with themselves before hand, and what minds soever they may seem to put on, when they shall be driven to make their wayes through the vollies of shot, having never been acquainted with the game before, it may either make them pinch courtesie through the strangeness thereof, or at least having tasted of that sauce (and finding it bitter) may spread rumours to discourage a whole Army; for oftentimes the fame and bruite of a repulse maketh others as fearful that but hear of it, as those that have been in the Action and born the blows themselves. How unlikely then it is, that you should profit your selves by that means or impeach your Enemy, may easily appear.

But let us come to examples, for it is not sufficient to say by experience of former invasions, *&c.* not alledging any. Where can it be remembered that a strong Enemy proffering to land, hath been prevented by the Frontier forces? I think few or none, who be avouched, unless the president of the Priest of Saint *Margarets* near *Dover* shall be admitted for one, of whom the old Fletchers retain a memorial in honour of their Bowes; who is said with his Bow and Sheaf of arrows to have kept down the *French* men that offered to land in a narrow passage up the Clift near *Dover*, where they found a gate fast barred and lockt to stop the same. And he standing over them, on the top of the Clift, played a tall Bow mans part, when as in these dayes the *French* had not any shot but some few Cross-bows, that could not deliver an Arrow half way up the Clift to him; and so it was given out that he kept them down till the Country was come down to the Sea side to repell them back to their Boats; or rather I suppose (my self knowing the place) when they saw the gate was so fast, as they could not suddenly break it open, they returned before their coming. But yet I must confess the Bow bare the bell, before the Divel (I suppose) sent the musquet, *&c.* out of Hell.

The Priest of Saint Margaret *with his Bow and Arrows.*

Who came for fresh water as was supposed.

But here lest the Authour be mistaken, he prefers the force of the Harquebuz and Musquet, far before the Bow, yet in judgement doth not disallow the Bow but rather judge the same to be a serviceable and warlike weapon, as well in Town as Field, and although it be not greatly pertinent to this question, yet it may be convenient to consider here, how and wherein good use may be made of this weapon: first in the field against the Horse-men, though it be shot at the highest random, only with the weight of the fall it galleth both Horse and Man; and though the wound be not mortal, yet both Horse and man are hereby made unserviceable then and long after; if they escape death. Secondly, in rainy weather when men come near together it is a good weapon. Thirdly in the night time it is a ready and a secret shot, *&c.* and the use of it may be good in the forcing of the Enemies Trenches, in sallying out of Town: or else, Fourthly, at an assault when all the defences are taken away in any Town, you may deliver your Arrows over the wall and shroudly gall your Enemy with the fall of them. Fifthly to shoot Arrows with wild fire, to burn gate or drawbridge, to fire thatched or shingled houses. When our *English* Army was before *Paris* those of our Commanders wished they had brought Bow men over with them; and I see no reason it should be wholly laid aside, for the worst Bow man that can but draw his Bow is better than a bad fire man.

The use of the bow bow serviceable.

But if we should not make use of our Bow in any of our warlik enterprises; it should be every Commanders care to chuse good fire men, for Ammunition is much wasted by the unskifulness of the Musquetteer, and execution not to expectation; and as we have an order established for our Musquet bore, I could wish the Mustermaster in every County would look so to it, that they may not be too big, as well as too little.

Mustermasters care.

But now touching landing let us see what may be conceived out of the for-

Examples and presidents of landing.

mer experience. Did not the Earl of *Warwick* notwithstanding the Duke of *Burgundies* great and puissant Navy which he had provided to joyn with *Edward* the fourth, for the impeaching the Earls landing from out of *France*; and the fleet being before the Haven in *Normandy*, out of the which the Earl must come; the Duke having also warned the King, into what part and Port of *England* the Earl meant to make his descent, whereby in all likelyhood he was or migt have been provided sufficiently to withstand the same; yet (I say) did it not so fall out that the Earl of *Warwick* escaped, their Fleet landed in *England*, and drove the King to flee for succour into the *Low Countries*, and enlarged *Henry* the sixth, and set him in his former estate? After this did not *Edward* the fourth with some small aid from the Duke of *Burgundie* given him, and that under hand, both of shipping men and money, transport himself into *England* again, and in Battel slew the Earl of *Warwick*, and his adherents, deposed *Henry* the sixth, resuming again unto himself the Kingdom of *England*?

Edward the fourth relanded in England *and deposed Henry the sixth.*

Have not the Kings of *England* many times entered *France*, by Navie; and *Scotland* during the time of Wars betwixt them? Did not Queen *Mary* land 5000 men in *Brittany* one of the most popular parts of all *France*, and there sackt and burnt *Conquet*, and other places, our men remaining on shoar two dayes and a night, burning and spoyling, and were not, or rather could not be resisted upon the suddain?

Queen Mary *landed* 5000. *in* Britany *and burnt* Conquet.

Have not our *English* (though but small) forces in Queen *Elizabeths* dayes landed in the *Indies*, at sundry times, sackt, and ransacked their Towns, brought away their Munition, with other great spoyles and riches, yet at their landing were not withstood? And did not our Army land in *Spain* and *Portugal* at sundry times, and in sundry places; they having knowledge a long time before of their coming, whereby the Country was or might have been in that readiness themselves would have desired, and yet by a temporizing course used against them they were driven to retire; both feeble and broken: whereas if they had been fought withall at their landing, and had won the field, there had been a great hope, they might have prevailed in that enterprise? Did not the *Spanish* forces also land in *Portugal* & his other Army by land, under the conduct of the Duke of *Alva* who by wining the Battel won the Kingdom withal, and drove the King quite out of his Countrey? And did not the *French* forces likewise land in the *Terceras* in despite of the Country? And did not the *Spanish* forces after reland, slay and drive all out again?

English *landed in the* Indies.

English *in* Spain *and* Purtugal.

The Spanish *Forces landed in* Portugal.

The French *in* Terceras.

The Spanish *relanded there.*

Infinite are the presidents of landing, and a rare matter to find any example of an Army coming to invaid, to be prevented of landing, by the Countries fury, and running down to the Sea side; and what Souldier (or man of War) would not undertake to land even a few men in comparison of a royal Army in any Princes Realmes and Dominions, spoile and burn at his pleasure, until such time they had assembled greater forces than the inhabitants of the Coasts.

Whatsoever a man cannot resist, he must give way unto. Reason and experience do plainly prove, that it cannot be withstood, but that a forceable Enemy will land. Therefore the best remedy will be to give him way, and withal to remember to do all things like wise men and Souldiers as hath been said already, by driving and withdrawing the Countries cattel and provisions that your Enemy may not be relieved and nourished.

Duke of Alva *against the Prince of* Orenge.

France against the Emperor.

Did not the Duke of *Alva* defeate the Prince of *Orenges* great Army, by forbearing to fight with him, and leaving him a vast Country to walk and way himself in? Did not the Constable of *France* defeat the Emperours attempt upon *Province*, by this only temporizing course? Did he not burn the Mills, destroy the Ovens,

Ovens, ſpoyle the fruit, *&c.* himſelf retiring to *Avignon*; there to joyn with his forces after that he had provided for the frontier Towns; leaving nothing but a waſt Country, for his Enemies to ſpend themſelves in; whereby he drove the Emperor in the end to make a moſt diſhonourable retreit? *Monſieur de Langey* doth alledge that example of the Conſtable of *France*, proving greatly his device and policy therein. Notwithſtanding there were divers who did not ſtick to blame him for that he did not ſeek to ſtop the Enemies paſſage, through the mountains, which they ſuppoſed he might have done very eaſily, and with few men. But he foreſeeing the miſchief that might grow by a ſmall foyl or loſs received at the firſt, thought it the ſafeſt way to prevent all dangers, by temporizing, until his forces were aſſembled in full ſtrength and his Enemies weakned; ſaying moreover, that it is a great point of wiſdome for a Prince, or Captain General, to defer fighting when the Enemies are entered in his Country: for ſaith he, if the battel ſhould be loſt through the encountring of them, the Country would alſo be in hazzard to be loſt, and this may appear by divers examples.

The King of Hungary *againſt the* Turk.

Firſt, the King of *Hungary* being aſſailed by the *Turk* in the year 1562. thought it better to hazzard the Battel and to fight with the *Turk* at his arrival, than to forbear and ſtand upon his guard, which was the cauſe he himſelf was ſlain, and a great part of his kingdom loſt. And did not *William* the Conquerour and King *Henry* the ſeventh become kings of *England* by reaſon the defendent gave them battel at their landing, and loſt the ſame.

William *the Conquerour, and* Henry *the ſeventh got the Crown of* England *by Battel.*

Obj. But ſome may here object, that the Parties and Factions within the land, were cauſe thereof. And doth any man think that a Forraign Prince is ſo void of Judgment as that he thinketh to prevaile by way of Conqueſt without a party? Did not the Duke of *Burgundie* get the Country of *Leidge*, by reaſon of ſome Battel he won againſt the the people thereof? *Philip de Comines* ſaith, that a man ought greatly to fear to hazzard his eſtate on a Battel, when he may otherwiſe avoid the ſame: for ſaith he, of a ſmall number of people loſt there followeth a great change to him that loſeth them, not ſo much by the fear they conceive of the Enemy, as in the little eſtimation they will have of their Maſter afterward, being ready ſtill to enter into mutinies, demanding things more boldly than they were wont; alledging further, that one Crown before, will do more with them, than three will do after. Whoſoever will read the Book of the actions of *Lewis* the eleventh King of *France* (who was both a very wiſe and valiant Prince) ſhall find, that after the great incounter between him and Count *Charles* the Duke of *Burgundies* ſon at *Mountleyrre*, notwithſtanding, that the conflict went ſo indifferent, as neither ſide knew almoſt by the ſpace of three or four hours after who had the Victory, ſo ſoon as each party had rallied their broken Troops, *&c.* having ſome good means ſo to do by reaſon of a great ditch and long hedge that was between their two Armies, where the fight firſt began, although the Kings power remained ſtill great, by reaſon of ſo many Princes, as he had aſſembled together, yet then, and ever after he determined, no more to venture ſo great a Kingdom as *France* was, upon the uncertain event of a Battel. And therefore the night following he diſlodged and retired to *Corbel*; after which time he carried all his Wars, with ſuch a Temporizing courſe, as thereby he wearied his Enemies, and became a mighty Prince, making his Army ſo great as his adverſaries at no time after durſt attempt to give him Battel. Although *Philip de Comines* doth write that our Nation hath been wonderfully fortunate in Battel, and are much addicted thereunto; yet he doth more allow of the politique and wiſe temporizing of *Lewis* the *French* King in forbearing to fight with *Edward* the fourth when he entered *France*, proffering him Battel near *Amyens*. The King conſidering how dangerous an adventure it was to his eſtate,

The Duke of Burgundie *won the Countrey of* Leigh *by Battel.*

Lewis *the eleventh aginſt* Charles *the Duke of* Burgundies *Son.*

Lewis *againſt* Edward the fourth.

if it should not succeed well with him, looking also back to the great thraldome and subjection, that his predecessors had brought the Kingdome of *France* into, under the *English* Nation, by such like rash acceptance of Battel, he determined to temporize, though it were to his charges, thereby to weaken the King of *England*, the winter season drawing then on: In the mean time sending great presents to those that were near about the King, and Victuals of free-gift to relieve his Army; condescending also to pay a yearly sum of 50000 Crowns into the Tower of *London*, thereby to hasten the peace, and to get our Nation to return. After all was concluded and the King returned home; one of the King of *Englands* men being with *Phillip de Comines* in discourse, he told him he had been at the winning of nine Battels, and how many said *Phillip* have you been at the losing? Only one said he; and that was at the last forbearance of my Master to fight with yours at *Amyens*; whereby we have gotten more shame unto our selves than honour by the first nine. When *Lewis* the King heard of this speech, he said, this is a shrewd boy, and sent for him to dine with him, and after gave him 1000 Crowns with other great promises to the intent he should be a means to entertain the peace, begun between the two Kings. What success had the *French* at the Battel at *Poytiers* and *Cressey*, who although they were in number far greater than the *English*, and in the heart of their own Country, yet they tasted nothing but the bitter effect of a lost field. And we by other such manifold examples might be warned not to commit the good estate of a Realme to so tickle and dangerous a trial as is the uncertain sway of a Battel. And now never to be forgotten, did not our *English* Navy defeat the great *Spanish* Fleet by this temporizing course? which had been so easie (as it was thought) to have been performed by main force, in boarding them at the first. Yet some would have this temporizing course not to be used at the beginning, but when all other means do fail: and then it may be too late to temporize when you have fought and received the foyl; and it is against the name of the word and thing it self to use it in the end when time is past. Infinite are the examples to confirme these temporizing courses, by meanes whereof great and huge Armies have in a short time been dissolved and come to nothing. As namely the *Germans* sundry times in *France*, and the Duke of *Parma's* Army in *France*, when he came to the relief of *Paris Anno.* 1590.

The Battels of Poytiers *and* Cressey.

Spanish *Fleet defeated.* 88.

Duke of Pama's *Army*

Lastly, The better to remove this old impression of rash encountring of an Enemy Invador, remember the unadvised encounter of the Duke of *Burgundie* who besieged a certain Town in the *Savoy*, called *Granson*, with a very great Army, to the relief whereof came certain *Switzers*, (though not great in number;) the Duke hearing of their approach, sent some forces to them to give them all annoyance possible, as also to prevent their entrie and descent into the Country (for the passage they should enter by was through a certain narrow straight betwixt certain Mountains) and himself followed with some greater forces to second them. And this was done by the Duke, contrary to the advice of his counsel who perswaded him, rather to attend their coming with all his forces in the place where they were; for the place both by Nature and also by Art was strongly enramped, and it was so that in all reason he could sustain no danger. To make it short, the Dukes Van-guard was not able to withstand the *Switzers* entrry, but retired; the Dukes rere-guard seeing this, supposing they had fled began also to fly; in fine his whole Army retired toward the Camp, although some behaved theselves very well in this retreit, yet when they came into the Camp they durst not defend it; but all betook themselves to flight, leaving their rich and pompous Camp and their Artillery to the spoyl of the poor *Switzers*, who slew but very few of his people for want of horsemen to follow the chase. The Duke, who the day before was lifted up to the skies in pride, through the seeking to himself so many great States and Princes, that desired to allie and confederate themselves with him in league and freindship, presently after the loss of this Battel found a great deal of alteration and change, for there fell from him four sorts of people, who became his Enemies.

The Duke of Burgundies *fall.*

Enemies. The rage of the Duke was still so great that he would not thus give over, but would trie a second Battel at *Mora*: Upon the loss whereof divers others of his Allies fell from him also. And lastly after the Battel of *Nansey* where he himself was slain, a great part both of his own proper Dominions, and of *Burgundie* it self, fell from his house also. Thus you may see what a long and evil tail a lost Battel hath; as *Lewis* the *French* King was wont to say. If you desire examples of greater Antiquity, you are referred to the reading of the *Roman* Histories; but because brevity is required, I will remember you only of this one; Namely of *Cæsar*, who never could attain to the sole government of *Rome*, until *Pompey* (opposing himself against it, on the behalf of the State and Senate of *Rome*) gave him Battel and lost it: after which he was driven to fly into *Egypt*, where *Ptolomy* the King sent his head unto *Cæsar*, whereby there were left none able to withstand. By the which he got not only the absolute government for himself, but also brought and reduced the free State of *Rome* to a *Monarchy*.

But if the defendant chance to win the Battel, then indeed he removeth the cause and endeth the danger. As the *Moors* against the King of *Portugal*, who landed without any resistance: But the defendants finding themselves the stronger as well in Foot as in Horse, thought it no danger to give Battel, which grew by temporizing, untill their power was come together: for it is most certain, that as long as you abstain from coming to fight, the Enemies shall alwaies be held in doubt of winning, and you shall be in no hazard of losing the Country, and your male-contents and evil disposed persons will be kept from revolt, who no doubt will see a Battel fought before they will shew themselves open Enemies; yea, whatsoever they had promised beforehand, as the *Portugals* did to *Don Antony*, and performed it not. By which dilatory manner of proceeding, you may be at choice either to accept or refuse the Battel, as shall be most for your advantage, when by time you have made your selves strong and your Enemies weak. And this defensive War, and these temporizing courses, we see that all Princes and men of War that are, or have been of late of Judgment do imitate and follow. As whosoever will Look into the Duke of *Parma*'s actions shall seldom see that ever he came to fight a set battel, but when all other meanes did fail to accomplish that which he intended. And no less noble and glorious is that victory holden, which is obtained by Counsel, device and policy, than that which is won by the sword, violence and Blood.

The Moors *against the King of* Portugal.

I have now answered to the question first proposed, & given the reasons on both sides, leaving my superiors to their better judgements. Although the people of this Nation heretofore ran headlong upon the invador to the Sea side, without sufficient armes, advice or command; such furious actions the discreet Souldier is against. But in these our later dayes the people being more civilized, better armed and disciplined; and the whole Nation in a better posture of defence; it may now be granted that in some cases, to deter and delay your fight may be dangerous, as in letting slip some notable advantage; from which you are not restrained, but only to be advised in this case, not to joyn Battel rashly and unadvisedly with the Enemy. The which (besides the danger of rash attempts) doth cut you off from advantages and supplies, that may be had, by time, deliberation, and counsel; for their is nothing in which true fortitude may be shewed more than in this action: for to fight, courage doth not naturally provoke; but to refrain upon good cause, is the advice of wisdome; and he that will fight upon every call of the Enemy when offered, shall be sure to do it to his disadvantage; and thereby shall shew that he hath no experience of Wars, and is ignorant of the chances and mutability of fortune, or as I may say more aptly, knoweth not how to use his fortune: yet what is the common voice of the Country? which heat and fury as it riseth suddainly, so may it be cooled quickly again. But that which increaseth and confirmeth courage best and maketh men resolute and constant indeed, is when they shall see themselves accompanied with numbers able to resist, instructed with knowledge how to use their armes and weapons, and fortified with order to be able to

If any advantage is offered not to temporize.

withstand and repel an Enemy: This is it, which will make a coward valiant: For as one saith, the fierce and disordered men, are much weaker than the fearful and ordered; for that order expelleth fear from men, and in the end disorder abateth fierceness; so then it is not fury that prevaileth in War, but good discipline and order.

The chief scope is to perswade a restraint of the violent and disorderly running down of the Country to the Sea side to fight and give Battel to the Enemy at his landing after the old custome, shewing the danger and inconvenience that may follow. And for the other part it is granted by all that it is perilous for a defendant Prince to hazzard his Crown at a Battel; and more dangerous for men untrained to encounter expert disciplin'd Souldiers. Put the case that Battel be given, and loss received; then if we have no strong Towns adjacent to give the Enemy stop, to make head and rally again, it will prove most perilous to us. Therefore moderately it may be concluded dangerous (unless advantage might be obtain'd) for any Prince to give an invading Enemy Battel.

And here by the way (occasion being offered) to speak of strong Towns; some there be of that opinion that a Country well peopled, that hath no, or few strong Towns, is in less danger of conquest than that Realm that hath many: because (say they) an Enemy cannot any way nestle himself, but that you may at all times force him to Battel at your pleasure. To that may be answered that a Battel being the thing that an invadour is most desirous of, and which a defendant ought to shun; your strong Towns in that case are most available for the defendant Prince in his own Country against an Invador; because he may onely with one strong Town weary an Invadours Army and consume it: especially if he be but able with a small force to encamp near his Town besieged: for the Invador is thereby restrained from assaulting the same, for fear the defendants Camp should assail him in the mean time. The which worketh all for the defendant, in winning of time to the weakning and ruin of his Enemies Army: the date whereof (as by daily experience is found) is not above twelve or thirteen weeks continuance; so as your strong Towns avail wholly for the defendant; and are dangerous only in *Civil and Intestine Wars*, for that such Towns revolting work the like contrary effect against their Lord and Master, as they did before for him: for examples & presidents of this, you may behold what the strong holds of *France*, and the *Low Countries*, and England it self did against their Lords and Soveraignes: Insomuch as we may truly say of them *They are a dangerous good*: Wherefore I think it matter of Joy to all loyal hearts that our most Gracious Soveraign hath a Kingdom so well replenished with a warlike people, whereby to be enabled at all times to front and give a stop to an Enemy Invadour: And as touching a rebellious number, I hope we shall never doubt or fear them, as long as they shall want skillful leaders and Governours to direct them; pay, armour, Munition, and other necessaries to uphold them; wherewith His now most Royal Majesty is plentifully furnished; the want whereof shall force Rebels in a few dayes to disperse themselves, who being once broken may presently be followed in gross; in such sort as they shall never be able to assemble and make head again. And what leader of skill and judgement will undertake such an enterprize in these dayes; and not forecast that a power and force assembled cannot long stand without rich and strong Towns to supply their wants; or at leastwise, without so much as is requisite to retain and keep an Army together in due order and obedience; without which there can grow nothing but confusion and ruin; be their numbers never so great.

In our late Wars.

To

THE

CONTENTS.

For the ſervice of the Horſe.

For the ſervice of the Foot.

FINIS.

MILITARY ARCHITECTURE,

OR THE ART OF

Fortifying Towns;

Together with the wayes of

DEFENDING

AND

BESIEGING

THE SAME.

By *ANDREW TACQUETT*, of the Society of *JESUS*, and Translated out of the Latine by *J. L.*

To the Right Honourable

AUBREY de VERE,

Earl of *Oxford*; Baron *Bolebec*, *Samford*, and *Badlesmere*; Chief Justice, and Justice in Eire of all His Majesties Forrests, Chaces, Parks, and Warrens on the South-side of *Trent*; Colonel of His Majesties Royal Regiment of Horse-Guards, Lord Lieutenant for His Majesty in the County of *Essex*, Knight of the most Noble Order of the Garter, and One of His Majesties most Honourable Privy Council.

My Lord,

Shall not be tedious in informing Your Lordship of the reasons which induc'd me to this Dedication. Your most Heroick Ancestors being alwayes the truest defenders of Loyalty, and eminentest Patterns of Valour; your Lordships particular disposition and affection to Martial acts, the Experience you have had in the Fortifications abroad, have Intituled you to the Patronage of these my Addresses, and given you the undoubted right to be a fit Judge of all Military designs whatsoever. And though the particular

particular favours and kindnesses which I have receiv'd from your Honourable Family (as owing my Education to the bounty of it) have sufficient force to oblige me to a most humble and grateful acknowledgment, yet in this case I laid aside those considerations, and had respect only to your Lordships self as a Souldier, furnish'd with all that may render you capable to examine either this, or any other Martial Treatise.

I am confident, My Lord, the Book in it self, how meanly soever by me Translated out of the Latine, *will not be unworthy your Lordships favourable aspect, it being the Easiest and Exactest of that Nature that ever yet was Extant, having been compiled from all Authors that have treated of that Subject by* Andrew Tacquett *of the* Society *of* Jesus, *for the use of his Pupil* Count d' Horne *of* Flanders. *The new Corrections of the* Count d' Pagan, *and* Van Ruse, *that we all so admire, but no body practises, is not here so much as spoke of; he thinking it best that men should be well grounded in the old wayes; afterwards for divertisement they may follow what Novelties they please. I shall not insist further on the praises of the Author, or obtrude him upon your Lordship by numerous commendations: If at your vacant hours you shall vouchsafe to cast an Eye upon him, I do not doubt but you will give him the esteem he deserves, and favourably accept the poor Endeavours of him who is willing to omit no opportunity of testifying himself,*

MY LORD,

Your Honours most Obliged humble Servant

John Lacy.

THE FIRST PART OF Military Architecture TREATING OF REGULAR FORTIFICATION.

CHAP. I.

Wherein is contained the Definition, Beginning, Progress, and Perfection of Military Architecture, &c.

Military Architecture is a Science how to defend and fortifie any place against the force of an Enemie.

Towns and Castles (says *Vegetius*) are either fortified by Nature, or by hands, or else by both. By Nature as being situate in some high abrupt place, or being encompass'd with the Sea, Lakes, or Rivers. The Mountains about *Cilicia* in *Asia*, and *Helvetia* of *Germany*, almost render them inaccessible.

The Rock *Aornis* baffled the force of *Hercules* and *Alexander*.

The Castles of *Namur*, and *Hermenstein*, and many others in *Europe*, are almost invincible by reason of the Rocks which lie underneath them. *Venice*, *Straltsound*, *Custrine*, and almost all *Holland*, are defended by the waters that flow about them. So that you may see Nature in her fortifying of Towns, either casts about them the Element of Earth or Water. And Art imitating Nature (as it uses to do) placed Walls and Rampars instead of Rocks and Mountains; and Moats or Ditches, where the Sea or Rivers have been wanting.

Fig. 1. But as all beginnings are wont to be, so this of fortification was altogether simple and unskilful. They rais'd their walls to such a height as might seem to deny the enemy an easie ascent by his Ladders. The breadth was such as would hold six or seven Rancks of armed men; nay *Curtius* reports the walls of *Babylon* were 32 feet broad. But this Structure had two faults in it, and both of them very dangerous. The first was that the defendants standing on their wall without any covert lay open to their Enemy. The other was that the Enemy approaching under their wall, was so secured by the wall it self, that he could not be hurt by the defendants that stood on high over him.

Fig. 2. These Errors at length they endeavour'd to remedie, by building throughout upon their wall a brestwork B C Z, the top of their brestwork they distinguish'd with Battlements Z Z Z, not joyn'd together, but left open at certain distances, so that the defendants, cover'd with these Battlements, could beat off the enemy through their open intervals; so was the first Error in some manner sublated.

Fig. 2. To mend the other they caused loopholes to be cut in the wall at a mans height from the ground, marked with the letter P P P.

Nor yet were these inconveniences perfectly taken away, for the Enemy lying within the triangles D E F, G K H, would escape the shot of the Townsmen.

Fig. 3. Therefore they began to look on a flancquing or side defence, and still keeping their battlements and loopholes they built round their work square Turrets that ran out beyond the thickness of the walls, and so they added to their fore-right defence (which was only then in use) a flancquing or side defence; but this same side defence was as yet imperfect, because the Enemy could be hid within the triangle I P K; besides square Towers were not thought able enough to bear the brunt of Engines and and battering Rams.

Fig. 4. Therefore slighting their square Turrets they made round ones; so the Triangle A C B, in which the Enemy was hid, became so much lessened, that now he could not traverse his battering Engines within it; and the Round form of Turrets was found to stand firmer than any other against the force of the batteries. And here the Art and endeavour of the Ancients rested, till Gunpowder being found, men began to imitate Thunder and Lightning. And indeed this last way of Fortification was far better than the former. Neverthelesse the business went yet suspected, for the Triangle A C B, was found large enough to shelter *Pioneers*, besides the flancquing defence F C, D E, could scowr only one point of the round Towers, B C A, because round bodies cannot be touched by right lines but in one point only.

At last Art conquered it self, and found out that way of defence which we now use, turning the Walls into Rampars, and the round Turrets into Bulwarks fitted with face and flancque; and enclosed the whole Fortification with right or streight lines. To conclude, it is brought so to pass, that the Enemy let him stand where he will, shall lie open to the Shot of the defendants, and all the parts of the Fortification mutually defend one another.

Being about to treat of this last manner of fortification, I will keep such Order, that when I shall have expounded the terms that are used in this matter, I shall then propose the Rules and Principles of the Art; and thus instructed, at last, God willing, we will fall upon the practice it self.

CHAP.

CHAP. II.

The Terms of Military Architecture are Expounded.

1. A Fortification is a Place having such a Circumference, whose each part receives from other parts a Flancquing or side Defence, besides the fore-right Defence they yield themselves. So that all parts mutually scowre one another. One part is said to scowr or flanque one another, when it can defend it with the parallel shot of a Gun. So the part of the Circumference X B C scowrs the part F G; the part A E F scowrs C D: So of the rest. *Fig.* 5.

2. To delineate a Fortification, is to describe the out-lines of the Fortification.

3. A Regular Fortification is built upon a Regular Figure, hath all its parts equal and like placed.

4. A Regular Figure, is that which hath equal sides and angles; such is the Figure H K R P M N, all whose sides K R, R P, P M, M N, N K, and angles N, M, P, R, K, are equal among themselves: About this a Circle may be circumscrib'd, that shall have the same Center H, as the Figure hath. The Angle of the Center is th at which is contain'd between two Semidiameters K H, R H. The Angle of the Circumference, or of the Figure, is that which was contain'd between the sides of the Figure, as M, P, *&c.*

5. An Irregular Fort, is that which is built on an Irregular Figure; an Irregular Figure is that which hath neither Sides nor Angles equal.

6. A Bulwork or Bastion, is that part of the Fort B D H L M which most of all runs into the field. *Fig.* 6.

7. A C, B D, Are the flanques of the Bulwork.

8. D H, C G, The face of the Bulwork.

9. B F, M F, The gorge or neck of the Bulwork.

10. F H, E G, The Capital lines.

11. A B, The Courtine.

12. If the flanque of the Bulwork be divided in the point 2, and on the inside you take 5, 3, equal to 2, B, and joyn the points 2, 3, the part 3 D, or that curved Line within it is called *Orillon*, or eare of the Bulwork; and the rest of it 3, 5, is called the *Flancq; Couvert*; but the use of these *Orillons* are almost out of date.

13. C Q, The flanque prolonged.

14. Q G, The front or surface.

15. B G, The fichant line of defence.

16. R G, The flanquing line of defence.

17. K B, The flanque of the Courtine, called by the French, *the second Flanque*; it is that part of the Courtine which lies betwixt the flanque of the Bastion D B, and the flanquing line of defence K G.

18. E F, the side of the inward Polygon or Figure.

19. G H, The side of the outward Polygon, or the distance of the Bastions.

20. P E, P F, The Radius of the inward Polygon, or Figure.

21. P G, P H, The Radius of the outward Polygon.

22. E P F, The Angle of the Center. *Vide def.* 4.

23. A E O, The Angle of the Figure. *Vide def.* 4.

24. N G C, The Angle of the Bulwork, called in French *Angle Flancque.*

25. K C A, I D B, The Angle of the flanque, and flanquing line of defence, called in French, *Angle de la flancquant & du flancq;*

26, C K A, D I B, The Angle of the flanquing Line of Defence and Courtine, called in French, *Angle flancquant interieur.*

27. A C G, The Angle of the flanque and face.

28. G T H, The Angle of defence, in French, *angle flancquant exterieur*; *Angle de tenailles.*

29. D S H, The Angle determining the flanque. *Angle forme flanque*

There are several sorts of Fortifications, as to their Magnitude.

30. *A Fort Royal,* Is that whose fichant line does not exceed a Musquet-shot, and is used most in fortifying Cities and great places.

31. *The middle sort of Fort Royal,* Is that whose fichant line is less than Musquet-shot, but the distance of the Bulworks more.

32. *The lesser sort of Fort Royal,* Is that whose Bulworks are distant just Musquet-shot.

Those that are less, are called *Castles, Forts,* &c. We shall expound the Orthographical terms, or the Profile, commonly called *the uprights,* in the 7th Chapter following.

CHAP. III.

The Canons or principal Rules of Fortification.

1. THe end of Fortification, is that few may resist many.

2. The form of the Fort must be such, that all its parts may receive an oblique flanquing-side defence, beside the fore-right defence they afford themselves.

3. Therefore each part of the Fortification, must flanque and be flanqued. The manner of flanquing is this: The face, which is the weakest part of the Fortification, is defended by the flanques of the Bulwork and Courtine, as also by the oppo- Fig. 5. site face: The flanque of the Bulwork are defended by the Courtine, and the Courtine by the Flanques. *Vid. fig.* 5.

Fig. 6. 4. The shorter and obliquer the defence lines are, so much the stronger and surer. Now the Lines of defence will be so much the obliquer, as the Angle of defence G T H, shall be acuter.

Fig. 6. 5. The Fichant line B G, A G must not exceed a Musquet-shot, that is 750 or 720 feet. The Bullet may be carried farther, but not to do execution at a mark. The Fichant line among all the Lines of the Fort is the chief, and doth it self determinate the bigness of all the rest.

Note. *When we shall make mention of feet, you must understand them to be* Rhyneland *feet.*

6. Above all, care must be taken to make the flanquing parts of the Fortification as large as you can.

7. Therefore let the flanque of the Bulwork be of a just bigness, and make the second flanque as large as you can: For that Fort is far the strongest, which keeping the Rest of the Maxims, hath also flanques in the Courtine.

8. Let the Courtine be of a just length, let it be more than the face, and the flanques of the Bulwork joyn'd, because it is the strongest part of the Fort.

Fig. 6. 9. Let the Angle of the Bulwork N G C, be able to resist the force of Canon, and consequently not less than 60 degrees; for experience hath taught us that such a one will suffice.

10. A Right Angle for the Bulwork is the best, but to gain it you must not omit or cut away too much of the second flanque.

11. The Angle of the Flanque and Courtine C A K, must alwaies be a right Angle: For so, as well the Courtine as the Face will be more largly flanqued and defended, and consequently more sure and commodious, and the Angle of the Face and Flanque will be bigger, and therefore stronger. *Fig. 6.*

12. Let the Gorge or neck-line A C, F H, be large, least the Bulwork be straitned. *Fig. 6.*

13. Let the quantity of the Bulwork be such as may receive a sufficient number of armed Men, and yield room enough for the traversing Guns, and performing other Military duties.

The Bulwork is chiefly straitned for these reasons; if you lessen the Face, and keep the same Angle for the Bulwork, and consequently increase the Flanques: Or if you retain the same Flanques, and increase the Angle of the Bulwork.

14. At length, that I may contract the Rules above-mentioned, and many others into one, that form of a Fortification will be the best, that hath the largest Flanques in the Bulwork and Courtine, the Gorge Lines very spacious, the Angle of the Bulwork a Right Angle, or near a right Angle; and the Fichant Line, at most, not to exceed a Musquet-shot.

That this form may be had in Regular Figures, the proportion of the Courtine, Face, Flanque and Neck, will be as follows.

15. Let not the Face be less than half the Courtine, nor bigger than the whole.

16. The Flancque must not be less than a fourth part of the Face, nor bigger than half the Face.

17. The Gorge Line must not be less than the Flanque.

In these three *Dogen* and *Goldman* agree: The reason of them you may see in the Account of the Fifth Chapter.

CHAP. IV.

Being an Explanation of the foregoing Maxims.

ALL the reason and proportion of our Fortification will rely on the Rules delivered in the last Chapter. Therefore 'twill be here necessary more fully to declare them; especially those which sometimes all Ingineers did not approve of. The first, second, and third want no exposition.

About the 4th and 5th, although now no body disagree, yet there was a time when men did doubt them. Some Military Architects, those chiefly that flourisht in the former Age, did order such a distance for the Bastions, that the Fichant Line, or the longest Line of defence, should not a little exceed a Musquet shot. The Reason they brought was, that the place might better be defended with great Guns than with Musquets: And therefore, because great Guns cannot be so well level'd against an Enemy that's near, they required a greater distance for their Bulworks, and so the charge would be the less, the Town being defended with fewer Bulworks. But this way, by all modern Ingineers, is neglected, who with one consent remove the Bulworks to such a distance, that the Fichant Line might be measur'd with a Musquet-shot. What reason our former Architects brought for their opinion, is plainly none at all. For both by Reason and Experience 'tis evident, Towns may be better defended with Musquets than with Cannons; for the use of great Guns is very costly, slow, difficult; the execution they do, very rare and uncertain, so that 'tis become a Proverb, *He is curst in his Mothers belly, that's kil'd with a Cannon bullet.* And if a great Gun should be made useless, by being dismounted, or by the death of the Gunner, or some other mischance, all the Flanquing defence is lost, to the great incouragement of the Besiegers. On the contrary, the use of Musquets is not costly, but easie, ready, quick, and sure. For who will deny, that an Enemy may not better be beat off with a thousand small Shot than one great Gun? A thing so clear needs no more arguments. Therefore let stand what we have appointed, the Fichant line to be measured by a Musquet-shot.

Nor do we exclude the use of great Guns from our defence; for in this modern way of Fortification, they may and ought to be admitted usefully: We only perswade, that the chief of the defence may rather be committed to Musquets than to Cannons.

What we ordered in the 6th. and 7th. Rules, is the chiefest concern in the whole business of Fortification. The Faces of the Bulworks, because they lye farther out than any of the other parts, are the weakest parts of the Fortification: The Flanque and Courtine are the strongest, for they lie farther from the Enemy, and being near to one another, stoutly defend themselves. Since then the Face is a place weaker than the rest, and which the Enemy most usually attaques, we ought with our chiefest care to help it.

Fig. 7. There are two sorts of Bulworks. In the first, the Face G V C, produced, falls upon the end of the Courtine F; for which reason the Face G C can only be defended from the Flanque of the Bulwork.

Fig. 5. In the second form of Bulwork, the Face G F produced, does not fall upon the end of the Courtine, but in another point of it X, so that it leaves out a part of the Courtine X B, which is called the Flanque of the Courtine, from which the Face may be as well defended and scowred as from the Flanque of the Bulwork B C. The first they follow, that would have the Angle of the Bulwork a right Angle, in all Figures above a Pentagon.

The latter the *Dutch* first receiv'd, and made use of; who judged it best for their advantage to add to their defence second Flanques in the Courtine, though with the loss of a right Angle even in a *Duodekagon*. Neither is there any doubt, but this method is far better than the former, since it doth not only sufficiently provide for the Angle of the Bulwork, which it never makes less than 60 degrees, but also increases the defence of the Faces often to twice as much as the former.

The Reason of the 8th Rule, which bids the Courtine be of a just length, is, that among all the parts of the Fortification the Courtine is the strongest: For it lies distant from the Enemy farther than any other of the parts, and placed betwixt two Bulworks, is very strongly defended. Now 'tis very agreeable to reason, that the strongest parts of the Fortification should be longer than the weaker: Yet do not extend the Courtine so far as to make the Fichant line above Musquet-shot, for that is against the 5th Rule. The fittest proportion will be, if with *Dogen* or *Fritach*, you give it 432 feet, or with *Goldman* 480 feet.

The 9th and 10th Cannon treats of the Angle of the Bulwork; where a right Angle is preferr'd before any other, provided it do not too much obstruct the rest of the Rules.

For the better understanding the Reason of this Rule, you must note, that right and obtuse Angles do resist the Cannon shot with their whole bodies, but an Acute one
Fig. 7. doth not with all his body. Let there be a right angled Bulwork F O B Q P; and
Fig. 6. another Acute angled M L H D B. Now suppose the Bullets to fall in B O, the Face
Fig. 7. of the right angled Bulwork F O B Q P, from the Guns planted in R, by perpendicular strait-lines R B, R S. Therefore because the two strait Lines R B, B Q, are both perpendicular to B O, by supposition, in the same point B they will make one strait Line R B Q, by the 14. *l.* 1. *Euclide*. From whence it is manifest, that the side of a right angled Bulwork B Q, objects its whole self against the perpendicular shot R B: and so consequently a right-angled Bulwork doth with his whole bulk oppose and resist all the perpendicular shots R S.

The

The same thing may be demonstrated by stronger reason in an obtuse Angle: But in an Acute Angle M L H D B, the perpendicular shots S H, S Q, being continued on, or protracted, in a little space falls within the Bulwork, and so it appears the Bulwork doth not object its whole body against the shot. From whence you may gather, that an Acute Angle is weaker than either a Right or obtuse Angle. Fig. 6.

These things being known, 'tis plainly manifest why a right Angle should be prefer'd before an acute Angle; that is, if it can be had without prejudice to the rest of the Maxims: And why it should rather be chosen than an obtuse one. These are the Reasons.

The first is, that keeping the same Flancques Q P, O F, and the same Gorge Lines P E, F E, the Bulwork will be very much straitned, which is against the 13th Rule; and the Angle of the shoulders P Q B made so much the less. Fig. 7.

The other and chiefest reason is, that the obtuser the Angle is, the lesser will be the Flanque of the Courtine, or else all lost.

Therefore a Right Angle, or one near a Right Angle, must be given to the Bulwork as oft as may be, but so that one clause in the Rule be not neglected, which forbids you to spoil the second Flanque for the desire of a right Angle: And because in a *Hexagon*, and the figures following to a *Duodekagon*, a Right Angle in the Bulwork will cut off the second Flanque in the Courtine, we judge it better, with most of the famous Engineers of this Age, to detract something from the Angle of the Bulwork, keeping notwithstanding a due strength for him, than to want the Flanque in the Courtine to the prejudice of our defence, which will be so much lessened. *Barleduc* and others followed the contrary; but most people now a dayes being taught by Experience, the School-mistriss of all things, have forsaken them.

The reason and sense of the rest of the Rules is so plain, that they need no farther Explanation.

CHAP. V.

The constitution of Regular Fortifications.

THe Definitions and Principles of the Science being now expounded, we will come to the thing it self.

That the Constitution of a Fortification may be found, some things ought to be given. Those things here are said to be given, which we take at our discretion, so that none depend on, or prejudice one another. Now from these *Data* once order'd, the proportion of the rest of the parts follows sure and determin'd according to the Reason of the things given. Therefore 'twill be the part of a skilful Ingineer to choose those *Data* which may best agree with the Rules establish't in the third and fourth Chapters, and make the parts agree which depend on them. Fig. 6.

Furthermore, because these *Data* may be varied without any prejudice to our Maxims of Fortification, the Constitution also of Fortification will be various. I shall choose and propose six of the best and most approved. The proportion of the Lines will serve for any form, the quantity for the *Royal* only.

The First Manner

Is *Goldmans*. Let the Face be half the Courtine in what Figure soever.

	Feet	
The Courtine	480.	
The Face	240.	
The Flancq; in A 4 Ang.	60.	*That is* $\frac{1}{4}$ *of the Face.*
in A 5 Ang.	80.	*That is* $\frac{1}{3}$ *of the Face.*

In the rest of the Figures up to a nine-angled Polygon 10 feet are alwaies added to the flanque, till in a Nonangle the Flanque becomes 120 feet, that is $\frac{1}{2}$ the face, which quantity is retain'd for the flanque in all the following figures.

The Angle of the Bulwork is made of half the Angle of the Figure, increas'd with 15 degrees. Therefore it will be

In a … angled figure	Degr.
4	60.
5	69.
6	75.
7	79. 17'9". or in decimals 79,286
8	82. 30. or 82.5. in decimals.
9	85.
10	87.
11	88. 38'. 11". or 88. 63.64. in decimals
12	90. or a right Angle, which is retain'd in all figures following.

From these *Data*, or things given, the proportion of the rest of the lines will arise, which the following Table shews you.

	Radius.	*Capital.*	*Gorge.*	*Flanque2.*	*Fichant.*
IV	494.5.5.8.	172.6.9.9.	109.7.0.6.	256.0.7.7	722.2.2.2.
V	595.2.9.3.	197.9.1.1.	109.9.0.2.	254.0.8.7	724.1.5.7.
VI	713.4.8.6.	209.9.7.6.	116.7.5.3.	262.7.2.1	724.9.0.9.
VII	833.8.5.8.	222.0.5.6.	121.7.9.3.	262.0.1.1.	726.2.5.4.
VIII	955.6.6.1.	233.9.6.4.	125.7.1.3.	256.9.4.2.	728.0.7.4.
IX	1078.5.0.8.	245.6.2.8.	128.8.7.0.	249.4.8.2.	730.3.1.7.
X	1212.6.0.7.	246.5.9.2	134.7.1.7.	258.9.8.8.	729.6.3.3.
XI	1347.0.8.3.	247.5.4.3	139.5.2.1.	266.3.2.1.	729.0.3.5.
XII	1481.8.8.6.	248.4.6.0.	143.5.4.0.	272.1.5.4.	728.5.1.5.

In this Table the figures before the separating line are Rhynland feet; the rest are 10ths, 100ths, 1000ths, parts of a foot, &c.

In this first manner of Fortification there are four things given besides the species of the Figure. *Viz.* The Courtine, the Face, Flanque, and Angle of the Bulwork, who themselves agree with our Rules, and also the rest of the Lines which follow from them; as the Gorge, second Flanque, and the flanquing and fichant lines of defence, which you will find to be true, if by the help of the *Trigonometrie* you calculate the quantities of each of the parts out of the *Data*, or things given; of which we shall speak in the following Chapter. I shall here only mention two things: That is, is, the second Flanque in this way will be larger than in any other, so as to exceed half the Courtine. And the Gorge line be alwayes above a 100 feet.

The Second Manner

Is *Dogens*. The face is 24 perches, or 288 *Rhynland* feet.
The Courtine 36 perches.

Therefore the proportion of the Courtine to the face is *sesquialter* or as 3, to 2. which is observ'd in all the following methods.

The Angle forming the flanque is 40 degrees always.

The Angle of the Bulwork is ½ the Angle of the figure increas'd with 15 degr. as in the first manner. *Goldman, Marolois* and *Fritach,* agree in the Angle of the Bulwork.

Note, that the Perch we speak of contains 12 *Rhynland* feet.

The Third Manner

Is *Dogens* second. It differs from the second in the last *datum* only, for it makes the Angle of the Bulwork equal to two thirds of the Angle of the figure, therefore 'twill be

			degr.
	4		60
	5		72
In a	6	Angle	80
	7		85. 42'. 51". or 85.71428 in *Decimals*.
	8		90. which will serve in all that follow.

	Rad.	*Capital.*	*Gorge.*	*Flanq;* 1.	*Flanq;* 2.	*Fichant.*
IV.	38. 50	19.73	9.23	7.74	7. 10	60. 80
V.	49. 05	20. 40	10. 83	9.09	8. 03	61. 10
VI.	60.00	21. 10	12.00	10. 07	8. 33	61. 34
VII.	70. 80	21.75	12.9	10. 83	8. 41	61. 54
VIII	82. 66	22. 32	13.63	11. 44	8. 39	61. 72
IX.	93.08	23. 15	13.83	11. 61	11. 10	61. 74
X.	103. 62	23. 83.	14. 62	11. 76	12. 91	61. 70
XI.	114. 26	24. 40	14. 19	11. 91	14. 19	61. 68
XII.	124.97	24. 88	14. 34	12. 04	15. 15.	61. 66

The numbers in this Table before the points are perches of Rhynland that contain 12 feet, the rest are 10ths, 100ths, of a perch,

The Fourth Manner.

Is *Dogens* third, *Fritachs* first.

Let the Courtine be 36 perches.

The face 24 perches.

The Angle of the Bulwork ½ the Angle of the Figure increased with 20 degr.

			Perches
	4		6.72
	5		7. 84
	6		8. 96
The *Flanque* in a	7	Angle is	9. 108
	8		10. 12
	9		11. 132
	10		12. 144 which is kept in all the following Fig.

The

The Fifth Manner

Is *Fritach's* second.
Let the Courtine be 36 perches.
The Face 24.
The Angle of the Bulwork half the Angle of the Figure increased with 15 degr. as in the first manner and the second.

			Perches
	4		8. 96
	5		9. 108
The Flanque in a	6	Angle is	10.12
	7		11. 132
	8		12.144 the same always in the following Fig.

Out of these *Data*, the proportion of the rest of the parts that follows, which the Table underneath will shew you.

	Rad.	*Capital.*	*Gorge.*	*Flanq*; 2.	*Fichant.*
IV.	38. 14	20.01	8.97	6. 14	*little exceeding 60 Rods or Perches.*
V.	48.08	21.03	10. 26	10. 51	
VI.	58. 19	22. 15	11. 08	11. 86	
VII.	68.47	23.31	11. 71	12.03	
VIII.	78.60	24.48	12.16	11.67	
IX.	90.31	24.64	12.89	12.95	
X.	101. 84	24.66	13.47	13.90	
XI.	113.38	24.76	13.95	14.63	
XII.	124.77	24.85	14.29	15.22	

The numbers before the points are perches, the rest are 10ths. 100ths. of a perch.

The Sixth Manner

Is *Dogen's* Fourth.
Let the Courtine be 36 perches.
The face 24.
The Angle forming the Flanque always 40 degr.
The Angle of the Bulwork as in the fourth manner. Therefore it will be

			degr.	
	4		65.	
	5		75.	
	6		80.	
In a	7	Angle	84.	17.9
	8		87.	30
	9		90.	And so always after.

All these several ways of Fortification agree with the Canons delivered in the 3 d. and 4 th. Chapters. *The Fourth* seems least in use (so I gather out of *Fritach* pag. 15.) *The Fifth* is more used. *The Second and Third* are much alike. Betwixt these (*viz.* the second and third) and the fourth, the *Sixth* is a mean, which according to *Dogen* is to be prefer'd before them. *The First* goes beyond all the rest for the largeness

largeneſs of the ſecond Flanque,and comes ſhort of all the reſt in the firſt Flanque ,the neck, the faces, and in the Angle of the Bulwork. Whence it is conſequent, he ſhould have his Bulworks leſs than any of the reſt. His Courtine is larger than the others by 48 feet. This ſeems to be leſs in uſe than any of the other.

The *Data*, or things given in the ſecond and fifth, differ about the Flanque, which in the fifth is bigger: For which reaſon it hath its Gorge line and ſecond Flanque leſſer. The third and fourth in their *Data's* differ about the Angle of the Bulwork and the Flanque. The Flanque in the fourth is leſſer: the Angle of the Bulwork is bigger, except in a *Hexagon*. Where, &c.

But all theſe wayes are approved; let every one take that which pleaſes him beſt.

And ſo have we order'd the conſtitution of each way in Fortification: But by what Art the quantities of the reſt of the Angles, and Lines depending on the things given, are found out of each of the things given; that is, by what method the Tables above were made, we muſt ſeek for in the following Rules.

How to find the Angles.

1. The Angle of the Center of any Regular Figure is had, if you divide 360 degr. by the number of its Angles. See the *Scholium* of the 16 *Propoſ.* of the fourth of *Euclid.* ſet out by me. *Fig.* 6.

	IV	V	VI	VII	VIII	IX	X	XI	XII
The Angle of the *Center*.	90.	72.	60.	51, 43′,38″.	45.	40.	36.	32, 43′,38″.	30.
The Angle of the *Figure*.	90.	108.	120.	128.34′,17″.	135.	140.	144.	147,16′,22″,	150.

2. The Angle of the Figure, or of the Circumference is found, if you ſubſtract the Angle of the Center from the right Angles, that is 180 degrees. For the Angle of the Center P, together with the Angles P E F, P F E, makes two right ones. 32. 1. but theſe are half the Angle of the Figure, and ſo joyn'd together make up the whole Angle of the Figure. Therefore the Angle of the Center, with the Angle of the Figure, makes two right ones. Therefore, &c.

3. The Angle of the Bulwork is found after this manner: By the foregoing Rule find the Angle of the Figure, and add to its half 15 degr.

4. The Angle G K A or C K A, will be diſcover'd, if you deduct half the Angle of the Bulwork from half the Angle of the Figure. For becauſe G H, E F are parallel, the Angle E G Q is equal to P E F; and G K A equal to C G Q. Therefore, &c.

5. The Angle A C K is had by ſubſtracting the Angle laſt found C K A, from 90 degr. For ſince C A K is a right Angle; A C K, C K A, muſt make another right Angle.

6. The Angle G T H will be found after this manner. Double the Angle C K A, which ſubſtract from 180 degr. the remainder is the Angle I T K, or G T H. For the Angles C K A, D I B, are equal by conſtruction; therefore C K A doubled, is equal to them both. Now theſe two Angles being known in the Triangle I T K, the third alſo will be known, *Euclid.* 32. 1. and the Angle I T K is proved equal to G T H, by the 15. 1.

7. The Angle A C G is diſcovered, if you ſubſtract A C K from 180 degr. for A C K, and A C G, make two right Angles. *Eucl.* 13. 1.

8. To find the Angle G E A, ſubſtract P E F, half the Angle of the Figure found in the ſecond Rule, from 180 degrees: For P E F, G E A, are equal to two Right Angles. 13. 1.

How to find the Lines.

1. The Lines AK, CK.

Fig. 6. In the Right angled Triangle A C K the Flanque A C is given; and the Angles C & K are found by the fifth and fourth Rules. Therefore the Sides AK, CK, will be found by Trigonometrie.

2. The Flanque in the Courtine, and the flanquing Line of defence.

The Face which is given being added to C K found out last, gives the flanquing Line of defence G K; and A K one of the Lines last found, being deducted from the Courtine that is given, leaves the Flanque in the Courtine B K.

3. The Lines G Q, Q C.

In the right angled Triangle G Q C, the Face G C is given; and the Angles are already found in the fourth Rule. For Q G C is equal to G K A; therefore G Q, Q C will be found.

4. The outward side of the Polygon G H.

To G Q doubled, add the Courtine which is given.

5. The Line A Q.

To the Flanque which is given, add the Line Q C, found out in the third Rule.

6. The Capitals G E, G Z.

In the right angled Triangle G Z E, the Angle E G Z is found; for it is equal to P E F, half the angle of the Figure; and the side Z E, or Q A, is found by the fifth Rule; therefore G E, G Z, are found.

7. The Gorge Line A E.

Substract G Z, found in the sixth Rule, from G Q, found in the third Rule, and there remains Z Q, or E A.

8. The side of the inward Polygon E F.

Add the Courtine which is given, to the Gorge line doubled, found out in the foregoing Rule.

9. The Radius P E, Y P.

In the right angled Triangle E Y P, the side E Y is found (for 'tis half the side of the Figure found out in the last Rule) and the Angle P E Y found in the second Rule of Angles; therefore the sides E P, Y P, will be found.

10. The bigger Radius G P.

Add the Capital to the lesser Radius.

11. The Fichant line of defence B G.

Out of the sum of the Squares of G R, B R, extract the Root, and that shall give G B. The demonstration is from the 47. 1. of *Euclid*. R B is found out in the fifth Rule. G R is had, if to Z R, or E B, the sum of the Courtine and Gorge line you add G Z, found in the sixth Rule.

And so you have the compleat constitution of Fortification. Nor will it now be difficult for one that is not altogether unskilful in *Trigonometrie*, which I have have taught in the third Chapter of my first Book of *Practical Geometrie*, to find all the Lines and Angles by the like method out of what *Data* soever.

CHAP.

CHAP. VI.

The delineation of Regular Fortifications, either on Paper, or in the Field.

SInce that in the foregoing Chapter the quantities of the Lines and Angles of Fortifications are determined; to delineate the same either on Paper or in the Field, there is nothing more required than what I have taught in my *Practical Geometrie*. Therefore in the tenth Chapter of my *Practical Geometrie* you'l find what you desire digested into ten Problems.

CHAP. VII.

An Explanation of the Orthographical Terms.

HItherto I have deliver'd the delineation of Regular Fortification: That is, I have describ'd the out-circuit of the Rampar only: But now I pass to the Orthography, in which all the parts of the Fortification, as to their height and thickness, are contain'd. The beginning, as it uses to be, is drawn from the Explication of Terms.

The Horizontal Line is A E S V Z.

The Orthography of a Fortification, is a Section of a Fortification made by a place per pendicular to the Horizon, showing the height, thickness and position of each part in the Fortification: It is shown in the eighth Figure. *Fig.* 8.

The Rampar A L I K E is a body of Earth surrounding the whole Fortification, it includes also the Bulworks.

The breadth or thickness of the base of the Rampar A E.

The thickness of the top of the Rampar L 3.

The outward sloaping, or rectination of the Rampar 3 E, called in French *penchant du Rempar Exterieur*.

The outward *Talu*, or Line forming the sloap of the Rampar E F, called in French *le Talu Exterieur du Rempar*.

The inward sloaping or rectination of the Rampar A L, *Penchant du Rempar Interieur*.

The height of the Rampar B L, *Haulteur du Rempar*.

The brestwork of the Rampar, in French called *Parapett*, 4 G I K 3. It is a bulk of earth surrounding the whole Fortification rais'd upon the Rampar to a mans height.

The thickness of the base of the Brestwork D 3.

The thickness of the top of the Breitwork O K: You must take no notice of the little line intercepted betwixt I T, I D.

The sloap or inclination of the top of the Brestwork I K.

The outward sloaping or rectination of the Brestwork K 3; 'tis in a direct or strait line with the outward sloap of the Rampar E 3.

The outward *Talu*, or Line forming the slope of the Brestwork 3 2; *Talu Exterieur du Parapett*.

The inward Sloap or reclination of the Brestwork T D, *penchant interieur du parapett.*

The inward *Talu* or Line forming the inward Sloap of the Brestwork D T, *Talu Interieur du parapett.*

The Step of the Brestwork D G, called in *French* Banquet.

The plain or Walk upon the Rampar L 4, in french *Terreplein.*

The Fauss Bray, or *Parapett des Rondes,* 5 N P Q R, it is a Brestwork rais'd round the Fort at the foot of the Rampar, principally used for the defence of Moats or wet Ditches, and in all things like to the upper Brestwork.

The plain or walk of the Fauss Bray E 5, or *Chemin des Rondes.*

The Bank-side of the Ditch R S, *Lisier.*

The Ditch S 87 V, *Le Fosse.*

The inward sloaping descent of the Ditch S 8, *Escarpe.*

The inward *Talu* or Line forming the inward sloap of the Ditch, S H, *Talu interieur du Fosse.*

The outward sloaping descent of the Ditch V 7, *Contrescarpe.*

The outward *Talu,* or Line forming the outward Sloap of the Ditch, V 5, *Talu exterieur du Fosse.*

The lower width of the Ditch, 87.

The upper width of the Ditch, S V.

The depth of the Ditch 8 H, 75. *profundeur du Fosse.*

The Couvert way, N 6, *Chemin Couvert Corridor.*

The Brestwork of the Couvert way 6 X, Y Z, *parapett du chemin Couvert.*

Its Base O Z, *peid ou base du parapett de chemin couvert.*

Its outward sloaping, Y Z.

Note, that this Orthographical Section is not drawn by the Courtine, but by the Face of the Bulwork; and so the Lines 87, S V, *do represent the width of the Ditch or Moat that washes the Bulwork, which you must always understand, when there shall any mention be made of the width of the Ditch.*

CHAP. VIII.

Wherein are determined the Orthographical dimensions or the Profiles of Fortifications, and first, those of the Rampar, and Brestwork rais'd upon the Rampar.

THe sole and main business of the delineation hitherto expounded, was truly to constitute or form the Rampars circumference, compleated with Faces, Flanque and Courtine, which indeed is the fundamental & principal work of all Martial Structures. But now to prescribe the dimensions of the Rampar it self, and the rest of its parts, as to their height and thickness, is the business of Orthography. Every Fortification consists almost of these parts, (*viz.*) Rampar, Brestwork, Fauss bray, Ditch or Moat, the Couvert way, and an out-Brestwork. Yet if the Ditch be dry, the Fauss-bray both may, and is wont to be omitted. In this Chapter we shall speak of the dimensions of the Rampar and Brestwork.

The *Spartans* in former times would not defend their City with Walls and Ditches: and King *Agesilaus* showing his armed citizens to one that asked why *Sparta* wanted Walls, said, that those were the Walls of *Sparta*. This was plainly a foolish and empty ostentation of strength, relying on no sound councel, but only rashness; which

the

the experience of all nations hath condemn'd, and which the *Spartans* had almost found fatal to themselves in the *Theban* War. But leaving this wee'l come to the purpose.

I. For the Stuff or matter to make the Rampar.

The Rampar must not be made of wood nor stone, but Earth; this is every where at hand, and ready to come by, and is easily heaped up to such a thickness that the Rampar may be Cannon Proof, besides, Earth by its yielding and giving way does sooner master and break the force of the Shot. Yet I do not prefer a bare Earthen Rampar before one cased with stone, of which I shall speak hereafter.

II. The height of the Rampar.

There is hardly any thing so destructive to a Fortification as a high Rampar. This errour hath been committed in most of the ancient Fortifications, especially those of the most famous cities in *Europe*; for these high Rampars flatter the sight, and make a show of Strength where there is none, when indeed they spoyl the whole defence, and betray the Town to the Enemy; and least so great mischief might be had *gratis*, the Treasury must be also drain'd to obtain it.

The fault of high Rampars consists chiefly in this, that they shelter the enemy when he draws near them from the Shot of the Townsmen. This to its own great loss, *Breda* hath taught us, when it was last besieged by the *Hollanders*.

Prince *Maurice* had fortified this Town with great care and expence, so that it might seem to be reckon'd one of the compleatest Fortifications of *Europe*; but the height of the Rampar flattering his sight, as I said, deceived him. The Inhabitants of *Breda* being afterwards besieged by *Frederick*, *Mauritius* his Brother, were not able from their high Rampar with all their Cannon to remove the enemy approaching nearer unto them, nor his Blinds stealing by degrees upon them; whence they were forced to cut holes in several places of their high Rampar that was rais'd at such great charges, and pull it down, and level it, to make a place for lower Batteries, from whence they might surer hit and break the fatal Blinds of the Enemy. But these high Rampars cannot be so mended, but they'l be marr'd worse in another point; for while they are cut in many places, the binding together and joynting of the work is loosned, so that 'twill easily fall if batter'd with the Enemies Cannon.

But a Rampar that rises to an indifferent height hath not this deadly inconvenience, as is manifest in it self; nay and Musquet Shot doth more Execution from a low Station than from a high one; For let there be two heights, A B the bigger, A C the lesser, and let the Line D E at the height of a man stand perpendicular upon the *Horizon*: Now it is clear the line or Shot which is directed from C to E, shall fall beyond that line or Shot which shall be directed from B to E, and intercepts a larger space on the Earth D F; whereas the other from B passing through E, intercepts only the space D G: Therefore more ground may be scowred from a low place than from a higher. *Fig.9.*

But perhaps those that are the Patrons of high Rampars will say they cannot be so easily climb'd, and that the Enemies approaches may better be discovered from them.

I answer the inconvenience now alledged must prevail, for an ordinary height will sufficiently hinder the ascent of the Enemy; and for discovering his approaches you may raise Cavalliers in the Bulworks.

III. The height is determin'd.

Therefore let not the height of the Rampar exceed 18 *Rhynland* feet, nor be less then 10 feet, for this would expose the City to the Enemies Shot; the other suffices, more would make you fall into the error spoken of before in the second number.

Engineers by reason of the several magnitudes of Fortifications, prescribe several heights, but meerly by guess.

In	IV.	V.	VI.	VII.	VIII.	&c. The height of the Rampar.
feet	12.	14.	15.	16.	18	

If Hills should hang over the Town, you must not for that reason raise your Rampar above 18 feet, but raise Cavalliers in your Bulworks, or præoccupate those higher places with Outworks.

IV. The Talu of the Rampar or Line forming the Sloape.

The Rampar must be so built that both without and within it may be sloaping, for a body of Earth cannot like a Wall rise to a perpendicle.

Fig. 8. The inward *Talu* A B, must be always equal to the height B L, that upon any sudden occasion the Souldiers might easily run up to their Rampar.

The outward *Talu* E F, is most commonly half the height, and it would be requisite to make it less if the Earth be firm: If the ground be very loose, it may be made equal to two thirds of the height; but if the outward *Talu* be too big, it gives the Enemy an easie ascent, as appear'd in the memorable taking of the Fort of *Schinkin*.

V. The upper thickness of the Rampar.

Fig. 8. The upper thickness of the Rampar L 3, must not be only such as may bear the force of Cannon, but ought to be so big, that after its Brestwork is set on, whose lower thickness must be 24 feet, (else not Cannon Proof,) together with the step or Banquet D 4 three feet broad, yet it may also have remaining a plain or walk called in French *Terreplein* 4 L, large enough for the traversing great Guns. Therefore 'twill be most an end 51 or 57 *Rhynland* feet; a thickness much exceeding this will be superfluous, and for no other use than draining the Exchequer. And here also your Engineers for the diversity of the figures prescribe several thicknesses, and meerly again by guess.

In	IV.	V.	VI.	VII.	VIII.	IX.	The upper thickness of the Rampar.
feet	36.	39.	44.	48.	51.	57.	

And because Rampars and their Brestworks ought to be Cannon proof, I will briefly add, how much ground a Shot can penetrate. A whole Cannon at 400 feet distance, with a Ball of 48 pound, shall strike 20 feet deep into firm Earth. A Demy-Cannon at the distance of 300 feet with a Ball of 24 *l.* shall enter 12 feet of firm ground. A Field piece at the distance of 200 feet, with a Ball of 12 *l.* shall pass through about 7 feet of firm ground. This *Goldman* reports. But if the ground be loose, it will penetrate far deeper. *Dogen* denies that 20 feet of any ordinary Earth can be pierced with whole Cannon Shot.

VI. The lower thickness of the Rampar.

Fig. 8. The lower thickness of the Rampar is found, if to the upper thickness L 3 or B F, you add the outward and inward *Talu's* A B and F E: 'Tis therefore for the most part six or seven perches, that is 72 feet, or 84 feet; but then the outward *Talu* E F, will be somewhat less than half the height. For the Quality of the Figure *Authors* order again by guess

In	IV.	V.	VI.	VII.	VIII.	IX.	The lower thickness of the Rampar.
feet	54.	60.	66.	72.	78.	84.	

VII. Of

VII. Of a Rampar Cased with Stone.

A Rampar cased with Stone is to be preferr'd before a bare one, 1. because it chiefly hinders nocturnal invasions, and sudden attempts, since the enemy cannot mount it without Ladders, the providing of which will be very troublesome, and the use as uncertain. 2. Because it hinders an open assault, since it cannot be attempted but by Ladders, which will be to no purpose, or by the ruines of the wall thrown down with Mines. 3. Because it is a stable and everlasting work; whereas a bare Rampar, unless it be continually repaired, falls to the ground.

They that disagree, reason after this manner. 1. That Walls battered with Cannon sooner fall than the bare Earth. 2. Their Stones beaten down fill up the Ditch. 3. That the pieces or Splinters of the stones flying about will hurt the defendants. The first I deny, if the Walls be very thick, or if (as I ordered) propt with an earthen Rampar. As to the second, 'twill be the same thing, or rather worse in a bare Rampar. The third is avoided, if you do not raise the wall to the top of the Rampar, which is observed in the Wall of *Antwerp*. This inconvenience will be much less if you make the walls of Brick.

VIII. The Brestwork of the Rampar.

Upon the Rampar there is always a Brestwork built 4 G, IK 3, whose dimensions are these following. *Fig.* 8.

1. *The inward height* T 4 must be always 6 feet, that it may conveniently shelter the Souldiers, who seldome exceed this measure.

2. *The outward height* 2 K must be 4 feet, for so not only the field and the out-Brestwork, but also a great part of the Ditch will be defended by the Rampar; and you may know how much, if you can come to the knowledg of C φ, which will be found after this manner; as I O is to O K, so is I C to C φ. The three first terms are known, therefore the fourth C φ must be known. Now from C V known, take C φ known, there will remain φ V also known.

3. *The inward Talu* D I must be always 1 foot; there is no need of a greater, since it lies from the Enemie, and is propt up sufficiently by the Step or Banquet G 4 D, neither is it exposed to the feet of men always running up it, as the inward side of the Rampar.

4. *The outward Talu* 2 3. must be always 2 feet; for since the outward side of the Brestwork K 3 lies in a streight Line, with the outward side of the Rampar 3 E, and K 2, 3 F, are parallel. 'Tis evident that the Triangles 2 K 3, F 3 E, are like Triangles. Therefore since in the fourth number we ordered the outward *Talu* of the Rampar E F, to be half the height of the Rampar F 3, 3 2 will also be half the height 2 K: But 2 K was appointed to be always 4 feet, therefore 3 2 will be always 2 feet.

5. *The upper thickness* O K, must be Cannon proof, therefore since a whole Cannon will scarce strike through 20 feet of Earth, 21 feet may suffice.

6. *The lower thickness* D 3 is composed of the two *Talues* D T 3 2, and the upper thickness O K; the two *Talues* taken together, make 3 feet, and the upper thickness 21 feet, so that the lower thickness will be 24 feet.

And here again our Engineers sport it, and for the variety of the Figures alter the thicknesses after this manner.

In	IV.	V.	VI.	VII.	VIII.	IX.	&c.
Lat. sup.	9	11.	12.	15.	17	21	feet.
Lat. inf.	12	14	15	18	20	24	feet.

The Step or Banquet is built at the foot of all Brestworks on the inside, and is 3 feet thick or broad, and 1 ½ feet high.

IX. The Terreplein or Walk upon the Rampar.

The Walk on the Rampar L 4 is found, if from the upper thickness of the Rampar L 3 you substract the lower thickness of the Brestwork D 3, and the thickness or breadth of the step D 4; wherefore since D 3 in number 8. was ordered to be 24 feet, and D 4 to be 3 feet, and in the 6 number L 3 was ordered to be 51 feet, or 57 feet, there remains for the Walk 24 feet or 30 feet. But if you have a mind to sport with the Engineers above, it will be

In	IV.	V.	VI.	VII.	VIII.	IX	&c.	The breadth of the *Terreplein.*
	21.	22.	25½.	27.	28.	30.	feet	

X. The Bank of the Ditch.

If the Rampar want a Fauss-bray, there will be left a Bank-side, or a space of Earth 6 feet broad from the feet of the Rampar to the Brink of the Ditch R S.

CHAP. IX.

The Orthographie of the Fauss-bray.

I. The End and necessity of a Fauss-bray.

EXperience hath taught us in the taking of many Towns in *Holland*, that so soon as the Out-works are taken in, the Moat without any great difficulty will be covered with Galleries, and so conquered; for the water in the Moat hindering the sallies of the besieged, the Builders of the Galleries can only be called from the opposite flanques, being safe before by reason of the necessary height of the Rampar which protects the Enemy lying so near under it from the Shot and sight of the besieged. Against so deadly an inconvenience the Brestwork 5 N P Q R is built, at the foot of the Rampar, which is called commonly Fauss-bray, or *parapet des Rondes*: And in this alone consists the safety of a Moat or wet Ditch. For from this the besiegers are beat off on all sides, with Shot almost quite level or *Horizontal*; And therefore surer to do Execution, as I shewed in the eighth chapter, number the second. Therefore the only End of a Fauss-bray, is the defence of a Moat, which help, a dry ditch doth not stand in need of, as shall be taught hereafter.

II. Its height and Structure.

Some *Architects* sharply contend, that such a height ought to be given to the Fauss-bray, as might make it able to command the Out-works. But the defence of the Out-works will better be perform'd by the Rampar it self; and as much as you shall add to the height of the Fauss-bray, so much will you diminish from the defence of the graft: Therefore let it not exceed humane stature. The rest of its Structure is the same in all things, as that of the Brestwork of the Rampar, delivered in the eighth Chapter, numb. 8.

III. The

III. The Walk of the Fauss-bray. Chemin des Rondes.

Betwixt the Rampar and the Fauss-bray is left a ſpace E 5, fit for the Beſiegers to Plant and Traverſe their great Guns, which we call *the Walk of the Fauſs-bray*; Its greateſt breadth is equal to two *Rhynland* Perches, and the leaſt is equal to one. When upon occaſion a Fauſs-bray ſhall be drawn about the antient Rampar of Cities, to be defended only by Muſquetiers, the breadth of the Walk may be taken ſomewhat leſs than a Perch. If you have a mind to proportion it to the Polygons, you may order it after this faſhion.

In	IV.	V.	VI.	VII.	VIII.	IX	The walk of the Fauſs-bray,
	15.	18.	20.	24.	24.	24.&c.	with its ſtep or banquet.

This Width will ſerve to plant Guns in, but not the biggeſt.

IV. The Bankſide or Liſier.

At the foot of the Fauſs-bray towards the Ditch, is left a ſpace of ſix feet R S, for the ſtrengthning and keeping up of the work, leaſt any of the Earth ſhould fall into the Ditch.

CHAP. X.

1. Whether a dry Ditch or Graft be better than a Moat.

THere is not a queſtion more frequent amongſt Engineers; and many now prefer the dry one. The inconveniences of a Moat are theſe; it keeps the beſieged in like Priſoners, that they cannot ſally out upon the Enemy, unleſs a Covert way and Out-breſtwork be rais'd beyond it at very great expences: And when the Out-breſtwork ſhall be taken, it cannot defend it ſelf, ſince there is no going on it but by little boats. Therefore the Galleries are eaſily brought over the Moat unto the Rampar, as Experience hath often taught the *Hollanders*, the water hindring the beſieged, that they cannot run down into the Ditch, with handy blows to throw down the Fatal Engine. This defect however, is ſupplied by building a Fauſs-bray, Ravelins and Half-moons, at vaſt expences, and the entertainment of a far greater Garriſon. Therefore a Moat is both of it ſelf weak, and keeps the Towns-men in like Priſoners, ſo that they cannot come to beat off the Enemy any other way than by firing at a diſtance, though they ſee him ſpring his Mines, and bring the laſt deſtruction to the Town; beſides, the Fauſs-bray is built only for the ſecurity of the Moat, as is the Out-breſtwork and the Couvert way, and in fine, all ſorts of Out-works; and it requires a far greater number of Souldiers to defend it.

A dry Ditch, ſafe in its own ſtrength, doth not need theſe chargable Out-works, eſpecially an Out-breſtwork it never wants: For as the Moat keeps in the Souldiers like Priſoners, the dry Ditch conveys them ſafe and unſeen on the Enemy. Neither have theſe that ſally any need of a Couvert-way, ſince the Ditch can hide them in its own bottom; nor have they any need of an Out-breſtwork, ſince the out-ſide of the Ditch it ſelf, *viz.* if it have ſteps made to it, is able to ſupply the place of an Out-

 breſtwork.

brestwork. Nay, there is no sort of Out-work required, since they are rais'd only to keep the Enemy from the Ditch and Rampar, which will be better perform'd by Sallies, which may be made safely through the dry Ditch. Again, a dry Ditch makes an easie and safe retreat for those that sally, when they are wholly pursued by the Enemy: But a wet Ditch would either exclude or drown them; for there is no passage from Out-work to Out-work, or from the Out-works to the principal Rampar, but what is made by little narrow wooden bridges, which can receive but few at a time; and if they are crowded too much, as commonly in such cases it happens, they yield to their weight, and are broken: As it fell out when *Breda* was last besieged, in the taking of *Gincken's* Horn-work, with the great loss of their stoutest Souldiers perishing in the waters. To conclude, since a dry Ditch can safely be without Half-moons, Ravelins, Horn-works, and Out-brestworks, and all other Out-works, or at least may neglect them far safer than a wet Ditch can; we must confess that the Town, if it were besieged, would be defended with a far less Garrison.

It plainly appear'd at the siege of *Mastreicht*, the sharpest of all the *Dutch* Sieges, how far a dry Ditch is to be prefer'd before a wet one. The ditches of the Town being partly wet, partly dry, the Prince of *Orange* consulted with his Captains which was best to fall upon; who resolved to attempt the dry one; but the taking of it was so slow and so difficult, that the Prince confess'd his error, and resolved, after that, never to try the taking of a dry Ditch before a wet one: That I may omit the rest of the actions in this most valiant defence. The Townsmen from the Ditch it self brought forth their Mines, to blow up the lines of Approaches, with such facility and success, that the Enemy was forced to spend five weeks to gain a Line of five Perches: Then with Skirmishes, Works and Countermines, they so tired the *Dutch* that besieged them, that the Prince despairing to bring his Line over the dry Ditch, was constrain'd to carry a Mine into the Town, under the bottom of it, which was very near forty feet lower than the level of the Town.

Notwithstanding, 'tis to be confess'd, the nocturnal attempts and surprises of the Enemy are better kept off by a wet Ditch than by a dry one; yet there is great danger from the water it self being once frozen, unless the Ice be always broke; as appear'd in the taking of *Wachtendonch* by the Dutch, and *Philipsbourg* by the Emperialists, by a surprise in the dark, over their Moats that were frozen.

Whilst these things are controverted on both sides, This is my opinion, that a dry Ditch is best against open Assaults, and the wet one best against Surprises: But because all surprises and suddain attempts may be prevented by the care and vigilancy of the Officers and Souldiers, but open force no other way but by force, it seems to me the dry Ditch is absolutely to be chosen, if the nature of the ground will permit it: Especially since a great deal of money is spared, which otherwise would have been spent in building the Fausse-bray and the Out-works.

II. The making of the Ditch.

Let the solidity of the Ditch be equal to the solidity of the Works that are to be rais'd, *viz.* to the Rampar, the Brestwork on the Rampar, the Fauss-bray, and the Out-brestwork, added together; therefore you must not take more earth out of the Ditch than will serve for making the said Works: For which reason all the dimensions of a Ditch cannot be determin'd, before the solidity of all the Works to be rais'd is known.

III. The upper Width.

The upper Width of the Ditch about the Bulwork S V must at least exceed the tallest trees, otherwise the Enemy would lay bridges over it, 120 132, 144 feet will be large enough; but if you will vary it according to the diversity of the Figures, you may order it after this manner.

In

In	IV.	V.	VI.	VII.	VIII.	IX.	X.
	72.	84.	96.	108.	120.	132.	144. feet.

IV. The Talu of the Ditch SH, V5, or Lines forming the Sloap.

The outward *Talu* V5 of a wet Ditch, and the inward SH, must be equal to the depth of it, which is now to be determin'd, so consequently the Angle HS8 will be half a right Angle.

V. The Depth 8H α π.

For the most part it is ordered to be ten or twelve feet; but it cannot be less than six feet, otherwise a wet Ditch might be waded over, and a dry Ditch would not cover a man standing. But why a Ditch having the Width s above-determin'd, and its depth ten feet, should supply earth enough to raise the Rampar and its Brestwork, the Fauss-bray and Out-brestwork: Thus I demonstrate. Measure the Orthographical Sections of the Rampar and its Brestwork ALIKE, the Fauss-bray 5NPQR; and of the Out-brestwork 6XYZ, and multiply their sum into the principal Perimeter of the Fortification, which will be known, if all the Courtines, Faces, Flanques, be added among themselves. But the Orthographical Sections, and the Perimeter of the Fortification must be measured with one and the same measure, and the product shall give a solid almost equal to the aggregate of the Rampar, and its Brestwork, the Fauss-bray and Out-brestwork. In like manner, the Ditch will be almost equal to the solid that shall be produced out of the multiplication of the Orthographical Section of the Ditch S87V, into the Perimeter that passeth through the middle point of its Width α: Therefore because the Ditch ought to be equal to the aggregate of the Works, 'twill be by the *Corrol.* of the 34th of the 11th of *Euclide*. As the Perimeter passing by α, is to the principal Perimeter of the Fortification; so is the sum of the Sections of the Rampar, &c. to the Section of the Ditch S87V, which is consequently known, because it is a fourth proportional to three quantities known. Now because SV is known, and its half Sα, that is αβ; for since SH is equal to H8, Sα will be equal to αβ, by the 4.6. *Euclid.* Therefore βα multiplied into Sα shall give the Triangle SβV; from which substract S87V, already known, and there will remain the Triangle 8β7 also known. Then as the Triangle SβV is to the Square of αβ, so is the Triangle 8β7 to the Square of πβ; wherefore since three terms are known, the fourth also will be known, which is the Square of πβ, whose root is the Line βπ, which substracted from βα (that is Sα) shall give απ the depth of the Ditch, which this way is found to be near ten feet. If you need any more Earth to raise batteries for Cannon and Cavaliers, make your Ditch something deeper about the Bulworks: If there be no Fauss-bray, nor Out-brestwork, yet 'twill be requisite to make the Ditch ten feet deep, especially if you intend it a dry one; the Earth that shall be over and above, will serve to raise Cavaliers and other Works, of which there is great use.

VI. The Width at the bottom of the Ditch 8,7.

This follows from the upper Width, the Angle forming the sloap, and the depth being already determin'd.

In	IV.	V.	VI.	VII.	VIII.	IX.
	52.	64,	76.	84.	96.	108. feet.

VII. The Properties of a dry Ditch.

1. It ought to be ſomething deeper than a wet one.

2. Its inward *Talu* SH muſt be leſs than a wet one half the depth, that is ſix feet, that it may be harder for the Enemy to climb up.

3. But it muſt not be leſs than ſix feet, leaſt the Rampar fall down.

4. You'l make the Enemy a great deal of work, if in the middle of the great Ditch you dig a leſs ω θ φ δ 16, 18, 20, feet broad, and 4 or 5. feet deep.

5. The outſide of the Ditch 7V muſt be made after the faſhion of a Breſtwork that may cover a man, and have two ſteps or Banquets for the eaſier getting up to it.

6. Sally-ports muſt be made in the Rampar, for the Townſ-men to deſcend into the Ditch.

CHAP. XI.

The Out-breſtwork and Covert-way.

I. Its Uſe.

A Dry Ditch may ſafely be without an Out-breſtwork; but a wet one altogether wants it: For ſince a wet Ditch doth not keep out the Enemy more than it keeps in the Towns-men, when upon occaſion they ſhould ſally out upon the Beſiegers, a Covert-way V6 was found neceſſary to be made beyond the Ditch, and a Breſtwork to protect it; by which means the Defendants could ſally ſafely out of their City over the Moat; and ſo the Enemy was kept from the Town, but the Towns-men were not hindred, when they pleas'd to fall upon the Enemy.

II. The breadth of the Covert-way.

Moſt commonly it is made equal to the walk of the Fauſs-bray 24 or 21 feet; for ſo much almoſt will be required here for traverſing great Guns, and performing other Military duties. If you have a fancy to vary it according to the diverſity of the Figures, uſe this Table.

In	IV.	V.	VI.	VII.	VIII.	IX.	
	12.	15.	15.	17.	21.	24.	feet.

III. The making of the Out-breſtwork.

1. Its height ♈Y muſt be ſix feet.

2. The inward *Talu* muſt be one foot, as in the reſt of the Breſtworks.

3. The outward ſloap of it Y Z muſt be ſo inclin'd, that being produced, it may paſs through 1. the top of the Breſtwork of the Rampar. There are many and great advantages from this form; for ſo all of it will be ſcowred from the Breſtwork of the Rampar, which would not have been, if the inclination had fallen from Y in 10. for ſo all the Triangle ♈Y 10. is obſcured from the ſight and ſhot of the Breſtwork of the Rampar.

4. To find this ſloap or inclination, the baſe ♈ Y muſt firſt be known; which is after this manner: The Lines I C and C9 are known; and therefore 9 I is known, and T 3 is alſo known, or C F and F λ is known; therefore C λ, or 9 Y is known, and ſo is

Y λ known; then by the 4. *lib.* 6. *Euclid.* as 19 is to 9 Y, so is Y λ to λ Z, to which if you add one foot, the whole base λ Z will be known.

The *Perimeter* of this Brestwork, or the Lines of it surrounding the whole Fortification, whether they be inward or outward, must be drawn parallel to the Faces only, so that they meet at a point opposite to the middle points of the Courtine, and make outward Angles; but if Ravelins are built before the Courtines, the Brestwork is drawn about them, but not about the Horn-works, if any should be built.

IV. Whether it be expedient to make a Ditch about the Out-Brestwork.

Some affirm it, and stand to it: But they do not consider, when they think to make this Brestwork stronger, that they quite over-throw the end it was made for; which was, that the besieged might safely sally out upon the Enemy, and in their return injoy a safe retreat; both which will be hindred by a Ditch made about it: Insomuch that if the Towns-men do not make it, 'twould seem fitter for the Enemy to make.

CHAP. XII.

An Orthographical Table of Regular Fortifications.

This Table is collected out of the doctrine of the four foregoing Chapters.

	Max.	*Med*	*Min.*
The breadth of the base of the Rampar A E.	84	72	60
The inward *Talu*, or line forming the Sloap AB.	18	6	14
The outward *Talu* E F.	9	8	7
The height of the Rampar B L.	18	16	14
The breadth on the top of the Rampar L 3.	57	48	39
The breadth of the base of the Brestwork 3 D	24	18	14
The inward *Talu* of the Brestwork D T.	1	1	1
The outward *Talu* of the Brestwork 3 2.	2	2	2
The inward height of the Brestwork T I.	6	6	6
The outward height of the Brestwork 2 K	4	4	4
The breadth of the top of the Brestwork K O.	21	15	11

Rhynland feet.

 The

The rest of the foregoing Table.

	Max.	*Med.*	*Min.*
The breadth of the step or Banquet D 4	3	3	3
The height of the step or Banquet 4 G	$1\frac{1}{2}$	$1\frac{1}{8}$	$1\frac{1}{8}$
The Terrepleine or Walk on the Rampar 4 L	30	27	22
The walk of the Fauss-br., or *chemin des Rondes* E 5	21	71	15
The Fauss-bray with its Banquet			
The border or bankside. *Lisier* R S	6	6	6
The upper width of the Ditch S V	132	108	84
The outward & inward *Talu's* of the ditch SH V 5	12	12	10
The depth of the Ditch H 8, α π	12	12	10
The Width of the bottom of the ditch 8 7	108	184	64
The Covert way V X	21	17	15
Its step or banquet			
The base of the out-brestwork λ Z	79	70	69
Its height	6	6	6

Rhynland feet.

For the base of the Out-brestwork, working according to the Rules deliver'd in the 11. *Chap. num.* 3. I find it to be

Max.	*Med.*	*Min.*
82.	$75\frac{1}{4}$.	69.

Therefore *Dogen* and *Fritach* are out in their account.

The first Column shews you the largest and strongest Orthography, which is able to sustain the greatest force of the Besiegers. The second is able to bear an indifferent Siege. The third is made against the least strength which is usually sent against Towns. But here we only treat of the Forts themselves; I shall hereafter give you the Orthography of Castles and Out-works. And again, I had no proportion or respect to the diversity of the Figures or Polygons, as many Engineers have; who for no reason, as I can tell, give to a *Pentagon* a different Orthography from that which they give to a *Hexagon* or a *Nonagon*. For a stronger or weaker Orthography is to be given a Fortification, not as it hath more or less Angles or Bulworks, but as it ought to resist a greater or less strength of an Enemy.

Note. *If the Fortification be made without a Fauss-bray, the Out-brestwork will have another Base, for it will be a fourth proportional to the three terms* I 9, 9Y, Y λ, *but the mean or middle term* 9 Y *will be less by the space* E R, *if the Fauss-bray be wanting, and then the base of the Brestwork* λ Z *will be*

max.	*med.*
65	50

CHAP.

CHAP. XIII.

Of the raising of Out-Works.

A Fortification formed according to its essential parts, is made stronger if it be surrounded with some Out-works. The chief of which is a Raveline, a Half-moon, a Horn-work, a Crown-work, and Tongs. I shall treat of each of them distinctly in the following propositions.

PROP. I.

I. The definition and form of a Raveline or Target.

A Raveline is a Bulk of Earth almost like a Bulwork cut off, except that it wants flanques; it is surrounded with water, and separated from the Fortification by the breadth of the whole Ditch. Such an one is F E G H, in the 10th. *Figure*, its faces are F E, G E. It wants, as I said, for the most part flanques, yet it admits of them when it is built before Gates, which then will be about 8 or 9 perches. Towards the Enemy it is built with a Rampar and Brestwork, and lies open towards the Fortification, least it might shelter the Enemie when he hath possest it, it is rais'd but a little height above the level of the ground, that it may be better defended from the main Fortification, and the plains the better scowred by it. *Fig.* 10.

Its Angle must not be less than 60 degr. nor more than a right Angle. The length of the faces is determin'd in Regular Fortifications, *numb.* 3. If they are applyed to the covering of a Courtine that is above its just length, observe this, that the faces must not be longer than the faces of the Bulworks, therefore they may be about 40, 50, or 60 paces.

II. Concerning their place, and how they are defended.

For the most part it is raised before Gates and Courtine, but never before the Bulworks. The 10th. *Figure* shews the Situation of it, as it lyes before a Courtine; 'tis best to have it of such a breadth as might cover the Courtine only, and not the flanques, for then 'tis defended by the faces and flanques of the Bulworks that it lies betwixt.

III, The making of it

Is various; but this is most approved. Raise an infinite perpendicle from the middle point of the Courtine S, from this Line on the other side of the Ditch cut off H E equal to $\frac{3}{4}$ or $\frac{2}{3}$ or $\frac{1}{2}$ of the Face; then from the point E draw streight Lines either to the ends of the Courtine A, B (and this will be the best form for the Raveline, for the whole Courtine is covered by the Raveline, and the Raveline it self not only scowred and defended by the Faces, but by the flanques of the Bulworks also) or to some other point of the flanque, *Fig.* 10

flanque, or to the ends of the flanque C D; those parts of these strait lines F E, G E, cut off from the Bank-side of the Ditch towards E, are the Faces of the Bulworks.

1. Another way. On the Centers A B, the extream points of the Courtine, with the distance of the same Courtine, describe two Arches intersecting one another in E.

2. Produce the marginal lines of the Ditch φ I, M L till they meet at the point H; then from the ends of the flanques C D draw strait lines to the point E, that may cut the marginal lines of the Ditch in F G, and F E G H shall be the perfect delineation of the Raveline; the faces are F E. G E, the Gorge Lines are F H, G H.

1. Another way, bisect the Gorge Lines of the Bulwork A R, B Q in the points O, P; then draw strait lines from the points O, P, by the ends of the flanques C, D till they meet one another in the point E.

2. Then produce the out-lines of the Ditch φ I, M L, till they meet in H, and cut the former lines in F G, so shall F E G H be the Ravelin required.

IV. The Orthographie and Ichnographie, or the Profile and Plain.

This Table following shews the height and breadth of each part. The third column shews the Orthographie of the Out-works of *Breda*; The first and fourth shews the Orthographie of the largest; The second and fifth of the middle size; the sixth shews the least; the four last Columns are taken out of *Dogen*. This Table doth not serve only for Ravelins, but for all manner of Out-works.

A Table for the building of Outworks.

	Max.	*Med.*	*Bred.*	*Stab.*	*Min.st.*	*Temp.*
The lower breadth of the Ramp.	40	36	44	36	24	20
The outward *Talu* of the Ramp.	3	2	6	3	2	2
The inward *Talu* of the Ramp.	6	4	8	6	4	4
The height of the Rampar.	6	4	8	6	4	4
The upper thickness of the Ram.	31	30	30	27	18	14
The base of the Brestwork.	15	15	16¾	13	10	8
The outward *Talu* of the brestw.	2	2	3¼	2	2	2
The inward *Talu* of the Brestw.	1	1	1	1	1	1
The outward height of the Brest.	2	2	5	4	4	4
The inward height of the Brestw.	6	6	6	6	6	6
The upper thickness of the Brest.	15	12	12	10	7	5
The height of the step.	1½	1½	1½	1½	1½	1½
The breadth of the step.	3	3	3	3	3	3
The Walk on the Ramp.	12	10	10[illegible]	11	5	3

Rhynland feet.

The

The rest of the foregoing Table.	*Max.*	*Med.*	*Bred.*	*Stab.*	*Min.st.*	*Temp.*
The border at the foot of the Ram.	3	3	6	3	3	2
The width of the Ditch.	48	30	42	30	24	16
The outward *Talu* of the Ditch.	10	8	7	8	6	4
The inward *Talu* of the Ditch.	10	8	7	8	6	4
The depth of the Ditch.	10	8	7	8	6	6
The width of the bottom of the D.	18	14	28	14	12	8

Rhynland feet.

PROP. II.

Of the Half-moon or Helmet.

I. Its definition and place.

HAlf-moons for the most part do not differ from Ravelins, unless it be in bigness; perhaps they had this name given them, because those which are built before Bulworks are Arch'd in the form of a crescent, on that side which lies towards the Bulwork. They are placed upon the Covert-way which is beyond the Ditch, so that their Capital line produced, cuts the Courtine into two equal parts. They are built also before the Angle of Bulworks (as I said) but the greatest use of them is in Irregular Fortification, as I shall shew hereafter.

II. Their Form.

Let not their Angle be less then 60 degr. nor more than 90 degr. Let their height be but indifferent, and not distant from the Rampar above Musquet-Shot, that they may be defended by the Rampar. When they are built on the Covert-way, their faces must be 25 or 30 paces; let the thickness of their Rampar be 15 or 20 feet, and they must be so large as to receive 100 or 150 Souldiers.

III. Their Delineation.

1. In the Angle of the Fauss-bray V as in a center, with the distance of the breadth of the Ditch V M, describe an Arch, and produce the Capital line infinitely, cutting the Arch in α.

2. On the other side of the Ditch cut off α X from the Capital Line produced, which is $\frac{2}{7}$ of the Face of the Bulwork, and from the points H and λ where the Gorge lines of the Ravelins intersect one another, draw unto λ the lines HX, λX.

3. Produce the faces of the Fauſs-bray φ V, φ V, till they cut the lines H X λ X, in ζ, δ and the Arch in β, γ or the Fichant lines of the Fauſs-bray continued on 2 V, 3 V, may determine theſe Interſections. So have you a half-moon delineated, placed before a Bulwork, whoſe faces are X ζ, X δ, and its flanques (but open) are ζ β, δ γ. The delineation of other half-moons is like that of Ravelins.

The Orthographie and Ichnographie, is had out of the foregoing propoſition, *Chap.* XIII. *numb.* 4.

IV. Its Uſe and Conveniency.

'Tis the weakeſt of all the out-works, ſince it cannot entertain a good quantity of Souldiers to defend it by reaſon of its ſtraits, and is alſo with more difficulty defended from the Fortification. Therefore theſe half-moons ſeem to be hurtful to the Fortification unleſs they be arm'd with theſe cautions; to wit, that Ravelins be built on both ſides, and that they conſiſt only of Faces, being altogether without flanques (otherwiſe being poſſeſt by the Enemie, they cannot be ſhot from the Ravelins) and at laſt let them be every where within Muſquet-Shot. Yet if all this were perform'd, 'twill be ſtill doubtful whether they are uſeful or not: Wherefore they ſeem not to be built without peculiar neceſſity.

PROP. III.

Of the Horn-Work.

I. Its Definition and Kinds.

Fig. 10. THat Outwork that runs fartheſt into the field with two ſtrait ſides objecting to the Enemy two half-Bulworks, is called *a Horn-work*: The tenth Figure ſhews an example of it. There are three kinds of Horn-works; the firſt hath its ſides inclining to one another towards the Field; the ſecond towards the Fortification; and the third's are parallel.

II. Its Place and Form.

They are built oppoſite to the Courtine, or the Angle of the Bulwork, beyond the Out-breſtwork: Yet they are better defended if they cover the Courtine, than if the Bulwork, eſpecially if the ſides, are parallel: For when they cover the Bulworks with parallel ſides, they receive no other defence than from the Courtine, and that to little purpoſe, ſince at ſo great a diſtance; beſides, after this manner the work would be too narrow: Yet if they are to be placed before Bulworks, 'tis altogether neceſſary the ſides ſhould incline to one another towards the Bulworks, that ſo they may not take in all the faces, but exclude ſome part of them from which they may be defended. See the Conſtruction in *Dogen*, pag. 160, 161.

If they are built before the Courtine, let their ſides be rather parallel, and perpendicular on the Courtine. If they cover the whole Courtine (as ſome will have it, and as we have expreſs'd in the Figure) their defence will be from the faces of thoſe Bulworks that the Courtine lyes betwixt. If it does not cover the whole Courtine, as others will have it, the defence of the ſides will be the greater; to wit, both from the faces of the Bulworks, and from part of the Courtine. Betwixt the Horn-work and the

the Courtine, there is commonly rais'd a Raveline; nay, before the work it self, betwixt each of its Horns, a Raveline, or rather an Half-moon may be built. To conclude, you will add a great deal of strength to this work, if you make some Retrenchments: But of that afterwards.

III. Its Delineation.

1. Let there be drawn two parallels E I, F K, for the sides of the Horn-work, from the Out-brestwork towards the field, at such a distance, that if they were produced towards the main Work, they might fall in a strait Line with the flanques of the Bulworks; or if you desire a less breadth for the Horn-work, let them fall within the flanques on the Courtine it self. But the ends of these sides must not be above Musquet-shot from the Rampar, wherefore they must not run beyond the Rampar above sixty *Rhynland* Perches: Yet these sixty *Rhynland* Perches use to be counted from the Out-brestwork, that so the approaches of the Enemy might be the more infested.

Joyn E F, on which make the Angles F E G, E F H twenty five degrees each; then bisect one of these F E G, with the right Line E L meeting with F H in C; then from E G cut off E D equal to F C, so will F C, E D, be the faces of the half Bulworks.

3. From the point D and C draw D A and C B, equal and parallel to E I and F K, for the flanques of the Horns, and joyn the Courtine A B, the proportion of the flanques D A and C B, to the faces, will be almost the same as uses to be in Regular Fortifications.

Also after this manner following, the Capital and Gorge lines, the Flanques and Courtine will be with more ease determin'd: For $\frac{1}{3}$ of E F gives the Capitals E N and F M; also $\frac{1}{3}$ of M N or E F gives the Gorge lines N A, M B, and there remains for the Courtine A B also $\frac{1}{3}$; the right Lines M E, N F, will determine the length of the Flanques rais'd from A and B; and so also the faces E D, F C will be found.

These things being done, a Horn-work is delineated, such as uses to be stretched before the Courtines in a Regular Fortification; the delineation of the rest will be performed almost by the like method, having alwayes a respect to the place.

Note. *That here is a twofold Practice in building Horn-works; 1. That the Courtine might be determin'd by the Faces. 2. The faces by the Courtine.*

IV. Its use.

If Ravelins, Half-moons and Horn-works, are built about a fortified place, the Fortification is accounted most compleat and perfect, whose use consists most in this; 1. They keep off the Enemy far from the Fortification. 2. They are taken with a great deal of difficulty; for they are defended from the Courtine, from the Bulworks, and from the adjacent Works, and some Lines from the Out-brestwork it self. 3. Being taken and possess'd, they can hardly be kept, because they lye open towards the Fortification. 4. Horn-works are most destructive to the approaches of the Enemy, and under their shelter the besieg'd may work counter, as occasion shall offer, &c.

PROP. IV.

Of the Tonges, in French Tenailes.

I. Their Definition and Kinds.

THey are Out-works that differ from Horn-works almost only in this, that instead of two half Bulworks they have only an external Angle; and this sort is called the single one: It is called the double one, when it hath two outward Angles with one Inward. The twelfth Figure shews the single one; the thirteenth the double one.

Now this outward Angle is that which is without the Figure, and whose sides incline inwards. The inward is that which is within the Figure, with its sides running outward.

II. Their Place.

The same as that of the Horn-works: Yet it will hardly be expedient to lay them before Bulworks, by reason of their weakness. Of which *Num.* 4.

III. Its Delineation.

You must describe a single one after this manner. Draw the sides A C, B D after *Fig.* 12. the same manner as in the delineation of Horn-works, which is already prescrib'd, unless these are wont to be shorter, *viz.* than forty or fifty Perches.

2. Joyn C D, which bisect in F; and from F let fall the perpendicular F E equal to $\frac{1}{4}$ of C D, and joyn C E and D E; so have you the simple external Angle.

Draw the double one after this manner: Having drawn the sides A C, B D, as *Fig.* 13. above, joyn C D; which being bisected in G, from G raise the perpendicular G E equal to $\frac{1}{4}$ of C D, and joyn C E and D E.

2. Produce E G to F, till G F be the half of G E; and the right Lines C E, D E being bisected in K and H, joyn F K and F H; so will A C K F H D B be the double Tonges, or double external Angle.

IV. Its strength and use.

They are much inferiour to the Horn-works, insomuch that they seem only then to be made use of, when some suddain occasion urges.

Moreover, the defect of these Tonges, and of all external Angles, is this; that about its very Angle it affords the Enemy a certain Quadrangular space, within which he need not be expos'd to the shot of the Defendants; this space is determin'd, if the outward sloaping surface of the Brestwork be conceiv'd to be produc'd till it cut the field; its capacity is almost equal to twenty three *Rhynland* Perches, which will be easily computed. Since then this sort of building is so much against the first Laws of Architecture, 'twill be almost necessary to raise a Raveline before it.

The Double Tonges, since they have a double external Angle K and H, will likewise double the defect already spoken of; wherefore they are less used.

PROP.

PROP. V.

Of the Crown-work.

I. Its Definition.

THat work is called a Crown-work, that hath on both sides two half Bulworks, and in the middle one or more whole ones. Therefore it is the part of some Regular Fortification; and seems to have this name given it, because it doth, as it were, incompass part of the Fortification. *Fig.* 14.

II. Its Place

Is the same as that of Horn-works; though the Crown-work can cover more of the Fortification than the Horn-work, and sometimes they are drawn about Horn-works. Their chiefest use is to inclose neighbouring places, that might infest the Town, as *Hills*, &c. and so prevent the Enemy.

III. Its Delineation.

Since 'tis most an end the part of some Regular Fortification, let the Engineer look, what Fortification is fittest for the place of the Polygon that is to be incompassed; which when he hath found, let him delineate so many Bulworks of that Fortification which is built on the observ'd Polygon, as the place requires; only this let him observe, that the Angles of the half Bulwork be not less than sixty, nor more than ninety degrees. Its Bulworks are wont sometimes to be less than those of the main Work. But let us expound more especially the construction of a Crown-work having one whole Bulwork.

The whole description is made after this manner. Let the Capital of the Bulwork be produced infinitely; or if the Crown is to be set before the Courtine, from the middle point of the Courtine raise an Infinite perpendicular; on the Capital produced set off from B to D forty *Rhynland* Perches; on the perpendicular of the Courtine you may reckon sixty or seventy; for so the sides of the Crown-work will be yet within the shot of a Musquet coming from the Bulworks of the main Fort.

Then at the point of D, of the right line B D, make the Angle B D I, half of some *Multangle* or *Polygon*, and on the other side the Angle B D K; then in the sides of these Angles from D to I and K, reckon 40 or 50 perches, at most 60; and laying a Ruler by the point I, to the flanque of the Bulwork F, as also from the point K to the other flanque E, draw strait lines till they meet with the Out-brestwork in M and L, so will the sides of the *Crown-work* be determin'd by the Out-brestwork.

But if the sides M I, L K, exceed 60 perches, that is, a Musquet-Shot, the Angles B D I, B D K, must be made less, (Yet so that the whole I D K may remain bigger than a right Angle) or certainly (which is thought best) the Line B D must be shortned.

Then see what Regular Figure's Angle is equal, or comes near to the Angle K D I: say for Example an *Heptagon* or seven-angled figure; therefore make within K D I one whole Bulwork and two half Bulworks of an *Heptagon*, by the help of your Tables.

If you would place more whole Bulworks in the middle, let the sides of the *Horn-work* be drawn forth, so that they do not exceed Musquet-Shot, and within these build part of a Regular Fortification, as hath been said above.

General Rules concerning Out-works.

1. Let them be within Musquet-shot of the main work.
2. Let not their height be more than what may conveniently serve to scowr the ground possest by the Enemy.
3. Let the Remotest be lower than the nearest.
4. Let a dry graft have no out-works, unless Horn-works, if you see occasion; let the wet one have Ravelins and Horn-works, but it will hardly admit of Half-moons without Dammage.

THE SECOND PART OF Irregular Fortifications.

Since most Cities are of an Irregular figure, 'tis evident what great use or rather necessity there is like to be of this Part; I shall comprehend all the matter briefly in the following Chapters.

CHAP. XIV.

The Parts of Irregular Fortification.

These works following serve for the fortifying Irregular places, *Ordinary Bulworks, double and Triple Bulworks, Forked Bulworks, Plain Bulworks, Half Bulworks, Ravelins, Half moons, Horn-works, Crown-works, Tonges, External Angles, Angular Tonges, Plain Moles, half plain Moles, the middle Defence or toothed, Retrenchments.*

Some of these *(viz.)* those that are wont to be used in strengthening Regular Fortifications, we have already expounded. And although their manner of building there delivered, be proper to Regular Fortifications, yet out of this 'tis easily understood how they are to be fitted to an Irregular place. Now these that are over and above, are to be explain'd in this Chapter.

1. *The Double or Triple Bulwork,* is a Moat or Bulk of Earth composed of several Bulworks placed one above another; 'tis shewn in the 15th. figure, and is built commonly in steep places, such as the sides of Hills, that when the Enemy coming up can be no longer touched from the lowest, he might be hot from the second, and lastly from the third; these are seldome used.

2. *Forked or cut Bulworks,* I call those whose Angle E is cut off, and chang'd into an external Angle F K G, after this manner in the 16th figure is the Mole or Bulk A C F K G D B; they are of use when the Angle of the Bulwork is too acute.

3. *Half-Bulworks,* you have in the *Horn-work,* fig. 10. and in the *Crown-work,* fig. 14. They are not only to be used in *Horn-works* and *Crown-works,* but also in many other

other places, as we shall say afterwards. Observe that the Angle of these be not too acute, and take care that their plain side be not destitute of defence.

4. *The external Angle*, is that which is made by two lines running inwards towards the Center of the place called in French *angle retire*; on the contrary, the *Inward Angle* is that which is made by the sides running forth towards the field from the Center of the place, called in French *angle Avance*. In the 17th. figure the outward Angles are, A, L, C, E, G, *&c.* The inward B, D, F, *&c.* The outward Angle, if it be not too obtuse, seems strong enough, since its sides do mutually scowr one another; and from this is had the defence of the Tonges and Forked Bulworks. We have above showed its defect. *Fig.* 17.

Some people extoll this so, as to think a place surrounded with outward and inward Angles, to be equal in strength to one that is fortified with Bulworks, but they are not to be heard.

1. For first, it always happens, that when a place is inclosed with External and internal Angles set alternately, some of the outward will be too blunt or obtuse; as A L, and some of the inward too acute, either of which is very hurtful. The last in this, that its Angle is liable to be cut off by the Enemies Canon. The other, in that it looses so much the more of its scowring defence the nearer it comes to a strait line.

2. The outward Angles likewise have this Essential inconvenience, that the Enemie drawing near the Angle it self, cannot be hot within a notable space, as we have shewn above, which fault the Bulworks are without.

3. These External Angles do lessen the *Area* of the place, and increase the circumference, both which is faulty.

5. *Angular Tonges*, are wont to be used in fortifying an acute external Angle, or a right one; but not so conveniently an obtuse one: with help of these you may mend the second fault spoken of above; you must build it after this manner. *Fig.* 18, 19.

Produce A B, E B, the sides of the Angle, 8 or 10 paces to K and N, and joyn K N; then draw K E, N G parallel to B A, B E, likewise C E, D G parallel to B E and B A, which may meet with the former in E and G. If all the space contained within the Lines C E K N G D be emptied and cleared, you have the Tonges sought for.

Some build it after this manner, omitting the Line K N, and slighting the Triangle F B N, they empty only the spaces C E F B, B N G D; yet the first seems to be prefer'd, because in it the defence is not only had from the flanques E K, G N, but also from K N, which is as it were a little Courtine; but the other wants this defence, and its sides B F, B N are almost useleless for defence. But if they are to be built with a wall, (as for the most part they ought to be) the labour is doubled and without profit, because F B and B N are bigger than F N, and as I said unuseful. On the ends of the sides of the Angle which is strengthened with the Tonges, half-Bulworks, X, Z, are always wont to be made. *Fig.* 19.

6. *Plain Moles*, serve for the strengthening obtuse outward Angles, less fit for acute and right ones: you shall build them after this manner. *Fig.* 20.

From the sides of the outward Angle E B D cut off the right lines B A, B C 25 or 30 paces, and raise the Perpendicles A H, C I equal unto them, and joyn H I; so will A H I C be the Plain Mole, whose flanques A H and C I, will scowr the sides of the Angle A E, C D, and these will be scowred by them. But the Front H I will be scowred by N E, M D the segments of the sides which the Front produced cuts off on both sides. Therefore the sides of the Angle ought to be so long that they may cut the Front prolong'd on both sides, and the parts N E, M D, must be of a considerable quantity, least otherwise the Front want its defence.

This work is better then the Tonges, because it enlarges the places, and is capable of great Retrenchments.

If you desire Orillons to it, or Ears, take H K, I L ⅓ of the flanques, and on these you must build them. The rest of the parts A K, L C, being each ⅔ of the flanques, will give the Covert flanques.

7. The 21 figure shews, *The half plain Mole*; 'tis of use when one side B E of the *Fig.* 21.

 External

External Angle is longer than the other, and so much longer that it exceeds Musquet-shot.

Fig. 22. 8. *Inward Angles, angles avance's,* may be taken in stead of Angular Tonges or the plain Mole, for the defence of External Angles, whether they are acute or obtuse. In the example let there be the outward Angle B A C: here it will be conveniently fortified by building the inward Angle D F E, where observe this, that the parts of the sides intercepted A D, A E must be always of such a bigness, that the remaining segments of the sides may not exceed Musquet-shot.

Fig. 23. 24. 9. *The middle or simple defences,* are shown in the 23, 24. figures They are of use when any side of a Fortification will not admit any other defence. Also in some peoples judgments, they may be used to purpose, about the out-Brestwork. Others had rather be without these middle or simple defences, because C D, E F, *&c.* are each of them scowred but by one flanque, C B or E D, *&c.* far otherwise then it is in Courtines, which are placed between two Bulworks.

Fig. 25. 10. *Retrenchment* is a part cut off from the whole work, which can be no longer defended, a d it is like the whole. The 25 figure shows the Retrenchment of Hornworks and Bulworks, after whose *Idea* the rest may be perfected.

Fig. 26. 11. Now there remains that we should expound the construction of plain Bulworks. Those are said to be plain Bulworks, that are not made upon Angles, but upon a right Line, and are used in the strengthening River-sides, and Courtines that are over long *&c.* Though when they are applyed to the fortifying of Courtines, their construction will be somewhat different from the rest, as will be said afterwards.

This Table serves for their construction to be made three several ways, the first is due to an *Hexagon,* the second to an *Octogon,* the third to an *Enneagon,* or those bigger than an *Enneagon.*

	Courtine.	*Gorge.*	*Flanque.*
Manner 1.	480. 0.0.0.	169. 7.0.6.	90. 0.0.0.
Manner 2.	480. 0.0.0.	169. 7.0.6.	110. 0.0.0.
Manner 3.	480. 0.0.0.	169. 7.0.6.	120. 0.0.0.

The construction will be after this manner.

Let there be given the right line A Z to be fortified after the second manner.

1. First look in the Table for the Courtine, you'l find it 480 *Rhynland* feet, which cut off from A Z, and let them be A B. In like manner look in the Table for the Neck line, you'l find it to be 169, 706. feet, which cut off twice from B Z, and let them be B C, C D; and mark the point C. Then again cut off the Courtine D E, and the Neck-lines E F, F G, and so proceed for the number of Bulworks you shall want.

2. In the Table seek the flanques, you l find them 110 feet, which raise perpendicularly from B to D, and let them be B K, D L, and joyn K L, which bisect in N, and from N raise the perpendicular N I equal to the Neck line C B; at last joyn K I, L I, and you'l have the plain Bulwork B K I L D, whose Angle at I is a right one. In like manner the rest will be made, the proportion of the rest of the parts will arise from this construction, which the Table underneath sheweth.

	The Face.	*The flanque of the Courtine.*	*The flanquing line of defence.*	*The fichant line of defence.*	*The angle of the Bulwork.*
1. *Manner.*	240	390	367. 2.7.9.	699. 6.8.9.	90 d.
2. *Manner.*	240	370	795. 5.6.3.	707. 3.5.3.	90 d.
3. *Manner.*	240	360	409. 7.0.5.	711. 3.7.0.	90 d.

CHAP.

CHAP. XV.

How an Irregular place may be regularly Fortified.

IRregular places may be ſtrengthened two wayes, *viz.* Regularly and Irregularly. An Irregular place is ſaid to be Regularly fortified, when it is ſo changed, as that it may become Regular; or if it cannot be produced to Regularity, a Regular Figure is circumſcrib'd about it. But an Irregular place is fortified irregularly when the Figure of the place is not reduced to a Regular one.

PROBLEME I.

Let it be proposed to fortifie an Irregular place Regularly.

1. DEſcribe the plain of the place to be fortified, and obſerve what Regular Figure it comes neareſt to, and reduce it to that you find neareſt. The Reduction muſt be ſo, that all thoſe parts of the old circumference that can be uſed, muſt be retain'd: The reſt are to be excluded with a new circumference, if the place be large; or included rather, if the place be only of a mean capacity. Now a place reduced after this manner, will be fortified according to the laws of Regular Fortifications.

2. But if the Figure of the place be ſo Irregular, as not to be reduced to a Regular, 'twill behoove you to circumſcribe about it a Regular Figure. But that you may know how many ſides the Figure circumſcrib'd is to have, meaſure the largeſt Radius of the place you intend to incloſe, then turn to the Tables of Regular Fortifications, and obſerve what Figures Radius, your Radius is equal to, or neareſt; and what Figures Radius you find it to be, that Figure you muſt circumſcribe.

CHAP. XVI.

How an Irregular Place having fit Sides and Angles, is to be Irregularly fortified.

SOme Angles of Irregular Place are ſaid to be fit, others unfit; as likewiſe ſome of the ſides are fit, and ſome unfit.

That is a fit Angle that is not leſs than ninety degrees; that which is leſs is unfit; for the Angle of the Bulwork ſet upon it would be leſs than ſixty degrees, if a due proportion were kept of the reſt for the parts. The external Angles alſo are reckon'd among the unfit.

That side is fit, that leaves for the Courtine not less than three hundred feet, nor more than five hundred feet, when the two Gorge lines belonging to a Square shall be cut off on both sides. That side is unfit that leaves more than five hundred, or less than three hundred feet. *Dogen* pronounces one side to be unfit, that is less than the side of a square Regular Figure: Therefore look in the Tables for the Neck-lines of a square Fortification, and cut them off at each end from every particular side; and if the remainder be no less than three hundred feet, or more than five hundred feet, the sides are fit.

PROB. I.

Let there be given an Irregular place Z, having fit Sides and Angles, which were required to be Irregularly fortified.

Fig. 27.

1. FInd out by help of an Instrument the least Angle of the Place, which let be A; then observe what Regular Figure's Angle of the Circumference is equal to this least angled, or next less. Let us order it to be the Angle of a Square.

2. Seek therefore in your Tables (Chap 5.) the Neck-lines that serve for a Square, which let be AH, A H, cut off from the sides: Seek also the flanques of a Square, which being rais'd perpendicularly from H, H let be H G, H G. Then bisecting the Angle A. with an infinite Right-line A Q, cut off from it the Capital line of a Square A F, likewise found in the Table, and joyn F G, FG: so you have H G F G H the Bulwork of a square Fortification. Where note, that if the least Angle be 100 degrees, or betwixt 110 or 108, you must give to the Flanques seventy feet.

3. If on the rest of the Angles you make Bulworks belonging to a Square, the Fortification will be compleat and perfect.

4. If the Courtine, and flanques in the Courtine, be in some places too little, there make the Bulwork of a Regular Figure next less, till your Courtine be long enough; you may also lessen the Angle of the Bulwork if the Flanques are too short, still preserving its just bigness spoke of in the *Maxims*, On the contrary, you may increase the Angle of the Bulwork, if the flanque of the Courtine be very big.

5. Very great Angles, to wit, such as are bigger than 150 degrees, shall be fortified as right sides; that is, you shall so fortifie each side of the Angle, as if it were one Courtine: The manner will be delivered afterwards.

6. The Bulworks being built after this form, by help of the least Angle; if the Courtine, and flanques of the Courtine, be of that length, that that they may be shortned, still preserving their due quantity, then 'twill be lawful to increase the Angle of the Bulwork by increasing either the Flanques or Neck-lines, or both together; and so will you take away any inconvenience that might be in this way; neither will there be any thing that *Dogen* can condemn; nor such need of that troublesome new invention of Lines, found by the Rule of Proportion.

PROB. II.

To do the same thing another Way.

1. MEsure each Angle of the place, and see what Regular Figure's, angles each angle is equal to, or next bigger.

2. On each Angle of the given place build Bulworks, with their Neck-lines, Flanques, Capital, taken from those Figures, unto whose Angles of circumference, the Angles of the given place shall come nearest.

The business shall be illustrated with an Example. Suppose the Angle A to be found next less than the Angle of a Square, on this build the Bulwork of a Square; then let the Angle B, be next bigger than the Angle of an *Hexagon*; therefore you must build on B the Bulwork of an *Hexagon*; and so for the rest.

3. But if, when the Bulworks shall be built after this manner, that is to say, on B that of an *Hexagon*, on C that of a *Pentagon*, it happens that the Courtine I. K is notably less than 300 feet, you must build on B the Bulwork of a *Pentagon*, and on C the Bulwork of a Square. If the Courtine be not yet 300 feet, you must also make on B the Bulwork of a Square; but if yet the Courtine be less than 300 feet, the side C B will be unfit. *Fig.* 27.

PROB. III.

To do the same yet another Way.

1. THe third manner is this; if the Angle of the Place differ notably from the Angle of the next Regular Figure, then with the same *Data* as are in any of the six manners of the fifth Chapter, find for each of the Angles A, B all the Angles and Lines as we did there in Regular Fortifications. *Dogen*, in pag. 204. seems to prefer for this purpose the third manner delivered in the fifth Chapter. *Fig.* 27.

2. On the Angle A, make a Bulwork with his Neck-lines, Capital, Flanques, which you found for the Angle A; in the like manner on the Angle B make a Bulwork, taking the Neck-lines, Capital and Flanques, which you found for the Angle B, and so in the rest of the Angles C D E.

3, If, after the Bulworks are thus order'd, the Courtine be found too short, you must help that fault almost after the same manner, as in *num.* 3. *Prob.* II.

4. At last, the Figure being fortified after this manner, according as the several circumstances may require, the proportion of the Flanques, Faces, and of the Angle of Bulwork, may be freely changed and altered, *&c.* provided you do not transgress the Canons establish'd in the third Chapter: *Dogen* hath Tables of this after *pag.* 200. This way is taken out of *Dogen*.

CHAP. XVII.

How an Irregular place, having unfit Sides and Angles, ought to be fortified.

PROB. *I.*

To fortifie the unfit Angles of the Irregular Place A.

Fig. 28. 1. IF the Angle S I B be only little less than a right one, build on it the Bulwork of a Square, and cut off its Angle Q, for it is less than it should be, and make a pair of Tonges, or the outward Angle N O P. Others, when the Angle is betwixt eighty and ninety degrees, had rather build before it a Horn-work. I judge it best to do both.

2. If the Angle B C H were less than eighty degrees, but bigger than sixty, surround it with a Crown-work. Others cut away the Angle it self, if it be near sixty degrees, and turn it to a pair of Tonges D F E: He doth best for a Fortification that joyns both.

3. If any Angle, as S G H, be less than sixty degrees, let the Figure of the place be changed, by drawing a new side G R C, that may make Angles of a just quantity with both the sides S G and B C.

4. 'Twill be lawful also to change an unfit Angle, provided not less than sixty degrees, into a whole Bulwork or half Bulwork, or into a Raveline, or Half-moon; or else to cut it off, and change it into Tonges or a Horn-work.

PROB. II.

To fortifie the external Angles of an Irregular Place.

Fig. 29. LEt there be given the outward Angle of an Irregular Place A B C, to be fortified.

1. If the ends of the Sides A and C are not distant from one another, neither less than 518 feet, nor more than 826, build whole Bulworks on A and C; as we taught in *Chap* 16. *Prob.* 1, 2. &c.

2. If the distance of the ends A and C be more than 826 feet, you must build before the outward Angle either a Raveline, or Hornwork, or else both. Likewise you may make in the sides middle or toothed defences (of which see *Chap.* 14. *num.* 9.) building over and above a Raveline.

Fig. 30. 3. If the distance of the ends A and C be less than 518 feet, make two half Bulworks for the defence of the sides A S and C R: But before the outward Angle you must build a larger sort of Raveline.

4. The

4. The best way of all to fortifie external Angles, is to inclose them within the Figure, by drawing a new side G C; and then the Angles B C G, S G C, and the side G C, may be fortified after the manner deliver'd in *Chap.* 16. if they are fit; if unfit, according to the method, partly already deliver'd in this Chapter, and partly to be deliver'd. *Fig.* 28.

PROB. III.

To fortifie the sides of an Irregular Fortification.

1. LEt the side that is too long be A B, measure the least Angle of the place A, and observe as above what Regular figures Angle of the circumference it comes nearest to; Let us suppose it comes nearest to the Angle of a *Pentagon*, and bisect the side A B in G; also cut off the Neck-lines of the *Pentagon* A O and B N, because we suppos'd the least Angle at A to be nearest that of a *Pentagon*. This being done, if the remainder G O, G N, be not less than 300 feet, or more than 500, you shall build on the middle point of the Courtine G, a plain Bulwork, according to the Method delivered *Chap.* 14. *numb.* 11. In which alter only this, that the Neck-lines G I, G H be taken equal to the Neck-lines A O, B N of the Bulworks set on the neighbouring Angles. *Fig.* 31.

2. If any side as A L be of so great a length, that being it self divided into equal parts L ϖ, ϖ θ, θ A, and having its Neck-lines cut off, A β θ ζ, θ λ, ϖ ω, ϖ φ, L δ, does leave its Courtines δ φ, ω λ, ζ β, not less than 300 feet, nor more than 500, you shall build more plain Bulworks on the side A L.

3. That side for which two Bulworks are too little, and three are too much, must be rather fortified with two great ones, than three little ones.

4. If the side too long will not admit of one plain Bulwork, the Courtine must be fortified with Ravelins and other works, but their Profile must be longer than ordinary.

Note, *That universally sides either too long or too short, may be corrected or not; they may be corrected when the sides that are too long, can be cut shorter; or when those that are too short can be produced. Besides you may make a new Angle on the side that is too long, that shall yield two sides of a fit quantity.*

PROB. IV.

To fortifie the sides of an Irregular place that is too short.

1. IF several sides are less than 300 feet, you must change the figure and fortifie it after some manner already delivered.

2. If the figure of the place will not admit of a change, either the Courtines must be fortified with Ravelins built before them, whose profile must be more than ordinary, or the Angles must be surrounded with Crown-works; they may be also changed into Tonges or Hornworks, or else they may be shelter'd with one whole Bulwork.

3. If the side to be fortified, having on each end the Neck-lines belonging to a square cut off, be less than 300 feet, Bulworks must not be built on the Angles adjacent to the second side, although they be fit, but shall be fortified with other Out-works;

 and

and if the Angles are betwixt 90 and 120 degrees, you must build before them Hornworks; or if more then 120 degr. you must object before the angles in the Ditch it self either Ravelins, or Retrench'd Bulworks.

4. The side that is too short, and those too long may be also mended; if you make Irregular Bulworks, whose Neck-lines are almost all set off on the longest side.

PROB. V.

How Ancient Cities are to be Fortified.

1. AN ancient Rampar if it be strong and surrounded with a Wall and Towers, must not be demolish'd; therefore you must inclose it with a new fortification, which must be Regular, if possible, or as near a Regular as might be.

Betwixt the New Fortification and the old Ditch there must be left a large *Pomœrium* fit for Military uses.

2. If the ancient Fortifications be of Earth, or can be mended without much cost and labour, then proceed according to the Rules of Irregular Fortification already delivered. Many French and Dutch Cities are fortified with Ravelins, Halfmoons, Hornworks, and other sort of works: which sort of building since 'tis to supply the place of Bulworks ought to be stronger than usual. They are likewise frequently fortified with a Fauss-bray, and the Brestwork of the Covert-way; and sometimes with a Ditch about this Out-brestwork, and with *Stakado's*.

Corollary.

Out of these three foregoing *Chapters*, 'tis understood by what Method all Irregular places are to be fortified, whether they labour with all the defects above mentioned, or not with all. Moreover, this is to be observed in the Fortification of every Irregular place, that you have the Plane of the place described on paper, that so you may the better see, what form of Fortification, and what works may best agree with the given place; and as the figure that is to be fortified proves Irregular, so commonly its Bulworks, Hornworks, Ravelins, &c. will have an Irregular figure, the place so requiring.

CHAP. XVIII.

SOmething of what is now to be said is also common to Regular places, but we shall conveniently dispatch them all together in this place.

1. Those places o're which rising Hills or neighbouring Mountains domineer, are unfit to be fortified. Either therefore the Hill is to be inclosed within the circuit of the walls, or if it cannot be inclosed, all care must be taken that the Enemy do not possess it: Which will be done by setting a new and strong Fortification upon it; or when this cannot be done, it must be by raising of *Cavaliers* or batteries in the Bulwork or Courtine, o're which the Hill seems to hang. If Castles or Cities are built upon Mountains where there may be danger of Mining, you must fortifie the foot of the Mountain with works.

2. The most convenient and safest place for the Gates, is betwixt the two Bulworks

in the middle of the Courtine, for they can be defended in no other place with so much security and facility. For the same reason Rivers cutting through a City, are received betwixt the two Bulworks.

3. To keep great Cities in their duty and obedience, there is nothing fitter than to joyn a *Cittadel* to that place which may most command the Town.

Concerning their building and scituation observe this, 1. Let them possess the strongest part of the City; wherefore if there be a Rock or Hill within the Town, there let them be built. So they have done at *Namur*, *Cambray*, *Naples*, and other places. 2. Let them be set against the chiefest avenues of the Towns, and let the gates be lyable to their command. 3. Let them be *Pentagons*, for this figure is fittest; for the square is weaker, and not so capacious: The rest of the figures above a *Pentagon*, are larger than needs, and are too costly. *Antwerp*, *Turin*, *Amiens*, *Vitri*, *Phallzbourg*, *Stenay*, and many other Towns, have Pentagonal *Cittadels*; *Millain*, *Perpignan*, and *Casall*, have *Hexagons*; *Manheim*, *Verdun*, *Blavett* have septangular ones. 4. They are so to be placed that they turn two of their Bulworks towards the Town, three to the field; And so that one of the Cou tines of the City A B, meet with the Courtine of the *Cittadel* T, betwixt the two Bulworks C and G, one of which looks towards the City, the other towards the Enemy, as you have it express'd in the 32 Figure. This last is not of little moment, for so the Bulwork G is stoutly defended from the Courtine of the Town; and the Courtine it self of the Town is scowred and defended by the *Cittadel*. From whence it appears, they very much erre, who remove the *Cittadels* far from the Towns. 5. Let them have at least two gates, one towards the Town, another towards the field, to receive in succours upon occasion. 6. Betwixt the *Cittadel* and the houses of the Town let there be a plane of a sufficient bigness. *Antwerp* shews you an example of a *Cittadel* compleat and perfect with all its numbers; for this commands the City with two Bulworks, with two more scowrs the *Scald* that flows by it; and with three, proudly domineers o're the field, and it is furnished with all the rest that may either appertain to its form or scituation. *Fig.* 32.

4. The sides of Cities that are wash'd with Rivers, may be fortified with slight works, to wit, with a single External or internal Angle, or with middle defences, terminated with half-Bulworks. You shall fortifie the sides with Hornworks fitted for the place, *vid.* fig. 33. Not only the mouths of Havens, but the sides that are longer then ordinary, are to be strengthened with Fortifications. If the city be distant from the River a Musquet-shot, it must be joyn'd to it by building a *Cittadel*. *Fig.* 33.

5. The Banck opposite to the Town, if it be within Musquet-shot, and in a friends Countrey, may be fortified with less Works; To wit, with an half sexangular Star, or with a plain Bulwork. But if it be in an enemies Countrey, or in a friends, out of Musquet-shot, you shall fortifie it with half a Regular *Hexagon*, whose sides must be protected with Hornworks and other works. You have an example in Fig. 34. The neglect of this was the loss of *Nimmeghen* on the *Vahal*. Of all this you may see farther in *Dogen Lib.* 2.

These few Rules following shall put an end to Irregular Fortification, of which there is great use in this Business.

I. Let the Irregular Fortification be reduced altogether to a Regular one, or as near it as can be.

II. Let it be round about as equal as possible can be, or equally firm.

III. A Fortification that is larger with the same circumference, is to be prefer'd before a less.

IV. Sides that bend inwards, that is, those that contain an External Angle, must be avoided, because they lessen the place, and are built at greater expence.

V. The Bulworks may be Irregular, and unlike ; for that sort of Fortification is counted handsomest that is strongest.

VI. The least distance of the Bulworks (according to *Dogen* pag. 188.) must be 60 *Rhynland* perches, the greatest 80.

VII. The Angle of defence on the Angle of the *Tenailles*, must be as oft as can be, opposite to the middle point of the Courtine.

VIII. Against Hills that hang over the Town, or against Rivers that flow into the Moat, rather object the Courtine than the Bulwork, for that is stronger than this.

THE THIRD PART.

Of besieging Towns, and how to defend them.

THere are five Acts proper to the Seige, Circumvallation, The Lines of approach and Batteries for Cannons, The Sappes, or the cutting through the out-brestwork, The Gallerie, and the breaking of the Bulwork by a Mine.

1. First, therefore the place that is to be besieged is to be so inclosed round about with a Rampar, fortified with all sorts of works, that no going out, nor coming in, may lie open to it. 2. You come to the out-brestwork under the favour of trenches depress'd beneath the *Horizon*, and drawn with various windings, so that they cannot be scowred from any part of the place besieged. 3. The out-brestwork in cutting through, you must no longer use Trenches drawn obliquely, but it must be done by the shortest cut, that is by a Line drawn directly. 4. The Graft must be fill'd with a bank made of earth and stones and Faggots, carried on thorough it to the Rampar, on which at last the Gallery is layd. If the Ditch be dry, sometimes the Gallery is carried under ground to the place appointed for the Mine. 5. Through the Gallery that is now finished, the Pioneers advance without any danger to the Rampar, where they dig a hole, and put in such a quantity of Gunpowder as may serve to break the great Bulk of earth that stands over it ; which at last being set on fire, and the Rampar broken, the Souldiers are led on through the Gallery to the breach, to enter the City that lyes open before them. This is the Sum of the Siege, whose parts I shall briefly expound, and every one distinctly by it self.

CHAP. XIX.

Of Circumvallation.

CIrcumvallation consists in Camps, Trenches, and works of all sorts. The very Camps also being a lesser kind of Circumvallation, doe comprehend the two last, to wit, Trenches, and varietie of Works.

PROP.

PROP. I.

The disposing of the Camp or Quarters.

1. THe Camp is to be form'd in those places that seem most convenient to let in an External Enemy.

2. It must not be made in a place that may be drowned.

3. Let there be so many, that relief may be readily sent from them, to all parts of the Circumvallation.

4. Let them be above Cannon shot from the Town, or at least so far off, as that they may fear little dammage from their Guns.

5. Let them be placed, if you can, by a River side.

6. The Camp, as likewise all the rest of the Circumvallation, must be fortified with Trenches, that is, with a Rampar round about it, and several other works.

PROP. II.

Of the Lines commonly called Trenches.

THese Lines of the Siege are a continual kind of Rampar, which surround as wel the Camp, as all the rest of the places about the Town besieged. Concerning these, Observe this.

1. Let them be twofold, one inward, built against the besieg'd, to keep them in, least with their Sallies they hurt the Beliegers; the other outward, to keep off any enemy that should attacque the Camp from without. Let the outward be stronger than the inward; nay, when there is but a small Garrison in the Town, these inward ones may be spared, or at least very slightly built.

2. These Trenches, especially the outward one, must not be extended above 750 feet upon a right Line: After every 750 feet, they must be fortified with several works cast before and betwixt them. These are wont to be used, Redoubts or little Turrets, Middle or toothed defences, outward and inward Angles, Little Tonges, Stars, square Forts with whole Bulworks, various Forts with half Bulworks, whole plain Bulworks, and half ones, Ravelins, half moons, Hornworks, Crownworks.

All this Trade of Works so various and so manifold, was used in no time more than in our age, nor in no place oftner than in *Holland*, at the Siege of *Hartogen Bosch*, at both the Sieges of *Breda*, *Mastricht*, and many others; most of those are already delivered in the foregoing propositions: we will expound those that remain in the following.

3. The Profiles and Ichnography of these Trenches is various, in respect of their place and danger; I'le give you three sorts of them used at the siege of *Hartogen Bosch*.

The Base of the Brestwork.	$7\frac{1}{2}$.	7.
The outward Sloap or *Talu*.	$2\frac{1}{2}$.	3.
The inward Sloap.	1.	1.
The inward height.	6.	6.
The outward height.	5.	5.

The upper part.	4.	3.
The width of the Step.	3.	3.
The heighth of the Step.	$\frac{1}{2}$.	$\frac{1}{2}$.
The Border or footing on the outside.	3.	3.
The width of the Ditch.	12.	8.
The outward *Talu* or Sloap of the Ditch.	4.	2.
The inward Sloap of the Ditch.	4.	2.
The depth of the Ditch.	5.	2.
The width at the bottom of the Ditch.	4.	4.

At the coming of the Royal Army, the *Dutch* made their Circumvallation stronger, they increas'd the Base of their Brestwork to 9 feet, making three Steps, whose widths added together made 9 feet; the height of the brestwork was likewise 9 feet, the width of the Ditch was 15 feet.

PROP. III.

To build a Redoubt or Turret.

IT is a most easie thing, since their form is simply square. Therefore describe on the earth a Line of 48 feet, and on it delineate a square; and what you require is done. The Ichnographie and Profile is after this manner.

Its Base.	14. or 20.
Its width a top.	4. or 6.
Its height.	8. or 10.
Its border or footing.	2. or 3.
The width of its Ditch.	15. or 24.
The depth of the Ditch.	5. or 6.

There is usually added to the Brestwork two or three Steps gradually placed over one another.

PROP. IV.

To delineate a Star.

Fig. 35. **To delineate a quadrangular one, work after this manner.**

1. DEscribe on the field a Line of 48 or 50 feet, and on it describe a square.

2. Bisect the side A B in C, and from C raise the perpendicular C D equal to $\frac{1}{4}$ of A C, or $\frac{1}{8}$ of the whole A B.

3. Joyn A D, D B, if this construction be made round all the sides, you'l have a quadrangular Star.

Fig. 36. **To have a Pentagonal Star, work after this manner.**

Describe a Regular *Pentagon*; and from the side A B bisected in C raise the perpendicle C D equal to $\frac{1}{3}$ of A C or $\frac{1}{6}$ of A B. Joyn A D, D B, and if you do the same round the figure, you will have a Pentagonal Star.

For

For a Sexangular one.

Describe A C E *&c.* a Regular *Hexagon,* let each of its sides A C *&c.* be equal to about 104 paces, at the ends of C H *&c.* make the Angles D A C, D C A, *&c.* 30 degrees each; And D A, D C will be each about 60 paces. *Fig.* X.

Their Ichnographie and Profiles are the same as that of Redoubts.

Your larger Stars are not in use.

PROP. V.

To delineate a square Fort with half-Bulworks.

1. DEscribe the square A B C D, whose sides must not be less than 120 feet, nor more than 180. *Fig.* 37.

2. Trisect the sides in E, F, L, M, Q, S, T, V.

3. To each of the sides add $\frac{1}{3}$ B I, D N, C O, A H; but for the Neck-lines take $\frac{1}{3}$ in the sides themselves, to wit, B L, D Q, C T, A E.

4. From the ends of the Neck-lines raise the perpendicular L K, Q R, T X, E G, each of which must be $\frac{1}{6}$ of the side.

5. Draw the right lines I K, N R, O X, H G.

So have you a Fort with four half-Bulworks.

PROP. VI.

To delineate a Fort on a Rectangular Paralellogram with half-Bulworks.

1. TRisect one of the lesser sides A B, and cut off $\frac{1}{3}$ of it from all the sides for the Neck-lines A F, B G, C O, D Q. *Fig.* 38.

2. Add also to each of the sides A K, B L, C P, D S, equal to $\frac{1}{3}$ of A B.

3. On the ends of the Neck-lines raise the perpendicles F I, G M, O N, Q R, equal to $\frac{1}{6}$ of the same A B.

4. Joyn K I, L M, P N, S R. I say 'tis done.

PROP. VII.

To delineate another sort of Quadrilateral Fort, with half Bulworks and double Tonges.

1. TAke the third part of the sides of the square A B C D, for the Neck-lines C P, A M, B N, R D. *Fig.* 39.

2. Add to the side C D on both sides $\frac{1}{3}$ C I, D K, but to the sides C A, D B likewise add $\frac{1}{3}$ A S, B T.

3. From the ends of the Neck-lines raise perpendicles equal to [illegible] PX, M L, N V, R Z, and joyn I X, S L, T V, K Z.

4. Bisect the side C D in E, and thence cut off E G, E H equal to [illegible] of the side; and thence again raise the perpendicle E F equal also to [illegible].

5. Joyn G F, H F, you have your purpose.

Fig. 40. There are built also square Forts with two whole Bulworks, and on the opposite side the double Tonges. See *Fig.* 40.

PROP. VIII.

To delineate a three-sided Fort with half Bulworks.

Fig. 41. 1. DEscribe an equilateral Triangle A B C, whose sides must be less than those of a Square.

2. Cut off from the sides the third part A I, B L, C K, for the Neck-lines.

3. From the end of the Neck-lines raise perpendicularly the sixth part of the sides I H, L M, K G.

4. Add to the sides of the third part B D, C E, A F, and joyn F H, D M, E G. you have your purpose,

The four Forts describ'd in the foregoing Propositions, are not to be built promiscuously, and for varieties sake, but with choise, and with respect to the place: And although they are much weaker than Forts with whole Bulworks, nevertheless they are conveniently made use of.

As to their Profile and Ichnography, you may give them the same as to Redoubts and Stars; or if they require a greater, you may give them that which was used in the siege of *Hartogen Bosch*; in which the base of the Rampar was 27 feet, the height 6, the upper breadth of the Rampar 18, the base of the Brestwork 8, the upper breadth of the Brest-work 4, the height of the Brest-work 6, the width of the Ditch 30 feet.

CHAP. XX.

Of Batteries for great Guns, and of the Approaches.

THE Circumvallation being finish'd, which is the first act of the Siege, deliver'd in the foregoing Chapter, you raise batteries for great Guns in certain places, and go towards the Out-brestwork, cover'd in oblique Trenches. Of these therefore in this present Chapter.

PROP. I.

To build an Offensive and Defensive Battery.

THere is a twofold Battery, offensive and defensive; the last is directed towards the enemy without; the first towards the besieged. You shall build an Offensive one after this manner. *Fig.* 42.

1. Multiply the number of Guns that are to be mounted by 12; the product shall give in feet the length of the Battery, for each Gun is distant from another 12. feet, and the two at the ends are distant from the Brestwork 6 feet each.

2. You'l have the breadth A D, if, to the length of a Gun mounted in his carriage, you add the spa e AF, ten or twelve feet for the recoiling of the peice; and the space F D, for traversing and passage.

3. Let the plat-form of the Battery be made sloaping downwards towards the Enemy, that when the Guns are recoil'd they may with more ease be brought back to their places: Let its entry behind be I, K; the way leading to it must not be very steep, but gently rising, that the Guns may with more ease be got in.

4. That part of the Battery that faces the Enemy, must be fortified with a Brestwork, whose Base you may make 12, 15, or 18 feet, its height 6; for the sides A D, B E a less width will suffice.

5. Let there be so many Ports in the Brestwork as there are Guns; let their height be three feet, their outward width four, their inward two; the outward width is more than the inward, that the Guns may scowr more of the field.

6. Behind the Battery you must describe a space D S N E equal and like the Battery; in it make a square hole, as M, whose side must be ten or twelve feet; in which the powder must be kept, and you must cover the mouth with leather, least any sparks should fall in. To conclude, as well about the Battery it self A E, as the space D N, you must make a Ditch eight or ten feet wide, six feet deep.

7. The first Batteries are wont to be raised at a Musquet-shot from the Town, afterwads near the very ditches; the general rule may be this, that the nearer they are the place, they do the greater execution.

8. The Defensive Batteries are not so full of work; their Brestwork, if it be made of earth, may be six or seven feet thick; the height is sufficient, if it cover a Gun in its carriage; instead of an earthen Brestwork they use commonly great wicker Baskets fil'd with earth.

PROP. II.

To direct the Lines of Approaches to a place Besieged.

1. ABout the distance of a thousand feet from the Town open the Trench $\alpha\kappa$, which you must carry on obliquely towards the place besieged, so that it may not be scowred from any part of it; which being continued some space you must dig a new one the other way, as $\kappa\lambda$, with the same obliqueness; and so by several turnings you proceed to the Out-brestwork it self, where at length the Approaches are finish'd, drawing two Trenches $\theta\kappa$, θ I longer than ordinary, and parallel to the place besieged. These two last Lines cover the Besiegers like a Brest-work, so that being so near at hand they frighten away the Defendants from guarding their Grast and Rampar. *Fig.* 43

 2. Although

2. Although the Approaches ought so to be carried on, that they may never be scowred from the Enemies Rampar, yet the Engineer shall take good heed he make them no more obliquer than needs, to the loss of time and expences. I think with two turnings you may alwayes come to the out-brestwork, a far shorter way than if more oblique lines had been made: For let there be drawn from the point where you began your Approaches, the right line $\alpha\ \beta$, which continued may fall a little without the Angle of the brestwork, and if another line be produced from β, which goes without the Angles of the out-brestwork, you will arrive at the out-brestwork in two turnings $\alpha\ \beta$, $\beta\ \theta$: but why this way of Approaches is less used, I think this to be the reason: That your long lines of Approach, if attempted, may be sooner carried and demolish'd by the Enemy, than those that are cut in and out with several windings.

3. At the end of every Line you must build Redoubts, after such a manner, that two may be flanqued by one; for this is the best situation of Redoubts: If one of the Lines be drawn longer than ordinary, you may also build Redoubts in the middle for its defence, all which the 43 Figure sufficiently expresses.

4. The earth which is cast out is thrown towards the Enemy, that it may be instead of a Brestwork to the Pioneers.

Let its Tower width be six feet, its upper twelve or fifteen, its least depth must be such, that may cover a standing man, with the height of its Brestwork joyn'd to it. The nearer they advance to the Town the deeper they must be: The width also must be increas'd, if there is occasion to bring stuff for the Gallery thorough the Trenches: They use frequently to make three steps to the Brestwork.

6. For the security of the Approaches, Batteries are to be built in convenient places.

CHAP. XXI.

The Sapp, or the cutting thorough the Out-brestwork.

Fig. 43. 1. THe Approaches being advanced to the out-brestwork, two longer Trenches, as I said before, ought to be drawn parallel to the place that is besieged, the Brestwork being built towards the Enemy; in these Musqueteers are to be placed, that they may hi nder the Enemy from showing his head above the Rampar.

2. These things being done, when you can no longer draw your Lines obliquely, 'tis necessary that from that longer Trench, which is parallel to the place you intend to attaque, you cut a strait Channel L H, commonly called a *Sappe*, thorough the out-brestwork, to the very ditch of the Fortification. Without doubt this work is full of dangerous chances: But the danger seems to be lessened by these means. 1. The Souldiers being placed in the Trenches θ I, $\theta\kappa$, by their continual firing hindring the Defendants. 2. The Brestwork and flanques of the Rampar are now so batter'd by the Cannon, that the Defendants can scarce stand upon their Rampar.

3. This Channel is made deeper than the rest of the Approaches, and is cover'd above with boughs, straw, hides, and other things necessary; that if a man cannot be protected by it from the shot, yet at least the Pioneers may be by this means withdrawn from the sight of the besieged.

4. This

4. This Channel is to be directed to that part of the Fortification which is design'd for the Mine; wherefore, if you besiege a Regular Fortification, you must not direct it towards the Courtine, or the Angle of the Bulwork, but to either of the faces of the Bulwork; For whosoever attaques the Courtine, is lyable to shot from both the Bulworks, and they very near; and whosoever attempts the Angle of the Bulwork, is also lyable to the shot of two Bulworks, though they lye farther off: Whil'st he that attaques the face can be hurt but from one only. But if the Courtine hath not on both sides its full defence. as it often happens in Irregular places not perfectly fortified, the *Sappe* and the attaque may be carried on to the middle point of the Courtine.

CHAP. XXII.

Concerning filling the Ditch, and carrying over the Gallery advanced.

THe *Sappe* L H being advanced thorough the out-brestwork and covert way unto the Ditch, all that remains is that you fill the Ditch with a solid bank of earth carried on quite over it, and that the Gallery be built upon this bank. *Fig. 43.*

1. The Ditch whether it be wet or dry is filled with stones, boughs, faggots, logs, and with sacks full of earth; but this Rubbidge that is cast in must be so ordered, that the bank may rise quite over the Ditch as high as the foot of the Rampar, and have such a breadth that the Gallery may conveniently be set upon it.

2. The bank being now finished, there is commonly so much earth brought thorough the *Sappe* and cast down on the bank, as may serve to make a kind of little hill betwixt the face of the Bulwork and the besiegers; then casting, with shovels longer than ordinary, the lower part of this heap of earth over the upper, this hill is turned over and over, and is rouled on by degrees to the face of the Bulwork.

3. This hill being rowled on some space, there are two gates erected at a little distance from one another; which are so joyned together with planks, as well on each side as at top, that no part of them lyes open. On that side which regards the Enemies Bulwork so much earth is cast up, as may make it Cannon-proof: The other side doth not need so much covering. Also the upper part will be sufficiently fortified against fire, if it be covered with a foot or a foot and half of Earth. In like manner the rest of the parts of this Gallery shall be continued till they come to the Rampar. The width of these gates is either 9 or 10 feet, the height 10 feet, the thickness of its beams or timbers 6 or 7 inches, half a foot.

4. This is the Theorie of Galleries, which you'l hardly describe easier than build. In the universal affair of the Siege there is nothing more dangerous than this enterprize: Nevertheless the danger seems to be lessened by these means. 1. That rowling hill of earth betwixt the face of the Bulwork and the Workmen, keeps their front safe. 2. The opposite flanque, as well that of the Bulwork as that of the Courtine, is so battered with Cannon, that the side of the Gallery cannot be broken from thence by the Guns of the besieged. Also from the Trenches of θ I, θ κ, the Musqueteers that guard the builders of the Gallery, are continually firing on every part of the Rampar. 3. They work most commonly in the night. 4. They secure their sides with faggot which they set upon cleft wood, commonly called candlesticks, by which means they escape many shots, and hide themselves from the sight of the Enemie.

CHAP. XXIII.

Of the Mine.

Fig. 43. THe Ancients also used Mines, but to a different end, and after a different manner. In this Age now that this Art may seem to have attained its perfection, the business is done almost after this manner.

1. The Gallery A A being brought over to the face of the enemies Bulwork, you design the place where you intend to put the powder. Then digging two or three turnings C E, E F, you come to the place appointed K by the conduct of a needle; the channel C E F G is made winding, that the powder might not so easily get out toward C. It is 4 feet or 4 ½ feet deep, 4 feet or 3 ½ feet wide, yet it is made narrower the nearer you come to the place appointed.

2. When you come to the place appointed K, there you dig a place to lodg the powder, whose height is commonly 6 or 7 feet, the side of its base 4 or 5 feet; here you put your Barrels of powder so as to set them close together in the place, for so the powder will be all lighted in a shorter time; and therefore does it effect the stronger. This also experience hath taught us, that the earth of the broken Bulwork will fall towards that part, toward which the greatest space was left between the Barrels and the Superficies of the place where they are put; therefore if you would have the Earth fall towards the Enemy, you shall put the powder nearer the side φ N, if towards *&c.*

3. One Barrel of powder will blow up 12 feet of earth; hence gather how many Barrels are to be put in. The powder must not be long carried in before you intend to put fire to it, otherwise it would grow moist, and be spoyled.

4. The mouth of the Mine C must be diligently stopped, only leaving in it a Trunck or hollow pipe full of powder for the Train, reaching the powder in K, that putting a match to it you may blow up the Mine at the time appointed.

As for the Attacque it self, which is ordered when the Mine is sprung and the breach made, I leave that to the Officers and Souldiers, to whom these things belong.

CHAP. XXIV.

Of defending Towns.

1. THe first beginning is to keep the enemy from the Town as far off and as long as you can. Therefore whatsoever without the works can put a stop to the Enemy, the Besiegers must possess and defend as long as they can.

2. They must use all their endeavour to hinder the approaches of the Enemy; therefore let them sally frequently (but warily, least they fall into snares to the irreparable loss of the Town) and rout and kill the Pioneers and Souldiers; Let them throw down the Lines that are finish'd, and if they cannot carry away their Guns, they must spike them up, by driving Nails in their Touch-holes.

3. Those outward works which they can keep no longer must be retrenched, (see what we said before of Retrenchments) but if they are utterly like to be lost, they must be blow'n up together with those that possess them.

4. The

4. The ſapping of the out-breſtwork muſt be intercepted by a counter and tranſverſe *Sappe*.

5. The filing of the Ditch and the building of the Gallery muſt be hindered at a diſtance by the continual firing of Muſquets, great Guns, hand Granadoes, and other fireworks; nor is there any other way if the Ditch be full of water. But if the Ditch be dry, then they muſt fall upon the builders of the Gallery with handy-ſtroaks, as well as with all that which I declared above. And the Gallery it ſelf muſt either be deſtroyed by fire, or blown up with a Mine.

6. But if notwithſtanding all this, the force of the Enemy prevailing, the Gallery is brought over to the Bulwork, and the Bulwork it ſelf be undermined. Againſt this plague no remedy remains, but to find out the place of the Mine. To do this they uſe ſeveral practiſes. Some by the motion of Peaſe leaping on a Drum-head well braced, do conjecture at the place of their digging; others boaring a very long Augur into the ground ſuſpected, and applying their ear to it, think to hear the ſtroakes of their digging; others uſe other ways to diſcover it. The moſt certain way is by countermining to ſearch the foundation of the Bulwork. The Mine being found, the powder muſt be carried out; but if the ſtreightneſs of time will not permit, it muſt be wetted, and a paſſage opened for the fire.

7. The Bulworks being blown up, if the Beſieged have no inward works remaining, the laſt refuge is, that ſince they can no longer reſiſt the Enemy with wall and Rampar, that they ſtop his paſſage with arms and hands as he is breaking in at the breach. Which ſince they are rather the parts of Captains and Souldiers than the Engineers, I leave the reſt to them, and put an end to this treatiſe.

FINIS.

A

New, Exact, and most Expeditious

METHOD

Of Delineating all manner of

FORTIFICATIONS

(*Regular* and *Irregular*)

As well from the *INTERIOR*, as from the *EXTERIOR POLIGONE*;

Being comprehended within the Two *Faces* or *Superficies* of a

MEDALL.

A New, Exact, and most Expeditious METHOD Of Delineating all manner of FORTIFICATIONS

Regular and *Irregular*, (as well from the *Interior*, as from the *Exterior Poligon*;) being comprehended within the Two *Faces* or *Superficies* of a *MEDALL*.

The use of the First Face or Superficies of the MEDALL as represented in Fig. A.

THe first *Face* or *Superficies* of the *Medall* serves to delineate all manner of *Fortifications* from the *Base* or *Exterior Poligon*; And that

1. From a *Pentagon* to a *Right Line*, as being the more perfect } Figures.
2. From a *Square* to a *Pentagon*, as being the less perfect } Figures.

1. *From a* Pentagon *to a* Right Line.

Having divided the given *Base* or *Exterior Poligon* A A (as in *Fig.* C,) into two equal parts in the point D; from that point D erect a *Perpendicular* D E of a sufficient length. Then take any measure whatsoever, (be it a Chain, Pole, Staff, or Stake out of a Hedge) and mark out 3, or 6, or 9, or 12, or 15, or 18, or 21, or 24, or 27, or 30 Lengths upon the Line A D in the point B; from which raise a *Perpendicular* B C equal to ⅓ of A B, so is C a *visual* point, through which is to be drawn the Line A F, cutting the *Perpendicular* D E in the point E; And E a *visual* point, through which is to be drawn the Line A N.

Which done, divide the *Perpendicular* D E into eight equal parts, and make either of the Lines E N and E F equal to nine of those parts. And then from the points N, and F, of the Lines A N and A F, let fall the *Perpendicular* N O, till it cut the Line A F in the point O. And so likewise the *Perpendicular* E P, till it cut the Line A N in the point P. Lastly, joyn the points A O N F P A, and so you have A O, and A P for the two *Faces*; N O, and F P for the two *Flancks*, and N F for the *Curtain* of that *Fortification*. And observing the same Method from all the *Bases*, the *Fortification* becomes entire, as in *Fig.* C.

2. *From a* Square *to a* Pentagon.

The Method of delineating from a *Square* to a *Pentagon*, is the very same with that from a *Pentagon* to a *Right Line*; Onely instead of marking out three Lengths upon the *Half-Base*, you are to mark out 15 for the Line G H. And instead of (1) you are to allow (4) for the *Perpendicular* H I. And lastly, instead of dividing the *Perpendicular*

dicular K L into eight parts, you are to divide it into five; and of those parts you are to set off seven both upon the Line L M, and upon the Line L R. And this is all the difference, as may be clearly seen in *Fig.* D.

The use of the Second Face or Superficies of the MEDALL, as represented in Fig. B.

THe second *Face* or *Superficies* of this *Medall* directs how to delineate any *Fortification* by the *Interior Poligon*; And that from a *Square* to a *Right Line*:

For Example.

The *Interior Poligon* D F O being given (as in *Fig.* E) first draw the Capital Lines A G, K T, and M Q of a sufficient length. Then by the foregoing Directions, describe a *Fortification* inward upon this *Interior Poligon* (as though it were an *Exterior*;) Which done, continue the *Courtains*, and so you have given you the two Lines A C, and K M, which you are to divide equally in the points B, and L. And from those 2 Points to draw the four Lines B D, B F, L F, and L O: As likewise from the two points, E and N, you are to draw the four Lines E G, E H, N T, and N Q; so as E G, may be parallel to B D, E H to B F, N T to L F, and N Q to L O; Or (which is the very same thing) make the *Angle* D E G, equal to the *Angle* A B D; the *Angle* F E H, to the *Angle* C B F; the *Angle* F N T, to the *Angle* K L F; and the *Angle* O N Q, to the *Angle* M L O.

Lastly, from the four points of Intersection, *viz.* G, H, T, and Q, draw the Lines G H, and T Q, which are the two *Bases* sought; upon which, by the foregoing Method, describe a *Fortification* Inward, and the Work is done.

Only whensoever the *Bases* (and consequently the two Faces of a *Bastion*) do not meet in a point, (as very rarely they will) the *Face* of the less *Half-Bastion* cuts off the *Face* of the greater *Half-Bastion*; which hath this good property among many other, that it often opens or enlarges the *Angle* of the *Bastion* very considerably. Thus in *Fig.* E, the *Face* R H cuts off the *Face* P T in the point S.

There is one thing observable in the Method both of the first and second *Face* of this *Medall*, which is this, That instead of taking three Lengths of any Measure for the Line A D, in *Fig.* C, and then setting off (1) for the *Perpendicular* B C, I might divide the *Half-Base* A D into 3 or 6, or 9 equal parts, and take ⅓ thereof for the *Perpendicular* D E, because the Line D E bears the same proportion to the Line A D, as the Line B C doth to the Line A B. So likewise, instead of taking 15 or 30 Lengths upon the *Half-Base* G K in *Fig.* D, for the Line G H, and setting off 4 or 8 of those parts in the *Perpendicular* H I, I might as well have divided the *Half-Base* G K into 15 or 30, and set off 4 or 8 for K L. For as K L is to G K; so is H I to G H.

But forasmuch as this last way is more difficult and tedious than the other before mentioned, That was made use of, and This laid aside.

FINIS.

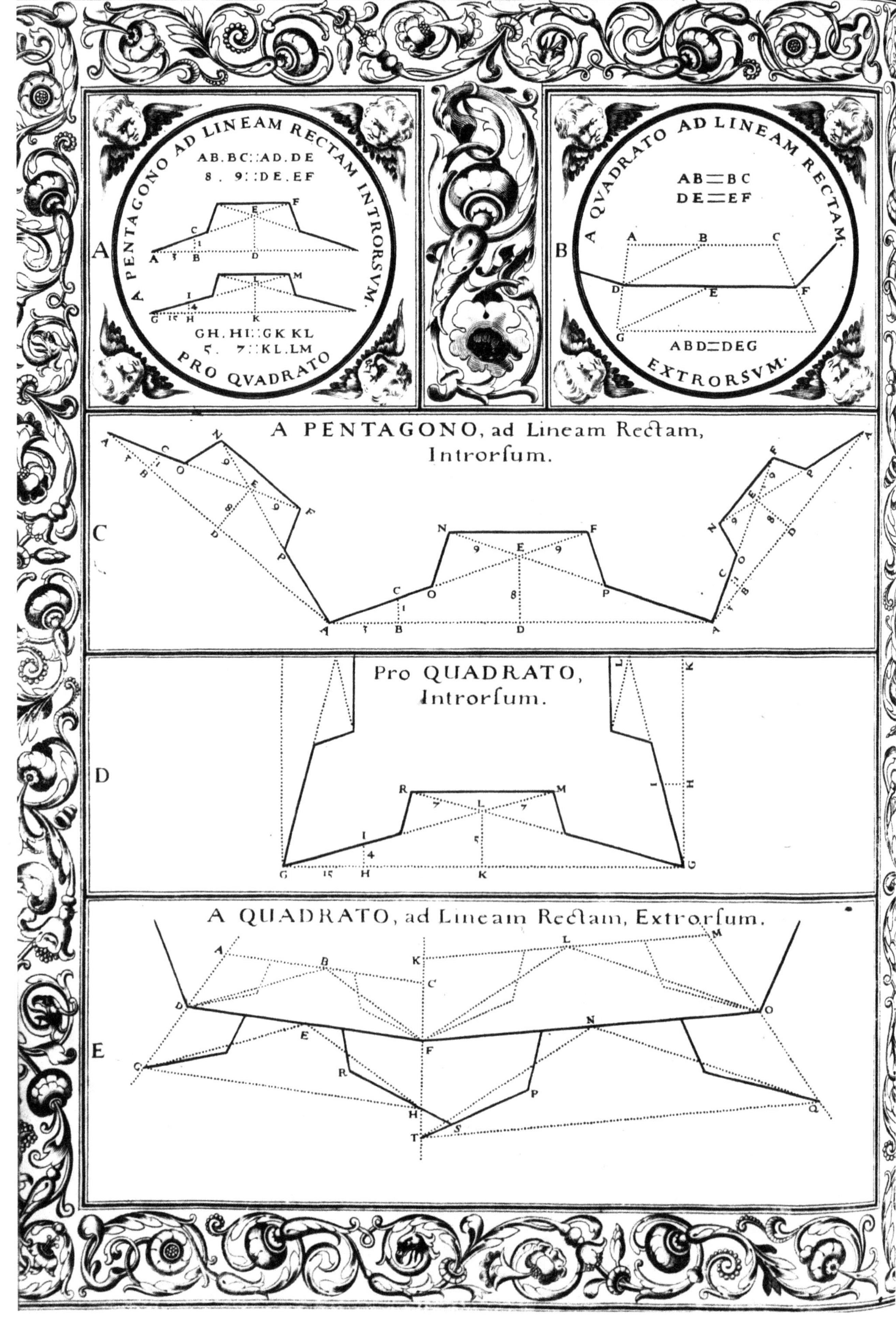
A PENTAGONO AD LINEAM RECTAM INTRORSVM.
AB.BC::AD.DE
8 . 9::DE.EF
GH.HI::GK.KL
5 . 7::KL.LM
PRO QVADRATO
A QVADRATO AD LINEAM RECTAM.
AB=BC
DE=EF
ABD=DEG
EXTRORSVM.
A PENTAGONO, ad Lineam Rectam, Introrsum.
Pro QUADRATO, Introrsum.
A QUADRATO, ad Lineam Rectam, Extrorsum.

A SECOND METHOD

(*Not inferiour to the former*)

Of Delineating any *FORTIFICATION*,

By the INTERIOR POLIGONE *given.*

LEt the *Interior Poligone* given be (A C) in the oppoſite ſuperficies of a *Medall* or (D F N V) in the adjoyning *Figure.*

Having delineated a *Fortification* inwards, and thereby gotten the ſecond *Interior Poligone* according to the foregoing Direction, *Page* 2. continue the Diſtance B E to a ſufficient length: For as the length of A C in any number of Parts, is to the Diſtance B E, ſo is the length of D F (being divided into the ſame number of Parts to the Diſtance E G. Then draw a Line X Y through the Point G parallel to D F, which Line X Y is the true *Baſe*, upon which is to be erected a *Fortification* by the Directions of *Pag*. 1. And this Method being continued from each reſpective *Poligone* given, the *Fortification* becomes perfectly *delineated.* For as H K, is to I L; ſo is F N, to M O. And ſo likewiſe as P R, to Q S; ſo is N V, to T W. Than which nothing can be more evident, as to the matter of truth and demonſtration; or more expeditious, as to the real practice and performance.

A Caveat to the Reader.

BUt to prevent any miſtake, which ſome perſons, either out of ignorance, or inadvertency, may run into, it will be convenient, to let the Reader underſtand, That although in *Fig.* C, *Pag*. 3. the middle *Baſe* (or *Poligone*) A A, is much longer than that on the left hand, and almoſt double to that on the right, that ſo it might appear to the eye to be ſufficiently *Irregular*, and alſo that it might reſemble the *Fortification* in *Fig*. E, where, without ſuch an inequality of *Baſes*, the Method of one *Face* cutting another, could not be ſo plainly expreſs'd, or ſo clearly diſcerned. (Otherwiſe it had been more eaſie to have made all the *Baſes* equal within that very ſame *Figure* C, than it was to make them ſo in this oppoſite *Figure* F.) Yet notwithſtanding this new Method takes it for granted, That all who pretend to make uſe of it, be ſo far inſtructed in the firſt Principles of *Fortification*, as to know, That when ever an *Exterior Poligone*, or rather a Ground-Plot, is given them, they are ſo to deſign and contrive it, That, if poſſible, all the *Baſes*, (if not the *Angles*) may be equal, That ſo there may be a perfect Harmony and Symmetry in all the parts thereof. This new *Rule* does likewiſe ſuppoſe, that he already knows, That, if it be practicable, each of his reſpective *Baſes*, (or *Exterior Poligones*) ought to be about 1150 Feet; but never leſs than 1024. nor yet more than 1280. That ſo the *Lines of Defence* may not be too ſhort on the one hand, nor exceed the Port of a *Muſquet* on the other. As likewiſe, that the *Angle* of his *Baſtions* be in no caſe whatſoever leſs than 60 *Degrees.* But now, where either the ſcituation of a Place, or the old Walls or Ramparts of a Town, or City, admit not any ſuch equality, either of *Baſes*, or *Angles*, there the *Hercotectonick* Laws do permit the *Engineer*, either to open, or ſharpen his *Angles*, or elſe to lengthen, or ſhorten his *Lines*, as he ſhall find it neceſſary.

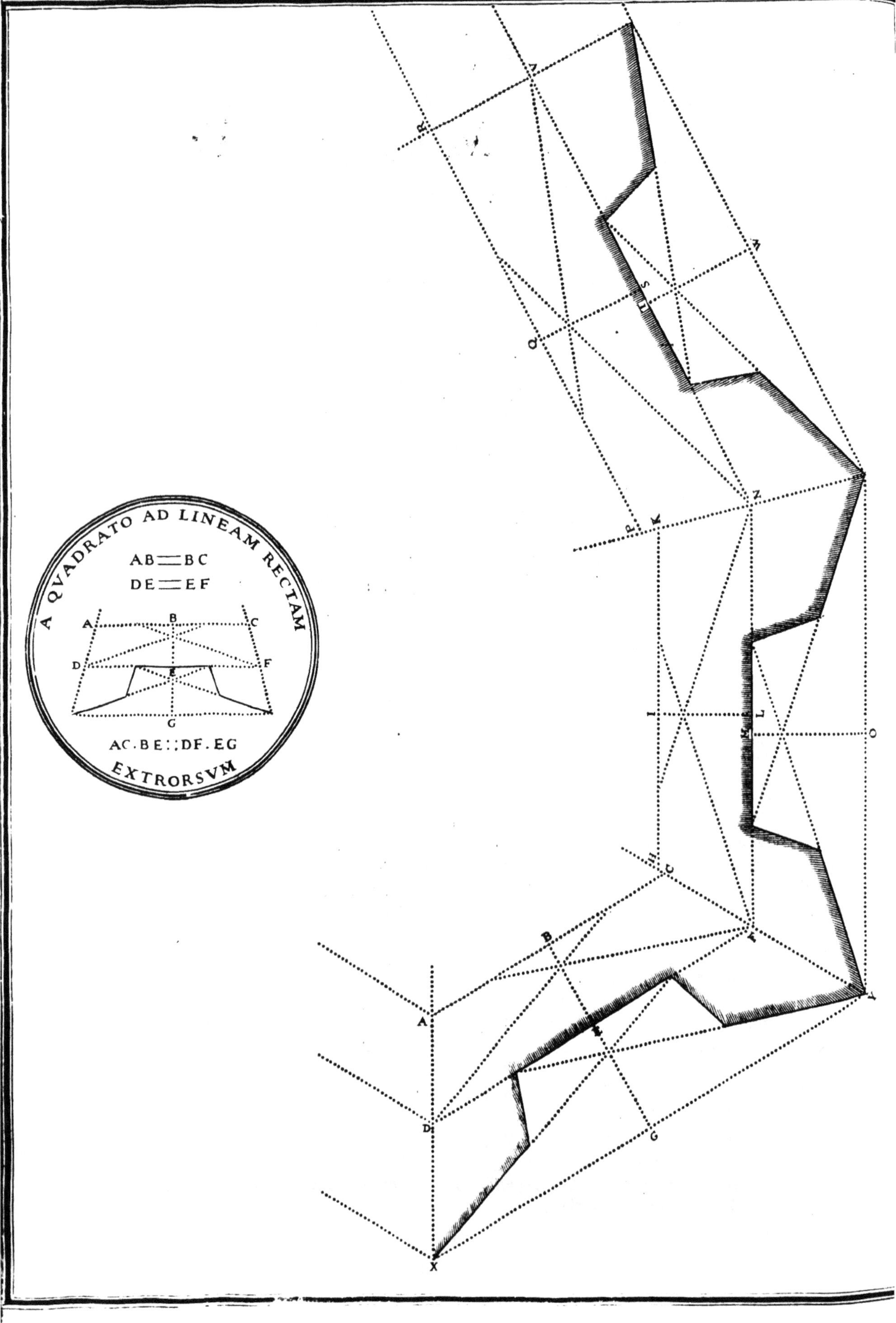
A QVADRATO AD LINEAM RECTAM
AB = BC
DE = EF
A B C
D E F
G
AC.BE::DF.EG
EXTRORSVM

THE COUNT of *PAGAN'S* METHOD

Of Delineating all manner of

FORTIFICATIONS

(*Regular* and *Irregular*)

FROM THE

Exterior Poligone.

REDUCED TO

Engliſh Meaſure,

And converted into

HERCOTECTONICK-LINES,

By *S. M.*

LONDON, Printed in the Year 1672.

ICHNOGRAPHICK Terms:

OR

Words of Art for Lines *in Fortification, neceſſary to be known.*

Lines	Engliſh.	*Latin.*	French.	*German.*
B D	Side of the Exterior Poligone.	*Latus Multanguli Exterioris.*	Poligone Exterieur.	*Beite der Bollwercks punčten.*
K N	Side of the Interior Poligone.	*Latus Multanguli Interioris.*	Poligone Interieur.	*Die Seite der Burgh.*
S B or S E	Radius of the Exterior Poligone.	*Radius Multanguli Exterioris.*	Le grand demidiameter.	*Des euſſerſten Bieleks halbe Mittellinie.*
S K or S P	Radius of the Interior Poligone.	*Radius Multanguli Interioris.*	Le petit demidiameter.	*Der Beſtung halbe Mittellinie.*
K B	Capital Line.	*Capitalis.*	Ligne Capitale.	*Haupt-linie.*
B F	Face.	*Facies Propugnaculi.*	La Face.	*Geſicht-linie.*
F L	Flanck.	*Ala Propugnaculi.*	Flancq.	*Die Streich.*
L Q	Curtain.	*Cortina, & Chorda.*	La Courtine.	*Ball.*
B Q	Line of Defence.	*Linea Defenſionis.*	Ligne de Defence.	*Behrlinie.*
C M	Diſtance between the Ext. & Int. Polig.	*Diſtantia Multangulorum.*	Diſtance des Poligones.	*Die weyts der beyden Biel-eck.*
K L	Shoulder.	*Collum.*	La Gorge.	*Hals Keel-linie.*
B C	Half-Baſe.	*Semi-Baſis.*	Demi-Baſe.	
H Q	Compliment.	*Complimentum.*	Complement.	

ICHNOGRAPHICK Terms:

OR

Words of Art for Angles *in Fortification, necessary to be known.*

Angles	English.	*Latin.*	French.	*German.*
KSN	Angle of the Center.	*Angulus Centri.*	Angle du Centre.	*Mittelpuncts eck.*
OKN	Angle of the Figure.	*Angulus Figuræ.*	Angle du Poligone.	*Keelpunct.*
RBF	Angle of the Bastion.	*Angulus Propugnaculi.*	Angle Flancque	*Bolwercks eck.*
BHD	Angle Flancking.	*Angulus Defendens.*	Angle Flanquant.	*Der Schutzwinckel.*
BFL	Angle of the Face and Flanck.	*Angulus Faciei & Alæ.*	Angle du Flancq & de la Face.	*Der winckel der Streichen und Gesicht-linie.*

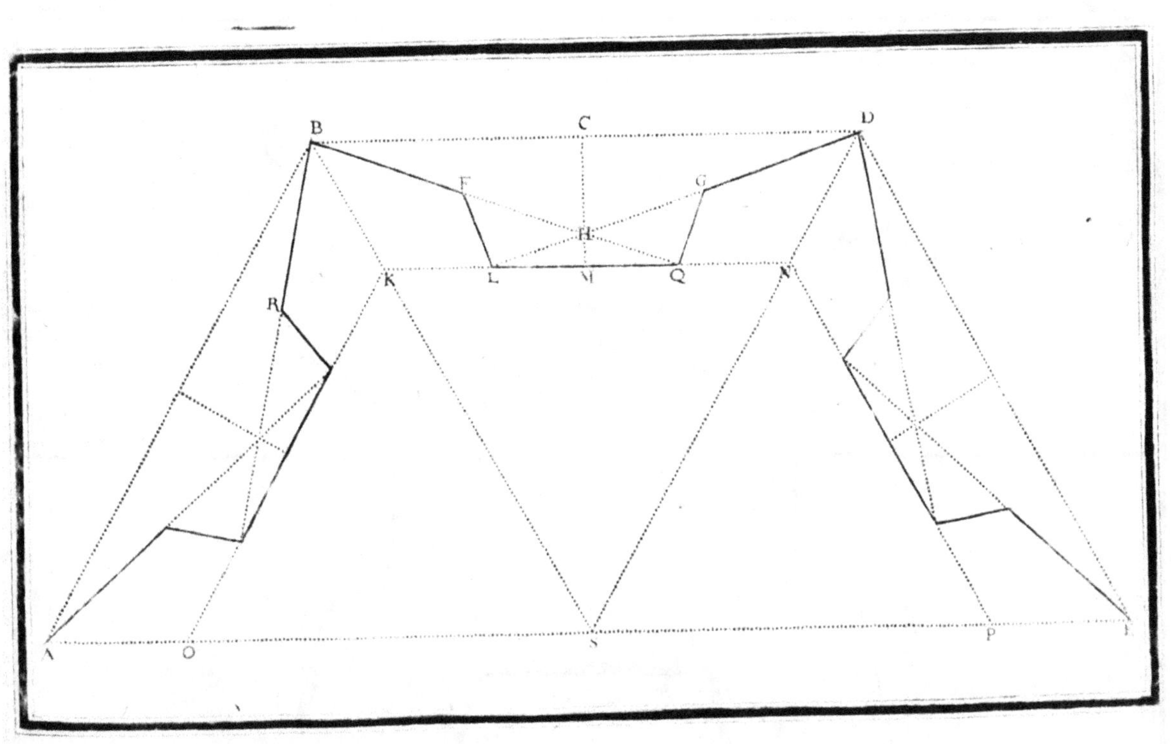

1. From a Pentagone, to a Right-line.

HAving divided the given *Base* (or *Exterior Poligone* C D in *Fig*. I. which suppose to be 575 *English Feet*) into two equal parts, in E; From the Point E raise a *Perpendicular* E L of a sufficient length. This done, enter the Number of the *Half-Base* (*viz*. 575) in the first Column of the *Hercotectonick Table*, (over which is *D. Base*, and look what number answers to it in the second Column, (over which is *Perp.*) and finding it to be 192. take from off your *Sector* or *Scale* 192, and set it on the *Perpendicular* E L, where it will terminate in the Point F. And then from either Point D and C of the given *Base* C D through the Point F, draw the Lines C G and D H of a sufficient length.

In the next place, enter the number of the same *Half-Base*, (*viz*. 575) in the third Column of the Table, (at the head whereof is *D. Base*) to which you will find the Number 351¼ answers in the fourth Column (over which is the word *Face*). This likewise you must find upon your *Sector* or *Scale*, and by it, determine the two Lines C I, and D K.

Lastly, enter the aforesaid Number 575 in the fifth Column of the *Table*, which you will find answered by 204½ for the *Compliment*; which *Compliment* (or 204½) must determine the two Lines F G and F H. Which done, joyn the Points C I H G K D; so have you C I and K D for the two *Faces*; H I and G K for the two *Flancks*; and H G for the *Curtain* of that *Fortification*. And observing the very same method from each *Base*, the *Fortification* becomes perfectly delineated; as in *Fig*. I.

2. For a Square.

THE Method for delineating a *Fortification* upon a *Square*, is the very same with that from a *Pentagone* to a *Right-line*; only the Proportions, and consequently the Numbers expressing those Proportions are different, as may be better seen in the second Part of the *Hercotectonick Table*, compared with *Fig*. II.

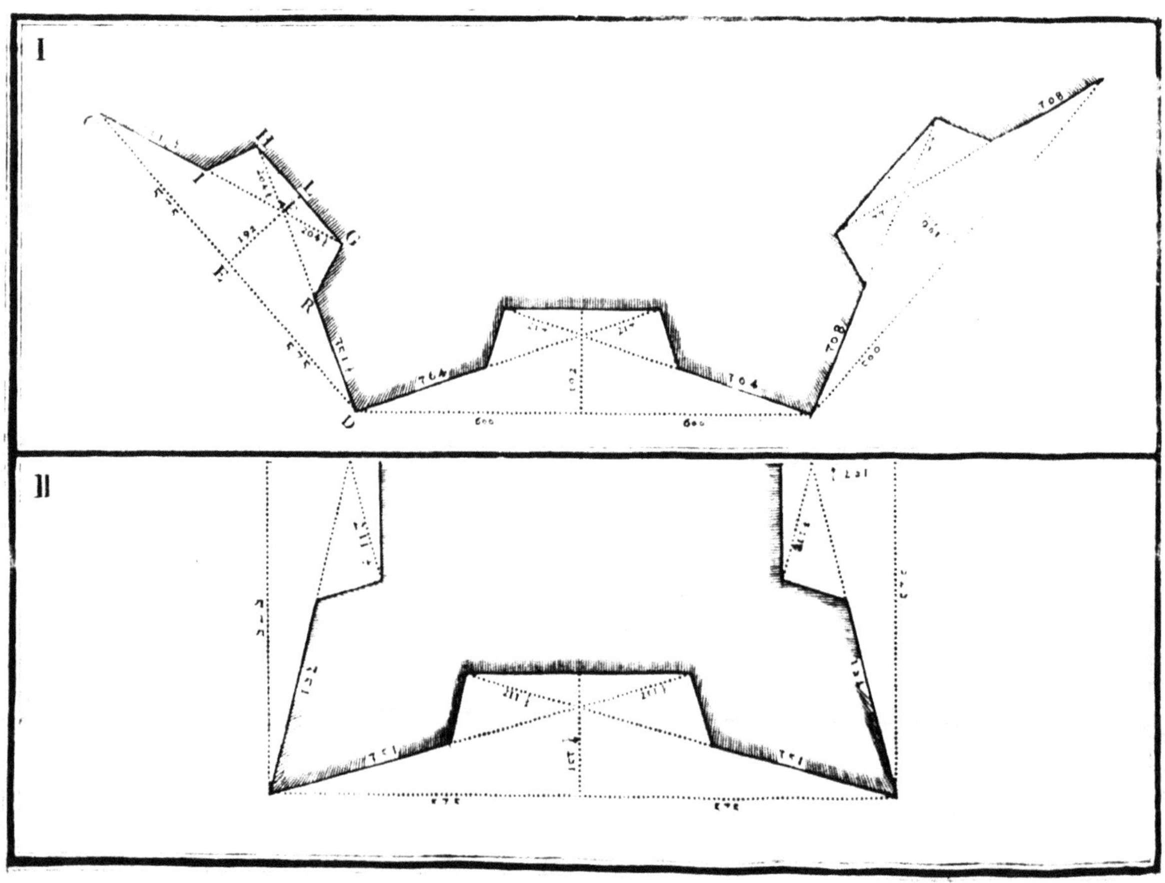

But now forasmuch as in Fortifying Cities, and other Irregular places, it often happens that the *Engineer* is constrained to make use of the old *Walls* and *Ramparts*, and consequently the *Courtines* must be the same with those *Walls*: Therefore the *Count de Pagan* thought it would be some help, to give a Rule to find the *Distance* between the two *Poligones*; which *Distance* is also found in the 8th. and 16th. Columns of the *Table*. For example, in *Fig*. I. E L (or the *Distance* between HG and CD) is 257 *Feet*, and four *Inches*; And in *Fig*. II. M N (or the *Distance* between OP and QR) is 207 *Feet*, and eight *Inches*: But as to this last particular, namely of *Fortifying* from the *Interior Poligone*, the *New Method* comprised in a *MEDALL*, is much more exact and expeditious.

LINEÆ *HERCOTECTONICÆ NOVÆ*, Augustissimo Principi CAROLO II, Magnæ BRITANNIÆ, &c. REGI; humillimè oblatæ à *Samuele Morlando, Equite Aurato et Baronetto nec non* Cameræ Regis Privatæ Adjuncto. Anno Salutis MDCLXVI.

Lignes DES FORTIFICAT: REGUL: & IRREGULIERES							
Base	Perp:	D. Base	Face	D. Base	Compl:	D. Base	Dist:
20	148	320	205	320	96	320	188¼
30	149	30	210	30	100	30	190
40	150	40	5	40	5	40	200
50	1	50	220	50	110	50	205
60	2	60	5	60	5	60	206
70	3	70	230	70	120	70	207
80	4	80	5	80	5	80	208
90	5	90	240	90	130	90	209
00	6	400	5	400	5	400	210
10	7	10	250	10	140	10	5
20	8	20	5	20	5	20	220
30	9	30	6 7	30	150	30	5
40	160	40	260	40	5	40	230
50	5	50	270	50	160	50	5
60	170	60	280	60	5	60	240
70	5	70	290	70	170	70	5
80	180	80	300	80	173	80	250
90	5	90	310	90	173	90	253
00	½ 190	500	320	500	5	500	4
10		10	5	10	180	10	5
20		20	330	20	5	20	6
30		30	5	30	190	30	7
40		40	340	40	5	40	8
50		50	5	50	200	50	9
60		60	350	60	5	60	260
70		70	360	70	210	70	
80		80	370	80	5	80	
90		90	380	90	220	90	
600		600	384	600	5	600	
10		10		10	230	10	
20		20		20	5	20	
30		30		30	237	30	
640		640		640		640	

LIGNES DES QUARREZ.							
D. Base	Perp:	D. Base	Face	D. Base	Compl:	D. Base	Dist:
512	135	512	288	512	211½	512	18
515	6	515	290	515	211½ 212 213 214 215	515	19
520	7	520	5	520	220	520	1
5	8	5	300	5	5	5	2
530	9	530	5	530	230	530	3
5	140	5	310	5	5	5	4
540	1	540	5	540	240	540	5
5	2	5	320	5	1	5	6
550	3	550	5	550	2	550	7
5	4	5	330	5	3	5	8
560	5	560	5	560	247	560	9
5	6	5	340	5		5	20
570	7	570	5	570		570	1
MQ 5	8	5	350	5		5	2
580	9	580	5	580		580	3
5	150	5	360	5		5	4
590	1	590	5	590		590	5
5	2	5	370	5		5	6
600	3	600	5	600		600	7
5	4	5	380	5		5	8
610	5	610	1	610		610	9
5	6	5	2	5		5	21
620	7	620	3	620		620	1
5	8	5	384	5		5	2
630	9	630		630		630	3
5	160	5		5		5	4
GQ 640	1	640		640		640	5
	2						6
	3						7
	4						8
	5						9
	6						22
	7						1
	8						2
	9						3
	170						4
	1						5
	2						6
	177						7
							8
							9
							23
							1
							2
							3
							4
							5
							6
							[illegible]

Of the Dimensions of the Bastions, Ramparts, Ditches, Half-Moons, Counterscarps, &c.

AS concerning the Measures and Dimensions of the *Count de Pagan's Bastions, Ramparts, Ditches, Half-Moons, Counterscarps*, &c. it would require more time than I can at this present afford, and a larger Volumn than I have design'd for this Treatise; forasmuch as the *Count* has given Names to many things, quite different from those in other Authors. I shall therefore leave the comparing those differences to those who are more at leasure, and only content my self to have set down some few of his Proportions, which are adjoyned to the opposite *Table* of *Plain-Angles*, which *Table* is of Excellent and Universal use.

The use of the Table of Plain-Angles.

WHen you would measure an *Angle* of any Field or Plot of ground; As for example, let the *Angle* to be measured be C A B in *Fig.* C. Take a *Chain* and measure 30 *Links* (it matters not of what length those *Links* be, so they be equal one to another) from A to C, and so from A to B. And at B and C stick up two sticks: And then measure with the same *Chain*, the distance between C and B, and finding it to be 20½, seek 20½ in the *Table* in one of the *Columns* over which is the word (*Bases*) and the Number of the next *Column* answering to it, is the true Number of *Degrees* and *Minutes* of the *Angle* sought, *viz.* 40° 00′. After the same manner, because the distance between I and K is 55 *Links*, the opposite *Angle* is 132° 55′.

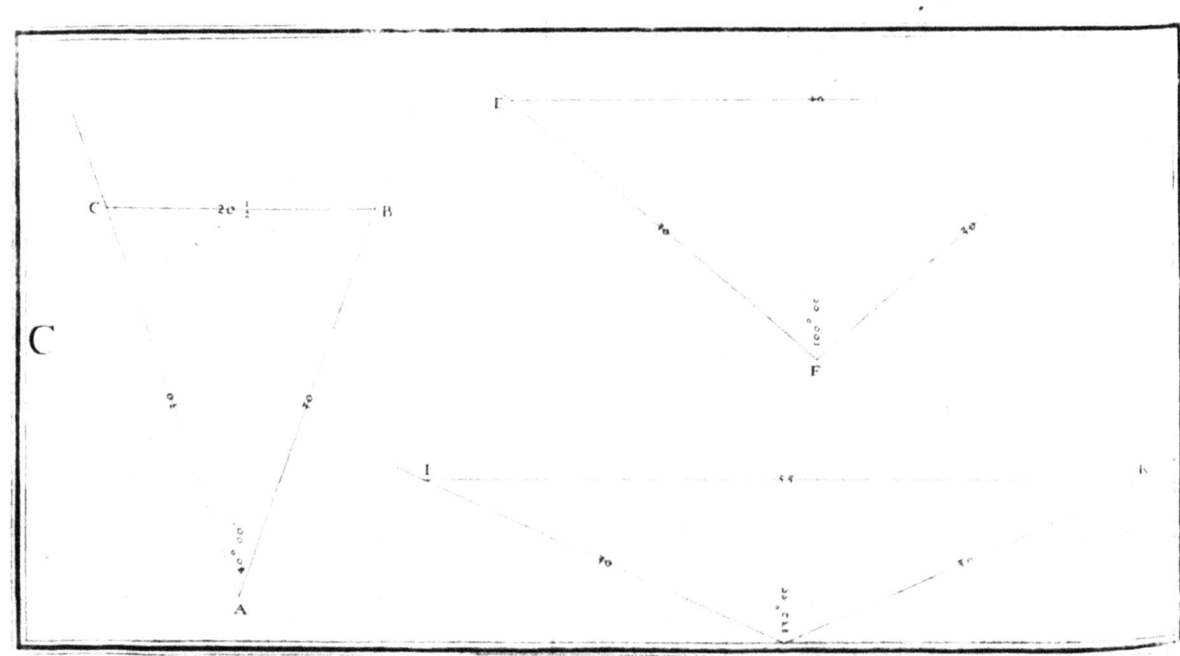

Again, ſuppoſe you deſire to lay out an *Angle* of 100° 05′. I firſt ſtick down two ſticks at the two ends or Terms of any given Line F E, (divided into 30 equal parts) in the Points F and E. Then faſtening a *Chain* of 30 *Links* (equal to thoſe 30 equal parts) at F, and one of 60 *Links* at E, I enter the *Table* of *Angles* with 100° 05′; and finding 46 to anſwer to it, where-ever the *Chain* of 30 *Links*, and 46 of the *Chain* of 60 meet, (as in *G*.) thence draw the Line F G, and you have what you deſire. And after the ſame manner may any *Angle* be laid out moſt exactly and expeditiouſly from 10 *Minutes* to 180 *Degrees*.

DES BASTIONS, DES RAMPARTS, ET DES FOSSEZ

	Pieds d'Angl:
Largeur des Ramparts	45
Largeur des Parapets	19
Hauteur de la 3 caſematte, du fond du foſsé	38½
Hauteur des Parapets au dedans	6½
Hauteur des Parapets au dehors	5½
Largeur du Grand Foſsé	102
Profondeur du Grand Foſsé	19

La largeur du Foſsé, compris entre le premier et 2 Rampart du Baſtion eſt diverſe, ſelon la Fortification, & le Poligone; et ſa profondeur 13 Pieds, ou plus. Et la largeur du Flanc retiré, 77 Pieds

DES DEMI-LUNES, ET DES CONTRESCARPES

1 Methode

	Pieds d'Angl:
Demi-gorge de la Demi-Lune	192
Face de la Demi-Lune	320
Largeur de la Grande Contreſcarpe	320
Largeur de ſon Foſsé	77
Largeur de la Petite Contreſcarpe	26

La Demi-Lune ſe forme touſiours ſur l'Angle Rentrant de la Contreſcarpe.

2. Methode

	Pieds d'Angl:
Largeur de la Grande Contreſcarpe	161
Largeur de ſon Foſsé	77
Largeur de la Petite Contreſcarpe	26
Demi-gorge de la Demi-Lune	128½
Face de la Demi-Lune	217½

Les Flancs de la Grande Contreſcarpe comprennent 3 Parapets, et peuuent auſſi contenir 6 Pieces de Canon.

LIGNE DES ANGLES PLANS touſiours compris par deux coſtez de trente Pieds.

Angles	Baſes	Angles	Baſes	Angles	Baſes	Angles	Ba[ſes]
	1		23		43		
	2		24		44	140	
	3	50	25		45		
	4		26		46		
10	5		27	100	47		
	6		28		48	150	
	7		29		49		
	8	60	30	110	50		
	9		31		51	160	
20	10		32		52		
	11		33	120	53		
	12	70	34		54	170	
	13		35	130	55		
	14		36				
30	15		37				
	16		38				
	17	80	39				
	18		40				
	19		41				
40	20		42				
	21	90				180	
	22						

The Figure of a most useful Instrument, by the help whereof any Poligone, from a Square to a Dodecagone, (which is as much as is required in any Fortification) may be described, not only with greater expedition, but likewise much more exactly than by any Sector, Scale, or other Instrument or Method whatsoever.

THE use of this *Instrument*, is only to lay it upon your Paper, and holding it fast with your left hand, to mark out any *Poligone* therein conteined with the point of a Needle, by its respective *Figures*, and so joyn the *Points*. And if you desire to describe a *Poligone* larger than the *Instrument*, (as is the *Dodecagone* in this *Figure*) it is easie to continue the Lines from the said *Pricks* to the *Circumference*: And if it be desired to have a *Poligone* less than the *Instrument*, the reason is the same.

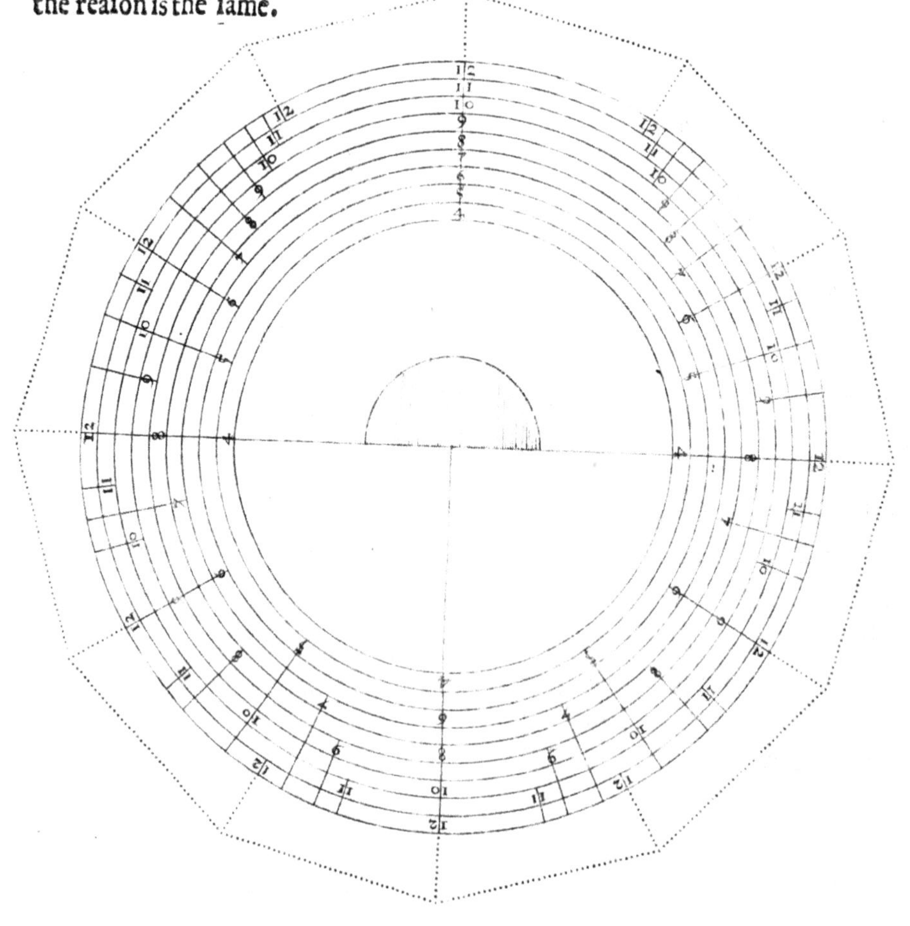

ARCHITEC: MILIT.

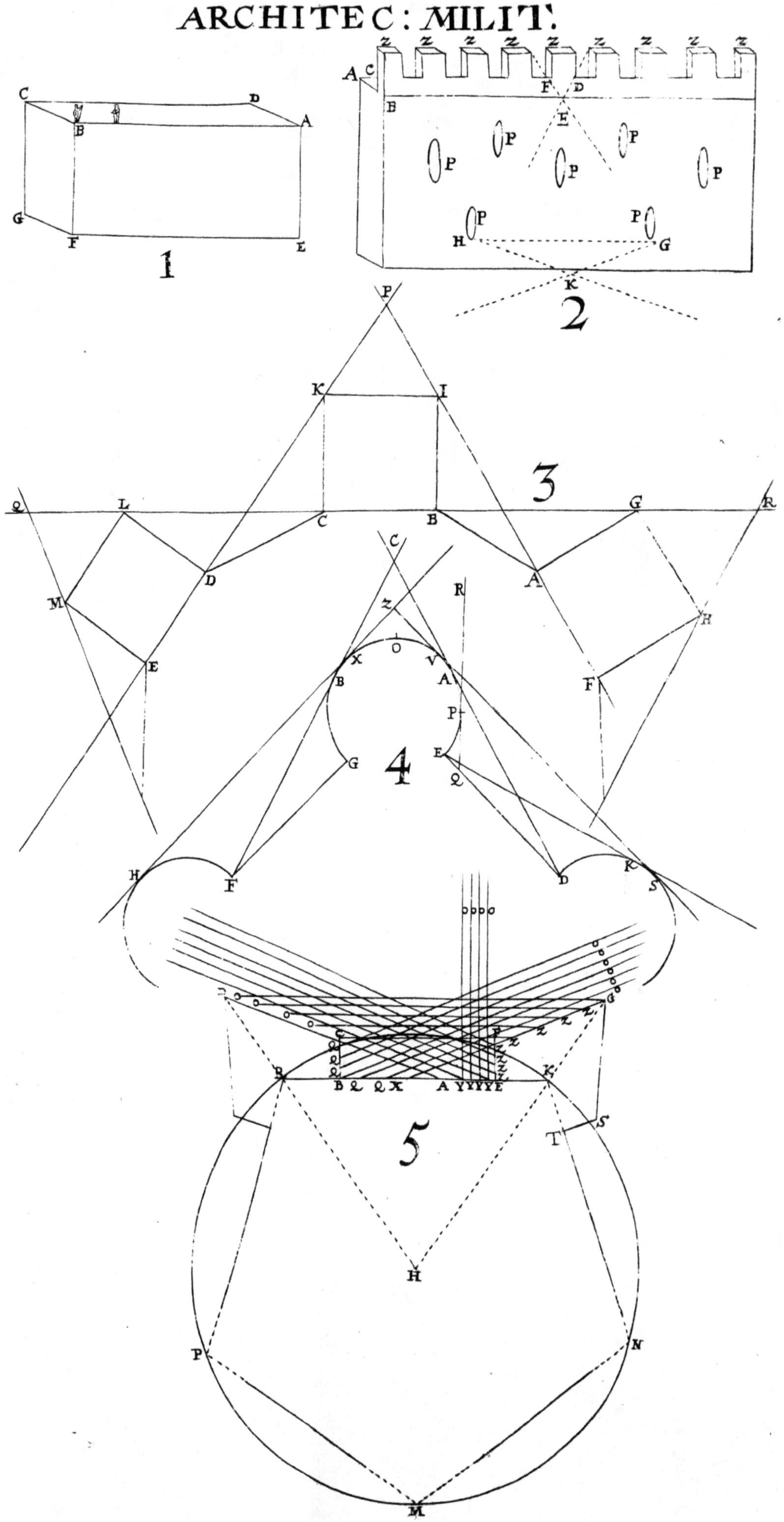

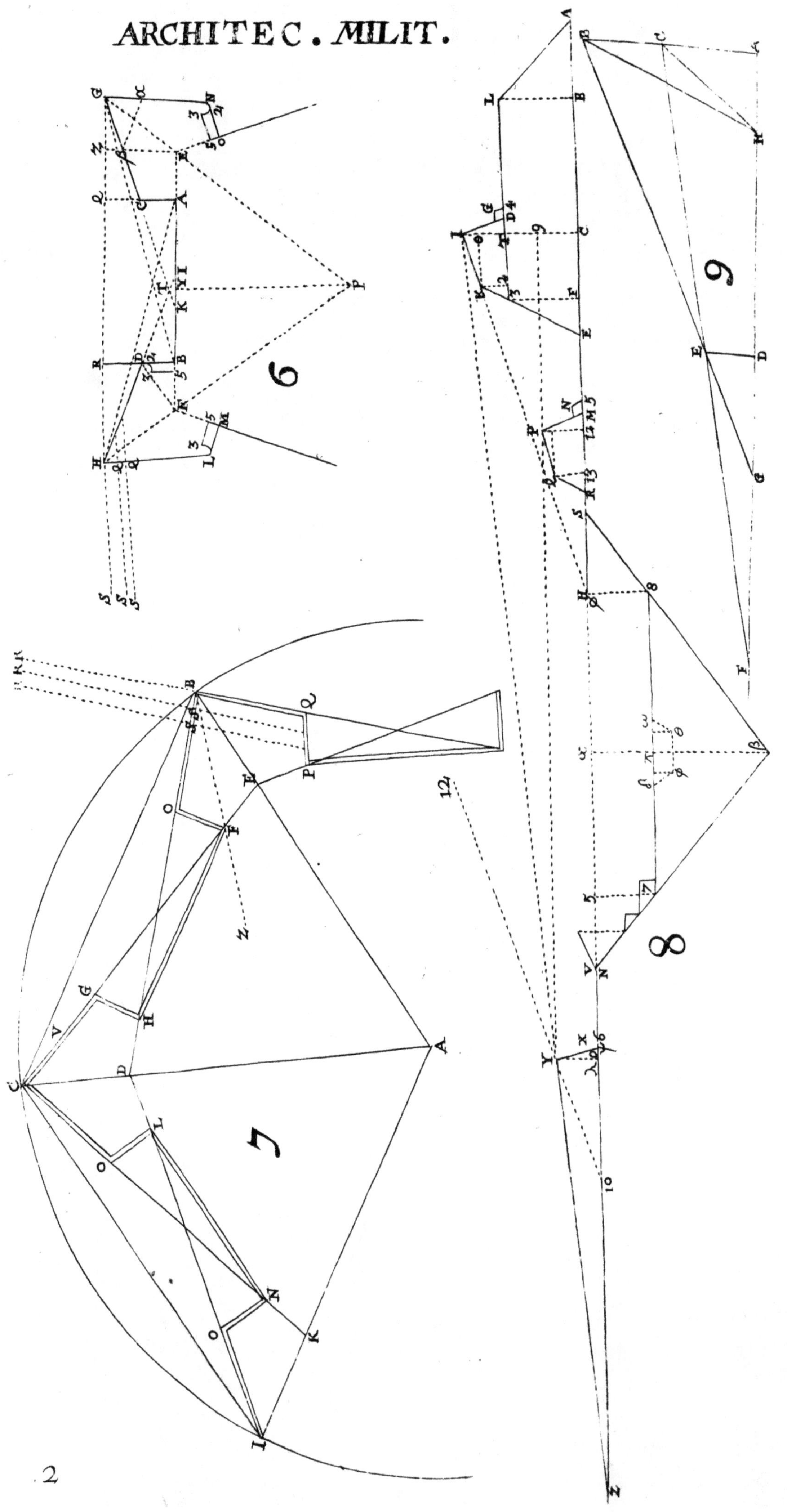
6
7
8
9

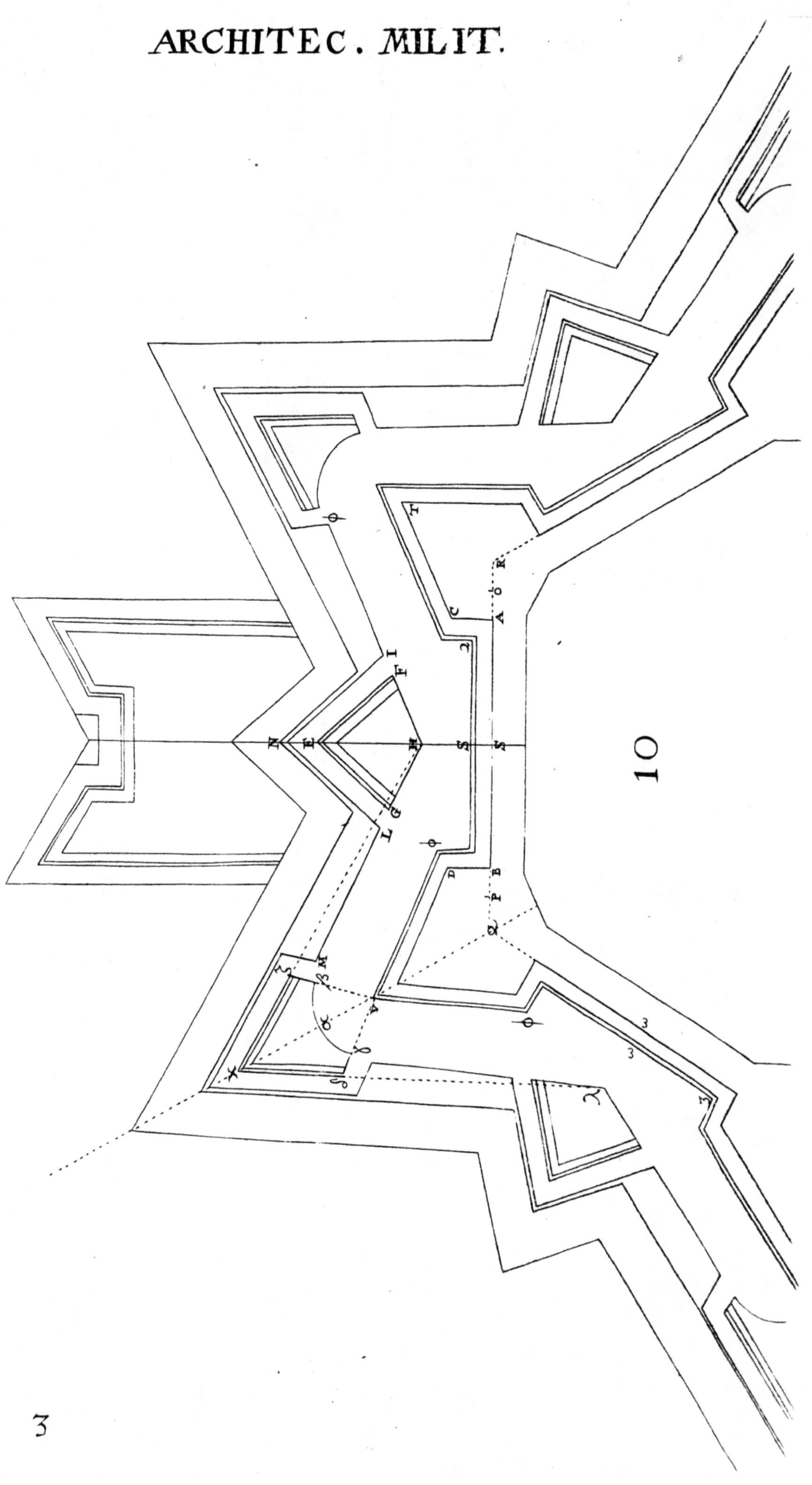
10

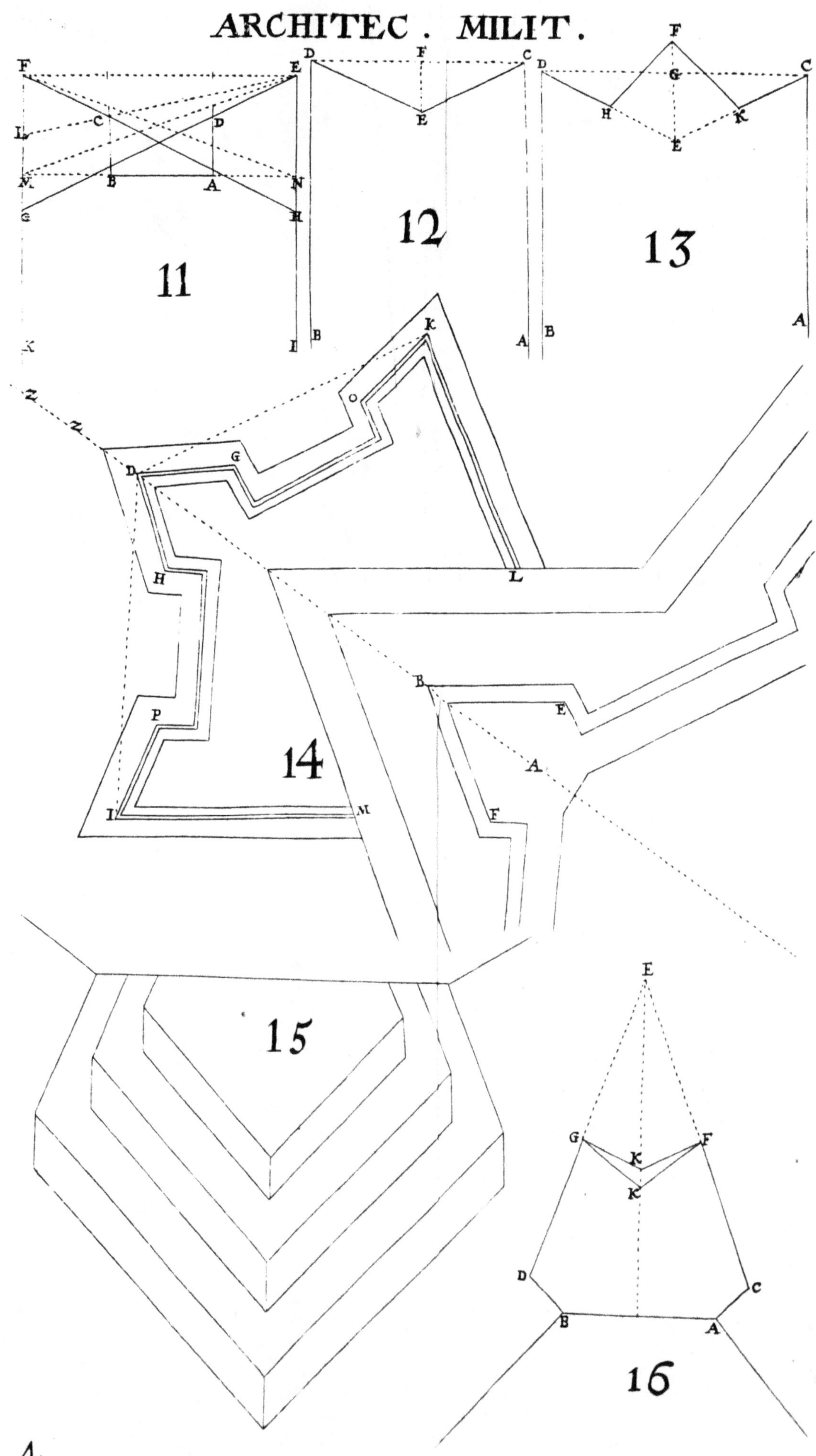
F
E
C
D
L
M
B
A
N
G
H
11
K
I
D
F
C
E
12
B
A
F
D
G
C
H
K
E
13
B
A
K
Z
Z
O
D
G
H
L
B
E
P
A
14
I
M
F
15
E
G
F
K
K
D
C
B
A
16

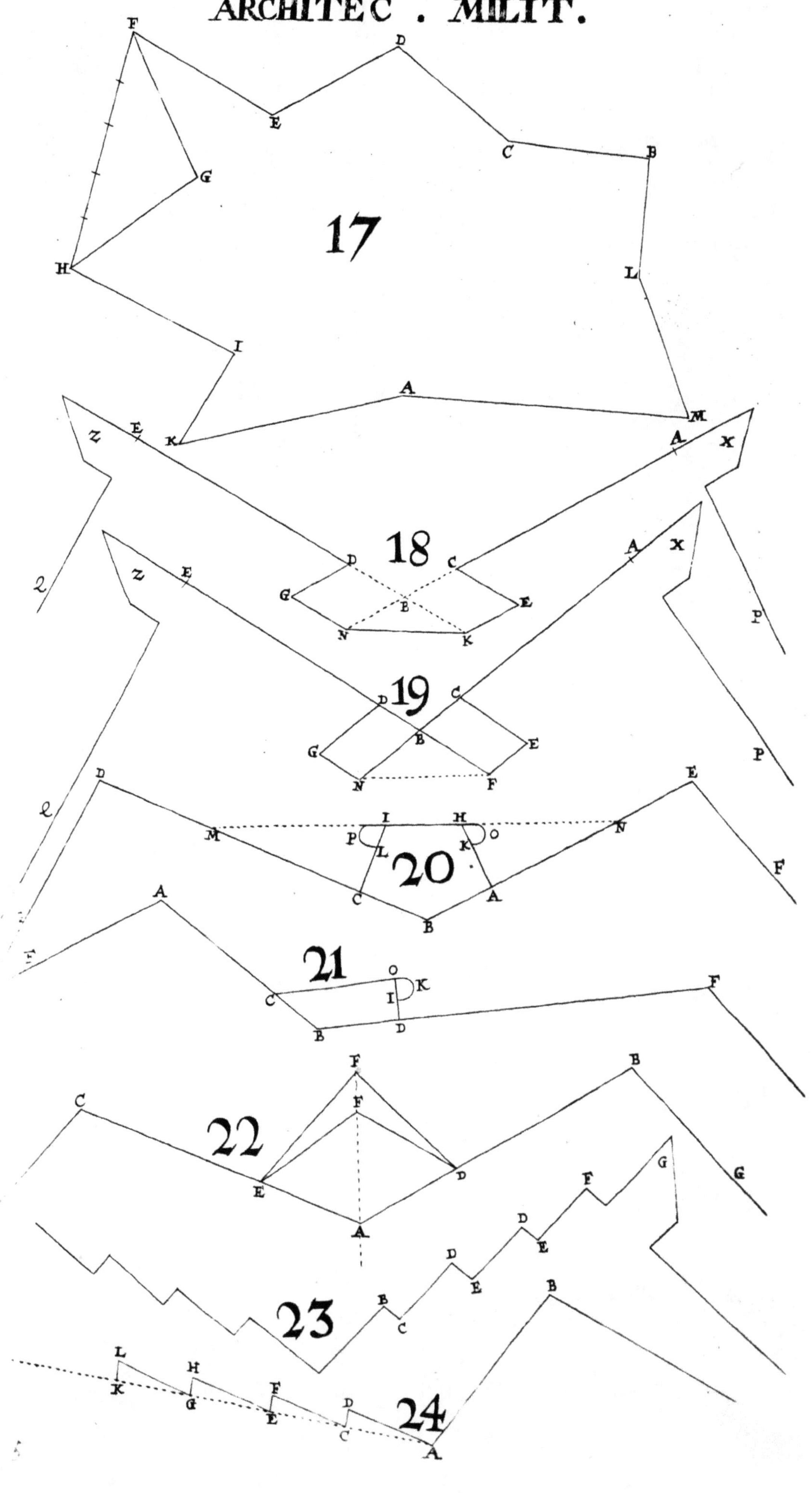
17
18
19
20
21
22
23
24

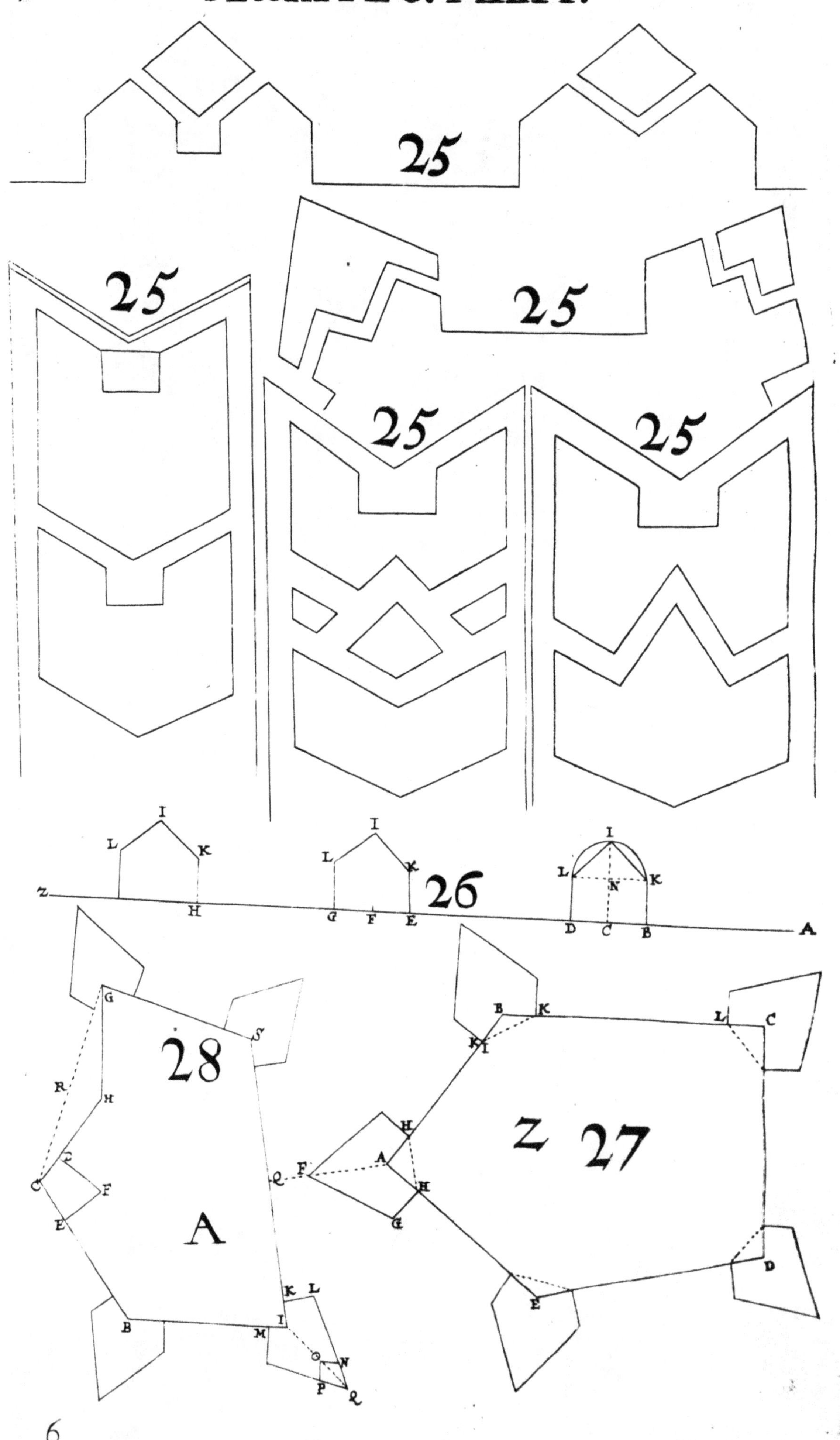
25
25
25
25
25
26
Z
A
I
L
K
H
G
F
E
D
C
B
N
28
27
A
Z
R
O
M
P
Q

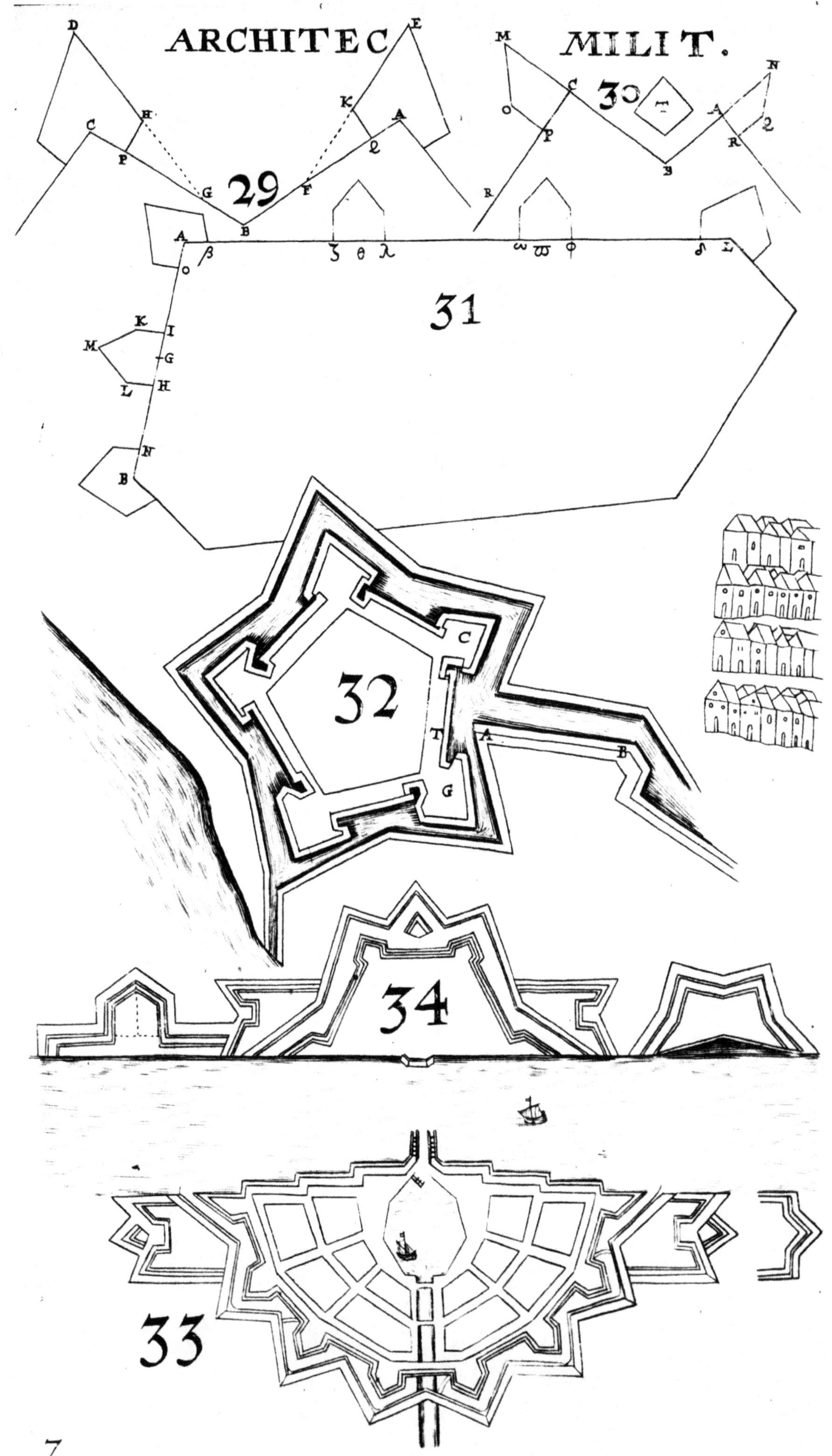
ARCHITEC MILIT.
29
30
31
32
33
34
D
H
C
P
G
B
E
K
A
F
M
O
N
R
T
A
B
β
ζ θ λ
ω ϖ φ
I
G
L
H
N
T
C
G

7

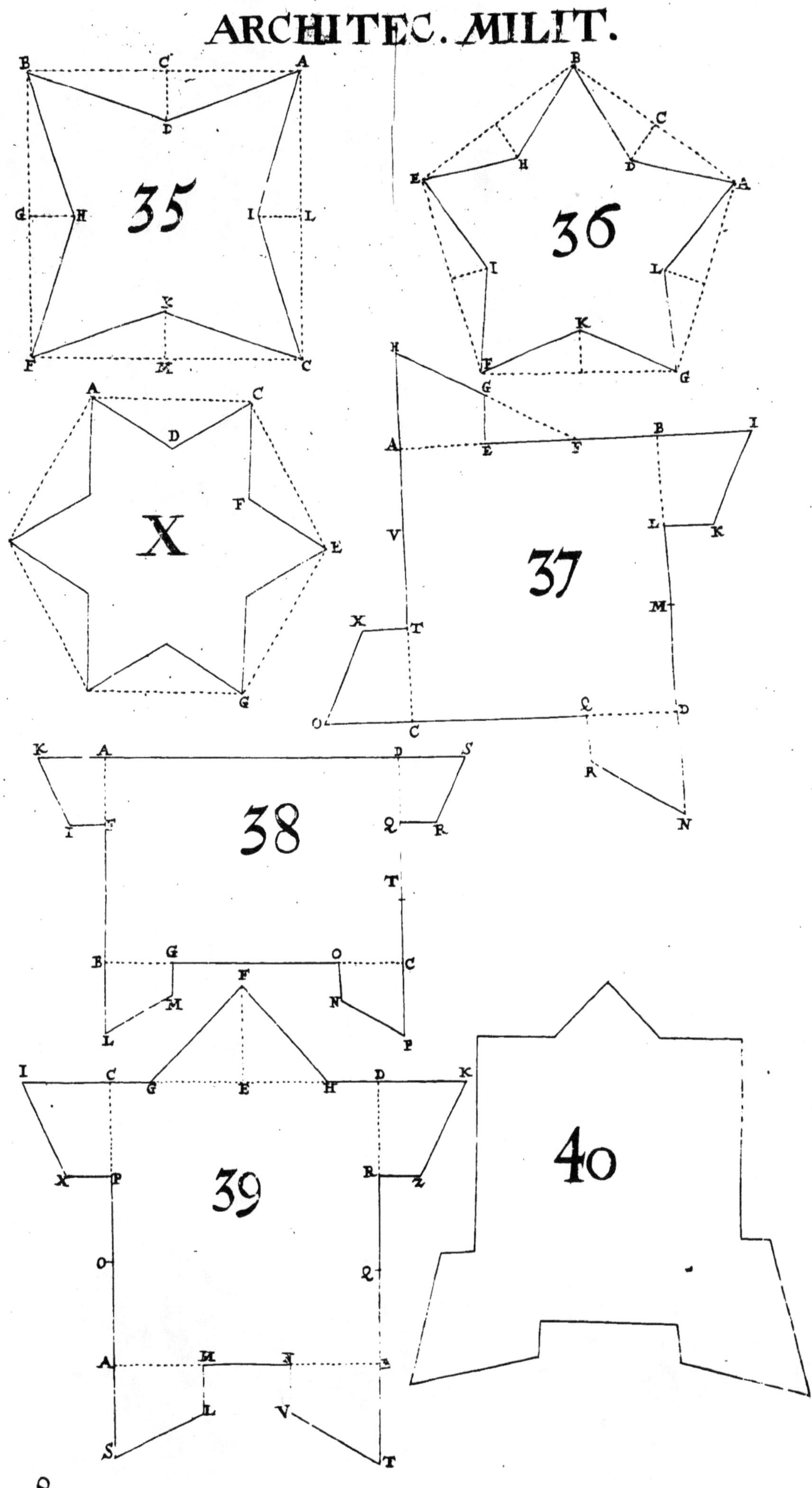
35
36
X
37
38
39
40

THE

Compleat Gunner,

IN

THREE PARTS.

PART I.

Shewing the Art of Founding and Casting Pieces of Ordnance, with the composition of Metal thereunto necessary.

The Composition and Matters of Gunpowders, the Several Sorts, Colours, and Operation.

PART II.

Discovers the necessary Instruments, and variety of Instructions to the compleating of a Gunner, with a Table of Squares and Cubes serving for the Resolution of Questions of Gunnery and other Arts.

AS ALSO

The way of taking Heights, Distances and Profundities, either with or without Instruments.

PART III.

Shews the Nature of Fire-works, the manner of Composing many that are Excellent and Useful both for Sea and Land, for the defence of our selves as well as the offence of our Enemies.

Translated out of *Casimir*, *Diego*, *Uffano*, *Hexam*, and other Authors.

To which is added the Doctrine of Projects applyed to Gunnery by those late famous Authors *Galilæus* and *Torricellio*, now rendred into English.

TOGETHER WITH

Some Excellent Observations out of *Mersennus* and other famous Authors.

of wise men not to censure any thing, without a good consideration and a perfect knowledge of the subject upon which they ought to ground their judgment: So also I hope you will not blame my Indeavours, when you have judiciously examined the same. I have divided it into three Parts, endeavouring that it might be imperfect in nothing that is necessary to this Art, or useful for a Gunner to know. I will assure you that I have no other end in publishing this Treatise, than what I have mentioned before.

I shall only crave your pardon for the faults that may be committed in the Printing, as being not there present at the Correction of any part of it, my occasions calling me other wayes: yet I hope their care was so much that the faults are not material, or at most not so much but your Courtesie may supply that defect. So I recommend this Work to your good reception, and bid you farewell.

W. T.

THE

THE Compleat Gunner.

CHAP. I.

Treating of the Earth necessary in making of Molds for the Casting of Pieces of Ordnance, With the manner of Casting, &c.

WE will not dispute of the first Invention of Guns, that is, whether it came from *Archimedes*, as the *Italians* do report, or from an *Englishman*, or from a *Monk*, for this knowledge matters not much to the Art, nor is it of any profitable signification to the Artist; especially considering, that Authors do not really consent in this thing. Our intent is therefore not to trouble the ingenious Students with vain uncertain repetitions, but to compose a compleat Piece of Gunnery, and therein to discourse from the beginning to the end, all that is necessary to be known or learned (after the knowledge of common Arithmetick) by one that intends to be a perfect Proficient in the said Art. We do suppose it therefore necessary for a Master Gunner to know first the making of Molds and casting of Pieces. Therefore I shall first begin to discourse of the property and Nature of the Earth fit for casting, or making Molds; for this is of great moment, considering that many, or indeed most Earths are not for this purpose; for the Earth fit for the casting of Pieces of Ordnance must be such as will not be melted or fuse, although it be put into a very great fire, but must remain firm and hard: and these Earths are generally of a Reddish, or Iron like colour, which is well known to many Potters, especially such as make *Chymical* Vessels. The Earth being obtained, it must be sifted and cast up after the usual manner, as men do in the making of Morter; then let it be moistned with an Alchalated Water (especially such as is made of Niter) for that purpose, and make it like paste; then, as is usual, let it be beaten up strongly with an Iron Bar; the more 'tis beaten the better it is: in the beating add one sixt part of Horse dung, and a proportionable part of Flox or Hair, and let it again be well beaten and incorporated, alwayes keeping a Moity of this Earth without Hair or Flox, which is for Ground-work; and these Compositions or Earth thus incorporated, you must reserve for the making your Molds for Pieces of Ordnance, according to the Rules prescribed in the next Chapter.

CHAP. II.

Of making Molds, and Casting Pieces of Ordnance, with the mixture of Metals, and allowance of Powder for proof.

AS a Maſter Builder when he intends the Building a Ship, makes firſt a Mold or Moddel of the ſame; ſo the Maſter Gunner, or he that takes in hand the buſineſs of Caſting Guns, muſt have a form or Model of his Piece intended made of wood, or ſuch other matter he may think moſt convenient, which then being brought to the Founder with an intent to be Caſt, muſt firſt be ſmeered all over with Palm Oyle, or inſtead of that, our Lard or Hogs-greaſe, then firſt cover it over with the ſaid earth thinly, and let it dry leiſurely, then lay on more, encreaſing it to ſuch a thickneſs, as you may judge convenient for your purpoſe; and it muſt be ſo made that it may be taken into ſeveral parts, ſo that the pattern may be taken out, and the Mold again exactly cloſed, and the outſide ſtrengthned with Iron plates as long as the Chace of the Piece is, and hooped together with Iron hoops to knock on and off. Then muſt there be made (with the ſame earth upon a ſquare Bar of Iron, bound round with a Cord that the clay may ſtick well) a form exactly round, of the faſhion of the concave of your Piece (whether you intend it a Cylender or a Chamber-board Piece) proportioned both in length and diameter, and it muſt be placed exactly in the middle of the concave; and when all is well joyned together, be ſure it be well polliſhed and ſmoothed, that the Metal may run the better, and be the clearer from flaws, holes, or clefts.

In the beginning of your work take care that your Mold be exactly proportionable as to heighth and ſubſtantialneſs of Metal, according to the nature of the Piece you intend. That is, the Canon double-fortified muſt be ſo caſt that the Diameter at Muzzle be but $\frac{7}{18}$ of the Diameter at Britch. The leſſer Cannon at Britch to be $\frac{3}{4}$ ſo big as the greater Cannon $\frac{9}{18}$ at Trunions, and $\frac{7}{18}$ at Muzzle, whereas ordinary fortified Cannons have at the Touch-hole $\frac{7}{8}$ at the Trunions $\frac{5}{8}$ and at the Muzzle $\frac{5}{8}$, all leſſer Pieces in that kind have $\frac{18}{18}$ at the Touch-hole $\frac{15}{18}$ at Trunions, and $\frac{9}{18}$ at Muzzle; and the ordinary fortified Culverins are fortified every way like the double fortified Cannon, and the leſſer Culverin like the ordinary fortified Cannon in all reſpects.

Great care muſt be taken in the Caſting of Pieces of Ordnance, that they be equal every way in proportion of Metals, that is, that the Cylender be in the very middle of the Metal, that it may be truely bored, otherwiſe your Piece will fail the Artiſt that ſhall uſe it, until the error be known.

In the next place let the Trunions be exactly placed in a Diagonal line with the Axis of the Piece; and they may be placed in their proper diſtance from the Muzzle and Britch, if you obſerve theſe Rules. Take the length of the bore of the Piece from Muzzle to Britch, divide that meaſure by ſeven, and multiply that ſum that cometh of the Quotient by three, the Product will ſhew you how many inches the Trunions muſt ſtand from the loweſt part of the concavity of the Piece.

And farther note, that the Trunions ought to be placed ſo, as $\frac{1}{3}$ of the Circumference of the Piece, may be ſeen in that place where the Trunions are ſet.

When all additional Patterns, as Britch, &c. be made and Luted in their proper place, all things at pleaſure being neatly added to the pattern, let the Mold then be fixt or placed ſo as is moſt convenient for the pouring in the Metal; ſo when the

the Metal is caſt, the perfect impreſſion will be made upon the ſuperficial part of the Piece, and the Cylender will keep the bore propoſed according to what you have preſcribed, the length of the Piece and its Diameter of the bore may be found by the following Table in the next Chapter. For the Metals generally uſed for thoſe Guns, generally called braſs Guns, they are mixtures, and many times varied as experience will give leave. Some of the chiefeſt do approve of this mixture, that is, to every hundred Weight of Copper 24 pounds of Tin, and 6 pounds of Lattin. Others to 100 *l.* of Copper, add 8 *l.* of Tin, and 10 *l.* of Lattin. Others to ever 100 *l.* add 20 *l.* of Bell-Metal, which is 25 *l.* of Lead and Tin to every 100 *l.* of of Copper. Some add Tin, Lead, Copper, and *Lapis Calaminaris* together; ſo every one follows ſuch wayes of Compoſition as doth moſt pleaſe his own Experience. The Copper and other better Metals being once melted, the Tin and Lead is added for the better and quicker fuſion; and the higher the Metal is in fuſion, the more ſolid and compact your Metal will run and ſettle. The Lattin doth incorporate and cauſe the Piece to be of a good colour, and the Tin doth ſtrengthen and bind the other matters together. Now a Piece of Ordnance being Caſt, before it comes to Service, it muſt be put to tryal; for which purpoſe there is uſed for proof, according to the weight of the ſhot, about two thirds, or four fifths of that weight in Powder, and for ſmaller Pieces more.

CHAP. III.

The Names of the principal Pieces of Ordnance uſed in England, their Weight, Length, Diameter of the Bore, Height and Weight of the Shot, allowance of Powder.

THe greateſt in uſe is the Cannon Royal, which is in weight of Metal about 8000 *l.* in length about 12 foot, carries a Shot of $7\frac{1}{2}$ inch. Diameter, and its weight is 58 *l.* of Iron, its bore is 8 inches, requireth for her charge in Powder, 32 *l.* 8 *z.*

Demi-Cannon of the greater ſize, called by ſome Cannon of Seven, whoſe weight of Metal is 7000 *l.* in length about 12 foot, carrying a Shot of $6\frac{3}{4}$ inch. Diameter, and its weight of Iron is 42 *l.* 10 *z.* the Diameter at bore is 7 inches, requireth for her charge in Powder 20 *l.*

Demi-Cannon great ſize, it's weight of Metal is 6000 *l.* in length about 12 foot, carrying a Shot of $6\frac{1}{4}$ inch. Diameter, and its weight in Iron is 34 *l.* the Diameter at bore is $6\frac{1}{2}$ inch. requireth for her charge of Cannon Powder 18 *l.*

Demi-Cannon ordinary, its weight of Metal is 5600 *l.* in length 11 foot, carrying a Shot of $6\frac{1}{2}$ inch. Diameter, its weight in Iron is 32 *l.* the Diameter at bore is $6\frac{1}{2}$ inch. requireth for her charge in Powder $17\frac{1}{2}$ pounds.

The loweſt *Demi-Cannon*, whoſe weight of Metal is 5400 *l.* being in length ſometime 10 and ſometimes 12 foot, it carries a Shot of 6 inches, the weight of that Shot in Iron is 30 *l.* the Diameter of the bore is $6\frac{1}{4}$ inch. it requireth for charge in Powder 14 *l.*

Culverin of the largeſt ſize, weighs about 4800 *l.* being in length 10 or 12. foot, it carries a Shot of $5\frac{1}{2}$ inch. Diameter, the weight of that Shot in Iron is 20 *l.* the Diameter of the bore is $6\frac{1}{4}$ inch, it requireth for charge in Powder 12 *l.* 8 *z.*

Ordinary whole *Culverin* weighs about 4500 *l.* being in length about 12 foot, it carries a Shot of 5 inches Diameter, the weight of that Shot of Iron is about 17 *l.* Diameter at bore is $5\frac{1}{4}$ inch. it requireth for charge in Powder 11 *l.* 6 *z.*

Culverin of the least size, weighs about 4000 *l.* being in length about 12 foot, it carries a Shot of $4\frac{3}{4}$ inch. Diameter, the weight of that Shot of Iron is 15 *l.* Diameter, at bore is 5 inch. charge of Powder is 10 *l.*

Demi-Culverin of the greatest size weighs about 3000 *l.* being in length 10 or 12 foot, carries a Shot of $4\frac{1}{4}$ inch. Diameter, the weight of that Shot of Iron is 12 *l.* 11 *z.* Diameter of the bore $4\frac{3}{4}$ inch. charge of Powder is 8 *l.* 12 *z.*

Demi-Culverin ordinary, weighs about 2700 *l.* being in length 10 or 12 foot, carries a Shot of $4\frac{1}{4}$ inch. Diameter, weight of that Shot of Iron is 10 *l.* 12 *z.* Diameter of the bore $4\frac{1}{2}$ inch. charge of Powder is 7 *l.* 4 *z.*

Demi-Culverin lower than ordinary, weighs about 2000 *l.* being in length 9 or 10 foot, carries a Shot of 4 inches Diameter, weight of that Shot 9 *l.* Diameter of the bore $4\frac{1}{4}$ inch. charge of Powder is 6 *l.* 4 *z.*

Saker of the oldest sort, of 1800 *l.* weight, being in length 9 or 10 foot, carries a Shot of $3\frac{3}{4}$ inch. weight of that Shot 7 *l.* 5 *z.* Diameter at the bore 4 inches, charge of Powder 5 *l.*

Saker ordinary, of 1500 *l.* weight, in length about 9 foot, carries a Shot of $3\frac{1}{2}$ inch. Diameter, weight of that Shot 6 *l.* 0 *z.* Diameter at the bore $3\frac{3}{4}$ inches, charge of Powder 4 *l.*

Saker of the lowest size, of 1400 *l.* weight, in length about 8 foot, carries a Shot of $3\frac{1}{4}$ inch. weight of that Shot 4 *l.* 12 *z.* Diameter at the bore 3 inches and a half, charge of Powder 3 *l.* 6 *z.*

Minion of the largest size, of 800 or 1000 *l.* length 8 foot, height of the Shot 3 inches, weight of the Shot 3 *l.* 2 *z.* height of the bore 3 inches, and one quarter, the charge of Powder, if of 800 *l.* two pounds and a half, if of 1000 *l.* three pounds and a quarter.

The ordinary *Minion* of 750 *l.* in length 7 foot, height of the Shot $3\frac{1}{8}$ inch. weight of the Shot 3 *l.* 4 *z.* height of the bore 3 inches, charge of Powder $2\frac{1}{2}$ pounds.

Faucons of 750 *l.* length 7 foot, height of the Shot $2\frac{1}{2}$ inch. weight $2\frac{1}{2}$ pounds, height of the bore $2\frac{3}{4}$ inch. charge in Powder $2\frac{1}{2}$ pounds.

Fauconet of 400 *l.* in length 6 foot, height of the Shot $2\frac{1}{8}$ inch. weight 1 *l.* 5 *z.* height of the bore $2\frac{1}{4}$ inch. charge 1 *l.* 4 *z.* of Powder.

Rabnet of 300 *l.* length 5 foot, height of the Shot $1\frac{1}{3}$ inch. weight 8 ounces of Iron, height of the bore $1\frac{1}{2}$ inch. charge of Powder 12 ounces.

Base of 200 *l.* length 4 foot, height of Shot $1\frac{1}{2}$ inch, weight 5 ounces, height of the bore $1\frac{1}{4}$ inch. charge of Powder 8 ounces.

There are other Pieces in use in our Nation, which are called Bastard Pieces; of which you shall have a particular account in its proper place.

CHAP.

CHAP. IV.

The Names of the Principal parts of a piece of Ordnance.

IT is necessary for him that intends to be a Gunner to understand, after the knowledg of the Piece in general, to know and learn every part and member of a Piece of Ordnance; for well understanding the same take these Instructions following.

All the outside of the Piece round about is called the superficial part of the same, or Surface of the Piece; the Inner part is called the concave Cylinder, and Soul of the Piece.

The full length is called the Chase of the Piece; so much of the Cylinder or concave of the Piece as contains the powder and Shot is called the Chamber or charged Cylinder, the remaining part to the small end of the Gun is called the vacant Cylinder.

The Spindle standing out, or Ears by which the Piece must hang in the Carriage, is called the Trunions; the space between the Trunions, the gravity of the Center.

The Pumel or Button at her Coyl or Britch-end is called the Casacabel or her Deck, the little hole the Touch-hole, all the metal behind the touch-hole the Breach or Coyl, the greatest ring at her touch-hole the Base Ring, the next ring or circle the reinforced Ring, the next the Trunion Rings, the next before the Trunions is called the Cornish Ring, the foremost next the Muzzle is called the Muzzle Ring, Lastly, all the rings, Circles, Eminencies, at her Muzzle, and so those behind the base Ring, are Frizes.

Let the Piece with its several names be placed by this Chapter. Fig. 1.

CHAP. V.

The Mounting of a Piece of Ordnance in its Carriage.

THe Gunners upon Land-Service, for the conveniency of mounting a piece of Ordnance, that is by any means whatsoever dismounted, have for their principal Services, a Screw, and a Ghynne, and their appurtenances (which you will find in their proper place) by whose help they are able to mount a Piece, and place him in his Carriage, whereby he may be able to perform the work intended. Which to perform artificially, observe these Rules.

Before you endeavour to mount your Piece, above all things have a great and diligent care that the Ghynne be very firmly set, so that it may not slip any way; but so placed, that the Pully or Truckle coming down from the head, fall just between the Trunions, or gravity of the Piece, whereof to be assured you may let fall down from the head of the Ghynne a Plummet with a Line, or for want of a Plummet any stone made fast to a Line, and so moving the Ghynne until the said Plummet fall just upon the Center of Gravity, which is between the Ears of the Piece, that the metal may fall near equal, or that an easie hand may poize it; and this care must be the more, if the Ground whereon the Ghynne stands be sandy or loose Ground, or the Earth be boggy soft, so that the feet may fail or sink in or give way, according to the greatneſs of the weight. For ſometimes it may be neceſſary to put planks or ſome ſolid thing under the Ghynne and Pins to ſtay them; but this as neceſſity ſhall require.

Now the Ghynne firmly placed and ſetled, the Gunner muſt get up by the Ladder, or ſome Steps, to the head or top of it, having the Rope in his hand, ſhall put it through the uppermoſt truckle of the head, and let it fall down to another man again, that he may catch it, that he may put it through one ſide of the Piece to faſten it into the Ears of the Piece, and ſo having put it through them he may draw it up, until he can give it him that is above, and then put it through the other hole of the Truckle, and give it to him that is under him, who muſt reach it again to him that is above, and ſo faſten it to the head of the Ghynne, giving it ſome turns until it come under the uppermoſt Truckle.

This done, he muſt faſten it with great diligence to the lower Truckle, by putting the Ears as through the Ring which is under the ſaid Truckle; after this begin to Hoyſe your Peice, and in the Hoyſing put a ſpar or ſome ſuch thing into the mouth of the Peice, ſo that thereby it may be governed, and may not ſway from one ſide to the other, which would be dangerous; for if it ſhould ſtrike againſt the Rouler or any one of the feet of the Gynne, it may break all, and ſo ſpoil both the work and the men tending upon it. Therefore I ſay, be ſure that thoſe who ſtand by the Spar be careful in guiding the Piece and keeping it ſteddy and right, until the weight of the Piece is well ſetled, a diligent Eye being had all this while, that neither the feet of the Gynne, nor Rope give way; and be ſure every part of the Rope draw equal, and that there be no Knicks, or that they be not tangled one amongſt another; and for that purpoſe, when they begin to hoyſe the Piece, blows muſt be given upon the Tackling until it be ſet tort, and all bear equal.

But if you ſhould perceive that the Ghynne or any part give way, preſently let your Piece ſink, and underlay and ſettle well the feet of the Ghynne, and that as gently as may be, to the end the Croſs beam or Rouler may not be disjoyned or broken.

Then wind it up carefully and very gently by the help of two men onely, and in ſuch a manner, as when one of the Leavers is brought down, it muſt be held there faſt until the other has got purchaſe, and then muſt this other alſo be brought down; this muſt be reiterated ſo often until it be ſo high that the Carriage may be placed under it, ſo that the Trunions may fall into the Sockets, or holes of the Carriage, and then Guide the Piece by the Spar, ſo that it fall eaſily in, and ſo reſt it ſelf in the Carriage, and then let it be well claſped over, and then locked in and faſtned with Forelocks, and ſo you may draw away your Piece where you pleaſe. On board Ships this Ghynne is not of uſe, it being the Boatſwains buſineſs to fix a Tackle that may be able to hoiſt up any Piece into its Carriage, the Slings one part muſt come about the Caſacabel, and the other part about a Billet, ſo made that it may fit in at the Muzzle, and by ſtrength of hands, or by help of a Windleſs, or Capſtain, it may be hoyſed up ſo that the Carriage may be brought under; ſo that the Gun being Loared, its Trunions may fall into the holes of the Carriage, which then claſp over with its Iron Claſps; let them be Forelocked, and then with Hand-Tackles be brought where you pleaſe.

See the Figure of the Gynne, and the Field and Ship-Pieces mounted in the Figure 11.

CHAP.

CHAP. VI.

The way to draw a Piece of Ordnance, with the necessary things thereunto belonging both for Land and Sea.

SEeing we have discovered the way of Casting a Piece, and Mounting it in its Carriage, it follows in the next place that in this Chapter we treat of, and shew the manner of drawing them from place to place, for Service; where care must be taken what the way is that you are to pass, for if the way be foul, moorish, and dirty, there is then required as many more Horses as in good wayes. That is,

For a whole Cannon of 8000 *l.* you may use 15 couple of Horses, besides the Tyllar.

For a Demi-Cannon of about 6000 *l.* you may use 11 couple of Horses, besides the Tyllar.

For a Piece of 4000 *l.* weight, you may use 8 couple of Horses, besides the Tyllar.

For a Field Piece of about 3000 *l.* use 6 couple of Horses, besides the Tyllar.

For a Saker of 1800 *l.* weight, you may use 4 couple of Horses, besides the Tyllar.

For a Piece of 1500 *l.* weight, you may use 3 couple of Horses, besides the Tyllar.

For a Faucon, two couple of Horses, besides the Tyllar. For a small Drake of about 250 *l.* one Horse will serve: and by the same Rule you may find how many Horses will draw any weight whatsoever.

Many times when Horses are wanting, men are made use of: Upon such occasions, you must divide your men into three drawing files, according to the greatness of the Piece; now to the end the Ranks may spread, and every man may draw equally alike, fasten to the end of the Carriage a Cross beam or bar, to which you must fasten the drawing Ropes, equally at such distance, that one may not impead the other, and let there be besure one to steer the Piece when you come to any winding or turning. If the drawing Ropes be long, 'tis necessary to cross it with Ropes, or some light peeces of wood like a Ladder, with two or more cross peeces; let them be made fast for the better and more steady drawing, and to every there must be a Neckline fastned to the Ropes, and so to cast over every mans Sholders, in manner as is used to draw our Western Barges: And you must know your proportion of men fit to draw any Piece of Ordnance, and that must be regulated according to the goodness or badness of the way, and so more or less men, allowing every man to draw about 50, 60, or 80 pounds; for 'tis supposed a man may draw in ordinary way 50 or 60 pounds, but in very good way more than 80 pounds; however 'tis good to have men enough. Let the Spunge, Ladle, *&c.* be made fast along the Piece to the Ring and Britch end. Sometimes by reason of the unevenness, steepness, or other defects of the way, it sometimes happens, that you may be forc'd to dismount your Piece, and remount it again; there 'tis necessary every Gunner have with him a Ghynne, a Wynche, and all appurtenances necessary thereunto. As to the Sea Gunner on board Ship, their occasions require no more than the Wynch, and their Piece being mounted according to the directions given in the former Chapter, then with one or two Tackles he bring the Piece to the place desired, where it ought to be well fastned in its place; for which purpose there is thereunto required Tackles and Britchins; and in case of foul weather, or that any of the Geer or Tackling be suspected, or by my much tumbling every thing hanging upon the Nail, for fear any Bolts should give way or draw, it is usual to nail down to the

Deck with Spikes, one Coyne behind each Truck, or at least the after Trucks, which to great Pieces are commonly dead Trucks; so that each Piece may have little or no play.

But in case any thing should give way in foul weather, then with all speed dismount the Piece as soon as possible you can, for fear of further mischief; for which purpose put in his way as he runs from side to side, Rugs, Pillows, Beds, *&c*, and stand ready with Crows and Handspikes, and with Tackles, to hitch or ketch him close and fast to any Ring by the Ship side, or such other place as best presents. As for the length of the Tackles useful, it is usually known thus; see how long the Piece is, and make the Tackles four times as long, and let the Britchin be twice the length of the Piece, and something more. The manner of drawing of Pieces by Man and Horse, you will see in the third Figure.

CHAP. VII.

To Prove or Examine the goodness of a Piece of Ordnance, whether it be Flawed, Hony-Combed, Crackt, Chamber-bor'd, &c. With the difference of Common, Legitimate, and Bastard Pieces.

IT remains necessary for this Chapter to treat, or shew the way to know, whether a Piece be serviceable or no, which is usually done in the first proof by Powder, which we intend not to Write of here, having mentioned it before, and more will be said, when we have shewed the composition of Powder. That knowledge of a Piece we here intend, is to examine a Piece, bought, or to be taken into Service, whether good or serviceable, or out of many Pieces to make choice of the best, or such as are freed from holes, flaws, cracks, honycombs, *&c*. And first to know if a Piece be free from crack, or have holes through, take a long stick, longer than the Piece, made of a Hoop-stick or otherwise, slit it at one end, so that you may put a short peece of Candle in it, then light the Candle, and put it into the Piece, and so putting it along easily, whilst another laying his Eye close to the Piece, do go along equally with the Candle, until the whole Piece be viewed, and so by help of the Light within side, the Eye without side will perceive whether there be any Flaws, Cracks, *&c*.

This may be done by the reflection of the Sun beams in at the Muzzle of a Piece, by help of a Looking-glass, or pollished Steel; but many times a Piece may be Flawed or Hony-combed, and cannot be discerned through the Piece, and then the best way to find them out is thus; make the usual search with two or three Springs, or in case you have them not, bend the Iron point of a Half Pike, then put it into the Piece up to the Britch end or bottom of the Cylinder, turning it round carefully and gradually, as you pluck it out, and if there be any Honey-combs, Cracks or Flawes, the end or bended point of the Half Pike will stick or catch at them.

To know whether the Piece be Chamber-bor'd, take a priming Iron that is small, or a piece of Wire, bend it a little at the end, but so that it may go down at the Touch-hole, and put it down so far as it will go; Then at the Touch-hole close by the Metal of the Piece, make a mark upon the Wire; then gently pluck it up upon one side of the Touch-hole, until the bended point stop upon the Metal or upper side of the Chamber; and then make another mark upon the Wyer, just by the Touch-

hole;

hole; then draw out the Wyer, and the distance between these two marks, is the height of the Chamber or bore of the Piece at Britch: take the height of the bore at Muzzle, and if this height at Muzzle agree with that taken at the Britch of the Piece, then is the Piece full bored; but if they differ, so much as the difference is, sheweth the tapering of the Piece, and according to this must your former be made for your Cartredges. There is another way to know whether a Piece be Chamber-bor'd, or Tapering, by the disparting of a Piece; which way we shall shew in its proper place, where we treat of disparting a Piece of Ordnance.

Now although we have mentioned in the former Chapters the most usual Pieces of Ordnance; yet, as I have said, there are other Pieces which are longer, or shorter, which are used, and are generally called by the name of Bastard Pieces, and they are distinguished from the common Legitimate Pieces thus; The Legitimate Pieces have their due length of Chace, and are proportioned according to the true height of their bore. Bastard Pieces are shorter Chases, such as the proportion of their bore doth require, and are therefore called Cuts of the same nature of the Piece they agree with in the bore; as those of Demi-Culverin bore, are called Demi-Culverin Cuts, &c. There are also Pieces called Extraordinary, which are such whose Chaces are longer than is usually for that bore.

Now we have well and duely understood how, not only to make, but also to examine and prove a Piece of Ordnance, in the next place shall follow their use, set down in due order: Wherein first 'tis necessary for us to treat of the nature of Gunpowder, and its various Compositions, with the Materials necessary thereunto, and afterward shew its use.

CHAP. VIII.

Of the Materials used in the Composition of Gunpowder; and first we will treat of the Original of Salt-Peter.

IT is believed by many in these latter times, that the Salt-Peter now in use, is not the Niter of the Ancients, but a new Invention used or found out for the Composition of Powder; And that theirs was only a Niter generated by nature, or that Salt that is coagulated of it self, without any humane Artifice, in the Caverns of the Earth, from whence they took it which nevertheless they divide into four different Species, to wit, *Armenian*, *Affrican*, *Roman*, and *Egyptian*; and this *Egyptian* holds its name by a certain Region in *Egypt*, in which is found great abundance. *Serapian* delivers to us, that the places from whence they drew their Niter were all one and the same, like them where common Salt is formed, in which the water running doth congeal, and condenseth like a vulgar Stone, from hence came it to be called stonified Salt, or Sal-Peter. The same Author doth affirm, that Niter was found of divers colours, *viz.* White, Reddish, Livid, or Lead-like, and all other colours it was able to take; he saith likewise that it was found in different forms; for some was found full of holes or caverns like a Spunge; others on the contrary were firm, close, sollid, shining, and Diaphanous as Glass, which being let fall easily will split in thin leaves, and is fryable in beating; and from its various appearances is judged its manifold vertues, in one more powerful than another, which is known by its operation.

From hence we see that which is to be found from the testimony of the best received Authors about the Mineral Niter, and in none is any mention made of Artificial Salt-Peter, or such as we at present make use of generally, which is called properly *Salt-Peter*, *Sal Nitre*, or *Halinitre*; yet is there very little difference between the Natural that useth to be brought to us, and the Artificial; for if we compare the vertues and operations of the one, we shall find them in our uses no way differing, as *Scaliger* testifies, saying that the ancient Niter is not much different from ours, particularly if we consider its tenuity and subtil part.

There is of the ancient Niter found upon the superficies of old Walls, exposed to the humidity; but particularly in Cellars and deep Caves, and in covered Vaults; it resembles perfectly a certain Brine, or white Gelly, or fine Meal, or in more proper speaking, fine Sugar, and is many times white as Snow; and this thus had, the vertues are to be commended, which I my self have taken the pains to collect, in the imitation of many others which I have often seen; which if now it be desired to prepare this Salt according to the method of our Art; It will be congealed into small little long Christals like Isicles, and it will be like that of the Ancients. But as 'tis impossible to find so great a quantity, as the continual use doth consume, and necessity doth excite to this day for the supply of all Wars, which have been great, and in few years consumed many great and vast places of the Universe: We are therefore constrained to this new subject, and are forced even to study and invent in these latter ages a new way to supply the want of the former, which being made with much labour and industry from the bowels of the Earth, and then purified and washed divers times to separate it from its more gross and Terrestrial parts, and taken from its first crudity, that its may shew its likeness of its Mother, it is in the end perfectly purified and brought to such a height, that it differs nothing to be of the same form and vertue of the ancient Salt-Peter.

Wherefore if I may be admitted to speak my thoughts upon it, I shall say openly and plainly, leaving none in doubt, the Ancients did indeed find natural growing Niter, which came out of it-self at the tops of Rocks, filling the clefts and holes, and there condensing into small Icicles, it hardens and petrefies. This Niter is natural; but since Art is the Imitator of Nature, as 'tis allowed by all, then you may not think it strange, if we can by a little of her aid, and by force of industry, attain to the perfection of her productions; nay, (if I may be bold to say it) such as shall surpass by far, the more perfect of her works. Do we not daily see an infinite of very principal Works brought to light, after a long and painful travel, which is not permitted nature to imitate, although she did imploy at the best all her secret and full strength to come to perfection. It may from hence therefore be concluded that our Salt made by the Art of Fire, is such as is every way agreeing with that of the Ancients, not any way differing one from the other; especially as to those uses we intend here. For if according to our method given in the next Chapter, I dare affirm, in all our uses it will truely imitate the natural, but the more, if it be purified and purged many times: So that at last it will come to be more excellent than the Ancient and natural Salt-Peter; which is plainly seen in the ordinary way of purifying Common Salt or Sugar, which by Art is so purged, that it comes to be far purer and whiter than 'twas before, in its first natural dress. And this we do suppose to be a sufficient argument, or reason, for us to judge that our Artificial Salt-Peter is not only as good, but far more excellent than the natural: Which being thus allowed, we will add only a few words of the properties of Niter, and so pass to its Artificial preparation. And first of the spetting quality and noise it makes in the fire, which *Scaliger* would have to be caused by its terrestrity that it holds in it self, which we cannot allow of, but rather judge otherwise; for if the Earthy part were the subject that made it make such noise, then the Earth it self might be adjudged to make a far greater noise, seeing it is also mixed with this Element, and yet we find it cracks not at all, being put in the fire; therefore by consequence this reason is void. Well then, is it of its rarity, which *Aristotle* calls χαυνόντα and συμφόντα, This cannot pass for a truth, since daily experience doth let us see that the Mushrooms, or Toad-stools, and many other things which are of a most rare thin nature, yet make no noise when put upon burning coals. Neither is the hardness that is joyned to these more subtil parts, the cause of the cracking; For we see that the Pumice-stone will not spet nor crack, nor make any noise in the fire, although it be of a substance sufficiently spungy and hard. There must therefore be another thing that must be the cause of this spetting, and all the noise that is made by Nitre, when it is embraced by the fire. The Divine *Præceptor*, in the 11 Section of his Questions saith, that the Salt cracks in the fire, because it contains in it much moisture, which being attenuated by the fire, and rarified in a high degree, converts all into Spirits, and an Airy nature; For in it there is contained more of a Spirit, than watery matter, which being brought to the fire, the two fiery Spirits mutually attract each other, and joyning together, do become Master of the lesser part the Water; for the fire of the Niter being fortified and put into action by the common fire, the Water is constrained from its bonds, and can stay no longer there, but must of a suddain depart, and in its way, by the violency of its departure, overthroweth all such obstacles as come in its way: And in this action the external air being strongly and violently agitated, by their refraction, it breaks with impetuosity or great violence, and from thence by consequence follows that hideous and fearful noise which commonly and ordinarily happens, in the combustion of Salt-Peter, and other Compositions mixed with it, whereof Salt-Peter is the greatest part.

CHAP. IX.

The Way of Preparing Salt-Peter from a Nitrous Earth.

THe Earth and matter of Salt-Peter is found commonly in great abundance, in obscure shadowed places, where no Rain nor any fresh water doth penitrate, nor likewise where the Sun by his rayes can communicate his heat; it is likewise drawn from Horse dung under Stables, and from covered places where great and small Cattle are shut up; likewise in such places as men use to piss in, or Jaqueses, or the like places; or in places where has been made great Fights, or where has been laid up together many dead Bodies, and earth thrown upon them: For from thence in few years may much Salt-Peter be drawn. I shall declare three several wayes whereby to ground your judgment with more certainty, concerning the goodness of the place from whence one would draw the Salt-Peter, which is most necessary to be known by all Salt-Peter men, or such as intend to mannage these Affairs.

The first is, that such Earth as you suspect to hold Salt-Peter, be put upon the Tongue, and if it prick a little sharply, it is a most certain sign you will not loose your labour in taking it to task; but on the contrary if it be not biting, or a little corrosive, it will not well answer your money and labour in preparing of it.

The second way to know a good Nitrous Earth is this: make a hole in the Earth with a sharp pointed thing, either of Wood or Iron. and in it put a peece of Iron red hot; after having stopt the hole, let it stand until it be quite cold, then draw it out, and if you find a little after about this Iron some Citrine marks, inclining a little after to a whiteness, you need not doubt that earth; but further assure your self 'tis very good to put to work.

The third way is, throw a little of that Earth upon burning Coals, and if you perceive it make any noise, and that it ſpets in the fire, or that clear and ſhining ſparks come from it, you may from thence judge that that Earth holds a forcible matter of that nature.

After you have found a proper Earth to draw Salt-Peter from, and that by ſome of theſe proofs you have teſtimony of its goodneſs and worth, let be taken of it a great quantity, or as much as you pleaſe; let it be carried to a place appointed for this purpoſe, then prepare to burn a good quantity of Wood, either of Oak, Aſh, Elm, Maple, or other ſorts of hard Wood, that you may have Aſhes; then take two parts of theſe Aſhes, one part of quick Lime, mix them well, and put this mixture by it ſelf, for ſuch uſes as I ſhall ſhew you anon.

Take then Veſſels of Wood, or Pipes, or Hogſheads cut in two parts, for they muſt be able to hold a good quantity of Water, make a hole at the bottom about one or two fingers breadth, put into the hole a ſmall wicker thing, or you may whelm over it an Earthen Diſh, after put Ruſhes all over the bottom (not excepting the hole) or in its place clean ſtraw; this Veſſel being thus fitted, diſpoſe of it in this manner; Set it ſo, that under may ſtand a leſſer Veſſel of Wood to receive the Liquor that ſhall diſtil down from the upper Veſſel; after put into the upper Veſſel about the height of a hand of this Salt-Peter Earth, which has been before for ſome time dryed in the Air; upon this Earth put the height of three or four fingers of the mixture made of Aſhes and quick Lime, and then again of the Salt-Peter Earth, after of the Aſhes about the ſame height as before; and continue this faſhion, putting Earth upon Aſhes, and Aſhes upon Earth, until the Veſſel be full within a hands breadth at the top, to hold the Water that is put in; this done put upon it freſh Water as much as ſhall be neceſſary, *viz.* ſo much as muſt ſurmount the Earth two or three fingers breadth, and look that it paſs through all the Earth, and run drop by drop through the hole at bottom of the Veſſel into the Tub ſtanding under, and you ſhall have a Nitrous *Lixivium*, according to the quantity of Water as you poured into the Veſſel; which if you judge is too little, you muſt reiterate the infuſion, and the ſecond time alſo the water paſſing through the Earth will carry with it a ſubſtance; And ſo the third time.

This done, put all the *Lixivium* into a Kettle of a ſufficient bigneſs, and let it be boyled upon the fire very eaſily, and moderately at firſt; after increaſe the fire to the conſumption of the Liquor, or a little more, keeping continually skimming it all the time it boyls. And when 'tis thus conſumed, pour it into wooden Veſſels that are broad, and cover them over with Cloaths, and let them ſtand until the pure part Chriſtalize into white Salt, and the feculent or more terreſtial part ſettle to the bottom. In the mean time continue pouring in of the *Lixivium* again into the Kettle, boyling and skimming it as before; and this do until all your *Lixivium* be boyled up and poured into wooden Veſſels to Chriſtalize.

Then from the wooden Veſſels, inclining them gently, pour all the *Lixivium* (leaving the ſettling at bottom by it ſelf) into your Copper as before, and boyl it up again with a good fire until half be conſumed, or until it begin to thicken, or until by putting a little upon a ſtone or peece of board, it do immediately congeal.

Then take it from the fire, and when 'tis a little cooled, pour it as before into wooden Veſſels or Boles, and put into each about a hand in height; then cover each Veſſel with courſe cloaths, put it into a cool place, and two or three dayes after you will find your Salt-Peter congealed and thruſt together in ſmall Chriſtals, like tranſparent Ice, ſticking to the ſides of the Veſſel, and likewiſe upon ſome ſticks for that purpoſe, provided the rinds being taken off and placed in the wooden Veſſels before the pouring in of the Liquor; get diligently together the Peter, as well that which ſticks to the ſides of the Veſſel, as that to the ſticks, in a Veſſel of wood proper to receive it, and cover it, and keep it dry. The remaining water you muſt boyl up as before, not forgetting to ſeparate it from its reſidence.

Whilſt 'tis boyling, it happens ſometimes that the Liquor may riſe and boyl over the Cauldron; to prevent that danger, have in readineſs other *Lixivium*, made of of three parts of Ashes, and one part of quick Lyme, as we spoke before, in which is dissolved *Roch Allum*, allowing to every hundred weight of *Lixiviun*, four pounds of Allum; and when it begins to rise, pour in a little of this from time to time; And by this means you will see that the water that was hastning to come over, will fall down; and that the common Salt and more terrestrial part will settle to the bottom.

The Earth remaining in the Wooden Tubs from whence the salt was drawn, must be put in some cover'd place made for that purpose, where neither Sun, Rain, nor any other water may come; and there it must be spread all abroad about a foot high: Then you must have in readiness Horse dung or the Excrements of all sorts of Beasts, great and small, and put off this upon the other, about the height of three or four foot; then take all that was skum'd from the *Lixivium* in boyling, and the water that is left and will not shoot, and the bottoms that are left in the wooden Vessel, where the Salt-Peter did shoot, and throw them away, as hurtful and useless, upon the Dunghil; throw likewise every day, or as often as you can, the Urine of men, and let it lye two years, and you shall have your Earth filled with Salt-Peter as before, with a greater aboundance: You may likewise throw upon your Dunghill, the Horns, Claws, and Hoofs of Beast, and then from this Earth it will be very easie to draw good Salt-Peter by the method we have prescribed.

CHAP. X.

To Clarifie and Refine Salt-Peter.

TAke as much Salt-Peter as you please, and being put in a Copper, pour upon it so much fair water as will dissolve it, that is about eight of Water, and three of Salt; and pour upon the same of the former *Lixivium*, prepared of Ashes, Quick-lyme, and Roch Allum; boyl it upon the fire until all the Salt-Peter be dissolved; that being done, have in readiness a Vessel of Wood sufficiently big, and so disposed, that another may stand under the same: which must, before it be so set, be peirced in the middle, and the hole covered over with an Earthen Dish: Let the uppermost Tub be filled five or six inches with fine clean sand; then let the Tub be covered over with a course cloath, and pour through the same into your Sand-Tub your dissolved Salt-Peter, and so it will distil by little and little into the Vessel which stands under; and so passing through the Sand, it will be discharged of all its superfluities, and will leave the most terrestial part, and such as is useless, in the Sand, which water again put into the Cauldron, and boyl it up as formerly, until it may be fit to congeal, and in the end pour it into wooden long flat Vessels as before, and in two or three dayes 'twill be shot into Christals as formerly; which if you would have purer, you must reiterate this work once more, or you may put upon this Peter, Lyme-water, filter it and boyl it up according to Art, and it will be pure.

Salt Peter may be purified thus; put your Salt-Peter in a Vessel of Copper, Iron, or Vernish't Earth (I like a Crucible best) which being put to a small fire, augment it gradually until all the Salt be melted and boyl'd; then take common Sulphur finely pulverised, and throw it upon the liquified Salt-Peter, which will quickly take fire and burn, and by the same means consume all the gross and viscous humours, with the terrestrial Salt remaining useless amongst the Salt-Peter, before the rectification; besides you may reiterate this work by putting on fresh Sulphur many times, until such time all the strange humours be quite consumed; in the end, the Salt-Peter being well melted and well purified, pour it upon well polished Marble or Plates of Iron, or Copper, or glazed Earth, and let it cool, and you will have a Salt-Peter congealed, almost resembling in colour and hardness the true Alabaster.

CHAP. XI.

How Salt-Peter Meal is made without any beating, for the making of Gun-powder.

SAlt-Peter well purified, must be put in a Kettle, upon a furnace over a fire, then moderately increase the fire with Bellows to such a degree of heat, until it begin to smoak and evaporate, until the Salt begin to lose its humidity, and obtain a whiteness, and so keep continually stirring it with a wooden or Iron Ladle, for fear it should return into its pristine form, and hereby will be taken away all its fatty greasiness that may be commixt. This being done, pour so much water into the Kettle as will cover the Salt-Peter, and when it shall be dissolved, and it has obtained the consistence of a thick Liquor; then with a wooden stick or Ladle keep continually stirring it without any intermission, until all its humidity be evaporated, and all be reduced into most dry white Meal.

CHAP. XII.

To make Salt-peter with the flower of Old Walls, of Caves, Cellars, Vaults, &c.

GAther together a good quantity of this Flower, which you may find upon the Surface of Old Walls, which are in moist places under the Earth; you may also make provision with a certain Salt which sticks to Lyme, or upon ruinated Walls; which Peter, one *Sardi* a *Roman* took notice of, was alwayes well practised at *Bruxells* in *Brabant*, as he confesseth in his fifth Book of Artillery, *Chap.* 49. First, see how much Salt-Peter matter you have; then take one fourth part so much of quick Lyme, pour upon it warm water, boyl it well, and clarifie it according to custom, then put your Salt-Peter matter into a Tub with a tap in it, and a little Earthen Dish before the hole of the tap within, pour into this Tub the Lye, and stir it well with a stick until all the Salt Peter be dissolved in the Water; then let it distil leisurely into a Vessel that stands under the tap; and at last being all dissolved and run out, put this water into a Kettle, and boyl it over the fire, until so much be consumed, that the remainder being dropped upon a Tyle-stone or Board, do congeal, and be of hardness, but not too hard; for if it be very hard, the water is burnt; but if too soft, not enough. When 'tis well boyled and scummed, take it from the fire, and proceed with it as in the tenth and eleventh Chapters.

CHAP. XIII.

How to examine the goodness of Salt-Peter.

PUt upon a Wooden Table, or any clean and smooth Board, a little Salt-Peter; then give fire to it with a live coal, and observe these Rules following, *viz.*

If it make the same noise in burning as the common Salt doth when it is thrown upon live coals, it is a sign it holds yet much common Salt.

If it hold a thick and fat scum, it is a sign 'tis fatty and viscous.

If after the Salt be consumed, there resteth yet crass and filthy matter upon the board, it is an infallible sign that the Salt contains yet a quantity of earthy matter, and so much the more, if you see much dregs after the combustion of the Salt-Peter is past; and therefore the less powerful and active.

But by contraries, if it render a cleer long flame divided into many streams, and that the superficies of the board remain neat without any filth; or that it be consumed so that nothing is left, but a white clean ash, without making much noise, or great trembling, you may then conclude that the Salt-Peter is good, and well cleansed, and in its perfect preparation.

CHAP. XIV.

The true way to purifie Salt-peter, and separating it from all offending and superfluous matter; as common Salt, Vitriol, Allum, and all fatty and viscous humours.

TAke Two pound of Quick-Lyme, Two pound of common Salt, One pound of Verdigrease, One pound of *Roman* Vitriol, One pound of Sal-Armoniack, beat them all together; after put them into an Iron Vessel, and pour upon them a good quantity of Vinegar, or in default of them, good clear water; and make a *Lixivium*, which you shall let rarifie and clarifie of it self, standing the space of three dayes; after put your Salt-Peter in a Kettle, and pour upon the same as much of this *Lixivium* as will well cover the Salt-Peter; put it upon a fire sufficiently moderate at first, increasing it until it boyl to the consumption of half; take it then away from the fire, and pour it by gentle inclination into a wooden Vessel, and throw away all the dregs and Salt which remaineth in the bottom of the Kettle: That done, let the Salt-Peter water cool, and continue your preparation as we have given before, where we treated of refining Salt-Peter.

CHAP. XV.

How to clarifie common Sulphur, and to know its goodness.

WE experience often, and without contradiction, that not only Salt-Peter is filled with terrestrial qualities, but Brimstone also, which is not only of a fatty & certain oleganious humour, but likewise a noysome quality which is in the compound, common to one and the other of its matters; from hence (if we desire to be curious in our work) we judge it may be necessary to purifie Sulphur, and to procure to it by power of clarification, a nature most sublime, subtile, fiery and volatile. The order and method that ought to be used in this, is thus; in Vessels of Iron or Copper, melt your Sulphur with a very gentle fire over Coals, well lighted, and not flaming; and when it is melted with a Ladle, skim neatly off all that riseth on the top and swimmeth upon the Sulphur; then not long after, let it be taken from the fire, and strained through a double Linnen Cloath into another Vessel, pouring it through at leisure; thus all the Oylie matter and crassy substance remains in the Cloath; but under in the Vessel will be a pure Sulphur, such as we have before spoken of.

To know the goodness of Sulphur you must do thus: Press it between two Iron plates, that are hot, and if in the running it appear yellow, without any bad odour, and that which remains be of a reddish colour, one may believe 'tis natural and excellent; so likewise 'tis a good sign, if when 'tis set on fire, it do freely burn all away, leaving little or no resident matter. For if Sulphur be pure and good, we do find that there is such a sympathy between it and fire, that the fire is desirous of the Sulphur for its nutriment, and that reciprocally the Sulphur is pleased likewise to be thus devoured and consumed by the Element of fire; so that if some fragment of it be put about some pieces of Wood, if this shall feel the fire at some distance, it seems as if it did attract it to it self, and doth sometimes unawares at a distance catch or take fire, if great care be not taken.

There is a certain kind of Sulphur which will not burn so freely as other Sulphur, nor send forth any ill scent, but being put upon the fire, melts no otherwise than common Wax; and this Sulphur is found abundantly near Mount *Ætna*, as *Carniola* of *Libavius* reports, in his first Book of the *Apocap. Hermel.* but this Sulphur is commonly red, as also is that which is found in the *Heil des Heim* (as *Agricola* mentions in his first Book, *Chap.* 22.) And upon the testimony of *John Johnson, Adm. Nat. Clas.* 4. *Chap.* 13. Sulphur is found likewise of divers other colours, as pale, Yellow, Green, as is many times to be seen and found sticking about Stones and Rocks: So, that a man may, without any great difficulty, take it from thence, and make it into a Mass.

That which is clear, perfectly yellow, not very hard, nor too much shining, is the very best. Yet there is another Sulphur which looks greenish, and hath never past the fire; and this is called *Sulphur Vivum*, and by some *Virgin Sulphur*, by reason Women and Maids had a custom to compose with it a certain *fucus* or Paint, with which they used to adorn their faces.

CHAP.

CHAP. XVI.

Of the third principal in Composition of Gun-powder, viz. Coal, and its preparation.

IN the Month of *May* or *June*, when all sorts of Trees are easie to peel, by reason in that time there comes out a sap, and they are fuller of humours than at any other time of the year, Cut then a great quantity of Hazle or Ash, the length of two or three foot, of the bigness of half your fist, taking away from them with a Bill all that is Superfluous, then take away the rind likewise; and of these make little bundles, and make them very dry in a warm Oven; then in a place chosen for that purpose, that is plain and even. set them upright one by another, and set them on fire; and after you see the fire well lighted, and that the fire hath reduced them all into burning Coals, cover them closely and diligently with watered earth, so that it may have no respiration, or that no Air may pass in; then, the flame being thus stifled upon the Coals, they will remain pure and whole, without being charged with much Ashes; then 24 hours after, you may take them away and keep them for to serve you in your business, and put them to such uses as we shall write of hereafter.

But if you have occasion for a small quantity only, take then of the Arms and Limbs of such Trees aforesaid, that is of Teil wood, of Juniper, of Ash, *&c.* Cut them in small pieces, and dry them well; then shut them in an Earthen Vessel, and lute the Cover on the top with Clay; then place Coals round about the Pot, and let it be all covered with Coals, leaving them so the space of a good hour, continuing the fire all this while in the same degree of heat; at last let it cool of it self, and when 'tis cold, open the pot, and take out the Coals for your use.

CHAP. XVII.

The wayes of Compounding or Making Gun-powder.

THe wayes of Compounding of Gun-Powder have been so commonly known, that not only such as are conversant in fireworks do understand the same, but others also; so that it is made a particular Trade: nay, that which is more strange, the Countrey people in *Polonia* have learned to prepare it with their own hands, without the use of any Artificial Engine, or Chymical Vessel. For I have seen many of the People of *Podolie*, and the *Ukrains*, which we call now the *Cossaques*, who prepare their Powder quite contrary to the common way, or that which is used by Fire-Masters. For they put Sulphur, Salt-Peter, Charcoal, all together in an Earthen Pot, a certain proportion of each; (which proportion one to the other they have learned by experimental practice) upon which they pour fair fresh water, which they boyl upon the fire until all the water is evaporated, and the matter become thick; then they take it from the fire, and dry it in the Sun, or in some warm place, as a Stove, or the like; then they pass it through a Hair Sieve, and reduce it into small Grains. There are others that take these Materials, and grind them upon a smooth flat Stone, or a smooth Earthen Dish, and then having moistned it, by their Skill they bring it into Grains; which powder brought to this degree of perfection, they serve their occasions with as much utillity and profit, as if it had been made by the hand of one of the most knowing or skilful Powder-makers in the world.

It is in my judgment, labour lost to speak more of these superficial wayes; but come to the order and method which is necessary and usually observed in the preparing of Gun-Powder: It shall likewise suffice me to propose in this Chapter some Compositions most excellent and best approved; which are these,

Compositions for Cannon Powder.		Compositions for Musquet-Powder.		Compositions for Pistol-powder.	
The first.		The first.		The first.	
Salt Peter	100 *l.*	*Salt-Peter*	100 *l.*	*Salt-Peter*	100 *l.*
Sulphur	25	*Sulphur*	18	*Sulphur*	12
Coals	25	*Coals*	20	*Coals*	15
The Second.		The Second.		The Second.	
Salt-Peter	100 *l*	*Salt-Peter*	100 *l.*	*Salt-Peter*	100 *l.*
Sulphur	20	*Sulphur*	15	*Sulphur*	10
Coals	24	*Coals*	18	*Coals*	8

You must first finely powder these compositions or mixtures, for Cannon or Musquet Powder, and after moisten them with fair fresh water or Vinegar, or with *Aquavitæ*; but if you will have your Pistol Powder stronger and more violent, you ought to stir it up several times whilst tis in the Morter, with this following liquor; that is, a water distilled from Rinds of Oranges, Citrons, or Lemons, by an Alymbeck, or any other Chymical Vessel; then let all be beaten and well brayed 24. hours, and then in the end reduce it into very fine small grains.

A Liquor for this purpose may likewise be made of twenty parts of *Aquavitæ*, and 12 parts of distilled Vinegar made of Whitewine, and four parts of Spirit of Salt-Peter, and two parts of water of Sal-armoniac, and one part of Camphire dissolved in Brandy-wine, or reduced into Powder with powdered Sulphur, or reduced with Oyl of sweet Almonds.

To Corn Powder well, you must prepare a Sieve with a bottom of thick Parchment, made full of round holes; then moisten the Powder that must be corned with its water, and make it up in Balls as big as Eggs; which put into the Sieve, and with it put a wooden Bowl, and when you have so done, sift the Powder so, as the Bowl rouling about the Sieve, may break the Clods of Powder, and make it pass through those little holes into Corns.

It is observed by Fire-Masters and Gunners, that Powder when it is Corned, is of much greater force and power, than in Meal; from hence 'tis concluded, that powder when 'tis put into a Piece of Ordnance, ought not to be pressed or beaten home too hard in the Piece; for thereby it will loose its form of grains, and thereby looseth a great part of its strength that it had, and is therefore not able to throw out the Bullet with so great a violence, as if the Powder had been gently thrust home to the Britchend.

CHAP.

CHAP. XVIII.

Of the several Colours which are to be given to Powder.

KNow first that all the blackness which you see in Gun-powder comes from the Coal; not that this colour is absolutely necessary to be conjoyned to its nature, or that it is absolutely necessary to be given to it, for its meliorating or making it more vigorous; this is not so; but by contraryes you may be permitted to give unto it any such colours as you shall think fit, without prejudice or hinderance of the Powder and vertue of it. For if instead of Coal you take rotten dryed wood, or Sawdust well dryed, or white paper moistned and dryed in a Stove and powdered, or indeed any other thing of a combustible nature, or that is well disposed to take fire (such as you read hereunder) and to this you may add a colour according to your fancie and pleasure; and you will infallibly have a Powder that will make the same Effect as the black powder. And for this purpose I shall lay down in this Chapter certain mictions, with which I served my self many times, and therefore known to be experimental truths.

White Powder.

Take Salt-Peter six pounds, Sulphur one pound, of Sawdust of the Elder Tree well dryed and powdered one pound, these mixed according to the directions in the former Chapter, there will be made a Powder of a white colour. Or thus,

Take Salt-Peter ten pounds, of Sulphur one pound, of the woody part when the Hemp is taken away, one pound, &c. Or thus,

Salt-Peter six pounds, Sulphur one pound, of Tartar calcin'd until it be brought to a whiteness, and the Salt extracted for use, one Ounce.

Red Powder.

Take of Salt-Peter twelve Parts, of Sulphur two parts, of Amber one part, of Red Sanders two parts, &c. Or,

Take Salt-Peter eight pounds, of Sulphur one pound, of dryed powdered Paper boyled up in a Water, wherein is Cinaber or Brazil Wood, and then again dryed, one pound.

Yellow Powder.

Take Salt-Peter eight pounds, Sulphur one pound, Wild or Bastard Saffron boyled in *Aqua Vitæ*, after dryed and powdered, two pounds, &c.

Green Powder.

Salt-Peter ten pounds, of Sulphur one pound, dryed Wood or Saw-dust boyled in *Aqua Vitæ* with some Verditer, then dryed and powdered, of this two pounds.

Blew Powder.

Salt-Peter eight pounds, of Sulphur one pound, of the Saw-dust of the Teil Wood boyled in Brandy Wine with Indigo, and after dryed and powdered, one pound.

CHAP. XIX.

Still Powder, or Powder without Noise.

THere are several that do Write many strange things concerning this Still Powder, or Powder, withou ut noise, or as some do give it the name, Deaf Powder, whereof they have treated prolixly; the which I think not convenient to do, by reason I am loath to tire the Reader with any such Discourse, as tends not much to Edification: I shall therefore put down certain mixtures, which I have known to be more excellent and best approved.

First way,

Take Common Powder two pounds, *Venus Borax* one pound; these being well powdered, mingled and incorporated together, must be made up into Corn Powder.

Second way,

Take common Powder two pounds, *Venus Borax* one pound, of *Lapis Calaminaris* half a pound, of Sal-armoniack half a pound; powder and mix them well, and make them up into Grains.

Third way,

Take common Powder six pounds, of Live Moles burnt in an Earthen Pot, of *Venus Borax* half a pound, mix them as before, *&c.*

Fourth way,

Take Salt-Peter six pounds, Sulphur eight pounds and a half, powder of the Second Bark of Elder Tree half a pound, common decripitated Salt two pounds; make Corn Powder of these according to the precedent order, or accustomed method.

To these known things, I shall add here a thing whereof you may make experience if you please; it being only taken from the Books of Authors, without any tryal made by me; which you may also find written in the natural Magick of *John Baptista Porta,* which is in our *English* Tongue, where he saith, that if you add burnt Paper in the Composition of Gun-Powder, or the double quantity of Hay seed well beaten; these will take away a great part of the strength, and will hinder it from making so great flame and noise.

Some do say that the Gall of a Pike doth the same effect, if it be mixed and mingled with the same; but we shall leave the belief of these things to the faith of such Authors as have experimented the same.

There

There are some wise and knowing men in this Art, attribute the cause of this noise, or as some do express it, this horrible noise, produced by a Cannon after the firing, not to the Powder, but to the beating and contusion of the Air which is inraged, or in a passion, by being so furiously endeavoured to be stifled or choaked by a strange and extraordinary movement, of which we have spoken more at large in the former Chapter, where we treated of Salt-Peter. Yet in favour of the Sons of Art, we shall nevertheless give you the opinion of *Scaliger*, taken out of his his fifteenth Book, in his *Exer. Exoter.* against *Cardan* of *Subtil. Exer.* 25.

Longe pejus illud cum sonitus causam a bellicis machinis editi, attribuis Sal Petræ; nam tenuissimum in pulverem comminutum cavernulas amisit.

CHAP. XX.

The proof or Tryal of Gun-powder.

It is accustomary for men skilled in these Arts, to try Powder three several wayes; that is, by sight, by touch, and by fire: And first, for the tryal by sight; it is thus,

If the Powder be too black, it is a manifest sign of too much humidity, or too much coal; now if it contain too much, as you suppose, rub it upon white Paper; if it black the Paper more than other good Powder use to do, it is a sign there is more coal in it than ought: for such Gun-Powder as is of a fair azure colour, or a little obscure, somthing bordering upon red, is the best sign, and the most assured testimony of good Powder.

Secondly, Gun-Powder its goodness is known by the touch, in this manner, crush some Corns under your fingers ends, and if they easily break and return to Meal without resisting the touch, or without feeling hard, you may assure your self from thence, that your Powder hath in it too much Coal.

If by pressing it a little hard under your fingers upon a smooth hard board, or upon a stone, you feel amongst it small grains harder or more sollid than the rest, which do in a manner prick the ends of the fingers, and do not yield to the finger but very difficultly, or hardly, you may infer from hence that the Sulphur is not well incorporated with the Salt-Peter, and by consequence the Powder is not well and duely prepared.

You may draw infallible proofs or conjectures of the goodness of Powder by its burning, if after you have made little heaps of Powder upon a clean and even Table, distant one from another about a hands breadth, you then put fire to one of them only; and if it take fire alone, and burn all away without lighting the others, and make a small thundring noise, or make a white clear smoak, and that it rise with a quickness, suddainly, almost imperceptible, and if it rise in the Air like a circle of smoak, or like a small Crown; this is an infallible sign the Powder is good, and perfectly well prepared.

If after the burning of the Powder there remain some black marks upon the Table, this then signifies that the Powder contains too much Coal, which has not been enough burnt.

If the board looks greasie, then the Sulphur and Salt-Peter is not enough cleansed, and by consequence it retains much of their terrestrial matter and oyly natures which were naturally conjoyned to their matters. If you find small grains, white and Citrine, it is a testimony that the Salt-Peter is not enough cleansed, and by consequence it retains much of its terrestrial matter, and of common Salt, and besides, the Sulphur hath not been well powdered, nor sufficiently incorporated with the two other matters of its Composition.

If two or three Corns of Gun-Powder be laid upon a Paper, distant about a fingers bredth one from the other, and you put fire to them, if the fire be good and strong, they will fire at once, and there will remain no grossness of Brimstone, or of Salt-Peter, nor any thing but a white smoaky colour in the place where they were burnt, nor will the Paper be touched. If small black knots, which will burn downward in the place where proof is made, remain after firing, they do shew that the Gun-powder hath not enough of Peter, and that it is of little force or strength.

Good Gun-Powder will not burn your hand, if it be set on fire there.

Gun-Powder that is very sharp or eager in tast, is not well purified, and will turn moist.

Amongst many sorts of Powder, to know the best, make a little heap of every sort at a distance one from another; observing well when you fire each heap, which of them doth soonest take fire, for that which soonest takes fire, smoaks least and clearest, and riseth quickly up close and round, and leaves little or no sign behind it, is the best Powder.

There are Instruments likewise invented for the tryal or proof of Powder, which the most part of Fire-Masters and Gunners are accustomed to use, which are described at large by other Authors; therefore we shall not here repeat the same; considering likewise, that we have found by experience a great fallacy in the same, for that one and the same Powder, in the same measure and quantities, hath raised the cover to different degrees of height.

CHAP. XXI.

To fortifie weak Powder, and amend that which is spoiled, and bring it to its full strength again; and to preserve good Powder from decaying.

WE call such Gun-Powder weak, which hath much degenerated from its first strength, and the force which it did acquire in its first preparation; as such as hath taken wind, wet, or air; for these do diminish the quantity of Salt-Peter, and actually separate the Sulphur and Coal.

There are two different wayes that these accidents do happen; that is, by being many years made, or lying in a moist place long; for in time the Salt-Peter alters and separates it self, being naturally subject to alter, and return into its first matter; for Salt-Peter in its beginning or original being engendered of water, or of a certain Saline humour, no otherwise than other Salts are produced of their own proper Brines, doth at last, or in a long time, separate it self from the Coal and Sulphur, and so return to a Brine water again, as it was in the original, and so abandons the other two matters that adhered to it, the Sulphur and Coals loosing nothing of their weight, seeing that no humidity that is attracted, can be able to dissolve them; but rather by the contrary, the Coal doth attract greedily, and becomes more ponderous.

If for the reasons aforesaid you desire to repair and restore the strength of Gun-Powder that begins to alter, or that hath quite lost its force, its defects may be amended three several wayes, &c. viz. The

The first is thus, make a Lye of two parts of *Aqua vitæ*, and one part of clarified Salt-Peter made into fine Powder, of good Vinegar made of good Wine half a part, of Oyl of Sulphur one eighth part, and as much Camphire dissolved in Brandy; these put together, do make a *Lixivium*, which must be strained through a large Strainer, and then with it you may amend your powder that is decayed, by moistning it with the same, very often, and drying it by the Sun in Wooden Vessels, and then putting it up in a dry place, free from any humidity or air, and then it will not in a long time again be damnified.

The second way to repair Powder is thus, examine how much your Powder weighed when it was first put into the Cask or Barrel, then see how much it doth now weigh after 'tis damnified (it being first dryed if it chance to be wet) then see the difference between these two weights, and add so much Salt-Peter to your decayed powder, mix it well, and make it up into Corns again, and preserve it as before.

The third way to restore the strength of Gun-Powder, is such as is most plain and commonly used amongst the Powder-men; they put upon a Sale-cloath or smooth place or board, a portion of damnified Powder, to which they add an equal weight of that which is new made, and then with their hand or wooden Shovel they mingle it well together; then they dry it in the Sun, and put it up into a Barrel again, and keep it in a dry and proper place.

Yet there is another way may be allowed, but this is almost the same with making new Powder, and it is thus; Take what quantity of decayed Powder you please, put it into Earthen or Wooden Vessels, pour upon the same three times so much hot water, stir it well about, and when it begins to be cold, or hath stood one hour or two, strain the water away, and to the feces put more water, stirring it well about, then let it stand and settle as before, and strain it from the feces, this do a third time, and you will have drawn out all the Salt-Peter; put these waters in a clean Kettle, and boyl it away until so much be consumed, as that a drop dropped upon a Stone or Iron do congeal, then pour it into some wooden Vessel that it may congeal into Salt-Peter; and that water as remains, you must boyl up again as before; and if need be, you must in the boyling skum what riseth on the top of the water. Having by this Art obtained the Salt-Peter out of the decayed Gun-Powder, you may according to the proportions given in the Composition of Powder, mix it with its remaining Sulphur and Coal, or fresh Sulphur and Coal, which is better; and after 'tis well mixed, Corn it according to the given Rules; then let it be well dryed, and put up into dry Powder Barrels, and let it be conserved in a dry place from Air or any Moisture.

Some do mend their Powder in this nature, they moisten it with Vinegar or fair water, beat it fine, and sift it and dry it, and to every pound of Powder they put one Ounce of Mealed Salt-Peter; then moisten and mix them well, so that neither may be discerned one from the other, but that they be perfectly incorporated, which you may know by cutting the Mass with a Knife, or breaking it: When it is well compounded, let it be Corned in manner as we have before prescribed.

If your Composition of Powder be made up with *Aqua vitæ*, and so made up into great Balls, and well dryed in a Stove, or in the Sun, and put into glazed earthen Pots, and close covered, you may keep it as long as you please, for age will not decay it.

There ought alwayes a care to be taken by Gunners or Fire-Masters, or such as have the charge of Gun-powder, to chuse if they can such places as are dry, and stand upon the best ground, free from dampness of the Air or any water possibly coming near. Every Gunner, *&c.* ought to take care that his Barrel be turned upside down, or any Carthredge ready filled; for if the Powder attract air, the Peter with the moisture it hath attracted, will in time seperate from the other matters, and sink to the bottom; so that the Powder in the upper part will loose its strength, which is prevented by turning and shaking them every fourteen dayes, and airing them at the Sun at convenient times. And as 'tis necessary a Gunner should have Carthredges filled for present Service, those ought also to be turned out and filled again every fourteen dayes more or less, as the Gunner in his judgment shall allow of.

CHAP. XXII.

Of the property and particular office of every Material in the Composition of Gun-powder.

WE ought infallibly to believe that Gun-Powder was not found out casually, or by fortune; but invented by a true knowledge, and by reasonable speculation in Natural Philosophy; considering that to this day no man hath opposed (notwithstanding many persons have made it their endeavour) or could find any other Materials like unto these, or of such a nature, which being well united and incorporated together, they are able to produce a fire so vigorous, fearful, powerful, and above all, so inextinguishable that the whole Universal matter is consumed in a moment; which is the more to be believed, since we make not much difficulty, particularly in this our Age wherein we live, to add many things to the invention of others, and that (as the Physitians say) all that had a beginning doth pass from imperfection to perfection. We desire therefore it may be permitted (since the Inventors have left us nothing in Writing) to propose here some Observations of Speculative truths, drawn from Experiment, which have been made about the strength, nature, effects, and Office of all the matters comprehended in the Composition of Gun-Powder, as well of the particulars, as all made up into one body. For I believe, that having insinuated into a perfect knowledge of the properties, and the affections, as well specificated as general, of all its Ingredients, no body more will fall into those Errors which are too often committed in the Art of *Pyrotechny*.

We must therefore know, that Gun-powder was not without reason composed of these three materials, to wit, Salt-Peter, Sulphur, and Coal, but to the end that one might remedy or supply the defaults of the others. And this is it which is easie to be comprehended in the effect of Sulphur; for this is naturally the very aliment of the fire, seeing it joyns with it so willingly and freely, and having once taken fire, is most difficult to put out, being no otherwise rightly than a flaming fire, or, to express it better, a pure flame; and therefore hath an aptitude to enflame the Salt-Peter, by its activity, more than any other kind of fire. But as the Salt-*P*eter lighted doth go promptly into certain windy exhalations, it hath thereby such a strength in it, that it would by its ventosity put out the flame which the Sulphur hath conceived, and by consequence deny it self of that which the Sulphur communicateth to it; hereby you may see, if one had made a simple composition of these two things only, that is, of Sulphur and Salt-Peter compounded well together, if fire were then applyed, they would in truth be suddenly enflamed, but they would soon after go out, that is, the fire will not continue to the Conflagration and Consumption of the whole matter, the reason whereof we have given a little before. It was therefore by good reason adjudged, that Coal well dryed and powdered, being adjoyned to these two materials in a certain proportion, was an excellent remedy for the supplying of this defect, seeing that Coal is of such a property and of such a nature, that if it be held to the fire, it will soon light and be reduced to a fire without any flame; And from hence it comes to pass, that the more it is agitated by the Air, or by wind, the more the fire augments, and will not go out, but conserve it self until the matter that nourisheth it is totally consumed, a little ashes only excepted. From hence it was concluded that a Composition made of these three Ingredients, such as is our Gunpowder, will conceive fire, and will be conserved, enflamed and consumed unto the last Atome. For it is most certain, that if we approach fire with it, the Sulphur which the fire extreamly loves is soon taken with it, and holdeth the same and introduceth it, not

only

only into the Salt-Peter, but the coal also at the same moment, without producing any flame. Now this fire (as we have said before) cannot be suffocated by wind, but on the contrary is enflamed the more, and takes new strength by the agitation of the Air. And as this Sulphur is a great neighbour of the fire either with or without flame, so it cannot hinder it from taking fire; and 'tis the flame of the Brimstone imbraces the Salt-Peter, and the Coal continues it. And by consequence these three materials joyned together, and well incorporated, and then lighted, produceth a fire, until all its aliment and substance be universally consumed and annihilated: Yet there must care be taken that none of these substances have any accidental defaults, either in humidity or disproportion, either more or less. We will conclude then all that we have said, that the true office of Sulphur in the Powder is to conceive the flame or receive the fire, and having received it, to communicate it to the other matters; and that the Coal hath a particular care to retain and consume it, and to hinder the fire (after it is once introduced by the Sulphur) from suffocating or going out by any windy Exhalation and great violence caused by the Salt-Peter; and lastly, that the most notable and particular office of the Salt-*P*eter is to produce and cause a most vehement and powerful ventosity or windy Exhalation. And in this which I have said, lieth all the truth of the strength, power and expulsive motion and activity of the Gun-powder; and by consequence Salt-Peter alone is the first and principal cause of all the admirable and astonishing Effects produced by Gunpowder; and consequently, the two other materials are alliated with the Salt-Peter for no other end than to make it break forth into fire and wind. For proof of this, if any one will make a Composition of Sulphur and Coal only, and with it charge a Piece of Ordnance, he will find that this will not move or thrust out a Shot of Iron or any other metal; the reason of this weakness is easie to be understood by our foregoing discourse, because the violent expulsion depends absolutely in the Salt-Peter, and in this only expulsive faculty, and not in any of the other matters. Yea I believe that one may prepare Gunpowder without Brimstone or Coal, rather than without Salt-*P*eter; or that a man may without much difficulty prepare other matters, that the one may do the office of Sulphur in kindling the matter, and the other that of Coal in Conserving it and keeping it without flame. But any other thing that hath such hidden natural properties to cause such a ventous Exhalation, so violent and capable to produce such prodigious Effects, as Salt-Peter, may not be produced.

CHAP. XXIII.

How to prepare Common Match and Extraordinary Match, that is such as will render no Smoak nor bad scent.

FIrst there must be made Cords of coarse hemp, or rather of Tow, about the bigness of half your thumb, or a good finger in Diameter; then take the ashes of Oak, Ash, Elm, or Maple, three parts, of quick Lyme one part, and make thereof a Lye after the usual manner; which being done, add to it of the Liquor drawn from Horse-dung neatly strained and leasurely exprimed through a strainer, or linnen Cloath, two parts, of Salt-*P*eter one part, and being all well mix'd, put into a Copper your Match Cords, and pour upon them your *Lixivium*, and make a small fire under the same, augmenting it gradually, until it be great, which you must keep boyling two or three dayes continually ; not boyling it dry, as some of our Writers prescribe, but supplying it continually with fresh *Lixivium*, for fear both Match and Kettle burn for want of Liquor; in the end having taken out the fire, take the Cords out of the Liquor, and wring them hard in your hands, rubbing off the moisture from them with a peece of Cloath, that comes forth in the wringing; then hang them in the Air or Sun upon long *P*oles to dry, and when they are well dryed, make them up in bundles, and carry them into a commodious place to keep for use.

But to make Match that will never have bad scent nor smoak, you must get a certain quantity of red Sand, or Gravel well washed, and purged from all its filth; put it into an Earthen pot that is not varnished, then put into the pot upon the Sand, your common Match, or any other made of Cotton, or the like matter, and coyle it in such manner, that there be half a fingers breadth of interval between every coyl of the Match, to the end they may not touch each other, but that the Match in its turning or Coyles have its sides equally distant one from the other; then throw again upon that a good quantity of Sand, and coyl in the Cord again as before: Continue thus your work until your pot be full, then cover the pot with a cover of the same earth, and close well the joynts with Lute made of fat Earth that no Air may enter; This being well and surely done, put lighted coals round about the pot, and let it stand in this posture some time, then take it away and let it stand until it be quite cold before you open it; When 'tis perfectly cold, take off the Cover, pour out the Sand, and draw out the match, for 'tis prepared, and will burn as we have said.

CHAP. XXIV.

Of the Square and Cube Roots.

WE have already in the Second Chapter of this Book shewn the way of molding and casting peices of Ordnance; if well understood, you cannot be ignorant in the way of Casting Shot. Therefore to avoyd any thing that might be tedious or unnecessary to the Students of this art, we will come to the most necessary things concerning Shot, that is, such as every Gunner ought to know. But because most of the propositions depend upon the knowledg of the Square and Cube Roots, which many (though otherwise knowing in most common Arithmetick) do not understand, I thought it good therefore to shew the Extraction of the Square and Cube Roots after a very easie way; with the necessary propositions in Gunnery, thereunto belonging.

A Table of	1.	2.	3.	4.	5.	6.	7.	8.	9.——-Roots.
Squares and	1.	4.	9.	16.	25.	36.	49.	64.	81.-——Squares.
Cubes.	1.	8.	27.	64.	125.	216.	343.	512.	729.—Cubes.

The Extraction of the Square Root.

Set down any number of figures as you shall think good, as, 2735716, then begin at your first right hand figure that is at 6, and make a prick under it, and so along every other figure as you may see here already done; and seeing the first prick to the left hand falls to be under 2, therefore seek in the Table above in the ranck of Squares

```
            1
        1 1 7 3 2           quotient
      2 7 3 5 7 1 6          (1654
      1 2 6 2 5 0 4          (1654
          3 3 3              -----
                              6616
                             8270
                            9924
                           1654
                           -------
                           2735716
                           -------
```

Squares for this number 2, or the nearest number less, which here we find to be 1, and over it we find the Root to be 1, which must be placed in the quotient, and likewise under the first prick to the left hand, then having 1 for a Divisor, and 1 for the quotient, say but the common Rule of Division, 1 times 1 is one, 1 from 2 and there remains 1; which sent over the 2, then double the quotient and it makes 2, which place between the two first pricks to the left hand that is under 7; then say how many times 2 in 17, (here you must be very cautious not to take too many) which here may be six times, place the 6 in the quotient as before, and under the second prick that is under 3, and divide as before, then double the quotient which is now 16 and it makes 32, place the 2 between the second and third prick, *viz.* under 5, and the 3 before it under the 6, so the 32 will stand under the 175 which is above; then say how many times 3 in 17, which you will find to be 5, place it in the quotient and under the third prick, and divide as before, always setting the Remainder over the head of its proper figures; then double the quotient again, which is now 165 and it makes 330, place the 0 between the two pricks as before, and place the figures before it to the left hand, as you see above, and the first figure to the left will be 3 which stands under 13; then say how many times 3 in 13, which will be 4, which place in the quotient, and under the fourth or last prick, and divide as before; so you will find no Remainder, which assures the number given to be a square number. The proof of these is known by multiplying the square Root found in it self (taking in the remains if any be) and it must produce that given number, otherwise it is false. Note how many pricks you have, and so many numbers must the quotient consist of.

If the number given be not a true Square, then a fraction will remain, which fraction you may find out the value thereof to a tenth, hundredth, or a thousandth part; *&c.* Doing thus set next to the right hand after the Sum proposed, two, four, or six cyphers, or more (for the more cyphers you put, the less is your Error) and every two cyphers will produce a fractional figure more than the Integers belonging to the proper quotient, which are tenths, hundredths, or thousand parts of a Unite, according to the number of cyphers added; that is, if you add two cyphers, then you find the tenths of a Unite *&c.* But the Square Root being not of so much use in Gunnery, as the Cube Root, we shall proceed no farther to Exemplifie the same, supposing it to be done already in the Treatise of Military Discipline.

The Extraction of the Cube Root.

Begin at your right hand, (as you did in Extracting the Square Root) and set pricks under every fourth figure, that is, leave two figures unprickt, or between the pricks, and so proceed to the left, until you have done as here you see, 7567873 2 (the number of pricks shew the number of figures that will be in the quotient.

Then see by the Table before in this Chapter the nearest Cube to the numbers standing over the first prick to the right hand, which is 75, I search in the Table of Cubes and find the nearest number to it in the Table of Cubes to be 64, and its Root 4, which must be set down in the quotient, and likewise its Cube 64 under the prick; and if that number doth not amount to so much as the number standing over the prick, then substract it from the same, and set the Remainder over head.

Then triple the quotient, and that triple you must set under the next number to the right hand, before that prick where you did last end.

Multiply that tripled number by the quotient, and set it down under the first triple, and that number let be your Divisor.

Then (as in common Division) must you look how many times the Divisor in the figures is standing over them, and place that in the quotient.

This done, Multiply your quotient by your Divisor, and set it under your Divisor, with a Line between.

Then multiply the last figure in the quotient by it self, and then in the triple, and set that figure under the former, one figure more to the right hand.

Lastly, Multiply the last figure cubically, and set that Sum also one figure to the Right hand; then add all these three multiplications together, and substract it out of figures standing over the first and second prick, and the Remainder set over them.

This done, again triple the quotient, and proceed exactly as before &c.

If your number be not an exact Cube, but some numbers remain whereof you desire to find the exact fraction, that is as near as possible may be, *viz.* to a tenth, hundredth, or a thousandth part &c. To find the tenths add three cyphers, the hundreds 6 cyphers, the thousands nine cyphers, at the Right hand of your figures, according to the directions given in finding the fractional of a square. But these Rules being somthing tedious to many men, we will for their encouragement and ease add a Table of Squares and Cubes whereby any man may find, by inspection only, the Square and Cube of any number of Inches, and parts of an Inch, to a tenth part, provided your number exceed not 100 inches, which will be found very necessary, and save much labour, as will appear by the following Examples. But first we will present you with the Table it self.

A Table

A Table of Squares and Cubes, very useful for the speedy Extracting of Square and Cube Roots, for the Resolution of Questions in Military Affairs: Whether for the Ordering of Battalions, or Gunnery, &c.

R	Aq	Ac	R	Aq	Ac	R	Aq	Ac
1	1	1	45	2025	91125	89	7921	704969
2	4	8	46	2116	97336	90	8100	729000
3	9	27	47	2209	103823	91	8281	753571
4	16	64	48	2304	110592	92	8464	778688
5	25	125	49	2401	117649	93	8649	804357
6	36	216	50	2500	125000	94	8836	830584
7	49	343	51	2601	132651	95	9025	857375
8	64	512	52	2704	140608	96	9216	884736
9	81	729	53	2809	148877	97	9409	912673
10	100	1000	54	2916	157464	98	9604	941192
11	121	1331	55	3025	166375	99	9801	979299
12	144	1728	56	3136	175616	100	10000	1000000
13	169	2197	57	3249	185193	101	10201	1030301
14	196	2744	58	3364	195112	102	10404	1061208
15	225	3375	59	3481	205379	103	10609	1092729
16	256	4096	60	3600	216000	104	10816	1124864
17	289	4913	61	3721	226981	105	11025	1157625
18	324	5832	62	3844	238328	106	11236	1191016
19	361	6859	63	3969	250047	107	11449	1225043
20	400	8000	64	4096	262144	108	11664	1259712
21	441	9261	65	4225	274625	109	11881	1295029
22	484	10648	66	4356	287496	110	12100	1331000
23	529	12167	67	4489	300763	111	12321	1367631
24	576	13824	68	4624	314432	112	12544	1404928
25	625	15625	69	4761	328509	113	12769	1442897
26	676	17576	70	4900	343000	114	12996	1481544
27	729	19683	71	5041	357911	115	13225	1520875
28	784	21952	72	5184	373248	116	13456	1560896
29	841	24389	73	5329	389017	117	13689	1601613
30	900	27000	74	5476	405224	118	13924	1643032
31	961	29791	75	5625	421875	119	14161	1685159
32	1024	32768	76	5776	438976	120	14400	1728000
33	1089	35937	77	5929	456533	121	14641	1771561
34	1156	39304	78	6084	474552	122	14884	1815848
35	1225	42875	79	6241	493039	123	15129	1860867
36	1296	46656	80	6400	512000	124	15376	1906624
37	1369	50653	81	6561	531441	125	15625	1953125
38	1444	54872	82	6724	551368	126	15876	2000376
39	1521	59319	83	6889	571787	127	16129	2048383
40	1600	64000	84	7056	592704	128	16384	2097152
41	1681	68921	85	7225	614125	129	16641	2146689
42	1764	74088	86	7396	636056	130	16900	2197000
43	1849	79507	87	7569	658503	131	17161	2248291
44	1936	85184	88	7744	681472	132	17424	2299968

R	Aq	Ac	R	Aq	Ac	R	Aq	Ac
133	17689	2352637	187	34969	6539203	241	58081	13997521
134	17956	2406104	188	35344	6644672	242	58564	14172488
135	18225	2460375	189	35721	6751269	243	59049	14348907
136	18496	2515456	190	36100	6859000	244	59536	14526784
137	18769	2571353	191	36481	6967871	245	60025	14706125
138	19044	2628027	192	36864	7077888	246	60516	14886936
139	19321	2685619	193	37249	7189057	247	61009	15069223
140	19600	2744000	194	37636	7301384	248	61504	15252992
141	19881	2803221	195	38025	7415875	249	62001	15438249
142	20164	2863288	196	38416	7529536	250	62500	15655000
143	20449	2924207	197	38809	7645373	251	63001	15813251
144	20736	2985984	198	39204	7762392	252	63504	16003008
145	21025	3048625	199	39601	7880599	253	64009	16194277
146	21316	3112136	200	40000	8000000	254	64516	16387064
147	21609	3176523	201	40401	8120601	255	65025	16581375
148	21904	3241792	202	40804	8242408	256	65536	16777216
149	22201	3307949	203	41209	8369421	257	66049	16974593
150	22500	3375000	204	41616	8489664	258	66564	17173512
151	22801	3442951	205	42025	8615125	259	67081	17373979
152	23104	3511808	206	42436	8741816	260	67600	17576000
153	23409	3581577	207	42849	8869743	261	68121	17779581
154	23716	3652264	208	43264	8998912	262	68644	17984728
155	24025	3723875	209	43681	9129329	263	69169	18191447
156	24336	3796416	210	44100	9261000	264	69696	18399744
157	24649	3869893	211	44521	9393931	265	70225	18609625
158	24964	3944312	212	44944	9528128	266	70756	18821096
159	25281	4019679	213	45369	9663597	267	71289	19034163
160	25600	4096000	214	45796	9800344	268	71824	19248832
161	25921	4173281	215	46225	9938375	269	72361	19465109
162	26244	4251528	216	46656	10077696	270	72900	19683000
163	26569	4330747	217	47089	10218313	271	73441	19902511
164	26896	4410944	218	47524	10360232	272	73984	20123648
165	27225	4492125	219	47961	10503459	273	74529	22346417
166	27556	4574296	220	48400	10648000	274	75076	20570824
167	27889	4657463	221	48841	10793861	275	75625	20796875
168	28224	4741632	222	49284	10941048	276	76176	21024576
169	28561	4826809	223	49729	11089567	277	76729	21253933
170	28900	4913000	224	50176	11239424	278	77284	21484952
171	29241	5000211	225	50625	11390625	279	77841	21717639
172	29584	5088448	226	51076	11543176	280	78400	21952000
173	29929	5177717	227	51529	11697083	281	78961	22188041
174	30276	5268024	228	51984	11852352	282	79524	22425768
175	30625	5359375	229	52441	12008989	283	80089	22665187
176	30976	5451776	230	52900	12167000	284	80656	22906304
177	31329	5545233	231	53361	12326391	285	81225	23149125
178	31684	5639752	232	53824	12487168	286	81796	23393656
179	32041	5735339	233	54289	12649337	287	82369	23639903
180	32400	5832000	234	54756	12812904	288	82944	23887872
181	32761	5929741	235	55225	12977875	289	83521	24137569
182	33124	6028568	236	55696	13144256	290	84100	24389000
183	33489	6128487	237	56169	13312053	291	84681	24642171
184	33856	6229504	238	56644	13481272	292	85264	24897088
185	34225	6331625	239	57121	13651919	293	85849	25153757
186	34596	6434856	240	57600	13824000	294	86436	25412184

R	Aq	Ac	R	Aq	Ac	R	Aq	Ac
295	87025	25672375	349	121801	42508549	403	162409	65450827
296	87616	25934336	350	122500	42875000	404	163216	65939264
297	88209	261980	351	123201	43243551	405	164025	66430125
298	88804	26463592	352	123904	43614208	406	164836	66923416
299	89401	26730899	353	124609	43986977	407	165649	67419143
300	90000	27000000	354	125316	44361864	408	166464	67917312
301	90601	27270901	355	126025	44738875	409	167281	68417929
302	91204	27543608	356	126736	45118016	410	168100	68921000
303	91809	27818127	357	127449	45499293	411	168921	69426531
304	92416	28094464	358	128164	45882712	412	169744	69934528
305	93025	28372625	359	128881	46268279	413	170569	70444997
306	93636	28652616	360	129600	46656000	414	171396	70957944
307	94249	28934443	361	130321	47045881	415	172225	71473375
308	94864	29218112	362	131044	47437928	416	173056	71991296
309	95481	29503629	363	131769	47832147	417	173889	72511713
310	96100	29791000	364	132496	48228544	418	174724	73034632
311	96721	30080231	365	133225	48627125	419	175561	73560059
312	97344	30271328	366	133956	49027896	420	176400	74088000
313	97969	30664297	367	134689	49430863	421	177241	74618461
314	98596	30659144	368	135424	49836032	422	178084	75151448
315	99225	31255875	369	136161	50243409	423	178929	75686967
316	99856	31554496	370	136900	50653000	424	179776	76225024
317	100489	31855013	371	137641	51064811	425	180625	76765625
318	101124	32157432	372	138384	51478848	426	181476	77308776
319	101761	32461759	373	139129	51895117	427	182329	77854483
320	102400	32768000	374	139876	52313624	428	183104	78402752
321	103041	33076161	375	140625	52734375	529	184041	78953589
322	103684	33386248	376	141376	53157376	430	184900	79507000
323	103329	33698267	377	142129	53582633	431	185761	80062991
324	104976	34012224	378	142884	54010152	432	186624	80621568
325	105625	34328125	379	143641	54439939	433	187489	81182737
326	106276	34645976	380	144400	54872000	434	188356	81746504
327	106929	34965783	381	145161	55306341	435	189225	82312875
328	107584	35287552	382	145924	55742968	436	190096	82881856
329	108241	35611289	383	146689	56181887	437	190969	83453353
330	108900	35937000	384	147456	56623104	438	191844	84027672
331	109561	36264691	385	148225	57066625	439	192721	84604519
332	110224	36594368	386	148996	57512456	440	193600	85184000
333	110889	36926037	387	149769	57960603	441	194481	85766121
334	111556	37259704	388	150544	58411072	442	195364	86350888
335	112225	37595375	389	151321	58863869	443	196249	86938307
336	112896	37933056	390	152100	59319000	444	197136	87528384
337	113569	38272753	391	152881	59776471	445	198025	88121125
338	114244	38614472	392	153664	60236288	446	198916	88716536
339	114921	38958219	393	154449	60698457	447	199809	89314623
340	115600	39304000	394	155236	61162984	448	200704	89915392
341	116281	39651821	395	156025	61629875	449	201601	90518849
342	116964	40001688	396	156810	62099136	450	202500	91125000
343	117649	40353607	397	157609	62570773	451	203401	91733851
344	118336	40707584	398	158404	63044792	452	204304	92345408
345	119025	41063625	399	159201	63521193	453	205209	92959677
346	119716	41421736	400	160000	64000000	454	206116	93576664
347	120409	41781923	401	160801	64481201	455	207025	94196375
348	121104	42144192	402	161604	64964808	456	207936	94818816

R	Aq	Ac	R	Aq	Ac	R	Aq	Ac
457	208849	95443993	511	261121	133432831	565	319225	180362125
458	209764	96071912	512	262144	134217728	566	320356	181321496
459	210681	96702579	513	263169	135005697	567	321489	182284263
460	211690	97336000	514	264196	135796744	568	322624	183250432
461	212521	97972181	515	265225	136590875	569	323761	184220009
462	213444	98611128	516	266256	137388096	570	324900	185193000
463	214369	99252847	517	267289	138188413	571	326041	186169411
464	215296	99897344	518	268324	138991832	572	327184	187149284
465	216225	100544625	519	269361	139798359	573	328320	188132517
466	217156	101194696	520	270400	410608000	574	329476	189119224
467	218089	101874563	521	277441	141420761	575	330625	190109375
468	219024	102503232	522	272484	142236648	576	331776	191102976
469	219961	103161709	523	273529	143055667	577	332929	19[illegible]100033
470	220900	103823000	524	274576	143877824	578	334084	193100552
471	221841	104487111	525	275625	144703125	579	335241	194104539
472	222784	105154048	526	276676	145531576	580	336400	195112060
473	223729	105823817	527	277729	146363183	581	337561	196122941
474	224676	106496424	528	278784	147197952	582	3387[illegible]4	197137368
475	225625	107171875	529	279841	148035889	583	339889	198155287
476	226576	107850176	530	28[illegible]00	148877000	584	341056	199176704
477	2274[illegible]9	108531333	531	281961	149721291	585	342225	200201625
478	228484	109215352	532	283024	150568768	586	343396	201230056
479	229441	109902239	533	284089	151419437	587	344569	202262003
480	230400	110592000	534	285156	152273304	588	345744	203297472
481	231361	111284641	535	286225	153130375	589	346921	204336469
482	232324	111980168	536	287296	153990656	590	348100	205379000
483	233289	112678587	537	288369	154854153	591	349281	206425071
484	234256	113379904	538	289444	155720872	592	350464	207474688
485	235225	114084125	539	290521	156590819	593	351649	208527857
486	236196	114791256	540	291600	157464000	594	352836	209584584
487	237169	115501303	541	292681	158340421	595	354025	210644871
488	238144	116214272	542	293764	159220088	596	355216	211708746
489	239121	116930269	543	294849	160103007	597	356409	212776073
490	240100	117649000	544	295936	160989184	598	357604	213847192
491	241081	118370771	545	297025	161878625	599	358801	2149[illegible]1799
492	242064	119095488	546	298116	162771336	600	360000	216000000
493	243049	119823157	547	299209	163667323	601	361201	217081801
494	244036	120553784	548	390304	164566592	602	362404	218167208
495	245025	121287375	549	391491	165469149	603	363609	219256227
496	246016	122023936	550	302500	166375000	604	364816	220348864
497	247009	122763473	551	303601	167284151	605	366025	221445125
498	248004	123505992	552	304704	168196608	606	367236	222545016
499	249001	124251499	553	305809	169112377	607	368449	223648543
500	250000	125000000	554	306916	170031464	608	369664	224755712
501	251000	125751501	555	308025	170953875	609	370881	225866529
502	252004	126506008	556	309136	171879616	610	372100	226981000
503	253009	127263527	557	310249	172808693	611	373321	228099131
504	254016	128024064	558	311364	173741112	612	374544	229220928
505	255025	128787625	559	312481	174676879	613	375769	230346397
506	256036	129554216	560	313600	175616000	614	376996	231475544
507	257049	130323843	561	314721	176558481	615	378225	232608375
508	258964	131096512	562	315844	177504328	616	379456	233744896
509	259081	131872229	563	316969	178453547	617	380689	234885113
510	260100	123651000	564	318096	179406144	618	381924	236029032

R	Aq	Ac	R	Aq	Ac	R	Aq	Ac
619	383161	237176659	673	452929	3048[illegible]1217	727	528529	384240592
620	384400	238328000	674	454276	306182024	728	529984	385828362
621	385641	239483061	675	455625	307546875	729	531441	387420499
622	386884	240641848	676	456976	308915776	730	532900	389017000
623	388129	241804367	677	458329	310288733	731	534361	390617891
624	380376	242970624	678	459084	311665752	732	535821	391223168
625	390625	244140625	679	461041	313046839	733	537289	393832837
626	391876	245314376	680	462400	314432000	734	538756	395446904
627	393129	246491883	681	463761	315821241	735	540225	397065375
628	394384	247673158	682	465124	317214568	736	541696	398688256
629	395641	248858189	683	466489	318611987	737	543169	400315553
630	396900	250047000	684	467856	320013504	738	544644	401947272
631	398161	251239591	685	469225	321419125	739	546221	403583419
632	399424	252435968	686	470596	322828856	740	547600	405224000
633	400689	253636137	687	471969	32424[illegible]703	741	549081	406869021
634	401956	254840104	688	473344	325660672	742	550564	408518488
635	403225	256047875	689	474721	327082769	743	552049	410172407
636	404496	257259456	690	476100	328509000	744	553536	411830784
637	405799	258474853	691	477481	329939371	745	555025	413493625
638	407044	259694072	692	478864	331373888	746	556516	415160936
639	408321	260917119	693	483249	332812557	747	558009	416832723
640	409600	262144000	694	481633	334255384	748	559504	418508992
641	410881	263374721	695	483025	335702375	749	561001	420189741
642	412164	264609288	696	484416	337153536	750	56[illegible]500	421875000
643	413449	265847707	697	485809	338638873	751	564001	423564751
644	414736	267089984	698	487204	339068392	752	565504	425259008
645	416025	268336125	699	488601	341532099	753	567009	426957777
646	417316	269586136	700	490000	343000000	754	568516	428661064
647	418609	270840025	701	491401	344472101	755	570025	430368875
648	419904	272097792	702	492804	345948408	756	571536	432081216
649	421201	273359449	703	494209	347428927	757	573049	433798093
650	422500	274625000	704	495616	348913664	758	574564	435519512
651	423801	275894415	705	497025	350402625	759	576081	437245479
652	425104	277167808	706	498436	351895816	760	577600	438976000
653	426409	278445077	707	499849	353393243	761	579121	440701081
654	427716	279726264	708	501264	354894912	762	580644	442440728
655	429025	281011375	709	502681	356400829	763	582169	444184947
656	430336	282300416	710	504100	357911000	764	583696	445933744
657	436649	283593393	711	505521	359425431	765	585225	447687125
658	432964	284890312	712	506944	360944128	766	586656	449445096
659	434281	286191179	713	508369	362467097	767	588289	451207663
660	435600	287496000	714	509796	363994344	768	589824	452974832
661	436921	288804781	715	511225	365525875	769	591361	454746609
662	438244	290117528	716	512656	367061696	770	592900	456533000
663	439569	291434247	717	514089	368601813	771	594441	458314011
664	440896	292754944	718	515524	370246232	772	595984	460099648
665	442225	294079625	719	516961	371694959	773	597529	461889917
666	443556	295408296	720	518400	373248000	774	599076	463684824
667	444889	296740963	721	519841	374805361	775	600625	465484375
668	446224	298077632	722	521284	376367048	776	602176	467288576
669	447561	299418309	723	522729	377933067	777	603729	469097433
670	448900	300763000	724	524176	379503424	778	605284	470910952
671	450241	302111711	725	525625	381078125	779	606841	472729139
672	451584	303464448	726	527076	382657186	780	608400	474552000

R	Aq	Ac	R	Aq	Ac	R	Aq	Ac
781	609961	476279541	835	697225	582182875	889	790321	702595369
782	611524	478211768	836	698896	584277056	890	792100	704060000
783	613089	480048687	837	700569	586376253	891	793881	707247971
784	614656	481890304	838	702244	588480472	892	795664	709732288
785	616225	483736625	839	703921	590589719	893	797449	712121957
786	617796	485587656	840	705600	592704000	894	799236	714516984
787	619369	487443403	841	707281	594823321	895	801025	716917375
788	620944	489303872	842	708964	596947688	896	802816	719323136
789	622521	491169069	843	710649	599077107	897	804609	721734273
790	624100	493039000	844	712336	601211584	898	806404	724150792
791	625681	494913071	845	714025	603351125	899	808201	726572699
792	627264	496793088	846	715716	605495736	900	810000	729000000
793	628849	498677257	847	717409	607645423	901	811801	731452701
794	630436	500566184	848	719104	609800199	902	813604	733870808
795	632015	502459875	849	720801	611960049	903	815409	736314327
796	633616	504358336	850	722500	614125000	904	817216	738763264
797	635209	506261573	851	724201	616265051	905	819025	741217625
798	636804	508169592	852	725904	618470208	906	820836	743677416
799	638401	510082399	853	727609	620650477	907	822649	746142643
800	640000	512000000	854	729316	622835864	908	824644	748613312
801	641601	513922402	855	731025	625026375	909	826281	751089429
802	643204	515849608	856	732736	627222016	910	828100	753571000
803	644809	517781627	857	734449	629422793	911	829921	750058031
804	646416	519718464	858	736164	631628712	912	831744	758550528
805	648025	521660125	859	737881	633839779	913	833569	761048497
806	649636	523606616	860	739600	636056000	914	835396	763551944
807	651249	525557943	861	741321	638277381	915	837225	766060875
808	652864	527514112	862	743044	640503928	916	839056	768575296
809	654481	529475129	863	744769	642735647	917	840889	771095213
110	656100	531441000	864	746496	644972544	918	842724	773620632
811	657721	533411731	865	748225	647214625	919	844561	776151559
812	659344	535387328	866	749956	949461896	920	846400	778688000
813	660969	537367797	867	751689	651714363	921	848241	781229961
814	662596	539353144	868	753424	653972032	922	850084	783777448
815	664225	541343375	869	755161	656234929	923	851929	786330467
816	665856	543338496	870	756900	658503000	924	853776	788889024
817	667489	545338513	871	758641	660776311	925	855625	791453125
818	669124	547343432	872	760384	663054848	926	857476	794022776
819	670761	549353256	873	762129	665336617	927	859329	796597983
820	672400	551368000	874	763876	667627624	928	861184	799178752
821	674041	553387661	875	765625	669921875	929	863041	801765089
822	675684	555412248	876	767376	672121376	930	864900	804357000
823	677329	557441767	877	769129	674526133	931	866761	806954491
824	678976	559476224	878	770884	676836152	932	868624	809557568
825	680625	561515625	879	772641	679151439	933	870489	812166237
826	682276	563559976	880	774400	681472000	934	872356	814780504
827	683929	565609283	881	776161	683797841	935	874225	817400375
828	685584	567663552	882	777924	686128968	936	876096	820025856
829	687241	569722789	883	779689	688465387	937	877969	822656953
830	688000	571787000	884	781456	690807104	938	879844	825293672
831	690561	573856191	885	783225	693154125	939	881721	827936019
832	692224	575930368	886	784996	695506456	940	883600	830584000
833	693889	578009537	887	786769	697864103	941	885481	833237621
834	695556	580093704	888	788544	700227072	942	887364	835896888

R	Aq	Ac	R	Aq	Ac	R	Aq	Ac
943	889249	838561807	963	927369	893056347	983	966289	949862087
944	891136	841232384	964	929296	895841344	984	968256	952763904
945	893025	843908625	965	931225	898632125	985	970225	955671625
946	894916	846590536	966	933156	901428696	986	972196	958585256
947	896809	849271123	967	935089	904231063	987	974169	961504803
948	898704	851971392	968	937024	907039232	988	976144	964430272
949	900601	854670349	969	938961	909853209	989	978121	967361669
950	902500	857375000	970	940900	912673000	990	980100	970299000
951	904401	860085351	971	942841	915498611	991	982081	973242271
952	906304	862801408	972	944784	918330048	992	984064	976191488
953	908209	865523177	973	946729	991167317	993	986049	979146657
954	910116	868250664	974	948676	924010424	994	988036	982107784
955	912025	870983875	975	950625	926859375	995	990025	985074875
956	913936	873722816	976	952576	929714176	996	992016	988047936
957	915849	876467493	977	954529	932574833	997	994009	991026973
958	917764	879217012	978	956484	935441352	998	996004	994011992
959	919681	881974079	979	958441	938313739	999	998001	997002999
960	921600	884736000	980	960400	941192000	1000	1000000	1000000000
961	923521	887503681	981	962361	944076141			
962	925444	890277128	982	964324	946966168			

CHAP. XXV.

The Use of these Tables in Gunnery.

QUEST. I.

By knowing the Diameter and Weight of any one Shot, to find the Weight of another Shot, being both of one and the same Metal.

THe Shot whose weight we know not, we must have in Diameter likewise, which is found thus, Gird the Shot with a Line, then divide that into twenty two equal parts, and seven of those is the Diameter or the height of the Shot.

But if you have a pair of Callapars by you, the best way is to take the Diameter with them. The fashion and form of taking the Diameter of a Shot, is as here you see in the figure following.

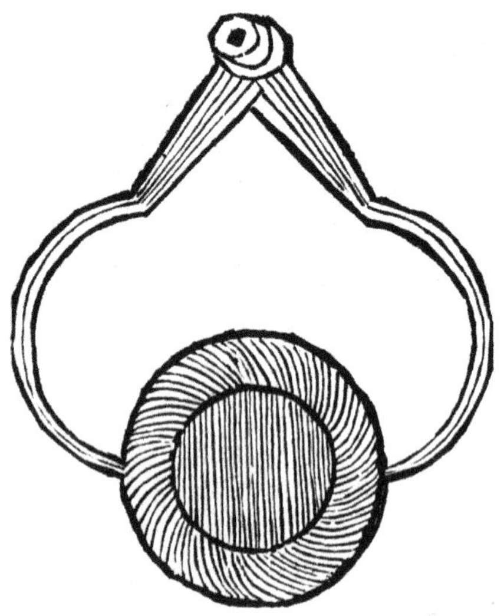

If an Iron Shot of 4 Inches Diameter weigh 9 *l.* what shall a Shot weigh whose Diameter is twice as much, that is, 8 Inches.

Cube each Diameter, then multiply the Cube of the Shot whose weight is required by the Diameter of the given Shot, and that Sum divided by the Cube of the known Diameter, the quotient is the Diameter of the Shot required.

Example.

Inch.	*l.*	*Inch.*		*l.*
If 4 weigh	9 what	8	Answer	72.
4	512	8		
16	18	64		
4	459	8		
64	4608	512		

1 2 (*l.*
4608 (72 The weight of the Shot of
644 8 Inches Diameter.
6

This question may also be performed by the former Table of Cubes, if you search in the Collum of Roots until you find your Diameters in a right Line with the same

under

under the word Cube, you will find the Cube answerable to the number given, thus; you will find the Cube of 4 to be 64, and of 8 to be 512, and this 512 multiplyed by the weight of the known Bullet, *viz.* 9 *l.* it makes 4608, which divided by 64, gives the weight of the Bullet to be 72 *l.* which was to be known.

QUEST. II.

Knowing the Diameter and weight of one Shot, to find the Diameter of a Shot that weigheth twice as much.

Suppose the known Shot was 4 Inches Diameter, and weigh 9 pound, and it were required to find the Diameter of a Shot, whose weight is twice as much, that is 18, find the Cube-Root of each Shots weight, then multiply the Diameter of the Shot whose weight is known, by the Cube of the Diameter of the Shot whose weight is required; and that Sum divided by the Cube of the Diameter of the known Shot and the quotient is the Diameter required. Example. By the former Rule, or by the Table, the Cube of the pounds will be found to be 2,08, and the Cube of 18 will be 2,62, now multiply this last number by 4, and it makes 9,48, which divided by 2, 08 will give in the quotient 5,03 for the Diameter required.

This question may very easily be wrought by the Line of numbers, thus; divide the distance between 9 and 18 into three equal parts, and that extent will reach from 4 Inches to 5,03 Inches, the Diameter required.

QUEST. III.

How the former question may be Resolved Geometrically.

Make a Square of the Diameter of the lesser Bullet, then draw a Line from Corner to Corner, and this Line thus drawn shall be the Diameter of a Shot twice the weight of the other; which if you divide into two equal parts, setting one foot of your compasses in the middle, you may draw a Circle, and that circumference will represent unto you a Bullet twice the weight of the lesser Diameter.

This work may be proved Arithmetically thus; the Diameter of the lesser Bullet is 4 Inches, the Square thereof 16, which being doubled is 32; and the square Root of this 32 is 5,65, and so much is the Diameter of the greater Bullet, which weighed 18 *l.* There ariseth here a difference between this way and the former, but this way is the most true; not but that both Rules are true in themselves, but the former depending upon finding the Cube Roots, which cannot be found much more exacter than what I have done, and so working by them, and they not being exact, causes the difference in the work.

QUEST. IV.

How to find the Diameter for the Weight of any Shot assigned.

Suppose a Shot of 27 *l.* be 6 Inches Diameter, how many Inches Diameter is a Shot of 64 *l.*

Find the Cube of 64 in the Table, and it will be found to be 4; which multiply by 6, and it makes 24; which divided by 3, the Cube of 27, and it gives 8 Inches for the Diameter of the Shot or Bullet which was required.

QUEST. V.

How this Question may Geometrically be resolved.

Mr. *Gunter* in his first Book, Section 4. hath shewed how to make a Line of Solids on his Sector; but this Rule shews us the proportion of the Diameters in Weight, having a Shot of one pound, two pounds, three pounds weight of Metal, or stone, &c. For if the given Shot be one pound, divide the diameter of that Shot into 4 equal parts, and 5 such parts will make a Diameter of a Shot of the said Metal, as is proposed, that shall weigh just twice as much. And divide the Diameter of a Shot that weighs just two pounds into seven equal parts, and eight such parts will make the Diameter of a Shot of 3 pounds weight. And Divide the Diameter of a Shot of 3 pounds, into 10 equal parts, and 11 of such parts will give a Shot of 4 pounds weight. And divide a Shot of 4 pounds weight into 13 parts, and 14 such parts will make a Shot of 5 pounds in weight. And divide the Diameter of a Shot of 5 pounds weight, into 16 equal parts, and 17 such parts will make a Diameter of a shot that will weigh 6 pounds. And so dividing the Diameter of a shot 6 pounds weight into 19 equal parts, and 20 such parts will make a Diameter of a shot that will weigh 7 pounds. Thus dividing each next Diameter into three equal parts more than the next less Diameter was divided into, and with one part added to the Diameter of a shot it will weigh just one pound more, and so may proceed infinitely.

A second way to Perform this work.

Find exactly the Diameter of a shot whose weight is just one pound, then describe a Circle whose Diameter shall be equal thereunto, and divide it into four equal parts, as *a b c d*, and draw the two Diameters *a c* and *d b* crossing the Center, and then take the distance *d c* in your Compasses, and lay it off from *e* to 2, and this will be a shot of two pounds weight.

Then take the distance *d* 2, in your Compasses, and set it off from *e* to 3, so will that distance be the Diameter of a shot of three pounds weight; and so you may proceed in the same manner at your pleasure; as you may see by the projection.

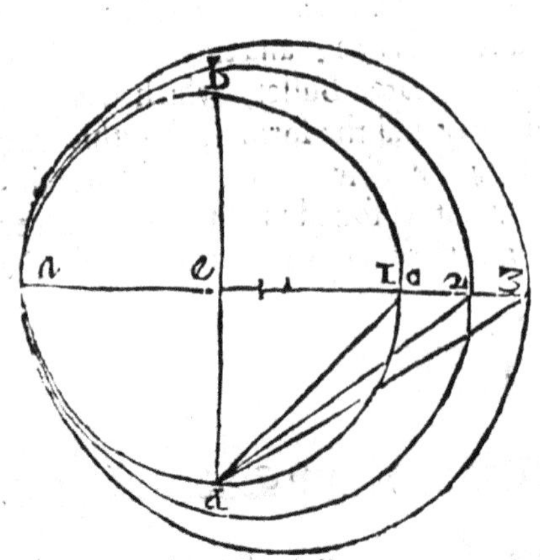

Likewise having the Diameter of a Shot of any weight, the double of the Diameter is the Diameter of a Shot that weighs eight times as much. So that if a Shot of four Inches Diameter weigh nine pounds, a Shot of eight inches Diameter will weigh seventy two pounds; as you may see by this following Table of the weights of Shot.

QUEST.

QUEST. VI.

If a Shot of three Inches and a half weigh six pounds, what will a Shot of seven inches and three quarters weigh.

You may for $3\frac{1}{2}$ put 3, 50. and for $7\frac{3}{4}$ put 7, 75. then you may Cube them the common way; then multiply the second by the third number, and divide by the first, the Quotient gives the content.

You may more easily work it by the Table of Cubes aforegoing; that is, against the Root 3, 50. you will find its Cube to be 42, 875; and against the Root 7, 75. you will find its Cube to be 46, 548. and this multiplyed by 6, and divided by 42, 875, will leave 65, 14. that is 65 pounds and $\frac{14}{100}$ parts of a pound. In this nature may any Fractions be wrought, even as easie as whole Numbers, especially if you reckon your Fractions the Decimal way, or bring them into Decimal Fractions by Reduction.

QUEST. VII.

The Proportions between Bullets of Iron and Bullets of Lead or Stone, that is, by knowing the Weight of an Iron Shot, to find the Weight of a Shot of the same Diameter made of Lead or Stone.

The Proportion between Lead and Iron is as 3 to 2, so that a Shot of two pound of Iron is the same Diameter as a Shot of 3 pounds of Lead.

Example.

If a Shot of Iron of $3\frac{1}{2}$ Inches Diameter weigh 6 pounds, what will a Shot of Lead of the same Diameter?

For $3\frac{1}{2}$ Inches put 3, 5, and say, if 2 give 3, 5, what will 3 give?

```
 35
---       (1
 15   105   52½ pounds.
 9    22
---
105
```

This $52\frac{1}{2}$ pounds is the weight of a Shot of Lead of 3 Inches and a half Diameter.

The proportion between Iron and Stone is as 3 to 8, so that a Shot of 12 pound of stone is as big, or the same in Diameter, as the like Shot of Iron that weighs 32 pounds; but some say the proportion between Marble and Iron is as 15 to 34.

A Bullet of Lead to the like of Marble is in proportion as 4 to 1.

The proportion between Lead and Brass is as 24 is to 19.

The proportion between Iron and Lead, as some say, is as 19 to 28.

The proportion between Iron and Brass is as 16 to 18.

By these Rules we may Calculate a Table very easily, to know if an Iron Shot be wanting, and a Shot of any of the other metals to be had, what height and weight either Shot of Lead Brass or Stone ought to be, to fit any piece of Ordnance; and by the same method we have here Calculated a Table, which doth shew the weight of any Shot of Iron, Lead or Stone; from 2 Inches to 9 Inches.

This is worthy to be observed, that you ought not to have so much Powder to Load a Piece that must discharge a Marble Shot, as an Iron Shot; but the proportion must be abated as the proportions between Stone and Iron doth allow of.

A Table of the Diameter and Weight of all such Shot as are generally used in England, from one to eight Inches Diameter, with the length of every Piece fitting to carry such a Shot.

The Names of the *Pieces* of *Ordnance.*	Diameter of the Bore.		Length of the Gun.		Weight of the Gun in pounds.	Breadth of the Ladle.		Length of the Ladle.		Weight of the Powder.		Diameter of the Shot.		The weight of the Shot.		He shoots point blank.
The	Inches.	Parts. [8	Feet.	Inches. [8	Pounds.	Inches.	Parts. [8	Inches.	Parts. [8	Pounds.	Ounces.	Inches.	Parts. [8	Pounds.	Ounces.	Paces.
A Base.	1	2	4	6	200	2	0	4	0	0	8	1	1	0	5	60
A Rabanet.	1	4	5	6	300	2	4	4	1	0	12	1	3	0	8	70
Fauconets.	2	2	6	0	400	4	0	7	4	1	4	2	2	1	5	90
Faucons.	2	6	7	0	750	4	4	8	2	2	4	2	5	2	8	130
Ordinary Minion.	3	0	7	0	750/800	5	0	8	4	2	8	2	7	3	4	120
Minion of the largest size.	3	2	8	0	1000	5	0	9	0	3	4	3	0	3	12	125
Saker the lowest sort.	3	4	8	0	1400	6	4	9	6	3	6	3	2	4	12	150
Ordinary Sakers.	3	6	9/9	0	1500	6	6	10	4	4	0	3	4	6	0	160
Sakers of the oldest sort.	4	0	10	0	1800	7	2	11	0	5	0	3	6	7	5	163
Lowest Demiculvering.	4	2	10	0	2000	8	0	12	0	6	4	4	0	9	0	174
Ordinary Demiculvering.	4	4	10/11	0	2700	8	0	12	6	7	4	4	2	10	11	175
Elder sort of Demiculvering.	4	6	12/13	0	3000	8	4	13	4	8	8	4	4	12	11	178
Culverings of the best size.	5	0	10/11	0	4000	9	0	14	2	10	0	4	6	15	0	180
Ordinary Culvering.	5	2	12/13		4500	9	4	16	0	11	6	5	0	17	5	181
Culvering of the largest size.	5	4	12/10	0	4800	10	0	16	0	11	8	5	2	20	0	183
Lowest Demicanon.	6	2	11	0	5400	11	4	20	0	14	0	6	0	30	0	156
Ordinary Demicanon.	6	4	12	0	5600	12	0	22	0	17	8	6	1/8?	32	0	162
Demicanon of great size.	6	6	12	0	6000	12	0	22	6	18	0	6	5	36	0	180
Canon Royal, or of	8	0	12		8000	14	6	24	0	32	8	7	4	58	0	185

QUEST. VIII.

How to make a Shot of Lead and Stone together (the Stone being first put into the middle of the Mold, in which the Lead must be afterwards Cast round about the Stone) to be of the like Diameter and Weight as an Iron Shot is of.

It is found by Experience that if you take five parts Lead, and one part of Stone, it will come very near the matter. By these Rules have we Calculated this Table.

It

It is found by experience, that if you take 5 parts *Lead*, and one part *Stone*, it will come very near the matter, wanting not above 3 Ounces, which is nothing, respecting the difference you shall find in *Pibble Stones.* Here you have a Table how much *Lead*, and how much *Stone* must be together, to make the equal of *Iron Shot*, from 1 *inch*, and to every half in the first and second Column to 8 *Inch. Diameter*; the third Column is how much *Lead*, the fourth how much *Stone*, the fifth how much weight both together.

Inches.	Quart.	Lead. Poun.	Lead. Ou.	Stone. Poun.	Stone. Ou.	Both together. Poun.	Both together. Oun.
1		0	$1\frac{2}{3}$	0	$0\frac{1}{3}$	0	2
1	2	0	$6\frac{1}{4}$	0	$1\frac{3}{4}$	0	8
2		0	14	0	4	1	2
2	2	0	12	0	8	2	4
3		3	2	0	10	3	12
3	2	5	0	1	0	5	0
4		7	7	1	8	8	15
4	2	10	8	2	2	12	10
5		14	7	2	14	17	5
5	2	19	4	3	12	23	0
6		25	0	5	0	30	0
6	2	32	0	6	0	38	0
7		40	0	8	0	48	0
7	2	48	0	10	0	58	0
8		59	0	12	0	71	0

Its use is thus; knowing the Diameter of the intended Shot, enter the Table in the first and second Columns, and against them, in the third and fourth Columns, you have the Weight of Lead and Stone, that will make a Shot of the same Diameter with a Shot of Iron, whose weight is in the fifth Column.

Example.

An Iron Shot of 2 inches Diameter, will weigh 1 pound, 2 ounces; If I enter this Table with 2 inches, in the first Column against it, I shall find that I must have 14 ounces of Lead, and 4 ounces of Stone, and this will make a Shot of 2 inches Diameter equal to the weight of the Shot of Iron.

QUEST. IX.

To find the sollid Content, and thereby the weight of any Iron Shot.

By the former Table or otherwise, find the Cube of the Diameter, which if you multiply by 11, and divide by 21, gives the sollid Content of that Bullet in inches and parts.

Now to know how many pounds weight any such body doth contain, multiply the sollid Content by 4, and divide that Sum by 16, it will shew how many pounds of Iron that Bullet weigheth, for an inch square of cast Iron weigheth 4 ounces.

CHAP. XXVI.

Questions about Pieces of Ordnance.

BEfore we come to work what we intend concerning a Piece of Ordnance, it is necessary to understand these Propositions following.

PROP. I.

Having the Diameter of a Circle, to find the superficial Content.

Multiply the square of the Diameter of any Circle by 785 398, and the product that shall come of that Multiplication is the Superficial Content.

PROP. II.

Having the Diameter of any Circle, to find the Circumference thereof.

The common way of proportions is, as 7 to 22, so is the Diameter to the Circumference; but more exactly it is done, if you multiply the Diameter by 3, 14,16, or it may be done thus, as 113 is to 355, so is the Diameter to the Circumference.

PROP. III.

Having the Circumference of a Circle, to find the Superficial Content.

Multiply the Square of the Circumference by 079, 578 will give the Superficial Content, or Multiply the Diameter by half the Circumference, and that Sum is the Superficial Content.

PROP. IV.

Having the Circumference of any Circle, to find the Diameter.

Multiply the Circumference by 318 308, gives the Diameter of that Circle.

PROP. V.

To measure the Frustrum of a Cone or Pyramid, knowing both the Diameters and length of the said Frustrum.

Multiply the Diameters one by the other, and add to them both their Squares, and that Sum divided by 785 39, the one third part of the Remainder is the Content of the Cone.

PROP. VI.

PROP. VI.

By knowing the weight of any one Piece of Ordnance, to find the weight of any other Piece of Ordnance.

If a Saker of 4 inches Diameter weigh 1400*l.* how much will a Cannon of 8 inches Diameter weigh, supposing they be equally fortified, (otherwise this Rule will not hold true) Cube each Diameter, or seek in the foregoing Table, and you will find the Cube of 4 to be 64, and of 8 to be 512, then say as 64 is to 1400 *l.* so is 512 to 12919 pounds, and this is the weight of a Cannon that is able to carry a proportionable Charge.

PROP. VII.

To find the sollid Content of the Concavity, Cylinder, or Soul of a Piece of Ordnance.

By the Rules given in the first of these Propositions, find the Superficial Content or Ayrea of the end of the Cylinder, which multiplyed by the length, will give the sollid Content.

PROP. VIII.

To find the sollid Content of the Soul or Concave of a Piece of Ordnance, if it be Tapering, or the Section of a Cone.

The working of this Proposition is the same as in the fifth Proposition, or you may for brevities sake, add both the Diameters together, and the half of that may be accounted the mean Diameter, by which you may find the Superficial Content by the first Proposition, which multiplyed by the length, gives the sollid Content.

PROP. IX.

How by knowing the weight of any one Piece of Ordnance, to find the weight of any other, being of the same shape.

With your Crallapars take the greatest thickness of the Piece whose weight you know, and likewise of the Piece whose weight you know not; then by the former Table find the Cube of each Diameter, then say, as the Cube of the Diameter of the Piece whose weight is known, is to the weight of the same *Piece*, so is the Cube of the Diameter of the *Piece* whose weight is unknown, to its weight sought.

But if the Pieces be not of one and the same Metal, after you have found the weight, supposing it to be the same Metal, then you must by the Rules given in the 24 Chapter, proportion the weight according to the Metal the Piece is of, whose weight you know not, and if the Piece whose weight you know, do differ in proportion, as if one be of Iron, the other of Brass, the proportion is as 16 to 18, *&c.*

PROP. X.

By knowing the weight of any one Piece of Ordnance, to find the weight of any other Piece of Ordnance, although differing in shape or form, knowing the Diameters at Britch, Muzzles, and length of the Pieces.

By the Rules given in the ninth Proposition, find the sollid Content of the *Piece* whose weight you know, supposing it to be a sollid body without a Chamber.

Then take the sollid Content of the Concave part, by Rules given in the seventh *Proposition*, if it be a Cylinder; or by the ninth *Proposition*, if it be Tapering. This latter Content that is of the Concave being deducted from the former Content of the whole *Piece*, gives the sollid Content of the whole Metal in the *Piece*.

Observe the same Rule in finding the sollid Content of the *Piece* whose weight is unknown; Cube both the sollid Contents, and say, as the Cube of the sollid Content of the *Piece* whose weight is known, is to his weight; so the Cube of the sollid Content of the *Piece* whose weight is unknown, is to his weight; but if they be not of one and the same Metal, we must work by proportions, according to the Rules given in the 24th. Chapter.

By these Rules, when Weights and Scales have been wanting, have I found out the weight of several *Pieces* of Ordnance; and if exact account be taken with good judgment and consideration had, of the difference of the Trunions and Britch end, especially if there be any great difference in the *Pieces*, you cannot erre much; for the Rule being demonstratively true, the operation truly done, cannot erre.

PROP. XI.

To find the weight of any Piece of Ordnance, where we have no other Piece of Ordnance, whose weight is known.

Find the sollid Content of the Metal according to the Rules given in the tenth *Proposition*; then multiply that by 4, and dividing that Sum by 16, will give the weight of the *Piece*, supposing it to be Iron; for it is generally allowed that one inch square of Iron will weigh just four ounces.

If the *Piece* whose weight you seek be not of Iron, but of some other Metal; then work by the Rules given in the 24th Chapter, for the difference of the weight of Metals.

CHAP.

CHAP. *XXVI.*

To know the Allowance or Proportion of Powder proper for any Piece of Ordnance.

THe general way is to allow for such Brass Pieces as are above 4000 *l.* five ounces and a half of powder to a hundred weight of Metal.

But for Culverin of Brass fortified of above 4000 *l.* about 3 ounces and a half compleat; yet there is used also generally for the proof of Shot three fourths or four fifths of the weight of the Iron Shot, but for the Service not above half the weight of the said Shot.

For Culverin, the whole weight of their Shot for proof and for action, is two thirds of its weight.

The Saker and Faulcon four fifths, the weight of their Shot; and for lesser Pieces the whole weight, and one third more for proof; but for action just its weight: but when they grow hot, a part must be abated according to discretion.

You must note, if you know how much Powder will Load a Brass Piece, three quarters so much will Load an Iron Piece of Ordnance.

SECT. I.

If Weights and Scales be wanting, and Ladles and the Cartredge not marked, yet to judg a reasonable Charge for any Piece of Ordnance.

The Allowance that may be made for Cannon is two thirds, the Diameter of the Cylinder for Culverin three Diameters, for the Saker three and a half Diameters, and for lesser Pieces four Diameters of the Cylinder, which length will also serve for the Cartredge.

SECT. II.

By the weight of Powder for any one Piece, to find the weight of Powder proper to any other Piece of Ordnance.

To perform this work you must find by the foregoing Table the Cube of the Diameter of the bore of the Piece, whose allowance of Powder you know; also the Cube of the Diameter of the bore of the Piece, whose allowance of Powder you desire to know: Then say, as the Cube of the known Piece is the quantity of Powder known, so is the Cube of the Diameter of the unknown Piece to the quantity of Powder proper to the unknown Piece.

SECT. III.

Practical Experiments concerning the Allowance of Powder necessary to any Piece in time of Service.

It is always necessary to take care in time of Service of over-loading a Piece, which Error many run into, only minding the bore of a *Piece*, and not minding whether the Metal will bear it, and so endanger themselves and other standers by. To avoid such errors observe these experienced Rules.

To a *Demy-Cannon* fortified of Brass about 4400, or a little more, there is allowed by the Tower 5 ounces and a half of Powder to every hundred weight of Metal; yet in time of Service Gunners do allow but 3 ounces ¾ to every hundred weight of Metal, which doth amount to 10 *l.* ¼.

Demy-Cannon Drake of Iron about 3800 *l.* is allowed by the Tower 3 ounces and a half of Powder to every hundred weight of Metal, which will be durable in time of Service; but there are Drakes of 4400 *l.* which must be allowed more, according to the proportion of their weight.

Culverin fortified Brass of 4600 *l.* is allowed by the Tower 3 ounces and a half of powder compleat to every hundred weight of Metal, which may be burnt in time of Service with very little abatement.

Culverin Drakes of 4000 *l.* or thereabouts of Iron, for these Pieces may be allowed in time of Service 3 ounces to every hundred weight of metal, but proportionably must be allowed for Pieces of greater or lesser weight.

The 12 Pounders fortified of Brass of 3200 *l.* for Guns of this weight and nature is usually allowed 3 ounces and a half for every hundred weight of Metal.

Demy-Culverin Brass of 3300 *l.* there is allowed by the Tower for Pieces of Ordnance of this nature 3 ounces and a half and somthing more, to every hundred weight of Metal, the which is approved a very sufficient Allowance.

Demy-Culverin Drakes of 2900 *l.* is allowed by most two ounces three quarters to each hundred weight of metal, which will be durable in time of Service.

Saker fortified Brass of 2000 *l.* is allowed 3 ounces and somthing more for every hundred weight of Metal, but there may be a small abatement in time of Service.

CHAP. XXVII.

To know whether a Piece of Ordnance be truly bored or no.

YOu must provide a Pike-staff, about a foot longer than the bore of the Piece, and at the end thereof fasten a Rammer head, that will just fill all the bore to the touch hole; and at the other end of the staff, you must bore a hole big enough to put through a Rod of Iron, which must hang from the same; and at the other end of the Rod must be made a weight about the bigness of a Saker Shot, this is done to make the Pike-staff and Rammer head to lie with the same side upward when they are taken out of the Piece, as they did when they were within the Piece; then you must put your Instrument thus prepared into the Piece, letting the Iron Ball (that is at the end of the Rod, which is put through the hole bored a cross the Pike-staff) hang perpendicular; then take your priming Iron, or some other bodkin, and put it down the touch hole to the Rammer head, making a mark therewith; this done, draw out your Instrument, and lay the same on a long Table, with the Iron Ball hanging off the end perpendicular, as it did when the Instrument was in the Piece; then observe, whether the mark you made upon the Rammer head when it was in the Piece, be just upon the uppermost part of the same, if it be, the bore of the Piece lies neither to the right hand nor to the left; but if you find it any thing to the right or left hand, so much lyeth the bore either to the right or left, and the Piece in Shooting must be ordered and charged accordingly.

But if you would know whether the bore lie more upwards or downwards, then bend a Wire at the very end, so that it being put in at the very touch hole, may ketch at the metal when it is drawn out, then put the Wire down the touch hole till it touch the

the bottom of the metal in the Chamber, then holding it in that place, make a mark upon the wire just even with the touch hole, after draw up the wire until it ketch at the metal on the top of the Chamber, and holding it there, make a mark as before; the difference between the two marks is the just wideness of the Chamber, and the distance between the first mark and the end of the Wire (having half the Diameter of the Chamber of the Piece substracted from it) will leave half the Diameter of the Piece, if the Piece be true bored; but if the Piece's number be more than half the Diameter of the Piece, the bore lieth too far from the touch hole, and the upper part of the metal is thickest, but if lesser, the lower part of the metal is thickest or hath most metal.

CHAP. XXVIII.

Of the necessary Instruments for a Gunner, with several other necessary things.

A Master Gunner intending upon service, ought most chiefly to be prepared with these Instruments, as Calabers, Compasses, height board, Sight Rule, Gunners Scale, and a Gunners quadrant; to divide as well into 12 as 90 equal parts, with a Geometrical Square, to make Montures, Levels, heights, Breadths, Distances, and Profundities, (of which you shall read more in the Second Part;) also with a little brass Level, Scales, Weights, Priming-Irons, Moulds to make Cross-bar Shot for Musquets, a Book of Accompts, and an Iron wire or Spring, and a Transome to dispart a Piece of Ordnance; that the Transome may go up and down according to the Diameter and thickness of the Piece, let the Transom be long enough to reach the base Ring, from the touch hole. In the next place he ought to be very expert in the knowledg of cutting out, making up, and finishing all sorts of Ladles, Spunges, Rammers, Cartredges, *&c.* For which purpose you may have Recourse to the foregoing Table. And because it may somtimes happen by reason of the steepness, badness and unevenness of the way, you may be driven to dismount and remount your Piece, e're you get up to the top of a Hill; therefore you must carry with you a Gynn and a Wynch, with all the appurtenances thereunto belonging; as wind Ropes, an Iron Goats-foot, with a Crow, Pins, Truckles, Pullies to help you at a dead lift.

CHAP. XXIX.

The making of Rammers, Spunges, Ladles, and Cartredges, Formers, Carriages, Wheels, Trucks &c. with the Height of Shot fit for any Piece.

FOr the better expedition of this work we have in the former Table shewed the length and breadth of each Ladle, always remembring that you cut each Ladle somewhat longer, that is, allowing so much more as must be fastned to the staff, or so much as the staff goes within the Plate.

The Buttons or heads of the Ladles must be near the height of the shot.

For Spunges, the bottoms and heads must be of soft wood, as Birch and Willow, and to be one Diameter and three quarters in length, and three quarters or very little less of the height covered with Sheeps skin, and nayled with Copper nayles, so that together they may fill the hollow of the Piece; Let the bottoms and heads of the Rammers be made of good hard wood, and the height, one Diameter of the Shot, and the length one third of the Diameter of the Shot.

To make Ladles for Chamber bor'd Pieces, open your Compasses to the just Diameter of the Chamber within one eighth part of an Inch, Divide that measure in two equal parts, then set the measure to one of them, and by that distance upon a flat or paper draw a Circle, the Diameter of that Circle is one fourth part shorter than the Diameter of the Chamber; Take three fifths of that Circle for the breadth of the Plate of the Ladle. But for Cannon, the length ought to be twice and two third parts, to hold at twice the just Diameter of the Powder. As for Example,

The Diameter of a Circle drawn for a Cannon whose Chamber bore is 7 Inches, containeth six and three quarters, the circumference whereof is 21 Inches $\frac{6}{7}$, and three fourth parts thereof is 12 $\frac{3}{4}$, and so much ought the Ladle to be in breadth, and in length 18 $\frac{2}{3}$ parts. By this Rule you may make a Ladle for any Taper'd Piece.

Take notice for a general observation, that a Ladle 9 balls in length, and two balls in breadth, will near contain the just weight in Powder, that the Iron Shot for any piece weigheth.

Lastly, for Cartredges, they are generally made of paper Royal or Canvas. Take the height of the bore of your piece without the vent of the Shot, and cut the cloath or paper of 3 such heights, for the Cannon in length 3 Diameters, for the Culverin 4 Diameters, for the Saker and Faulcon *&c.* half of the height of their proper bores, and leaving in the midst at the top or bottome one other such height, to make a bottom for the Cartredge, cutting each side somthing larger for Sewing, glewing, or pasting them together; you must have a great care to augment the goodness of your powder, and likewise the heating of your Piece, and so augment or diminish the quantity of Powder.

Let your Former be made to your Ordnance to the height of your Shot, and a convenient length longer than the Cartredge ought to be, and tallow it over first that the paper may slip off, and then put your paper on your Former. If you make your Cartredge of Canvas, half a Diameter more is allowed for seams, but if you make it of paper, half or three quarters of an Inch over-plus for pasting will serve, being lapt once about the Former; having the bottom fitted upon the end of the Former, which must be hard and close pasted by the lower side of the Cartredge, then let the lower end of the Cartredge be pasted down hard round about the bottom, and let them be well dryed before you fill them, and mark them how high they must be filled.

And if you have no Scales nor weights by you for Cannons, put two Diameters and a half for the height the powder must come, for Culverin 3 Diameters, for Saker 3 and a half Diameters, for lesser Pieces four Diameters of the Cylinder.

For Carriages of Pieces of Ordnance for Land service the Rules are given thus, one and a half the length of the Cylender is the length of the Carriage, and in depth four Diameters of the bore of the Piece at the fore end, in the middle three and a half, and at the end next the ground two and a half, let the thickness be the Diameter of the Shot, the wheels should be one half of the length of the Piece in height, but for Saker and Minion you must exceed the former proportion by one twelfth part, the Faulcon and Faulconet by one sixth part.

The Naves, the Cheeks called Limbres, and wheels, are usually made of Elm, but the Transoms, Axeltreees, Fore-Carriage and Cross beams, are made of Oaken Timber.

For drawing of Guns by men in case horses be wanting, there is usually allowed to every sixty, eighty, or a hundred weight of metal to one man, according to the nature of the ground whereon they are to be drawn.

As

As for Sea Carriages, they are so well known to every Carriage-maker that they need not to be spoken of.

As for fitting Shot to each *Piece*, it is the opinion of most Gunners, that every Piece of Ordnance ought to have its Shot within one quarter of an Inch of the Diameter of the bore; others do say, that the one and twentieth part of the Diameter of the Piece's Cylender is more proper and correspondent for all sorts of Pieces whatsoever; Every man may make choice of that which by experience he finds best.

CHAP. XXX.

How a Gunner ought to charge a Piece of Ordnance.

HAving shewed the compleat making of Pieces of Ordnance, and the preparing of powder and Shot, with the due allowance of powder fit for every Gun, with all the Instruments and Materials necessarily belonging to a Piece, as to its Rigging and Loading; It remains now, that we go *Artist like* to work to charge a Piece, and order all things for the best conveniency, and that the less danger may follow when you come to Action or Service; and for that purpose having planted your Piece upon the plat-form, have in readiness powder, Bullets, Linstocks, Scowrers, Rammers, and the rest of your things. Stick up your Linstock to Leeward of you; then to work with your Piece. First, cleer your *Piece* within with the Scowrer, and see that the touch hole be clear, and not stopped, and so clear, that no dirt or filth be in the same; Then let him that is by to assist, (for a Piece cannot be mannaged by less than two) bring the Budg-barrel with the powder just before the mouth of your Piece, put then your Ladle into the same and fill it, and if it be over-full, give it a little jog, that the overplus may fall down again into the barrel; after this, put it gently in at the mouth of the Piece, even until the end of the Ladle be thrust up to the Britch end of the *Piece*; then must you turn the Ladle gently and softly, and let it lie within the Chamber of the piece, drawing out your Ladle almost to the Muzzle of the *Piece*, put it back again to take up the loose corns, which were spilt by the way, and to bring them up to the Charge of powder; this done, the Gunner must draw out his Ladle, and take out of the Budg-barrel a second Ladle full, (by our former Rules given he must know the quantity of powder that his *Piece* will require) and so putting it in the *Piece* up to the former Ladle-full, then you may draw it out, and do as you did before, that no loose corns may lie in the bottom of the *Piece*; and in drawing out his Ladle, he must have a care that he let not fall any powder upon the ground; for it is a thing uncomly in a Gunner, to trample powder under feet. Then take a wisp of Straw, Hay, or any other thing, and put it hard in at the mouth of the *Piece*, then turn your Ladle end for end to come to the Rammer, thrust it into the *Piece* after the wisp, and drive it up with it, and it will carry all the loose corns which possibly may be scattered in the Mold of the *Piece*; having driven the wad up to the powder, give it two or three gentle shoves to make it lie close only, but drive it not too hard least you break your powder too much, which would hinder its force. The wisp or wad being close to the powder, draw out the Rammer and put in the Bullet, which rowle gently in the *Piece* up to the wad that was before put in to keep up the powder; the Shot being in, put in a second wad after the Bullet, and thrust it also home to the Bullet. Always remembring whilſt the powder is putting in and wadding up, one be ready at the touch hole and keep it ſtopt with his thumb, that no powder fly out at the touch hole, but that it be likewiſe filled with powder, which may be ſupplyed out of his powder-horn.

The Gunner that Loads a Piece is to be very careful, and indeavour always not to ſtand before the muzzle of his Piece whilſt he is loading the Piece, but on one ſide of the ſame, leaſt a danger or miſchief might happen to him. And thus the Piece having its due Charge of Powder and Bullet, he muſt cover the touch-hole with an Apron made of Lead, or for want of that, with dryed Sheep-skin; then let him level his piece and ſet away the Budg-barrel of powder with the reſt of his things, in ſome hollow place under the ground covered over ſafe; he muſt then attend the Gentleman of the Ordnance, or other chief Commander, their Order or Command, before he give fire.

Touching the Charges of Pieces, I have given full inſtructions neceſſary thereunto, with the weight of powder and Shot for any piece. But to ſay ſomething here touching the quantity of powder, proper for a Load; we do find ſome difference amongſt Authors; Some whereof do maintain, that there ought to be allowed to every Piece for its Charge ſo much powder as half the weight of the Bullet; others are of the opinion, that the more powder is put into a *Piece*, the ſwifter and farther the Bullet will flye, urging many reaſons to prove it. But experience, the Miſtreſs of this Art inſtructeth us better, for if a *Piece* be loaden with two thirds of the weight of her Shot in powder, it ſends the Bullet or Shot going more ſwiftly, and will carry it farther, which hath been very many and often times tryed, ſo that at this time, 'tis without contradiction.

Again, others do maintain, that if one ſhould forcibly Ramme the Bullet, then the powder might take fire before it caſt forth the Bullet, and then would cauſe the Bullet to flye farther than otherwiſe it would do; but you muſt conſider in ſo doing, you either endanger the breaking of the piece, or elſe the making it crooked and unſerviceable; becauſe your ordinary Pieces will not bear ſo great a Charge of powder. This hath been tryed by the Sea ſide before his Excellency *Prince Maurice*, of famous memory, where firſt one and the ſame *Piece* was Loaden with ten pound of fine powder, to ſee how far She would carry the Bullet; the place being marked where the Bullet reſted. The *Piece* was loaden again with nine pounds of powder which ſhot as far as when the *Piece* was Loaden with ten pounds of powder. But laſt of all, this piece of Ordnance being Loaden or Charged with 7 pounds of the ſame powder, it carried her Bullet further than the two former Shots; whence one may obſerve that a piece of Ordnance may be over-Charged, and therefore a good Gunner ought to have a ſingular care to give unto his *Piece* her due meaſure and Charge.

CHAP: XXXI.

Of the Office and Duty of a Gunner, with all his Properties, Endowments and qualifications.

HE that intends to be a Maſter Gunner, and would not abuſe himſelf nor others of the ſame profeſſion, muſt be qualified according to our Inſtructions following, *viz.*

He ought to be well skilled in Arithmetick, and to underſtand the Extraction of the Square and Cube Roots, and to have knowledge in Geometry, according to our Inſtructions

Instructions in the second part, whereby he may be able to take heights, depths, breadths and lengths, and to draw the plot of any piece of ground, to make Mines and Countermines, Rampars, Baskets of earth, and such like things used in time of war, as well offensive as defensive.

He ought most chiefly upon Land-Service to be well skilled in the making *Plat*formers, with Defences, Troniers, Gabbions, Loops, *Parapets* of Earth, and Faggots of 23 or 24 foot high; two foot high of Earth, bed upon bed, unto eleven foot high, and after three foot *Terra plene*, to raise the Tronniers and Loops, so that for the Cannon it be three foot wide in the Barbe, and within twelve foot wide, without the lower part thereof to descend Scarp-wise, the better to discover the Enemies avenues and offend them more freely, for avoiding the blast and Smoak and ruine it would else make: for Culverin two foot and a half within, and nine foot without will serve; and for less *Pieces* the less measure.

If the Battery be to be made with Gabbions, they being filled with Earth without Stones, moistned and Rammed 7 foot in Diameter, three Ranks between two *Pieces*, if the place will permit, or two at least; and three Rows also one before the other, setting one between two, so that if one Rank will have three, the second will have two, and the third one; but it will be hard to make a safe Battery with Gabbions, Cannon or Culverin proof.

Concerning *Plat*-forms. Let the platform for a Cannon have thirty foot for reverse, and 27 foot for a Demy-Cannon, and he ought to see that his plat-forms be even, or rising one foot for 20 foot backward the better to stay the Reverse, and facilitate the bringing the piece when Loaden to the Loop. The platform ought to be made clean, that no stones or other things lye in the way for the wheels to run upon, whereby may be hindered the true intent of his Shot.

He must before any service is, examine his Piece of its goodness or defect; according to our former Instructions given in this behalf, he must also be furnished with all necessary things for his Artillery, the particulars thereof we have mentioned in the 29 *Chap.* but because it takes not up much paper we will repeat them here again, *viz.*

Wheels, Trucks, Axeltrees, Ladles, Rammers, Spunges, Worms, Tampions, height-board, Auger-bit, fitness and roundness of the Shot, Chane-Shot, Cross-bar Shot *&c.* Canvas or strong paper for Cartredges, Calabers, Compasses, Sight Rule, Gunners Scale, Quadrant, Scales, Weights, priming-Irons, and Aprons to cover the Touch hole.

Before he come upon Service, he ought to examine and prove the goodness of his *Powder* and Match, and examine it according to the Rules given where we treat of the Examination of the goodness of *Powder*.

A Gunner ought to be most careful to see that the *Powder* be placed safely from danger of his own, as also the Enemies Ordnance, and to be furnished with artificial Torches, Dark Lanthorns, with all sorts of Fire-works, of which you shall have a particular account in the Treatise of Fire-works at the end of this Book.

He must have by him his Gyn and Winch, Hand-Spikes, Crowes, to mount and dismount Guns at pleasure as occasion may serve, also Coynes, Budge-Barrels, *Powder* Baskets to carry Shot to your *Piece*, to keep his Linstocks well armed with good Match.

He must alwayes have by him a Ruler, Scale, Compasses, to measure the Diameters or Bore of every *Piece*, and likewise the length of the Cylinder within, the better to fit her with due Shot and *Proportion* of *Powder*.

He must learn by such Instructions as we have already given, the Names, Length, Weight, and Fortification of every *Piece* about the Chamber, and to tell readily how much *Powder* is a due Charge for every *Piece*, and what Shot is necessary. How many *Persons* must attend in time of Service, how many Horses or Oxen will draw a *Piece* of Ordnance, and in case they be wanting, how many men will serve. How many pound weight of Shot one man may drive before him in a Wheel-barrow from place to place.

A Gunner ought chiefly to Charge and Discharge a *Piece* of Ordnance Artist like; and when he opens, or orders to be opened the head of a *Powder* Barrel, let no Iron Tool be used thereunto for fear of taking or striking fire; for that purpose therefore it is usual to have wooden Mallets, which will prevent such dangers.

Every Gunner before he beginneth to make a Shot, ought to consider that a wad of Hay, or of untwisted Ropes, will make the Shot shoot wide of the Mark.

He ought to consider whether the Trunions be placed in their due place in the Carriage, whether the Carriage have its due length, whether one wheel be not higher than the other, or whether one wheel doth not reverse quicker or sooner than the other, for these will cause the Piece to erre, and to shoot wide of the Mark.

Every Gunner ought to consider, that if his Piece lye point blank or under Metal, then he ought to put in a sufficient wad after the Shot, to keep it close to the Powder; for if it should not be close, great danger might follow; for if the Shot should lodge any distance from the Powder, then in the firing of that Piece it would break off in that very vacant place between the Shot and the Powder, and so do dammage to himself or standers by. If your Piece be mounted, you then use no wad at all after the Shot.

Every Gunner ought to have standing by him some Tubs of water to wet his Spunges in, whereby to cool his Piece in time of Service, as also to be ready upon occasion to put out any Fire that might happen in time of Service.

Every Gunner ought to try whether his Piece is truely bored or not; if it be not, he is to take it into consideration, and to order his proportion of Charge, according to the thinnest part of the Metal, to prevent all danger.

A Gunner ought to take his Observation of the Mark or place he intends to direct his Shot to, just over the middle of the bore within the Piece, for by this means he may be able, by his Skill, to make a true Shot in a bad Piece.

A Gunner, that he may the better direct his Shot to the place desired, ought to consider the difference of the Metal of the Piece at Britch and Muzzle, and thereby truely how to dispart a Piece, be it either true bored or not. Of disparting a Piece, I shall shew how it may be done several wayes in the following or second part of this Gunnery; where we come to the practical part of the Art in handling a Piece of Ordnance upon all occasions.

THE

THE Compleat Gunner.

THE SECOND PART.

CHAP. I.

The Description and use of the Geometrical Quadrant, for the taking Heights, Distances, Depths, &c.

First, you must make a common simple large Quadrant thus with your Ruler, draw the Line A B, and with the Distance A B in your Compasses upon the Center A describe the Arch B D, then with the Distance A B, setting one foot of your Compasses in B, set it off upon the Arch B D, and it will reach to L, divide the Arch B L into two equal, parts and that will be at F; The distance O L, being set upwards from L, will reach to D, so then drawing the Line A D, will make the Quadrant A B D, and the Arch B O L D will be divided into three equal parts; now every one of those parts must again be divided into three equal parts, and every one of them into 10 equal parts, so will your Quadrant be divided into 90 equal parts, called Degrees.

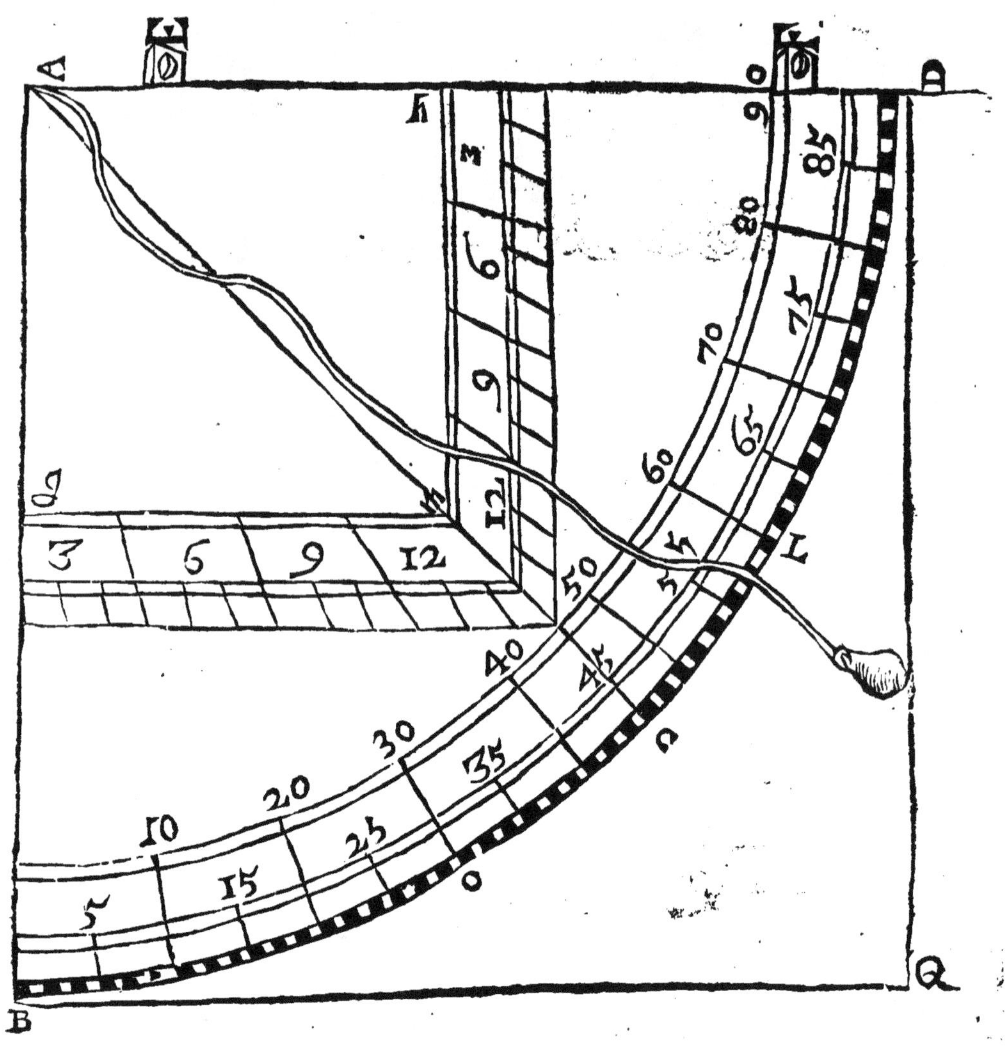

Of the Scale.

From any part of the Lines A B and A D, at equal distance from the point A, as at *g* and *h*, raise two perpendicular Lines which will meet in the point *m*, which we divide here into 12 equal parts, but may be divided into 100 or a 1000 equal parts at pleasure, and the more parts they are divided into, the more exact will your work be; let these Lines *g m* and *h m* be marked into the Divisions from the point A.

Let two sights of Brass be placed upon the Limb of your Quadrant, at the places marked E and F.

Let the Division upon the Line *h m*, being next the sights, be termed right shadow; the Division upon the side *g m*, left or contrary shadow.

Let a Line with a Plummet be fitted to your Quadrant falling from the Center *A*, as you see in your Figure.

CHAP.

CHAP. II.

The Use of this Quadrant in taking the Perpendicular or direct height, by help of the Suns shadow.

CՕnvey the left side of the Quadrant Geometrically towards the Sun, the Thread and Plummet having their free course, moving it up or down until both your sights have received the Sun-beams; then if your Thread be found in the twelfth part, all things that are upright or truly perpendicularly elevated, are equal in height with their shadows.

If the Thread with the plummet be observed to cut any of those parts next the sights, called right shadow, between *m* and *h*, then every upright thing is more than the shadow, by such a proportion as 12 exceeds the parts where the Thread was found.

If the Thread fall upon the first division, then 12 times the shadow is the height. If it fall upon the second Division, 6 times the shadow is the height. If it fall upon the third Division, 4 times the shadow is the height. If it fall on the fourth Division, 3 times the shadow is the height. In the fifth Division twice and two fifths of the shadow is the height. In the sixth twice, in the seventh once, and five sevenths in the eighth Division, one and a half in the ninth, one and a third in the tenth, one and a fifth part in the eleventh, once and the eleventh part of the shadow is the height on the twelfth part, then the length of the shadow is the height, as we said before.

Or in few words it may be done thus, Multiply the length of the shadow by 12, the product divided by the parts in which you found the Thread, your quotient sheweth the height.

But if the part cut be on the contrary shadow, that is, if the Thread fall between *g* and *m*, augment then the length of the shadow by the parts declared by the plummet, and the increase divide by 12, and the product is the Altitude.

Example.

In the Foregoing figure it is plainly to be perceived, when the figure falleth upon the 12 Division, the shadow is equal with the thing it self; In the 6 of the right, it is but half, in the 6 of the contrary it is twice the height, and so to conclude, as the side in the right exceeds the parts, so doth the Altitude the shadow; and the contrary in the contrary shadow. Behold the figure 6 where you will find the Thread cutteth 6 parts of the contrary shadow upon the Quadrant, the shadow B C then being 210 foot, multiply (as I have said) the length of the shadow 210 foot by 6, the parts cut by the Thread, and it makes 1260, and that divided by 12 riseth 105, which is the Altitude of such a body, that casts a shadow of 210 feet.

Also the height of any unknown thing may be known by taking the length of its shadow, and the length of the shadow of any staff set upright whose length is known, saying, as the length of its shadow is to its height, so the length of the shadow of the unknown thing is to its height.

CHAP. III.

Without Shadow or any Supputation by your Quadrant Geometrical, to take heights approachable.

Lift up ingeniously your Quadrant exactly made towards the thing to be measured, looking diligently through both sights backward or forward, as occasion is given, until you see the top, so that your Line or Thread fall just upon the middle or 12 Division; now if you measure your distance from you to the foot of the Object, which is the point directly under the top, then have you the Altitude of the highest summitie to the right point or base in height equal with our standing, adjoyning with it the height of your eye downwards.

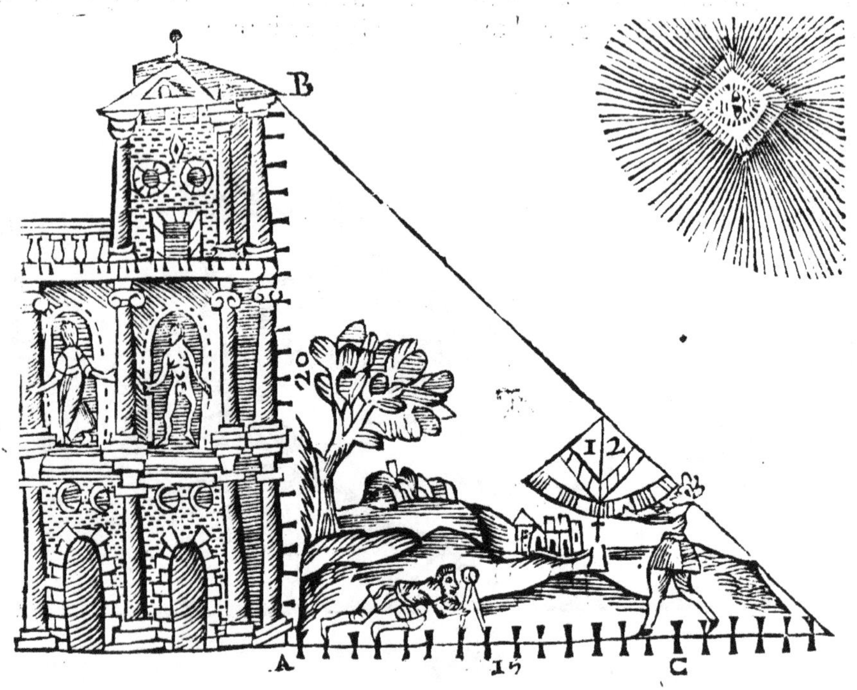

CHAP.

CHAP. IV.

With the Aid of two Stations to find out Inapproachable heights.

SEek two Stations going hither and thither, yea, toward or from the thing you intend to measure, so that in the one place the thread may fall just in 12, and at the other Station in 6 points of a right shadow; then if you double the Distance of both places, the Summitie shall appear from that part of the thing measured, which is equal in height with your Eye; or if your standing be even with the Base, joyning to that double distance the height of your eye, you have the whole Altitude from the ground, &c. If the one Station cause the Thread to fall in 12, and the other in 8 of a right Shadow, then triple the Distance between the two Stations, so have you the height also: Or if the one be in 12, and the other in 9 of right shadows, then quadruple the distance, the one under 12, and the other under 6 of the contrary shadow, and the place between both Stations is equal with that you measure, ever understanding from your Eye upwards.

CHAP. V.

How by the Quadrant, with Calculations, speedily to find all heights accessible.

YOur Quadrant, as in the former Figure, handsomly elevated against or towards the thing to be measured, perceiving through both sights just the top, mark well the Division or points crossed by your Thread, whether it be of the right shadow, then multiply the distance between you and the foot of the Object by 12, and divide that Sum by the parts cut upon your Quadrant, which your Thread manifesteth; and the remainder is the height of the Object from your Eye.

there put the fourth ſtaff. All this performed, ſeek out the diſtance between the firſt ſtaff and the Second, and that name your firſt diſtance; then the diſtance between the firſt and third, name your ſecond diſtance; Again, the diſtance between the third and fourth ſtaff is the third diſtance. Deduct your firſt diſtance from the third, ſo remaineth the Diviſor; then multiply your third diſtance by your ſecond, and the product divide by your Diviſor, the quotient ſheweth the true length from the third ſtaff to the fortreſs or mark deſired: for plainneſs behold the figure.

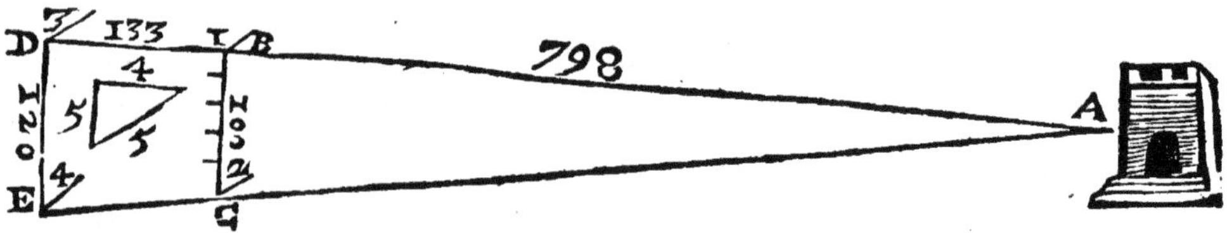

Example.

Here this Letter A repreſents the Caſtle, being the diſtance to be meaſured; B is your firſt ſtaff; C the ſecond ſtaff, differing from B the firſt Orthogonal 100 foot; D the third ſtaff, being diſtant back from the firſt in a Right line with the mark A 133 foot; E is the fourth ſtaff, running ſidewiſe Orthogonally, or in a Square, from the third, until the fartheſt part of your length A, is perceived in a right Line with the ſecond ſtaff at C; and this diſtance D E let be 120 foot. Now by Subſtraction take 100 from 120, there remaineth for a Diviſor 20; then multiply 133 by 120, ſo riſeth 15960, which divided by 20, and there cometh 798 foot, the true diſtance between D and A, from which if you abate A B 133, there remaineth B A your propounded diſtance.

But foraſmuch as this concluſion is to be done without Inſtrument, and here Orthogonal motions ſidewiſe is required, it ſhall be requiſite alſo to declare how an Orthogonal or Right angle is upon a ſudden to be made; ye ſhall therefore (according to *Pythagoras*'s Invention mentioned among the Definitions at the beginning of this Book) take 3 Staves, Cords, or ſuch like, making the one 4 ſuch parts, as the other is 3, and the third 5; This done, conjoyn their ends together, and the angle ſubtended of the longeſt ſtaff is a right, which firſt placed at B, and after at D, directing one of his comprehending ſides to A, the other ſhall guide you to C and E; or if you deſire with more expedition to diſpatch, and not to tarry the proportioning of Cords, or ſuch like, to this *Pythogarick* Rule, take any 3 Staves, Sticks, or Threads, and conjoyn them, making a Triangle, it matters not of what form or faſhion they be, then placing one angle thereof at B, turning one ſide to A, direct your ſelf ſidewiſe to the other, alwayes remembring to place the ſame angle at D, and departing ſidewiſe again in like manner, in all the reſt do as before is declared. Thus uſing any mean diligence, yuo ſhall moſt exactly meaſure any diſtance.

CHAP.

CHAP. VIII.

With Halbeards, Pikes, or any Staves, having no other Instrument, you may measure the Distance between any two Towers, Castles, or other Marks, lying in a right line from you, not coming near any of them.

YOu must first (as we have declared in the last Chapter) prepare a Triangle, with joyning any three Staves, or such like, together, which you must (at your standing) place in such sort, that one of the sides containing the Angles, may lye directly toward the Mark: Then setting up a Staff, Pike, or other Mark there, depart sidewise, as the other side of your Angle shall direct you, so far as you list, the more ground the better, and there set up your second Staff or Mark; then go directly back from your first Staff (alwayes keeping it exactly between your sight and the Mark) as many score again, or Pike lengths, as you list, setting up a third staff; this done, you shall place the same Angle you used at your first Staff now again at your third staff, in all points as it was before; the one side of the Angle lying directly toward the first Staff, the other side will shew you whither you shall go to place your fourth Staff; for passing still in a right line with that side of your Angle, you shall at the last find the second justly scituated between you and the farthest Mark, and there set up the fourth Staff; then remove your Angle again to the second Staff, and placing there as before, the one side even with the first Staff, pass on in a right line with the other, until you come directly between your nearest Mark and the fourth Staff, and there pitch up the fifth.

 Now

Now you must measure how many Paces, Halbeards, or Pikes length, are between your first and second Staff, deducting that from the distance between the third and fourth, and this Remainder shall serve you for a Divisor; then multiply your distance between the second and fifth Staff by the distance between the third and fourth, the product divide by your reserved Divisor, and it yieldeth in the Quotient the true distance between these two Marks. See the foregoing Figure.

Example.

Let A B be the two Marks, whose distance I would measure; my standing place where I set up my first Staff, I; in the middle, my Triangle made of three Staves, Halberds, Bills or any such like things, K L M; the Staves or Halberds of which I make my Triangle N, which I first place at C, secondly at D, thirdly at E; and note, at C and D the scituation of the Triangle is all one, but at E it somewhat differeth, as you may behold in this Figure, which I would have you note, lest haply you be deceived in your practice.

C E the distance between the first and third, deducted from D F the distance between the second and fourth, there remains H F your Divisor; which measured, I admit 50 Halberds lengths, the distance between G E 30 Halberds lengths, the space between D F 100 Halberds length, now 100 multiplyed in 30 produceth 3000, which divided by 50, leaveth in the Quotient 60. I conclude therefore the distance between A and B to be 60 Pikes lengths.

This one thing is to be taken notice of especially, that whatsoever you mete the space G E withall, that you use the same in measuring H F; and as for D F it matters not what you measure it withall, for your Quotient shall bear the same denomination. Preciseness is to be used in placing of your Triangle, and in measuring E G, and H F, otherwise error may ensue; especially if D F be but a small distance, and the Angle at B very sharp. There needeth in this matter no further admonition, small Practice will resolve all doubts.

CHAP. IX.

To measure the distance between any two Forts, Castles, or other places, howsoever they be scituated, though there be Rivers, or such like Impediments between, that you cannot approach nigh any of them; and that without an Instrument also.

LEt your Angles, as before hath been said, be prepared of any three Staves, &c. you shall first at pleasure set up one Staff, and applying thereunto your Angle in such sort, that the one containing side lye directly to one of the Marks (which here for distinction sake I will call the first) go backwards too and fro until you find your second Mark precisely covered with your Staff, noting what part of the line or side subtending the Angle it cuts by your line visual, and there make a fine notch or mark upon that subtending Staff; which done, you shall go sidewise from the first erected Staff, as the other containing side of your Triangle will direct you, so far as you list, and

and then set up your second Staff; yet pass on from thence in a right line with that containing side of your Angle that riseth from your Staves, and cometh somewhat toward the Mark, and go so far until you spy your self justly between your third Staff and your first mark, there set up your fourth Staff, then resort to your Angle again, and standing behind the second Staff, note whether a right line from the Angle to that notch (before made on the subtendent Staff or side of the Triangle) will direct you, for that way precisely shall you go on until you come in a right line with the second and third Staff, and erect there the fifth Staff; this done, measure the distance between the second and third Staff, reserving that for a Divisor; then multiply your distance between the first and third Staff, by the distance between the fourth and fifth Staff, the product divide by your reserved Divisor, and it yieldeth in the Quotient the true distance between the two marks.

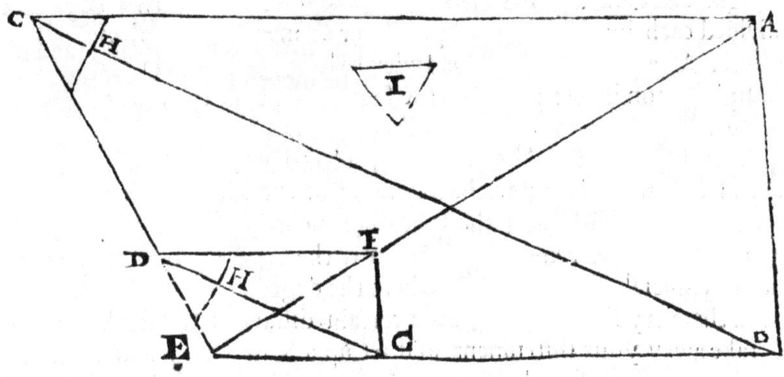

Example.

Let A B be the distance I would know, C my first Station where the first Staff is erected; I my Triangle made of three Staves, and placed at the Station, and directed with one of the containing sides to A which is the first mark, as you may see in the Figure, and with the other side to D and E the second and third Staves; H is the notch or mark upon the side subtended to the Angle, where the line visual from D passeth to the second mark B; my Triangle now I scituate at D, as it was before at C, the one contained side lying even with the erected Staves, the other directed to my fourth Staff F, placed in a right line with E the third Staff, and A the first mark. Again, my line visual proceeding from D to H, the notch in the subtended side of the Angle is extended to my fifth Staff G, scituated exactly between E the third Staff, and B the other mark: This done, I measure the distance between my second and third Staff, finding it 20 foot, likewise between the fourth and fifth Staff, and find it 72 foot, finally between the first and third Staff 65 paces; so that according to the Rule before given, multiplying 65 by 72, I have 4680. which divided by 20, yieldeth in the Quotient 234, and so many paces is there between A and B.

I have not set out the Figures in just proportions answering to these numbers, for that is not requisite, but in such form as may best open and make manifest the scituation of the Staves and Triangle, wherein consists all the difficulty of this Practice.

CHAP. X.

How you may readily find out the distance to any Tower, Castle, Forts, &c. by help of the former Quadrant.

LEt the Quadrant be made upon a ſquare Board as is there marked A D B Q. Let D B be divided into 90 Degrees or equal parts; and inſtead of the 12 equal parts, or right and contrary ſhadows, *g m* and *h m*, let the two ſides D Q and B Q be divided each into 1200 equal parts, or as many as you pleaſe, and marked from the Center A, and have a Ruler or Index to be moved round upon the Center A, having two ſights upon it, ſet juſt upon the feducial line of the Index, and let it be divided into ſuch equal parts as the Lymb B Q, or D Q.

Let this Inſtrument thus fitted be handſomly placed upon its Staff, or otherwiſe, lay the feducial of your Index upon the beginning of the Degrees of the Quadrant, and turn your whole Inſtrument (the Index not moved) till you may eſpy through the ſight your mark, then remove your Index to the contrary ſide of the Quadrant, placing the line feducial on the ſide line where the degrees end, and look through the ſights, and in that very line ſet up a mark a certain diſtance, the farther the better; this done, take away your Inſtrument, and ſet up a Staff there, and remove the Inſtrument to the mark you eſpyed; ſet your Index on the beginning of the Degrees, moving your whole Inſtrument, till you find through the Sights the Staff at the firſt Station, then remove your Index (your Quadrant keeping its place) till you may again eſpy through the Sights your mark; which done, note the Degrees cut by the line feducial, and then work thus, upon ſome even ſmooth Superficies, whether it be Board, Plate, or Paper: Draw firſt a ſtreight line, and open your Compaſſes to ſome ſmall diſtance, call that ſpace a ſcore, and make ſo many ſuch diviſions upon your Line as there is ſcores between your Stations; then upon the end of your line raiſe a perpendicular, and fixing one foot of your Compaſſes at the other end, opening it to what wideneſs you pleaſe, draw an Arch riſing from the ſame line that repreſents your Stationary diſtance, and dividing it into 90 equal parts or Degrees (as you was taught in the making your Quadrant) extend from the Center to the number of Degrees cut by your fedueial line, a right line, until it concur with the perpendicular before erected; then ſee how much of that ſpace (which repreſenteth the ſcore in dividing your Stationary diſtance) is contained in the perpendicular; ſo many ſcore is the mark off from your firſt Station, and by dividing the Hypothenuſal line, you may find the Diſtance from the ſecond Station.

Example.

A the firſt Station, C the ſecond, D the mark, A C 80 paces, Degrees of the Quadrant cut by the line fedueial at the ſecond Station is 71 d. $\frac{1}{2}$, and H is the unity or meaſure repreſenting one ſcore, E F 4 parts, G F 12, G E 12 $\frac{2}{3}$, or thereabouts: Thus may you conclude the mark to be diſtant from the firſt Station 12 ſcore paces; the Hypothenuſal line or diſtance of the mark from the ſecond Station, 12 ſcore and 13 paces.

See the Figure.

To perform this Work by Calculation.

In the foregoing Figure, B is the place to be measured, A the mark where I first disposed my Instrument, from it I go Orthogonally to C, the Index suppose cuts there 400 in the right side of your square; the distance between B and C, I have supposed 80 paces; wherefore multiply 1200 by 80, and there cometh 96000, which divided by 400, declareth unto me 240 paces, the true length from A to B. Or by dividing 1440000, the square of 1200, with 400 the parts cut, you shall produce in the Quotient 3600, your proportionable part found by the Rule of Reduction, which augmented in 80, yieldeth 288000, and that divided by 1200, bringeth in the Quotient 240, which is the length A B agreeing with the former operation.

But if you would find CB, or the Hypothenusal line, being the distance between the second Station and the mark; then by the former Table of Squares, or with your Pen, find the Square of A C, and the Square A B the distance already found from the first Station, these two Squares added together, the Square Root of that Sum is the distance C B, *viz.* 253 paces; or if the Sum of the Square of A B and A C be sought for in the Table of Squares, you will find against it 253 paces, the length of C B, which was to be found; for the Square of A B more, A C is alwayes equal to the Square of C B, and the Square of C B less, the Square A C is equal to the Square of A B.

CHAP. XI.

To measure the distance between any two marks that lye in one right line from the Eye.

THis may be resolved by the former Proposition, measuring how far either distance is from your self, and then deduct the one from the other; or thus, another way, the side of your Geometrical Square directed towards them, depart Orthogonally, as is before declared, 100 or 200 paces at your pleasure, but the more the better; then place your Inſtrument again, turning the ſide of it towards the firſt Station, remove then the Index to either marks, noting what parts at either place the Index doth cut of the Scale; and if the Index at both times falls on the left ſide, deduct the leſſer from the greater; with the number remaining, augment this diſtance between your Stations, and dividing by the whole ſide of the Scale, your Quotient is the diſtance. If the Index fall on the right ſide at either time, then muſt you by the Rule given in the Ninth Chapter, reduce them into proportional parts; or if at one time it fall on the left ſide, and at another time on the right, then ſhall you only reduce the parts cut on the right ſide; which done, deduct as before is ſaid, the leſſer from the greater, and with the remainder multiply your diſtance Stationary, the product divided by 1200, yieldeth how far one mark is beyond another.

Behold the Figure.

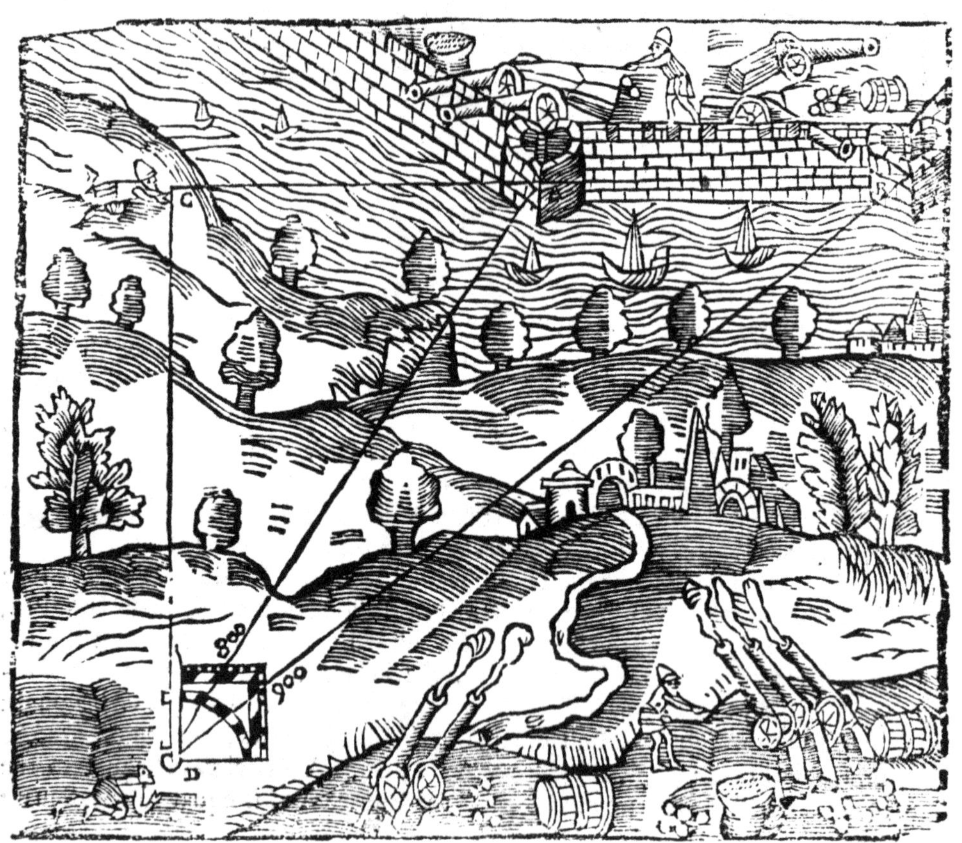

Example.

Admit A B the marks in a right line from C your firſt Station, D the ſecond Station Orthogonally ſcituated from C, where your Square being placed, ſuppoſe your Index firſt cut 800 parts on the left ſide, and after 900 parts on the right ſide; you muſt divide the Square of 1200 by 900, as was taught in the former Chapter; ſo will your Quotient amount to 1600, from which if you withdraw 800, the parts cut on the left ſide, there will remain 800, which multiplyed by 200 paces, the diſtance Stationary C D, there amounteth 160000, this divided by 1200, yieldeth in the Quotient 133 1/3; therefore the diſtance from A B, your mark, is 133 paces, 1 foot, and 8 inches.

CHAP.

CHAP. XII.

To measure the Distance between any two marks lying in one plain level ground, howsoever scituated, without Arithmetick.

THis at two Stations may be done, as we have done before; but we will here suppose but one Station, knowing the distance from that Station to each place, and the Angle it makes with each Station; then by help of a pair of Compasses, and any line of equal parts, this is most easily wrought, as is well known to small Practitioners in this Art, it being also the 4th Question in Right-lined Oblique Triangles.

I did intend to shew the working of every one of these Questions by Logarithms; but considering a Gunner hath not alwayes such Tables by him (and if he have them and understands right-lined Triangles, doubtless he may easily apply them to this work) I therefore thought what I have done in this case to be sufficient.

CHAP. XIII.

The Description of an Instument, whereby to plot out any Coast, Country, City or Garrison, and to take the distance to every Remarkable Object.

THis Instrument is four square, with a Circle in the middle, divided into 360 equal parts or degrees. Let the division of the square be from 1 to 100, or as many as you can; you must also have fixed to it an Index, with sight upon the same, as you may see by the Figure following in the next Page. It is called a Circumferenter or Geometrical Square.

To draw a Plot of any Coast or Country in such sort that you may readily tell how far any place is distant from you, or one from another.

YOu must ascend some high Tower, Hill, Cliff, or other place, from whence you may commodiously behold on every part those places you intend a Plot of, there set up your Instrument upon its staff, and in such sort place it by help of your Needle, that the four Semi-Diameters stand due East, West, North, and South; then turn your Index to Town, Village, Haven, Road, or such like, espying through the Sights the middle or most notable mark in them, noting withall in a Table by it self the degrees cut by the Index in your Instrument, which we call the Angles of position, and so make a Table of the first Station. Then search out with

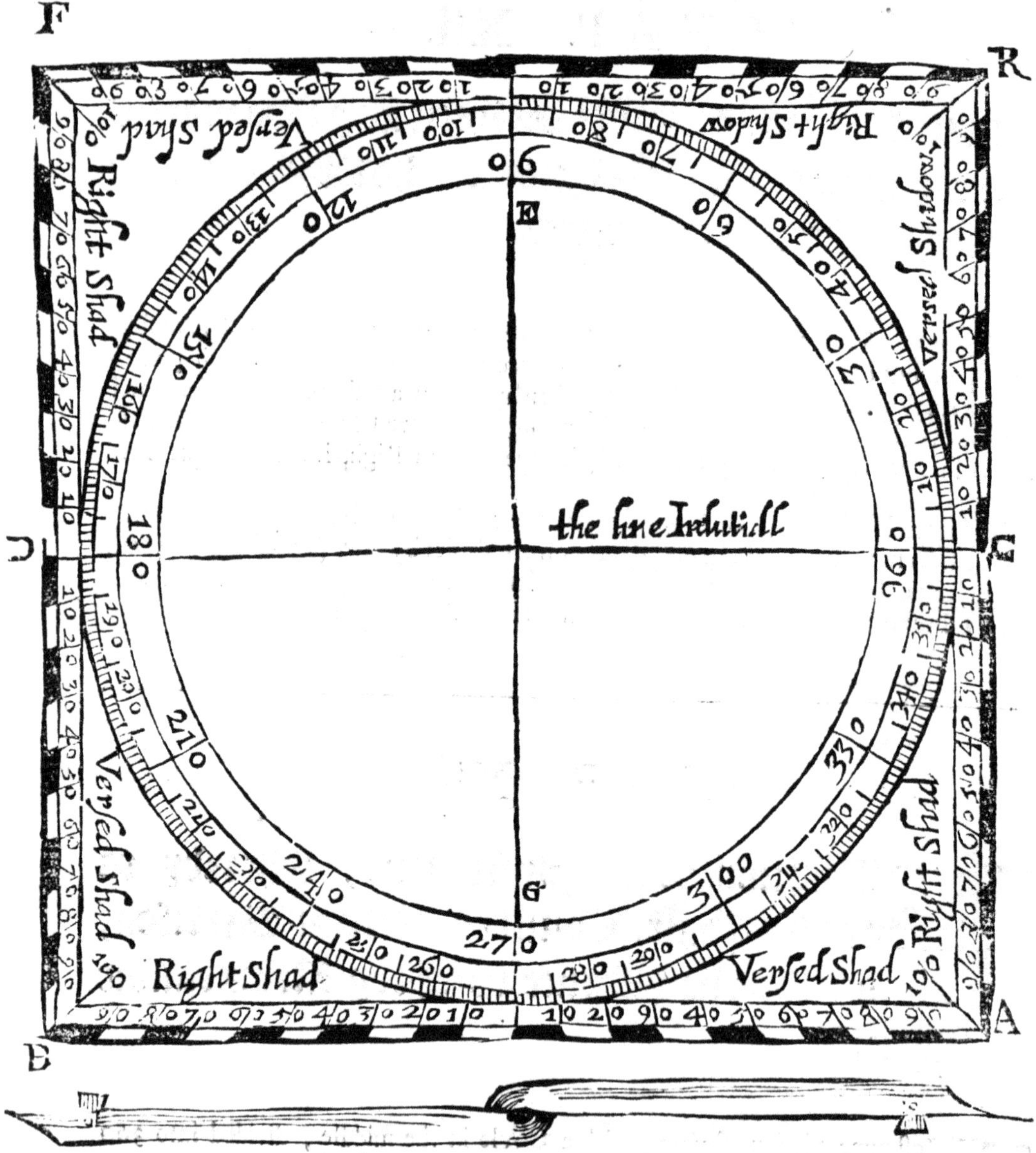

with your Eye, viewing round about, ſome other lofty place, from whence you may behold again all theſe places, for that ſhall be your ſecond Station, and turning thereunto the Index of your Inſtrument, note what degree it toucheth; this done, remove your Inſtrument thither, and place it in all reſpects as 'twas before, and turning the Diameter or Index of your Inſtrument to every place, eſpying through the Sight all ſuch marks as you ſaw before, noting again the degrees cut, or Angles of poſition, writing the names of every place, and its degree by it; ſo have you a Table alſo of your ſecond Station; with theſe Tables you ſhall reſort to ſome plain ſmooth ſuperficies of Board, Parchment, Paper, or ſuch like, and thereon deſcribe a large Circle, divide it into 360 degrees, like to the Circle of your Inſtrument; then from the Centre thereof to every degree noted in your firſt Table, extend ſtreight lines, writing upon every one of them the name of his place; and upon that line that repreſents your ſecond Station fix one foot of your Compaſſes, opening the other at pleaſure; and draw another Circle, and divide it alſo into 360 degrees, and from the Center thereof extend right lines to every degree noted in your ſecond Table, writing as before upon every one of them the name of their places or marks; finally, you ſhall note diligently the concourſe or croſſing of every two like lines, making thereon a a star or such like mark, with the names of the places thereunto belonging. Now if you desire to know how far every of these Towns, Villages, &c. are distant from each other, you shall do thus, measure the distance between your Stations by Instrument or otherwise, as you have been before taught, and divide the right line between the Centers of your Circles into so many equal parts or portions as there are Miles, Furlongs, or Scores, between your Stations; then opening your Compasses to one of those parts, you may measure from place to place, alwayes affirming so many Miles, Furlongs, or Scores (according to the denomination of that one part whereunto you opened your Compasses) to be between place and place, as you find by measuring there are parts.

Example.

There is a Sea Coast having sundry Harbours, Towns, Villages, Castles, and such like scituated thereon, whose Plot in due proportion I require, with the exact distances of every place one from the other.

Having therefore elected a lofty seat, from whence I may behold all these places (my Instrument scituated as is declared) removing the Index to a Castle that is farthest, being a Castle standing in the mouth of a Haven, having received it through my Sights, the line fiducial of my Index cutteth 30 degrees; then I remove it to the next, being a Village or Fish Town, and the Index cutteth 50 degrees, and so round to all the rest; and thus I shall have the Table of my first Station, as followeth,

The Table of my first Station.

	Deg.
The Castle.	30
The Village.	50
The City.	75
The Eastern Head of the Bay.	95
The Western Head of the Bay.	97½
The Fort within Land.	130.

This done, I behold another Hill or high place; from whence I may in like manner view all those places, and turning my Index thereunto, I find the Line fiducial lying upon 180 Degrees; then carrying my Instrument thither, and placing it in all points there, as it was at the first Station, I turn my Index again to my first Mark or Castle, and find it to cut in 15 Degrees, at the second 25, &c. as you may see in this second Table.

The Table of my second Station.

	Deg.
The Castle.	15
The Village.	25
The City.	40
The Eastern Head of the Bay.	50
The Western Head of the Bay.	55
The Fort within Land	80.

With these Tables I repair to a Paper, Parchment, &c. and by the former Rules draw the Figure following.

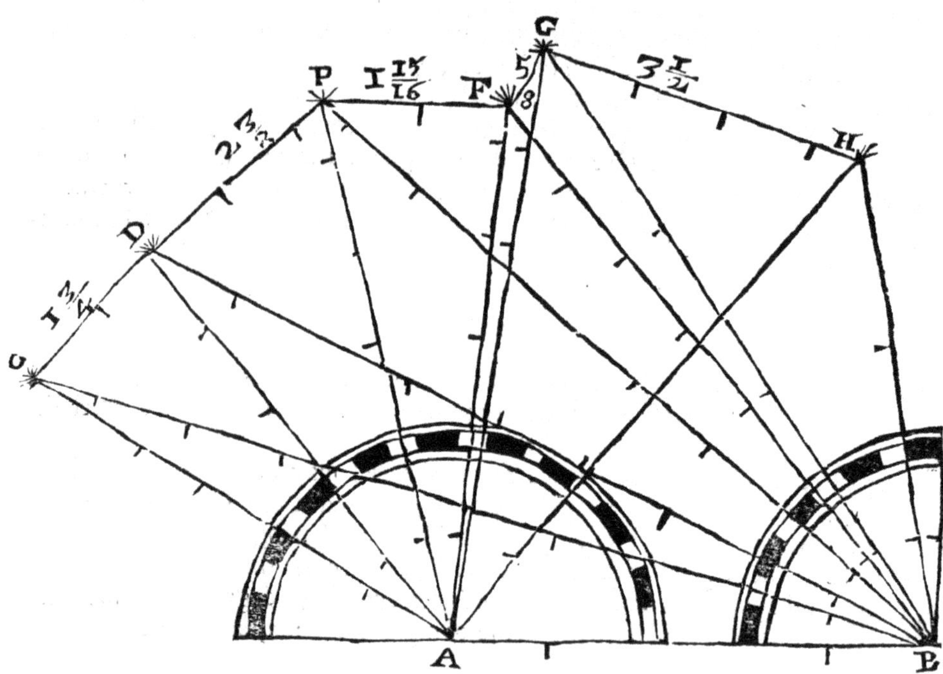

Having thus compleated your Plot, and found the diſtance between A and B to be 5 miles, make a Scale according to that diſtance, divide it into miles and parts, and with it you may meaſure your diſtance from place to place, or the diſtance from any of your Stations to each place, according as you have occaſion.

Thus paſſing or changing your Station, you may make ſeveral Plots, containing the true proportion and diſtance of Towns, Villages, Ports, Roads, Hills, Rivers, and all other notable places throughout a whole Realm.

Thus I ſuppoſe we have writ all ſuch propoſitions of meaſuring of heights, diſtances, and profundities, *&c.* as may be neceſſary to our work. We will next come to the more Practick part, of mannaging a Piece of Ordnance to do the beſt Service.

CHAP. XIV.

The Deſcription and uſe of the Gunners Scale.

THis Scale is made according to the Diameter of our *Engliſh* Ordnance, not above 8 inches long, being the Diameter of a Cannon Royal; they are generally made of Box, Pear-tree, or Braſs, any well ſeaſoned Wood that will not warp may ſerve: Upon one ſide I have ſet the names of all ſorts of Ordnance; and in the Angle of meeting with the names, is the Angle at the Bore; and between that and the next leſs Diameter, is the common length of ſuch a Piece; and upon the ſtep of bredth is the number of paces theſe Pieces ſhoot point blank; and right in the Angle of meeting, betwixt the two Diameters, with the Angle of meeting with the names, is firſt the weight of the Gun, the breadth of the Ladle, the length, weight of the Charge of Powder, the Diameter of the Shot, weight of the Shot, and a line of inches, and tenth parts of an inch. The Backſide is alſo divided into inches and quarters of inches, and over them is ſhewed the weight of every Iron Shot anſwerable to thoſe inches, with the weight

weight of the like Bullet in Lead and Stone; each being diſtinguiſhed. You may alſo if you pleaſe have upon this ſide the Gunners Quadrant, and ſuch other things as you ſhall think fit, as you may ſee in this Figure following, where all things are diſtinguiſhed by their Names, and need no more Explanation.

You will obſerve by this Inſtrument, that the Ladle is but 3 Diameters of the Shot in length, and $\frac{1}{3}$ part of the Circumference, from the Cannon to the whole Culvering, and the charge of Powder will be found to be about 2 Diameters of the Piece; from the Culvering to the Minion, the Charge may fill 2 Diameters and a half; and from the Minion to the Baſe 3 Diameters; but of this matter we have ſpoke at large in the firſt part of this Book; but there having left out the Table of Periors and Drakes, I thought good here to inſert it.

A neceſſary Table of Periors and Drakes proportioned.

Names of Pieces.	Height of the bore in inches.	Length in Diameter.	Weight in met.pound.	Weight of Powder.	Length of the Ladle.
Canon Perior.	9. 10. 12.	8	3500	3, $3\frac{1}{2}$ 4	3
D. Canon Drake.	$6\frac{1}{2}$	16	3000	9 *pound.*	$4\frac{1}{2}$
Culvering Drake.	$5\frac{1}{2}$	16	2000	5	$4\frac{1}{2}$
D. Cul. Drake.	$4\frac{1}{2}$	16	1500	$3\frac{1}{2}$	$4\frac{1}{2}$
Saker Drake.	$3\frac{1}{2}$	18	1200	2	$4\frac{1}{2}$

CHAP. XV.

How to make a true Diſpart of any true bored Piece of Ordnance.

KNow firſt, that to diſpart a Piece of Ordnance, is no otherwiſe than to bring the Diameter at Muzzle to be equal to the Diameter at the Baſe Ring; in true founded Ordnance, half of the Diameter of the Cylender is the diſpart; but more generally it may be done thus, Gird the Piece round about the Britch with a thred, after do the like by the Muzzle Ring, lay theſe two ſtrings ſtreight upon a Table at length, and make two marks for the length of each ſtring; divide the diſtance between each of theſe two marks into 22 equal parts with your Compaſſes, and 7 of them are their Diameters; then meaſure how much each Diameter is in length, and ſubſtract one Diameter from the other, then take the juſt half of the difference, and that is the true diſpart of your Piece in inches, and part of an inch.

But theſe Diameters are better and more artificially taken with a pair of Crallipars, as we have ſhewed before in taking the Diameter of a Shot, and then meaſured upon your Scale of inches and parts, will give you the true Diameters of the Piece both at Britch and Muzzle, with which work as above.

Alſo you may find the true diſpart of a Piece thus; Put a ſmall Wyer or priming Iron in at the Touch-hole of the Piece to the bottom of the Concave; then mind what part of that Iron is even with the Baſe Ring, and make a mark there; then take it out and apply it to the Muzzle, and place it upon the lower edge of the Concave of the Piece as upright as you can, and mind what part of the Iron or Wyer is even with the upper part of the Muzzle Ring, and there make a mark; for the difference between these two marks, is the true dispart of the Piece: or after you have placed your Iron upon the Muzzle as before, cause a dispart to be raised so high as that mark which was made upon the Iron when 'twas put down the Touch-hole.

If from the top of the dispart a fine thread or line be carried to the Muzzle Ring, you will see how high you may make a dispart at the Trunions,

Or thus a dispart may be made at the Trunions; lay a peece of soft Wax upon the Trunions, and let one raise it high, or depress it, until that the Metal at the top of the Base Ring, the Wax between the Trunions, and the dispart of the Muzzle, be all three of one height precisely; but the former way with a thread is more exact.

A Piece of Ordnance may be disparted thus; take two sticks (each of them must be longer than the Piece) and also make a Plummet of Lead to hang in a small thread made fast to one end of the stick, which lay cross the top of the Base Ring, to and fro, until the Plummet descending from the end thereof, may just touch the side of the Metal of the said Ring; then keeping fast the stick in that place, hang your Plummet down by the other side of the stick, until it on the otherside just touch the Metal of the Base Ring; when you have done, cut off the stick just in that place by which the Plummet descended, perpendicularly, and this length is the just Diameter of the Base Ring; after this manner you must proceed to take the Diameter at the Muzzle. Then lastly, set these two sticks together even at one end, and mark their difference in length or height; for just half of that difference is the dispart of that Piece.

I would advise all Sea Gunners upon some occasions to use Disparts between the Trunions of their Pieces, made of a just height, on purpose to serve that place, by the method we have even now prescribed, and let them be tyed about the Piece with a twine, because else at every Shot they will be to seek, when upon a suddain they should use them, and they will much avail and stand them in great stead. I could express other wayes, only I think these sufficient.

CHAP. XVI.

How to give Level with a Piece of Ordnance to make a Shot at any Mark assigned.

SEt your dispart on the Muzzle Ring, just over the Center of the mouth of the Piece, which you may best do by putting a stick cross the bore, and dividing it into two equal parts; then with a Plumb line hanging over the mouth of the Piece, being guided by the divided stick, you shall have good aim where to set your Dispart; this being done, go to the Base Ring, if the Piece be true bored, then find which is the highest part, and middle of that Ring; but if the Piece be not true bored, then find which part of the Base Ring is just over the Cylender, and take that for your true line: when you have found out the dispart, and placed it, and also found what point in the Base Ring is to answer to it, then make some very small mark on the Base Ring in that place, hold your head about two foot from the Base Ring, and there you may best observe, as the Piece is traversing, when you are in a direct line with the mark; this done, give one of your men order to raise and fall the Piece with his Hand-spike as you shall appoint him, until you can, holding your head two foot from the Britch of the Piece, with your eye perceive the mark at the Base Ring, and the top of the dispart in a direct line with the mark you must shoot at; at that instant stop the motion of the Piece with a Coyn, that it may remain as you have directed it; then Prime your Piece, and give fire.

Before

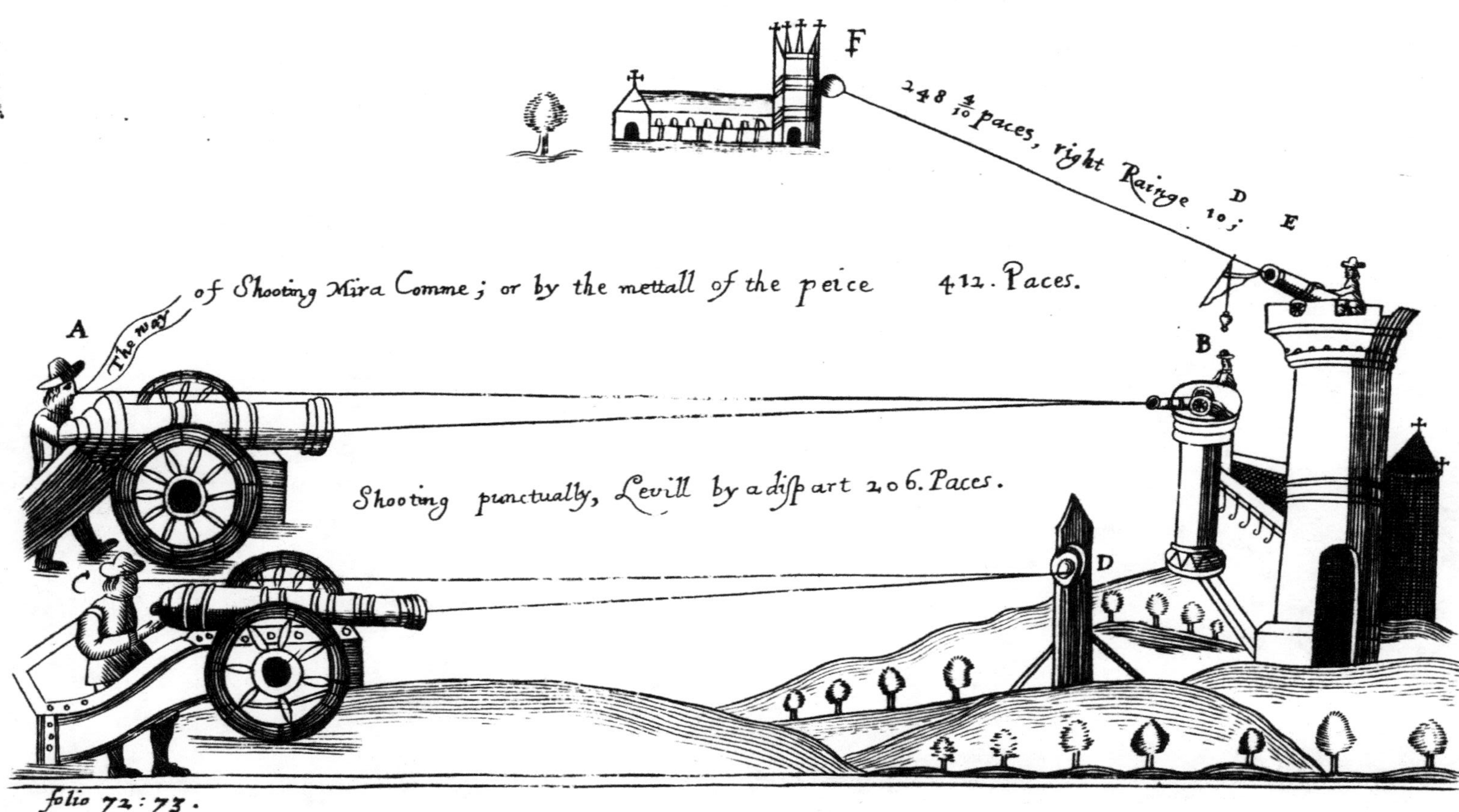
F
$248 \frac{4}{10}$ paces, right Rainge 10;
D
E
A
The way of Shooting Mira Comme; or by the mettall of the peice 412. Paces.
B
Shooting punctually, Levill by a dispart 206. Paces.
C
D
folio 72: 73.

Before you place your Dispart, you are to take notice whether the ground be Level whereon the Wheels of the Gun stand, or if they be not one higher than the other, and if the Trunions stand just over the Axeltree of the Wheels or no; whether one Trunion lye higher on the Carriage than the other: whether the Gun be truely placed in the Carriage or not; that is, that it be not nearer one side than the other: whether the Carriage be truly made according to the direction we have already prescribed in the first part; whether the Axeltree be placed just cross the Carriage or not.

CHAP. XVII.

How, if a Shot do carry to the right or to the left, under or over the mark, by reason of some known fault, to amend it in making the next Shot.

After you have made one Shot, and find the Piece carry just over the mark, then do all that has been taught again, and when your Piece lyes directly against the mark, observe how much the last stroak of the Shot is above the mark, so much longer make your dispart, that the top of it may be just seen from the Britch of the Piece, in a direct line with the stroke of the Shot; when it is of this length, then level your Piece with this new dispart to the assigned mark, Give fire, and without doubt it will strike the same.

If the first Shot strike under the mark, then bring the Piece in all points as before to pass, mark how much of the dispart is over the stroke of the Shot, and cut it just so short, as being at the Britch you may discern the top of it, with the mark on the Base Ring and stroke of the Shot in a just right line, and when you perceive it is of such a length, level the Piece to the assigned mark, as at the first, then Prime and Give fire.

If the first Shot strike on the right hand of the mark, to mend it you must level the Piece as formerly; you standing behind the Britch of the Piece, observe the stroke of the Shot over the dispart, and that part of the Base Ring as you at that instant look over in a right line towards the dispart, and the stroke of the Shot, set up in that place a Pin with a little soft Wax on the Base Ring; so this Pin will be in a right line with the dispart and stroke of the Shot: This being done, level your Piece to the mark assigned by this Pin and the dispart, and without question you will make a fair Shot; for when you level by the Metal of the Base Ring where the Pin is placed, and the mark of the Piece standing at that direction, look over the top of the dispart from the notch in the Base Ring, and you shall find it to lye just so much to the left, as the former Shot struck to the right, from the assigned mark, which should in all likelyhood now strike the mark.

But if a Shot be both too wide and too low, then you must use both the directions above taught, to make the next Shot: first regulate the dispart by cutting it shorter, according as the Shots mark is lower than the assigned mark; when this is done, then proceed to my directions to mend shooting wide, and these things performed with care and diligence, cannot choose but mend a bad Shot.

CHAP. XVIII.

Of shooting at Random at a Mark beyond the right line of the Pieces reach, or right Range of a Shot; and the Way of framing a Table of Randoms, by help of the Gunners Quadrant.

FOr the effecting of this matter, we must have a Quadrant with a Thread and Plummet (which is described in the first Chapter of this second Section) to one side of this Quadrant; so that one end of the Ruler may go into the Cavity of the Piece, and let a Piece of Lead be fastned to the end of the Rule, to make it lye close to the bottom of the Metal within, the Quadrant hanging without, and the Plumb-line swaying or hanging down from the Center of the Quadrant, perpendicular to the Horizontal line; for the *Quadrant* being thus placed, you may mount a Piece to what degree you shall find fit to shoot by.

Now every one that will learn to shoot at Random, must draw his Piece on a level ground, where first shooting level, he must observe that distance in feet or paces, then mount his Piece to one degree, and mark where that shall graze; thus finding the distance of every degree from the level to the tenth degree, by these distances make a Table, to which annex the degrees against the distance; by which Table you may (using the Art of Proportions) find how far another Piece will convey her Shot from degree to degree, and in Loading your Piece for this work you must have your Powder exactly weighed, and likewise the Wad, and let the Piece cool of it self, and this you must do every time; and if the Piece be mounted, there needs no Wad after the Shot; also you must have a special care of the strength of the Powder, and let the Powder equally, and with the same force and strength be pressed home, as near as possible you may.

CHAP. XIX.

An effectual Way to make a Shot out of a Piece of Ordnance at Random.

HE that intends to be expert at these things, ought principally to endeavour, at one time or another, to obtain so much liberty of his Superior Commanders, as to make two, three, or more Shot with the Piece he chooseth, or intends for most Service; then must he measure the distance from the Platform to the first graze of the Shot; and must apply it to the Table, which I have here inserted, being the experience of such as have been knowing Gunners. But first I shall set down Mr. *Nye* of *Worcester*'s Experiment, not as he is Mathematician, as he writes himself (which Title none of our Learned Mathematicians of *England* do assume) but as he was a Practical Gunner, and made these several experiments upon four several degrees of Mounture, *viz.* 1 deg. 5 deg. 7 deg. 10 deg. from thence was found these Randoms.

At

At 1 degree, the Shot did light from the Piece or place of ſtanding 225 paces.
At 5 degrees, the Random was 416 paces.
At 7 degrees, the Random was 505 paces.
At 10 degrees the Random was 630 paces.

And by theſe Experiments a Table may be framed according to this Rule. As the known degree of Mounture, is to the number of paces the Piece carries; ſo is the number of degrees propoſed, to the diſtance required.

A Table of Randoms.

Degrees.	Paces.
0	206
1	225
2	274
3	323
4	370
5	416
6	461
7	505
8	548
9	589
10	630

The uſe of this Table will plainly appear in one onely Example.

Suppoſe you make tryal of your Piece of Ordnance, according to the method preſcribed in the laſt Chapter, and find that at 6 degrees of Random upon a level ground, the Shot is conveyed 619 paces, and you are to ply your Piece againſt a place which lyes beyond the point blank, the diſtance being 498 paces, to know the degree the Piece muſt be elevated too, do thus; in this Table of Randoms againſt 6 degrees, there is 461 paces; then ſay as 619 paces is to 461, ſo is 498 to 375; which number, or the neareſt to being ſought, in this Table is 370, and ſtands againſt 4 degrees, but becauſe it is not exactly the ſame number, you muſt find out the part of a degree or minute, by a Table of proportional parts; but if the mark you ſhoot at be lower or higher than your Platformer, then you muſt add or ſubſtract ſo many degrees or minutes from the degrees and minutes found, and the remainder is the degree you ought to mount your Piece to.

Now that we may be underſtood well, we muſt know that there are two ſorts of Ranges or Motions of a Shot, of which you may ſee more in Chap. 20. the one is called the Right Range, and the other is termed the Curved or Crooked Range, and theſe two there termed a Compound Range, is called the Dead Range; that is to ſay, the whole diſtance from your Platform from whence the Shot was made, to the place where the Bullet firſt grazes; yet the perpendicular deſcending of the Bullet is alſo called the Natural motion, as you may ſee by the figure hereafter placed. Captain *Hexham* in his Book of Gunnery, ſhews how by finding out the Random of a Cannon for the firſt degree of Mounture to find the Random for every degree to 45 degrees, which is the utmoſt Random, after this manner; Firſt, find out how many paces the Cannon will ſhoot, being laid level by the Metal (which he accounts for one degree of Mounture) divide this diſtance by 50, then multiply the *Quotient* by 11, and that will bring out the number of the greateſt digreſſion or difference between Range and Range, which being divided by 44, the *Quotient* will ſhew the number of paces which the Bullet will loſe in the other Ranges from degree to degree. *Example.* A Battering Cannon being laid by the Metal, will ſhoot his Bullet (as he ſaith) 1000 ordinary paces, two foot and a half to each pace; which being divided by 50, the *Quotient* will be 20, which multiplyed by 11, is 220 paces, which is the number of the next digreſſion made in the ſecond degree : which 220 divide by 44, the number of the remaining degrees yields 5, which is the number of paces to be diminiſhed in each degree; and by this Rule this Table is framed.

A Table of Randoms to 45 Degrees, accounting 2 Foot ½ to the Pace.

The Degrees of Mounture.	*Paces*	*diff.*	The Degrees of Mounture.	*Paces*	*diff.*
0	0775	225	23	4685	110
1	1000	220	24	4795	105
2	1220	215	25	4900	100
3	1435	210	26	5000	95
4	1645	205	27	5095	90
5	1850	200	28	5185	85
6	2050	195	29	5270	80
7	2245	190	30	5350	75
8	2435	185	31	5425	70
9	2620	180	32	5595	65
10	2800	175	33	5560	60
11	2975	170	34	5620	55
12	3145	165	35	5675	50
13	3310	160	36	5725	45
14	3470	155	37	5770	40
15	3625	150	38	5810	35
16	3775	145	39	5845	30
17	3920	140	40	5875	25
18	4060	135	41	5900	20
19	4595	130	42	5920	15
20	4325	125	43	5935	10
21	4450	120	44	5945	5
22	4570	115	45	5950	

But this Table of *Alexander Bianco* for all forts of Ordnance, I do account as one of the beft.

A Table of Randoms for the fix points of the Gunners Quadrant.

	1	2	3	4	5	6
Faulconet.	375	637	795	885	892	900
Faulcon.	550	935	1166	1254	1309	1320
Minion.	450	765	954	1026	1071	1080
Saker.	625	1062	1325	1425	1487	1500
D. Culvering.	725	1232	1537	1653	1725	1740
Culvering.	750	1275	1590	1710	1785	1800
Demi-Canon.	625	1062	1325	1425	1487	1500
Canon of 7.	675	1147	1431	1489	1606	1620
Double Canon.	750	1275	1660	1710	1785	1800

The ufe of this Table is thus; having refolved upon what point of Mounture, look in this Table for the name of the *Piece*, and right under that point againft the name of the *Piece*, that is in the common Angle, you fhall find the number of paces of her Random fought.

CHAP.

CHAP. XX.

How to find the right Range of any Shot Discharged out of any Piece, for every Elevation by any one right or dead Range given for the Piece assigned.

THe right Range of every Piece being discharged in a level, or parallel to the Horizon, is allowed by some not to exceed 185 paces, that is 5 foot to a pace, yet some reckon much more, but then they account ordinary steps or paces of two foot and a half; and Batteries made with such Pieces are usally made at 100 or 120 such paces, at which distance they do the best execution.

The utmost Random likewise of any Piece that is from the Platform to the first graze of the Bullet, I find by some to be about ten times the distance of the right Range; and accordingly I have so set it down in the Table.

As for the Ranges to the other degrees and points of the *Quadrant*, I find these Tables in Good Authors.

A TABLE OF

Right Ranges, or Point Blanks.		Randoms, or the first Graze.	
The Degrees of the Pieces Mounture.	*The Right Range in Paces, 5 Foot to a Pace.*	*The Degrees of Mounture.*	*The Paces of the Random, 5 Foot to a Pace.*
0	192	0	192
1	209	1	298
2	227	2	404
3	244	3	510
4	261	4	610
5	278	5	722
6	285	6	828
7	302	7	934
8	320	8	1044
9	337	9	1129
10	354	10	1214
20	454	20	1917
30	693	30	2185
40	855	40	2289
50	1000	50	2283
60	1140	60	1792
70	1220	70	1214
80	1300	80	1000
90	1350	90	

This Table is rather proportional than real, and doth best agree with greater Ordnance; but by help of it, working by the Rule of proportion, you may know the Random of any Piece of Ordnance; by first (as we have said before) making one Shot, and measuring from your Platform that distance. You may make a Table for your Piece thus,

Suppose a Saker being mounted to 5 degrees, shoot the Bullet 416 paces, how far will it shoot being mounted 10 degrees?

As 722 the Tabular distance for 5 degrees of Mounture, is to 416 paces the distance found,

So is the Tabular distance for 10 degrees of Mounture, 1214. to the distance required, which will be found to be 699, 5 paces.

Now if you desire to know how much of the Horizontal line, is contained directly under the right line of any Shot, called the right Range, made out of any Piece at any elevation.

First, know that in plain Triangles, the violent motion or right line of a Shot is supposed to be the Hypothenusal, the Angle of Mounture to be the Angle at Base; these are given, and the Horizontal line is the Base which is to be found; there the proportion will run thus;

As the Radius 90 deg. is to the number of paces in a right Range;
So is the Sine Complement of the Angle of Mounture, to the Horizontal Base, or the right line which lyes parallel to the Horizon under the way of the Shot.

CHAP. XXI.

Of the violent, crooked, and natural motion or way of a Shot, from the time he is discharged, until it is descended.

BY the third and fourth propositions of the second Book of *Tartagilia*, his *Nova Scientia*, he sheweth that every body equally heavy, as a Shot in the end of the violent motion thereof, being discharged out of a Piece of Ordnance, so it be not right up or right down, the curved Range shall joyn with the right Range, and to the natural course and motion betwixt them both, which distinct motions you may see in the last foregoing figure.

In the 17 proposition of the same Book, he proveth that every Shot equally heavy, great or little, equally elevated above the Horizon, or equally oblique or level directed, are among themselves like, and proportional in their distance, as the figure following sheweth, as A E F is like and proportional in right and crooked Ranges unto H I, and in their distances or dead Ranges A F unto A I.

And in his 4th and 6th propositions of the same Book, he proveth that every Shot made upon the level hath the mixt or crooked Range thereof equal to the Arch of a Quadrant 90 degrees; and if it be made upon an elevation above the level, that then it will make the crooked Range to be more than a Quadrant: And if that be made imbased under the level, that then the crooked Range thereof will be a Quadrant.

And in his 9th proposition of the same Book, he shews, that if one Piece be Shot off twice, the one level, and the other at the best of her Random at 42 ½ deg. Mounture, that the right Range of the length is but the ½ of the dead range of the best Random. He that desires a further Demonstration of these Propositions, may peruse his said second Book *de Nova Scientia.*

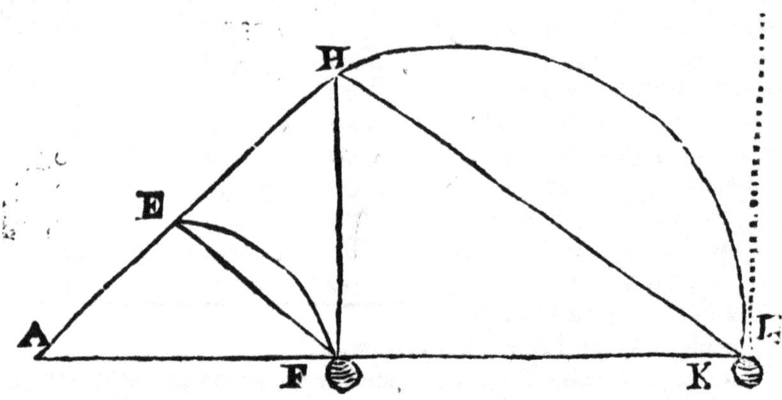

CHAP.

CHAP. XXII.

The making of a Gunners Rule, which will serve for the elevation of a Piece, which is sometimes better than a Quadrant; and the dividing it into degrees by help of a Table, fitting it for any Piece from 5 foot to 14 foot long.

BEcause the *Quadrant* cannot be conveniently used at all times, especially when the wind blows hard, and, being near the Enemies Guns, the Plumb-line is too long before it stands still; to remedy this, the Gunners Rule was invented, the figure hereof is as followeth; it must be 12 or 14 inches long, according as the Gun will require, it must have a long slit down the middle thereof like the Eye-Vane of a *Quadrant* or back Staff, the head thereof make circular or a little hollow, as you see in the figure the Instrument is described standing, at 'tis to be placed upon the Britch of a Piece of Ordnance; in the middle of the small narrow slit you must place a Lute string or a well twisted Silk with a Bead running upon the same to be set to any number of inches and parts, or to such a degree of the *Quadrant*, as you must mount your Gun unto; and on the one side of the slit you must place a division of inches, and let every inch be divided into 10 parts, and then it will serve for all sorts of Guns; but if it be for a particular Gun, then on the other side you may place the degrees and parts, when you shall find by the length of your Piece, how many inches and parts of an inch goes to a degree; but to use it with all sorts of Ordnance, let it only be divided into inches and parts.

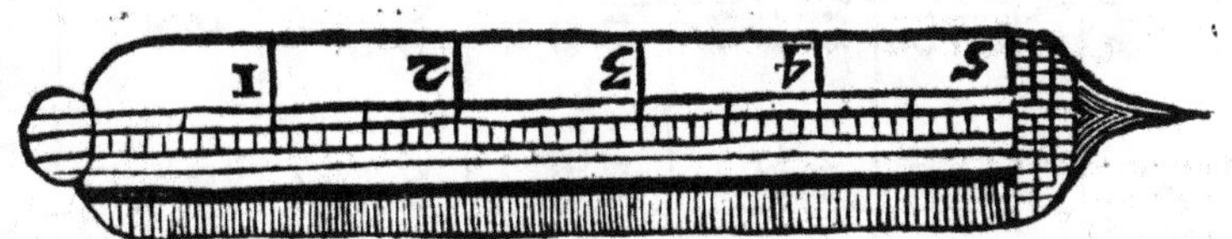

To fit this Rule for one Gun only, here is the Rule for the decimation of the degrees, note, this Table hath 11 Columns, the first shews the length of the Piece in feet and half feet, the other 10 Columns in the head are 10 degrees, and under is inches and the 100 parts of an inch, from 1 degree to 10 degrees; and so you may take them out of the Table, and put them on your Ruler.

The len. of the *Piece.*	1 *Degree.*		2 *Degrees*		3 *Degrees*		4 *Degrees*		5 *Degrees*		6 *Degrees*		7 *Degrees*		8 *Degrees*		9 *Degrees*		10 *Degr.*	
Feet and ½ Feet.	*Inch.*	100	*Inch.*	100	*Inch.*	100	*Inch.*	100	*Inch.*	100	*Inch.*	100	*Inch.*	100	*Inch.*	100	*Inch.*	100	*Inch.*	100
4 Foot long.	1	3	2	6	3	8	4	11	5	14	6	16	7	19	8	82	9	25	10	28
5 Foot and half.	1	14	2	28	3	42	4	56	5	70	6	84	7	98	9	12	10	26	11	40
6 Foot long.	1	22	2	44	3	66	4	88	6	10	7	38	8	58	9	78	11	8	12	29
6 Foot and half.	1	36	2	72	4	8	5	44	6	80	8	17	9	53	10	89	12	25	13	63
7 Foot long.	1	47	2	94	4	41	5	88	7	35	8	82	10	30	11	77	13	24	14	73
7 Foot and half.	1	58	3	14	4	71	6	28	7	85	9	42	10	99	12	55	14	14	15	71
8 Foot long.	1	68	3	36	5	4	6	72	8	40	10	8	11	76	13	44	15	12	16	82
8 Foot and half.	1	79	3	58	5	37	7	16	8	95	10	74	12	53	14	32	16	12	17	92
9 Foot long.	1	89	3	79	5	68	7	58	9	47	11	37	13	27	15	18	17	8	18	98
9 Foot and half.	2	00	4	0	6	0	8	0	10	0	12	10	14	2	16	3	18	4	20	4
10 Foot long.	2	10	4	20	6	30	8	40	10	30	12	61	14	73	16	84	18	56	21	8
10 Foot and half.	2	21	4	41	6	69	8	88	11	81	13	28	15	48	17	68	19	89	22	10
11 Foot long.	2	31	4	62	6	93	9	24	11	56	13	88	16	22	18	51	20	82	23	14
11 Foot and half.	2	42	4	48	7	26	9	68	12	10	14	53	16	95	19	37	21	80	24	21
12 Foot long.	2	53	5	6	7	59	10	12	12	65	15	18	17	71	20	25	22	78	25	33
12 Foot and half.	2	63	5	20	7	89	10	52	13	15	15	78	18	41	21	4	23	67	26	33
13 Foot long.	2	74	5	48	8	82	10	96	13	70	16	44	19	48	21	92	24	68	27	40
13 Foot and half.	2	84	5	68	8	52	11	36	14	20	27	4	19	88	22	72	25	56	28	42
14 Foot long.	2	95	5	90	8	85	11	80	14	75	17	70	20	65	23	60	26	56	29	53

The use of this Table in graduating the Rule is very plain; for if your Piece of Ordnance be 8 foot long, and you would mount your Piece two degrees, seek for 8 foot under the title length of the Piece, and in the common Angle against the length of the Piece under two degrees you will find 3, 36, to make a degree; that is 3 inches and 36 parts of an inch, divided into 100 parts, and to this you may set your Bead.

The

The use of the graduated Rule is thus: having loaded your Piece, and brought your Piece of Ordnance in a right line with your mark, the dispart being placed upon the Muzzle Ring, in like manner place your Rule upon the Base Ring, and let one standing by hold it, for the foot of it let it be fitted round to the Gun; so you may be sure to place it right, and you may estimate on its perpendicular well enough; now having before the distance to the mark you intend to shoot at, and admit you have found it to be 461 paces, and the first Shot you made for practice out of that Piece conveyed her Shot at two degrees of Mounture 274 paces; then by our former Rules and the Tables of Randoms, there I find 461 against 6 degrees, which is the degrees I must mount my Piece to reach 461 paces.

Then to find by this Table how many inches and hundred parts of an inch 6 degrees will require, look in the Table above, and find on the left hand in the first Column the length of the Piece, and just under the degrees (as is aforesaid) you shall find the inches and parts of Mounture, to which set your Bead on your string, that is in the sight, to so many inches and parts as the Table gives; then mount the Piece higher or lower, until you bring the Bead to the top of the dispart and mark, all in one line; stop then the Piece in such a position with a Coyn, then prime and give fire.

If you will shoot by the Metal of the Piece without a dispart, then substract the height of the dispart out of the inches found by the Table, and to the remainder mount your Piece.

If you have no *Quadrant* nor a Ruler, and would make a good Shot, look in the Table, and find the length of the Piece and the inches that you ought to raise your Piece unto, then cut a peece of stick just of that length, and set it upon the Base Ring, and bring the top of that stick, the top of the dispart, and the mark, all in a right line with your eye, and you will make as good a Shot as if you had a Rule and Bead, or *Quadrant*.

If you will have no dispart, take your dispart and measure it upon the aforesaid stick at the Base Ring, and from it cut off the length of the dispart, and the remainder use upon the Base Ring.

But if the Mounture should be so small that the inches of the dispart should be more than the inches answerable to the degrees of Mounture; then cut off from the dispart so much as 'tis longer than the other, and place it upon the Muzzle Ring, and bring the upper part of the Base Ring, the dispart, and mark, in a right line with your Eye, and you will this way make a level with a stick without Instrument, as well as if you had Ruler or *Quadrant*.

CHAP. XXIII.

How to make a Shot at the Enemies Light in a dark night, and to make at a Company of Horsemen or Footmen passing by, and also to make a good Shot at a Ship Sailing; and how a Shot lodged in a Piece, so that it will not be driven home to the Powder, may be shot out without hurt to the Piece.

TO shoot by night at the Enemies Lights, dispart your Piece with a lighted and flaming Wax Candle, or with a lighted Piece of Match, that with your Eye you may bring the Base Ring, the fired Match on the Muzzle Ring, and the Enemies Light, in a right line, or mark; then give fire, and you will make a good Shot.

Gen. I am also of your opinion, and hold it for good, yet I fear this will not be so soon done, and is sooner spoken, than executed, and that before you can bring your approach and sap so far, it will cost you warm blood; and a great many mens lives, if you have a stout Enemy within to deal withal, and one that is very Vigilant, and careful to stand upon his Guard, and his defence.

Capt. 'Tis true, this cannot be done without danger, and the loss of men, but he that is fearful must stay at home, and not come into the Wars where there is neither place nor time, which doth free or exempt him from danger: yet the danger is not alwayes so great, especially in such places, where you have Earth enough to work with, to cast up your sapps, and to heighten and deepen your Approaches, which will show you the way, for the more higher you find the ground in Approaching to the edge of the moat, the deeper Trenches you may make, and cover your self by casting up of blinds continually, to keep you from the sight of the Besieged; and it is better, when you have brought your approach as it were under them, than if you were 200 or 300 paces distant from them.

Gen. I pray you Good Sir, how would you plant, and divide these 18 Pieces of Canon?

Capt. I would make a great Battery with 8 of them to beat upon a right line, either upon a Curtain, or the point of a Bulwark (which the General shall find fittest) Two Batteries with each 3 Canon to play slope-wise from the great Battery; as the ninth plate, and 28 and 29 figures shows, and two Batteries, with two half Canon a Piece, to play as it were cross-wise upon the breach. And thus you see your 18 Pieces planted upon 5 Batteries, as you may observe in the 9th. Plate, and the two Figures of a Curtain and of a Bulwark following.

Gen. Good Sir tell me I pray you how many shot will these 18 Pieces of Canon make in 10 hours, and how much powder will they require.

Capt. In 10 hours they may make some 1500 shot, and will require a matter of 25000 pound weight of powder, that is 150 barrels full, each barrel containing 160 pound weight in it.

Gen. You make your account then that every Piece in the space of 10 hours is to shoot 80 shot, that is 8 shot an hour for every Piece.

Capt. You may make 10 shot in an hour if you please, if your Pieces be renforced; but as for your ordinary Pieces, they have not metalline substance enough to bear it: considering also that after you have made 40 shot out of a Piece, it will be so heated, that it must have a cooling time, which must be at least an hour, for otherwise your Piece being grown over hot, it may cause danger.

Gen. Methinks that 80 shot for a Piece in so long a time were too little, having often heard, that in that while, a Piece may well be shot off 130 times; can you give me your resolution upon this?

Capt. I will tell you Sir what hapned once in the Island of *Bomble*, Anno 1599. we planted a Piece by a mill, by which we did annoy the Enemy very much, so that they were forced to make a Battery, and planted a whole Canon, and a demy-Canon upon it, seeking to dismount ours. Now shooting with this Piece from four of the clock in the morning, till eleven toward noon, this Piece had a cooling time the space of two hours, and about one of the clock we began to play with it again, and continued shooting with it till 4 a clock in the afternoon; but this Piece being not able to endure the force aud heating of so many shot, we were constrained to leave off with it: and yet ceased not shooting with our other Pieces from another Battery by command from *Don Lewes de Valasco*, General of our Ordnance, and shooting cross-wise with some other of our Pieces, we put the Enemies two Pieces to silence in the space of an hour; a Souldier of ours standing by, was curious to keep a tally of the number of all the shot we made from the morning till four a clock in the afternoon, and shewed me 80 notches, which deducting the two hours cooling, our Piece planted at the Mill made 8 shot in an hour, which was as much as could be required of it.

Senior Diego Uffano *give your Translator leave to interrupt you a little, and so to conclude this discourse. If you remember at the Seige of* Ostend, *which you mention often in in your Chapters and Dialogues, you were without, and I was within the Town, that on the seventh of* January, Anno 1602. Stilo Novo, *After Sir* Francis Vere *of famous memory (who defended and kept the Town against you) had deluded you with a* Parley, *only to gain time, and to make up our Canon and Sea-beaten works along the skirt of the old Town, his Highness the Archduke resolved to assault us, and that morning began to batter* Sand-hill *and* Schotenburgh, *to make a breach for you against that night, with intent to Assault us (as you did) and to have entred the Town, and have put us all to the Sword, the Relation whereof you shall hear in the end of this Book. Now you had placed and planted your 20 Pieces of Cannon to batter them in this manner, 8 from your Battery at the foot of the* Downs, *8 from a Battery on the right hand of the* Downs, *6 from your pile Battery, 6 more which you had made upon the Sand, and as it were raised out of the Sea: the first shot upon the breach in a right line, and the other two slope-wise, as your two figures following do demonstrate. These 20 Pieces of Canon towards noon had a cooling time, for a matter of some 2 hours, just as you have said; and afterwards you began to batter the breach and old Town again, till it was almost twilight, and then they cooled again, till you were ready to give us an assault; and before you fell on, as I do well remember, you shot off one of your Cannons with a hollow Bullet, which flew over the Town and made a great humming noise, as a warning Piece to the* Count of Bucquoy, *who lay on the East-side, that you were then ready to fall on, and that he should do the like, this was your Signal. Now* General Vere *knowing well your intent, gave order to the Gentleman of our Ordnance who had the guard upon* Sand-hill, *that he should keep a true Tally, and an account of all the shot you made that day, with your 20 Pieces of Cannon upon the breach and the old Town, which being cast up, there were found to be made that day from morning till night 2200 shot, which was found to be an 110 shot for every Piece, and 11 shot an hour for every Piece, which is more than 8; but I verily believe your Pieces were renforced.* This by the way, and so I return again to your own Dialogue.

Gen. (Good Sir) I pray show me how you would batter the point of a Bulwark (as the figure 28 following demonstrates,) and give me some reasons aswel defensive as offensive.

Capt. I am willing to give your Lordship content, and say, If I were to batter the point of a *Bulwark* or a *Bastion*, I would have the same number of battering Canon, and planted in the same form and manner as they were for the Curtain, and to shoot sloap and cross-wise also; and if your approaches were advanced so far, they should be planted upon the very brink of the moat and upon the *Counterscharfe*, I would plant 4 of them so, that they should dismount the Enemies Canon in their *Casemates*, or any, if they had sunk them in their *Falsebray*, which should wait upon that occasion.

Gen. I am of your mind, and prefer such a battery before all others, who are of the opinion that they had rather choose a Curtain than a Bulwark to be battered.

Capt. You have heard my reasons for that, and see the figures following traced out to you. But as for your *Bulwark* the *besieged* may cut it off (as you may mark in the figures of *Retrenchments* and *Cuttings off* in the second part of this book) for indeed it will be a hard matter to force an Enemy out of a Bulwark, who is resolved to loose it by peecemeal and degrees; and there is not so much danger in assaulting of a Curtain, which being once well battered and beaten down with your Ordnance, you have an easier way and entrance to fall on with your Troops of men, to enter the Town or Fortress; but for the defence which is made from your Flanking Bulwarks, or your Casemates, you must make Batteries upon the brink of the moat against them, (as is said) to dismount the Enemies Pieces, and to flanker with your Ordnance the Parapets of the Bulworks to beat them about their ears, that the Bulworks may lye the more open to you, and I think this way is the least danger.

Gen. But the Besieged, their cuttings off, may they not be made aswel upon a Curtain as upon a Bulwark.

Capt. No, for the Rampire being thinner, you have neither so much ground, nor the like accommodation in a Curtain as in a Bulwark; and indeed, a Governour

If you make a Shot at a Company of Horse passing by, take a *Piece* that will reach the way the Horse or Foot are coming in a right line, then let your Gun be so loaded with *Powder* as it may presently take fire, and let your Shot be fit for your use; then take notice of some Hillock or some turning cross way for the mark, and when the Enemy comes near to that way in a right line with your Gun, give fire; but for shooting at a Ship upon the River, you must put your *Piece* to some eminent mark on the other side of the River, and when the Head of the Ship shall begin to be between the *Piece* and the mark, then give fire.

But if by some mischievous accident a Shot is lodged in the concavity of a *Piece*, and there sticks, and will not go home to the *Powder*, or come out; then the Gunner, to save his *Piece* from breaking, must imbase the mouth of the *Piece*, or put it under the line of level, then put in at the Touch-hole fair warm water at several times, so that it may run out at Muzzle or Mouth of the *Piece*; and when all the Salt-*Peter* is washed from the *Powder*, which is known by the taste of the Water, then let the Gunner clear the Touch-hole, and put in as much *Powder* as possible he can, and prime and give fire, and it will serve to draw out the Shot.

But when a Shot hath lain long in a *Piece* until he is grown rusty, and so sticks fast, put strong Vinegar warm into the mouth of the *Piece*, and with the Rammer strike the Shot until it doth move; then put in Vinegar until it run clear through the *Powder* and Shot; prime as before, and give fire with good *Powder*, and if it do not run through after it hath stood three dayes, clear the Touch-hole, prime and give fire.

A man may also shoot farther than ordinary in one and the self same *Piece*, if the *Powder* be gently driven home, and wadded accordingly; then the Shot being compassed with Paper, Leather, Oakam, or such like, to fill close to the *Powder* with a good Wadd, putting after it a Tampion of Cork, and with a Spunge moisten it with Oyl, annoint the vacant Cylender, and so Barricado the *Piece* that it may not reverse in the Discharge.

CHAP. XXIV.

A Discourse by way of Dialogue between a General and Captain, concerning the Assaulting a Town or Work, &c.

General. HAving brought your Approaches near unto a Town or a Fortress, whether would you choose a Bulwark or a Curtain to be battered with your Ordnance?

Captain. A Town may be assaulted in divers places; sometimes you assault one side, when as you make your Battery on another; sometimes you choose a Bulwark, otherwhiles a Curtain to be battered, with this intention, to take in the Town as soon as possible may be. As for me, if I were to take in a great Town which is populous, I had rather choose to batter a *Curtain*, than a *Bulwark*, which hath a high catt, or mount upon it: especially, seeing that in great Towns the Bulwarks lying one far from another, they do show the skirt of the Curtain very open.

Gen. Why would you rather choose a Curtain than a Bulwark?

Capt. Because your Bulwarks are alwayes stronger, and better fortified than your Curtain, and being it is the principal strength of a place, and better furnished with Platforms, Flanks, &c. it will require more time, labour, and charge to batter, than your Curtain.

Gen.

Gen. But what General is so ill experienced, as to labour to batter a Curtain, having two strong Bulwarks on both sides of him, to flanker him when he is to put over his Gallery, and to give an assault upon the Curtain: peradventure for his labour and pains, he may be well beaten.

Capt. Soft (Good Sir,) Suppose that after a great deal of labour and pains you have battered a Bulwark, and falling up to the breach to assault it, you find it cut off, an Enemy lodged in it, must you not then begin to sap forward again, to make a new battery? whereas on a Curtain there is not that means of cutting it off, as upon a large Bulwark.

Gen. Have you ever seen the experience of it?

Capt. *Yes Sir, the Prince of* Orange *took in the* Bosch *by a Bulwark, and also* Breda, *but* Mastrick *was taken in by making a breach, and springing of a mine, upon the Curtain between* Jonger *Port and a Bulwark*; howsoever the Town of *Cortes* upon the frontiers of *France*, was first battered by the *Arch-duke of Austria* upon the point of a Bulwark, near unto the very joynt of the Curtain, where a high and a strong turret stood, which did annoy us much, so that we could not advance forward, but were constrained to leave off our approach on that side, and began to make a new Battery for a breach in a Curtain on the Field-side, where there lay a strong Bulwark to defend it, which did our men a great deal of harm; but howsoever, with great difficulty and much ado, we took in the Town that way, by lodging our selves in the Curtain. Likewise the City of *Cambray* was battered, and taken in upon a Curtain, for all there were two strong Bulwarks that flankered it, which if we had run our line upon a Bulwark, we should not have forced it so soon; yea such an occasion might present it self, that a General may be forced to batter both the one and the other, or to find out some secret way by undermining a wall, and blowing it up with powder.

Gen. This is for your great Towns; but what say you to a Castle, a Cittadel, or some narrow Fortress, how will you go to work to take in those with the best advantage?

Capt. As for your Forts, and Castles, it is much better to batter them upon a mount or a Bulwark, than upon a Curtain: my reason is this, that in these your Bulwarks lying close one by another, will flank one another with the greater force, and hide the Curtain much better to defend it, so that one cannot so easily force it, if the said defenses be not taken away.

Gen. Go to then; a Town then being to be battered, either upon a Curtain or a Bulwark, how many Pieces of Ordnance would you have to do it, and, how and in what manner would you place, and plant your Ordnance upon your batteries to make a good breach?

Capt. To effect this, I would have 18 Pieces of Canon and half Canon, *(for lesser Pieces for Battery are now grown out of use.)*

Gen. Whether would you choose more whole Canon or half Canon?

Capt. To batter a place well either upon a stony or earthy wall, you may assure your self, the more whole Cannon you have, the greater and the more sufficient your breach will be: for your great battering Pieces do spoil and beat down any thing, which doth meet with their great force and violence: *Howsoever of late years experience hath taught at divers Seiges that your half Canon which are more portable, having good store of them, will do the business aswell as your whole Canon.*

Gen. But at what distance would you make your Batteries, for these 18 Pieces of Canon, and how near unto the place, which you intend to Batter.

Capt. I would counsel a General to approach as near unto that place as possible may be, and make his Batteries some two or three hundred paces one from another, and that if it were possible to advance covertly the Approach and sap, even up to the Counter-scharfe, and very brink of the Moat, to prepare a way for his Gallery: not only to Batter that place being at hand with the greater force, but also to keep in, and hinder an Enemy from Sallying out upon the Besiegers, to discover and dismount their Ordnance in *Casemates*, or if they have sunk any in their Walls or False-bray, and so to terrifie them, that they dare not stir out.

of a Town, or of a Fortress, if he were put to his choice, had rather to be assaulted on a Bulwark (than on a Curtain) by cutting it off into the form of a half moon, that he might make a new resistance, and defend it with a less number of men. Besides, in a Bulwark the Besieged have this advantage over the Assailants, which is very dangerous for them, that they may make a Mine within the bowels of their Bulwark when an Enemy shall attempt to assault it, and thinking to enter the Breach and take the Town, they may be blown up into the Air by a Countermine; the like also may happen to the Besieged, the Assailants springing their Mine also in a Bulwark, when they think they stand upon their best defence.

Gen. May not the like be done also in a Curtain?

Capt. No, it will not take the like effect as in a Bulwark; for a Breach being once made in a Curtain, for as an Enemy may assault it at large, so they may bring a greater number of men to fight, to help to defend it; whereas in a Bulwark they are pen'd up and straightned in a narrow place, which may be cut off, and will require a fewer number of men to defend it, whereas those which are to force it, must be constrained to bring up a great many men to assault, who in an instant may be in danger of blowing up.

Gen. Your reasons (Good Captain) are not to be slighted; but as for me, I hold it safer, to batter and assault the breach of a Bulwark, than of a Curtain. For though the besieged may cut it off, and defend it with a fewer number of men, yet the Assaulters have this advantage over the Besieged defendants, that they have more place and elbow room, and may find a less resistance than in a Curtain, seeing that one may make as a great a breach in a Bulwark as in a Curtain, because your Ordnance may beat it flat, and level with the ground; and choosing rather a Bulwark: I will herewith conclude this discourse, and now shew you the figures both of the one, and of the other in this following plate.

CHAP. XXV.

Containing the demonstration of Morters, and the use of them.

YOur great and small Morters, are not only serviceable in a War offensive, by shooting and casting of great Granadoes, as of 100, 150, 170 pound weight, and smaller of 40, and 50 pound; but also by casting of Fire-balls, Stones, old Rubbidge, and Pieces of Iron, into Cities, Towns, and Fortresses; and may be used also defensively, to be shot from Towns and Forts into any Enemies works, and approaches; especially they are of singular use, when an Enemy hath covertly approached, and lodged himself under some Bulwark, Tower, or Turret, and is a beginning to undermine them; which if they do, you may plant one of these Morters at a reasonable distance, on the inside of your Wall, and shooting your Granado, as it were bolt upright into the air, by its natural fall, it may light just into the Enemies works, and there with great violence breaking among them, it will make them cry, fly, and forsake the place; you may also fire them out of a place, by casting good store of Hand Granadoes down among them, and so annoy them, that the work will be too hot for them.

Two of these Morters are represented unto you, in the Plate and Figures following number. Now for the shooting away of your great Granadoes or Fireballs, you must ever remember, but to take $\frac{1}{5}$ or $\frac{1}{7}$ parts of fine Powder of the weight of your

Granado

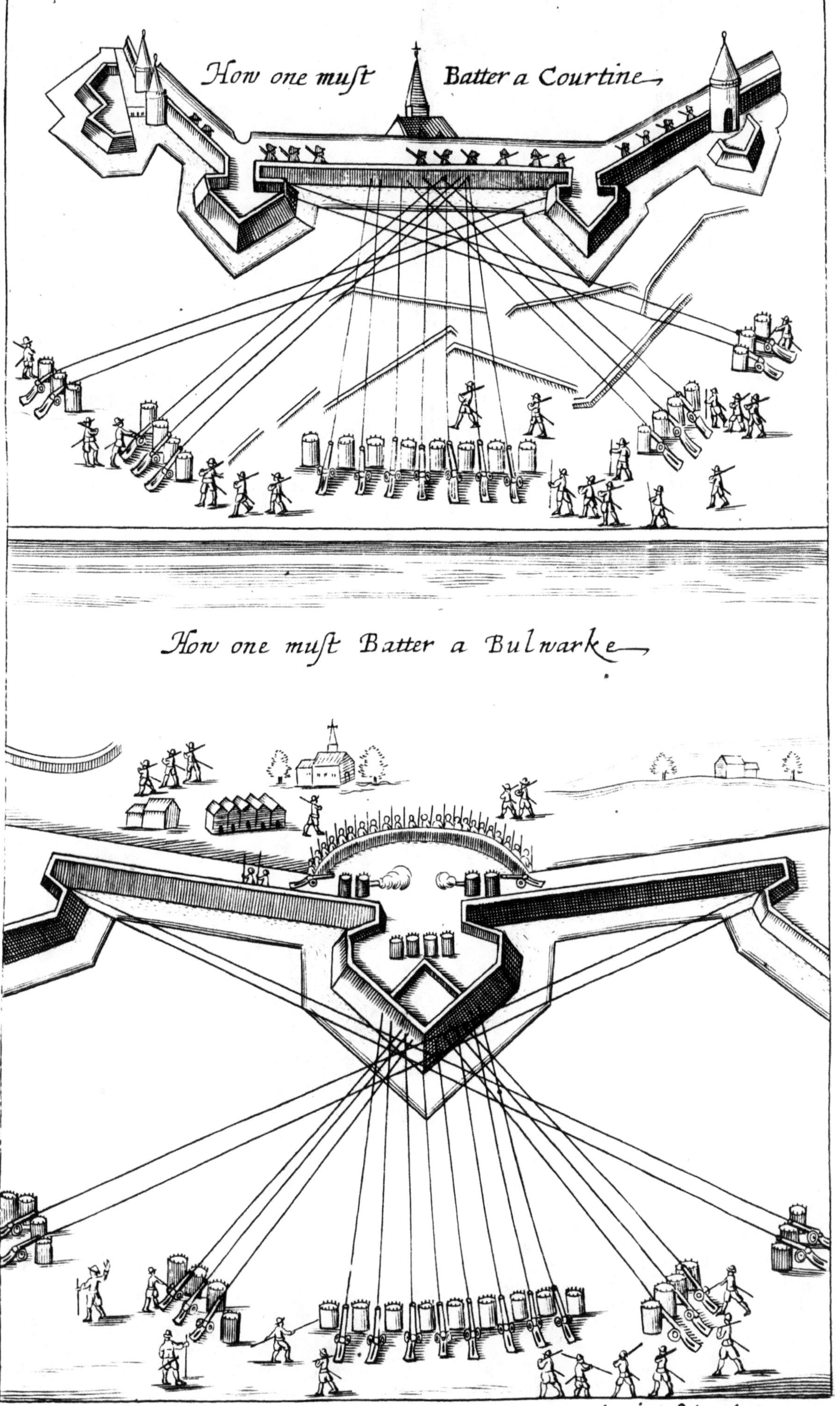
How one must Batter a Courtine
How one must Batter a Bulwarke

betwixt 86 and 87

Granado or thing which you ſhoot; but if you are to ſhoot away a Bullet without any Fire-works in it, or ſome maſſie ſtone, or ſuch like ſolid thing, then you muſt take but half the weight of it in fine Powder, which, having given fire to the Morter, will ſend it going merrily.

The uſe of them is not to ſhoot in a right line, as other Ordnance do, but in an oblique line, as you may ſee by the two Figures following, unleſs your Morter be mounted to 90 degrees, mounting them uſually above 45 degrees, namely to 60, 70, 80, and ſometimes more or leſs, as the diſtance and fall of your Granado or Shot ſhall require.

Having before ſhown you the making and uſe of the Quadrant, it remains now that I come to the charging and uſe of a Morter; now before you put in your Powder, it muſt be well ſponged and cleared, whether you charge it with looſe Powder, or Cartouch, turning the mouth almoſt bolt upright; the Powder being put into the Chamber, you muſt ſtop it with a Wadd either of Hay or Oakam, and after a Tampkin of ſome ſoft wood, and this with the Powder that was put in firſt, it muſt fill up the whole Chamber thereof, that there may be no vacuity between the Powder and the Wadd, or between the Wadd and the Shot; this done, the ſhot ſhall be put in at the mouth, with another Wadd after it; but you muſt have a care that your Morter be not much mounted, leſt your ſhot flyes out too ſoon, and the Wadd between the Tampkin and the ſhot will not only ſave the ſhot from the Tampkins breaking of it, but alſo is to avoid vacuities which may endanger the breaking of the Piece by ſecond expanſions.

Now then having reſolved of the premiſſes, touching your Piece, Shot, and Powder, as abovesaid, and upon the diſtance and mounture of your mark, as the Rules and Tables following ſhall direct you, then for the bending and diſpoſing of it to the aſſigned mark; lay firſt a ſtraight Ruler upon the Mouth of your Morter, and upon it place a Quadrant (as you may ſee by the Figures) or ſome other Inſtrument croſs-wiſe, to ſet the Morter upright, for ſhuning of wide ſhooting, and then placing them fore-right to elevate it into the reſolved degree of Mounture, to avoid ſhort or overſhooting, accordingly as the Tables following will teach you; for having made one ſhot, you may thereby proportion the reſt, conſidering whether you are to ſhoot with or againſt the wind, or whether it blows towards the right or the left hand, whether weakly or ſtrongly, and ſo accordingly to give or abate the advantage, or diſadvantage, which judgment and diſcretion will induce you thereunto, and the help of the Rules following.

Now we will come to the uſe of a Morter, and that in this example following; Suppoſe an Enemy be approached to the *Baſis*, or foot of a Wall or a Bulwark, and there is a rooting, and begins to make a Mine, and having Chambred his Powder, intends to blow it up, and that there is no other means left you, to repulſe and hinder their egreſs and regreſs into it; but by ſhooting out of your Morters ſome Granadoes, Fire-Balls, Stones, and Rubbiſh among them, or at leaſt by caſting many Hand-Granadoes down upon them. To do this either by force or policy, it behoveth a good Canonier or Fire-worker, to know firſt (as hath been taught) how far his Morter will carry a Granado, or any ſolid thing elſe, which ſhall be ſhot out of it, being ſet upon ſuch and ſuch a degree and elevation as the Morter Figure will ſhew you. As for Example, take your aim level with the mould or mouth of your Morter, noted A upon the Quadrant, and it will carry 200 paces, where you ſee the Granado falls upon the letter A; but your morter being elevated to the mark B, it then will carry its Bullet 487 paces; if to the ſecond C, then 755 paces; if to the third D, it will carry 937 paces; if to the fourth E, then 1065 paces; if to the fifth elevation F, then 1132 paces; if to the ſixth G, which is in the midſt of the Quadrant, and lyes then upon its higheſt elevation, it will carry 1170 paces, as you may ſee by the ſeveral falls of the Bullets upon every Letter. The ſecond Figure ſhews you a Morter caſting a Granado upon a Caſtle, as you may ſee by the Example.

Another Table of Diego Uffanoes for Morter Pieces, with their Randoms made for every degree, between the Level and 90 degrees, as followeth.

Deg.	Pac.	Deg.	Deg.	Pac.	Deg.	Deg.	Pac.	Deg.
0	100	89	16	392	73	31	539	58
1	122	88	17	406	72	33	543	57
2	143	87	18	419	71	34	549	56
3	364	86	19	432	70	34	552	55
4	285	85	20	445	69	35	558	54
5	204	84	21	457	68	36	562	53
6	224	83	22	468	67	37	568	52
7	243	82	23	479	66	38	573	51
8	262	81	24	490	65	39	477	50
9	280	80	25	500	64	40	580	49
10	297	79	26	510	63	41	582	48
11	314	78	27	518	62	42	583	47
12	331	77	28	524	61	43	584	46
13	347	76	29	526	60	44	582	
14	363	75	30	534	59	45	582	
15	377	74						

THE

THE Compleat Gunner

THE THIRD PART.

OF ARTIFICIAL FIREWORKS.

He number of artificial Fire-works which are practised as well in Armies upon Land in the attacquing and defence of places, as in defence of Ships at Sea, whereby warlike Executions may be performed, are many and various, according to the ingenuity of the Fire-Master: And the wayes of preparing them are so many, as it is impossible for us in this room we have allotted to prescribe all that are known. We shall therefore be contented to make choice of some of the best and principal things among so great a number, but more particularly of some most admirable inventions; and we shall give a Chapter to every kind of Fire-work, considering they differ among themselves both in fashion and effect, and every one hath its name which is particularly applyed to it. But before we begin with our composition we shall begin with the particulars, and their preparation unto this work, whereby they may be the more exalted, and have the greater efficacy. The more principal materials, that is, Peter, Charcoal and Sulphur, are mentioned at large in my first part of Gunnery, and therefore we shall proceed.

CHAP. I.

To prepare Oyl of Sulphur.

TAke a good quantity of clarified Sulphur, (the way of Clarification we have shewed before) melt it over a very gentle fire in an Earthen or Copper Vessel, then take old red Tyles that have been already used in buildings, or if you cannot find such, take new Tyles that are well baked, and that have not taken dirt, break them in pieces as small as a Bean, and throw them into melted Brimstone, then mingle your Brimstone with the remaining fragments of the Bricks, until they have drank up all the Sulphur, then let them be put into a Limbeck upon a Furnace to distil, and after the Oyl is drawn according to a Chymical order it will be very excellent, and above all, have a very combustible quality, proper to the Compositions of artificial fires.

To prepare Oyl or Balsam of Sulphur.

Fill a long body of Glass full of Sulphur well powdered, then pour upon it Oyl of Turpentine, or Oyl of nuts, or Juniper, in such a quantity that the oyl with the Sulphur may fill but the half part, place it in an Iron Kettle, with Sand round about it, and a small heat for 8 or 9 hours, and you will see that the Oyl of Turpentine will convert the Brimstone into a red Oyl, as fiery and combustible as before.

There are those that take the following matter to the preparing the oyl of Sulphur, to the end it may be rendered more combustible, *viz.* Sulphur 1 *l.* of quick Lyme half a pound, of Sal-armoniac 4 ounces.

Above all this, the Chymists know how to prepare a certain oyl of Sulphur, (which they call a Balsam) of which the virtues are so admirable, that they admit not any body, either living or dead, to be touched with putrifaction, but will conserve it in so perfect and entire state, that neither the pernicious Influences of the celestial bodies, nor that corruption which the Elements produce, nor that which reduces things into their Principles, can any way damnifie it, if anoynted with it. There is also from it prepared a certain fire (as *Tritemius* teacheth) with flowers of *Sulphur*, *Borax* and *Brandy-wine*, which will remain many years without extinguishing of it self. Others that are knowing, do attest that a Lamp may be filled with such like Oyl, from whence all that are within the Light of it, will appear as if they had no heads.

There is another way of making Oyl of Sulphur which is very admirable and excellent, which is prepared thus. Incorporate well together an equal proportion of Sulphur and Salt-Peter, reduce them into most subtile Powder, and pass it through a fine sieve, then put them into an Earthen Pot that hath never been used, and pour upon them Vinegar made of *White-wine* or *Aqua-vitæ*, as much as will cover the Powder; Close the Pot in such manner that no air may any wise enter, and put it thus in any hot place so long time until all the vinegar be digested and vanished. Lastly, take that matter which rests in the Pot, and draw from thence an oyl, by Chymical Instruments proper to this work.

CHAP. II.

The preparation of the Flowers of Benjamin.

TAke Benjamin a certain quantity of ounces, put it into a Gourd or a Limbeck glaſs, and cloſe it well with a blind head (as they call it) then have in readineſs an earthen veſſel, ſet it upon a Tresfoot, or for the more certainty upon a ſmall Furnace, place it in your glaſs body, and compaſs it well about with fine Sand or aſhes ſo high as the matter is in the glaſs; after make a moderate fire under it, for fear the Limbeck heat too ſoon, and be too hot, for that will make the flowers become citrine or yellow, when they ought to be as white as Snow. Obſerve when you ſee the flowers begin to raiſe a vapour or ſmall fume, continue your fire in that ſame degree the ſpace of one quarter of an hour; after you ſhall ſee the flowers riſen unto the internal Superficies of the blind head, then take it away carefully, and put to it another that ſhall be quite cold, and put that which you have taken off upon a white paper until it be cold, then gently with a Feather or wooden Spatula, cauſe the flowers to come forth of the blind head, and gather them together carefully: thus you may add a third or fourth blind head, and in time many, until all the Benjamin ceaſe to fume.

Benjamin may be made into flowers another way, thus; put into a glazed pot a certain quantity of ounces of Benjamin, and place it upon warm aſhes, and when you ſee it begin to fume, cover the veſſel with a Cornet of paper made in the form of a Cone, and a little larger than the orifice of the pot, leave it there about one quarter of an hour, after take off the Cornet, and take the flowers and gather them together; then put upon the veſſel another Cornet of paper, and let it ſtand as long as before; take it off, and gather the flowers to the former, and continue thus putting Cornet after Cornet, until your flowers be entirely evaporated.

CHAP. III.

The preparation of Camphire.

TAke Juniper Gumm (which is called ſomtimes) Sandarach, white varniſh, or Maſtick moſt ſubtilly powdered 2 *l.* white diſtilled vinegar as much as is neceſſary to cover the Gumm in a glaſs, ſet it deep in horſe-dung the ſpace of 20 days; then take it and pour it forth into another glaſs Veſſel with a wide mouth, and let it ſtand thus in digeſtion a whole moneth, and in it you ſhall have Camphire congealed in form of a Cruſt of bread, and which hath in ſome meaſure the reſemblance of the veritable or true Camphire. The Camphire hath ſuch a love for the fire, that being once lighted, it goeth not out until it be quite conſumed. The flame that comes from thence is very clear, and of a very agreeable odour; after it hath remained ſuſpended in the air ſome time it vaniſheth inſenſibly. The cauſe that produceth all theſe rare effects from Camphire, is by reaſon its parts are extream ſubtil and airy.

I do add to all this, that it may be eaſie to reduce Camphire into Powder, to make it uſeful in artificial fireworks, if a man crumbles it and beats it gently, rouling it with Sulphur. The oyl of Camphire, which ſerves alſo for the ſame effect, is made by adding a little of oyl of ſweet Almonds, and ſtir them well together in a braſs Morter, and peſtle of the ſame metal, until all be converted into oyl of a greeniſh colour.

Or a man may put it into a Glaſs Viol which muſt be cloſe ſtopped, provided alſo that the Camphire be true and natural, and not a Cheat; then put that Glaſs into a warm Furnace, and draw it out, when you ſhall ſee all the Camphire turned into a pure clear oyl, which will burn with an admirable vivacity.

CHAP. IV.

Water of Sal-armoniac.

TAke Sal-armoniac 3 ounces, Salt-Peter 1 ounce, reduce them into a moſt ſubtil Powder, and mix them well together, after put them into a Limbeck, and then pouring on them ſome of the beſt and ſtrongeſt Vinegar, you may diſtil the ſame into a water with a ſmall fire.

CHAP. V.

Of a certain artificial Water which will burn upon the Palm of your hand without doing any harm.

TAke *Oleum Petroli*, and of *Terebinthi*, and of *Calx vive*, of Mutton fat, and of Hogs Lard, of each equal parts, beat them well together, until they be well incorporated, then cauſe them to be diſtilled in warm aſhes, or upon burning coals, and you ſhall draw from thence an excellent oyl.

CHAP. VI.

To prepare Fire-Spunges.

TAke of the oldeſt and greateſt Toad-ſtools which grows at the Root of Aſh, Oak, Birch, and Fir-tree, with many other Trees which produce them freely; get a good parcel, ſtring them, and hang them in the Chimney, and leave them to macerate; being well mortified and macerated, take and cut them in pieces, and then beat them with a wooden Mallet; this done, boyl them over a ſmall fire in a ſtrong Lye, and a ſufficient quantity of Salt-Peter, until all the humidity be evaporated: At laſt, having put them upon a Plank or even board, put them in a warm Oven, and let them well dry there; having drawn them from thence, you muſt beat them with a wooden Mallet as before, until it become wholly ſubtile and ſoft; being thus prepared, you muſt keep them in a commodious place to ſerve you upon occaſion.

CHAP.

CHAP. VII.

How to prepare Match or Tow for Artificial Fires.

MAke Cords of Tow, Hemp, or Cotton, which you pleaſe, of two or three twiſts,not made too hard,put them in a new Earthen pot Verniſhed, pour upon them Vinegar made of good white Wine four parts, of Urine two parts, of *Aqua vitæ* one part, of Salt Peter purified one part, of Cannon Powder reduced to Meal one part: Make all theſe Ingredients boyl together upon a great Fire, to the Conſumption of all the Liquor; then ſpread upon a great ſmooth Plank or Board, the Meal or Flower of the moſt excellenteſt Powder that you can get. Having drawn your Match out of the Pot, roul them in the Powder, and then dry them in the ſhade or Sun, for it matters not which, and the Cords or Match that are thus prepared will burn very quick.

Francis Jouchim Prechtelin, in his ſecond part of his Fire-works *Chap.* 2. deſcribes a certain Match, which is extream ſlow in burning, and is thus made; take Maſtich two parts, Colophonia one part, Wax one part, Salt-Peter two parts, Charcoal half a part, then, having melted all and mixed them well upon the fire, take a Match made of Hemp or Flax of a ſufficient bigneſs, and draw it through this Compoſition, making it go down to the bottom of the Veſſel, drawing it often through, until it hath gotten the bigneſs of a Candle, and when you deſire to uſe it, light it firſt, and when it is well lighted blow it out, and there remains none but a burning Coal.

CHAP. VIII.

Of certain Antidotes excellent and approved againſt the burning of Gun-powder, Sulphur, hot Iron, melted Lead, and other like accidents, drawn from the particular Experiments of Cozimu Nowicz.

SECTION. I.

BOyle Hogs greaſe in common water, over a moſt gentle fire, the ſpace of ſome time; then take it from the Fire, and let it cool, and after expoſe it to the fair and clear weather three or four nights; after having put it into an Earthen pot, melt it again upon a ſmall fire, and being melted, ſtrain it through a Cloath into cold water, after waſh it many times with good clean and freſh water, until it come as white as ſnow; this done, put it into a glazed pot to ſerve you at your occaſions. The uſe is thus, you muſt annoint the burnt part as ſoon as you can, and you will ſee a quick and admirable effect.

SECT. II.

Take Plaintain water, Oyl of Nuts of *Italy*, of each as much as you please.

SECT. III.

Take Mallows water, Rose water, Plume Allum, of each as much as is necessary, and mix them well together with the white of an Egg.

SECT. IV.

Take a *Lixivium*, made of *Calx Vive* and common water, add to it a little Oyl of Hempseed, Oyl Olive, and some whites of Eggs, mingle all well together, and annoint the burnt place with this Composition. All these Oyntments cure burnings without causing any pain. These I have often experimented upon my self.

Some Receipts from divers Authors.

Take Oyl of Olives, Oyl of sweet Almonds, Liquid Vernish, each one part, juice of Onions two parts, with these chafe the part affected.

If there be already blisters raised and Ulcerations in the parts, this following Oyntment is most excellent.

Boyle a great quantity of the second Rind of Elder tree, in Oyl of Olive, then pour it through a Linnen cloath; add to it a little after two parts of Cerus or burnt Lead, of Lytharge of Gold, of each one part, put them into a Leaden Morter, and then stir them about and mix them so, that they become in the form of a Linament.

Take melted Lard, pour it into two Ounces of Morrel water, and one Ounce of Oyle of Saturn, then mingle them well together: this Remedy is soveraign.

Take the Mucilage of the Roots of Henbane, and of the Flowers of Poppies, of each one Ounce, Salt Peter one Ounce, mingle them all with Oyl of Camphire, and make a Linament according to Art.

Or take the juyce of Oynions rosted in embers two Ounces, Nut Oyle one Ounce, mingle them all well together.

Or take of the Leaves of Ivy two m. or handfuls well beaten up with Plantain water, Oyl Olive one pound, make all boyl with four Ounces of good white Wine, until the Consumption of the whole Wine, at the end of the decoction add Wax as much as is necessary, to give him the form and consistency of a Linament.

Again, take old Lard, let it be melted over the flame, and poured into two Ounces of the juyce of Beets and Rue, of the Cream of Milk one Ounce, Mucilage of Quince-seeds and Gum Tracanth, of each an Ounce and a half, mix them well together, and make thereof a Linament. This remedy is none of the worst, we took it from *Joseph Quercetanus, in libro Sclopetrio.*

CHAP.

CHAP. IX.

Of Hand Granadoes.

THe Hand Granadoes respecting their form, are Globically or perfectly round and hollow in their interior part in manner of a Sphere; they are called Hand Granadoes, or Handy Granadoes, because they may be grasped in the hand, and thrown to the Enemies; and if we should dwell upon the denominations of the Latine, we may call them as they do, *Granades Palmares*, they are commonly of the bigness of a Bullet of Iron of 5, 6, and 8 *l.* they weigh sometimes 1 *l.* and sometimes one pound and a half, some are of two pounds, and others of three pounds; there is given to these sort of Globes the names of *Granadoes*, by reason of the great resemblance they have with the Fruit *Punique*, which we call *Pom-granad*; for as these do shut up in their rinds a great quantity of grains; so our Military Globes are filled with a number of Grains of Powder, almost innumerable, the which having received the Fire, do break into a thousand and a thousand shivers, leaping against the Enemy, and piercing if it could all such things as it meets opposing its violence. They are generally made of Iron or Copper, carrying in its Diameter about three Ounces, being about the length of a Barly Corn in thickness of Metal; they are filled commonly with Gun-Powder, and sometimes of other Compositions, there is added to its Orifice a small Pipe commonly called a Fuse, which is filled with a matter or Composition that is slack or slow in burning, but nevertheless very susceptible of the Fire, and capable to hold fire some time, for fear that it should break in the hands of those that mannage it, and intend to throw it.

There is amongst Fire-Masters accounted three sorts of Hand Granadoes, the first and most common are made of Iron; others are made of Brass, allayed with other Metals in the melting; the third sort is of Glass.

If you cause them to be made of Iron, take such as is most fragile, and as little wrought as possible you can get; if you will cast them of Copper, you must allay six pound of Copper, with two pounds of Tyn, and half a pound of Marcasite, or you may put one part of Tyn with three parts of Lattin or of *Auricalque*. Those that are made of Iron are in thickness about the ninth part of the Diameter; those that are made of Brass must have one tenth part of the Diameter in thickness of Metal. Lastly, such which you cause to be made of Glass, must have one seventh part of their Diameter in their thickness.

The largeness of the Orifice in which you must put in your Fuse made of Wood, whose upper part must be about $\frac{2}{9}$ the Diameter of the Granado, and the small hole in the Fuse should have the largeness of $\frac{1}{18}$ of the same Diameter, the rest of the capacity of the Shell must be filled with well grain'd Powder, the length of the Fuse must be about $\frac{2}{3}$ of the Diameter, and the top must be broad, and a little rounding like a Hemisphere, the hollow and inner part of the Fuse must be about $\frac{1}{9}$ Diameter at the small or inner end, and $\frac{1}{6}$ at the outer end: Men do generally fill the void place with Powder ground most subtilly, which must be moistned with Gum-water, or dissolved glue, that it may joyn the better. As for the Fuses, they must be filled or charged with one of the Compositions hereunder written; afterward you must fasten it well and close with Tow or Okham, and the Pyrotechnian Lute which the *Germans* call *Kit*, which is made of four parts of Ship Pitch, two parts of Colophonia, one part of Terebinthe, and one part of Wax; you must put all these Ingredients in a glazed Vessel, and melt them upon a small fire, then mix and mingle them well together.

Compositions for Charging the Fuses of the Hand Granadoes.

Powder	1 l.	*Salt-Peter*	1 l.	*Sulphur*	1 l.
Powder	3 l.	*Salt-Peter*	2 l.	*Sulphur*	1 l.
Powder	4 l.	*Salt-Peter*	3 l.	*Sulphur*	2 l.
Powder	4 l.	*Salt-Peter*	3 l.	*Sulphur*	1 l.

Another sort of Granadoes.

I shall here represent you with a Hand Granado, which may be hid at the entring of a passage, or any such place where we suppose the Enemy must come: This Granado hath two holes opposite, passing just cross the Diameter, in which must be fastned a Fuse of Wood or Metal with holes in several places, and all about it within let there be beaten Powder, and through it you must pass a common match, lighted at one end, and at top let there be a third hole, by which it must be charged with a good grain'd Powder, which must be close stopt again with a Tampion, and then is your Granado prepared. I suppose it not necessary to say much of the use of this Granado, and since it is so easie to be understood by what we have said, and that the occasion you will have of such things will forge your Inventions enough to put them in practice.

CHAP. X.

How and where a man ought to heave Hand-Granadoes.

ACcording to the definition which we have given of them, it is most evident, and I suppose no body will doubt, that they are to be taken in the hand, and that we must grasp them to throw them at the Enemy. It is said before that this kind of Arms is as well defensive as offensive; therefore we shall not rest upon the proof of these things; those that have been at the managing of them must instruct them that are ignorant.

We shall say only this, that the Places where these Hand Granadoes are used at Sea, are where Ships are Board and Board to clear the Enemies Decks, so that the way may be cleared there. Upon Land Service they are used immediately after the good and happy success of a Mine which hath made a great overture in a Rampire, overthrowing one part of the Wall, Bulwark, or Bastion, to give place to the Assailants, to do their endeavour to get into the breach; it is there that the Besieged as well as Besiegers may make use of these Hand Granadoes; 'tis there where you shall see the more generous of both sides armed with Fire and Flames, defending valiantly the quarrel of their Prince, the interest of their Party, their Liberties and their Lives. They are imployed also upon other occasions, to wit, when the Besiegers are come up to the Walls of the Rampire, and so well placed, that making winding Stairs in the thickness of the Platform, they mount insensibly by retact; so that the Besieged cannot any way hinder by the defence of their Flanks, nor be kept safe by the Rampires themselves. Upon these occasions I say, the Besieged ought to pour down a quantity a quantity of Hand Granadoes from aloft, or from the top of the Walls, upon their under-miners.

And ſometimes they are alſo thrown at a diſtance greater than ordinary, according to the occaſion; but when this cannot be done by the natural ſtrength of a Soldier, without the aid of ſome artificial Inſtrument, the Maſters in this Art have invented certain ſmall Engines, made like unto one of our Ducking-Stools, with a Rope at one end to pluck it down by force, and at the other end a hollow place to lay the Balls in that are to be thrown, and with this Engine well contrived, one may throw upon the Enemy, not only Hand Granadoes; but alſo a quantity of other Artificial Military Fires, as gliſtring or ſhining Globes, Bombards, Fire-pots, and many other ſuch like things, of which we ſhall ſpeak in their place, may be thrown at a greater diſtance than is poſſible by the hand only.

This Inſtrument is not very difficult to make, it may eaſily be comprehended by what we have ſaid. I ſhall only advertiſe you of one thing, that the longer the arm of the Engine is on that ſide that is to hold the Granadoes, more than the other part to which the Rope is faſtned, the greater force the Engine will have; but you muſt underſtand this meaſure to be made from Axes or Iron Rolls, upon which the Arm moves.

CHAP. XI.

Of gliſtring or bright ſhining Fire-balls.

DIſſolve upon the fire in a Braſs or Earthen Veſſel an equal portion of Sulphur, black Pitch, Rozin, and Turpentine; then take a Ball of Stone or Iron, that the Diameter be far leſs than the Diameter of a Cannon, or Morter Piece, for which you intend this Globe; plunge this Shot in this melted matter until it be all over cover'd with the matter about its exterior part, draw it from thence, and role it gently in Corn Powder, that done, cover it all over with a Cotton Cloath; then plunge it again in your Compoſition, and reiterate the rolling it in Powder, as before, then cover it a ſecond time with another Cotton Cloath; and thus continue dipping your Bullet, and wrapping it about with Cloath, until your Shot has acquired a juſt bigneſs, exactly to fill the Orifice of the Engine, remembring that the laſt Coat of the Shot muſt be of Corn'd Powder: Being then thus prepared, it muſt be put into the Cannon or Morter Piece naked, without any other thing compaſſing it, immediately upon the Powder in the Chamber, which muſt make the Bullet come forth; Then give fire freely to your Piece, to throw the ſhot where you intend it.

CHAP. XII.

Of Balls which Cast forth so great a smoak, that they blind whomsoever they come near.

IT is accustomed to do great execution by favour of the night, in occurrences of War, as well as in many other occasions: I mean not here to speak of the darkness of the night, for that is naturally effected by the first Causer of all things, from the order that he hath established amongst the Beings; but I intend only here to treat of the darkness that is made Artificially, and particularly such as may be produced and made to last a little time in a close or narrow place, according to the Rules of our Art, to be made for the blinding of the Enemy, which would force into our beings, and would attaque us by main strength, in a design to take away our Lives, Honour, and Goods; or when we have a design to facilitate the passage for the Assailants, in confounding or oppressing the Besieged in their Forts, with a cloudy and thick fume, in such a sort that one may take them as amazed Fish in troubled waters. For this purpose are Globes prepared, which whil'st they are on fire, produce a smoak so vehement and unpleasant, and in so great aboundance, that 'tis impossible to withstand the incommodity without bursting asunder; see here the Method. Take Ship Pitch in the Stone 4 *l.* Liquid Pitch 2 *l.* Colophonia 6 *l.* Sulphur 8 *l.* Salt-Peter 36 *l.* melt all these Drugs upon burning Coals in any vessel whatsoever, adding after 10 *l.* of Coal of Sawdust made of the Pine or Firr-Tree 6 *l.* Crude Antimony 2 *l.* incorporate and mix them very well together; then put into this melted matter Tow, Hemp, and Linnen Cloaths a great quantity, and boyl them well in this Composition, and when they have drank up all the matter, then form them into Balls of such a bigness as you please, so that it may be cast with the hand, or with the Engine mentioned in the last Chapter, according as you shall find most convenient. And this is our true way to make Night at Noon-day, to obscure the Sun it self, and to blind the Eyes of the Enemies for some time. And this is the most lawful way that one may follow, because it shews its original from natural things, and we may believe that it is alwayes sufficient justice, so that the Wars where such things are practised, be not unjustly enterprized.

CHAP. XIII.

Stink Balls.

STinking Globes are made to annoy the Enemy by their stinking vapours and fumes disagreeable to Nature; nay so unsufferable to the Nose, and to the Brain it self, by its most violent stink, that by no means it can be endured. The preparation is as followeth, Take of Powder 10 *l.* of Ship Pitch 6 *l.* of Tar 20 *l.* Salt-Peter 8 *l.* Sulphur Colophonia 4 *l.* make all these Ingredients melt at the fire by a small heat, in an Earthen or Copper vessel, and all being well melted, throw into the melted matters 2 *l.* of Coal dust, of the cuttings or filings of Horses Hoofs 6 *l.* *Assafœtida* 3 *l.* *Sagapenum* 1 *l.* *Spatula fœtida* half a pound: Mingle and incorporate them well together; then

then put into this matter Linnen or Woolen Cloath, or Hemp or Tow, so much as will drink up all the matter, and of these you may make Globes or Balls of what bigness pleaseth your self best, according to the method and order as we have heretofore prescribed.

The Globes or Balls may be made Venomous or Poysonous, if to their Composition be added these things following, *viz.* Mercury sublimate, Arsenick, Orpiment, Cinaber, to which may also be added many other Poysonous matters, which I shall forbear to mention, considering every one by Nature is apt enough to learn to do that which is mischievous.

CHAP. XIV.

Of the Shooting of Shot made red hot in the Fire.

IT is a practice that hath been practised in former times to shoot red hot Fire-balls, and was counted of great defence, as you may find amongst many other things in the Works of *Diodorus Siculus*, where he sayes, *Tyrios immisse in Alexandri Magni machinamenta massas magnas ferreas candentes*: Out of many Authors may be proved the customary use in former times of Shooting red hot Pieces of Iron, which we shall not dwell upon, but come to the Practice. First, you must Charge the Piece of Ordnance according to the customary manner, his due proportion of Powder, upon this Powder you must put a Wooden Cylender or Fidd, of a just and equal wideness with the bore of the Piece, which must be driven very stiff home to the Powder, and for your better security, you must put upon this another wad made of Straw, Hay, or of Oakam, or Tow; this being done, let the Piece be laid a little under Metal, and then cleanse the vacant place or hollow of the Piece with a Spunge, so that all the Grains of Powder that are there, may be taken away. This being done, lay your Piece to bear with the place you intend to shoot at, according to the method we have given in the second Part of Gunnery, and let your Piece thus remain until you have put in your red hot Bullet: your Bullet must be sure to be exactly round, and not so high, but that it may run freely down in the Piece to the wad, the Shot being red hot, take it out of the fire with a pair of Tongs made for that purpose, and put it into the Piece, and give an attentive Ear, for as soon as the Shot is supposed to be up to the Wad, give immediately Fire to your Piece of Ordnance.

There are others which put into their Pieces Boxes made of Plate, of Iron or Copper. Others do put into their Pieces Potters Clay, and upon them the fiery Bullet, which with a quick hand they thrust home with a Rammer, which ought to be defended from fire by lining the Rammer head with Copper. But these are more perillous; and therefore we account that method above to be the best, and most free from danger.

CHAP. XV.

To Arm Pikes to defend a Ship or any other place.

TO arm Pikes, to defend a ſhip, or breach, or to enter the ſame, or to ſtick in the ſides of a ſhip, or other place, take ſtrong Canvas, and cut it in length about a foot, or 14 inches, and ſix inches high in the Center, and let the ends be both cut taper-wiſe, then faſten the Canvas at both ends with ſtrong twine, and fill it with this receipt.

Powder bruiſed 8 parts, Peter in Roch 1 part, Peter in meal 1 part, Sulphur in meal two parts, Rozen Roch three parts, Turpentine 1 part, Verdigreaſe $\frac{1}{2}$ part, Bole-armonick $\frac{1}{3}$ part, Bay ſalt $\frac{1}{3}$ part, *Colophonia* $\frac{1}{6}$ part, Arſnick $\frac{1}{8}$ part, mix them very well together, and try them in the top of a Braſs Candleſtick, when the fire doth burn furiouſly with a blew and greeniſh colour, then fill the Canvas, and roul it over, being firſt armed with ſtrong twine all over, with this liquid mixture molten in a pan, Pitch four parts, Linſeed Oyl 1 part, Turpentine $\frac{1}{3}$ part, Sulphur 1 part, Tarr $\frac{1}{3}$ part, Tallow one part; and as ſoon as this is cold, bore two holes in each of the ſame next the Iron an inch deep, with a ſharp Iron Bodkin, filling the ſame with fine bruiſed powder, and putting in every hole a little ſtick of two inches long, which are to be taken out when you would fire the ſame; this compoſition will burn furiouſly.

And remember you cut off the ſtaff ſome three inches from the work, and put thereon a braſs ſocket of five or ſix inches long, and then cut the end of your ſtaff to fill the ſocket, for when you fire your work, you may ſtick it in the ſide of a ſhip, and pull the ſtaff out again, ſo will not the work be ſo eaſily avoided, as when the ſtaff was on, and hangs at length, becauſe the very weight of the ſtaff, and length thereof, will be a means to weigh down the work, or that the enemie may come, and thereby pull it out, or beat it off quickly; let the Compoſition and work contain in weight about 7 pounds, then will it do execution, and work a better effect, than if it were of leſs weight, by much, by reaſon the compoſition elſe would be waſted, before it comes to effect its Execution.

To burn the ſayls of Ships a pretty diſtance, or to fire Thatch'd houſes, Corn-ſtacks, or any other combuſtible matter apt to burn, when you cannot come to the ſame; it is good to have certain ſtrong Croſs-bows to bend with Racks or Gaffels, and ſo ſhoot Arrows armed at the heads with Wild-fire, made of the compoſition as above, and about three inches in length, and one inch and a half in the Diameter, tapred as afore in all points: or you may have long bows, but then let your Arrows be alſo longer, which for divers ſervices may do great good.

CHAP. XVI.

To charge Trunks with Balls of Wild-fire.

TO charge Trunks to ſhoot little Balls of wild-fire, either to offend or defend, you muſt firſt charge him with two inches of good Powder, and then with a Ball of wild-fire a little lower than the concave of the Trunk, let the Ball be bored through croſs-ways, and primed full of fine powder. Laſtly, with ſlow receipt, then with powder, then with a Ball again as aforeſaid, until you have filled the ſame within $\frac{1}{4}$ of an inch of the mouth, which would be filled up with fine powder and receipt mixed together. Some do uſe to have at the mouth two Iron ſtirts to ſtick them in the ſide of any thing, or or to defend ones self from the Enemy from taking it off with a thrust while they do Execution.

To make the Ball.

The Ball of Wild-fire must be thus made, Take untwisted Match, Tow, and Hemp, the which would be moistned in *Aqua-vitæ*, or boyled in Salt-Peter water: then take of bruised Powder six parts, of Salt-Peter one part, of Brimstone finely beaten one part, of coal made of light wood moistned with a little Linseed-oyl and Turpentine wrought together, one part: then lay the Tow or Oakam, abroad in thickness of the back of a knife, and as broad as a great Oyster-shel, put into the same as much as you can grasp together in your fist, and tying the same hard with a pack-thread, coat it over with molten Brimstone, and when you would use the same, bore it through with a Bodkin, and fill the holes full of fine powder bruised.

To make Bullets of Wild-fire to shoot out of a Trunk, which will be as hard as a Stone.

Take Sulphur in meal six parts, of Rozen in meal six parts, melting the same in some Pot over a slow fire: then take stone pitch one part, of hard wax one part, of Tarr $\frac{1}{4}$ part, of *Aquavitæ* $\frac{1}{2}$ part, of Linseed Oyl $\frac{1}{2}$ part, of Verdigrease $\frac{1}{4}$ part, of Camphire $\frac{1}{8}$ part, melting all these together. Likewise stir into the same of Peter in meal two parts, and taking it from the fire, put therein four parts of bruised powder, working the same well together in your hands, and roul it round of the bigness you mean to make your balls of, boring two holes through the same cross-ways, which must be primed with bruised powder. These balls being cold, will grow very hard, and fired will burn furiously.

To make Hedg-hogs.

To make Hedg-hogs, or balls, you must fill them with the same receipts you do your Arrows, and Pikes, and let them be five inches in the Diameter, and well armed with twine before you coat them, and after boared two holes, and primed with fine powder: then put in two sticks, and using them, pull them out again, and at the said holes fire them. The spikes end of Iron must be like Deaths Arrow heads, five or six stirts a piece to hang in the sayls, or stick in or upon any place assigned; and remember in the arming, to leave a noose to throw him being fired, out of your hand.

To make Powder-pots.

They are made of black Potters clay, or thick glass, round Bottles with ears to tye matches, lighted at both ends, the pots or glasses are to be filled with dry fine powder, and thrown upon the decks, or other where, which will much prejudice the Enemy, and many times fire their own Powder-chests.

ARTIFICIAL FIRE-WORKS FOR RECREATION.

AMongst all Artificial fires that have been put in practice many years, the *Fuzees* (which the Latins call *Rocheta*, and the Greeks *Pyroboli*) have always had the first Rank; (nevertheless this Greek word doth not well agree with the Etymologie of the word *Rocheta*) seeing that κυρoβολ signifies properly *Tela ignita*, that is, burning darts or Arrows, the Italians call them *Rocheta* and *Raggi*, the Germans *Steigen de Kasten*, *Ragetten*, and *Drachetten*, the Poles *Race*, the French *Fuzees*, the English *Rockets*, or *Serpents*. If we consider the invention of them, it hath been of so ancient standing, that the construction is now very common and familiar amongst all the *Pyrobolists* and Fire-masters; the which, although it appears very easie in it self, yet there is in it labour, and requires that he that applyes himself to this work should not be careless, but on the contrary take all the care and diligence that possibly he can have for the preparing of such perilous things, considering likewise the expences and losses are irreparable after the experiment made; and seeing that nothing can be put in practice in publick Recreations without these *Fuzees*, therefore I think I am something obliged here to shew the true way of preparing them, with their particular use.

CHAP. I.

How to make Rockets.

I Intend not here to write the Construction of Moulds fit for this purpose, but rather leave the more curious Students herein to the works of *Casimier Siemienowicz*, Lieutenant General of the Artillery in the Kingdome of *Polonia*, in his great Art of Artillery written in the French Tongue and Printed at *Amsterdam*, and also in our Countrey-men Mr. *Bate* and Mr. *Babington* &c. That which I intend to do, is to teach you how they may be made by hand, or by help only of a Rouler to Roul the Paper upon; let it be turned to the thickness you intend, only let the Rouler be 8 times the Diameter in length. If it be three quarters of an inch in thickness, the length will be three inches. Roul your Paper hard on the Rouler until the thickness be one inch and a quarter Rouler and all; then glue the uppermost paper, and the Case is made. On the choaking or contracting the paper together at one end, within one Diameter of the end, except only a little hole, about one quarter the Diameter of the bore thereof, to contract these Cases on this manner, do thus, wet the end about one inch in water, then put the Rouler in again, and tye a great packthread about the wet within three quarters of an inch of the end, put another thing almost of the same Diameter with the Rouler in at the wet end about half an inch, hold it there, get some other

other body to draw the packthread together, you holding the Rouler and Rammer, one put down to the end within one inch, and the Rammer which must be little less than the Diameter to meet with that end within half an inch, in which the contract or choaking must be; the packthread having drawn it together, tye it fast on that place, take out the Former, let it dry, and it is done; when the hole is contracted together, make it so wide as is before taught, with a round bodkin, which you must provide for that purpose.

CHAP. II.

How to make Compositions for Rockets of any size.

THese ways which I will teach you I take them not upon trust out of every Author, but such as are men of known experience, as that *Casimier* before spoken of, and others of the like repute. And first, for Rockets of 1 ounce, you must use only Cannon-powder dust being beaten in a Morter, and finely sifted, and this will rise swift, and will make a great noise, but carries no tayl: Those of most beauty in their operation are made of 1 ounce of Charcoal-dust, eight ounces of Powder, this Composition will hold for Rockets of one, two, or three ounces; but for those of four, take three ounces of Charcoal-dust, to one pound of Cannon-powder dust, continuing that Rule until you come to Rockets of ten ounces, and from thence to Rockets of a pound; for there used to be one pound of Powder-dust to 4 ounces of Charcoal-dust. But for better satisfaction observe these Rules.

For Rockets of one pound.

Take Powder 18 *l.* Salt-Peter 8 *l.* Charcoal 4 *l.* Sulphur 2 *l.*

For Rockets of two or three pound.

Take of Salt-Peter 60 *l.* Coal 15 *l.* Sulphur 2 *l.*

For Rockets of four or five pound.

Take of Salt-Peter 64 *l.* Coal 16 *l.* Sulphur 8 *l.*

For Rockets of six seven or eight pound.

Salt-Peter 35 *l.* Coal 10 *l.* Sulphur 5 *l.*

For Rockets of nine or ten pound.

Salt-Peter 62 *l.* Coal 20 *l.* Sulphur 9 *l.*

For Rockets from eleven to fifteen pound.

Salt-Peter 32 *l.* Sulphur 8 *l.* Coal 16 *l.*

For Rockets from sixteen to twenty pound.

Salt-Peter 42 l. Coal 26 *l.* Sulphur 12 *l.*

For Rockets from thirty to fifty pound.

Salt-Peter 30 *l.* Coal 18 *l.* Sulphur 7 *l.*

For Rockets from sixty to a hundred pound.

Take Peter 30 *l.* Sulphur 10 l. Coal 10 *l.*

CHAP. III.

To fill the Rockets with this Composition.

PLace the mouth downwards where it was choaked, and with a knife put in so much as you can of the receits provided for that size at one time; then put down your Rammer, which must be longer and narrower than the Former or Rouler upon which you made the Cases, and with a hammer of a pound weight, give three or four indifferent knocks,. then put in more composition with your knife, until it be full, at every time knocking the like as before with the Rammer, until the composition come within one diameter of the bore of the top, there put down a peece of pastboard, and knock it in hard, prick three or four little holes therein, then put fine pistol powder in almost to the top, and upon that another cap of paper, upon which put a peece of leather, that it may be tyed on the top of the Rocket, and fast glued on, then get a streight twig, and bind it upon the Rocket with strong packthred; it must be no heavier, than being put upon your finger, two or three fingers breadths from the mouth of the same, it may just ballast the Rocket; then it is prepared for use.

CHAP. IV.

How to give fire to one or more Rockets.

SEt your Rockets mouth upon the edge of any peece of timber, battlement of a wall, top of the Gunners carriage wheel, or any dry place whatsoever, where the rod or twig may hang perpendicular from it, then lay a train of powder that may come under the mouth thereof, give fire thereunto, and you have done. But if you would fire more Rockets than one, that as one descendeth, the other may ascend by degrees, make this composition following of *Roch peter* 8 ounces, *Quick Brimstone* 4 ounces, and fine Powder dust 2 ounces, which lay in a line from one Rocket to another, they being placed ten inches or a foot one from another, give fire to this composition, and it will work your desire, by causing one to mount into the air when the other is spent; but before you place your Rockets, remember to prick them with the bodkin.

CHAP.

CHAP. V.

Divers and sundry Compositions for Stars.

A Composition for Stars of a blew colour mixed with red.

TAke of *Powder mealed* 8 ounces, *Salt-Peter* 4 ounces, *Quick Brimstone* 12 ounces, Meal all these very fine, and mix them together with two ounces of *Aqua-vitæ*, and half an ounce of Oyl of *Spike*, which let be very dry before you use it.

Another Composition which maketh a white and beautiful fire.

Take *Powder* 8 ounces, *Salt-Peter* 24 ounces, *Quick Brimstone* 12 ounces, *Camphire* 1 ounce, Meal these Ingredients and incorporate them: Now to meal your *Camphire*, take a brass pestle and morter, wet the end of the pestle in a little of the Oyl of Almonds, and it will meal to powder, then keep it close from the air, else it will become of no use.

Another white fire which lasteth long.

Take *Powder* 4 ounces, *Salt-Peter* 16 ounces, *Brimstone* 8 ounces, *Camphire* 1 ounce, *Oyl of Peter* 2 ounces, Meal those that are to be mealed, and mix them according to the former directions.

CHAP. VI.

The manner of making Stars; and to use them.

TAke little four square peeces of brown paper, which fill with the composition you approve of best, of the three last taught: so double it down, rouling it until you make it round, about the bigness of a nut, or bigger, according to the size of your Rocket, that you intend them for, prime them, withdrawing thorow them Cotton-week, and they are prepared.

You may also make them after this manner, you must have a rouler which must be as big as an ordinary arrow, which shall be to roul a length of paper about it, and with a little glue past it round; when it is dry draw out the rouler, and fill it by little and little, with a thimble; still thrusting it down, every filling of a thimble, with the rouler; which being filled, cut it in short pieces, about half an inch long; then having in readiness either hot glue, or size, mingled with red lead, dip therein one end of your short peeces, lest they take fire at both ends together, and because that it may not so easily blow out: these being thus finished, set them to dry until you have occasion to use them: and then putting the open end in powder on the top of the Rocket, in that place after the first pastboard, or cover, is placed in a Rocket; next the composition, where I taught you before to put powder for to make a report:

which now you must leave out to place in these Stars; after this manner make two or three holes in that pastboard, which prime with powder-dust: and thereupon put a little Pistol powder, to blow the Stars out when the Rocket is spent: after the powder, put as I have said before, the open ends of these Stars, down upon that powder: when you have put them so close as they can stick one by the other, put a little small-corned powder on the top of them, to run between them, and put another tyre of Stars upon that, and in like manner a third tyre upon them, till you come to the top of the Rocket-case, there put a paper over the head of it, and tye it close about the top, that none of the powder come from under or between the Stars.

How to prepare the Cotton-week, to prime the first sort of Stars.

Take Cotton-week, such as the Chandlers use for Candles, double it six or seven times double; and wet it thoroughly in *Salt-peter* water, or *Aqua-vitæ*, wherein some *Camphire* hath been dissolved, or for want of either in fair water, cut it in divers pieces, roul it in mealed powder, dry it in the Sun, and it is done.

CHAP. VII.

How to make silver and golden Rain, and how to use them.

NOw I shew you the order of making golden Rain, which is after this manner; you must provide store of Goose-quills, which being provided, you must cut them off so long as they are hollow, the composition to fill these must be made thus; two ounces of cole-dust to one pound of powder well mixed; having filled many of these quills, you shall place them in the same place as I taught you to put the powder and Stars, first putting a small quantity of Pistol powder under them, to blow them out when the Rocket is spent: upon this put your quills, as many as will fill the top of the case, with the open end downwards; so soon as the Rocket is spent, you shall see appear a golden showre, which by some is called golden Rain: The like way you may make silver Rain, filling the quills with the Composition for white Stars.

CHAP. VIII.

How to make Fisgigs, which some call by the name of Serpents, and to use them.

YOu must provide a small rouling pin, about one quarter of an inch in thickness, upon which roul seven or eight thicknesses of paper: fill them four inches with powder dust, sometimes putting between the filling a little of the Composition for Rockets of 10 ounces: and at the end of four inches choak him; fill two inches more with

with Pistol powder; then choak the end up: at the other end put in a little of the mixture for Stars, and choak between that and the composition, and you have done: put divers of these with the Starry end downwards, upon the head of a Rocket, as you did the quills, with powder to blow them out; when the Rocket is spent, they will first appear like so many Stars; when the Stars are spent, taking hold of the powder dust, they will run wrigling to and fro like Serpents; and when that Composition is spent, they will end with every one a report, which will give great content. I shall have occasion to speak of these Fisgigs in other Fire-works.

CHAP. IX.

How to make Girondels, or (as some call them) Fire-Wheels.

A Fire-Wheel is often required in great Works for pleasure, and therefore I have thought fit and necessary, to set down their description, as well as of all other sorts of Fire-works; First, you must make a Wheel of Wood, so big as you please, to make Girondels, and unto these bind Rockets very fast of a mean bigness, with the mouth of one towards the tail of another; thus continuing until you have filled your Wheel quite round, which done, cover them with paper pasted very curiously, that one taking fire, they may not take fire all together; and daub Sope upon them quite round, leaving the mouth of one of them open to give fire thereto; for the first Rocket having burned, will give fire to the next, keeping the Wheel in continual motion, until they be all spent: there may be bound fire Lances to these Girondels, either upright, or neer, overthwart, which will make to appear diversity of fiery Circles; Your care must be, to place the Girondels at a convenient distance, from other Fire-Works, lest they should cause confusion, and spoil all your Work.

CHAP. X.

How to represent divers sorts of Figures in the Air with Rockets.

I Have taught you to make a report upon the head of a Rocket, and also to place golden or silver Hair or Rain, or Stars, or Fisgigs, which when you have divers Rockets to make for a great Fire-work, let one be with a report, the next with Stars, another with Gold Hair, or Rain, one with Silver Hair or Rain, for standing just under the Rocket it appeareth like Rain, but being aside hand, like Golden or Silver Hair: and upon the head of another Rocket place the Fisgigs, which when the Rocket is spent will first appear like so many Stars, after they are ended, they will shew like Serpents wrigling to and fro, and lastly, give every one his report.

It is a rare thing to represent a Tree or Fountain, in the air, which is made by putting many little Rockets upon one great one, passing all the rods of the little ones thorow wires, made on purpose upon the sides of the great one, or some other way, as your industry will discover; now if the little ones take fire while the great one is mounting up, they will represent a Tree, but if they take fire as the great one is descending or turning down again towards the ground, then they will be like a fountain of fire; if there be two or three little Rockets amongst others, that have no rods, they will make divers motions contrary to the rest, very pleasing.

If before you put the Fisgigs upon the head of a great Rocket, you with a small string tye them together, a foot of line between; when they are on fire in the Air you will see very great variety of Figures, because as they wriggle to and fro, they will pull one another after them, to the speculators great content: it will be pleasant if you tye them not altogether, but three or four, which will in the firing of them, be distinguished from the rest, with great variety.

CHAP. XI.

How to make a Rocket, which firing it out of your hand, shall continually be in agitation, either on the earth, or in the air.

HAving prepared a Rocket with a report in the head, such as I taught you first to make, tye it to a bladder, so that the end of the Rocket may come to the mouth of the said bladder, and bind it over very strongly, then firing it out of your hand, cast it away from you, it matters not which way, so it will come to the ground; there, by reason of the bladder, it cannot stay, but presently rebounds upwards, moving to and fro, until all be spent: there is another sort, and that is a small rocket, put into a bladder, and so blown up round about it, and tyed about the neck thereof, which will have delightful motions.

CHAP. XII.

Of the many defects in Fuzees, how they may be avoided, and of such things as ought to be observed in their good Construction.

THe first and most notable defect which is observed in Fuzees, is that after they are lighted or risen into the Air the height of 1, 2, or 3 Perches, they break, and do dissipate without making their entire effects.

The second, which is little better, is after it is remaining suspended upon the nail it consumes but very leisurely, without going away or raising it self in the Air.

The third is, when they are raised in the Air, they describe only an Arch of a Circle like a Rainbow, and return upon the earth again before the Composition in the Fuzee be consumed.

The

The fourth is when it moves in a ſpiral manner, whirling in the Air without obſerving an equal motion; that is not right as it ought to be.

The fifth is when it mounts ſloathfully and negligently, as if it diſdained or refuſed to elevate it ſelf into the Air.

The ſixth and laſt is, that the Caſe or Cartouch remains hanging upon the Nail quite empty, and the Compoſition doth riſe and diſſipate alone into the Air. There is many other vexations and inconveniencies which may give trouble to the Practitioners in theſe Arts with vain expence, which would looſe too much time to repeat: It will be ſufficient if you take notice of theſe which are principal, whereby, if by ill fortune you be faln into any of theſe defaults, you may correct your error eaſily, and then immediately correct thoſe faults. And for this purpoſe, obſerve the rules given in the next Chapter.

CHAP. XIII.

Infallible Rules by which you may make Fuzees, or Rockets, without any default.

FIrſt, that they have their height proportionable to the Diameter of their Orifice, as we have before declared.

Secondly, the Cartouch ought to be of wood, or glued or paſted paper, not too thick, nor too thin.

Thirdly, they ought to be made of ſtrong paper of indifferent dryneſs, properly rouled and well compacted cloſe upon the Former.

Fourthly, the necks ought to be bound about very ſtrongly and firm, in ſuch a ſort, that the knot of the thred, and the folds of the Cartouch, may not lye amiſs one upon the other.

Fifthly, all the Materials of the Compoſition muſt be exactly weighed according to the proportion of the Orifice of the Fuzee that you would charge, and alſo well beaten and ſifted particularly; after, having weighed them again, and mixed them in one body well together, you muſt pound them again, and paſs them through the Sieve as you did before.

Sixthly, that the Salt-Peter and Sulphur be powdered and clarified as much as poſſible may be, and the Coal perfectly well burned and exempted from all humidity, and made of wood that is light and ſoft, as the Teile, the Hazle, and the branches of the Willow Tree; and on the contrary, 'tis neceſſary to have a care, that you make not uſe of ſuch Coals as are made of Birch, Oak, nor Maple, becauſe they contain in them much weighty and terreſtial matter.

Seventhly, matters for Rockets or Fuzees ought to be prepared immediately before they are intended for uſe, and not before.

Eighthly, the matters of Compoſition ought to be neither too dry nor too moiſt, but moiſtned a little with ſome Oliganious matter, or with a little Brandywine.

Ninthly, there muſt be put into the Cartouch alwayes an equal quantity of the Compoſition at a time, and ſo beat it down alike; and thus do until it be filled.

Tenthly, you muſt beat the Compoſition alwayes with the Rammer right up, or perpendicularly, and take care that in the beating it be not made crooked.

Eleventhly, You muſt ſtrike down the Compoſition with a wooden Mallet, that is of heſt proportionable to the bigneſs and thickneſs of the Rocker, and alwayes with an equal ſtrength, and juſt number of ſtroaks, every time you put in any of the Compoſition.

Twelfthly, in Cartouches made of paper, you must put in round peeces of wood hollowed; but in those that are made of wood, you must put such as are smooth, without any channel or hollowing, to the end that it joyn the better to the sides of the Fuzee, where it must joyn firmly, as well without as within.

13. The Fuzee must be peirced with a Bit or Awl that is convenient, in such a sort that the hole be not too big nor too straight, nor too long nor too short.

14. The hole must be made the most streight and perpendicular that may be possible, and just in the middle of the Composition, to the end that it lean not to any one side, more than to the other.

15. The Fuzee must not be peirced before it be intended for use, and after it is pierced you must handle it tenderly, only with the ends of your fingers, for fear of deforming it.

16. The Pearch or Stick to which you fasten the Fuzee, ought to be proportionable as well in length as weight; it must not be crooked nor winding in any manner, neither unequal, nor full of knots, but streight as possible can be made, and must therefore be made smooth, and streightned with a Plain, if need requires.

17. After they are Charged, they must not be laid into too dry a place, nor in a place too moist, for the one or other of those accidents may hurt them; therefore let the place be temperate.

18. When you would use them and put them into action, hang them upon a nail perpendicular to the Horizon.

19. You must not think to raise a bundle of a great weight, or that has too great a disproportion to their strength, you must adjoyn them together so rightly, that all together may have a proper form, and reasonable to pass into the Air, and to elevate it self on high without any difficulty, and in such a sort, that those bundles may not by any means give hinderance or stoppage to their rising in a streight line; and take care most exactly that the Fuzee be not so big, but that they may retain as near as you can a Pyramidal or Conical form, when all its weight that may be is adjoyned to it.

20. Men ought to shun as much as possible those nights that are rainy, moist, and when the Sky is darkned with black clouds, as being very incommodious and offensive to the Fuzees. And more than that, avoid impetuous Stormy winds, and the Whirl-winds hinder no less than the first.

21. You may not reject above other causes, the different effects which are produced by sundry Fuzees (although they be charged with one and the same Composition) no otherwise than thus, that they were not made with an equal diligence either in the Charging or Peircing, or in the other Circumstances, which you were obliged to observe; or in this, that it may be some may have been kept in a more moister place than the others, where they have acquired too much moisture, which causeth to them, effects much different one from another, as well in Rising as in Consuming.

22. If you would make appear in the Air streams of fire, or a quantity of burning sparks or stars, or long large rayes to dart from the Fuzees; there is accustomed to mix with the Composition some small quantity of powdered Glass grosly beaten, filings of Iron, Sawdust. One may also represent fire of divers colours, as we have shewed before in the fifth Chapter; but more particularly thus; if you put a certain portion of Camphire in your Composition, you will see in the Air a certain fire which will appear, white, pale, and of the colour of Milk; if you put Greek Pitch, which is a light yellow Pitch used in Plaisters, called *Pix Burgundy*, it will represent unto you a red flame, and of the colour of Brass; if you put in Sulphur, the fire will appear blew; if Sal-Armoniack, the fire will appear Greenish; if from Crude Antimony, the flame will be Red, Yellowish, and of the Colour of Honey; if the filings of Ivory be added, they will render a Silver-like, White and shining flame, yet something inclining to a Livid Plumbous colour; if the powder of Yellow Amber be added, the fire will appear of the same colour, with the Citrine; lastly, if black Pitch be added, it will throw forth an obscure smoaky fire, or rather a smoak that is black and thick, which will darken all the Air.

CHAP.

CHAP. XIV.

Of Odoriferous Aquatick Balls.

CAuse to be made by a Turner, Balls of wood, hollow within, about the bigness of a Wild Apple, which you must fill with some one of these Compositions hereunto annexed, and they being all prepared and charged, you may throw them into the water after they are lighted, but it ought to be done in a Chamber or close place, that the fume may be the better kept together, and this must be done with some small end of our Match made of prepared Flax or Hemp, to the end that the Composition which is shut up in the Globe may take fire with the greater facility.

The Compositions are these that follow, viz.

Take Salt-Peter, Storax Calamite, one Dram; Incense one ounce, Mastick one ounce, Amber half an ounce, Civet half an ounce, of the Sawings of Juniper wood two ounces, of the Sawings of Cypress wood two ounces, Oyl of Spike one ounce; Make your Composition according to the Art and Method given. Or,

Take of Salt-Peter two ounces; of Flower of Brimstone, Camphire, half an ounce; powder of yellow Amber half an ounce, Coals of the Teile tree one ounce; Flower of *Benjamin*, or Assa sweet, half an ounce; Let the matters that may be beaten be powdered, afterwards well mingled and incorporated together.

CHAP. XV.

Compositions to Charge Globes or Balls, that will burn as well under as above water.

FIrst, take Salt-Peter reduced into fine meal 16 *l.* Sulphur 4 *l.* of the sawings of wood which hath been first boyled in a Nitrous water, and afterwards well dryed, 4 *l.* Of good Corned powder half a pound, of the powder of Ivory 4 ounces. Or thus,

Salt-Peter 6 *l.* Sulphur 3 *l.* of beaten powder 1 *l.* Filings of Iron 2 *l.* of Burgundy pitch half a pound. Or thus,

Salt-Peter 24 *l.* of beaten powder 4 l. Sulphur 12 *l.* of Sawdust 8 *l.* of yellow Amber half a pound, of Glass beaten in gross powder half a pound, of Camphire half a pound. For that which concerns the manner of preparing all these Compositions; it differs nothing from what we have prescribed in the making of Rockets, only 'tis not necessary that the materials be so subtilly beaten, powdered nor sifted, as for those *Fuzees*, but nevertheless to be well mixed one among another. Care must be taken that they be not too dry when you charge the Globes or Balls, and for that purpose they may be moistned with Linseed-oyl, Oyl of Olives, Petrole, Hemp-seed, Nuts, or any other fatty humour that is receptible of fire.

Note, that amongst all these Compositions of matters that will burn in the water, which I have here proposed from my own particular experience, every one may make them as pleaseth himself best, provided he always take the materials in proportion one to the other, as they ought. But neverthelefs I fhall counfel you to experience from time to time your Compofitions, for the greater furety, before you expofe them to the publick view of the world. It is alfo amongft the reft very neceffary that you learn the force and ftrength of every material you put into the Compofitions, whereby you may at your pleafure know how to alter and vary your proportion, as you fhall judg fit.

CHAP. XVI.

Of Stars and fiery Sparks, called by the Germans Stern-veuer and Veuerputzen.

I Have fhewed the Compofition of Stars in Chap. 5. I have alfo fhewed the way of making them up, and their ufe, and alfo I have fhewed the manner of giving to them various Colours, as in the 22 Rule of the 13 Chapter, where I had an intent to fay no more of thefe things: But finding in Mafter *Cazimier*'s Artillery thefe Compofitions, which I judge may prove very excellent; therefore I thought good to infert them, that I might leave out nothing that might make more perfect any thing we treat of.

Firft, you muft know that between fiery Sparks and Stars there is this difference, that the Stars are greater, and are not fo foon confumed by the fire as the Sparks are, but do fubfift longer in the Air, and do fhine with greater fubftance, and with fuch a light, that by reafon of their great fplendor, they are in fome manner comparable with the Stars in the Heavens. They are prepared according to the following Method.

Take Salt-Peter half a pound, Sulphur two ounces, Yellow Amber powdered one Dram, Antimony Crude one Dram, of beaten Powder three Drams. Or,

Take Sulphur two ounces and a half, Salt-Peter four ounces, Powder fubtilly powdered four ounces, Olibanum, Maftick, Chriftal, Mercury fublimate, of each four ounces, White Amber one ounce, Camphire one ounce, Antimony and Orpiment half an ounce; All thefe materials being well beaten and well fifted, they muft be mixt together with a little Glue or Gum-water, made with Gum-Arabick or Tragacant; then make them into fmall Balls about the bignefs of a Bean or fmall Nut, which being dryed in the Sun, or in a Pan by the fire, may be kept in a convenient place for fuch ufes as we have fpoken of in the fifth Chapter of this Book. You muft only remember, that when you would put them into Rockets or Recreative Balls, they muft be covered on all fides with prepared Tow, of which we have fhewed the way of preparing in the feventh Chapter of the firft Part of our Fire-works.

Sometimes Fire-Mafters are accuftomed to take in the places of thefe little Balls, a certain proportion of melted matters, of which we have fpoken in the firft Part of Fire-works; But if thefe do not pleafe you, by reafon of their fwarthy colour, but you rather defire to fee them yellow, or inclining fomewhat to white, then take of Gum-Arabick or Tragacant four ounces, powder it and pafs it through a Sieve, of Camphire diffolved in *Aqua-vitæ* two ounces, Salt-Peter a pound and a half, Sulphur half a pound, Glafs groffly powdered four ounces, White Amber an ounce and a half, Orpiment two ounces, make all thefe Ingredients into one mafs, and make Globes of them as before. I Learned this, faith my Author, from *Claude Midorge*.

For

For the method of making Sparkles in particular, it is thus; Take Salt-Peter one ounce, of this Liquid matter half an ounce, of beaten Powder half an ounce, of Camphire two ounces; after you have beaten all these materials into powder, every one by it self, put all of them into an Earthen Pan, and put upon them the Water of Gum Tragacanth, or Brandy-wine, wherein you have dissolved some Gum Tragacanth or Arabick, until it be of a good consistency; that done, take an ounce of Lint, which has first been boyled in Brandy-wine or Vinegar, or in Salt-Peter, and after dryed again, and the threads drawn out; then put it into the Composition, and mix them well together, so well and so long until it has drank up all the matter; of these Compositions make little Balls in the form of Pills, and of the bigness of great Peas, which you must roul in mealed Gun-powder, and dry them, whereof you may serve your self, according to the method we have prescribed.

Besides these, there are certain odoriferous Pills prepared, which are employed in small Engines and fiery Inventions, which are shewed in Chamber Roams, or close Cabinets, these are commonly prepared of Storax, Calamite, Benjamin, Amber, white and yellow, and of Camphire, of each one ounce, Salt-Peter three ounces, of Coals made of the Teil Tree four ounces; beat all these Ingredients to powder, then incorporate them well together, and moisten them with Rose Water, in which is dissolved Gum-Arabick or Tragacanth, to make thereof little Balls; at last, having fashioned them, expose them to the Sun or to the fire to dry.

THE DOCTRINE OF PROJECTS APPLYED TO GUNNERY.

By thoſe late famous *Italian* Authors

GALILÆUS AND TORRICELLIO.

Now rendred in *ENGLISH.*

TO THE INGENIOUS Student.

IT being well known among the Learned, that the late famous Merſennus *of* France,*a moſt diligent Collector and Publiſher of the choiceſt Mathematical inventions of that time, hath among his Phyſico-mathematical Reflexions, and Mechanicks, divers material Experiments and Theories relating to the Art of Gunnery, it was thought fit for the Readers benefit to cauſe the ſame to be tranſlated, and ſubmitted to his cenſure.*

Moreover that Author giving all his diſtances in feet, or paces of three feet, or fathoms of ſix foot; It was thought likewiſe expedient to put the Reader into a capacity of reducing the ſame to our Engliſh

 meaſure,

measure, to which purpose there being an accurate experiment, made some time since by the most learned and Reverend Doctor John Wallis *Savilian Professor of Geometry at* Oxford, *take an account thereof, as the Doctor communicated the same to a friend of his here, namely, that he hath formerly compared the* French *and* English *foot very exactly, both measures being as he was assured very exact to the Standards of each Nation, and he found the* French *foot to contain of ours* $12\frac{4}{5}$ *Inches (not missing so much as* $\frac{1}{100}$ *part of half an Inch.)*

OF THE Swiftness OF SOUND.

The swiftness of Sound is greater than the swiftness of Bullets shot off, and finishes 230 fathoms in the space of one second minute.

Hosoever would try the swiftness of Sounds by night, and by day, either in valleys, woods, or mountains, either with or against the wind, or when it is rainy or fair weather, shall find in all respects as I have tried it, that there will be alwayes the same swiftness of Sound.

But after that you have searched out a second by 230 fathoms, he that shoots off a lesser Gun, may again retire 230 fathoms, so that he may be gone back from you 460 fathoms, the same or the like Sound in passing over that way will spend two seconds; which when it shall be five times multiplied by us, that we should hear the Sound 1150 fathoms, the flash by night breaking forth from the mouth of the Gun is alwayes seen at that distance before the Sound is heard five seconds of time. And seeing we make a *French* league to be 2500 fathoms, and the circuit of the Earth 7200 of such leagues, you may easily conclude in what time the sound does pass over one whole or several leagues, for the swiftness of the sound is not diminished by its debility, whenas the last part of the Sound that may be heard does emulate the swiftness of the first.

The Sound of the Gun therefore will pass over a league in the space of 11 seconds, seeing a league contains 11 times 230 fathoms (the space passed over in a second minute) less onely by 30 fathoms, which are here scarce worth consideration, because that they are passed over by the Sound in the seventh part of a second.

From which many things may be gathered; first, that a Souldier attentive my decline or shun the shot of a Gun at one hundred fathoms, is he foresaw the flash of it; which I thus demonstrate: It is evident from observation, that a Bullet in flying 100 fathoms does at the least spend a second of time, and the Sound of it in passing of them does at the most spend but half a second. Therefore the Souldier from the fire seen (if Vision can be in an instant) hath a whole second wherein he my easily go three or four paces before that the bullet can fly so far; also there remains to him half a second from that point of time in which he hears the Sound, until the coming of the Bullet: although I would not advise any one to try that, unless he first fortifie himself with a shield, helmet, and all other kind of Armour, that he may be out of all danger. But any one may try it behind a wall, to which the Sound will come before the Bullet.

Secondly, from the Sound and fire observed, may be known how much the Guns are distant that are shot off against the besieged, or besiegers, even as to the ingenious Gunners there will not be wanting matter to promote their Art.

Thirdly, by hearing the Sound of Thunder, and seeing the lightning go before may be known how far it is off, so that if the Thunder be not changed from the place where the lightning was seen; for how many seconds (whether measured by the pulse, which exactly continues a second, or by a Pendulum or any other Watch) there are between the Lightning and the Sound, so many 230 fathoms are to be reckoned; so that if you number five seconds it may be distant from you half a league; if ten seconds a whole league, whether the distance shall be upright, or sideways and oblique, for it matters nothing.

Fourthly, If by the turnings and windings or Circles in the air a sound in the same manner may be considered, and caused, as we see circles extended in the water struck with the finger or a little stone, as all almost believe, and if from the swiftness of bodies in like manner moved we my ghess at their crassitude, thickness and weight, we may say that water is 1380 times thicker and heavier than air; for as much as the Semidiameter of Circles of the Water in any manner struck, which is, made in a second of time, scarce exceeds a foot, in which time the semidiamiter of Circles in the air, made also by any percussion is 1380 foot, that is 230 fathoms; which proportion of gravities come very near to observations by him mentioned. There is yet one thing that may cause some doubt, which is, that the Sound of greater Guns moves more slowly than of lesser, whereas our Geometer in the siege at *Theodonis* observed that their Sound was heard, from the fire seen, after thirteen or fourteen seconds of time, when yet he was scarce half a league distant from those Guns; And the Sound according to that which hath been before said, may pass over a whole league and more in that time: Wherefore the Sound of those Guns doth seem to be different from that of lesser Guns.

The Author having by this discourse argued that the Sound of Guns is heard at the distance of above 16 miles a minute (which is almost as swift as the *Copernicans* suppose the Earth to move in its diurnal revolution about its Axis) it was thought fit to subjoyn hereto the Authors latter thoughts of the same Argument, published three years after.

OF

OF THE SWIFTNESS OF SOUND,

And force of Bullets ſhot out of Guns.

WHen I have oftentimes conſidered that the Sound paſſes over 230 fathoms in the time of a 2d or ſixtieth part of a minute, and that there ſeem to ariſe ſomeed doubt, whether there ſhould be that Swiftneſs of the Sound of greater Guns, as there is of leſſer, with which I tried; at length it was obſerved that in the ſpace of eleven ſeconds, the Sound of the greater Guns of the Kings Armory, have paſſed from the ſame Armory, after the flaſh was ſeen, as far as our houſe, or the *Vicennian* Convent, whilſt for obtaining the ſurrender of *Pouploon* the Guns were ſhot off by night.

But when with a fathom I found that it was 3524 fathoms from Port Saint *Anthony* to the gate of the aforeſaid Convent, where the ear was, and to the wall of the *Vicennian* Caſtle firſt meeting it, near 2500 fathoms, 'tis certain firſt that it is a juſt league of 2500 fathoms from the Garden walk of the Armory, from whence the Guns are wont to be ſhot off, to that Caſtle: for if any thing in the paſſage muſt be diminiſhed that diſtance will well enough equal it, whereby the corner of the Garden is more diſtant, or the walk by *Sequana* nearer from the Caſtle, than Port Saint *Anthony*.

It is evident therefore that the Sound runs over more than 230 Fathoms in each ſecond, to wit, 320 in every ſecond, which make 1920 foot; which ſince any one can prove by his own experiments, I need not ſay more thereof.

But ſome may imagine that hence perhaps muſt be concluded that greater Sounds paſs more ſwiftly, which diſagrees with divers obſervations. But when ſometimes theſe experiments ſhall be repeated, that I may number the ſeconds, I ſhall advertiſe, for as much as I conjecture that there is no ſwiftneſs of ſound greater than that, which I have proved of 230 fathoms for a ſecond; for in theſe ſmall matters I do not approve that common ſaying, He that acts by another, ſeems to act by himſelf; who want not opportunites may obſerve for their own ſatisfaction.

But now we ſhall add ſome thing concerning the ſwiftneſs of Bullets ſhot out of Guns. When therefore at the Marqueſſe of *Doraiſons* four leagues from the *Sextian* waters, I commanded a Braſſe Gun nine foot long, whoſe name was the *Marchioneſs*, commonly called *la Marquiſe*, (whoſe Bullet was two pounds and an ounce, but quantity of Powder, ſuch as is wont to be in the uſe of leſſer Guns, the weight of one pound) to be levelled horizontally, with a plum line I found that the Bullet ſhot off Horizonitally, in the time of five ſeconds had paſſed over 630 fathoms or 3780 foot, and had reached the horizon, or fell to the ground, as was evident by the huge quantity of duſt raiſed by the blow.

Moreover that point of Earth which was firſt ſtruck by the Bullet was depreſſed under the horizon of the Gun 27 fathoms, for otherwiſe the Range ſhould not have been ſo great before its fall to the earth, which meets ſo much the more ſlowly by how much it is the more depreſſed under the Horizon of the Gun ſhot off, and I preſume I have attributed a leſſer ſwiftneſs to the Guns than is juſt, unleſs yet the Bullets of the greater Guns shot off with very fine powder, which we used, may exceed the swiftness of Bullets shot from Harquebuzes; of which thing I do not yet pass judgement, till experiment, shall bring some further evidence: but I shall propound some things newly observed.

Now therefore of the Bullet which I made trial of, I affirm that the swiftness was so great that, at least, in each second minute it could pass over 126 fathoms.

I said, at least, because the observers know that the force on the Bullet doth go before the excussion or flash of the powder, and the perceiving thereof; so that half a second may well be attributed to this time. Moreover in the first second the Bullet passes more swiftly, in which time I doubt not but it passes over 150 fathoms; Lastly, if by reason of that tarrying which happens betwen the smiting of the Earth until the dust is seen to rise, we should augment that swiftness by so many fathoms as it could pass over in half a minute, to wit 70, and that the swiftness be supposed almost equal for the time of five seconds, and in each second of that time that it passes over 140 fathoms, that is, if the point of the Earth first struck were 700 fathoms distant from the Gun, it would reach it in the time of five seconds. Then the swiftness of the Bullet may be determined from what hath been said, to be 130 fathoms, at least, in the time of a second: which also agrees with the experiments of Bullets shot from lesser Guns: to wit, they pass an hundred fathoms in the same time as the Sound of the Gun hath the same passage.

For if, behind a wall that is to be struck by the Bullet, the ear be attentive, in the same instant the sound and the percussion of the Bullet is heard, as if the very Bullet had caused that Sound; which doubtless you shall find to be true as I did if you try: although it will be worth the labour to prove it, not only with that most refined powder, which they are wont to use who shoot at a mark for a wager, but also with the courser sort of Powder for great Guns, that it may be observed whether it causes any sensible difference of the swiftness.

Whatsoever powder you use, the least swiftness of the Bullet, may be defined in the first second an hundred, the greatest 150 fathoms, if you put but so much Powder into the Gun as is necessary for a good shot; for if you put in but a few grains which can scarce shoot the Bullet off, another thing is to be said.

I add that a Bullet shot vertically or Perpendicularly upright from the aforesaid Gun in its ascent and descent, spends 36 seconds: which if it spend so much time in its Rise as in its fall, and that a heavy body descending in the time of 18 seconds alwayes keeps the same proportion in hastening its descent which it keeps in the four first seconds, the Vertical ascent shall be 648 fathoms, forasmuch as a Bullet of six pound Weight of that Gun, which the Illustrious Knight *Hugenius* caused to be shot off at the *Hague* upon my request, in its ascent in the time of 16 seconds passed over 512 fathoms, which falling, pierced three foot into the Earth.

But two things there are which may lessen the space of the ascent; first, that perhaps the bullet may not spend so much time in its ascent as in its descent, because Arrows in ascending pass over the same way in three seconds of time that in descending they do in five seconds: furthermore should we imagine to shoot with the mouth of the Gun towards the Earth, the Bullet would pierce deeper into the Earth, than by its mere fall, as it happens in Arrows: whence there arises in me no small suspicion that the eyes in the ascent of the Bullet are deceived, to wit that the Bullet was even falling when it was yet esteemed to ascend: which also may be imagined of Arrows, which perhaps had began to descend when they should seem to be inverted, that the point which went before ascending should likewise descending antecede: which you may conclude of from the small blow of the Bullet descending, unless you may contend that the stroke made by the Bullet shot upright from the mouth of the Gun and falling upon the Earth very near, is greater indeed than the stroke of the same Bullet shot from the greatest height, and that not by reason of the greater swiftness, but by reason of the air so unawares intercepted and oppressed, that it may much better

better turn over or bore through the Earth, than when it is prepared for the last motion by the Bullet falling slowly.

Which indeed can be known by Rocks and Mountains 600 fathoms high, to wit, one standing on the top shall observe what time the Bullet that is shot off at the foot of the Mountain, shall spend in coming to the top or any other place of the Mountain, and a sign being given shall warn the leveller of the Gun of the time, or from it shall learn the time of the ascent and descent: from which cutting off the time of the ascent shall conclude how much shorter it shall be in the time of the descent; which also may be observed by an iron Bullet red-hot shot off in the night, whilst it can be seen light to the greatest height: however it is I think fit to add the observation of that Holland Gun, which being levelly or horizontally shot off, carried a Bullet of six pounds 398 paces, before it first touched the Earth, taking a pace for three foot; after this Space it made eight leaps, and at length it ceased at 1750 paces: we have here expressed the distance between each leap, as likewise the distance of each grazing from the Gun.

	Between leaps	Paces.
The passage in the air was		398
	392	
The first leap		790
	275	
The second leap		1065
	179	
The third leap		1244
	150	
The fourth leap		1394
	81	
The fifth leap		1475
	73	
The sixth leap		1548
	78	
The seventh leap		1626
	124	
The eighth leap		1750

Moreover a middle range of 45 degrees was 3225 paces, whose half if we take it for an upright or vertical shot, will be 3225 foot, or $537\frac{1}{2}$ fathoms, for which before we counted only 512. Hence it comes to pass that we may judge that a vertical shot in the ascent doth not proceed by the same or equal and proportionable degrees of swiftness, by which it falls in its descent, for at least there are wanting 25 fathoms, by which 512 differ from 537, although that way of him that levelled the Gun, in counting by common paces, restrained to no rule, cannot be so certain, but that the other may differ from it, so that it cannot with undoubted certainty be reduced to our defined fathoms.

Whoever therefore would certainly try, let him have a chain or wheel for counting of fathoms or any other determinate measures, as is done in the passage of the league of 2500 fathoms from the *Bastilian* Tower erected right over against Port Saint *Anthony* as for as the walls of the *Vicennian* Castle that first meet.

There remaines one thing that may diminish the upright height, to wit, that the Bullet spends more seconds in the descent than it ought, after it comes to the point of equality, after which it doth not any more augment its own swiftness: so that not only 16 seconds are to be reckoned for the descent of the Holland Bullet, but perhaps 20, and 12 are to be counted for the ascent.

For although in moderate heights of 40 or 50 fathoms, the access to the point of equality, in leaden Bullets may not be sufficiently observed, it does not thence follow that it comes not to such a point, in greater heights of an hundred or more fathoms; yea experience proveth the Contrary.

Let there be taken a Corken Bullet which is at least 70 times lighter than a leaden one, yet both them almost in the same time make a three foot space, although perhaps the Corke attains its point of equality within 50 foot.

But whether a leaden Bullet 70 times heavier, can pass over a seventy fold space, that is, 3500 foot, before it comes to its point of equality, which little differs from the height to which Bullets arrive that are vertically shot out of Guns, although I cannot yet conclude, yet it seemes probable enough to me. Moreover the force will never be augmented after the arival at that point, if the greater force shall be argued from only the greater swiftness. But note, it hath been observed by a Noble man who related it to me, that a field Gun 18 foot long, and cut shorter foot by foot, did alwaies curry its shott the further till it came to be eleven foot long, and then it began not to give so great a Range.

To which may be added from the experience of some in small Guns, that if it be over charged with Powder, part of the Powder will blow out of the Gun without firing. Morever if the Bullet be not quite rammed home it will pierce the further, and the Gun recoyle the more.

Also that where the Gun is found most to furr with many shootings off with Powder, there it ought to be cut off, the remainder being the proper length requisite.

It hath been related that a ship becalmed and tormented with the Cushee Piece of a Galley, that lay in a manner out of shot, was at the last reached by the industry of a Mariner, who wrapping up a much lesser sized Bullet than the Bore of the Gun made use of required, in a good Wad did shoot as far as the Galley, thereby retaliating the Injury received.

Of the Depression of shot below the Marke.

I Have often took care that a Gun should be shot off commonly called an Harquebuz, at the space of an hundred fathoms from the mark, that is, six hundred foot, which make three hundred common paces, and found that the Bullet was depressed under the mark-line eight or ten foot, which would scarce have made a greater space, if it had fallen perpendicularly down at the same moment of time it was left off.

Again at the the Marquess of *Doraisons*, a Bullet shot off, in the space of five seconds of time fell 27 fathoms beneath its horizontal line or marke; and whereas perchance the rising of the dust, and the perceiving of it might make us lose a second of time, and that we retain only four seconds, then in each second the Bullet should be carried $157\frac{1}{2}$ fathoms (surely not more) yet it ought to have descended 32 fathoms, if it descends so much horizontally shot off as it would naturally fall were it not shot off, and therefore it either loses some thing of its descent by reason of its being shot off, or in running 360 fathoms, it spends not so much as four whole seconds of time, but rather about $3\frac{1}{4}$.

We add that something is by this means abated from the swiftness of the fall for the space of 27 fathoms which the Bullet in shooting off did descend, or fall below the marke: so that all things considered, I would not as yet start from that opinion, which holds that two heavy bodies, to wit, two Bullets, whereof one may fall perpendicularly from its place above the Horizon, and the other be forced horizontaly, shall both in the same moment of time arrive at the ground or Horizon: for example, if the pit of the aforesaid *Marquess* be 27 fathoms deep, as indeed it is, if I rightly remember, or also a little deeper, 32. a Bullet shot into the fields inclosed between the Sextian waters, will hit the horizon, the same moment

Of this there is a controversie between Borellius *who published a Treatise* de vi percussionis, *the which was writ against by* Honorato Fabri *in his Dialogues of Motion.*

ment, that the like Bullet falling, ſhall the ſuperiour ſuperfice of the aforeſaid point of the water.

There is another thing that I may ſuſpect, whether or no the ſurveyour hath accurately enough meaſured the horizontal depreſſion; however it be, you ſee with what difficulties experiments are hedged in, and how much natural knowledge is indebted to them, who are enriching the ſame with exact Obſervations.

But note that the air that meets the bullet that is ſhot off does ſo much hinder or diminiſh its motion,as much as a wind of the ſame ſwiftneſs with the Ball,blowing continually againſt the ſame in a vacuum.

* For is it not the ſame impediment, or deſtruction of the ſame force, if the bullet beats the aire or is beaten of it? But when I ſaid it was known by experience, that water does ſo much the more deſcend, by how much the ſlower it moves horizontally, and the ſame may ſeem to be concluded of other projected heavie bodies; I advertiſe that obſervations are not yet made ſo exact as that any thing of this nature ſhould be too poſitively aſſerted.

Of the Impediment of the Air.

IN regard that Bullets ſhot from Guns do about the end of their motion utter a more vehement noiſe or hiſſing than about the middle or onwards; there is no doubt to be made but that they move more ſlowly, and the force decreaſing as the ſwiftneſs, *Merſennus* concludes that the Curved range line deſcribed by a Bullets motion cannot exactly deſcribe a Parabola, but however the Theory is tolerable, admiting the firſt violence to move in the touch line of a Parobola, and it is likely the greater Mountures cauſe the greateſt difference, becauſe, there is ſo much the more Air beaten and removed by the paſſage of the ſhot.

But yet it is moſt hard to find out, how much the Air hinders; for although it ſeems to hinder ſo much, as the wind agitating the air with the ſame ſwiftneſs, ſtrikes upon the Bullet ſhot off; yet we are Ignorant of the force of that wind compared with the force of the Bullet ſhot off; unleſs we may appeale to our other experiments in which is ſhewn that the air is at leaſt a thouſand times lighter than water: and ſeeing that a leaden Bullet is eleven times heavier than water of the ſame bulke, a leaden Bullet will exceed the weight of the air 11000 times: and therefore the air agitated by the ſame ſwiftneſs of the Bullet, meeting with the bullet, ſeems to take away the 1100 part of the ſwiftneſs from the Bullet ſhot off. Which impediment truly is ſo light, that in the deſcription of the Parabole it ſcarce ought to be conſidered.

Thoſe things are very excellent which the famous *Torricellius* hath ſet forth in his approved Treatiſe,to which *Merſennus* referrs his Reader.

Experiments OF SHOOTING.

Wherein is explained various observations concerning Guns; And what might happen to bullets shot off in a vacuity, diverse waies compared with those which are obstructed in the Air.

WHenas I made trial about the shooting of Bullets in Guns only of an indifferent bigness (which we commonly call Harquebuzes) which in the ascent and descent together spend 22, 23 or 24 Seconds of time, *Peter Petil* a man most skilful and accurate in observations whilest he lived at *Francopolis*, found (at my request) the Range of a shot, out of a great gun, at the elevation of 22 degrees, whose iron Bullet weighed 33 pounds and $\frac{1}{3}$, to be 1900 fathoms, which the Bullet flew or passed over in the space of 20, 21 or 22 seconds; the Gun being placed at 8 fathoms in the Castle above ground or Horizon; from which place a Bullet of 12 pounds which so many pounds of gun-pouder shot off at the elevation of 16 degrees above the horizon, spent in the air 16 seconds.

Besides, a Culverine of 12 foot long and horizontally levelled being 6 fathom high above the Horizon of the ocean and shot off, the Bullet, whose diameter was almost five Inches, continued 8 seconds of time in the air; when yet another Bullet whose diameter was 6 Inches and $\frac{1}{3}$, also horizontally shot off out of an other Gun 12 foot and $\frac{1}{3}$ long, spent only 6 seconds in the air; another Gun shot off at the Elevation of 15 degrees, its Bullet spent 24 seconds in the Air.

An Iron Culverine of 10 foot long, whose Bullet, had a diameter of almost four inches, horizontally levelled, and standing 9 fathoms above the surface or brim of the Sea, spent only three seconds, in its horizontal Range, after which grazing five times above the Ocean, spent four other seconds.

Three daies also before the taking of *Theond*, *Robervallus* our Geometer observed, the Bullets of Guns shot off from the City against our Souldiers, for the most part to spend only 14 seconds of time in the air, after which there was a hissing increased more and more until the force and motion of the Bullet was almost quite extinguished, and that after the shot had flew almost half a league.

Which being supposed it may be Theorically concluded, how great the shoots ought to be at whatsoever elevation above the horizon, if they be in such Proportion one to another, as shots in a Vacuity, no Medium hindring; that is, for example, if the range of 45 degrees be double the height of the Perpendicular or vertical shot in a space not hindring, so is the range of 45 in the air to the vertical in the air, and so of the rest; which observations only will teach; which yet are most difficult in the greater sort of Guns or Bows, especially the perpendicular, whose height we can scarce certainly know, unless some rock might be found high enough, to whose top, or some certain place, the Bullet or Arrow may come, the height of which top or place we may afterwards measure.

No Towers surely are high enough; and by the time of the descent or fall of the Bullet, to conclude a place may be found to which bullets, darts, or other things that are cast upright or vertically ascending, do come, doth therefore fail, because they do not observe the same rule of swiftness in descending; as is evident from darts, to which seeing it happens in their ascent or rise of 50 fathoms to be slackned in their descent or fall, something like this may be also thought to happen to Bullets, to wit, when they descend from the height of a thousand fathoms.

But you may avoid these difficulties: for if from that rock in the *Dolphinate*, whose height

height 'tis said is 600 fathoms or more, a stone or bullet of Iron or any other matter be let fall, * the time of its falling being noted, as for example, if in the space of 18 seconds it fall from the height of 648 fathoms (as truly it should fall, if the spaces be in Duplicate *ratio*, or as the square of the times in the whole descent) then we have rightly judged before of the vertical altitude or perpendicular shot (which the Bullet of an indifferent Gun reaches) that is the height of 288 fathoms; which yet I cannot credit; otherwise the middle shot or range of 45 degrees of that Gun at least would be double to that perpendicular or vertical one, that is to say, it would be 576 fathoms, whenas I found it not 400 fathoms.

Experiments of this kind the Reader will doubtless find, as also others about Pendulums *in the* Opuscula Posthuma *of* L. Bap. Batiani.

Besides these observations I shall add those which the industrious *Galeus* an Engineer to divers Dukes in whose presence he made them, writ with his own hand and gave me, which that you may more easily understand, let the greater Gun K, which we commonly call a Cannon, be parallel to the Horizon, and let the eye be taking aim by the points I and O, the horizontal shot being supposed O P, or in the figure beneath, S X, or, T V, he sayes that the remainder of the rang which bends till it touches the horizon in the point λ, is almost equal to the horizontal shot, that is, that there is almost as much space made by the bullet from that point, from which it begins to bend towards the horizon, until it touch it, as it had made before the bending of it.

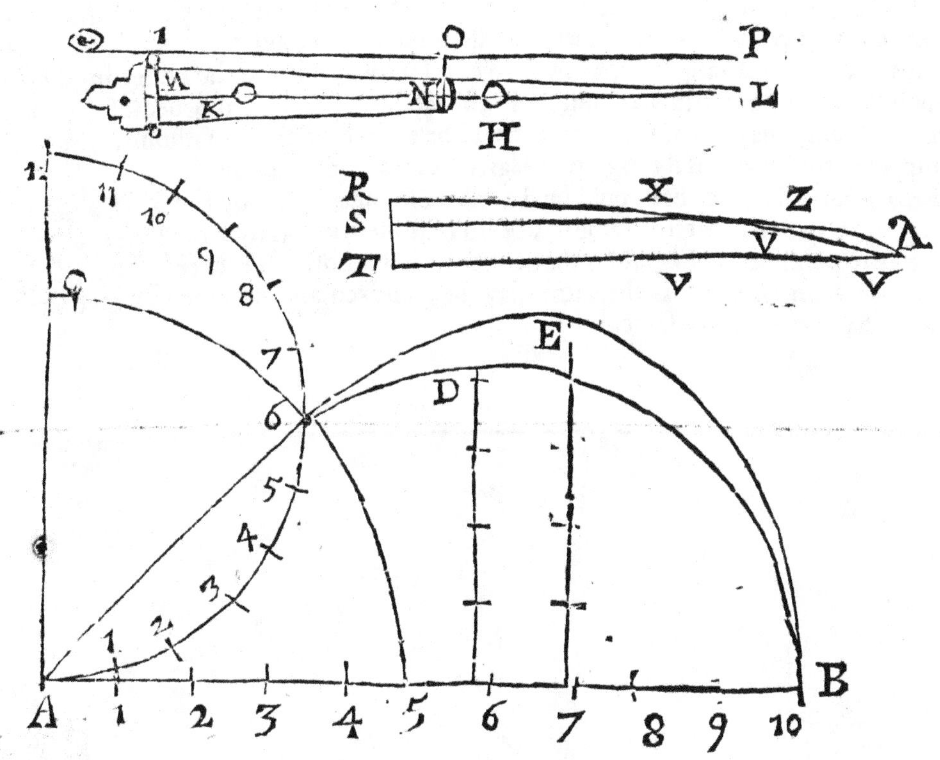

But now let us suppose that horizontal shot O P, or T V, removed to the lower figure in which let A B be the horizontal plain, and let the the aforsaid horizontal shot be A I, *Galeus* contends that the middle range of 45 degrees, which is the longest of all, is eleven fold the length of the horizontal shot O P, or A I: And in those Guns which are half the weight of the foregoing greater Guns, to be in respect of A I, as 10 and $\frac{1}{2}$ is to 1, and in lesser Guns as 10 to 1 that is our figure, as A B in respect of A I; in which the middle range is A G E B; for that is the middle range which passes through the middle of the quadrant φ 5, which they call the sixth point, because it is the middle part of the half circumference A, 1, 2, 3, 4, 5, 6, 7, 8, 9, 10, 11, 12, divided into 12 equal parts; which joyned to the quadrant φ 5, may be useful for levelling the gun at any elevation above the horizon, if it shall be divided not only into 12 parts, but also into an 180 degrees.

And hence he concludes that the dead or exact Horizontal Shot or range, that is in the figure, R λ I to be in Proportion to the middle range as 1 to 6; or in lesser Guns, as one to five; which dead Horizontal ranges is to the range of an Elevation of one degree, as five to six, or more exactly as 55 to 67, or as 14 to 17.

But when the recoyling of the greater Gun is hindred, the dead Horizontal range will be greater by a seventh, eighth, ninth, or tenth part, than that range which is made with recoyling; in lesser Guns it will be a twelfth or a fifteenth part less.

Moreover he asserts that the middle range A 6 E does proceed righton without arching by the line A G, which may be almost equal to A 5, that is, almost 5 fold or $4\frac{1}{2}$ the Horizontal shot: then not only that it does ascend to the point D, so that the greatest height of the middle range may be fourfold the Horizontal, and be over the line A C sixfold the same which some affirm; but he by observation saies is false against *Tartaglia*; affirming that the greatest altitude must be F E, answering the point 7, that is seven distances of Horizontal range from the gun A, that F E may be almost five fold the Horizontal range.

Galeus did likewise well conjecture that the Curve for the middle range does come near to the Curve of an hyperbolical or parabolical line, and that not by force of reason, but only from observations. Moreover the greatest range at forty five degrees elevation he makes 16200 foot, that is 2700 of the *French* fathoms; who because he used feet less than ours, you might account it for 2500 fathoms, that the said range may answer to our league, and that the bullet might pass through the air in near half a minute, or 30 seconds of time: and because the dead Horizontal range may be $\frac{1}{6}$ of the utmost, it will be 2700 foot or 450 fathoms, which being supposed the Horizontal range will scarce exceed 200 fathoms.

Mersennus in this place hath published a table of ranges made by the said *Galeus*, but it being apprehended that the same is not so near the truth as that of *Torricellio*, or another here published in *English* by the antient well known Teacher of the Mathematicks Mr. *Henry Bond*; that the same may be preserved and become more common in use we have inserted the same.

Two

Two Tables of
RANGES
According to Degrees of *MOVNTVRE.*

By H. Bond.

The first Table.

deg		deg	
1	8758	47	2113
2	7813	48	2150
3	7077	49	2189
4	6482	50	2230
5	5991	51	2272
6	5581	52	2317
7	5234	53	2363
8	4932	54	2412
9	4669	55	2463
10	4440	56	2516
11	4237	57	2572
12	4055	58	2633
13	3889	59	2695
14	3741	60	2762
15	3606	61	2832
16	3483	62	2908
17	3370	63	2989
18	3266	64	3075
19	3279	65	3168
20	3080	66	3268
21	2996	67	3376
22	2978	68	3493
23	2845	69	3621
24	2776	70	3762
25	2712	71	3916
26	2651	72	4086
27	2593	73	4276
28	2538	74	4489
29	2486	75	4732
30	2437	76	5006
31	2391	77	5303
32	2344	78	5690
33	2300	79	6263
34	2260	80	6641
35	2221	81	7274
36	2183	82	8059
37	2146	83	9061
38	2111	84	10430
39	2077	85	12330
40	2044	86	15140
41	2012	87	19850
42	1981	88	29250
43	1952	89	37480
44	2007	90	00000
45	2041		
46	2076		*Finis.*

The Second Table.

deg		deg	
1	1.142	47	4.736
2	1.280	48	4.653
3	1.413	49	4.570
4	1.543	50	4.487
5	1.669	51	4.403
6	1.792	52	4.318
7	1.911	53	4.234
8	2.028	54	4.148
9	2.142	55	3.062
10	2.253	56	3.976
11	2.361	57	3.889
12	2.467	58	3.800
13	2.572	59	3.712
14	2.674	60	3.622
15	2.774	61	3.532
16	2.872	62	3.440
17	2.968	63	3.347
18	3.063	64	3.253
19	3.156	65	3.158
20	3.248	66	3.061
21	3.339	67	2.963
22	3.428	68	2.864
23	3.516	69	2.762
24	3.603	70	2.659
25	3.689	71	2.554
26	3.774	72	2.448
27	3.858	73	2.339
28	3.941	74	2.228
29	4.024	75	2.114
30	4.105	76	1.998
31	4.186	77	1.880
32	4.267	78	1.758
33	4.347	79	1.634
34	4.426	80	1.506
35	4.505	81	1.375
36	4.584	82	1.241
37	4.662	83	1.102
38	4.740	84	0.960
39	4.818	85	0.812
40	4.895	86	0.661
41	4.972	87	0.504
42	5.050	88	0.342
43	5.127	89	0.174
44	4.985	90	0.000
45	4.902		
46	4.819		*Finis.*

The use of the first Table, by Example.

1. Suppose a peece curry a shot 763. paces at 13. degrees of *Mounture*, What is the Horizontal Range? Multiply the Number against 13. degrees, which is 3889. by 763. and from the product cut off 2 figures towards the right hand, leaves the paces of the Horizontal Range desired.

The use of the second Table, by Example.

2. Suppose a peece Curry a shot 374 paces at the Horizontal Range; How many paces shall it Curry at 16. degrees *Mounture?* Multiply the Number against 16. degrees, which is 2. 872 of this second Table, by 374. and from the product cut off 3. figures towards the right hand, leaves the Number of paces desired.

3. Having the paces of any degree of *Mounture* to find how far that shall curry a shot at a greater degree of *Mounture*. Example.

Suppose a peece Curry a shot 543 paces at 11. degrees *Mounture*; How may paces shall it curry at 10. degrees *Mounture*? First multiply the Number against 11. in the first Table, which is 4237, by 543. and Multiply that product again by the Number found in the second Table against 19. degrees, which is 3. 156. And from the Last product cut off 7. figures towards the right hand, and the remainder are the Number of paces desired.

1. By the peeces *Mounture*, and the paces she curries a shot at that *Mounture*, to know how many she curries at level Range, by the direction aforesaid.

2. Having the level Range of a peece, to find how many paces that shall curry at a *Mounture* given, by the directions aforesaid.

3889	2.872
763	374
11667	11488
23334	20104
27223	8616
296(7307	1074(128

3. Having the paces that a peece Curries at one *Mounture*, to find how many paces it should curry at a greater *Mounture*, by the directions aforesaid.

4237	2300691
543	3.156
12711	13804146
16948	11503455
21185	2300691
2300691	6902073
	726(0980796

 The

The Ranges of Spouts or Squirts compared with the Ranges of Bullets shot out of Guns.

FOr as much as a Bullet spends a greater time in its fall than its rise, like darts; or the descent is not so swift, that it should always hasten in that degree whereby in three or four seconds, we have found its swiftness to be increased, which I suppose to be confirmed from this reason, because a bullet descending cannot have so great a power to smite, as it hath ascending, so that approaching the Earth it is not so swiftly moved, as when it comes from the mouth of the Gun, for when the swiftness of any thing projected is equall, it equally strikes.

Therefore I account Spouts useful, seeing they bring us to the knowledg of shooting, of which otherwise we could not judge, by reason of the difficulty of trial which is most easily discerned in tubes: for because any one may compare in a little time what ever shot he pleases with another, to wit, a middle Range with a vertical, or Perpendicular one as to time and height, that this may be the better understood, in the following figure let the Cock be A above the Horizon A B, and let the altitude of the tube be A 12, whose vertical Squirt is A Φ, Experience teacheth us that the length of the middle Squirt A B, is double to the Vertical A Φ. *Former Figure.*

But to what height the middle Squirt ranges, whether to D or E, which also you may understand of Bullets shot from Guns, there is none hitherto hath observed: but it is one half of the vertical Φ A, wherefore the point D or E is higher than it ought to be, and whatever is said by the ingenious, may be corrected by spouts.

There are other things also that want inquiry into; for example, how it can come to pass, that a bullet shot out of the mouth of a Gun from O to P comes right on, when in that time it flying along the line O P a hundred fathoms ought to fall towards the center of the Earth 12 foot, if the horizontal motion of a thing violently projected hinders not its natural motion, as many imagine in a vacuity or place that does not impede.

For although that can partly be explained by the diversity of the lines, which is found in Guns, to wit the line R X Y, which follows the outside of the Gun, and that which they call *Linea animæ* S Z, which passes thorough the axis of the hollow M N to the aforesaid side, is in no wise parallel: because, to wit, the bullet K or H levelling at L may ascend to the side line I L, or the point S passing to Z may ascend to the point X of the side line R Y: yet another thing is to be added, when what is aforesaid is not true, when the eye of the shooter takes not aim by the line I L or R X but by the line M N or S X: for then the bullet K does not descend so much, as it would if it were left to it self in the air.

Add, that the water out of the Cock fitted to the Horizontal Squirt doth not descend so much, as it would if left to it self; for it is manifest by Experience, that the Horizontal Squirt of 30 foot, which continues two seconds, descends not so much as eight foot, when according to the law of bodies of equal weight, it should be 48, or at least by reason of the resistance of the air breaking the water it ought to descend 30 foot.

FINIS.

THE PREFACE.

GALILÆUS *in his 4th. Dialogue of Motion, hath largely treated of æquable and accelerate or increasing Motions, as also of that of Projects, or things shot, and thence derived several Propositions or Conclusions, and hath likewise made several Tables touching the Amplitudes or Base Lines, and the Altitudes or Heights of the* Semiparabola's *or* Curves *described by the Motion and Ranges of Projects. The which Doctrine the late Famous* Torricellio *of* Florence, *having with great Judgment much advanced and facilitated, applying the whole to the* Art of Gunnery; *that the benefit of his pains might redound to the* English *Reader, that is especially Delighted or Exercised in the Affairs of* Mars, *it was thought fit to render the same into* English.

THE DOCTRINE OF PROJECTS APPLYED TO GUNNERY.

PROPOSITION.

The Impetus B A (that is, as much as is that of the moveable naturally falling from B to A by the * Definition) as also the Direction A I, according to which the Projection is to be made with the said Impetus being given: it is required to find the Amplitude, Altitude, and the whole future Parabola of this Projection.

* Which Definition is; *when we name an* Impetus *given, we determine it in spaces, according as* Galilaus *useth*; Exemp. Grat. When we say, let the *Impetus* given be A B, then we mean, let the *Impetus* given be so much as is requisite to throw the Project from A to the highest point of the perpendicular B; or, which is the same, as much as is the *Impetus* of a moveable naturally falling from B to A.

Horow A and B draw the Horizontal lines A D, and B L, and describe the Semicircle A F B about the Diameter A B, which shall somewhere cut the line A C, seeing that A D is a Tangent. Let the Section be in F, and draw the Horizontal line F E, and prolong F G equal to F E; then by G let fall the perpendicular L G D; then about the Diameter G D, by the points G and A, describe the *Parabola* A G, which can be but one, by the precedent * *Lemma*; nor can there any other *Parabola* be described about the Diameter

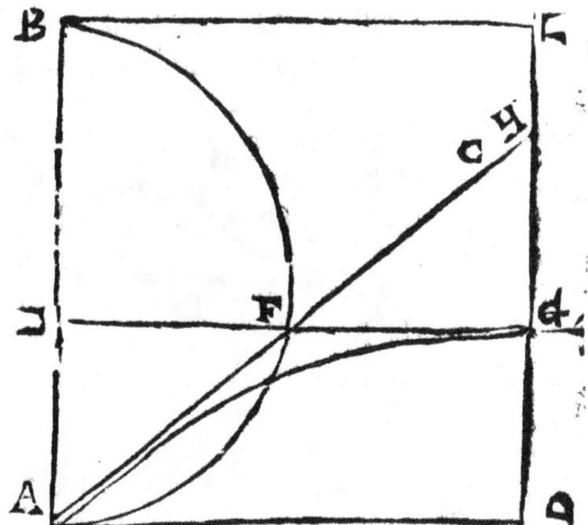

* *Which* Lemma *was; that about the Diameter* G D, *thorough the* Vertex G, *and any assigned point* A, *there cannot be described more than one* Parabola. *Lemm. of Propos. VIII.*

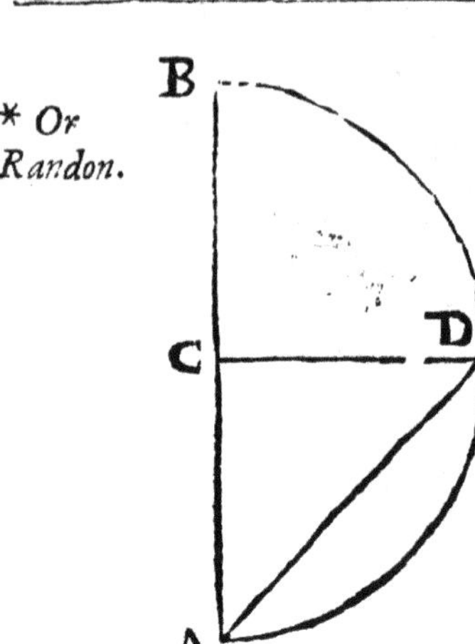

** Or Randon.*

7. We will therefore make a Corollary of that which to *Galilæus* was an arduous Theorem, to wit, that the Semi-right * projection is the greatest of all those made by the same *Impetus*. For, if you suppose the Angle C A D to be Semi-right, C D shall be the Semi-Diameter; that is the greatest of all the Sines that can be given in the Semicircle.

8. It is manifest also, that the whole Amplitude of the Semi-right *Parabola* is double to the line of the Sublimity, or the *Impetus* A B: for it hath been demonstrated to be Quadruple of the right line C D, that is double to A B.

PROP. II.

I incite this Proposition, as being also cited in the ensuing Discourse.

The Impetus **and Amplitude being given, to find the direction according to which the** Parabola **was made; as also to find the Altitude.**

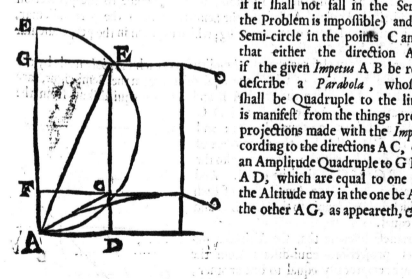

LEt the given *Impetus* be A B, and let A D be the fourth part of the Amplitude given. About A B describe the Semi-circle A C B, and erect D C E, (which if it shall not fall in the Semi-circle, the the Problem is impossible) and let it cut the Semi-circle in the points C and E. I say, that either the direction A C or A E, if the given *Impetus* A B be retained, shall describe a *Parabola*, whose Amplitude shall be Quadruple to the line A D, this is manifest from the things preceding. For projections made with the *Impetus* A B, according to the directions A C, or A E, have an Amplitude Quadruple to G E, or F C or A D, which are equal to one another; and the Altitude may in the one be A F, as also in the other A G, as appeareth, &c.

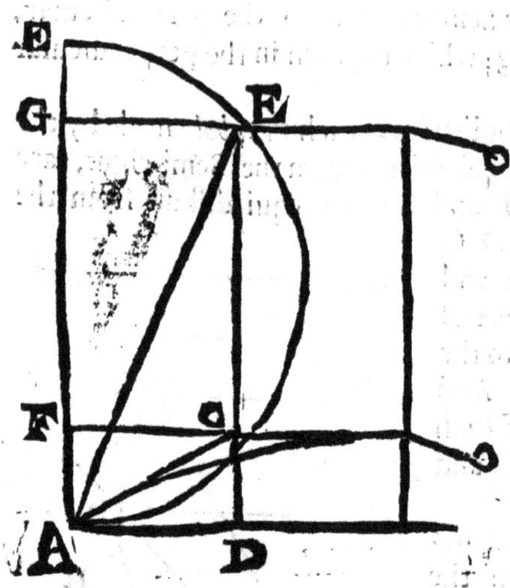

In

In this place I have thought fit to insert the Tables following: the first Classis of which containeth three Tables, the same with those of *Galilæus*, which we placed *Part.I. Dial.4. Page* 241. of this present Tome, but different in many of the Numbers, as being desumed from the Tables of Sines and Tangents, whereas *Galilæus* Calculateth his with much labour, according to the Principles of his Doctrine of Projective motion, laid down in that his fourth Dialogue. The second Classis consists of two Tables added by *Torricellius*, the one of Durations, the other of Elevations or Randons: the Explanations and Calculations of which are annexed to them by the Author, but here omitted on the account of brevity.

this is the *Parabola* sought. For the directive line of this *Parabola* is A I, seeing that it toucheth the *Parabola* in A, for E G, or A D, is double to F G by construction; and therefore D G, and G I are equal: wherefore A I is the Tangent to the *Parabola*.

Again, I say, that this *Parabola* is described by the *Impetus* given; for A E, E F, and E B, or those three lines equal to D G the Altitude, G F the Semi-base, and G L are in continual proportion. Wherefore G L is the sublimity, by the V. Proposition of * *Galilæus*, and its Corollary.

De metu Projectorum.

Then thus: the *Impetus* of the *Parabola* A G in the point A, is as much as that of the Cadent naturally falling from L to D, (by X. of *Galilæus*) that is, from B to A, or of the Project ascending from A to B: therefore the *Parabola* hath in the point A the *Impetus* that was given: wherefore that is done which was required.

But because this Proposition is of great moment, for clearing of those that follow, we will prove it another way.

Let the same *Impetus* A B, and the same direction A F C be given: the *Parabola* made by this projection is fought, describe as before, a Semicircle about the Diameter A B, which shall cut A C: seeing that A D is a Tangent. Let it cut it in F, and drawing the Horizontal line E F G, so as that E F and F G may be equal, describe, or conceive a *Parabola* to be described along by the points A and G about the Diameter G D. I say, that this is the *Parabola* of the Project, if it be thrown from the point A, according to the Direction A C, with the *Impetus* A B. Now if the moveable do not run along this same *Parabola* it will run along some other; as suppose A P: let the Vertex, or the highest point of this *Parabola* A P be found, and let it be P.

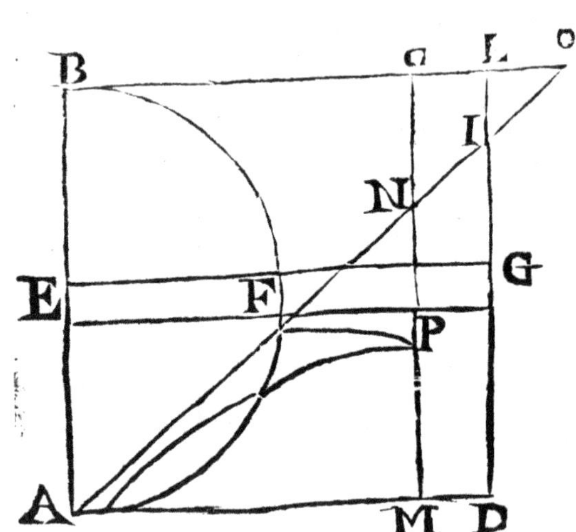

First, it is manifest that the point P cannot be in the line L D; because since the line A C toucheth each *Parabola*, that I D the common *Axis* should be cut into two equal parts in two points by the Vertex's of the *Parabola*, is absurd. Nor can it be in the line E G: for drawing the Diameter, suppose M N, thorough the Vertex, that M N should be cut into two equal parts by the line E G, is absurd: for only I D, of all the lines parallel unto it in the angle C A D, can be cut into two equal parts.

Now let the point P fall any where at pleasure, and draw the Horizontal line P R S: for as much as P N and P M are equal, by the II of * this, N R and R A, P R and R S shall be equal. And because the *Parabola* A P hath the *Impetus* B A; that is, O M, the Point O shall be its sublimity: and for that reason the lines O P, P R, and P M shall be in continual proportion; and the Rectangle O P M equal unto the square P R: and changing the lines with their equals, the Rectangle B S A shall be equal to the square S R: therefore the R is in the point Periphery of the Semicircle: which is absurd; for the right line A F shall meet with the Periphery in two several points: wherefore, &c.

Which second Proposition is, that the sublime point of the Range of any Project [P] doth cut the Perpendicular [M] intercepted betwixt the Horizon and line of direction, into two equal parts.

COROLLARIES.

COROLLARIES.

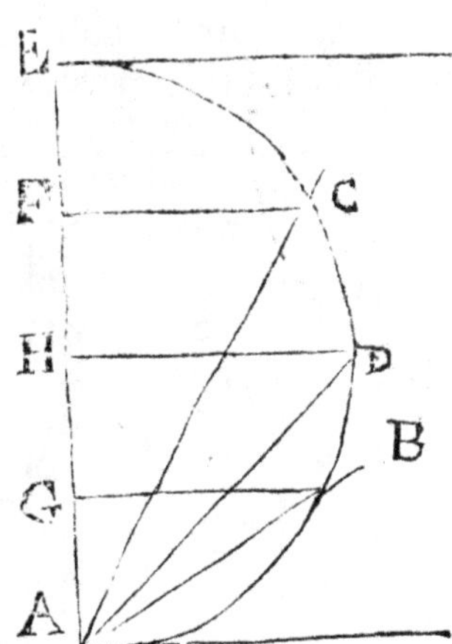

First, Hence is manifest, that the *Impetus* of any Machine being given, as for example E A, if there be described about E A the Semicircle A D E, one may assign the Altitudes and the Amplitudes of all the projections that can be made by the same Machine. For example; the *Impetus* E A remaining still the same, let projections be made along the lines of several elevations A C, A D, and A B. The projection made according to the direction A C, shall ascend as high as to the Horizontal line F C prolonged: and the projection made along the direction A D, shall have its Apex in the line H D prolonged: and of the projection made according to the line A B, the greatest Altitude shall be in the Horizontal line G B prolonged.

2. In the Book of *Galilæus de motu naturaliter accelerato*, it is proved, that projects thrown with the same *Impetus* out of A, if born up by plains of several inclinations, do alwayes arrive unto one and the same Horizontal plain. But here it appeareth, that the several ascensions of projects do vary when they are thrown thorough the pure Air, without any fulciment put under them, according to several elevations. For the moveable shall less ascend, which is emitted along the line A B less elevated, than that which shall be projected along A D more elevated.

3. It is manifest also, that no Altitude can in such sort ascend, as that it may reach unto the Horizontal parallel that is drawn thorow E the highest point of the perpendicular projection.

4. It is also manifest, that all Amplitudes do alwayes encrease from that projection which is called the point blanck Randon, until you come to the projection made at the Semi-right Angle. And from the Semi-right unto the perpendicular, they alwayes diminish until they come to nothing; which hapneth in the perpendicular projection, which hath no Amplitude.

5. From whence we may observe, that the Amplitudes of each *Parabola* made by the same *Impetus*, the elevations of which are equi-distant from the Semi-right, are equal to each other. For, since the lines A B and A C are equi-distant from the Semi-right elevation, the Arches D B and D C shall be equal, as subtending equal Angles: and consequently the B A and C E, the remainders of their Quadrants shall be equal: therefore also the Sines of them, B G and C F, shall be equal. And for the same reason, the whole Amplitudes of each *Parabola*, which are Quadruple to the Sines B G and C F, shall be equal.

6. It is manifest likewise that the Altitudes and Sublimities of projections equi-distant from the Semi-right, are reciprocally equal to one another, that is, the Altitude of the one is equal to the sublimity of the other.

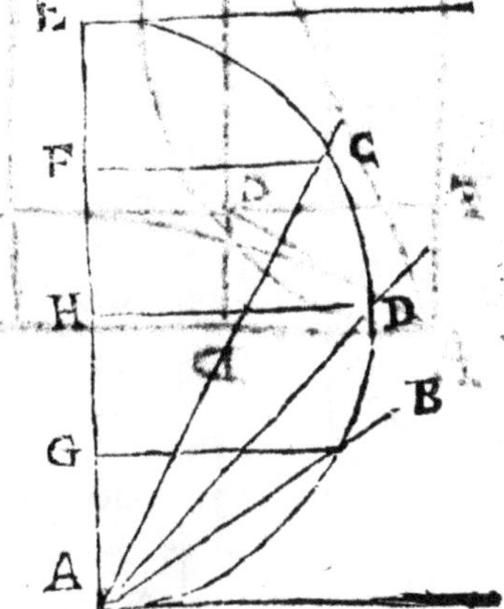

TABLE I.

The Amplitudes of the *Semi-Parabola's* describ'd by the same *Impetus*. The greatest Amplitude is supposed to be of 10000 parts; and the Numbers of the Table are double to the right Sines of the arches of the elevation.

Degr. of Elevat.	*Ampl. of Semi-P.*	*D. of Elev.*
1	349	89
2	098	88
3	1045	87
4	1392	86
5	1736	85
6	2079	84
7	2419	83
8	2756	82
9	3090	81
10	3420	80
11	3746	79
12	4067	78
13	4384	77
14	4695	76
15	5000	75
16	5299	74
17	5592	73
18	5870	72
19	6157	71
20	6428	70
21	6691	69
22	6947	68
23	7193	67
24	7431	66
25	7660	65
26	7880	64
27	8090	63
28	8290	62
29	8480	61
30	8660	60
31	8829	59
32	8988	58
33	9135	57
34	9272	56
35	9397	55
36	9511	54
37	9613	53
38	9703	52
39	9781	51
40	9848	50
41	9903	49
42	9945	48
43	9976	47
44	9994	46
45	10000	45

TABLE II.

The Altitudes of the *Semi-Parabola's*, whose *Impetus* is the same with that of the precedent Table. The greatest Altitude is supposed to be of 10000 parts; and the Numbers of the Table are double to the halfs of the versed Sines of the Arches of the Elevation.

D. of Elev.	*Altit. of Semi-P.*	*D. of Elev.*	*Altit. of Semi-P.*
1	3	46	5174
2	12	47	5349
3	27	48	5523
4	49	49	5696
5	76	50	5868
6	109	51	6040
7	149	52	6210
8	194	53	6378
9	245	54	6545
10	302	55	6710
11	364	56	6873
12	432	57	7034
13	506	58	7192
14	585	59	7347
15	670	60	7500
16	760	61	7650
17	855	62	7796
18	955	63	7939
19	1060	64	8078
20	1170	65	8214
21	1284	66	8346
22	1403	67	8470
23	1527	68	8597
24	1654	69	8716
25	1786	70	8830
26	1922	71	8940
27	2061	72	9045
28	2204	73	9145
29	2350	74	9240
30	2500	75	9330
31	2653	76	9415
32	2808	77	9494
33	2966	78	9568
34	3127	79	9636
35	3290	80	9698
36	3455	81	9755
37	3622	82	9806
38	3790	83	9851
39	3960	84	9891
40	4132	85	9924
41	4304	86	9951
42	4477	87	9973
43	4651	88	9988
44	4826	89	9997
45	5000	90	10000

TABLE III.

The Altitudes and Sublimities of the *Semi-Parabola's*, whose Amplitudes are equal, *Viz.* alwayes 10000 parts; the Altitudes are the halfs of the Tangents of the Angles of the Elevation; and the Sublimities are the halfs of the Tangents of the Complements of the Elevation.

D. of Elev.	*Altitudes.*	*Sublimities.*	*D. of Elev.*	*Altitudes.*	*Sublimities.*
1	87	286450	46	5178	4828
2	175	143186	47	5362	4663
3	262	95406	48	5553	4502
4	350	71503	49	5752	4346
5	437	57150	50	5959	4196
6	525	47572	51	6175	4049
7	614	40722	52	6400	3906
8	703	35577	53	6635	3768
9	792	31569	54	6882	3633
10	882	28356	55	7141	3501
11	972	25723	56	7413	3373
12	1063	23523	57	7699	3247
13	1154	21657	58	8002	3124
14	1247	20054	59	8321	3004
15	1340	18660	60	8660	2887
16	1434	17437	61	9021	2772
17	1529	16354	62	9404	2659
18	1625	15388	63	9813	2548
19	1722	14521	64	10252	2439
20	1820	13737	65	10723	2332
21	1919	13025	66	11230	2226
22	2020	12375	67	11779	2122
23	2122	11779	68	12375	2020
24	2226	11230	69	13025	1919
25	2332	10723	70	13737	1820
26	2439	10252	71	14521	1722
27	2548	9813	72	15388	1625
28	2659	9404	73	16354	1529
29	2772	9020	74	17437	1434
30	2887	8668	75	18660	1340
31	3004	8321	76	20054	1247
32	3124	8002	77	21657	1154
33	3247	7699	78	23523	1063
34	3373	7413	79	25723	972
35	3501	7141	80	28356	882
36	3633	6882	81	31569	792
37	3768	6635	82	35577	703
38	3906	6400	83	40722	614
39	4049	6175	84	47572	525
40	4196	5959	85	57150	437
41	4346	5752	86	71503	350
42	4502	5553	87	95406	262
43	4663	5362	88	143186	175
44	4828	5718	89	286450	87
45	5000	5000	90	*Infinita.*	∞

TABLE IV.

The Durations or *Impetus* of Projects made by the same *Impetus* compared to the Horizon. The greatest Duration or *Impetus* is supposed to be of 1000 parts; and the Numbers of the Table are the right Sines of the Elevations.

Degr. of Elevat.	*Dur. or Impet.*	*D. of Elev.*	*Dur. or Impet.*
1	75	46	7193
2	349	47	7314
3	523	48	7431
4	698	49	7547
5	872	50	7660
6	1045	51	7771
7	1219	52	7880
8	1392	53	7986
9	1564	54	8090
10	1736	55	8192
11	1908	56	8290
12	2079	57	8387
13	2250	58	8480
14	2419	59	8572
15	2588	60	8660
16	2756	61	8746
17	2924	62	8892
18	2090	63	8910
19	3256	64	8988
20	3420	65	9063
21	3584	66	9135
22	3746	67	9205
23	3907	68	9272
24	4067	69	9336
25	4226	70	9397
26	4384	71	9455
27	4540	72	9510
28	4695	73	9563
29	4848	74	9613
30	5000	75	9659
31	5150	76	9703
32	5299	77	9744
33	5446	78	9781
34	5592	79	9816
35	5736	80	9848
36	5878	81	9878
37	6018	82	9903
38	6157	83	9925
39	6293	84	9945
40	6428	85	9962
41	6561	86	9976
42	6691	87	9986
43	6820	88	9994
44	6947	89	9998
45	7071	90	10000

TABLE V.

The Degrees of Elevation to which the Piece is to be mounted, that the Amplitude of the Projections may be made of the given measure. We suppose all the Projection to have the same *Impet.* that is to be made by the same Piece, & that the greatest is 4000 paces.

Spaces, or equal encreases of the Projection.

Spaces.	*Deg. of Elevat.*		*Complement.*		*Spaces.*	*Deg. of Elevat.*		*Complement.*	
10	00	17	89	43	510	15	20	74	40
20	00	34	89	26	520	15	40	74	20
30	00	52	89	08	530	16	00	74	00
40	1	09	88	51	540	16	21	73	39
50	1	26	88	34	550	16	41	73	19
60	1	43	88	17	560	17	02	72	58
70	2	00	88	00	570	17	23	72	37
80	2	18	87	42	580	17	44	72	16
90	2	35	87	25	590	18	05	71	55
100	2	52	87	08	600	18	26	71	34
110	3	09	86	51	610	18	48	71	12
120	3	27	86	33	620	19	10	70	50
130	3	44	86	16	630	19	22	70	26
140	4	01	85	59	640	19	54	69	06
150	4	19	85	41	650	20	16	69	44
160	4	36	85	24	660	20	39	69	21
170	4	54	85	06	670	21	02	68	58
180	5	11	84	49	680	21	25	68	35
190	5	29	84	31	690	21	49	68	21
200	5	46	84	14	700	21	13	67	47
210	6	04	83	56	710	22	37	67	23
220	6	21	83	39	720	23	02	66	56
230	6	39	83	21	730	23	27	66	33
240	6	57	83	03	740	23	52	66	08
250	7	14	82	46	750	24	18	65	42
260	7	32	82	28	760	24	44	65	16
270	7	50	82	10	770	25	11	64	49
280	8	08	81	52	780	25	38	64	22
290	8	26	81	34	790	26	06	63	54
300	8	44	81	16	800	26	34	63	26
310	9	02	80	58	810	27	03	62	57
320	9	20	80	40	820	27	33	62	27
330	9	38	80	22	830	28	03	61	57
340	9	56	80	04	840	28	34	61	26
350	10	14	79	46	850	29	06	60	54
360	10	33	79	27	860	29	36	60	21
370	10	51	79	09	870	30	14	59	46
380	11	10	78	50	880	30	50	59	10
390	10	29	78	31	890	31	27	58	33
400	11	47	78	13	900	32	05	57	55
410	12	06	77	54	910	32	45	57	15
420	12	25	77	35	920	33	28	56	32
430	12	44	77	16	930	34	13	55	47
440	13	03	76	57	940	35	02	54	58.
450	13	22	76	38	950	35	54	54	06
460	13	42	76	18	960	36	52	53	08
470	14	01	75	59	970	37	58	52	02
480	14	21	75	39	980	39	16	50	44
490	14	40	75	20	990	40	57	49	03
500	15	00	75	00	1000	45	00	45	00

The use of the Precedent
TABLE.

SUppose that the greatest Range, namely the Range made at the elevation of the sixth point of the Quadrant by a Culverin, be, for example, 4000 Geometrical paces, I desire with the same Piece to make a shot in such manner that its Range may be just 2360 paces long. I take the fourth part of 2360, which is 590, and I look upon the Table, and find against that Number, that the elevation to be given to the said Piece is 18 Degrees and 5 Minutes, or Gr. 71. and Min. 55, its Complement. And I say, by the things demonstrated, that the forementioned Piece with one of these two Elevations, shall carry the Ball 2360 paces distance above the Horizon. But those Elevations which exceed the sixth point of the Quadrant, are not inserted for the use of* Artillery, but only for Morter-Pieces, Rams, and Granadoes. It is to be noted, therefore, that with that same first Elevation the Ball will make a low Range, but swift, as the line marked A, and with a great Horizontal *Impetus*, proper to make breaches in Walls, or give other lateral impulses. But with the other Elevation it shall describe the Range B, which shall be slow in its Horizontal motion, but with sufficient perpendicular *Impetus* at the last, proper to batter Vaults, Roofs, and to make other breaches perpendicular to the Horizon; or to cast things to any determinate mark, as, *v. gr.* little Baggs imbaled with Cord, full of Sulphur, Salt-Peeter, or Meal, or Balls with Letters or other things within them. In a word, both those Elevations that are equally distant from the sixth point, will carry the Ball unto the same place: but yet with this difference, that with the first and least Elevation it shall fall to the Earth (as Gunners speak) Grazing; and with the second and greater Elevation, it shall descend almost plumb, or perpendicular.

That is, all long Pieces.

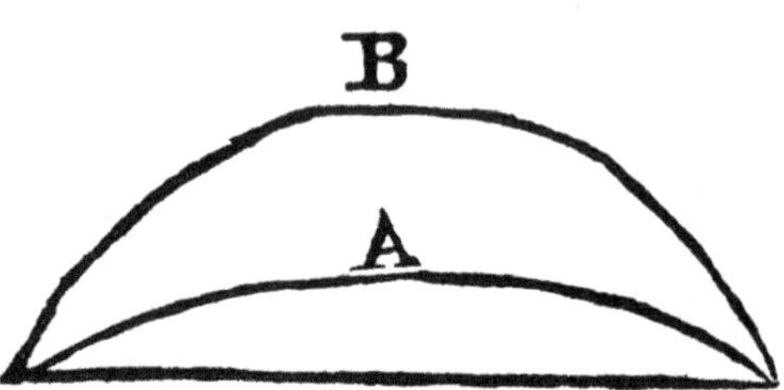

I know that its very seldom, and perhaps never found, that the greatest Range of a Piece of Ordnance is just those 4000 Paces, as it seemeth to have been supposed in the Calculating of our Table, and also in those of *Signiore Galileo*, so that the said Table might seem unuseful: but we shall shew, that the supposed number of 4000 doth not therefore serve to any great particular Machine, to the end it might serve to all in general. It is necessary therefore to take notice, that that same supposititious Number of 4000, is not of Paces, or of Ells, or of Yards, or of any other determinate measure, but of abstracted parts, such yet, whatever they are, as being convertible into any kinds of possible measures, they do make the Table general, as well for the Culvering, as for the Mortar-Piece or Cross-Bow. And to give an example how it may be adapted and applyed to all the Species of Artillery, and how the Abstract parts may be reduced into Geometrical paces, we will do thus.

The greatest Range of a Canon, by experiment made thereof, is found to be, suppose 2300 paces; and I would with the same Piece make a shot that should be 860 paces, I do thus: If the greatest Range 2300 give 860, I ask what the number 1000, the greatest of the Table will give? I work and find 374: which number being sought in the Table, is found to be betwixt 370 and 380. Therefore taking the part proportional according to my Judgement, I find the Arch of its Elevation ought to be *Grad.* 11. very near, or its Complement *gr.* 79. And thus it is cer-

tain,

tain, that that same Piece which being mounted to six points did carry 2300 paces, being elevated *gr.* 11. or 79. of the *Quadrant*, shall carry 860 paces, as we did desire.

PROBLEME.

How by a Shot made casually, one may find the greatest Range of an Ordnance.

LEt a Piece be directed according to the Mounture A C; of which let the Elevation be the Angle B A C, whatever it is. And the said Angle being measured with the *Quadrant*, let it be found; for example, *gr.* 30. then let off the Piece, and let the Shot reach to the point B: and let the line A B be carefully measured, which suppose to be *v. gr.* 2400 Geometrical Paces, I say that these two things being given, namely the Elevation, and the length of the casual Range A G B, you have therewithal given the line A D, which is the half of the greatest Range, according to what hath been demonstrated in the last Corollary of the first Proposition, *De Motu Projectorum*.

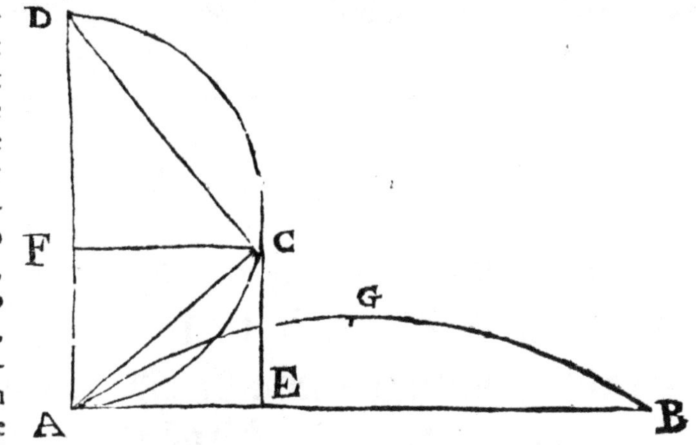

The Angle of Elevation C A B *gr.* 30, being given, the right Angled Triangle E A C shall be given in Specie: and because A B is given in paces, A E shall be given, which is the fourth part thereof, namely 600 paces. Let us therefore, to find the quantity of A D, work in this manner by Calculations and Sines.

Say, if as the Right Sine 86602 of the Angle A C E, *gr.* 60. that is, of the Complement of the Elevation, is to the side A E, which is 600: so is the whole Sine 100000 to a fourth number 693: and thus the Hypothenuse A C shall be 693 Paces. But because that the right angled Triangle A C D is given in Specie, begin again and say, as the right Sine 50000 of the angle A D C, which is equal to the angle given of the Elevation E A C, is to the right Line A C, which is found to be 693 paces, so is the whole line to a fourth number 1386. And thus the right line sought A D, shall be 1386 paces. But because A D, being the line of *Impetus* or Sublimity, is equal to half the greatest Range; if we double 1386, we shall make the number of 2772 paces; for so much shall be the length of the desired greatest Range of that Gun, which being elevated to the Randon of *gr.* 30, is found to carry 2400 paces.

But with much more brevity, and at one single working, we may perform the same thus. Suppose the whole Sine to be C F, then F A and F D shall be the Tangents, one, of the angle of elevation, and the other of its Complement. Say, therefore, as the whole Sine is to C F, which is 600: so is 230940 (which is the sum of both those Tangents) to a fourth number 1386. And thus the right line A D is found, as before, 1386 paces: which being doubled, will give the measure of the Semirect, or greatest * Randon, as you well call it.

*Or the best of the Randon.

COROLLARIES.

1. BY way of Corollary it may be advertised, that this is the manner of arguing from any Range of a Piece, how much the same should be to shoot upwards by a perpendicular line; which shall be as much as the line A D found out by way of Calculation.

2. The same line A D, directs us from what Altitude it would be requisite to let fall a Cannon Bullet, that it may arrive at the Earth with the same *Impetus* that the Cannon it self conferreth, alwayes allowing for the impediment which the Crassitude of the Air may occasion, which acknowledge must be sensible for to vary the demonstrated Propositions of Ranges, but much more for to obstruct this effect.

PROBLEME.

How with the sole Table of Sines we may know the greatest Altitude, to which the Ball hath attained passing through the Air in a Range, the Elevation and length of the said Range being given.

IN the precedent Figure, let there be given the angle of the Elevation C A B, and the length of the Range A B: it is required to know the greatest Altitude to which the Ball hath arrived thorough the Air: and this shall be E C. Take again A E 600 paces, that is, the fourth part of the whole length A B: and then say, as 86602 the Sine of the Angle A C E, the Supplement of the Elevation, is to A E, 600 paces, so is 50000, the Sine of the Elevation E A C to a fourth number: and we shall find 346 paces for measure of the Altitude C E, that is, of the greatest Altitude to which the Ball had attained in its passage through the Air.

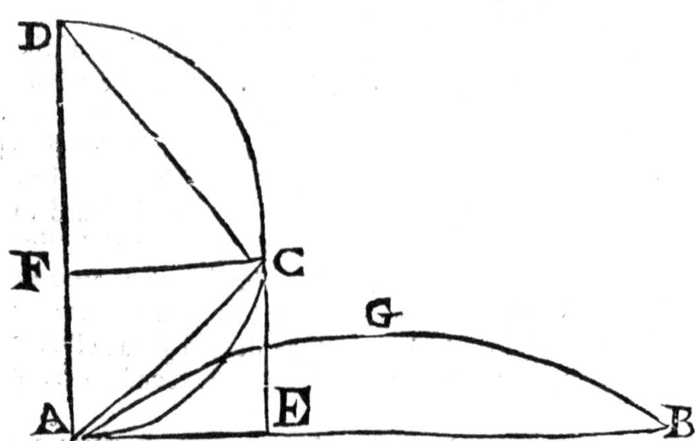

It

It is to be noted, that great Guns are not alwayes used so as that the Ball goeth to determine in the same Horizontal plain from which it did depart, as *Galileo's* and our Tables do suppose. Therefore being to shoot upon the side of a Hills declivity or aclivity, as also being to shoot from the summity of a Rock upon the Horizontal plain that is below, there hath no man as yet reduced the measures of these Ranges to an Art. The Table of them might be calculated, but every one will perceive, that it being to be composed by every grade of the Pieces Elevation or Mounture, and by every grade of the Hills inclination, and by every pace of the Hills Altitude, the Multiplication would be almost infinite. We will therefore only give you the general Rule for calculating those Ranges when they shall occur.

A *Piece* with the direction A B, maketh the Range A C D: but I would shoot along the inclined plain A C; and I desire to know what A C, the length of the Range of that shot upon this plain, shall be.

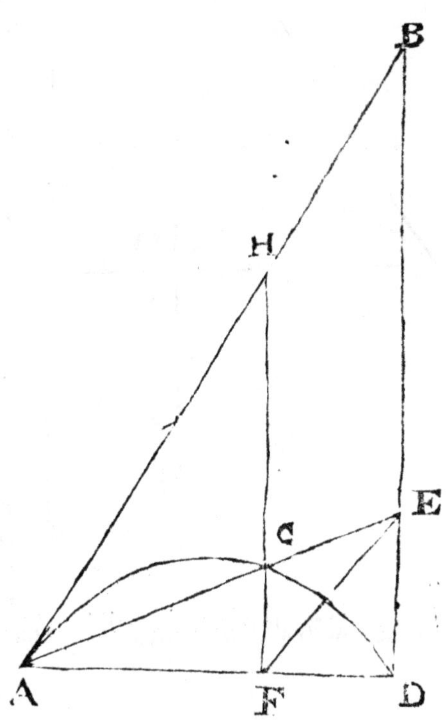

Draw B D by the point D, and H F by the point C, perpendiculars to the Horizon; and draw a line from F to E; which by the things demonstrated, is parallel to A B. Measure with some Instrument the angle D A E, that is the Hills Elevation, and, by the Table of Amplitudes, you shall find the length of the Horizontal Range A D. Then say, as D B the Tangent of the angle of the Pieces, Elevation is to B E, which is the difference of the Tangents of the two angles D A B and D A E known, (one being the Elevation of the Piece, the other the Elevation of the Hill above the Horizon) so is D A known, in paces, to a fourth number: and the right line F A shall be found in paces. Then say again, as the whole Sine is to that fourth number, which is the measure of A F in paces, so is A C the secant of the angle F A C, to a fourth number: and thus you shall know the number of paces that measure the line A C, that is, the length of the Range that that Piece will make upon the plain A E, when you shoot upwards.

But when from the point A it is required to shoot downwards by a descending Hill, as A B, we shall find the quantity of the Range A B, that is, the place where the Ball falleth, in this manner. Let the direction A E, that is, let the angle of the Pieces Elevation be given; also let there be given the angle of the Hills inclination C A B. Let us imagine the Horizon to be A C, and let us draw B E and H D F perpendiculars to the same: and conjoyn or draw a line from C to H, which line shall be parallel to A E. Now upon the Table of Amplitudes we shall find how many paces A D is, but we seek the quantity of A B. Therefore make the calculation thus; as F D the Tangent of the angle of the Pieces Elevation is to D H, the Tangent of the inclination of the plain; so is A D, known in paces, to a farther number. And this shall be the measure of D C in paces; and thus the whole line A C shall be known in paces. Then say again, as A C the whole Sine is to A C known in paces, so is A B the Secant of the angle C A B to a fourth number: and this last number shall be the measure sought of the right line A B in paces; that is, the length of the Range upon the descending plain A B. It happeneth also many times, that we are to shoot at plains perpendicular to the Horizon, as at the Walls of Cities, or Towers, or other wayes; therefore also in this case we will subjoyn the Computation for finding the Altitude of that point in the said Wall where the Ball is to hit.

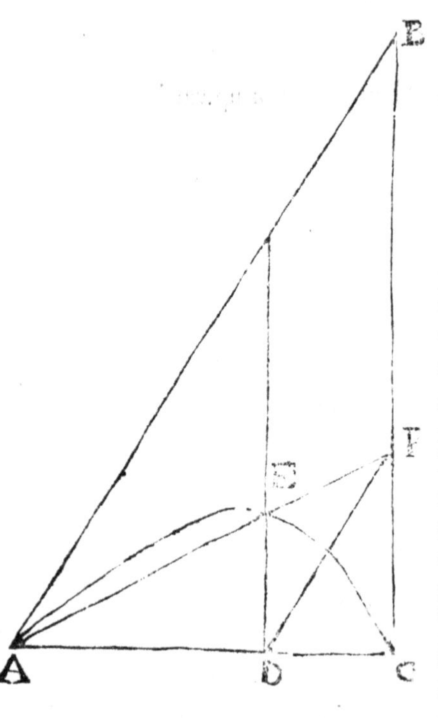

Let the Direction of the Piece be the Line A B, and the Horizon A C, and the Wall of the Tower D E perpendicular to the Horizon: and let the distance A D be known in paces. Let us suppose that the Ball passeth freely without hitting the Wall, and falleth upon the Horizon in C. The Table of the Amplitudes giveth the quantity of A C, but we seek the Altitude D E. Draw C B perpendicular to the Horizon, and D F parallel to A B, and then draw a line from F to A, which shall pass thorow the common Section of the *Parabola*, and of the Wall, as may be collected from the things already demonstrated. Now say, as C A the length of the Horizontal line is to C D the difference betwixt the lines A C and A D already known, so is B C the Tangent of the angle of the Elevation of the Piece, to C F the Tangent of the angle F A C. Again say, as the Sine Total is to A D known in paces, so is the last found Tangent of the angle F A C to a fourth number: which shall be the desired measure of the right line D E in paces. And thus we have

have found the point E in which the said shot would stick. The same calculation may be also deduced. Although the Wall D E be not perpendicular, but scarfed, as those of the modern Fortresses; but fearing to procure you more trouble than benefit, I will refer the care of that to the Geometrician that hath a mind to undertake it.

The Amplitudes of the *Parabola's*, of which *Galileo*, and also we do treat, suppose that the Range terminates not upon the plain of the Field, but in that Horizontal plain that passeth by the Muzzle of the Piece. The other is only true when the Peice is placed with its Carriages in a Trench, so that the mouth of the Piece lyeth exactly level with the ground. But because this is not usual, and because the Ranges do determine in the Horizon that toucheth the lower parts of the Wheels, we will Geometrically enquire how much a level Range, or Horizontal Range may be prolonged by means of the Altitude of the Muzzle of the Piece above the plain of the Field. It seemeth that the Semidiameter of the wheels, and the thickness of the Metal do cause the Muzzles of ordinary Artillery to be above the Horizontal Site about two Braces. I suppose therefore the Muzzle of the Culvering to be at A, and let the Horizon be B C; and let the Altitude of the Muzzle be the right line A B, supposed to be two Braces; and let the Range A C D be the level Range. The right line B C is sought; let the Semirect Range, or the best of the Randon of the same Piece, be the *Parabola* A E F; and let it be supposed that A F be 5000 Geometrical paces, that is a 15000 Florentine Braces. Describe the usual Semi-circle of the first Proposition A H I, and having drawn A L equal to A I apply L D. The right line A I, by the things demonstrated, shall be the *Impetus* of the *Parabola* A E F, or of A C D (for they are Ranges of the same Piece) therefore A L shall be the fourth part of the right side of the *Parabola* A C D: therefore L D shall be double of L A: but A F hath been demonstrated to be also double of A I; therefore L D and A F are equal; and there are three lines given, that is, L A 7500. L D 15000. and A B 2. And therefore, working by the Rule of three, as the right line L A is to A B known; so is the square of the right line L D to another number: we shall find 60000; which shall be the square of the right line B C; and extracting the Square root thereof, we shall find the line B C to be 245 Braces. We conclude therefore that that Machine which maketh its greatest Range of 15000 Braces, in case it shall have its Muzzle raised above the Horizon, will make its level Range, that is, without any Elevation or Mounture, to be in all 245 Braces long. Next, how much every other Range not level, but inclined upwards or downwards, by occasion of the Altitude of the wheels, or of a Bastion, or of a Mount, or of any other scituation that raiseth it above the Horizontal plain, may be prolonged, shall be found thus.

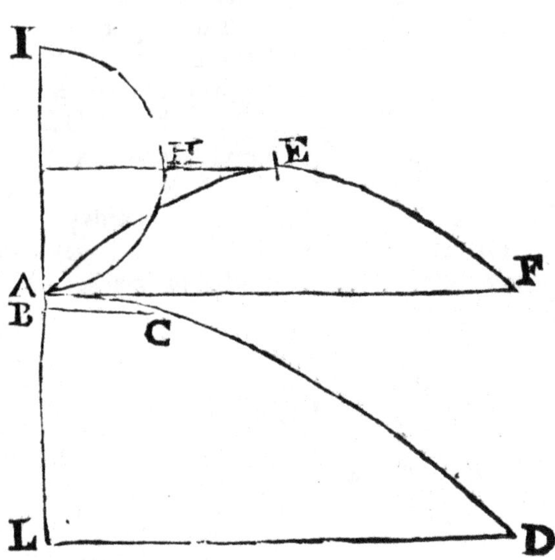

It is certain, that being to shoot from the top of a Rock, or of a Castle placed in the top of an Hill, or from any whatever high place above the Horizontal Plain of the Field that lyeth below, the Ranges will prove much longer than those noted upon the Table of Amplitudes; and this difference shall be so much greater, by how much the scituation of the Artillery shall be higher above that Horizontal plain in which the Balls are to hit, and the Ranges to determine.

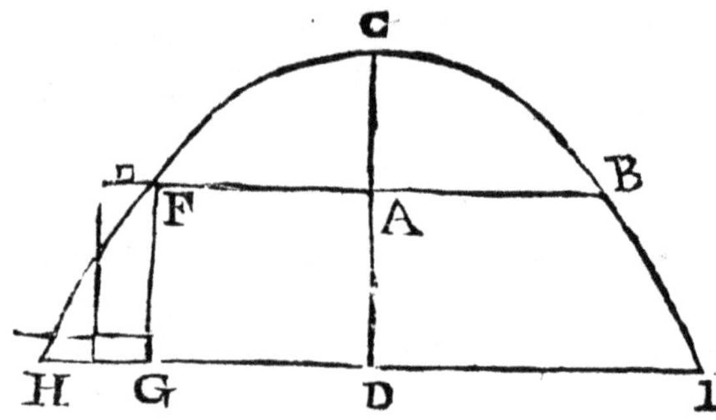

Let the height of the Hill or other place be G F, and from the point F, let a line be drawn upon the plain of the Field G E: and let us suppose the Horizon to be F B : now having made the Range F C B E at an Elevation, the measure of G E is sought.

By the Table of Amplitudes, we find the quantity of A B, and by the Table of Altitude, we find A C, the height of the *Parabola*. And for the working of the Computation, it may be performed sundry wayes.

Let the number of A B be squared, and divide that square by A C, and the *Quotus* shall be the right side of the *Parabola* F C B : Then multiply that *Quotus* by C D, and the square Root of the Product shall give D E.

Or we may work thus:

Draw the number D C into C A, and the square Root of the product shall be the mean proportional betwixt D C and C A. Then say, as C A is to the fore-mentioned Root, so is A B to another number. And this fourth number shall again be D E.

Or lastly, in this manner:

Say, as the number C A, the Altitude of the *Parabola* in the Table, is to the number C D, the Altitude of the *Parabola* and Range together, so is A B the Semi-Amplitude of the *Parabola* in the Table to another fourth number.

Then take the number that is mean-proportional betwixt that last number and A B, for that mean-proportional shall give you the said D E. And for as much as D G, equal to A B is known, the whole line G E shall be known.

But some might alleadge, that from the Mount G F, it may perhaps be required to play with Guns oftner downwards than upwards; therefore it would be necessary to know by a Geometrical Rule, the length of Ranges, which is done in this manner. Let the Range to be made downwards be that marked F H, with any whatever angle of inclination beneath the Horizon : G H is sought. Imagine with your self that the Range is to be made above the Horizon with the self same inclination; and by the precedent Rules, the quantity of D E is found as above, or D H, from which if we take the part already known F A, or D G, there shall remain known the quantity required G H. But if *gr.* 40 being given for the Elevation of the Range A B C, and the Base A C 1600 Paces, we would know all the different Altitudes of the Ranges of the Ball upon any point of the line A C, work thus: Having divided A C in the midst, and erected D B, this shall be the Supream Altitude, and shall be found in the Table of Altitudes and Amplitudes working in this manner. In the Table of Amplitudes right against *gr.* 40. of Elevation, I find the line A D to be 9848 parts : but in the Table of Altitudes I find the line B D to be 4132 parts. Then, by the Rule of Three, I say; if A D 9848 give 800 paces according to the supposition, how many paces shall D B, which is 4132 parts, give? and I find, that the right line B D is 336 paces. Now let any point be proposed, as E, over which you would know the Altitude of the Range of the Ball, that is the line E H. Let the right line A E be supposed 1000, and E C 600 : and work the Rule of three again, in this manner. If the square of A D, which

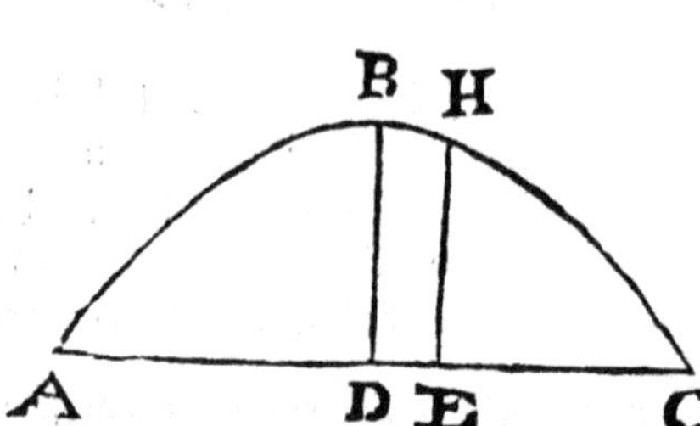

which is 640000, give the Rect-angle of the right lines A E and E C which is 600000, what shall the number B D (which was found to be 336) give? and I find 315 paces. Therefore the Altitude of the *Parabola* over the point E, was 315 paces; which is that that was sought.

It shall suffice to have hinted this little for the Calculating of some varieties that may happen about these Ranges. Other cases may be put, like to these, and particularly those of their conversions; but from the knowledge of these, those may easily be deducted: and the Ingenuity of any Geometrician, applying himself thereto, shall find less difficulty in resolving many of these Problems of himself, than in undergoing the length and obscurity of our explanations. Therefore we will proceed to the making of the *Quadrant*, the which seemeth really appropriated, nay, made by Nature on purpose for to measure Scientifically and Geometrically the Ranges of Projects.

Of the Quadrant.

LEt us now come to practice; and by help of an Instrument, let us resolve some of the Propositions above demonstrated. We will make a Military *Quadrant*, which with invariable certainty sheweth (at least to Geometrical Philosophers, if not to practical Gunners) what Mounture or Elevation ought to be given to any Piece, to the end that the length of the Range may prove to be of such a certain measure. We will also resolve, by help hereof, all Problems that can be framed about the shooting of Artillery, which were heretofore promised by *Tartaglia*, and reduced into Tables by *Galileo*, with something over and above. Military Industry did find that the use of a Machine so noble, and of so great consequence as the Canon, would be too much confined, and of too little benefit, if it could not be made use of save only at that small distance to which it carrieth a point blank, or in its level Range, without giving it with the *Quadrant* the advantageous assistance of some elevation. It was therefore enquired how a man might do that with the same Piece, which of it self did not carry more than 200 or 250 Geometrical paces, he might shoot 400 and also 600 paces, and more and more, until he come to the length of the greatest Range that can be made by that Piece. The Invention was thus: They began to help the Piece by Elevation, that is, they directed it not straight upon th' object which it was to hit, but, holding it in the very vertical of th' object, they elevated it above that right line which goeth from the Piece unto the object: and this they did sometimes more, and sometimes less, according as the force of the Shot was to be greater or lesser: An Artifice that from the very beginning of the world hath been known even to artless Boyes. We see that when they with a Ball of Snow, or other matter, do aim to hit a mark that is very near, they throw it directly at the mark: but being at another time to aim at one which standeth farther off, or being to throw Stones at each other, they do not throw Horizontally, or directly at their Adversaries, but turning the cast half way into the Air, without having ever had any other consideration, they do all throw at the elevation of the fifth, and also of the sixth point of the Military Square to them unknown: But Gunners, in process of time, have found an Instrument, that doth with facility measure these Elevations.

Nicolo Tartaglia of *Brescia*, a famous Mathematician, did invent a Square with unequal sides joyned together with the *Quadrant*, which hath for more than a hundred years past, been generally used, and is still the only Regulator of Gunners, not only to manage great Guns, and to raise them to those Mountures which they call Randons, but also to level them in the Point-blank Ranges; *Tartaglia* divided that Quadrant into 12 equal parts, beginning the Numeration of them from the lesser [or shorter] side; he also subdivided each of those into other 12 equal parts, naming those first

Points, and these second Minutes of the *Quadrant*. We will insert the figure of the Quadrant, and shew how it measureth the Elevation [Mounture or Randon] of the Piece.

Her Concave, Cilinder, or Bore.

Let the Canons * Soul be A B, fixed at some certain Mounture: put into the Muzzle thereof the greater of the *Quadrant* C A: so that it be applyed to the lower side of the said Soul, and let the Plummet fall in D. I say that the Angle E C D, that is the arch E D, is the measure of the Elevation of the Piece. Draw an Horizontal line A F, the angles at the point G shall be right: But the angle A C F is also right. Therefore the angles C A F, and F C G are equal by the 8 of the sixth of *Euclid*. Or thus; Draw thorough C the Horizontal line. If H I now from the right angles H C D and A C E there be taken the common part A C D, there shall remain th' Angle E C D of the *Quadrant*, equal to the angle of the Piece under the Horizon H I, or above the Horizon A F, which is the same as being alterne.

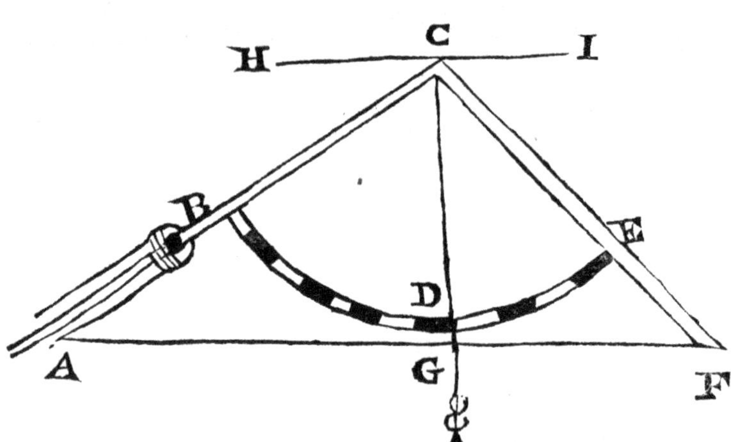

By the help of this *Quadrant* Gunners have with long observations composed such a *Praxis*, as that they know how many points they are to mount *v. gr.* a Culvering of 40 pound Ball to hit a mark distant; for example, 700 Geometrical paces, or at any other distance.

But the truth is, the observations are so fallible, and the Gunners so few that have made them, and made them exactly, that the use of Artillery, taking from it the Range of Point Blank, must needs have very little of certainty in it.

If one would collect some certain Science touching th' ordinary Quadrant, it would be necessary to make the Experiments not only with all sorts of Balls, and with all the varieties of Powder, but in all kind of Pieces, as also in all those that being the same *in specie*, are of different grandeur; and lastly, at all possible degrees of Elevation. A Multiplication that almost runs up into infinity. And we observe that these Experiments ought to be all made one by one; for it is not true, that by way of proportion one may from three or four Ranges of a Canon made at several elevations, argue to any others, no not of the same Canon, laden with the same Powder and Ball. That this is so, may be demonstrated by help of the Tables made by *Signiore Galilæo*, and by us. For example, That Canon which being elevated at the sixth Point, curryeth its shot 4000 paces, elevated at one Point, ought to curry the sixth part, at two points the third, and at three points the half of that Range. But the thing falls out far otherwise: For being elevated to one point, it curryeth 1032 instead of 666, which is the sixth part of that same greatest Range 4000: at the second point (and note that with this Mounture, Pieces carry alwayes the half of the greatest Range) in our case will curry 2000 in stead of 1333, which is the third part: At the third point it will curry 2824, instead of 2000, which is the half of the greatest Range: at the fourth point it will curry 3464 instead of 2666: At the fifth point it will curry 3860, in stead of 2333, which are 5 sixths of that greatest Range: See therefore how that increasing equally the Mountures of the Piece, that is shooting first at one point only, then at two, three, four, *&c.* unto the sixth, the increases of the lengths of the Ranges do not increase equally, that is with the same proportion wherewith the

* Randons

* Randons increase. But the first point currying 1032, the second increaseth above it 968, the third increaseth 824, the fourth 640, the fifth 396, the sixth 140. Therefore to derive some rule from the Experiments, it were necessary to make them exactly, at all the Grades of Randons, in all sorts of Pieces, with all varieties of Powders, and different matters of Balls; and happily one might say, it were necessary also that every Gunner made them by himself. Things almost impossible to reduce unto Rules, from which any certainty might be gathered, if the Theorick and Geometry had not given us a manifest Science thereof, by means of that one sole Proposition of *Galileo*, in which first of all men he hath advertised and taught us, *That Pro ects do all move in a Parabolical Line*. Upon this supposition we will ground the Instrument promised: and though by the impediment of the *medium* the *Parabola's* become too deformed, or by many other accidents the Ranges prove very inconstant, yet it sufficeth us to have given indubitable satisfaction to the School of Mathematicians, if not to that of Gunners.

Or Mountures.

Before we set down the making of our square, which consisteth only in describing one single Semi-circle, we will divide the ordinary *Quadrant* into unequal points, so as they may not measure the Randons of the Piece, but the lengths of the Ranges, which is that that serves to our purpose. Thus we shall be assured, that the Gun, if it shall be elevated to one point of the said *Quadrant*, shall carry to such a distance, whatever it be: and elevated to two points, shall precisely double that Range: and if to three, it shall carry three of those spaces; if to four and a half, it shall carry four and a half; if to five and a quarter, it shall carry five and a quarter; and thus until you come to the sixth point, shall the points of the Quadrant in the Instrument, and the spaces of the Ranges in the Field, alwayes increase in the same manner, and with the same proportion, and from the sixth to the twelfth point, they shall go in the same manner decreasing. The construction and demonstration is Geometrically taken from the proposition which we have made the First of this our Book of Projects, which by the Amplitude given, teacheth us to find the Elevation. And it serveth in common for whatsoever sort of Artillery and Mortar Pieces, and for any sort of Ball or Powder.

Let the sides of the Quadrant be A B the greater and A C the lesser; then making A the Center, describe the *Quadrant* C D E, upon which the unequal points are to be marked or set off: and about the Diameter A C draw the Semi-circle A F C; and having drawn F G perpendicular to A B, and Tangent to the Semi-circle, divide A G into six equal parts to find the six points of the *Quadrant*, and then again, each part into 12 to find the Minutes, (if the size of the Instrument shall admit of this second division) now let one of the six parts be G H. Draw H M I parallel to G F, cutting the Semi-diameter in the points M and I, and then from the Center A, draw the right line A F D, and D shall be the sixth point of the square: draw A I L, and L shall be the fifth point of the square: draw A M N, and N shall be the seventh point; and so of all the rest. Note, that the division will be the more exact, if after you have found the 1, 2, 3, &c. points, you do by the Transportation or setting of them off, design the ninth, tenth, and eleventh.

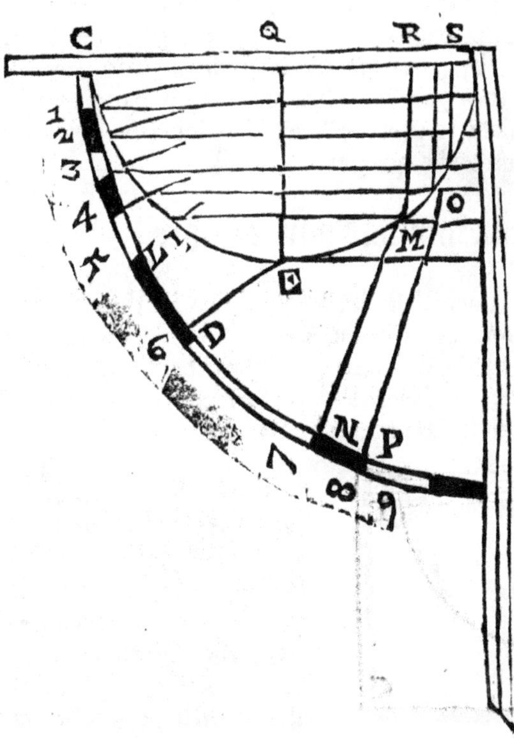

The half points, quarter points, and Minutes, are found in the same manner by subdividing each of the portions of the line A G into two, into four, or into twelve parts, which raising perpendiculars from the points of the Divisions: Those perpendiculars shall cut the Semi-circle, and by the points of the Sections shall the Diameters be drawn in the Quadrant, and these shall cut the Quadrant in the parts desired, of Half points, Quarter points, or Minutes.

Of Mounture. Now it is manifest by our I. Proposition, that if the line of the * direction, or of the elevation of the Piece shall be A O, or A P, the Amplitude or length of the Range shall be as the Quadruple of the S O; and if the direction shall be A M, or A N, the Range shall be as the Quadruple of R M: and if the elevation were according to the line A F D, the Range shall be as the Quadruple of Q F: but the lines S O, R M, and Q F, by our construction do equally exceed: And, therefore, likewise their Quadruples, or the Ranges aforesaid, shall equally exceed one the other.

The use of the aforementioned Division made in the ordinary Quadrant.

LEt there be propounded any Piece of Artillery, or Mortar-Piece; and with it let there be one single Experiment made, that is, let it be elevated to any point, as for example to the fifth. Let it off, and measure the length of the Range, and let it be found, *verbi gratia,* to be 2000 parts; this done we may know how far the same Piece will carry, being charged in the same manner, and elevated to any what-ever other Point or Minute: which shall be easie by the Rule of three, the points in this Instrument, as well as the length of the Ranges, being proportional. The *Praxis* is this; I desire to know how far the sixth point carrieth, I thus say, If five points give 2000 paces, how much shall six points give? and I find 2400 paces. I say then that the shot of that Piece at the sixth point, that is at the greatest Range, will carry 2400 of those parts, at which of the fifth point it carried 2000.

And take notice by the way, that instead of performing this operation with the points 7, 8, 9, 10, 11, and 12, It may be done with their Complements, which are 5, 4, 3, 2, 1, and 0.

But if it were required (which importeth much more) that we should elevate the aforesaid Piece in such sort, that the length of the Range ought to be; for example, 1300 paces, we are to work thus. If 2000 paces were made by 5 points, or to say better, by 60 Minutes of the Quadrant, by how many points shall 1300 paces be made? the working will be 2000. 60. 1300. 39, and we shall find that for to make the Range of 1300 paces, it would be necessary to give the Piece the Mounture of 39 Minutes of the Quadrant, or of three points and a quarter.

The manner how to Compose our Square.

BUt if we would frame an Instrument, which shall not only measure the length of the Ranges made at several Randons, but also the Altitude of the *Parabola*, the duration or time of the flight [or Range] the sublimity, and the other things demonstrated in the aforesaid Book of Projects, all this shall be performed with the sole and simple Semi-circle of I. Proposition. But let us proceed to the making of it.

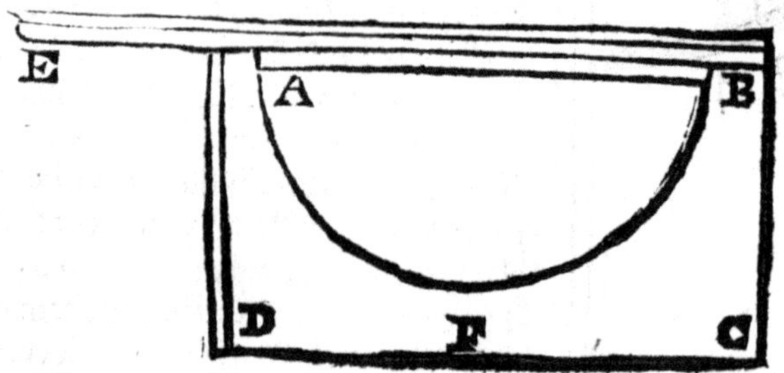

Take the Rect-angled Plate A B C D, of Brass, or other solid Matter, having the side A E long, for the applying of it to the Piece. Upon the Diameter A B, draw a Semi-circle A F B, which shall be the Semi-circle

circle of Propofit. I. *De Projectis*; and in B place the Thred and Plummet, and divide the Semi-circle A F B into 90 equal parts, which ſhall be the 90 degrees of the Quadrant; or into 144 equal parts, which ſhall be the equal Points and Minutes of the ordinary Quadrant. Let us now demonſtrate Geometrically, that this ſquare is convenient to meaſure, with exceeding plainneſs, the lengths and the Altitudes of the Ranges, the times of their Durations, the ſublimities of the *Parabola's*, and the Elevations of the Pieces. And then we will ſet down the Diviſion of the Lines thereupon, without the need of any Table for the uſing of the ſame.

Let us, as in the ſubſequent Figure, place the ſquare afore-named E A B C D in the mouth of any Piece, E A at pleaſure, and let the Plummet fall upon the point F of the Semi-circle A F B, divided into 90 equal parts. It is certain, in the firſt place, that the Arch B F meaſureth the Elevation of the Piece E A above the Horizon. For we having by the Diviſion of the Semi-circle into 90 parts only, valued every two degrees for one; we have made the Arch B F to be the meaſure of the Angle B A F, that is, of the Elevation of the Piece above the Horizon; which Horizon ſhall ever be the line A F. I ſay moreover, that if we ſhould ſuppoſe the line A B, Diameter of the Semi-circle, to be the *Impetus* of the aſſigned Piece, or the half of the greateſt Range, the line F H, perpendicular to the Diameter, ſhall be the fourth part of the Amplitude or length of the Range; B H ſhall be the ſupream Altitude of the *Parabola*: A H ſhall be the ſublimity; and B F ſhall be the time of the Ranges Duration.

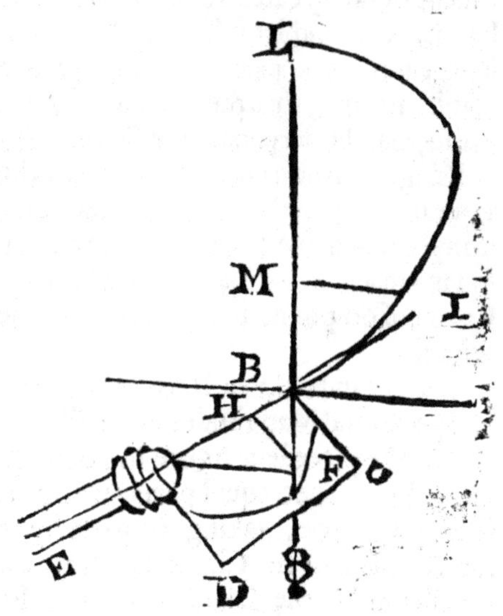

That this is ſo, ſhall thus be demonſtrated (having reference to the I. Propoſition of Projects, and its Corollaries.) Let the line of the direction A B I be prolonged indefinitely, as alſo the perpendicular F B L; then by imagination take B L of ſuch a length, that it may be really equal to half the greateſt Range of our preſent Piece. And about the Diameter B L, let there be imaginarily drawn the great Semi-circle B I L; cutting the Circumference B I in any point I; and draw the Horizontal line I M. It is manifeſt, by the afore-cited Propoſ. I. of Projects, that the line M I ſhall be the real fourth part of the length of the Range; as alſo, that D M ſhall be the (not imiginary, but) real Altitude of the ſaid Range; and ſo the other meaſures in the Semi-circle B I L, ſhall be all true and real. Now obſerve, that the Triangle H B F is like to the Triangle B I M, as being right-angled, and having two angles at the Point B. Therefore the ſame Propoſition ſhall be between all the ſmall and imaginary meaſures of the ſquare A C, as is between all the true meaſures in the imaginary and great Semi-circle B I L; that is, the lines, A B, B F, F H and H B, ſhall be to one another in the ſame proportion reſpectively as L B, B I, I M, and M B. Therefore, as to arguing in the proportions, we may without any error, as well make uſe of thoſe feigned proportions upon the ſquare, as of the true ones, imagined in the Amplitude of the Air.

It remains now that we ſhew how this Doctrine, which hath hitherto been a meer Speculation, may now be reduced to Manual practice, and that with facility. Every one ſeeth that for our obtaining knowledge of the quantity of the lines A B, B F, F H, and H B, and their proportions in the precedent Figure, it would be neceſſary that all the aforeſaid lines were divided into moſt Minute parts with ſome common meaſure. To this purpoſe, therefore, we will divide the Diameter A B, and Semi-Diameter E D, into equal and very ſmall parts, as appeareth in the following Figure; (upon which let us deſcribe the imaginary ſquare) and then let us give to each diviſion of

Fffff the

the circumference, its guides parallel to those Diameters, that so in them the number and quantity of the lines which shall be Indices of the length and Altitudes of the Ranges, may be read or found : And in the point of the angle of Semi-circle B, place the Thread and Plummet.

As to the number of parts into which the Diameter A B is to be divided, it shall be left to the choice of every one ; but yet it will be convenient to make choice of the number 2000, for that it will facilitate the Arithmetical operation.

It is to be noted, that if any one will make a square , as hath been said, on purpose for one kind of Artillery onely, he shall without the least trouble of Calculation, have the measures of all its Ranges.

The Division of this square is to be made *a posteriori*, in this manner. Make an Experiment of the greatest Range of that same Piece to which you would have the square to be adapted, and let it be found *v. gr.* to be 3000. Then divide the Diameter of the square into 1500 parts, and the perpendicular Semi-diameter into 750 equal parts ; that is, imagine that the Diameter A B 1500, is the half of the greatest Range 3000 ; as also, that the perpendicular Semi-diameter E D 750, is the fourth part of that greatest Range. And thus, every of the other Elevations being afterwards given, as soon as we shall apply this Square to the Muzzle of the Piece, we shall immediately see how many paces is the length, and how many the Altitude of the Range, *&c.* And this square made *v. gr.* for a Canon of 60 pound Ball, would be also good for every other Canon of 60 pound Ball, that should be the same in length , and other proportions, with that.

It's true indeed, that if we would make the square universal, to serve indifferently for all Species and Magnitudes of Artillery , we must then do thus. Divide the Diameter A B in the precedent figure in 2000 equal parts : also let the Semi-Diameter E D be divided into 1000 equal parts, (we by reason of the smallness of the figure have divided it only into 100, taking the parts by ten and ten.) This done, let there be drawn by the Divisions of the Circumference, cut into equal degrees , as is usual, the guides parallel unto the Diameters , that so one may upon those Diameters read or find the quantity of the right lines , as they shall happen to be.

Now let a Piece of Ordnance F G, unknown, be given. Then make the previous Experiment in this manner. Apply the square to the Muzzle of it, and let the thread fall in any place , as in I. Then find by the means of its guide , the quantity of I O upon the divided Semi-Diameter , and keep it in mind, and then shoot off the Gun, and measure the Range , which suppose to be , for Example, 1250 paces : charge the Piece again in the same manner , and give it a different Mounture, so that the thread may fall elsewhere, as in M : the length of this Range is sought. Say thus : If the number of I O give the length 1250 paces, how many paces shall the number of M L, that is found upon the divided Semi-diameter give? and you shall in like manner find the length of that Range numbred in paces.

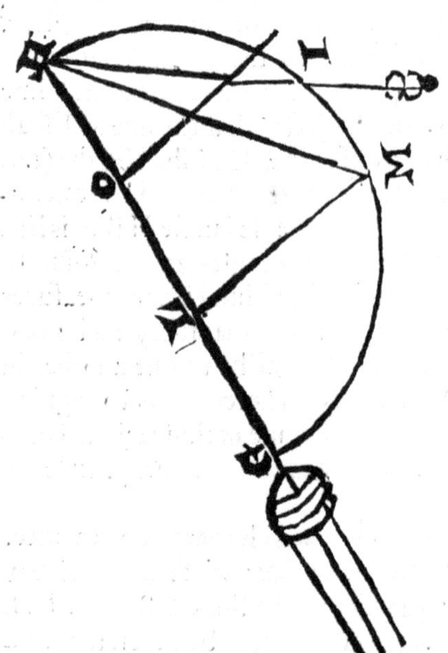

If you desire the Altitudes , and not the lengths of Ranges, then make the same working as before, but not with the lines I O and M L, which give the lengths , but with H O and H L, which give the Altitudes. And if we would have the sublimities , it would be necessary to work with G O and G L. But , which more importeth, if any one after the previous Experiment hath been made, shall desire that the same Piece may make an assigned Range, in length, *v. gr.* 2200 paces,

we

we are to find what elevation ought to be given to the Piece. Work thus: If the 1250 paces of the previous Experiment give I O numbred, what shall the 2200 paces give? and you shall find a number, which suppose for example, to be ascribed on the square unto the line M L. the Peice Therefore is to be raised to such a Randon, that the thread may pass thorow the point M; and then the Range shall be 2200 paces.

The times or durations of the Ranges are given by the Lines H I and H M: and to find the *Quantity* of these it may be done two wayes. First, by way of calculation: For the square of the time H I (in the precedent Figure) is alwayes equal to the two squares of the Altitude H O, and of the fourth part of the length I O. Secondly, by making to all the Divisions of the Perifry B, C, D, (in the present Figure) from the Center A the circular guides B E, C F, D H: for A H being thus divided into very small equal parts, it shall measure all the right lines, A B, A C, and A D, which are the times of the Ranges.

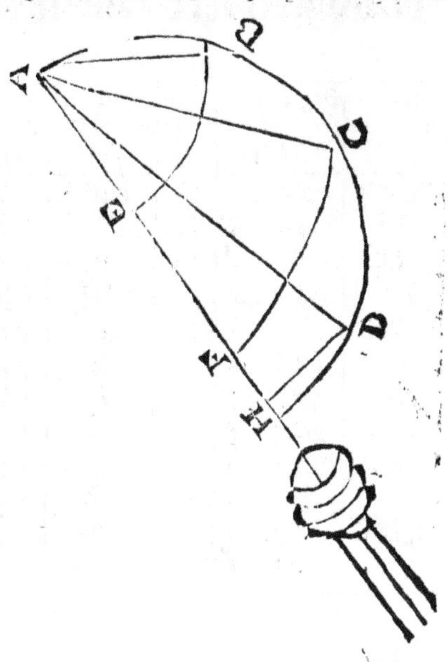

Yet we confess as to Military use, the Amplitudes or lengths of Ranges, only seem to Import; and they are of great moment: the rest are all accessary curiosities, which serve much more to the pleasures of Geometry, than to the occasions of War; therefore he that would have the square made only for this respect of Longitudes, may take the Semicircle A B C of Brass (as in the present Figure) having its side A D, and with the Semicircle E B, divided into most minute and equal parts, beginning the numeration from the point E; and may give moreover to all the points of the Perifry F, G, H, I, their guides G H, and F I parallel to A C: And thus he hath divided and numbred upon E B all the lines F N, and G O, which serve for the Amplitudes or Longitudes of the Ranges.

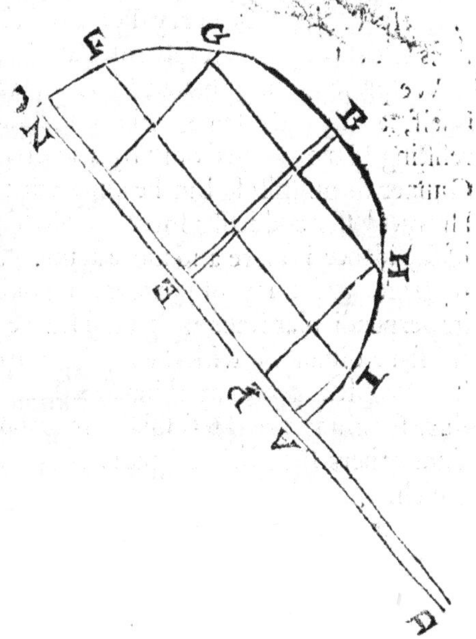

A Table which sheweth how many Degrees and Minutes of the Ordinary Quadrant inserted Page 20. each Point of one Square, the Points of which are unequal, doth contain.

Points unequal of the Square	Degrees of the ordinary Quadrant		Points unequal of the Square	Degrees of the ordinary Quadrant	
half	02	23	half	56	46
I	04	48	VII	61	47
half	07	15	half	65	42
II	09	44	VIII	69	26
half	12	19	half	72	10
III	15	00	IX	75	00
half	17	50	half	77	41
IV	20	54	X	80	16
half	24	18	half	82	45
V	28	13	XI	85	12
half	33	14	half	87	37
VI	45	00	XII	90	00

For Example, It is demanded where the Division of the one seventh unequal point doth fall. Look upon the present Table, right against the number VII, and you find that it falleth upon *gr.* 61. and *min.* 47. of the ordinary *Quadrant*.

BUt since we are fallen upon the consideration of the Motion and *Impetus* of Projects, we cannot balk th' occasion of adding somthing concerning the variety of their Forces in battering upon resisting Superficies, somtimes with greater, and somtimes with lesser Angles of Inclination. *Galilæo* considereth th' *Impetus* of these Projects in every Point of their *Parabola*, and measureth how much it is in its self, that is, in respect of that Plane in which it doth perpendicularly hit.

We presupposing that an *Impetus*, when it is upon the act of striking, is, as to it self, alwayes the same, will consider and measure how much it is in respect of the resisting Plane, varyed only by the diversity of th' Angles of Incidence. There is no Gunner so unskilful, but he knoweth that Cannon Bullets in hitting a Wall, have alwayes lesser and lesser force (if all things else be alike) by how much the Angle of Incidence is more and more acute. So that if the said Cannon with sixty pounds of Iron, and forty of Powder, not only pierceth, but beateth down a Courtin, with its perpendicular Range, it shall scarce hurt it (though it have the same Charge, and the same distance) with the Projection of the Range, which they call * Grazing. The Probleme, for any thing that I know, is unhandled. Therefore if we shall produce somthing that is less subsistent, and not purely Geometrical, either admit it till some others shall better handle the Doctrine, or wholly reject it, it matters not which.

*Di striscio.

SUP-

SUPPOSITIONS.

1. WE will ſpeak only of the Ranges of Great Guns; therefore, Let us ſuppoſe, that that portion of the Line which the Ball maketh a little before, and a little after its blow, be as it were a Right Line. I know that we treat of a Line really curved; but being (if it were entire) in length more than three thouſand Geometrical paces, we may take a yard, or a foot, or an inch thereof, without any ſenſible error, to be a Right Line.

2. Let us ſuppoſe ſecondly, that the Forces or *Impetus*'s of Projects are as the Spaces which they paſs or curry in the ſame Time; that is, If the Spaces A, B and C ſhall be paſt by the Moveable in the ſame Time; the *Impetus*'s or Forces in ſtriking, ſhall be as the Spaces A, B and C reſpectively. *Galil. 2. de Motu æquabili.*

3. But if the ſame Space ſhall be paſt by the Moveable in divers Times, the *Impetus*'s or Forces of the Moveable in battering ſhall have the Proportion reciprocal of their Times. That is, If the ſame Space D ſhall be paſt one while in the Time E, and another while in the Time F; the Force of the firſt ſhall be as F, and of the ſecond as E. *Galil. 3. de Motu æquabili.*

4. Let us ſuppoſe, in the next place, that all the Ranges have, as to themſelves, the ſame *Impetus*: which will happen if the Piece being fixed alwayes in the ſame place with the ſame Charge, the ſame Mounture, and Diſtance, &c. the obliquity of the Wall be only varied.

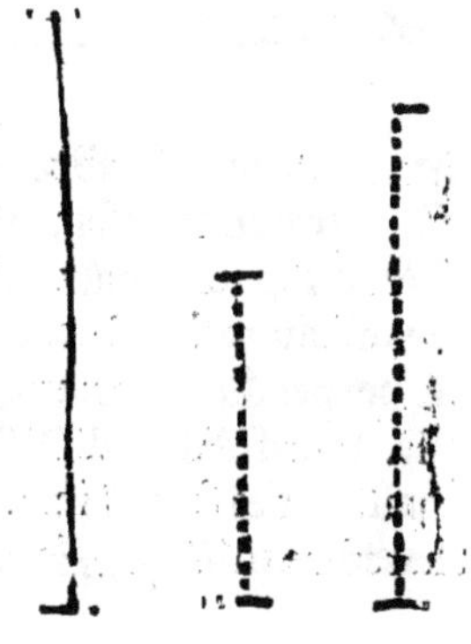

This ſuppoſed; when a Cannon Bullet approacheth to the oppoſed Wall, the Line and Direction of the Range is either perpendicular to the Wall, or not. If it be perpendicular, the Percuſſion operateth with ſuch a certain force: which we will prove to be the greateſt that that Range can have. If it ſhall be at Oblique Angles, as the Line A B unto the Wall B C, I do note that in reſpect to the Wall BC, there are in the Line of the Project A B, two Motions compounded together: that is, one of approximation perpendicular to the Wall, the other of paſſage lateral, or parallel to the ſame. The perpendicular Motion is both repreſented and meaſured by the Line A C; the parallel Motion by the Line C B: for both the Spaces A C and C B are paſſed by the Ball at the ſelf ſame Time.

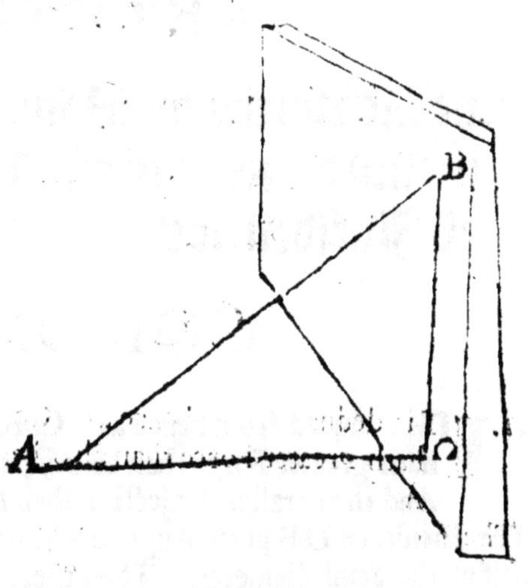

Now obſerve, that of theſe two ſorts of *Impetus*, one onely is to the purpoſe, for encreaſing the Forces to make a breach in the Wall, and to drive the Ball into it; to wit, the *Impetus* of the perpendicular Lation A C. Th'other, although it were infinite, will never encreaſe the force of the Project againſt the Reſiſtance of the Wall, unless the perpendicular Lation be withall accelerated. Nay, if the Horizontal Motion were simple and alone, without any mixture with the perpendicular Motion, what other would the Ball do but run equi-distant unto the Wall, without ever touching it, so far would it be from breaking it, although it were a very thin Glass? When therefore, the Direction of any Projection being given, we shall know how much of this perpendicular *Impetus* entereth into the Composition of the Motion, we shall also know the Activity or Moment of the Project towards the Resistance of the opposite Wall.

Let the Line of any Incidence at pleasure be A B upon the Plane B F taken with any what-ever Inclination: but withall, let the portion A B be so small, that it may be taken for Right. Draw A C perpendicular to the Plane, and conjoyn C B. So much, therefore, of Parallel Motion shall be in the Line A B, in respect of the Wall B F, as is the Line C B. But of this we make no accompt; for being multiplyed, it doth not help, and diminished it doth not weaken the Moment, if the other *Impetus* do remain unaltered and the same. Of Perpendicular Motion in the same there shall be as much as the Line A C: and the force of the percussion shall be greater and lesser, according as A C, greater or lesser, shall be past in the same Time.

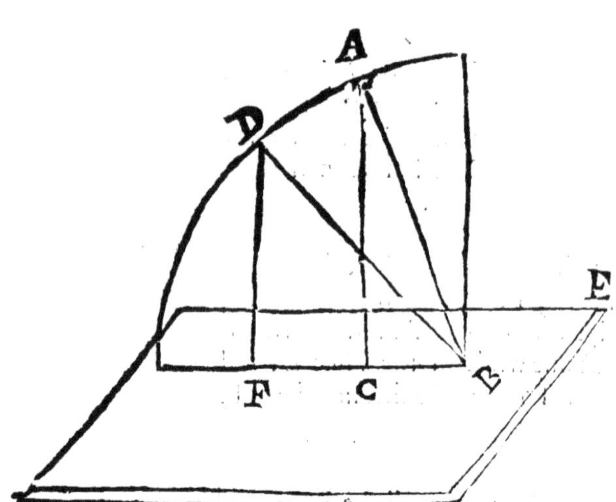

Let us suppose, now, that the force of th' Evidence A B be as A C. To know the force of any other Incidence D B, let D B be taken equal to B A, and having drawn D E perpendicular unto the Plane, the force of this Incidence shall be as that same Line D E. For if A B and D B are equal, and are the Ranges of the same Piece, they shall be past in the same Time. Therefore A C and D E, are also past in the same Time: Therefore th' *Impetus*'s, as to the Wall, are as A C to A D. We will therefore infer, that,

By Supposit. 2.

PROPOSITION.

The Activities or Moments of Ranges differently inclined, are as the Right Sines of th' Angles of Incidencies.

COROLLARIES.

1. IT is deduced from hence as a Corollary, that the Perpendicular Incidence A B, hath greater Force than all others, the force of it being as the Whole Sine. And the parallel Projection shall have no force, its force being as the No-Sine. The Incidence D B at th' Angle of *gr.* 30 hath half of the total force, its Sine being the half of the Semi-diameter. The others, likewise, according as they shall have greater or lesser Right Sine, shall have greater or lesser force.

2. The

2. The Forces of Projections have reciprocally the same proportion that the Sides of the Triangle have, which shall be formed upon the Plane by the Lines of the Incidencies.

Let a Projection be made along the Line A C, and another along the Line A B. And let the Plane of the Triangle A B C be perpendicular to the Wall. Because now the Space A C is past by the Ball in the Time A C; and the Space A B, that is (the parallel Motion deducted) the same Space A C, is past in the Time A B, the Forces shall be reciprocal to the Times: that is, the force along A C shall be as A B, and along A B, shall be as A C.

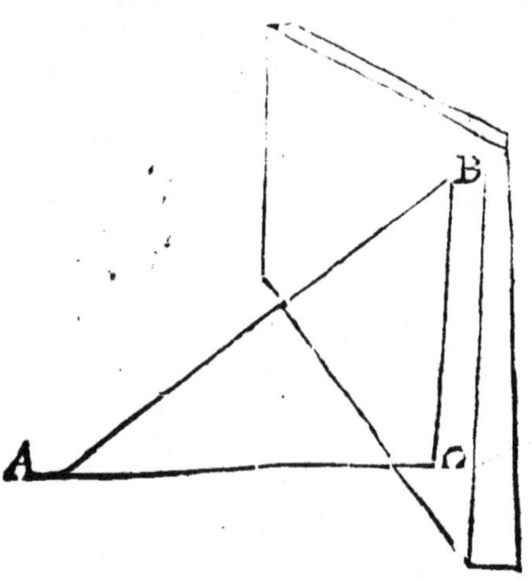

By Suppos. 3.

3. Projects shall then have the same force in battering, when the *Impetus*'s shall be as the Secants of the Complement of the Incidencies.

Let the *Impetus* along the Perpendicular A B, be as A B; and let it have such a certain force. To th' end that the *Impetus* along the Inclined A C may have the same force, I say that the *Impetus* along A C, ought to be unto the *Impetus* along A B, as A C is to A B: which A C is Secant of the Angle B A C, Complement of the * Inclination.

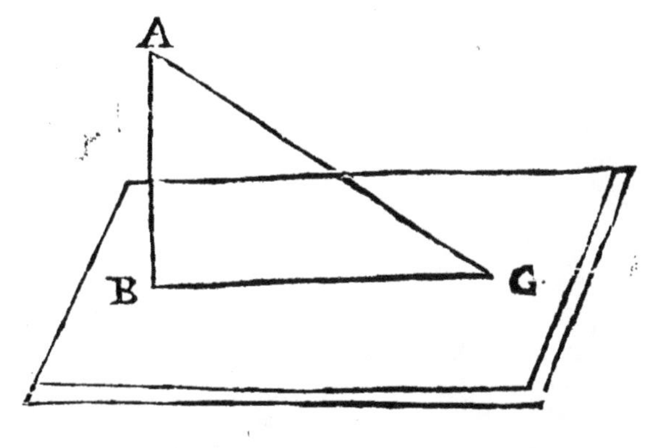

Or rather of the Incidency.

For if the *Impetus*'s along A B and A C shall be as the Spaces A B and A C, the Moveables shall, in the same Time, pass the two Lines A B and A C, that is, the same perpendicular Approximation A B. Therefore they shall have the same force against the Wall. *By Suppos. 2.*

4. Moreover, if with such a Piece, and along the Line C B, the Ball shall but just enter wholly into the Wall, then along all the more elevated Lines, it shall not only wholly immerge into the Solidity, but shall still make deeper impression or entrance, because it hath greater force. But because each of the less elevated shall have lesser force, none of them shall enter wholly into the Wall, nay some shall rebound and fly back.

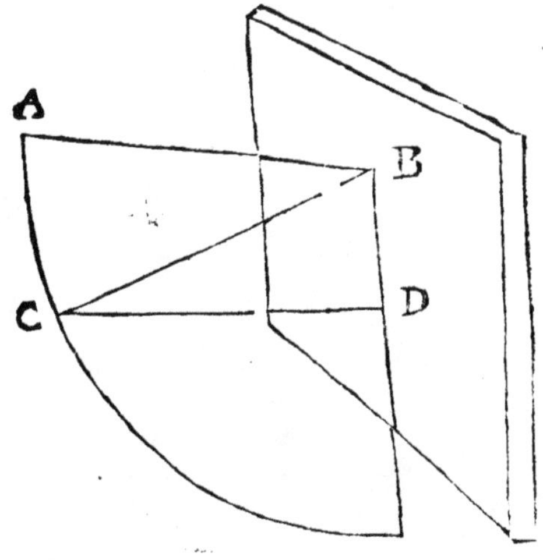

Yet let all this be spoken abstracting from a certain Effect of Pliancy or Refraction that Projects produce in passing with Inclination from the Rare *Medium* to the Dense, the Line incurvating contrary to that of the Refraction of Light, and visible Species.

FINIS.

Printed in the USA
CPSIA information can be obtained
at www.ICGtesting.com
LVHW072315201123
764112LV00138B/3178